RULE OF LAW VS MAJORITARIAN DEMOCRACY

What is more paradoxically democratic than a people exercising their vote against the rule of law and democracy? What happens when the will of the people and the rule of law are at odds?

Some commentators note that the presence of illiberal political movements in the public arena of many Western countries demonstrates that their democracy is so inclusive and alive that it comprehends and countenances even undemocratic forces and political agendas.

But what if, on the contrary, these were the signs of the deconsolidation of democracy instead of its good health? What if democratically elected regimes were to ignore constitutional principles representing the rule of law and the limits of their power?

With contributions from judges and scholars from different backgrounds and nationalities this book explores the framework in which this tension currently takes place in several Western countries by focusing on four key themes:

- The rule of law: presenting a historical and theoretical reconstruction of the evolution of the rule of law;
- The people: dealing with a set of problems around the notion of 'people' and the forces claiming to represent their voice;
- Democracy and its enemies: tackling a variety of phenomena impacting on the traditional democratic balance of powers and institutional order;
- Elected and non-elected: focusing on the juxtaposition between judges (and, more generally, non-representative bodies) and the people's representation.

Rule of Law vs Majoritarian Democracy

Edited by
Giuliano Amato,
Benedetta Barbisan
and
Cesare Pinelli

•HART•
OXFORD • LONDON • NEW YORK • NEW DELHI • SYDNEY

HART PUBLISHING
Bloomsbury Publishing Plc
Kemp House, Chawley Park, Cumnor Hill, Oxford, OX2 9PH, UK
1385 Broadway, New York, NY 10018, USA
29 Earlsfort Terrace, Dublin 2, Ireland

First published in Great Britain 2021

A catalogue record for this book is available from the British Library.

Library of Congress Cataloging-in-Publication data

Names: Amato, Giuliano, editor. | Barbisan, Benedetta, editor. | Pinelli, Cesare, editor.

Title: Rule of law vs majoritarian democracy / edited by Giuliano Amato, Benedetta Barbisan and Cesare Pinelli.

Other titles: Rule of law versus majoritarian democracy

Description: Oxford ; New York : Hart, 2021. | Includes bibliographical references and index.

Identifiers: LCCN 2021024061 (print) | LCCN 2021024062 (ebook) | ISBN 9781509936847 (hardback) | ISBN 9781509948376 (paperback) | ISBN 9781509936861 (pdf) | ISBN 9781509936854 (Epub)

Subjects: LCSH: Rule of law. | People (Constitutional law) | Democracy. | Populism.

Classification: LCC K3171 . R859 2021 (print) | LCC K3171 (ebook) | DDC 340/.11—dc23

LC record available at https://lccn.loc.gov/2021024061

LC ebook record available at https://lccn.loc.gov/2021024062

ISBN: HB: 978-1-50993-684-7
ePDF: 978-1-50993-686-1
ePub: 978-1-50993-685-4

Typeset by Compuscript Ltd, Shannon

Table of Contents

List of Contributors

Paolo Alvazzi del Frate is Professor of Legal History at the University of Roma Tre, Italy.

Giuliano Amato is a judge of the Italian Constitutional Court, and Professor Emeritus at the EUI in Florence and at the University of Rome *Sapienza*, Italy.

Benedetta Barbisan is Professor of Comparative Constitutional Law at the University of Macerata, Italy and Visiting Professor of Law at the Georgetown University Law Center, USA.

Moreno Bertoldi is Special Adviser to the Ambassador and Head of the Economic and Financial Section at the Delegation of the European Union to the United States.

Gian Primo Cella is Professor Emeritus of Social Theory and Economic Sociology at the University of Milan, Italy.

Simone Chambers is Professor at the University of California, Irvine, USA.

Justin Collings is Associate Dean and Professor of Law at Brigham Young University Law School, USA.

Antonio Cucinotta is Associate Professor of Comparative Law at the University of Messina, Italy.

Malgorzata Gersdorf is Full Professor of Labour Law at the Faculty of Law and Administration, University of Warsaw, Poland, and was Chief Justice of the Supreme Court of the Republic of Poland from 2014 to 2020.

Barbara Grabowska-Moroz is Research Fellow, Rule of Law Research Group, CEU Democracy Institute, Budapest.

Dieter Grimm is Professor of Law at Humboldt University Berlin and Permanent Fellow at the Wissenschaftskolleg zu Berlin (Institute for Advanced Study), and a former Justice of the Federal Constitutional Court of Germany.

Gábor Halmai is Professor and Chair of Comparative Constitutional Law at the European University Institute, Italy.

Piero Ignazi is Professor of Comparative Politics at the Department of Political and Social Sciences, University of Bologna, Italy.

Dimitry Kochenov is Head of Rule of Law Research Group, CEU Democracy Institute, Budapest and Professor of Legal Studies at the Department of Legal Studies, CEU Vienna.

Luigi Lacchè is Full Professor of Legal History at the University of Macerata, Italy.

Lord Jonathan Mance is former Deputy President of the UK Supreme Court.

José Luis Martí is Associate Professor of Legal and Political Philosophy at the Department of Law, Pompeu Fabra University, Spain.

Yves Mény was President of the European University Institute in Florence, Italy from 2002 to 2009, and President of the Board of Directors at the Scuola Superiore Sant'Anna in Pisa, Italy from 2014 to 2018.

Jan-Werner Müller is Professor of Politics at Princeton University, USA.

Gianfranco Pasquino is Senior Adjunct Professor of European and Eurasian Studies at the Johns Hopkins University SAIS-Europe, Italy, and Professor Emeritus of Political Science at the University of Bologna, Italy.

Mateusz Pilich is Associate Professor of Private International Law at the Faculty of Law and Administration, University of Warsaw, Poland.

Cesare Pinelli is Professor of Constitutional Law at University of Rome *Sapienza* School of Law, and Substitute Member of the Venice Commission, Italy.

Wojciech Sadurski is Challis Professor of Jurisprudence at the University of Sydney, Australia.

Michele Salvati is Emeritus Professor of Economics at the University of Milan, Italy.

Alberto Torini is Research Fellow at the Department of Law, University of Roma Tre, Italy.

1

Introduction

GIULIANO AMATO*

THIS BOOK DEALS with something the lovers of democracy generously hope would never happen. Indeed, years ago nobody expected it to happen. The adjective 'majoritarian' simply indicated one of the features of democracy, due to which, one way or another, the Government should rely on the will of the majority. However, such will being the fundamental pillar of any democratic form of government, we took it for granted that the rule of law was more than compatible with it. Respecting human rights and setting limits against the abusive use of power, first of all an independent judiciary, are the main implications of the rule of law. Are they not inherent to the notion of democracy itself, which is much more complex than respecting the will of the majority? In this sense any democracy should be both majoritarian and liberal. What has happened that has created tension between the rule of law and majoritarian democracy? Why is the will of the majority becoming intolerant towards the precepts of the rule of law?

It is not occurring everywhere in our western societies, nor has this unexpected trend had the same intensity in every country where it has gained ground. Only in two European states, namely Hungary and Poland, can we speak of majoritarian democracies in the new sense. In most other states there are political parties supporting majoritarian democracy as a prospect and frequently gaining a good share of the electorate by doing so. Here, liberal democracy is still in place, despite running a new and disturbing risk. In any case, a more or less profound intolerance of the rule of law has entered into our societies.

The most general explanation that is given goes to the economic and social consequences of globalisation in our western societies, accompanied by the ongoing technological revolution. The longstanding compromise between capitalism and liberal democracy, based on high employment and on the reasonable expectation of an increasingly equalitarian social structure, is over, because the circumstances that made it possible in the twentieth century are over. Now loss of jobs, reduction of income and paralysed economic and social ladders have entered the lives of the many, while the few are receiving an increasing share of the produced wealth. The many are

* Italian Constitutional Court.

dissatisfied with the pre-existing elites that have allowed globalisation to create such damages without defending them at all; those who live in Europe are also dissatisfied with the European Union, which they see as a transmission belt of globalisation; and several of them are ready to follow the leaders who preach closure against the world and closure against any newcomer who is perceived as a stealer of jobs and life opportunities. Whenever these feelings are shared by the majority, the impact upon the rule of law is inexorable. It is an undisputable fact that they lead both to a lesser respect for individual and minoritarian rights and to a distrustful wariness towards the institutions, not least of all the judiciary, whose task is to control and curb the power of the majority.

This is precisely what is occurring in Hungary, where majoritarian democracy is already a *fait accompli*. However, even though the economy has played a paramount role, the transformation is not due to the economic consequences of globalisation. The main reason has been the regime change, that has increasingly disappointed the citizens precisely for its economic and social impact. After communism, democracy was expected to bring not only more freedom, but also economic prosperity and material improvement. To the contrary, vis-à-vis a new class of 'plutocrats' (who have certainly enjoyed a remarkable material improvement) most of the others, mainly those with a low level of education, have been losing jobs and income. In this context, Prime Minister Viktor Orban, who was born a liberal, discovered and is now successfully practicing illiberal democracy.

On the assumption that liberal democracy, with all its protection of individual rights, promotes the selfish interests of the individuals, illiberal democracy proudly stands for the general interest of the nation, for the values mostly shared inside its community and for the protection of all those who live upon their work and accept the responsibility to work. Quite obviously this peculiar brand of democracy is not only illiberal, but also majoritarian and, as such, identifies the voice of the majority with the voice of the people, that no institution is entitled to contradict. Not surprisingly, in this new Hungary the traditional family prevails over other forms of family unions, minorities are not protected and immigrants are not allowed to enter. Nor is it surprising that institutional checks and balances are weakened to the advantage of governmental control.

Poland is arriving at a similar outcome, both in terms of values and in terms of institutional setting, for reasons that have nothing to do with the economy and therefore widen the horizon of the tensions between the rule of law and majoritarian democracy. In the Polish case, the electoral appeal and the power of the current majority are based on the defence of the traditional values of a society still embedded in its conservative Catholicism, against the assault of the tolerant principles, the expanded individual rights and the transgressive (but admitted) habits of our western societies. What has become ordinarily accepted in these societies throughout decades of civil and social developments sounds foreign and hostile to many members of a society that has not undergone a similar renovation. Furthermore – and most interestingly in relation to our purposes here – the rejection directly involves the case law of the two European Courts (the European Court of Justice and the European Court of Human Rights), that have codified the abandonment of traditional principles to the advantage of new and advanced individual rights. Therefore, in the Polish case the conflict transparently is between majoritarian democracy and what the supranational guardians of the rule of law have been defending (or introducing?) in our legal systems.

This last observation brings us to a further and disturbing reason to be considered in order to explain the conflict: may it also be that, beyond the economy and independently of it, the rule of law itself contributes to its own rejection? For sure the rule of law, by widening individual liberties far beyond their original range, has contributed to nurturing the reaction in the name of traditional values and also of national identities. Furthermore, when the *grund norm* becomes 'nothing above the will of the people', the main interpreters of the rule of law, the courts, fall under a well-known and widespread criticism: where does their legitimacy come from, as long as nobody has elected them? Even more so when European Courts are under fire: justice is generally administered in the name of the people (so several Constitutions assert). There is no demos in Europe. In the name of what people do these courts exercise their function?

The case of the UK is exemplary. Brexit has been promoted to the end of 'taking back control' and one of the main adversaries to be neutralised was the European Court of Justice with its binding decisions. Undoubtedly the case of Brexit is an extreme one. However, in the continent the attention paid to the defence of national identities vis-à-vis a rule of law coming from the supranational order has also been higher and higher. It is a fact that national courts, and first of all constitutional courts, have been visibly adapting their role. Throughout the previous decades they had become the national terminals of that supranational order, accepted as the source of hierarchically superior norms and decisions. Recently they have increasingly been instances of control of the judicial decisions adopted at that level, in the name of national identities and principles they have defined as fundamental and therefore untouchable. It has to be said that the German *Bundesverfassungsgericht* has always asserted the existence of this red line, despite its flexibility in assessing the enduring distance from it of individual European decisions. However, these days this position is much more widely supported, also on the basis of the explicit safeguard the Lisbon Treaty offers to national identities. Other courts, such as the Italian Constitutional Court, have expressed their readiness to erect national 'counter-limits' against European decisions contrary to their national fundamental principles. Outside the Union, in the wider Europe of the ECHR, the amended Russian Constitution, that already proclaims its 'highest legal force', will openly deny validity to international treaties and decisions that 'contradict' its clauses.

Must we conclude that the game between majoritarian democracy and the rule of law is over? At the moment, as far as Europe is concerned, it would be, to say the least, a hasty conclusion. First of all, the two Member States, Poland and Hungary, that have adapted their institutional frameworks to the demands of their newly formed majoritarian democracies, are still challenged by the institutions of the European Union. Some of their new arrangements, namely the reduction of judicial independence, are irrefutable violations of the Treaties. This is a still open controversy and it is not at all unlikely that ultimately the two majoritarian democracies will have to submit to the core of the rule of law. Secondly, the new attitude of our national courts vis-à-vis the European ones is not at all settled. The path of a reasonable balance between the demands of national identities and the demands of the rule of law seems to be where they will try to go from here. We will return to this later on, but surely they cannot ignore that their own authority would be heavily diminished and eventually cancelled, should they appear completely subjugated by the will of the people.

However, our future is not at all certain nor easily predictable. I would exclude the extreme prospect in which the rule of law is deprived of its historical and essential meaning while the rule by law (by whatever law the majority adopts) takes its place. Not only it is very unlikely in Europe, where the rule of law is a founding principle both of the Union and of the Council of Europe, but it is hard to foresee also in the wider world. The rule of law frequently happens to be more of an unaccomplished aim than a reality; furthermore, when entering into a variety of legal and cultural contexts 'universal' values necessarily multiply their own facets. Nonetheless, would anybody dare to openly challenge the Universal Declaration of Human Rights, whose clauses transparently enshrine single and eventually all the components of it?

We cannot expect an undisturbed continuation of a rule of law which, even though codified by many of our national legal systems, is an essential part of a supranational order whose commands enter into such systems by decisions of supranational courts. In times of surge of national communities defending and prioritising their demands and their overall identities, when these communities feel ignored or not sufficiently considered, the risk of rejection (or, to say the least, of not compliance) is very high. Are there remedies to avoid or at least to reduce this undesirable effect? The first one, not at all new, is the margin of appreciation that mostly the European Court of Human Rights always has recognised as regards its Member States in controversial matters, upon which our national communities have diverging views. Before asserting that same sex couples are entitled to have their union registered, the Court has waited until a wide (even if not unanimous) consensus existed in the Member States.

Let us be clear: the judicial use of the margin of appreciation is not a form of political opportunism. On the contrary, it directly goes to the fundamental issue raised by the rule of law as interpreted and enforced by supranational courts. We all agree that there cannot be democracy without the rule of law. Can there be rule of law without democracy? Where does its legitimacy (and the legitimacy of the corresponding courts) come from in a supranational order in which there is no demos and therefore no democracy? The only possible answer is that it comes from the demoi whose representatives have stipulated the Treaties and the Charters where the rule of law is embodied and have consequently accepted the jurisdiction of the respective courts. That being so, let us assume that one of these courts is deciding upon a controversial issue in relation to which only one individual state still dissents from the wide majority of the others. The (not sufficiently explored) issue is whether the Court could ignore the margin of appreciation, just because it would go to the benefit of only that state. It is a fact that in our domestic arenas we expect our own national courts to defer to the appreciation of their respective parliaments, whenever they have to decide on delicate matters where conflicting values play a paramount role. In such cases, the necessary balancing is for the representatives of the people, not for the judges. National judges are not entitled to supersede that balancing act unless it is manifestly unreasonable. Nor are they entitled to step in, while enduring divisions prevent a parliamentary decision on the matter, unless some right or principle protected by the Constitution is patently violated, due to this lack of action.

Is a supranational court entitled to infringe these boundaries to the detriment of no more than one of the national communities under its jurisdiction, just because all of the others agree with its solution? As long as its jurisdiction is conferred and accepted by each and all of the Member States and by all the corresponding demoi, one might argue that there is no reason for one of them to be differently treated in a context where majority voting does not apply. Nor is it an answer that in the US the Supreme Court decided in 2015 (in *Obergefell v Hodges*[1]) that same sex couples had the right not only to be registered, but to get formally married like any other couple, despite several Member States being still contrary to such an extended equal treatment. However controversial such a decision might have been in the US, the fact of the matter is that there is a federation there, there is a federal demos, and there is a federal Constitution that is supreme.

The underpinnings upon which our European Courts are installed are quite different. Their work aimed at the harmonisation of our national legal systems upon the basis of common principles is highly deserving. Furthermore – and here I refer to the Court of Justice of the European Union – the Europeanisation of our common constitutional traditions has greatly contributed to creating a precious cross-fertilisation among the cultural identities of the Member States. Facing the current conflicts, it can also nurture a further step that has actually been suggested. Namely, in cases where constitutional identities are at stake, courts could turn to article 2 of the Treaty (where the 'values common to the Member States' are enshrined) instead of relying on article 4 (where the features of national identities that 'the Union shall respect' are listed). Should the European Court of Justice pave the way and some, leading constitutional courts proceed in the same direction (as a few of them – such as the Italian one – have already done), the temperature of the identity-based conflicts would hopefully be lowered. However, the fact remains that legitimacy both of the European Court of Human Rights and of the European Court of Justice comes from all the under signatories of the Treaties that provide for their jurisdiction. The principle of conferral, conferral by the Member States, is still the basic norm of our European treaties and organisations.

The sensitive question on the margin of appreciation vis-à-vis the dissent of only one Member State may also remain open to further discussion. In any case, in the described context an appropriate (and not approximate) recognition not only of the common features, but also, when needed, of the specificities of national identities is more than recommended. With a proviso, that has to be clear: there are unsurmountable limits to such flexibility. When the rule of law is at stake, there are boundaries that cannot be crossed. Recognising a national margin of appreciation makes sense when confronting not unanimous views on the family, on parenthood, on giving life or giving death to others and on similarly moral issues. It is not the same when the representatives of the people, in order to make their decisions immune to any independent control, manipulate the judiciary and/or submit constitutional courts themselves to the will of the Executive. Or, even worse, when the Executive, seizing

[1] 576 U.S. 644 (2015).

upon the opportunity offered by an emergency, receives from its majority powers manifestly disproportionate to the needs of the emergency. Here no margin of appreciation is admissible. Here the rule of law is bluntly violated and any court, national or supranational as it might be, is under the obligation to declare it; whatever the consequence.

An adequate balance between uniformity and the recognition of diversities will prove essential, not only to preserve the rule of law and its principles vis-à-vis the demands stemming from majoritarian democracy, but also to lower national hostilities against the outside world and first of all of the European Union. This lesson is being learnt by the European institutions in a time when much of the discredit and of the hostility against them has been due to the excess of uniformity of their regulations and directives. United in our diversities, which is not only the motto, but the founding principle of the Union, this would have required a much less simplistic pathway: namely, on the one side a wider use of mutual recognition (according to which national regulations remain also in the integrated market, as long as all of them comply with some common principles); on the other side not only directives, but also regulations that, whenever possible, the states are allowed to adapt to their specific contexts.

Of course, we must be aware that the suggestions advanced here typically correspond to the requirements of the damage reduction theory: nothing less, but also nothing more. More can be accomplished only by removing the roots upon which in most of our countries the appeal of majoritarian democracy relies in order to gain ground. Is it an attainable aim? Perhaps it is, but the arena is the widest of all, namely the globalised economy that has been the main reason for the widespread anxieties and dissatisfactions to which we owe the new brand of majoritarian democracy. This crucial role of the economy has been the starting point of our reflections here. It should not be surprising that, in concluding, we are back to such a role.

Among the scholars who study the economy, nobody thinks the developments ahead of us will ever restore the conditions that allowed our western societies in the past century to have high employment, increasing incomes, social mobility and bright prospects for the future Does this mean that low salaries, uncertain jobs, reduced social mobility and increasing inequalities (with all the social reactions they bring with themselves) will remain as permanent features of our societies? Here the answers are much more diversified and, even though under new and different conditions, a not so gloomy future is not excluded at all.

It is not only Pope Francisco who says that an economy which is more egalitarian, more mindful of the overall interests of our societies and, in other words, more sustainable is not only desirable, but achievable. The Business Roundtable released in August 2019 a statement in which 181 CEOs of primary American companies expressed their commitment to deliver value to customers, to invest in employees, first of all compensating them fairly, and to support the communities where they work. Furthermore, scholarly doctrines are changing. Keynes might not return to be as influential as he was before the neo-liberal advent, but nowadays proactive policies aimed at reducing inequalities, promoting education and a newly balanced welfare, not to speak of preserving human life in the planet, are more and more widely recommended. Even more so, after the catastrophic impact of the coronavirus pandemic.

Post neo-liberal policies are actually envisaged. Can they also be practised? What our societies and our governments have done in coping with the effects of the coronavirus has irrefutably demonstrated that they can. However, whether they can become ordinary policies is yet to be seen. Also to be seen is whether they can be successful in restoring economic and social conditions that allow the majority of our citizens to feel satisfied and confident again. Only at that point will the rule of law and its territory be safe.

We don't have the answers to these doubts. Nobody does. Our only possible conclusion is that the tension between the rule of law and majoritarian democracy does not necessarily lead to a final disruption of the rule of law: first, for the already mentioned resilience of the rule of law itself, secondly because the (though limited) remedies we have focused upon could produce a sustainable balance, and finally because majoritarian democracy might eventually turn out to be a temporary phenomenon.

The only non-hypothetical conclusion we may draw is that democracy, and with it the rule of law, is strong and easily accepted and practised in the good times, while it meets many more difficulties in the bad times. Arguing that, due to this, democracy is just a regime for the good times would be too much. However, those who happen to rule a democratic country while the bad times are arriving, should be sufficiently alert as to take immediate action on behalf of the weakest segments of their society before it is too late, before others intervene and wipe them out in the name of majoritarian democracy.

The rulers of the old times, before democracy was introduced, were well aware of the risk of revolts whenever the supply of foods was becoming scarce. This is why the price of bread and its own distribution had always been subject to public regulation. In ancient Rome already in the year 123 BC the first *lex frumentaria* was adopted, according to which bread wheat was to be sold by the state to all Roman citizens at a fixed and lower price. The *Assisa Panis et Cervisa*, an English code establishing special rules for the sale of bread, was issued in 1266 and remained in force in the London area until 1815. So it was in several other European states and cities and whenever, due to acute and unexpected shortages, the price was not promptly lowered, bread riots were the almost inevitable response (Alessandro Manzoni made the bread riot of Milan in 1628 famous in his novel *I promessi sposi*).

Democracies should never forget this lesson. The price they are currently paying to their majoritarian version is largely due to the fact that in the years following the outburst of the economic and financial crisis of 2008 the lesson was totally ignored.

FURTHER READING

On democracy and populism:

I Krastev, 'The Age of Populism. Reflections on the Self Enmity of Democracy' (2011) *European View* 11.

L Diamond, 'Facing up to Democracy Recession' (2015) 26(1) *Journal of Democracy* n 26.

B Milanovic, *Global Inequality. A New Approach for the Age of Globalization* (Harvard University Press, 2016).

M Lilla, *The Once and Future Liberalism. After Identity Politics* (Harper Collins, 2017).
S Levitsky and D Ziblatt, *How Democracies die. What History Reveals About Our Future* (Penguin, 2018).

On Poland:
W Sadurski, *How Democracy Dies (in Poland): A Case Study of Anti-Constitutional Populist Backsliding* (Sydney Law School, Legal Studies Research Paper n. 18/01, 2018).

On Hungary:
A Biro-Nagy, *Illiberal Democracy in Hungary: The Social Background and Practical Steps of Building an Illiberal State* (Cidop, 2017).

On the rule of law and democracy in the global context:
M Bussani, 'Deglobalizing Rule of Law and Democracy: Hunting Down Rhetoric Through Comparative Law' (2019) 67 *American Journal of Comparative Law* 701.

On the rule of law as enforced by supranational courts:
D Lasting and J Weiler, 'Judicial Review in the Contemporary World – Retrospective and Prospective' (2018) *I-CON, International Journal of Constitutional Law* 2.
LD Spieker, 'Framing and Managing Constitutional Identity Conflicts: How to Stabilize the Modus Vivendi Between the Court of Justice and National Constitutional Courts' (2020) 57 *Common Market Law Review* 361.

Specifically, on the margin of appreciation:
A Legg, *The Margin of Appreciation in International Human Rights: Deference and Proportionality* (OUP, 2012).
P Agha, *Human Rights Between Law and Politics: The Margin of Appreciation in Post-National Contexts* (Hart Publishing, 2017).
JH Fahner, *Judicial Deference in International Adjudication* (Hart Publishing, 2020).

Cases:
The *Bundesverfassungsgericht* and the defence of national prerogatives: Lisbon Urteil, 30 June 2009.
The Italian Constitutional Court between common constitutional values and national counter-limits: ord. 26 January 2017 n.24 on the *Taricco* case.
The European Court of Human Rights and same sex couples: *Oliari and others v Italy*, 21 July 2015.
The US Supreme Court and same sex couples: *Obergefell v Hodges* 576 U.S. 644 (2015).

Part One

What is the Rule of Law About?

2

Rule of Law between the Seventeenth and Nineteenth Centuries

PAOLO ALVAZZI DEL FRATE AND ALBERTO TORINI*

PREMISE

THE CURRENT LEGAL definition of the rule of law taken as a reference is the one formulated by the United Nations in 2004 under the Report of the Secretary-General. According to this definition, the rule of law represents

> a principle of governance in which all persons, institutions and entities, public and private, including the State itself, are accountable to laws that are publicly promulgated, equally enforced and independently adjudicated, and which are consistent with international human rights norms and standards. It requires, as well, measures to ensure adherence to the principles of supremacy of law, equality before the law, accountability to the law, fairness in the application of the law, separation of powers, participation in decision-making, legal certainty, avoidance of arbitrariness and procedural and legal transparency.[1]

In this chapter, we intend to focus on the historical perspective trying to restore the original meaning of the term, in order to outline its development, in particular during the eighteenth and nineteenth centuries, a crucial period for political and legal thought due to the affirmation of constitutionalism in Europe and North America.

I. THE RULE OF LAW: THE MEANINGS OF THE TERM

Sometimes, political and legal terms, when used in a non-juridical debate, risk losing their real essence and simplifying themselves in a generic and non-scientific meaning. Certainly, the expression 'rule of law' runs said risk.[2] Indeed, it may simply refer to

* Both University of Rome 3. Although the article was devised and discussed jointly by the two authors, the premise and sections I–V were written by Paolo Alvazzi del Frate and sections VI–X by Alberto Torini.

[1] UN, *Report of the Secretary-General. The rule of law and transitional justice in conflict and post-conflict societies*, (S/2004/616), III.6. 'The rule of law – according to Tamanaha – means that government officials and citizens are bound by and abide by the law'; BZ Tamanaha, 'The history and elements of the rule of law' (2012) *Singapore Journal of Legal Studies* 233.

[2] By way of example, as it is stated by Martin Krygier 'the rule of law is today the beneficiary, sometimes the victim, of enormous rhetorical enthusiasm. No one is against. Once upon a time, and not too long ago,

the 'respect for legal rules', whose use is 'trivialized and ritualized',[3] regardless of its historical genesis which, only separately considered, is able to clarify the meaning of such an expression. In light of the above, the political speech about the rule of law principle has incorporated, even in their significant diversity, the German *Rechtsstaat* and the French *État de droit*.

Certainly, the current meaning of this expression has changed more and more in order to become broad, symbolic and full of emotion. It can be summarised with the guarantee of the rights of freedom and the principle of equality of people before the law.[4]

It is certainly very difficult to properly define the content of the expression rule of law, since it is characterised by vague and sometimes misleading different meanings. The rule of law includes different legal and political principles, put together by the intention of establishing 'government by laws and not by individuals'. This means the replacement of the 'government of individuals', considered arbitrary and potentially despotic, with the 'government of laws', characterised by the compliance with formal legal rules.

The origin of the principle of rule of law is ancient, but only in the sixteenth and seventeenth centuries did it become more clarified, initially in the English political-juridical culture and afterwards it was established in North America and continental Europe in the eighteenth century.

Preliminarily, it has to be noted that through the doctrine of the rule of law it has been possible to oppose freedom to absolutism, to claim the importance of rights by arguing the autonomy of individuals against the oppression arbitrary power. Therefore, the doctrine of the rule of law is a fundamental element of legal history, the study of which is essential in order to understand the development of the society.

The analysis shall necessarily move from the eighteenth century, which was characterised by the cult of reason and by an exasperated rationalism. This period – according to Pietro Costa's words – corresponds to a 'deep change in the political lexicon which took place in Europe during the Enlightenment', a phenomenon that had already started in the seventeenth century.[5]

The British expression 'rule of law', the German one *Rechtsstaat* and French one *État de droit*, make reference to partially different concepts and principles, aimed, however, at achieving the same purpose, namely the overcoming of absolutism, due to the affirmation of citizens' rights of liberty and equality.[6]

it had a lot of enemies': M Krygier, '*On the Rule of Law. History, Politics, Theory* by Brian Z. Tamanaha' (2005) 32(4) *Journal of Law and Society* 657–66.

[3] J Chevallier, *L'État de droit*, 3rd edn (Montchrestien, 1999) 8. The *État de droit* 'omniprésent dans le discours politique, il est devenu l'un de ces mots "passe-partout", "omnibus", qui recouvre des significations variées … son usage tend à se banaliser et à se ritualiser'.

[4] See P Craig, 'Formal and substantive conceptions of the rule of law: an analytical framework' (1997) 21 *Public Law* 467–87.

[5] P Costa, 'The Rule of Law. A Historical Introduction' in P Costa and D Zolo (eds), *The Rule of Law. History, Theory and Criticism* (Springer, 2007) 77.

[6] The rule of law has been the subject of almost exterminated literature, among which, please consider the following most recent works: BZ Tamanaha, *On The Rule of Law: History, Politics, Theory* (CUP, 2004); T Bingham, *The Rule of Law* (Penguin, 2010); J Waldron, 'The Rule of Law' in EN Zalta (ed),

The first and most known definition of rule of law is certainly the one provided by the historian and jurist Albert Dicey (1835–1922)[7] who, in 1885, highlighted three fundamental aspects of the principle in the British legal system: (1) 'the absolute supremacy or predominance of regular law as opposed', with the fundamental consequence that an individual may 'be punished for a breach of law, but he can be punished for nothing else';[8] (2) 'equality before the law';[9] and (3) the law of the Constitution is 'not the source, but the consequence of the rights of individuals, as defined and enforced by the Courts'.[10]

The notion of rule of law was therefore issued with specific reference to the British legal system and its political and legal culture. However, the need to eliminate arbitrariness in the exercise of public powers and to ensure fundamental rights of freedom were felt almost everywhere in Europe. This spread particular interest and attention towards the British legal culture which, further to the Glorious Revolution of 1689, definitively acquired the principles of liberalism and progressive democratic development as an indispensable reference of its political-juridical system.

The expression 'rule of law' became general during the nineteenth century and was adopted in various European languages through specific formulations that represented a more or less faithful translation of that principle, although based on different legal conceptions.

In particular, the German expression *Rechtsstaat* – issued in the 1830s by Robert von Mohl (1799–1875)[11] and developed by Georg Jellinek (1851–1911), Otto Mayer (1846–1924) and Rudolf von Jhering (1818–92) – appears significantly different from the British one.[12]

Through the principle of rule of law, it is intended to guarantee rights and freedoms already existing in the society and duly protected by customary customs and common law against any arbitrary acts by the state. Differently, with reference to the culture of *Rechtsstaat*, the state adopts an act of 'self-limitation', whereby it spontaneously reduces its powers and accepts being subject to control of legality by the jurisdiction.

In other words, while under the British system the state is created in compliance with law, according to the German perspective the right is created by the state and it

The Stanford Encyclopedia of Philosophy (Spring 2020 Edition), (https://plato.stanford.edu/entries/rule-of-law/). For the Italian bibliography, see G Pino and V Villa (eds), *Rule of Law. L'ideale della legalità* (Il Mulino, 2016).

[7] Before Dicey – and it is the same author who affirms this – William Edward Hearn (1826–88) used the expression 'rule of law' in the volume *The government of England. Its structure and its development* (Longmans, 1867).

[8] AV Dicey, *Introduction to the Study of The Law of the Constitution (1885)*, 8th edn (Macmillan, 1915) 120. The rule of law 'excludes the existence of arbitrariness, of prerogative, or even of wide discretionary authority on the part of the government', ibid.

[9] 'The rule of law in this sense excludes the idea of any exemption of officials or others from the duty of obedience to the law which governs other citizens or from the jurisdiction of the ordinary Tribunals', ibid.

[10] Dicey (n 8) 121.

[11] According to the work of 1832 *Die Polizeiwissenschaft nach den Grundsätzen des Rechtsstaates* (*The police science according to the principles of the constitutional state*).

[12] G Gozzi, '*Rechtsstaat* and individual rights in german constitutional history' in P Costa and D Zolo (eds), *The Rule of Law: History, Theory and Criticism* (Springer, 2007) 237–59; O Jouanjan, *Figures de l'État de droit: le Rechtsstaat dans l'histoire intellectuelle et constitutionnelle de l'Allemagne* (Presses universitaires de Strasbourg, 2001).

does not pre-exist to it. This is why, as it is properly observed by Giuliano Amato, in the European ideological system, 'the English one is the most liberal of liberalisms'.[13]

The French version of the *État de droit* emphasises even more the role of the state and of the law, as 'expression of the general will', as stated in article 6 of the Declaration of the Rights of Man and of the Citizen 1789.[14] According to the French perspective, the regulatory monopoly by the state law is affirmed and jurisdiction plays a secondary role, limited to mere application of the legislative rules and therefore of the will of the legislator.[15]

Also, considering the variety of political-juridical conceptions, the rule of law principle was firmly established as a characteristic and fundamental feature of western juridical culture. Indeed, this does not imply an underestimation of the very serious crisis experienced in the twentieth century with the spread of European totalitarianisms (fascism, nazism and communism). However, despite this (which – from a historical point of view – we can consider an, albeit long, parenthesis) the rule of law remains a value to be achieved, a tendential principle to which the western legal systems aspire.

II. THE EIGHTEENTH CENTURY: THE HISTORICAL CONTEXT

The development of absolute states in the sixteenth and seventeenth centuries had caused a progressive centralisation of power in Europe, against the role and functions of the traditional representative and jurisdictional bodies of the medieval tradition. We mainly refer to the crisis of the General Estates (*États généraux*) and the Parliaments (*Parlements*) in France, but absolutist attempts also occurred – as known – in the UK and culminated in the seventeenth century Revolutions, although to a lesser extent, Spain, Portugal, the Italian and German states and the Empire also experienced similar phenomenon.[16]

The main powers available to absolute sovereigns inevitably reduced the role of the classes and bodies that traditionally limited and controlled the action of European governments. While medieval systems guaranteed a certain stability and continuity of policies, since they were founded on *iurisdictio* and on the guarantee of the *status quo*, during the modern age this balance disappeared, favouring more incisive reform interventions and more radical changes to the consolidated structures. After a first phase of 'empirical absolutism' (in the sixteenth and seventeenth centuries), largely unaware of government action, a phase of 'enlightened absolutism' took over in continental Europe in the eighteenth century (also called *Polizeistaat* in German, Police state in English, *État de police* in French). Absolutism therefore initiated a broad policy of economic and social reforms and the strengthening of the state, inspired by the Enlightenment doctrines.

[13] G Amato, *Forme di Stato e forme di governo* (Il Mulino, 2006) 44.
[14] Article 6, 'Law is the expression of the general will'.
[15] See Chevallier (n 3) 22–43.
[16] See P Anderson, *Lineages of the Absolutist State* (NLB, 1974).

In the eighteenth century the development of the functions of the states and of the powers available to the rulers had significant consequences from a political and legal point of view. Public power found itself in the position to act through higher intensity and efficacy towards the social and economic reality, reducing and, in some cases, eliminating the role of traditional 'intermediate bodies'. The articulated legal systems of the *Ancien Régime* experienced a significant phenomenon of simplification and reduction of social articulations. Therefore, the traditional limits to the powers of the sovereign gradually faded, allowing a more incisive reform action.

Such evolution characterised the territories of the Empire (with the sovereigns Maria Theresa, Joseph II and Leopold II), Prussia (with Frederick II) and, to a lesser extent, France and Spain. The UK, after the Glorious Revolution and the Bill of Rights of 1689, had a different route characterised by a greater institutional continuity and stability, which allowed it to carry out important and gradual reforms without changing the substantial respect for its historical tradition, typical of that culture. The complex and heterogeneous situation of the Italian states was largely extraneous to this phenomenon of simplification, with the exception of the territories belonging to the Austrian Empire (Lombardia and Veneto regions) or in any case under its influence such as the Grand Duchy of Tuscany (with Pietro Leopoldo).

During the eighteenth century, Europe therefore appears as a reality in transformation, where the aspiration for a profound reform under the banner of simplification and rationalisation of the legal systems is strongly felt and promoted by the doctrines of the Enlightenment. Not to be overlooked, however, is the importance of the tradition which still exercises a significant cultural and social influence.

In the last decades of the century, the two great revolutions, in America and France, marked a significant fracture and the definitive crisis of the model of the enlightened absolutism. Afterwards, it was no longer possible to re-introduce the idea of a paternalistic and enlightened power, although still absolute, capable of leading a route of radical reforms, completely excluding the population from public life.

III. AGAINST THE REASON OF STATE (RAGION DI STATO)[17]

The rule of law, based on superior and binding legal rules applicable to everyone, was first opposed to the Reason of State which, on the contrary, theorised the total freedom of political action.

The rule of law principle was elaborated in British culture and practice, while in continental Europe, in particular in Italy and France, the Reason of State was affirmed (in Italian *Ragion di Stato*, in French *Raison d'État*).

According to the doctrine of the Reason of State, whose theorisation is mainly due to the Italians Niccolò Machiavelli (1469–1527) and Francesco Guicciardini (1483–1540) – the sovereign had to be considered free from any legal and moral

[17] Hereinafter, through the expression 'Reason of State' we refer to the translation of the Italian concept of '*Ragion di Stato*'.

constraint as he represented the only authority capable of understanding and pursuing the 'common good' (*bonum commune*), intended as the interest of the collectivity.[18] This theory necessarily moved from the clear separation between morality and politics, through a complete autonomy in favour of the latter. The figure that historically interpreted in full this autonomy and in a very symbolic way was certainly Cardinal Richelieu (1585–1642), minister of Louis XIII, king of France.

From a long-term perspective, it can be argued that the rule of law intended to reconcile politics and law with the transparency of documents and the moral evaluation of the action of public authorities.

IV. LIMITING ABSOLUTE POWER

Is it possible to introduce legal limits to the sovereign's power? This is the fundamental question that jurists and philosophers seemed to ask themselves in the seventeenth century and, even more, in the eighteenth century. During the Middle Ages, power appeared naturally limited by the generalised acknowledgment of universal authorities, the Pope and the Emperor, and by the adoption of the so-called common rights (*iura communia*) by Roman and canon law. Differently, in the modern age, the crushing of the traditional political scheme led to the emergence of almost absolute powers (from the Latin *legibus soluti*) which recognised no authority above them (*auctoritas superiorem non recognoscens*), disavowing the idea of 'limitation of power'. In this regard, the maxim of the French law of the *Ancien Régime* is significant, stating that 'what the king wants, the law wants' (*Qui veut le roi, si veut la loi*)'.[19] The authority of the king was therefore identified with that of the law.

Absolutism – the political and legal doctrine prevalent in the modern age – claimed the full freedom of sovereign power and the overcoming of the bonds that medieval tradition had established. This does not mean that the states of the modern age reach the absoluteness of monarchical power. Instead, it was a 'tendential' phenomenon, a doctrine and a sort of programme to be implemented. Among the greatest theorists of absolutism, we remember the French Jean Bodin (1529–96) and the English Thomas Hobbes (1588–1679).

The affirmation of absolute and unrestrained power led jurists and philosophers to theorise, by reaction, the need to establish effective limits to that power. The genesis of political liberalism and the rule of law doctrine therefore arise from the need to legally limit absolutism and also to subject sovereign power to compliance with legal rules. In technical terms, this meant establishing the hierarchical superiority of one legal source over the other and, in particular, of the 'Constitution' with respect to the legislative act of the king. Consequently, a legislative act contrary to the Constitution (higher than it) would have been void and therefore null.

[18] See M Senellart, *Machiavélisme et raison d'état* (PUF, 1989).

[19] A Loysel, *Institutes coustumières: ou manuel de plusieurs et diverses reigles, sentences, et proverbes tant anciens que modernes du droict coustumier et plus ordinaire de la France* (Abel L'Angelier,1607) 1, tit. 1.

V. THE FIRST STATEMENT: THE ENGLISH CONSTITUTIONAL MONARCHY AND THE DOCTRINE OF JOHN LOCKE

Which were the fundamental milestones in the concrete affirmation of the rule of law?

Without any doubt, the first milestone can be found in the conclusion of the troubled period of the English revolutions, from the Petition of Right 1628, to the Habeas Corpus Act 1679 and to the Bill of Rights 1689. The result was the stable affirmation of the principle – already proclaimed in the Middle Ages with the *Magna Carta Libertatum* of 1215 – according to which every public authority is subject to respect for fundamental law, that is the British Constitution. The latter represents a higher law towards the royal will (or Royal Act) and also towards the legislation (or Parliamentary Acts).

After the previous theorisations of Edward Coke (1552–1634), Samuel Rutherford (1600–61) and James Harrington (1611–77), the cornerstone in the evolution of the principle is undoubtedly the doctrine of John Locke (1632–1704). It was the founder of the liberal doctrine and was deemed as the constant reference of every reflection on the rule of law, Locke firmly anchors his doctrine to the principle of Liberty and Property according to which there is an inseparable link between the freedom of individuals and the protection of private property. Locke's doctrine affirmed the need for humankind 'to be under no other restraint but the law of nature':

> freedom of men under government is, to have a standing rule to live by, common to every one of that society, and made by the legislative power erected in it; a liberty to follow my own will in all things, where the rule prescribes not; and not to be subject to the inconstant, uncertain, unknown, arbitrary will of another man: as freedom of nature is, to be under no other restraint but the law of nature.[20]

According to Locke, the higher law was thus identified with 'natural law', superior to men and their laws.[21] There was therefore a double level of legality: one with respect to the legislation created by men and another with respect to natural law. With Locke's doctrine and the system of the constitutional monarchy, the modern conception of the rule of law was inaugurated, which gradually spread throughout Europe in the eighteenth century.

VI. MONTESQUIEU: LIBERTY AND SEPARATION OF POWERS

Montesquieu (1689–1755) – as known – continued and developed principles partially already enunciated by Locke: we make reference to 'liberty and property' and the rule of law. As Locke, he identifies the 'separation of powers' as the most suitable principle to guarantee liberty and supremacy of the law.[22] The concentration of legislative,

[20] J Locke, *Second Treatise of Civil Government*, Ch IV, s 22 (1690).

[21] See F von Hayek, *The Constitution of Liberty* (University of Press, 1960) Ch XI, 170–75.

[22] See the classic book of E Carcassonne, *Montesquieu et le problème de la constitution française au XVIIIe siècle* (Puf, 1927); JN Shklar, *Montesquieu* (OUP, 1987); and ThL Pangle, *Montesquieu's Philosophy of Liberalism: A Commentary on the Spirit of the Laws* (Chicago University Press, 1989).

executive and judicial powers provides a single body with excessive influence and inevitably causes tyranny.[23] This is Montesquieu's famous conclusion:

> there would be an end of everything, were the same man or the same body, whether of the nobles or of the people, to exercise those three powers, that of enacting laws, that of executing the public resolutions, and of trying the causes of individuals.[24]

A particular function was attributed by Montesquieu to the judiciary power, capable of ensuring compliance with the law maintaining at the same time a 'neutral' or even 'null' role.[25] In this respect he affirmed that judges 'are no more than the mouth that pronounces the words of the law, mere passive beings, incapable of moderating either its force or rigour'.[26]

Montesquieu's doctrine was based on the interpretation of the British system. This was certainly a schematic reading, exaggerated and unrealistic, but logical and coherent in its formulation.

The influence of Montesquieu's doctrine was of significant importance.[27] Although Locke defined the fundamental characteristics of the rule of law and inaugurated the doctrines of political liberalism, Montesquieu clarified and rendered universal the theory of the separation of powers. Such a theory, it is perhaps useless to remember, is still in force today and represents the basis of the principle of rule of law.

VII. THE AMERICAN REVOLUTION

The American Revolution certainly represented a fundamental step in the evolution of the principle. Born in British culture and legislation, the rule of law has perfected and defined itself with specific features in North American constitutionalism.

These revolutionary events can be considered, from a certain perspective, as an act of loyalty to the British Constitution. In the name of the rule of law, American revolutionaries rebelled against the homeland that they believed guilty of repeated violations of constitutional rules.

In particular, such revolutionaries claimed the right to be regularly consulted in tax matters through an explicit and formal representation in the Parliament of London. Such approach was based on the well-known principle of 'no taxation

[23] 'When the legislative and executive powers are united in the same person, or in the same body of magistrates, there can be no liberty; because apprehensions may arise lest the same monarch or senate should enact tyrannical laws, to execute them in a tyrannical manner. Again, there is no liberty, if the judiciary power be not separated from the legislative and executive. Were it joined with the legislative, the life and liberty of the subject would be subject to arbitrary control; for the judge would then be legislator. Were it joined to the executive power, the judge might behave with violence and oppression', Montesquieu, 'Spirits of Laws (1748)', XI/6, in *The Complete Works of M. de Montesquieu* (London 1777) I, 199.

[24] ibid.

[25] 'Of the three powers abovementioned, the judiciary is, in some measure, next to nothing', ibid 204.

[26] ibid 208.

[27] 'His formulation of the separation of powers, the emphasis he placed on the judiciary as the preserve of the rule of law, his statement of legal liberty, and his insight that there is a complementary connection between the surrounding culture and the law, are of enduring moment' Tamanaha (n 6) 53.

without representation' whose origins may even be traced back to Chapter 12 of the *Magna Carta Libertatum*[28] in 1215.[29]

What were the violations attributed to the Government of King George III? American settlers believed that the imposition of taxes on settlers themselves was illegitimate because it was not discussed, nor approved by taxpayers but unilaterally decided by the Parliament of London where deputies representing them did not sit.

Therefore, if taxation according to the English Constitution was necessarily based on the approval of taxpayers, taxes such as the Stamp Act 1765 were to be consequently considered illegitimate. This is why the origin of the American Revolution, based on loyalty to British constitutional principles, is believed to represent a claim to the rule of law theorised by British legal and political culture. In reality, rather than a real revolution, the American one brought a reaffirmation of British constitutional principles.

Certainly, the innovative aspects of American constitutionalism should not be overlooked. First and most significant, we recall the convening of 'constitutional conventions' such as the Philadelphia Convention of 1787, charged with drafting the Constitution of the USA.

The convening of a constituent assembly did not appear in the eyes of American settlers as a violation of legality but as a reaffirmation of it. If, as stated in the Declaration of Independence of 1776, 'a long train of abuses and usurpations … evinces a design to reduce them under absolute despotism' it becomes necessary to 'throw off such Government, and to provide new Guards for their future security'.

Therefore, once again, the rule of law would have forced Americans to act to restore the legality violated by the despotic Government. Independence and the new Constitution would have established a new legality and a new Government.

In the publications of the revolutionary age, it is essential to remember the famous *The Federalist* by Alexander Hamilton (1755–1804), James Madison (1751–1836) and John Jay (1745–1829).

The objective of *The Federalist*'s writings was certainly to guarantee respect for citizens' rights of freedom, thanks to the adoption of the federal Constitution.

More specifically, Alexander Hamilton recalled the principles of the rule of law and stated that the Constitution was aimed 'to secure the public good and private rights against the danger' of the oppression of the majority 'and at the same time to preserve the spirit and form of popular government'.[30] The concern for the protection of minorities was evident, a protection which was at the same time to be reconciled with respect for the democratic principle of majority rule.

[28] Chapter 12: 'Nullum scutagium vel auxilium ponatur in regno nostro, nisi per commune consilium regni nostri, nisi ad corpus nostrum redimendum, et primogenitum filium nostrum militem faciendum, et ad filiam nostram primogenitam semel maritandam, et ad hec non fiat nisi racionabile auxilium; simili modo fiat de auxiliis de civitate London' (No scutage nor aid shall be imposed in our kingdom, unless by the common council of our kingdom; excepting to redeem our person, to make our eldest son a knight, and, once, to marry our eldest daughter, and not for these, unless a reasonable aid shall be demanded).

[29] As it was observed, 'Magna Carta symbolized the fact that law protected citizens against the king', Tamanaha (n 6) 26.

[30] J Madison, A Hamilton and J Jay, *The Federalist Papers* (Liberty Fund, 2001) n 10, 45.

In order to guarantee pluralism, *The Federalist* identified – as observed by Brian Tamanaha[31] – three fundamental principles: (1) representative democracy, considered an effective antidote to the populist tendencies of direct democracy; (2) the separation of powers that would act not only between federal powers (legislative, executive and judicial) but between state power and federal power; (3) finally, the *judicial review of legislation* considered as the fundamental guarantee for the correct functioning of the entire system. In this perspective, the task of the judges becomes 'to declare all acts contrary to the manifest tenor of the Constitution void'.[32]

Already in *The Federalist* there were principles that efficiently summarise the contribution of American constitutionalism in the evolution of the rule of law: 'a written constitution, democratic elections, explicitly articulated individual rights, the separation of powers, and judicial review of legislation'.[33] This is because it is necessary to ensure 'the government of laws, and not of men'.[34]

The following evolution of the principle in American legal culture was based on the reinterpretation and enrichment of new meanings of the constitutional provisions by the case law of the Supreme Court. This is, in particular, in relation to the principle of equality.

VIII. THE 'MANIFESTO' OF THE RULE OF LAW: THE FRENCH DECLARATION OF RIGHTS OF 1789

The French Revolution of 1789 represented the consecration and universalisation of the rule of law principle. The Declaration of the Rights of Man and of the Citizen of 26 August 1789 represented the real and proper 'manifesto' of the rule of law. This Declaration widely inspired the 1948 United Nations Universal Declaration of Human Rights.

Differently from the federal Constitution of the US and other North American legal texts of the time, whereby the contingent character and the specific and historical vindication were predominant, the French Declaration was addressed to all humanity in order to establish permanent and immutable principles and rules, based on natural law. It was therefore a text inspired by a universalistic aim. This explains the success, spread and longevity of the French Declaration.

From the first articles of the French Declaration the solemnity and universality of the words of the French ruler are clear: 'men are born and remain free and equal in rights' (article 1), 'the goal of any political association is the conservation of the natural and imprescriptible rights of man. These rights are liberty, property, safety and resistance against oppression' (article 2).

[31] Tamanaha (n 6) 54–55.

[32] 'Without this, all the reservations of particular rights or privileges would amount to nothing', *The Federalist*, n 78, 403.

[33] Tamanaha (n 6) 55.

[34] As affirmed by John Marshall on the basis of a definition by John Adams in order to sustain the need for the *judicial review of legislation*: 'the government of the United States has been emphatically termed *a government of laws, and not of men*. It will certainly cease to deserve this high appellation, if the laws furnish no remedy for the violation of a vested legal right': J Marshall, *Marbury v Madison*, 1 Cranch 137, 163 (1 February 1803).

The definition of liberty is very well known: 'liberty consists of doing anything which does not harm others: thus, the exercise of the natural rights of each man has only those borders which assure other members of the society the fruition of these same rights' (article 4).

The role of the law is strictly connected with liberty and represents the guarantee for the benefit of liberty itself. The law, which 'has the right to forbid only actions harmful to society. Anything which is not forbidden by the law cannot be impeded, and no one can be constrained to do what it does not order' (article 5) is defined according to article 6:

> The law is the expression of the general will. All the citizens have the right of contributing personally or through their representatives to its formation. It must be the same for all, either that it protects, or that it punishes. All the citizens, being equal in its eyes, are equally admissible to all public dignities, places, and employments, according to their capacity and without distinction other than that of their virtues and of their talents.

Deep within the rule of law, according to the liberal perspective that shares the French Revolution with the Anglo-American legal culture, the relationship between liberty, law and private property can be found. Therefore, individuals cannot be deprived of their liberty and property except according to a provision of law: 'No man can be accused, arrested nor detained but in the cases determined by the law, and according to the forms which it has prescribed' (article 7). Under criminal law perspective, the law should 'establish only penalties that are strictly and evidently necessary, and no one can be punished but under a law established and promulgated before the offense and legally applied' (article 8).

Based on the presumption of innocence, any kind of mistreatment towards prisoners was strictly prohibited: 'any man being presumed innocent until he is declared culpable if it is judged indispensable to arrest him, any rigor which would not be necessary for the securing of his person must be severely reprimanded by the law' (article 9). Freedom of speech and religion were granted: 'No one may be disquieted for his opinions, even religious ones, provided that their manifestation does not trouble the public order established by the law' (article 10). Also freedom of press was guaranteed: 'the free communication of thoughts and of opinions is one of the most precious rights of man: any citizen thus may speak, write, print freely, except to respond to the abuse of this liberty, in the cases determined by the law' (article 11).

Private property, defined as 'an inviolable and sacred right', shall not be violated except according to a provision of law and upon payment of a proper indemnity: 'no one can be deprived of private usage, if it is not when the public necessity, legally noted, evidently requires it, and under the condition of a just and prior indemnity' (article 17).

The rule of law according to the French Declaration of 1789 becomes synonymous with legality and constitutionalism. In this respect, article 16 provides the most important enunciation stating 'any society in which the guarantee of rights is not assured, nor the separation of powers determined, has no Constitution'.

Therefore, while according to the American version of the rule of law the protection of citizens' liberty is mainly entrusted to the jurisdiction and, first of all, to the Supreme Court due to the judicial review of legislation, in the French one,

Constitution and law identify themselves with liberty and represent the fundamental guarantee of freedom.

In the French perspective, the judge is entrusted with a secondary role, of mere 'syllogistic' application of the law, based on Montesquieu's view of the judge as the *bouche de la loi*. At the same time, the ruler emerges as an omnipotent and infallible legislator, since he is the position to interpret the general will (*volonté générale*). As stated by Jean-Jacques Rousseau, 'the general will is always right and tends to the public advantage'.[35]

IX. THE CRISIS OF THE RULE OF LAW

In the first half of the twentieth century, due to the spread of political liberalism, the rule of law became increasingly widespread. This can be linked to the theorisation of the *Rechtsstaat* in Germany and the *État de droit* in France that took place in those years.

It was a phenomenon of self-limitation of the state, whereby the functioning of public powers and relationships between citizens and public bodies were also governed by law, excluding any form of arbitrariness.

Such an approach represented the model for the modernisation of European legal systems.

It should be remembered that the rule of law was based on the formal affirmation of rights and liberties and it was in line with the individualistic and liberal needs that were predominant in this period.

With the spread of anti-individualist socialist and Catholic movements in the second half of the nineteenth century, the lack of 'negative liberties', intended as liberties granted to the individuals against the potential interference of public authorities, began to be highlighted.

How could a merely formal model that did not affect the substance of the existing inequalities guarantee the effectiveness of the rights of freedom?

The contrast with an abstract model spread and the liberal conceptions was criticised by conservative doctrines and by socialist and revolutionary thought.

The request for 'negative liberties' – as defined by Isaiah Berlin in the 1950s – was forcefully asserted.[36] Such freedoms were based on the concrete participation of citizens in the life of the society and aimed at the full realisation of themselves.[37]

[35] J-J Rousseau, *The Social Contract* (1762) II/3. As the French jurist Raimond Carré de Malberg (1861–1935) well noted, the law in the US does not have the same strength as the French one because it is not invested with that sacredness that it has in France, precisely because it does not represent the expression of the general will. In the US, only the Constitution is considered as work of the general will, while the ordinary laws 'are not the result of the work of the people, but a creation of the legislature, that is, the work of a simply constituted authority that exercises its competence by virtue of a delegation made by the people in the constitution', R Carré de Malberg, *La loi expression de la volonté générale* (Economica, 1931) 109.

[36] I Berlin, 'Two Concepts of Liberty' (1958) in *Four Essays On Liberty* (OUP, 1969) 118–72.

[37] As affirmed by Berlin, 'the positive sense of the word "liberty" derives from the wish on the part of the individual to be his own master', Berlin, ibid 131.

With the occurrence of the twentieth century and the advent of totalitarianisms, the pure liberal model ended, although the subsequent political and juridical evolution was still unknown.

X. EPILOGUE

The totalitarianisms of the twentieth century and the catastrophes of World War II imposed a general reflection and rethinking on legal systems and guarantees of fundamental freedoms.

The purely formalistic approach, suggested by the continental models of the *Rechtsstaat* and the *État de droit*, had proved to be dramatically useless. In that paradoxical perspective, even a totalitarian system (like Fascism or Nazism) would appear to be compliant to a *Rechtsstaat*, since it respected the legal rules that it had given itself. It appeared necessary to introduce new limits to the legislator and new international guarantees.

Therefore, in the face of the post-war rubble, the foundations of a new approach to the rule of law and the protection of freedoms were laid with the Universal Declaration of Human Rights of 1948. The history of the rule of law took a new and unknown path.

3

Rule of Law Metamorphoses in the Twentieth Century

LUIGI LACCHÈ*

I. HISTORY AND/OF RULE OF LAW

THE TWENTIETH CENTURY has been without a doubt a large and conflict-ridden stage on which to 'represent' issues, changes, challenges and new horizons of rule of law. The complexity and vastness of this panorama makes it impossible even to think of providing a comprehensive overview. I therefore cannot hope to do more than simply outline a number of key 'moments'. In particular, I would like to highlight three major 'phases'. I mean first of all the 'setting' of rule of law 'models' during the first decades of the twentieth century, then the experiences, in some countries, of the authoritarian/totalitarian regimes regarding the rule of law tradition, and finally the fashioning of our current conceptualisation of rule of law after World War II, interwoven as it has been with two main phenomena: the democratic/welfare state[1] and the Constitutional state.[2]

A preliminary consideration has to do with the semantic complexity[3] of the concepts, forms and rhetorics of the rule of law. Over time they have been marked by important transformations, but the coexistence and the tension between old and new meanings has certainly played an important role. Current politico-legal theory tends to emphasise the conceptual equivalences of the main historical paths (English and American Rule of Law, German *Rechtsstaat*, French *État de droit*, Italian *Stato di diritto* and so on), the aim being to consolidate a controversial 'common' core of principles, legal and political institutions. The English formula rule of Law – depending also on the dominant use of English language on a global scale – inevitably tends to level different historical and conceptual paths, thereby giving the impression that this category is genetically compact. Convergence of principles and linguistic

* University of Macerata.

[1] See for a general overview FG Castles et al (eds), *The Oxford Handbook of the Welfare State* (OUP, 2012) and B Greve (ed), *The Routledge Handbook of the Welfare State* (Routledge, 2013).

[2] See NW Barber, *The Constitutional State* (OUP, 2010).

[3] On this aspect see P Costa and D Zolo, 'Preface' in P Costa and D Zolo (eds), *The Rule of Law: History, Theory, and Criticism* (Springer, 2007) Part IX.

standardisation help to give rise to this effect. If we are to fully grasp the complexity of the category it is important to be aware of the wider background.

This approach will impart greater depth to the concept, but also enable us to better address current readings of the notion of rule of law, bringing out differences, tensions and even outright rejections. The universalisation of the rule of law[4] (based on the European/American matrix) has to deal with new perspectives – connected to other legal systems and regions in the world[5] – that tend to relativise the original sources, while acknowledging the existence of a common core (incorporating a series of principles and rights) and many 'local' variations. Substantive and formal approaches to rule of law, non-derogable or derogable rights are highly controversial matters.[6] The profound importance of the political ideal of the rule of law (a sort of compendium and the *logo*, perhaps, of an entire politico-constitutional civilisation) is perhaps matched by the sheer difficulty of saying precisely what it means and how it works. A historical approach can offer some useful insights and, indeed, help us to avoid a decontextualised perception.[7] In this sense, not only is there a fundamental gap between formal and substantive concepts but there is an equally important heuristic difference between the history and the theory of rule of law.

II. RULE OF LAW IN THE TWENTIETH CENTURY: A COMPLEX AND POLYSEMIC LEGACY

In 1921 the distinguished scholar and politician James Bryce, in his *Modern Democracies*, underlined the global tendency, in spite of concomitant problems and threats, to spread democracy, free government and rule of law. The end of World War I, with the victory of 'democracy' over autocratic regimes and the new liberal-democratic constitutions approved after 1919, bore witness to the growing success of the 'rule of law' discourse. 'We see backward populations, to which the very conception of political freedom had been unknown, summoned to attempt the tremendous task of creating self-governing institutions. China, India, and Russia contain, taken together, one half or more the population of the globe, so the problem of providing free government for them is the largest problem statesmanship has

[4] C May, *The Rule of Law: The Common Sense of Global Politics* (Edward Elgar Publishers, 2014).

[5] See R Gosalbo-Bono, 'The significance of the rule of law and its implications for the European Union and the United States' (2010) 72 *University of Pittsburgh Law Review* 280.

[6] See eg BZ Tamanaha, 'The Rule of Law for Everyone?' (2002) 55 *Current Legal Problems* 97; R Peerenboom, 'Varieties of Rule of Law: An Introduction and Provisional Conclusion' in R Peerenboom (ed), *Asian Discourses of Rule of Law: Theories and Implementation of Law in Twelve Asian Countries, France and the U.S.* (Routledge Curzon, 2004) 1; R Kleinfeld, 'Competing Definitions of the Rule of Law' in T Carothers (ed), *Promoting the Rule of Law Abroad: In Search of Knowledge* (Carnagie Endowment for International Peace, 2006); G Palombella and N Walker (eds), *Relocating the Rule of Law* (Hart Publishing, 2009); M Ellis, 'Toward a common ground definition of the rule of law incorporating substantive principles of justice' (2010) 72 *University of Pittsburgh Law Review* 191–215; A Bedner, 'An Elementary Approach to the Rule of Law' (2010) 2 *Hague Journal on the Rule of Law* 48–74, see https://core.ac.uk/download/pdf/15605763.pdf; Costa and Zolo (n 3) Parts IV, V and VI; C May and A Winchester (eds), *Handbook on the Rule of Law* (Edward Edgar Publishing, 2018) Part I Defining the rule of law.

[7] For some methodological aspects see BZ Tamanaha, *On the Rule of Law: History, Politics, Theory* (CUP, 2004); P Costa, 'The Rule of Law: An Historical Introduction' in Costa and Zolo (n 3) 73.

ever had to solve'.[8] New hopes were on the horizon. Bryce was right to identify this trend, within precisely that historical conjuncture. After World War I the rule of law seemed to extend its range. Yet shortly afterwards, between the 1920s and the 1930s, things changed with the rapid emergence of a number of different political regimes (URSS, Italy, Portugal, Austria, Hungary, Germany, Spain) which departed in various ways from the rule of law.

James Bryce – a colleague and a friend of Dicey – probably had in mind the evidence relating to British rule of law. At the beginning of the twentieth century rule of law served to identify a series of principles and institutions closely related to the history of modern constitutionalism. For a long time – one might say – such a 'thing' did indeed exist in British historical experience ('the law of the land', 'the rule of common law', 'government limited by law') but the category took on its current 'dimensions' in the second half of the nineteenth century, when this historico-constitutional experience better found in Albert Venn Dicey[9] the Victorian legal theorist – influenced by the Irish professor and politician William Edward Hearn – the main architect of the formula rule of law 'canonised' in his highly successful book *Introduction to the Study of the Law of the Constitution*, published for the first time in 1885 and then amended and expanded in several later editions. Alexis De Tocqueville had found it hard to know quite how to describe the 'real significance of the "Rule, supremacy, or predominance of law" as "one of the most marked peculiarities of English life"'.[10] So, according to Dicey, it was therefore a pressing matter to 'determine precisely what we mean by such expressions when we apply them to the British constitution'. Rule of law – as a characteristic of the English Constitution – encompassed at least 'three distinct though kindred conceptions'.[11] Dicey observes that this expression is first of all contrary to arbitrary power, to the effect that 'no man is punishable or can be lawfully made to suffer in body or goods except for a distinct breach of law established in the ordinary legal manner before the ordinary Courts of the land';[12] secondly, that 'every man, whatever be his rank or condition, is subject to the ordinary law of the realm and amenable to the jurisdiction of the ordinary tribunals';[13] finally, the third meaning concerns the fact 'that the constitution is pervaded by the rule of law on the ground that the general principles of the constitution (as for example the right to personal liberty, or the right of public meeting), are with us the result of judicial decisions determining the rights of private persons in particular cases brought before the Courts'.[14]

[8] J Bryce, *Modern Democracies* (The McMillan Company, 1921) I, see https://oll.libertyfund.org/titles/2084#Bryce_1427-01_70.

[9] See HW Arndt, 'The Origins of Dicey's Concept of the "Rule of Law"' (1957) 31 *Australian Law Journal* 117–23; RA Cosgrove, *The Rule of Law: Albert Venn Dicey Victorian Jurist* (The University of North Carolina Press, 1980) 66; BJ Hibbitts, 'The Politics of Principle: Albert Venn Dicey and the Rule of Law' (1994) 23 *Anglo-American Law Review* 1; Costa and Zolo (n 3); E Santoro, 'The Rule of Law and the "Liberties of the English": The Interpretation of Albert Venn Dicey' in Costa and Zolo (n 3) 73; JWF Allison, 'Turning the rule of law into an English constitutional idea' in May and Winchester (n 6) 167.

[10] AV Dicey, *Lectures Introductory to the Study of the Law of the Constitution* (The Oxford Edition of Dicey, I, JWF Allison (ed)) (OUP, 2013) 97 (187 10th edn).

[11] ibid 97 (188 10th edn).

[12] ibid.

[13] ibid 100 (193 10th edn).

[14] ibid 115 (196 10th edn).

Dicey – if we follow the evolution of his thought and of the various editions of *The Law of the Constitution* – had already recognised, as early as 1885, 'that in most European countries the rule of law is now nearly as well established as in England'[15] but nevertheless there is 'something' that foreign observers – even those as acute as the viscount De Tocqueville – could not altogether grasp. The English Constitution's rule of law was 'different', Dicey insisted, and for several reasons, but crucially perhaps because 'there runs through the English constitution that inseparable connection between the means of enforcing a right, and the right to be enforced which is the strength of judicial legislation'.[16] In England – in marked contrast to other countries – constitutional rules 'are not the source but the consequence of the rights of individuals, as defined and enforced by the Courts … thus the constitution is the result of the ordinary law of the land'.[17] Dicey's quarrel with French *droit administratif* underpinned his sense of the cardinal differences between the English and the continental understanding of 'rule of law'.[18]

The English Constitution rests on two pillars: the sovereignty of Parliament and the rule of law. They together withstood each and every attempt to assert arbitrary executive power. The political supremacy of the King in Parliament and rule of law ensured the balanced development of the British Constitution. Dicey had little or no confidence in 'abstract' written and rigid Constitutions. For him it was an 'easy' matter to declare solemnly rights and freedoms but this did not guarantee their efficacy in the concrete life of peoples, 'preferring [as he did] to rely on the slow, incremental process of common law decision-making, judge by judge, case by case'.[19]

According to this vision, the notable characteristic of the American 'variant' of rule of law ought properly to be regarded as its 'osmosis' with the judiciary and judge-made-law. Judges were there as the guardians of the written Constitution, thanks first to the invention and then the implementation of the judicial review of legislation. Despite such differences, the culture of judicial protection was a dominant factor shared on both sides of the Atlantic. Judicial interpretation and legal culture placed the principle of legality within a common framework and helped to maintain a considerable distance from the *Rechtsstaat* tradition.

At the beginning of the twentieth century this distinction was still full of meaning. Indeed, I believe that a common core of liberal-constitutional principles is not sufficient to establish an overlap between rule of law and the *Rechtsstaat*. The differences are substantial and have considerable consequences.[20] Subsequent developments – dating from the aftermath of World War II – cannot be invoked to establish

[15] ibid 98 (189 10th edn).

[16] ibid 117 (199 10th edn).

[17] ibid 199 (203 10th edn).

[18] On the development of Dicey's thought regarding rule of law and *droit administratif* and its enduring effects see more widely S Cassese, 'Albert Venn Dicey e il diritto amministrativo' (1990) 19 *Quaderni fiorentini per la storia del pensiero giuridico* 5–82.

[19] T Bingham, *The Rule of Law* (Allen Lane, 2010) 5. Dicey had also developed very clearly his idea of the English Constitution in the manuscript '[General] Characteristics of Existing English Constitutionalism' (1897) and in the manuscript 'Historical Constitutions and NonHistorical Constitutions' (1900), in AV Dicey, *Lectures on Comparative Constitutionalism* (The Oxford Edition of Dicey, II, ed by JWF Allison) 17–28, 171–91.

[20] Compare, for contemporary insights, CL Blaau, 'The Rechtsstaat Idea Compared with the Rule of Law as a Paradigm for Protecting Rights' (1990) 107 *South African Law Journal* 76–96; JY Morin, 'The Rule of Law and the Rechtsstaat Concept: A Comparison' in E McWhinney, J Zaslove and W Wolf

the previous existence of a common core.[21] This is one of the more important consequences of the 'lesson' from history. Here differences are more important than identities and similarities.[22]

In Germany the neologism and the autochthonous formula *Rechtsstaat* took shape over several decades. The liberal concept after 1848 was inserted, thanks to the extraordinary development of public law doctrine, within a framework having political ends (to establish a 'compromise' between constitutional liberalism and the *Monarchisches Prinzip* apparatus).[23] In the relationship between state and law, the former became the pivot of the system. The law of the state is the principal pillar, and not the judicial courts' interpretation/creation of law, by contrast with the UK and the US. The *Rechtsstaat* 'universe'[24] – state under the rule of law[25] – was based, irrespective of the different variations, on the development of the state's self-limitation theory and 'subjective rights'. This state-centric vision was limited and supported by the law, but the protection of individual rights and freedoms was guaranteed in the main by the internal machinery of the legislative power and the administrative state (administrative jurisdiction). At the beginning of the twentieth century and at least up until the collapse of imperial Germany, the *Rechtsstaat* was at the same time the most impressive achievement of German legal doctrine and the representation of a special link between state and law regarded as a liberal way of achieving a balance between the power of the state and individual rights and property. The British historical idea of Constitution – more than the rule of law as such – served as a bridge with the liberal jurists of Continental Europe. In this sense there was the possibility of creating in Europe a common framework[26] based on the supremacy of the 'neutral' state-nation law over the political supremacy of the people's sovereignty, on constitutional balance mechanisms and on the idea of a more effective and concrete protection of rights.

Rechtsstaat must be seen in connection with the evolution of the French *État de droit* or the Italian *Stato di diritto*. Any specificities that may exist do not preclude the possibility of considering these experiences within a more general interpretative model. The transformation process from the *État légal* to the *État de droit* – to summarise what was fundamentally at stake in the French debate[27] – shows a broader

(eds), *Federalism-in-the-Making: Contemporary Canadian and German Constitutionalism, National and Transnational* (Kluwer, 1992) 60–86; D Mockle, 'L'État de droit et la théorie de la rule of law' (1994) 35 *Les cahiers du droit* 4, 823–904; R Grote, 'Rule of Law, Rechtsstaat and État de droit' in C Starck (ed), *Constitutionalism, Universalism, and Democracy* (Nomos, 1999) 269; NW Barber, 'The Rechtsstaat and the Rule of Law' (2003) 53 *University Toronto Law Journal* 443.

[21] In this way eg N MacCormick, 'Der Rechtsstaat und die rule of law' (1984) 39 *Juristen Zeitung* 67 and H Hofmann, 'Geschichtlichkeit und Universalitätsanspruch des Rechtsstaats' (1996) 65 *Archiv für Rechts- und Sozialphilosophie* 9. See the observations of G Gozzi, 'Rechtsstaat and individual rights in German constitutional history' in Costa and Zolo (n 3) 237.

[22] See M Loughlin, *Foundations of Public Law* (OUP, 2010).

[23] On this evolution see Gozzi (n 21); Costa (n 3); Gosalbo-Bono (n 5).

[24] O Jouanjan (ed), *Figures de l'État de droit. Le Rechtsstaat dans l'histoire intellectuelle et constitutionnelle de l'Allemagne* (Presses Universitaires de Strasbourg, 2001).

[25] M Stolleis, *A History of Public Law in Germany 1914–1945* (OUP, 2004) 7.

[26] See M Fioravanti, 'Lo Stato di diritto come forma di Stato. Notazioni preliminari sulla tradizione europeo-continentale' in R Gherardi and G Gozzi (eds), *Saperi della borghesia e storia dei concetti fra Otto e Novecento* (il Mulino, 1995) 161–77.

[27] MJ Redor, *De l'État légal à l'État de droit. L'evolution des conceptions de la doctrine publiciste française, 1879–1914* (Economica, 1992). For a wide comparison, see L Heuschling, *État de droit, Rechtsstaat, Rule of Law* (Dalloz, 2002).

trend under the aegis of public law scholars – in which we find a juridical reflection on the limits to popular sovereignty, parliamentary omnipotence and the tyranny of the majority.

III. A TURNING POINT: RULE OF LAW IN THE COURSE OF THE 1920S

Rule of law during the nineteenth century mirrored a liberal vision dominated by a 'simple' idea: the state prevails over all that is public, the individual holds sway over property and contractual freedom. These two separated spheres saturated the whole social space. Nevertheless behind this image or facade a different reality was forming very quickly, following industrial take-off, economic changes, social challenges. While jurists were building the *Rechtsstaat*, societies were for their part becoming more and more complex. Social and economic associations, mutual aid companies, trade unions, working class parties began to 'fill' the space between state and 'atomistic' individuals. This pluralistic constitution of society required of the state that it provide answers and offer the first welfare solutions. Three key concepts – collectivism, solidarity, legal pluralism – allowed jurists to develop a new approach to the rule of law. World War I was an extraordinary catalyst of unanticipated issues and challenges. After the end of hostilities the germs of change, already visible between the nineteenth and twentieth centuries, became evident to all. The concept of rule of law could not be left untouched.[28] The European debate on the 'crisis' of the modern state was one of the aspects of this challenge: how was one to manage the 'collective' dimension, democracy and the masses without breaking down this 'wonderful creation of law'?[29] The Bolshevik revolution of 1917 heralded new horizons, while the Weimar Constitution in 1919 was the first controversial response to the post-war reorganisation of the rule of law in a socio-centric manner. In general, *Rechtsstaat* was required to keep abreast of the times, through social and political reform.

The 1920s represent a very important turning point both for 'reforming' the *Rechtsstaat* according to the new democratic and social constitutions and, conversely, for giving rise to the new 'totalitarian' idea of the state.

In that same period Hans Kelsen made an important contribution to the constitutional transformation of *Rechtsstaat*. At the base there was the traditional relationship between state and law but legislation was now no longer the centre of the system, the 'gold standard' of supremacy. It was but one level, one of the procedural mechanisms in the setting up of the legal order. Kelsen's *Stufenbautheorie* and the centrality of the Constitution seen as the apex of the state, the higher law, allowed for both legislative and administrative powers to be controlled by a judicial body, breaking the myth of the untouchable sovereignty of the legislative power. This reflection considered and

[28] HS Jones, *The French State in Question. Public Law and Political Argument in the Third Republic* (CUP, 1993); C Laborde, *Pluralist Thought and the State in Britain and France, 1900–25* (Palgrave Macmillan, 2000); for Germany M Stolleis, *Origins of the German Welfare State Social Policy in Germany to 1945* (Springer, 2013); for Italy M Fioravanti, *La costituzione democratica. Modelli e itinerari del diritto pubblico del ventesimo secolo* (Giuffrè, 2018).

[29] This is a famous sentence of Santi Romano in *Lo Stato moderno e la sua crisi*, an inaugural speech given at the University of Pisa (Tipografia Vannucchi, 1909) 8.

served to insert into the general theory of the constitutional state the oldest problem of the continental modern state, namely, the 'position' of judicial power within the state organisation. 'Mediocrity of the judge, infallibility of the law' had been the ideal slogan of the *État légal*, according to the French formula, in the aftermath of the Revolution. During the nineteenth century the rule of law in continental Europe was intended to be more an *État légal* than a fully equipped *État de droit*. An Italian liberal constitutional law scholar, Attilio Brunialti, wrote in 1870 that the hallmark of Anglo-Saxon nations was precisely the rule of law. They gave the judiciary an extension '[…] which in the eyes of the continentals violated that absolute separation: it is in homage to this truth, that the Anglo-Saxon recognises this power, the only interpreter of the constitution, and the administration is subjected to the power of the courts in the same way as the lowliest citizen: the conclusion is that England and the United States made the judiciary a real political power'.[30]

This line of thought featured only marginally in the nineteenth century debate. The idea of the centrality and supremacy of law remained firm. Dicey's politico-constitutional analysis of the law of the Constitution in England based on judicial legislation and the enforcement of the courts did much to define the specificity of rule of law. The American experience of the judicial review of legislation was the new graft on to the Anglo-Saxon tree of rule of law. But these two dimensions, different though sharing one and the same legal culture, were not able between the nineteenth and the twentieth century to alter the predominant, legicentric (at times attenuated by historicity and by constitutional liberalism), vision of the European *Rechtsstaat*.[31] A deep-rooted mistrust of the power of the judges still made itself felt despite the attempts to refine the *État de droit* framework, as for example in the case of Raymond Carré de Malberg, at least so far as *Sollen* was concerned.[32]

In Kelsen, judicial review is the consequence of a novel concept of constitutional *Rechtstaat* based on a system's hierarchical structure. Kelsen's theory, elaborated

[30] A Brunialti, 'La funzione politica del potere giudiziario' (1870) V *Archivio giuridico* 401. cf L Lacchè, 'Il potere giudiziario come "potere politico" in Attilio Brunialti' in L Lacche, *History & Constitution. Developments in European Constitutionalism: the comparative experience of Italy, France, Switzerland and Belgium (19th–20th centuries)* (Vittorio Klostermann, 2016) 439. Tocqueville's echo is evident: 'So the Americans have given their courts an immense political power; but by forcing them to challenge laws only by judicial means, they have greatly diminished the dangers of this power', *Democracy in America* (Liberty Fund, 2012) Vol 1, Ch 6 *Of Judicial Power in the United Stated and its Action in Political Society* 174.

[31] For the French debate see A Laquièze, 'Le contrôle de constitutionnalité de la loi aux Etats-Unis vu par les penseurs libéraux français du XIXème siècle' (2002) 4 *Giornale di storia costituzionale* 155–71.

[32] See G Bacot, *Carré de Malberg et l'origine de la distinction entre souveraineté du peuple et souveraineté nationale* (Edition du CNRS, 1985); Redor (n 27); O Beaud, 'La souveraineté dans la "Contribution à la théorie générale de l'État" de Carré de Malberg' (1994) 5 *Revue du droit public et de la science politique en France et à l'étranger* 1264 ff; C Schönberger, 'De la souverainété nationale à la souveraineté du peuple. Mutations et continuité de la théorie de l'Etat de Carré de Malberg' (1996) 4 *Revue française de l'histoire des idées politiques* 297–316; C Schönberger, 'Penser l'État dans l'Empire et la République: critique et réception de la conception juridique de l'État de Laband chez Carré de Malberg' in O Beaud and P Wachsmann (eds), *La science juridique française et la science juridique allemande de 1870 à 1918*, (Presses Universitaires de Strasbourg, 1997) 255–71; J Hummel, *Le constitutionnalisme allemand (1815–1918): le modèle allemand de la monarchie limitée* (Puf, 2002) 123–27; E Maulin, 'Carré de Malberg et le droit constitutionnel de la Révolution française' (2002) 328 *Annales historiques de la Révolution française* 5–27; P Brunet, *Vouloir pour la nation. Le concept de représentation dans la théorie de l'état* (L.G.D.J, 2004); A Laquièze, 'État de droit and National Sovereignty' in Costa and Zolo (n 3) 261.

also through his experience as a prominent 'drafter' of the Austrian Constitution of 1920,[33] made the Constitution the new sovereign and the Constitutional Court the 'brand' of the new figure of the state. He inserted certain pillars of the 'traditional' *Rechtsstaat* into a hierarchically structured system oriented through new concepts.[34] Constitutional justice was the 'missing piece' serving to really render Constitution – and rule of law – wholly binding. It completed the architecture of the *Rechtsstaat* and at the same time it fulfilled – at least formally – a very important political purpose. If parliamentary laws were 'constitutional' (or otherwise) they could offer minorities concrete protection against the liberticidal attempts of the majority. 'The specific constitutional form, which ordinarily consists in the fact that the revision of the constitution requires a reinforced majority, signifies that some fundamental issues can be resolved only with the agreement of the minority; the simple majority, at least on some matters, does not have the right to impose its will on the minority, in the sphere of guaranteed constitutional rights. Any minority – of class, religious or national – whose interests are in any way protected by the constitution has an eminent interest in the constitutionality of the laws'.[35]

IV. MISUSING THE 'RULE OF LAW'

Kelsen, during the 1920s, sowed the seeds but it would seem fair to say that in certain contexts political circumstances and economic crisis served to weaken or even arrest the foundational process of the new democratic constitutional state. Looking at the evolution of democracies, James Bryce – as I mentioned above – underlined in 1921 the possibility of taking into consideration this positive trend, but the 1920s were not destined to go down in history as the generalised and ultimate achievement of rule of law, beset as the latter was by various tensions and even threats to its very existence. In this context Italy with its *Stato liberale di diritto* (liberal *Rechtsstaat*) turned out to be an important laboratory. The Fascist movement – against the strong advance of the workers' movement and liberal political fragmentation – affirmed the need to 'save' the foundations of the national state, even resorting for this purpose to intimidation and violence. In the first years – at least until Matteotti's murder and the beginning of 1925 – many people belonging to the liberal ruling class thought that fascism could be a movement compatible with the Italian *Rechtsstaat* tradition. While the soviet regime, after the revolution, was seen as a radical, new form of state born after the collapse of the tsarist autocracy, the Fascist regime became a paradigm for the passage from the rule of law to a dictatorship resting on a majoritarian will.

[33] Constitutional justice was his 'maximum personal contribution' (*Hans Kelsen zum Gedenken*, Schriftenreihe des Hans Kelsen Instituts, 1 (Wien, Europaverlag, 1974) 50) to this text. The Austrian Constitutional Court, of which Kelsen was also a judge, was at the time an institution unique in Europe. cf G Schmitz, 'The Constitutional Court of the Republic of Austria 1918–1929' (2003) 2 *Ratio Juris* 240–56; G Bongiovanni, 'The rule of law and constitutional justice in Austria. Hans Kelsen's contribution' in Costa and Zolo (n 3) 292; S Lagi, 'Hans Kelsen and the Austrian Constitutional Court (1918–1929)' (2012) 9 *Revista Co-herencia* 16, 273–95.

[34] See Costa (n 3) 115.

[35] H Kelsen, 'La garantie jurisdictionelle de la Constitution' (1928) XXXV *Revue de droit publique et science politique* 202.

This specious argument that Fascism had won power through democratic elections – so that these latter, representing the majority of the Italian nation, might serve as a sort of bill of indemnity for the violences perpetrated – was often recalled to highlight how rule of law could be exploited to overcome the rule of law itself.

Not by chance Fascism was marked by a mass militia-party of revolutionary nationalism able to achieve and keep power illegally and to abolish a number of institutions of rule of law (parliamentary democracy itself, the separation of powers, political freedoms[36]) but conserving ambiguously a set of relationships with certain elements of the previous and much reviled liberal state.[37] The rise and affirmation of Fascism produced – according to one of the major 'architects' of the regime, Alfredo Rocco – the *transformation of the State*[38] but without a formal, decisive, break with the liberal state.[39] In the first decades of the twentieth century the *Rechtsstaat* concept was already set to change: *democratic* and *social* were becoming the new dimensions of the state facing legal pluralism and social conflicts. As regards several different aspects 'fascist state' and *Stato di diritto* found themselves coexisting – depending upon the various phases through the regime passed – in the accounts given by the great majority of scholars and in the wider public debate.[40]

The main strategy employed by the public law doctrine, more or less 'integrated' as it was into the fascist institutions, was above all else to ensure a 'compatibility' between the notion of *Stato di diritto* and the fascist state. To achieve this aim it was necessary to minimise or refuse the liberal, atomistic, dimension in terms of the separation of powers, public liberties and political pluralism. The purely formal principle of legality, and an 'emphasis' on the authoritarian organisation of corporatism and the 'administrative constitution' of the state, made it possible to conceive a fascist *Stato di diritto* subjected to the concept of the ethical state,[41] yet at the same time distinguished from the *Rechtsstaat* rooted in the nineteenth century but also from the German propensity to overcome – after the Nazi seizure of power – the boundaries of liberal individualism through the category of *Volkgemeinschaft* (People's community).

Nevertheless, before the advent of Nazism, the controversy between Kelsen and Schmitt on 'The guardian of the constitution' already illustrated the opposing arguments deployed to legitimate or repudiate the dismantling of the liberal rule of law.[42]

[36] See E Gentile, *The Struggle for Modernity. Nationalism, Futurism, and Fascism* (Praeger, 2003).

[37] S Panunzio, *Lo Stato di diritto* (Il solco, 1922).

[38] A Rocco, *La trasformazione dello Stato. Dallo Stato Liberale allo Stato fascista* (La Voce, 1927) 7.

[39] L Lacchè, 'The Shadow of the Law: the Special Tribunal for the Defence of the State between Justice and Politics in the Italian Fascist Period' in S Skinner (ed), *Fascism and Criminal Law: History, Theory, Continuity* (Hart Publishing, 2015) 15–33.

[40] Fundamental are the works of P Costa, *Lo stato immaginario. Metafore e paradigmi nella cultura giuridica italiana fra Ottocento e Novecento* (Giuffrè, 1986); P Costa, 'Lo "stato totalitario": un campo semantico nella giuspubblicistica del fascismo' (1999) XXVIII *Quaderni fiorentini per la storia del pensiero giuridico*, on the relationships between '*stato totalitario*' and '*stato di diritto*' 75–90; see also M Caravale, *Una incerta idea. Stato di diritto e diritti di libertà nel pensiero italiano tra età liberale e fascismo* (il Mulino, 2016).

[41] Costa (n 3) 127–29.

[42] See L Vinx (ed), *The Guardian of the Constitution: Hans Kelsen and Carl Schmitt on the Limits of Constitutional Law* (CUP, 2015); O Beaud and P Pasquino (eds), *La Controverse sur 'Le guardien de la constitution' et la justice constitutionnelle. Kelsen contre Schmitt* (Éditions Panthéon-Assas, 2007); D Diner and M Stolleis (eds), *Hans Kelsen and Carl Schmitt: A Juxtaposition* (Bleicher Verlag, 1999).

As we have seen, the judicial review of laws became for Hans Kelsen the new pillar of the pluralistic constitutional state, transforming and 'incorporating' a number of liberal state foundations. For Carl Schmitt, however, the nineteenth-century rule of law was no longer able to lead back to political unity the conflicting pluralism of the legislative state (the Weimar Republic was, finally, the negative paradigm) and it was necessary therefore to found the 'total' administrative state (*der Totale Staat*).[43] *Rechtsstaat* was an outdated political concept now filed away as something from the past. For Schmitt all political concepts, having a polemical meaning, were bound to a concrete situation: *Rechtsstaat* was at the beginning of 1930s simply 'crap', a sort of generic passepartout evoked to defame its alleged 'enemies'.

In the German debate we can see highlighted the radical and rapid transition to a new horizon, that of the *Führerstaat* seen as a political regime grounded on the fundamental bond between *Führer* and *Volk*. Conservative authors like Otto Koellreutter[44] sought to affirm that *Rechtsstaat* – once detached from its bourgeois origins – was a concept that was still meaningful but in the sense of a national-social state, linked to the *Obrigkeitsstaat* (authoritarian state), whereas Carl Schmitt for his part emphasised the radical transformation of the legislative state in favour of a new 'state of justice' – based on the administrative bureaucracy – able to affirm the 'concrete order' of the people embodied by the *Führer*:[45]

> The quarrel over the question of whether the new State should remain a Rechtsstaat was thus a tactical skirmish during the first phase of the consolidation of the regime. It took place not only between national conservatives and 'revolutionaries', but also between those National Socialists who were demanding the complete elimination of the old state, and those who believed that tactical lip service to the 'Rechtsstaat' was (still) called for.[46]

The debates on the *Stato di diritto* in fascist Italy and on the *Rechtsstaat* in pre-Nazi and Nazi Germany[47] manifest different strategies in abusing the semantic and rhetorical ambiguity of those concepts.[48] Both references fulfilled several different functions in dealing with the legacy of the common core of rule of law: separation between state and society, individualism, parliamentarianism, protection of rights,

[43] C Schmitt, 'Die Wendung zum totalen Staat' in (1931) December *European Review*, then in *Positionen und Begriffe im Kampf Weimar – Genf – Versailles 1919–1939*, 4th edn (Duncker & Humblot, 2014).

[44] O Koellreutter, *Grundriss der allgemeinen Staatslehre* (Mohr, 1933). See also H Lange, *Vom Gesetzesstaat zum Rechtsstaat* (Mohr, 1933).

[45] See P Caldwell, 'National Socialism and Constitutional Law: Carl Schmitt, Otto Koellreutter and the Debate over the Nature of the Nazi state, 1933–1937' (1994) 16 *Cardozo Law Review* 399–427; O Beaud, 'La critique de l'État de droit chez Carl Schmitt' (1993) 24 *Cahiers de philosophie politique et juridique de l'Université de Caen, L'État de droit*, 111–25; W Schuller, 'Der Rechtsstaat bei Carl Schmitt. Der Einbruch der Zeit in das Spiel' in R Morsey et al (eds), *Staat, Politik, Verwaltung in Europa. Gedächtnisschrift für Roman Schnur* (Duncker & Humblot, 1997) 117–33; C Hilger, *Rechtsstaatsbegriffe im Dritten Reich. Eine Strukturanalyse* (Tübingen, 2003) 33 ff.; R Car, 'Rivoluzione nazionale e Stato di diritto nel pensiero di Otto Koellreutter' (2013) 1 *Sociologia* 29–4.

[46] Stolleis (n 25) 351. See also M Stolleis, *The Law under the Swastika. Studies on Legal History in Nazi Germany* (University of Chicago Press, 1998) 87 ff; 102 ff.; M Stolleis, 'Que signifiait la querelle autour de l'État de droit sous le Troisième Reich?' in Jouanjan (ed) (n 24) 373–83.

[47] AJ De Grand, *Fascist Italy and Nazi Germany. The 'Fascist' Style of Rule* (Routledge, 1995).

[48] cf A De Martino, 'I rapporti tra la dottrina italiana e quella tedesca durante il fascismo intorno allo stato di diritto' (2018) 1 *Rivista AIC*.

division of powers. The Fascist *Stato di diritto* was the 'mirror' of a composite political-constitutional regime, a sort of intricate juxtaposition, a mosaic, of various authoritarian and totalitarian institutions and experiences. Paradoxically, the Fascist *Stato di diritto* – a 'performative' oxymoron – became, to a greater extent in fact than the Nazi experience, a 'model' or at least a reference point for other, very different, authoritarian regimes.[49]

The principle of legality was a 'patina' useful for those concerned not to seem to have broken radically with the liberal-authoritarian legacy. In the criminal law and justice system the difference between the two regimes was all too evident. The Nazi scrapping of the principle '*nullum crimen sine lege*' – replaced by that of '*nullum crimen sine poena*' – and of the prohibitions upon non-retroactivity of the law and analogy disclosed a radical break with the liberal rule of law tradition within the new Führerstaat framework.[50] In Italy, Fascism did not follow the extremist path of Nazi Germany. Although in 1939 legal philosopher Giuseppe Maggiore proposed to subvert systematically the principle of legality,[51] his remained an isolated case. According to Piero Calamandrei, Nazism and Fascism both attacked the rule of law. The Nazis openly destroyed legality, while the Italian fascists set out to falsify it.[52] The difference lies in the relative intensity and scope of the action taken. So, after the fall of Fascism some criminal law scholars elaborated the so-called 'brake theory', arguing that they had been able, thanks to the adoption of the technical-legal approach, to limit the 'Fascist orientation' and to safeguard the 'liberal core' of Italian liberal penal doctrine and hence the rule of law.[53] For this reason it was sufficient, they argued, to remove the Fascist patina in order to recover the liberal background and the corresponding legislation. However, the 'brake' theory seems unconvincing, as does the attempt of many legal scholars who were active during the Fascist period to entrench themselves in a supposed position of 'neutrality' by virtue of their having purportedly adhered to the technical-legal approach. Such arguments referred to the kinds of legal formalism adopted by Rocco's codes, which can be regarded as a sort of shelter behind which they sought to hide, in order not to be tainted by the wrongful policies of the regime.

[49] SU Larsen (ed), *Fascism outside Europe: the European impulse against domestic conditions in the diffusion of global fascism* (Social Science Monographs; New York, Distributed by Columbia University Press, 2001); C Iordachi (ed), *Comparative fascist studies: new perspectives* (Routledge, 2010).

[50] See G Werle, *Justiz-Strafrecht und polizeiliche Verbrechensbekämpfung im Dritten Reich* (de Gruyter, 1989).

[51] With the following definition: 'Every fact that offends the authority of the state is also a crime, and is worthy of punishment according to the spirit of the Fascist revolution and the will of the Duce, the sole interpreter of the will of the Italian people. This fact, unless provided for by a specific criminal law, is punished according to analogy'.

[52] P Calamandrei, 'La crisi della legalità' (1944) in P Calamandrei, *Costituzione e leggi di Antigone. Scritti e discorsi politici* (La Nuova Italia, 1996) 6–7.

[53] P Piasenza, 'Tecnicismo giuridico e continuità dello Stato: il dibattito sulla riforma del codice penale e della legge di pubblica sicurezza' (1979) X 3 *Politica del diritto* 290 ff; M Sbriccoli, 'Le mani nella pasta e gli occhi al cielo. La penalistica italiana negli anni del fascismo' (1999) 28 II *Quaderni fiorentini per la storia del pensiero giuridico moderno*, 821–22, 829, 843, 846; L Lacchè, '"Sistemare il terreno e sgombrare le macerie". Gli anni della "costituzione provvisoria": alle origini del discorso sulla riforma della legislazione e del codice di procedura penale (1943–1947)' in L Garlati (ed), *L'inconscio inquisitorio. L'eredità del codice Rocco nella cultura processualpenalistica italiana* (Giuffrè, 2010) 271–304.

It is more evident that the 'constitution' of the Third Reich can be identified with its rapid settling upon a racist 'regime of injustice' (*Recht im Unrecht*), despite some elements of continuity with the *Rechtsstaat*.[54] In Fascist Italy, contrary to some appearances, the principle of legal certainty did not perform the same functions that it would have done in a liberal-democratic legal system. The principle dictates that one cannot be subjected to penal sanctions unless these are previously provided for by law. During the Fascist regime, however, laws were promulgated without wide, democratic parliamentary debate, but instead as the will of a single party, the Fascist Party, which since the beginning of the dictatorship had trampled on every kind of political opposition. This then was the 'law' – legal, but not legitimate – to which the principle of legality referred.[55]

V. POST–WORLD WAR II CONSTITUTIONAL RULE OF LAW: A NEW PHASE, OLD ISSUES

The vicissitudes of the interwar rule of law had laid bare the various shortcomings of the 'wonderful creation of law' (Santi Romano). Totalitarian and authoritarian regimes had been able to take advantage of the 'darker sides'[56] of the refined architecture of the *Rechtsstaat*. The liberal state under the rule of law was transformed into the dictatorial 'dual state',[57] showing thereby how mythical the 'monolithic' principle of legality actually was. In the liberal orders the twin track of rule/exception, law/discretion played already a 'constitutive' role, permitting the structural coexistence of legal and discretionary prerogative measures.[58] The forms of duality or hybridity made it possible to falsify or misuse the rule of law tenets. Positive formal law did in fact prove unable to resist a range of authoritarian measures. On the contrary, the principle of legality was 'used' to 'legitimate' – on the basis of a mass consensus[59] – violence, political repression and the abominable promulgation and implementation of racial laws.

The abyss into which the rule of law fell during the interwar decades occasioned the formulation of at least two main issues after World War II: first of all that of the

[54] 'It may seem paradoxical to speak of law and despotism in the same breath, for to do so raises the dilemma of the existence of "law" in a system that is on the whole "unlawful" and "unjust" or at least commits many unlawful acts […]' (Stolleis, *The Law Under the Swastika* (n 46) 5).

[55] G Neppi Modona and M Pelissero, 'La politica criminale durante il fascismo' in L Violante (ed), *Storia d'Italia*, Annali XII, La criminalità (Einaudi, 1997) 831; G Neppi Modona, 'Principio di legalità e giustizia penale nel periodo fascista' (2007) XXXVI *Quaderni fiorentini per la storia del pensiero giuridico* 983; MA Cattaneo, 'Il diritto penale tra fascismo e stato di diritto' in F Lanchester and I Staff (eds), *Lo stato di diritto democratico dopo il fascismo ed il nazionalsocialismo* (Giuffrè, 1999) 275.

[56] C Joerges and N Singh Ghaleigh (eds), *Darker Legacies of Law in Europe: the Shadow of National Socialism and Fascism over Europe and its Legal Traditions* (Hart Publishing, 2003); K Hite and P Cesarini (eds), *Authoritarian Legacies and Democracy in Latin America and Southern Europe* (University of Notre Dame Press, 2004); A Costa Pinto and L Morlino (eds), *Dealing with the legacy of the Authoritarianism. The 'Politics of the Past' in Southern European Democracies* (Routledge, 2011).

[57] E Fraenkel, *The Dual State. A Contribution to the Theory of Dictatorship* (OUP, 1941).

[58] Lacchè (n 39). For France see MO Baruch, 'Vichy and the Rule of Law' (2008) 6 *Bulletin du Centre de recherche français à Jérusalem*, see https://journals.openedition.org/bcrfj/2992.

[59] S Skinner (ed), *Ideology and Criminal Law. Fascist, National Socialist and Authoritarian Regimes* (Hart Publishing, 2019).

difficult and ambiguous transition towards the new democratic and constitutional regimes; secondly that of the reconstruction of a 'new' form of rule of law, one capable of innovating radically as regards its contents, mechanisms and tools. Whether or not Nazi and Fascist law – to evoke both of the more complex experiences in Europe – were indeed 'law', in any case the need to effect a profound metamorphosis of the state under the rule of law seemed to be urgent.

After the war, democratic Constitutions and the Universal Declaration of Human Rights began to frame this radical change, thereby bringing to the fore different legal and cultural backgrounds. British and American rule of law, Weimar social constitutionalism, Kelsenian doctrine, natural law references, and, indeed, new legal concepts afforded the 'materials' to build or to improve rule of law as a complex of principles. The opening statements from the Preamble to the Universal Declaration evoke 'the recognition of dignity and of the equal and inalienable rights of all members of the human family', with the peoples of the United Nations finding reaffirmed in the Charter 'their faith in fundamental human rights, in the dignity and worth of the human person and in the equal rights of men and women', thereby putting human rights under the protection of the rule of law. What remained of the liberal *Rechtsstaat* legacy had to be rethought in the light of this epistemic turn.

The alpha and omega now became the human person. His/her dignity, equality and liberty are inalienable values, being ontologically prior to the state and its law. These fundamental values find in the law of the Constitution the conditions under which they may exist and be protected. The Constitution of a democratic state is 'rigid', first and foremost, inasmuch it contains and proclaims a core of intangible shared fundamental principles defended against each and every kind of violation. This approach is designed to overcome the 'ambiguity' of the *Rechtsstaat* so as to prevent 'disregard and contempt for human rights that have resulted in barbarous acts which have outraged the conscience of mankind'. Constitutional inviolability is the reference concept. Of course, there is not merely one single path. Traditions and historical foundations reemerge. But some common trends may be identified. Post-war constitutionalism recovers the ancient 'culture' of the limit. The inviolability of fundamental rights requires the raising of high barriers. Anglo-Saxon rule of law – for a wide range of reasons – had manifested an 'intrinsic' force. Dicey had already highlighted this historical dynamic: the English Constitution had inseparably connected rights with the means of enforcing them by the courts through the incremental process of common law decision-making. The Americans, sharing this strong cultural background, entrusted to the judges and the Supreme Court the judicial review of legislation, an extraordinary invention of modern constitutionalism. Other kinds of limits and checks and balances contributed to enforce rule of law but judicial protection was probably the most important pillar.

On the European continent the *Rechtsstaat*, considered basically as a legal and administrative state, encountered serious difficulties when attempting to follow this same path. As we have seen, political sovereignty and a legicentric perspective were strictly linked. After World War II it was likewise not a simple matter to change this deep-rooted doctrine. After all, it was only during the twentieth century that American ordinary courts and the Supreme Court had implemented the protection of individual rights and above all of the rights of minorities,[60] 'a history closely connected to the role that the United States took on at the international level in the battle against the spread of totalitarianism in Europe'.[61]

The constitutional engineering of the second post-war period connected the principle of inviolability of fundamental rights with the dynamics of constitutional justice. The Austrian Kelsenian 'model' (more than the American experience)[62] was only the starting point but the new Constitutions (eg, German, Italian, French) grafted several new branches on to the trunk of constitutional justice, in order to overcome the omnipotence of the legislator and limit the threat posed by Leviathan to the freedom of the individual and of the minorities. The new kind of democratic Constitution recognises and organises pluralism and coexistence between distinct groups and political parties; it provides tools for the resolution of conflicts; it seeks to balance the democratic track (people's sovereignty and political will) with the juridical supremacy of the Constitution. The correct formation of political will cannot be left in the hands of variable political majorities. Constitution is the condition of sustaining and preserving pluralism, and the 'device' serving to contain the risk of arbitrariness on the part of the majority. Fundamental rights do not protect individuals only, but minorities also. A reinforced majority can be required to review the Constitution, meaning that the main issues can only be resolved by means of a certain degree of constitutional collaboration with the minority. The sphere of inviolability of constitutional rights is predicated upon the constitutionality of the laws, and in the case of conflict the judicial review of legislation is the only way to find a solution.

A number of different post-war constitutional experiences tend to confirm the rule of law notion. Nevertheless, we must consider this phenomenon to be a 'process' linked to time, space, traditions and historical backgrounds. A wide range of different factors affect the concrete functioning of rule of law based constitutional democratic systems. Constitutional justice can assume various forms, and judicial and 'political' dimensions, depending upon the Constitution's characteristics, upon political relations and upon the overall constitutional setting of the form of government and so on. Post-war rule of law incorporates a number of principles and fundamental values (no arbitrary power, the supremacy and independence of law under the Constitution rule, non-discrimination, respect for universal human rights ...) and the notion has been merged into some constitutional texts.

Many Constitutions, starting with the German one, introduced the notion into the text itself.[63] The Portuguese Constitution of 1976[64] and the Spanish Constitution

[60] RM Cover, 'The Origins of Judicial Activism in the Protection of Minorities' (1982) 91 *Yale Law Journal*, 1287–1316.

[61] B Casalini, 'Popular Sovereignty, the Rule of Law, and the "Rule of Judges" in the United States' in Costa and Zolo (n 3) 203.

[62] For the original perspective, see H Kelsen, 'Judicial Review of Legislation: A Comparative Study of the Austrian and the American Constitution' (1942) 4 *The Journal of Politics* 183–200.

[63] '... [t]he constitutional order in the states must conform to the principles of the republican, democratic and social state under the rule of law', German Basic Law (*Grundgesetz*), art 28, § 1.

[64] Article 2 (Democratic state based on the rule of law): 'The Portuguese Republic is a democratic state based on the rule of law, the sovereignty of the people, plural democratic expression and political organisation, respect for and the guarantee of the effective implementation of the fundamental rights and freedoms,

of 1978[65] further strengthened the formula. The specific reference to rule of law became a sort of 'brand' for the democratic transitions that took place. This was the case with some of the former Soviet Union countries and those states that had previously been members of the 'Soviet bloc'. All over the world, in the last decades, the rule of law has doubtless gained space and relevance but the formal constitutional declaration of principles, rules and remedies is never enough to guarantee in actual fact the principles of the supremacy of the law, equality before the law, fairness in the application of the law, the separation of powers, participation in decision-making, legal certainty, avoidance of arbitrariness, and procedural and legal transparency. So, rule of law enforcement is always a very complex 'process' depending on a wide series of conditions and site-specific features.

After all we have ascertained that British rule of law, American rule of law, German *Rechtsstaat*, French *État de droit*, Italian *Stato di diritto* and so on were, for a long time, distinctive paths marked by a number of different doctrines and final achievements. Their background rested on a multiplicity of cultural traditions, constitutional cultures, 'anthropological' attitudes. Only after World War II and a drawn-out process of 'convergence' has it become possible to identify in the lemma rule of law a communicable common core.[66] In Europe, in particular, rule of law implementation in the individual states has made it possible to elaborate a series of core elements.[67]

Once again the key element must be identified with the judicial enforceability and the reviewability of decisions of public authorities by independent courts. In 1986 the European Court of Justice referred to the European Community (EC) as 'a Community based on the rule of law'.[68] Two decades later the Court has opined

and the separation and interdependence of powers, with a view to achieving economic, social and cultural democracy and deepening participatory democracy'.

[65] 'Consolidate a State of Law which ensures the rule of law as the expression of the popular will' (Preamble); 'Spain is hereby established as a social and democratic State, subject to the rule of law, which advocates freedom, justice, equality and political pluralism as highest values of its legal system' (s 1.1).

[66] 'The Rule of Law has become "a global ideal and aspiration", with a common core valid everywhere. This, however, does not mean that its implementation has to be identical regardless of the concrete juridical, historical, political, social or geographical context. While the main components or "ingredients" of the Rule of Law are constant, the specific manner in which they are realised may differ from one country to another depending on the local context; in particular on the constitutional order and traditions of the country concerned. This context may also determine the relative weight of each of the components' (Council of Europe, European Commission for Democracy through law (Venice Commission), Rule of law checklist, adopted by the Venice Commission at its 106th Plenary Session (Venice, 11–12 March 2016) 9, B § 34.

[67] 'The Union is founded on the values of the respect for human dignity, freedom, democracy, equality, the rule of law and respect for the human rights, including the rights of persons belonging to minorities. These values are common to the Member States in a society in which pluralism, non-discrimination, tolerance, justice, solidarity and equality between women and men prevail.' (Article 2, Treaty on European Union). In its report, the Commission concluded that, despite differences of opinion, consensus exists on the core elements of the rule of law as well as on those of the *Rechtsstaat* and of the *État de droit*, which are not only formal but also substantive or material (*materieller Rechtsstaatsbegriff*). These core elements are: (1) Legality, including a transparent, accountable and democratic process for enacting law; (2) Legal certainty; (3) Prohibition of arbitrariness; (4) Access to justice before independent and impartial courts, including judicial review of administrative acts; (5) Respect for human rights; and (6) Non-discrimination and equality before the law.

[68] Case 294/83 *Les Verts v Parliament* [1986] ECR 1339, § 23. See ML Fernandez Esteban, *The rule of law in the European Constitution* (Kluwer Law International, 1999); L Pech, *The Rule of Law as a*

that 'Access to justice is one of the constitutive elements of a Community based on the rule of law and is guaranteed in the legal order based on the Treaty in that the Treaty has established a complete system of legal remedies and procedures designed to permit the Court of Justice to review the legality of measures adopted by the institutions [...]'.[69] The centrality of the role of judges in contemporary legal pluralism asks first of all for 'a recognition of the methods used for the interpretation of rules and the plausibility and reasonableness of the very rules of the other legal systems'.[70]

In conclusion, what is the legacy that the twentieth century has bequeathed to us in terms of rule of law? There are of course many profiles, but one is the ongoing endeavour (and tension) to find and preserve an effective balance between democracy and rule of law, namely between people's will and the constitutional/legal machinery of limits to protect and guarantee human dignity, fundamental rights, pluralism and all kinds of minorities. This balance was the result, as I have tried to show, of very dramatic events and of a huge intellectual effort.

Our critical horizon does not seem to be preoccupied by dictatorship or the putative advent of new totalitarianisms. The pitfalls are far more nuanced and subtle. The European Union is once again an interesting 'laboratory'. Liberal democracies can be called into question under pressure from illiberal and populist forces. The problems come when one tends to consider only one of the two pillars: people's sovereignty and the majority principle seen as the legitimate sanction to erode the second pillar, the democratic state under the rule of law. The 'majoritarian democracy' – as in Poland or Hungary[71] – tends to weaken first of all the independent

Constitutional Principle of the European Union (New York University School of Law, The Jean Monnet Working Paper, 2009), see http://jeanmonnetprogram.org/wp-content/uploads/2014/12/090401.pdf; A Magen and L Pech, 'The rule of law and the European Union' in May and Winchester (n 6) 235.

[69] Case C-131/03 P *RJ Reynolds Tobacco Holdings Inc v Commission of the European Communities* [2006] E.C.R. I-7795, 7837. On the constitutive idea of justice ('Europe is united through a specific European idea of justice', 520), see now U Müßig, *Reason and Fairness. Constituting Justice in Europe, from Medieval Canon Law to ECHR* (Brill Nijhoff, 2019).

[70] F Viola, 'The Rule of Law in Legal Pluralism' in T Gizbert-Studnicki and J Stelmach (eds), *Law and Legal Cultures in the 21st century. Diversity and Unity* (Oficyna, 2007) 124.

[71] On these two cases, within a now vast literature, P Lendvai, *Hungary: Between Democracy and Authoritarianism* (Hurst, 2012); A Von Bogdandy and P Sonnevend (eds), *Constitutional Crisis in the European Constitutional Area: Theory, Law and Politics in Hungary and Romania* (Hart Publishing, 2015); P Krasztev and J Van Til (eds), *The Hungarian Patient: Social Opposition to an Illiberal Democracy* (CEU Press, 2015); B Bugarič, 'A Crisis of Constitutional Democracy in Post-Communist Europe: Lands In-Between Democracy and Authoritarianism' (2015) 13 (1) *International Journal of Constitutional Law* 219–45; B Greskovits, 'The Hollowing and Backsliding of Democracy in East Central Europe' (2015) 6(1) *Global Policy* 28–37; A Ágh, 'The Decline of Democracy in East-Central Europe: Hungary as the Worst-Case Scenario' (2016) 63 5–6 *Problems of Post-Communism* 277–87; B Pająk-Patkowska and M Rachwał (eds), *Hungary and Poland in Times of Political Transition: Selected Issues* (Faculty of Political Science and Journalism Press, Adam Mickiewicz University, 2016); N Bermeo, 'On Democratic Backsliding' (2016) 27 (1) *Journal of Democracy* 5–19; A Pap, *Democratic Decline in Hungary: Law and Society in an Illiberal Democracy* (Routledge, 2017); M Bogaards, 'De-democratization in Hungary: diffusely defective democracy' (2018) 25(8) *Democratization* 1481–99, see https://doi.org/10.1080/13510347.2018.1485015; W Sadurki, *Poland's Constitutional Breakdown* (OUP, 2019).

judiciary and the constitutional courts,[72] but also independent media, civil society organisations and local governments. The main argument used by the political majority is the supremacy of the 'will of people' against the (non-elected) institutions called upon to preserve checks and balances, and endeavouring to limit the majority's 'limitless' power. Political populism recasts older questions. The tension between 'democracy' and rule of law is a permanent preoccupation. The current phase outlines new challenges and metamorphoses, which themselves require innovative and brave solutions.

[72] But we have to consider the analysis of the wide- ranging role of the judiciary and constitutional courts in the practice of governance in the European Union context: see A Stone Sweet, *Governing with Judges: Constitutional Politics in Europe* (OUP, 2000); O Gerstenberg, *Euroconstitutionalism and Its Discontents* (OUP, 2018).

4

Rule of Law and Democracy

DIETER GRIMM*

I. TENSION AND INTERDEPENDENCE

THE RELATIONSHIP BETWEEN democracy and the rule of law is characterised by both tension and interdependence.[1] The tension exists because each principle has the tendency to overwhelm the other. Democracy tends to set aside legal bonds if they collide with the actual will of the majority. The rule of law tends to fetter politics and reduce it to the implementation of the law. Driven to the extreme, both threaten to be self-destructive, democracy because it can end up in a dictatorship of the majority, the rule of law because it can end up in immobility. The interdependence finds its reason just in this threat. Each principle has to be balanced by elements of the other one.

The modalities of the accommodation vary with the concept of the two principles. Both the rule of law and even more so democracy, are ambiguous, contested and variable notions. There is not *the* democracy and *the* rule of law.[2] However, for the purpose of this article, it is unnecessary to unfold the whole variety. It seems sufficient to distinguish two broad notions, one more formal and simplistic, one more substantive and ambitious, and to neglect all the subcategories.[3] Both share a few basic elements, but differ for the rest. The substantive notions combine the two principles from the outset, while the relationship is less obvious with the formal ones.

* Humboldt University, Berlin.

[1] Democracy and the rule of law are mostly treated separately, but see for the relationship JM Maravall and A Przeworski (eds), *Democracy and the Rule of Law* (CUP, 2003); L Morlino and G Palombella (eds), *Rule of Law and Democracy* (Brill, 2010).

[2] See eg for democracy D Held, *Models of Democracy*, 3rd edn (Polity, 2006); M Schmidt, *Demokratietheorien*, 6th edn, (Springer, 2019); for the rule of law RH Fallon, '"The Rule of Law" as a Concept of Constitutional Discourse' (1997) 97 *Columbia L.R.* 1; R Grote, 'Rule of Law, Rechtsstaat and Etat de droit' in C Starck (ed), *Constitutionalism, Universalism and Democracy: A Comparative Analysis* (Nomos, 1999); M Rosenfeld, 'The Rule of Law and the Legitimacy of Constitutional Democracy' (2001) 74 *Southern California L.R.* 1307; L Heuschling, *Etat de droit, Rechtsstaat, Rule of Law* (Dalloz, 2002).

[3] See U Volkmann, 'Die zwei Begriffe der Demokratie' in K Hofmann and K Naumann (eds), *Europäische Demokratie in guter Verfassung?* (Nomos, 2010) 14; J Raz, 'The Rule of Law and its Virtue' in J Raz, *The Authority of Law* (Clarendon Press, 1979) 179, 210.

II. DEMOCRACY'S RELATIONSHIP WITH THE RULE OF LAW

The formal and the substantive concept of democracy share a number of features that distinguish them from non-democratic systems. Both start from the assumption that the people are the ultimate source of all public power. Popular sovereignty is the legitimating principle of democracies. The people possess the constituent power and they retain influence on the exercise of the constituted power. Democracy thus stands in opposition to political systems that legitimise public authority not by consensus, but by a certain pre-established truth, be it religious or secular, or by the superior quality or insight of a person like the monarch or a group of persons like an aristocracy or a certain movement or party. It also stands in opposition to systems that attribute the original power to the people, but allow that it is handed over unconditionally to an omnipotent leader, so that the first use of popular power is also the last.

Moreover, both basic types of democracy must acknowledge that, at least in rather vast and complex societies as they exist today, the people cannot govern themselves, but need representatives and agents who act on their behalf and in their interest. The relationship is conceived as one of 'master and servant' or 'principal and agent'. This does not exclude direct interventions of the people in form of a plebiscite or referendum. But they will always remain exceptional. The mass of problems that have to be solved by political decisions almost daily can only be handled by institutions and persons specialised in politics and public administration. Because of this necessity, representative democracy is not a minor form of democracy, compared to plebiscitarian democracy.[4] Variability exists only with regard to the combination of these elements. Democracy can be more or less representative, but it cannot be not representative.

If this is the condition under which democracies, other than monocratic systems, operate, the central democratic problem is the mediation between the inevitable plurality of opinions and interests in society and the mandatory unity of state action. This problem is solved by a chain of delegation. In a democracy, the power to govern is power delegated by the people. It is delegated to persons who represent the people and whose decisions are ascribed to the people and have binding force on it. In this sense, it can be said that in a democracy the addressees of the bonds are at the same time their authors.[5] Democracy is self-government by the people, but it is self-government by ascription, not in the sense that those who actually govern and those who are governed are identical. This difference has to be bridged by adequate mechanisms. Delegated power needs organisation.

The central mechanism to determine the representatives of the people who exercise public authority is the election. It is difficult to imagine a democracy as characterised here without elections. However, before elections can be held, a number of questions have to be answered. It must be determined for which institutions elections

[4] See E-W Böckenförde, 'Demokratische Willensbildung und Repräsentation' in J Isensee and P Kirchhof (eds), *Handbuch des Staatsrechts III*, 3rd edn (CF Müller, 2005) 31.

[5] See J Habermas, 'Über den inneren Zusammenhang von Rechtsstaat und Demokratie' in J Habermas, *Die Einbeziehung des Anderen* (Suhrkamp, 1996) 298 (English version: *The Inclusion of the Other* (MIT Press, 1998)).

are held and who may vote and who may be elected. Likewise, it has to be decided in which intervals elections will take place and how the precincts are apportioned. Furthermore, guidelines as to how the election is conducted must be developed. Of utmost importance is who counts as elected. The democratic answer to this question is: the one who got the majority of votes. But as far as seats in Parliament are concerned, this cannot be ascertained without a determination how votes translate into mandates.

Moreover, the election cannot take place without the prior selection of candidates. Since a pre-established will or interest of the people exists only for some theories of democracy, but not in social reality, where rather an immense variety of opinions and interests will be found, the election presupposes a reduction of this variety to a comprehensible number of alternatives among which the voters may choose. To form such alternatives and to present them to the electorate is usually the function of political parties. Parties are organisations rooted in society, but striving for influence within the state. They unite persons of similar views and interests, condense the views and interests to a platform or programme and select candidates who stand for this programme and compete to be entrusted with the power to rule for a limited period of time until the next election may mix the cards differently.

The dependence of elections on these preconditions makes a prior agreement on them necessary. In order to exclude the possibility of manipulations, this agreement must be as precise as possible and binding for the parties, the candidates, the voters and the staff who manage the election. Since elections may lead to a change of government if the people so wish, the conditions of transition must be determined. As agreements on the conditions of gaining and losing power are often difficult to reach, it makes sense to conclude them for a series of future elections instead of negotiating them before every election anew. All this points in the direction of a legal regulation, and since there is no democracy without elections and no election without a set of binding rules, democracy depends, at least in this respect, on the rule of law.

But the demand for regulation does not end with the election. It is an inbuilt risk of representative democracy that the representatives emancipate themselves from the needs and expectations of the people and pursue interests of their own. This is why, before the representatives are entrusted with the power to rule on behalf of the people, the people formulate the conditions under which they are to govern and compliance with which conveys legitimacy on their acts. These conditions must be binding for the representatives. This means that they have to adopt the quality of law because only the law can convey collectively binding force on the rules and extend them beyond the parties to the agreement and beyond the moment of adoption. In addition, they must enjoy primacy over their political acts. They are rules about ruling and as such not at the disposition of those to whom they are addressed. These are precisely the distinct features of constitutions.[6]

Within the elected organ, the need for rules about decision making repeats itself. In a democracy, the criterion is once again majority. However, majority is a purely numerical criterion unrelated to any substantive quality. This explains the intensive

[6] See D Grimm, *Constitutionalism. Past, Present, and Future* (OUP, 2016) 22.

debate about the justification of the majority principle.[7] The theories vary. Some authors believe that the majority principle leads to better results. For others, the decisive argument is the minimum of oppression: the smaller number of people must live with decisions that they do not support. Again others argue that the majority rule is the only rule in which political equality can be expressed. But all agree that for practical reasons, the majority principle is unavoidable.[8] Just as there is no democracy without election, there is no democracy without the majority rule, however this principle is justified and however it is concretised.

In this aspect as well, democracy depends on the rule of law. It guarantees that the conditions set by the people for the acts of their representatives are respected by them. But the importance of the rule of law for democracy does not exhaust itself in this aspect. Just as the people expect that their representatives respect the constitution, the elected representatives who have a mandate from the people to take collectively binding decisions for society depend, for their part, on the vast executive, administrative and judicial staff's compliance with the decisions adopted in the democratic process. The principle of legality which guarantees this is mostly viewed from the perspective of the individual. It excludes arbitrary treatment. But it is also a necessary condition of democracy. Democracy is doomed to fail if the decisions adopted in the democratic process are not faithfully executed on the level of application and law enforcement.

These preconditions of democracy can hardly be denied even by a minimalist or radical democrat. They are common to all notions of democracy. They may be formulated in many different ways, but they cannot be left unregulated. However, this is more or less the end of the commonalities between a more formal and a more substantive understanding of what democracy is about. The formal notion is satisfied if the people elect their representatives and if the representatives take their decisions according to the majority rule. The rule of law is democratically acceptable insofar as it organises the formation of the majority will and guarantees its implementation. In its formal understanding, democracy is largely identified with majority rule. It can be called formal because all the legal prerequisites of democracy are of an organisational or procedural nature. They do not contain any substantive requirements.

Yet, it is not sufficient to say that substantive requirements are absent. For a formal understanding they would be incompatible with democracy because they limit the scope of the majority principle. For the formalist notion of democracy, whatever the majority decides in due form is binding for society. Such an understanding does not make a constitution superfluous, but the constitution is confined to organisational and procedural provisions. It would not contain fundamental rights whose function is precisely to constrain the majority rule. As the deputy Crenière put it already 1789 in the debate of the French National Assembly on the Declaration of Rights: There is only one fundamental right, namely the right to participate in the formation of the general will.[9] The general will is identified with the will of the majority. Substantive rights would allow the minority to prevail over the majority.

[7] See E Flaig, *Die Mehrheitsentscheidung* (Ferdinand Schöningh, 2013).

[8] Recently, the old idea of a lottery found new interest, but it is suggested only for specific purposes or offices, not in general. See eg H Buchstein, 'Democracy and Lottery Revisited' (2019) 26 *Constellations* 361.

[9] Archives parlementaires de la Révolution francaise VIII, 451.

But is such a position tenable? All notions of democracy would agree that elections can express the popular will only if they are free and equal. Hence, at least this material precondition of a democratic election should be exempted from majority vote. Otherwise, democracy cannot protect itself against being abolished by majority vote. A purely formal notion of democracy gives those forces a chance who do not share the basic assumption of democracy that the general will has to be formed under conditions of a plurality of opinions and interests and that this pluralism is not only empirically given, but normatively legitimate. To the contrary, these forces pursue an absolute truth or pre-existing will vis-à-vis which freedom cannot be permitted. If they win a majority in a free election, they use the legislative power unimpeded by substantive requirements to perpetuate their rule and transform the democratic into an authoritarian system.

However, when the necessity of guaranteeing free elections has been accepted even by a formal understanding of democracy, a further question will arise, namely when an election can be said to be free. Here again, more formal and more substantive answers exist. A formal notion of free elections would be satisfied if the voter has a choice. The minimal choice is one between yes and no to a uniform list. But this comes very close to a mere acclamation, like advocates of an identitarian notion of democracy describe it as the adequate role for the people.[10] In a representative democracy, the plurality of opinions and interests in society should find an expression on the ballot and allow the voter to choose among various candidates or parties and thereby among different political concepts of or strategies for the common good.

But this would still be a very thin notion of freedom because it leaves everything out that precedes and follows the election. In the period of time before an election, freedom has a double point of reference. It refers to the competitors for public office and to the voters who choose among them. Since it is the function of the competing political parties and candidates to transport views and interests of citizens into the process of political decision making, free elections mean that the alternatives presented to the voter may be formed freely, which implies that everybody must have the right to set up a party or group that strives for certain goals and to nominate candidates who promise to implement them if they are elected. Free means furthermore that the parties have the same chance to attract support for their candidates and views from the electorate. This freedom matters particularly in the election campaign.

Regarding the election campaign, free elections mean foremost state neutrality vis-à-vis the competitors.[11] The campaign is the forum where parties and candidates try to convince the voters that their ideas and projects would serve the country better than those of their competitors. They seek a mandate from the people to transform their party programme into political measures through the legislative and financial means of the state. The state, more precisely: those organs of the state whose composition depends on elections, the Parliament and the Government, are the object of

[10] See C Schmitt, *Verfassungslehre* (Duncker & Humblot, 1928) 83 (English version: *Constitutional Theory* (Duke University Press, 2008)).

[11] See D Grimm, 'Die politischen Parteien' in E Benda, W Maihofer and H-J Vogel (eds), *Handbuch des Verfassungsrechts*, 2nd edn (De Gruyter, 1994) 599.

that competition. The decision belongs alone to the people. This puts the state into a passive position regarding the campaign. It may not itself influence the chances of the competitors and the outcome of the election. Taking sides and lending state support to certain competitors while withholding it from others would distort the people's will.

That state neutrality is a condition of free elections becomes even more evident if one acknowledges that, in a representative democracy, the activity of the state is driven by the majority party or parties. They dominate the legislative process, they form the Government and they dispose of the financial and coercive means of the state. State influence on elections would therefore be influence of the ruling party in its own favour and to the detriment of the competitors. Consequently, the ruling party must be prevented from using its legislative majority as well as the resources of the state for purposes of its re-election. A sharp distinction between the organs of the state and the officers and parties who temporarily fill the positions personally is a precondition of democracy. Representative democracy based on elections is incompatible with an identification between the ruling party and the state.

However, the state is not the only menace to a free election campaign. The outcome of elections is of immense interest to private actors in various social systems. Therefore, they try to improve the chances of those parties or candidates of whom they expect sympathy for their interests. The support can be given by arguments, but also by money or by payment in kind. There is nothing objectionable about this practice as such. The neutrality that is expected from the state does not apply to societal actors. A democratic problem results, however, from the different strength of the actors. Especially economic interests can usually count on a superior influence, thanks to their financial resources.[12] This distributes the chances among the competitors unequally and relativises the equal right to vote. Therefore, freedom of the election requires a regulation of campaign financing in the interest of equal opportunities.

Regarding the voters, free elections mean before all that they have a chance to inform themselves freely. Free information has a retrospective and a prospective aspect. Retrospectively, it must be possible to form an opinion on the performance of the outgoing Government that seeks re-election. This requires transparency of government activities. Prospectively, it means free information about the candidates, their programmatic views and their affiliations. Both aspects presuppose an open public debate about political matters. Such a debate cannot develop without the service of media of mass communication, which transmit opinions voiced in society, contribute opinions of their own, thus furnishing the necessary basis for opinion formation and becoming the starting point for new communications. The media system can render this service only if it is itself free.

The time after an election is in reality a time between two elections. For a formal understanding of democracy, this time is of little interest. The election has determined the representatives of the people and the formation of the Government. It is now the business of politicians to use the power that was given to them. The majority

[12] See for the US where this is a particularly urgent problem: RC Post, *Citizens Divided* (Harvard University Press, 2014); L Lessig, *Republic, Lost: How Money Corrupts Congress* (Twelve, 2011).

has its way. If the majority misuses its power or neglects the expectations and interests of the population, they will be driven out of office in the next election. The threat to lose the election is seen as a sufficient incentive for the rulers to be responsive to the views and demands of the citizens. Further precautions are unnecessary. For a more substantive understanding of democracy, this time also counts. Democracy does not exhaust itself in periodic elections but culminates in them.

The actions or omissions for which democratic governments are held accountable extend over the whole legislative period. The opinion about the majority's performance and the opposition's critique is formed during that period. What finally leads to a mark on the ballot is the result of a continuous observation and discussion of the politicians' performance, a comparison between promises and deeds, the evaluation of alternatives. For this to happen, the elected representatives of the people and the institutions of Government must be embedded in an ongoing discursive process in which opinions and interests may be articulated by individuals and social groups, while the Government explains its measures and the opposition criticises them and offers alternatives. The public discourse is what fills the democratic representation with life.

Like with the election campaign, this continuous public discourse can only be generated and upheld by the media of mass communication. The importance of the media system for democracy can hardly be overestimated. A democratic polity will only be as good as its media system. The media, in turn, can contribute to a vibrant democracy only insofar as they have access to the information that a democratic society needs to conduct its own affairs and as they can publish and comment on them free from external domination or pressure. However, because of the importance of media for political success and failure, the freedom of the media is constantly endangered. The threat is routinely expected from the state and the political parties that dispose of its means. But freedom of media and freedom of information as its corollary is also endangered by private forces who control influential parts of the media system and use it to promote their interests.[13]

These preconditions of a democracy based on free elections cannot be guaranteed by democracy itself. To the contrary, they are specifically endangered by democracy. In a democratic system, the question who may govern for a certain period of time and thus get the chance to implement his programme for the common good, depends on winning the election. This is the imperative under which party politics work. From their point of view, everything that improves their chances seems rational. The best opportunities present themselves to those who are already in power and want to stay there. They dispose of the means of the state, legislative as well as financial, and will be inclined to exploit them for party purposes, to frame the election laws in a way that favours their party, use the resources of the state to promote party goals, influence media reporting, and the like. Under a purely formal notion of democracy all this would not be objectionable.

After the experience of the collapse or self-destruction of democracies in the first half of the twentieth century, the soil was prepared for a better protection of

[13] See eg C Edwin Baker, *Media, Markets and Democracy* (CUP, 2002).

democracy as such as well as its preconditions. However, this could be reached only by turning to a more substantive understanding of democracy. As a safeguard against self-destruction, so-called eternity clauses on the line of article 79, section 3 of the German Basic Law were adopted in many recent constitutions.[14] They shield democracy against constitutional amendments that would abolish or severely damage democracy. In addition, early defence lines were established in the form of the possibility to ban parties or associations that attempt to overthrow the democratic order.[15] Strict legal rules try to prevent the use of these means from becoming a threat to democracy.

The preconditions of democracy are mainly protected by fundamental rights. Fundamental rights are an important element of the rule of law as it is seen today. They restrain majority decisions, but they do so in the interest of individual self-development and collective self-government and are thus compatible with a more substantive notion of democracy. For some of these rights, the relationship with democracy is obvious. Freedom of speech, freedom of the media, freedom of information, freedom of association and freedom of assembly have a direct impact on political competition, public discourse and opinion formation. They help in providing society with an unvarnished picture of the state of affairs, put issues and problems on the agenda, which are neglected by government and established parties, keep the political debate open for criticism and alternative views and demand responsiveness from the political class.

Some of these rights will fulfil their function for democracy if they are understood in the traditional way as negative rights that prevent encroachments upon the liberties by the state. For others, this would be insufficient. This is particularly true for freedom of media. Democracy, understood in a substantive way, can only be as vibrant as the media which are providing the information necessary for fuelling and maintaining the public discourse.[16] This essential function of media for democracy is not adequately reflected in a purely individualistic interpretation as freedom of the media owners and journalists. It is not just a subcategory of free speech, amplified by technical means. It is a different type of rights. Its object is the function that the media render to individual opinion formation and democratic government. Freedom of media is a functional right and protects individual freedom only insofar as the owners and journalists act in accordance with this function.[17]

The guarantee must therefore extend to the media system as such. To fulfil its democratic function it has to be understood, next to an individual entitlement for media actors, as an institutional guarantee of a free media system. This guarantee requires on the one hand, state abstention from control of the media, on the other hand state action in the interest of an all over media freedom. As a potential foe of

[14] See Y Roznai, *Unconstitutional Constitutional Amendments* (OUP, 2017).

[15] See G Cappocia, *Defending Democracy* (John Hopkins University Press, 2005); M Thiel (ed), *The 'Militant Democracy' Principle in Modern Democracies* (Routledge, 2009).

[16] See N Luhmann, *Die Realität der Massenmedien*, 2nd edn (Westdeutscher Verlag, 1996); C Substein, *Democracy and the Problem of Free Speech* (Free Press, 1993); J Lichtenberg, *Democracy and the Mass Media* (CUP, 1990).

[17] See D Grimm, 'Freedom of Media' in A Stone and F Schauer (eds), *The Oxford Handbook of Free Speech* (OUP, 2021).

media freedom, the state has to refrain from actions that would unduly limit media reporting. As a friend of media freedom, it has to take action in order to ban those menaces that emanate from private actors. This positive duty will usually be fulfilled by legislation. It implies that that the positive dimension of media freedom may require restrictions of the negative dimension, yet only in the interest of a greater overall freedom.

However, the importance of fundamental rights is not limited to those rights that are directly connected to the political process. Fundamental rights that do not directly protect political participation, but the private sphere of the citizens, their home, their personal communication, their religious beliefs, their professional activities, their leisure time etc, can also have an influence on democracy. One is not free as a political subject if one is not free as a private person.[18] If only political participation were protected against intrusions by the state or pressure by fellow citizens, people could not be free of fear that their political engagement might entail sanctions or disadvantages in the private sphere. The constitutional protection of personal data evolved as a result of this insight. In this sense, one can say that all fundamental rights contribute to democracy.

There is, however, still a deeper sense in which the majority rule depends on the recognition of fundamental rights. Where there is a majority, there is also a minority, whose demands and expectations remain unfulfilled in the democratic process. For democracy, it is crucial that they can nevertheless feel included in the democratic society and are willing to obey the law in spite of their disagreement. This willingness is essentially supported by the obligation of the majority to respect, for its part, the political and private rights of the minority and give it the opportunity to prevail with its opinions and demands in the next election. Structural minorities that do not see a chance to ever find attention for their views and interests and are even menaced in their personal way of life are a threat to representative democracy.

It would, however, be too narrow to recognise fundamental rights only insofar as they assist and support the democratic process. The majority of fundamental rights are in the first place guaranteed in the interest of individual self-development and self-fulfilment, which, in turn, presupposes freedom. These rights are ends in themselves, not means in the service of an external purpose, be it democratic or other. It is in principle up to the individuals if and how they use their freedom. Limitations of that liberty are indispensable because every liberty can be used to the detriment of others or society at large as well as legitimate state interests. But limitations of fundamental rights need a justification that may be derived from the protection of the same liberties of others or from other liberties or interests of society as a whole.

Democracy, in turn, appears as the political system that is best compatible with individual freedom. The two complement each other mutually. Democracy fulfils the claim of citizens endowed with political and personal rights to decide directly or indirectly through their elected representatives how they want to be governed and under which laws they want to live. Under conditions of social and ideological pluralism, democratic procedures convey legitimacy on the results. Equal rights establish

[18] See Habermas (n 5) 301 ss.

conditions under which democracy is able to reach results that are generally acceptable. Thus, individual self-development and collective self-government go hand in hand. In this sense, Habermas can call fundamental rights (and the rule of law, of which they are part) and democracy as co-equal.[19]

III. RULE OF LAW'S RELATIONSHIP WITH DEMOCRACY

Like the two basic concepts of democracy, the two concepts of the rule of law share some elements. The fundamental feature of any rule of law concept is that public power is exercised by law and in accordance with law. Exercising public power by law means that wherever the state regulates private behaviour, it has to be done in the form of law. Exercising public authority according to law means that the state uses its power in conformity with the law. Not only the horizontal relationship among private persons, but also the vertical relationship between private persons and the state is subject to law. The requirement of a legal basis for its actions prevents the state from converting power into orders or measures straightaway. Thus, governing under the rule of law is the opposite of arbitrary rule.

The notion of law implies a certain degree of generality. Laws differ from individual commands. Individual commands are addressed to a certain individual or group of individuals with regard to a certain existing or imminent situation. It exhausts itself in the act of compliance by the addressees or implementation by the law enforcement agencies. To the contrary, a law or statute is directed to an indefinite number of people and covers an indefinite number of future cases, even cases that were not or could not have been foreseen when the law was adopted. It applies wherever the conditions laid down in the law are given and vis-à-vis everybody who falls under these conditions. Preferences or disadvantages on personal grounds are excluded. Equal treatment under law is an essential element of the rule of law.

The first element alone, governing by law, would not be enough to establish the rule of law. It does not sufficiently distinguish a rule of law-abiding system from a dictatorial or totalitarian system. Such systems also rule by law, but the law is used as an instrument to govern, while the state is not willing to submit itself to the law. In the absence of the second element, it is neither guaranteed that the state respects the law that regulates its own behaviour nor that the law which regulates private behaviour is applied equally. Consequently, arbitrariness is not ruled out. The requirement that the state does not only rule by law but also according to law does not only apply to the executive, administrative and judicial agencies of the state. It is also mandatory for the highest organs of the state.

The law binds the state as long as it is in force. But compliance with the law cannot be taken for granted. It can hinder politicians from pursuing certain goals or taking certain actions which they find useful or urgent. Compliance with legal norms may have undesirable consequences. Adherence to the law may then appear as empty formalism which thwarts the achievement of substantive justice. A state that overrides legal requirements under such circumstances may even have public opinion on

[19] Habermas (n 5).

its side. But it could not claim to respect the rule of law if it is unwilling to comply with the law, even when it is unpopular, inconvenient, or annoying. If certain provisions of the law shall not apply in exceptional situations like a catastrophe or war, the permission must be contained in the law itself, for instance in the form of emergency provisions.

If the state wants to remedy an unsatisfactory legal arrangement, it may amend the law for the future, but cannot disregard it now. Once it becomes accepted that there are reasons to ignore the law under exceptional circumstances, it is only a small step away from disregarding the law for all sorts of illegitimate purposes: because it does not correspond to one's subjective sense of justice; because the outcome in a particular case seems undesirable; because it saves money; because it avoids trouble with those in power; because it helps in the struggle with political opponents or rivals, etc. The rule of law is based on the assumption that legal certainty is an intrinsic value, regardless of whether the outcome of compliance with the law is seen as good or bad, useful or harmful.[20]

The conditions for such an attitude are not equally favourable in all political systems. The reason lies in a fundamental difference regarding the legitimation of the state. There are states that see themselves in the service of a supra-individual truth or value, be it religious or secular, which antedates the law and claims absolute validity. There are other states which do not identify themselves with a particular truth but acknowledge a plurality of truth claims in society. Here, the place of the absolute truth is taken by individual autonomy, that is, a freedom value. While the latter states derive their legitimacy from a consensus of their populace, the former derive it from that truth. Political rule is legitimate insofar as it maintains the truth. The other states are based not on one single truth that is binding for all, but on the consensus of its citizens as to the conditions of peaceful coexistence despite disagreement about the good and just.

For the rule of law this difference is significant, because states that see themselves in the service of an absolute truth have greater difficulties in adhering to rule of law principles than pluralistic ones. They do not view the law as an autonomous system that follows a logic of its own, different from the logic of the political, the economic or the religious system, but develop a purely instrumental relationship to positive law. The law is submitted to the truth. If truth claims conflict with legal requirements, these systems usually give preference to the truth. The application of the law is conditioned on compatibility with the truth. Pluralistic societies with competing ideas of the common good and justice are more prone to accept the rule of law because the law is the product of a political process that follows established rules and can be changed at any time.

For a rule of law-bound political system, the regularity of government action, which excludes arbitrariness, is a value in itself, independently of the content of the law, because it makes government actions predictable for those who are affected by them and allows citizens to organise their behaviour in such a way that they do not come into conflict with the state. Rational planning in personal as well as in economic or other professional matters depends on trust in the law. Stabilising expectations has

[20] See A von Arnauld, *Rechtssicherheit* (Mohr Siebeck, 2006).

become one of the most important functions of the law.[21] If this is an intended effect of the rule of law, it becomes clear that retroactive laws are problematic, just because they submit acts to legal consequences like criminal punishment, which, at the time of the action, were not part of the law so that it was impossible to foresee them and to organise one's behaviour accordingly.

Obviously, the submission of the state to law only makes sense if the law has a regulatory content capable of binding state authorities effectively. This is particularly important in areas where the individual is intensely affected by state actions, such as in criminal or police law. Blank checks to government power cannot develop a binding effect. Neither do laws consisting of vague and open-ended phrases produce sufficient binding force. For this reason, it is meanwhile accepted as part of the rule of law that laws have to be clear enough to allow the addressees to know what to do and what to let. One has to admit, however, that the degree of certainty depends on the subject matter that is regulated. The turn from the liberal state with its limited function to guarantee individual freedom and societal self-regulation via the market to the welfare state and the increasing use of prevention necessarily lowers the standard of legal certainty.[22]

The formal concept of the rule of law contents itself with these aspects. Its formality consists in that the law as instrument and condition of rule has to be passed in due form in order to develop binding force. The due form includes that the competent organ adopted the law in the prescribed procedure. Likewise, publication of the law is an indispensable formal element of the rule of law, because a secret law does not put its addressees in a position to behave accordingly. For the formal concept, the rule of law is identified with the principle of legality. It is indifferent regarding the content of the law. As such, it corresponds with the formal concept of democracy. All questions of content are left to political determination. The question of whether the law is just or justifiable is irrelevant for a purely formal concept of the rule of law.

Understood in a formal sense, the rule of law does not depend on any democratic element. It is compatible with the majority principle, but can exist independently of democracy. As a matter of fact, the rule of law antedated democracy and co-existed with non-democratic systems, provided that they were willing to submit political power to legal rules. In Europe, this was already the case in the late eighteenth century when some absolute monarchs under the influence of the enlightenment agreed to rule according to law, while maintaining the exclusive power to make the law. Later on, when they granted constitutions and thereby moved away from absolutism, the rule of law was entrenched on a constitutional level. It could no longer be revoked unilaterally. Still, these constitutions were not based on popular sovereignty, so that the rule of law owed its existence to the will of the ruler to bind himself.

[21] See N Luhmann, 'Die Funktion des Rechts: Erwartungssicherheit oder Verhaltenssteuerung?' in N Luhmann, *Ausdifferenzierung des Rechts* (Suhrkamp, 1981) 73; N Luhmann, *Das Recht der Gesellschaft* (Suhrkamp, 1993) 131 ss.

[22] See D Grimm (ed), *Wachsende Staatsaufgaben – sinkende Steuerungsfähigkeit des Rechts* (Nomos, 1990).

Even in its formal understanding, the rule of law is no small achievement, because it excludes arbitrary government. But it is a limited achievement, because all questions regarding the content of the law are left open. One of these questions arises because the state, which is subject to the law, is at the same time the source of the law. In the absence of further rules, it is consequently up to the state to decide when and to what extent it will be bound. Where a law is lacking, no constraints apply. The state can exploit such gaps for all sorts of political purposes. From a formal point of view, this would not be objectionable. For a more substantive understanding, the rule of law means also that the state may pursue certain goals or use certain means to reach these goals only on the basis of a statutory authorisation – the so-called reservation of the law.

The reservation of the law might look like an additional formal requirement, but it is of substantive nature because the criteria for determining which type of state action requires an authorisation by law are necessarily substantive. This was already recognised by the pre-democratic constitutions of the nineteenth century. They stipulated that any encroachment upon the citizens' liberty and property required a basis in law. Although these constitutions were not based on democracy as legitimating principle, they accepted a democratic element insofar as elected Parliaments existed without whose consent no law could be passed. As a consequence, limitations of fundamental rights were possible only if the representatives of the people had agreed to them in a law. This is now generally accepted as part of the rule of law. Any state act that prohibits, limits or burdens the use of a fundamental right requires statutory authorisation.

But even if this is recognised, the protective value of the rule of law remains limited as long as the content of the law is left to political discretion. Under such conditions, the rule of law is compatible with oppressive, exploitative and discriminatory legislation. This weakness was already well known in the beginnings of constitutionalism. But the liberal advocates of the early constitutions found the justness of the law sufficiently guaranteed through the consent of the elected representatives in matters of liberty and property. It was assumed that the holders of fundamental rights would not give their consent to laws that restricted individual liberties unduly. Thus, the form of a parliamentary law was the means to protect the substantive values on which the system was built.

This assumption has been refuted by history. In many countries with constitutions of the nineteenth century, whether democratic or pre-democratic, the laws allowed the exploitation of the working class, based on the liberal principles of freedom of contract and freedom of property. This could happen because the election of a representative body was in most cases not based on universal suffrage, but privileged the wealthy and the educated classes, whereas the interests of the unpropertied and uneducated classes were not represented. But the full consequences of this narrowed concept of the rule of law came to light only through the decay of the liberal legal culture during the totalitarian regimes of the twentieth century. Experiencing first hand that the law can also become a tool for gross injustice gave the final incentive to a turn from the formal to a material understanding of the rule of law.

A state devoted to the rule of law in a substantive sense is therefore not only one in which public power is submitted to law, whatever its content may be, but one in which the law reflects certain notions of justice. Obviously everything then depends on the question of what notions of justice guide the legislative process. Here again, the distinction between political systems based on a pre-existing truth or an absolute value and political systems based on individual freedom matters. In the former systems, the rule of law, if accepted at all, applies under the reservation that the law is compatible with the pre-determined truth. In the latter systems, the rule of law applies unconditionally. Consequently, criteria for the justness of the law can only be derived from the law itself, yet from a law that ranks higher than statutory law, namely the constitution.

The modern constitutional state tries to guarantee the justness of the law by a number of substantive principles, most of them part of the bill of rights. This presupposes, however, that fundamental rights are binding for the legislature. This was not always so. Throughout the nineteenth century and deeply into the twentieth century, fundamental rights, although being entrenched in the constitutions, had no impact on legislation. They could be limited by law, and from this it was concluded that they were not above but below the law. They were thus reduced to prohibitions for the executive to interfere with fundamental rights without a basis in law. The legislature was only bound by the formal provisions of the constitution, not by the substantive principles. It needed the experience that formal provisions alone were not sufficient to prevent evident injustice in the form of law to give up this doctrine.

Nowadays, it is constitutional standard that the legislature is bound by fundamental rights. These rights were primarily enacted in the interest of individual freedom vis-à-vis the state. As such they were subjective rights or individual entitlements with vertical application and negative effect. They prohibited certain state actions and were consequently fulfilled by omitting these acts. The principle of proportionality strengthened this negative or defensive effect considerably. Meanwhile, it carries the main burden of rights protection in many legal systems and has become an integral part of the rule of law.[23] Over time, the scope of protection was gradually expanded beyond the classical meaning through the jurisprudence of constitutional courts or courts with the power of judicial review. In the course of this development, each of the three classical elements of rights – subjective, vertical, negative – was complemented by a new element.[24]

The first step led to an understanding of fundamental rights, not only as subjective rights, but also as objective principles or legal expressions of values. As such they form the highest guidelines for the political and social order. This understanding served as basis for the conclusion that their impact was not limited to the vertical dimension. Rather, a horizontal dimension was added according to which their

[23] See A Barak, *Proportionality* (CUP, 2012); M Cohen Elya and I Porat, *Proportionality and Constitutional Culture* (CUP, 2013); G Huscraft, BW Miller and G Webber (eds), *Proportionality and the Rule of Law* (CUP, 2014).

[24] The German Constitutional Court was leading in this respect, see D Robertson, *The Judge as Political Theorist* (Princeton University Press, 2010) 11, 40. For an overview see D Grimm, 'The role of fundamental rights after sixty-five years of constitutional jurisprudence in Germany' (2015) 13 I-CON 9; D Grimm, 'Return to the Traditional Understanding of Fundamental Rights?' in Grimm (n 6) 183.

influence extended also to private law relationships. If the application of private law affected a constitutionally guaranteed freedom, it had to be interpreted in the light of this right. Finally, the negative effect was accompanied by a positive effect which obliged the state to take action when the freedom guaranteed by a fundamental right was not menaced by state action, but by actions of private actors.

These menaces have increased considerably with the unparalleled progress in science and technology and the commercial use of its results. They can only be mitigated by the state. But as they grow out of private activities that are themselves protected by fundamental rights, laws are needed to address the risks. If the legislature were permitted to remain passive in this conflict of constitutional rights, the most assertive interests would tend to prevail over the interests of those in need of protection. In a similar vein, it is meanwhile accepted that the guarantee of fundamental rights extends also to those material means without which a liberty would be an empty shell. Taken together, it is a substantive understanding of individual freedom after the experience that a purely formal understanding was insufficient to reach the ultimate end of rights, namely individual autonomy.

However, fundamental rights alone are not a sufficient guarantee of the justness of the law. They draw limits to and impose directives on the legislature. But they do not furnish a blueprint that the legislature simply has to implement. Society cannot be ordered by a handful of rather general and abstract principles. Laws are indispensable and fundamental rights leave room for legislative discretion. The question of which law is just or serves a society best will always be contested in a pluralist society. Therefore, the law draws its legitimacy in addition to the compatibility with fundamental rights from the democratic process, in which those who are submitted to the law participate in its formation. For this reason, democracy must be understood as a condition of a materially understood rule of law.

Under the rule of law, the law is binding for the state. But the law does not enforce itself. It depends on the willingness of its addressees to follow it, and, if the willingness is missing, on enforcement mechanisms. This holds true not only for autocratic or theocratic regimes, but also for pluralistic societies and democratic states. Therefore, it is of paramount importance to ask what the state organs have to expect when they choose to ignore the law. If individuals act illegally the state may intervene with its police and judicial powers. But if the state itself breaks the law, there is no higher authority to enforce the law. The rule of law is therefore dependent on the existence of devices within the structure of the state, which monitor the lawfulness of government actions. In common law countries, these devices have always existed. The executive could be sued in court. In countries with an absolutist past, the state was able to evade this kind of judicial scrutiny.

It took some efforts until the continental judiciary regained the power to review the legality of state acts in the nineteenth century.[25] In most countries, the result of these efforts was not the expansion of the competencies of the ordinary courts like

[25] See A Gaillet, *L'individu contre l'Etat* (Dalloz, 2012); A Gaillet, 'Le Conseil d'Etat français: histoire d'une exportation difficile en Europe' (2013) 26 *Revue Française de Droit Administratif* 793.

in the common law model, but the establishment of special administrative courts, and took even more time until their jurisdiction became comprehensive. There are, however, still many countries in which citizens lack the means to challenge government acts that affect them – on the highest as well as on the lowest level. In states that derive their legitimacy from an absolute truth rather than from consensus, the lack of administrative justice tends to be the rule. As all experience teaches us, the rule of law is on shaky ground without the possibility to have administrative acts reviewed by courts.

If the rule of law is not defined in formal but in substantive terms, it does not exhaust itself in the legality of the administration. Rather, the legislature, too, is submitted to the legal constraints that are laid down in the constitution. However, the adherence of the legislature to the constitution cannot be determined by administrative courts. If the legislature should not be allowed to ignore the constitution with impunity, its actions must also be subject to judicial review. In the US, this conclusion was already drawn soon after the constitution had been adopted. In the rest of the world, this insight has found gradual acceptance only after bitter experiences with blatantly unjust regimes. The second half of the twentieth century saw the triumph of constitutional adjudication, with judicial review of legislation at its core.[26] Today, judicial review is widely regarded as an integral component of the rule of law. It is its apex, as one can read from time to time.

But from the very beginning, there have also been concerns about the compatibility of judicial review with democracy, especially in the country where judicial review was invented, the US.[27] As a matter of fact, it is a consequence of judicial review that judges can declare majority decisions of the elected representatives of the people null and void if they find them incompatible with the constitution. If fundamental rights are attributed, not only a negative, but also a positive function, it may even occur that the legislature is compelled to do something that it deliberately wanted to avoid. In a formal understanding of democracy, judicial review would be acceptable, if at all, only with regard to the organisational and procedural requirements for legislation. Submitting legislation to a content-based control would mean that it is not the people who rule through their elected representatives, but unelected and not accountable judges.

However, it would not be difficult to defend judicial review if it were not more than applying those limits for government, which the people themselves have laid down in the constitution. But many constitutional provisions, in particular the guiding principles and fundamental rights, are rather vague and open-ended. Their

[26] See C Neal Tate and T Vallinder (eds), *The Global Expansion of Judicial Review* (NYU Press, 1995); M de Visser, *Constitutional Review in Europe* (Hart Publishing, 2014); W Sadurski, *Rights Before Courts. A Study of Constitutional Courts in Postcommunist States of Central and Eastern Europe* (Springer, 2005); S Gardbaum, *The New Commonwealth Model of Constitutionalism* (CUP, 2013); R Sieder, L Schjolden and A Angell (eds), *The Judicialization of Politics in Latin America* (Palgrave, 2005); T Ginsburg, *Judicial Review in New Democracies. Constitutional Courts on Asian Cases* (CUP, 2003); AHY Chen, *Constitutional Courts in Asia* (CUP, 2018); CM Fombad (ed), Constitutional Adjudication in Africa (OUP, 2017).

[27] See B Friedman, 'The Birth of an American Obsession: A History of the Countermajoritarian Difficulty' (2012) 112 *Yale L.J.* 153.

application to cases is not fully determined by the text of the constitution. There is a gap between the abstract and general norms of the constitution and the concrete and individual cases, which has to be bridged by interpretation. However, interpretation is not just discovering a meaning that has been deposited in the text of the norm from the moment of its adoption. Rather, their meaning with regard to a specific case is to a certain extent created by the judges in the process of interpretation. However, if done correctly, this is a legal, not a political operation.[28]

Therefore, the democratic acceptability of judicial review depends on the character of constitutional interpretation. Is it a political or a legal operation? This, in turn, depends on the nature of the viewpoints and arguments permissible in constitutional interpretation. If it is done in a responsible way, only legal arguments may be used to determine the meaning of a constitutional provision with regard to a concrete case. It may be debatable what counts as a legal argument and what does not, but this is an intra-legal debate, and there is no doubt that political or, for that reason, economic or religious arguments are unacceptable. The argument of the critical legal studies movement and its contemporary followers that legal arguments serve only as an ex-post camouflage of what is really going on, rejects the relative autonomy of the legal system and, in spite of its asserted realism, does not draw a realistic picture of judicial behaviour.[29]

If this is accepted, judicial review can be reconciled with democracy, provided that democracy is understood in a substantive way. What remains, however, is a democratic risk. This risk exists because every expansion of the scope and function of fundamental rights by way of interpretation limits the discretion of the legislature and shifts the balance from the democratically legitimised and accountable branches of government to the judiciary. The more constitutional law courts produce, the less space remains for the democratic process. Thus, the apex of the rule of law can turn into a threat to democracy. But there is also a rule of law risk if judicial review were absent. When ordinary law is violated, be it by citizens, or be it by the administration, there is a whole apparatus with the power to enforce the law. In the case of constitutional law, this is different.

Constitutional law applies to the highest authorities of the state. Hence, the addressee of the law and the guarantor of the law are identical. This explains the specific vulnerability of constitutional law compared to ordinary law. There is ample historical evidence that fundamental rights play no significant role in the absence of constitutional adjudication. If they are interpreted as positive rights that oblige the legislature to take action, it is particularly easy to resist a court ruling by simply remaining passive. However, this risk seems to weigh heavier, whereas the democratic risk can be mitigated if it is agreed that the democratic principle puts limits on judicial review, albeit they are difficult to transform into precise rules. Ultimately, the political power to amend the constitution serves as a counterweight against constitutional courts that overstep their boundaries.

[28] See D Grimm, 'What Exactly Is Political about Constitutional Adjudication?' in C Landfried (ed), *Judicial Power* (CUP, 2019) 307.

[29] See Robertson (n 24) 13–20; Grimm (n 28).

However, the judiciary will not be able to render its service if courts are not independent, but integrated in the political chain of command.[30] It is an essential part of the rule of law that laws, once they are enacted, are shielded from political control and obtain an autonomous status, that is: that they will be interpreted and applied according to legal, not political criteria. This is the only way to guarantee that the political branches are bound by law. The guarantee for this is the separation of powers.[31] Separation of powers is more than a distribution of public functions among various governmental departments. It adds the independence of each power within its functional area to this division. Again, that is difficult to accept for countries that are committed to an absolute truth. Absolute truths demand hierarchy; separation of powers limits hierarchy.

As this shows, the rule of law as we understand it now is composed of several layers.[32] It is not a matter of all or nothing, but of more or less. Not all levels were achieved at the outset. Many were only won after bitter setbacks and hard struggles. Today these levels still differ from country to country. Some adopt it, not because of its intrinsic value, but as a means for other purposes, like the attraction of foreign investment. Yet, each additional step means a step forward compared to the previous level. Even the minimum concept of making the law binding on the administration – irrespective of the content of the law – is progress compared to arbitrary rule. However, the realisation of the rule of law becomes more demanding with each additional level and will meet with resistance, often in the name of democracy.

IV. NEW THREATS

It may now have become clearer why the relationship between the two notions is characterised by tension and interdependence. The degrees vary with the concept of the two principles. While in a formal understanding the rule of law can exist independently of democracy, even a formal understanding of democracy depends on the rule of law at least insofar as the democratically formed will of the legislature has to be followed by those who have to execute it. Obedience by the administration cannot be guaranteed by democratic means. It needs the rule of law, whereas a more substantive understanding of democracy implies necessarily the rule of law. Vice versa, a substantive understanding of the rule of law implies democratic law-making as a necessary element of its legitimacy.[33]

While, after the seminal changes of the year 1989, it seemed as if democracy and the rule of law had established themselves as a universal model for the organisation

[30] See eg J Ferejohn and L Kramer, *Judicial Independence in a Democracy* (CUP, 2006); S Shetreet and C Fiorsyth (eds), *The Culture of Judicial Independence* (Martinus Nijhoff, 2011).

[31] See C Möllers, *The Three Branches* (OUP, 2013).

[32] See D Grimm, *Stufen der Rechtsstaatlichkeit, Juristenzeitung* (Mohr Siebeck, 2009) 596 (English version in Dirk Ehlers e.a. (eds), *Constitutionalism and Good Governance* (Nomos, 2014) 141; also in (2011) 1 *European-Asian Journal of Law and Governance* 5.

[33] See J Habermas, *Faktizität und Geltung* (Suhrkamp, 1992), esp 166 ss; J Habermas, 'Inklusioin – Einbeziehen oder Einschließen? Zum Verhältnis von Nation, Rechtsstaat und Demokratie' in Habermas, *Die Einbeziehung des Anderen* (n 5) 154; Habermas, 'Zusammenhang' (n 5) 293.

and legitimation of public authority, the beginning of the twenty-first century sees a backlash in many parts of the world. Political parties and populist movements turn away from pluralist democracy and the substantive rule of law concept. Democracy is redefined as purely majoritarian or identitarian. The rule of law is regarded as an impediment to the implementation of the alternative model of democracy. The historical experience that had led to the concept of democracy and the rule of law described here is losing plausibility. The price is paid by those values that inspired the achievement of constitutionalism from its very beginning until today.

5

EU Rule of Law: The State of Play Following the Debates Surrounding the 2019 Commission's Communication

BARBARA GRABOWSKA-MOROZ AND
DIMITRY VLADIMIROVICH KOCHENOV*

I. INTRODUCTION

IN THIS CHAPTER we analyse the state of the debate on the Rule of Law challenges and developments in the European Union following the release of the 2019 Commission Communication 'Strengthening the Rule of Law: A Blueprint for Action'[1] and explain why the shortsighted approach of the Commission gives rise to worry. All the boxes seemed to be ticked during the 'discussion' exercise; yet the outcome has seemingly brought the Commission nowhere.

This latest round of the debate on the Rule of Law in the EU was originally initiated in April 2019 when the Commission published its Communication 'Further strengthening the Rule of Law within the Union. State of play and possible next steps'[2] and concluded in July 2019 with the publication of the blueprint for future Rule of Law action. Discussion took place at the time when the EU is facing the most serious Rule of Law crisis since its founding.[3] This crisis has been tackled with recourse to Treaty

* Both at CEU Democracy Institute, Budapest. This research was carried out as part of the RECONNECT project, which has received funding from the European Union's Horizon 2020 research and innovation programme under grant agreement No 770142 and further develops the analysis offered in D Kochenov, 'Elephants in the room: The European Commission's 2019 Communication on the Rule of Law' (2019) 11 *Hague Journal on the Rule of Law* 423. The authors are grateful to Emma Schulte for her assistance.

[1] European Commission, 'Strengthening the Rule of Law within the Union. A blueprint for action' (Communication) COM (2019) 343 final.

[2] European Commission, 'Further strengthening the Rule of Law within the Union: State of play and possible next steps' (Communication) COM (2019) 163 final.

[3] KL Scheppele, D Kochenov and B Grabowska-Moroz, 'EU Vlaues Are Law, after All' (2020) 39 *Yearbook of European Law* 1; M Smith, 'Staring into the abyss: A crisis of the Rule of Law in the EU' (2019) 25 *European Law Journal* 561; D Adamski, 'The social contract of democratic backsliding in the "new EU" countries' (2019) 56 *Common Market Law Review* 623; L Pech and KL Scheppele, 'Illiberalism within: Rule of law backsliding in the EU' (2017) 19 *Cambridge Yearbook of European Legal Studies* 3.

instruments such as Article 7 TEU as well as via the route of political innovation[4] and, crucially, in courts.[5] Article 7 TEU predictably showed numerous shortcomings – mainly political ones – with respect to enforcing the EU values.[6] Despite milestone CJEU rulings regarding the supranational Court's competence to engage with the independence of judiciary[7] there is a sense that those might not be sufficient to solve the problem of Rule of Law backsliding – intentional demolition of the separation of powers in Member States by those in power.[8] The Commission's Communications and public consultations demonstrate what the available options to tackle the ongoing crisis are in the eyes of the Commission and what tools could be deployed to make the EU's response more effective. A clear vision of how to get out of the current impasse is, however, missing entirely: the Commission did not provide a convincing strategy on how to tackle constitutional capture plaguing several Member States.

II. THE RULE OF LAW DEBATE OF THE COMMISSION – SCOPE, TOPIC, OUTCOME

In April 2019 the European Commission published a communication 'Further strengthening the Rule of Law within the Union: State of play and possible next steps.'[9] The Commission acknowledged that 'the Union's fundamental values and principles, including the Rule of Law, are under pressure and need particular attention.'[10] This view had been expressed already in 2013 by Commissioner Vivienne Reding, who stated that 'the testing moment for the Rule of Law always comes in times of crisis'.[11] She referred to three situations perceived as Rule of Law

[4] D Kochenov and L Pech, 'Better late than never: On the European Commission's Rule of Law Framework and its first activation' (2016) 54 *Journal of Common Market Studies* 1062; E Hirsch Ballin, 'Mutual trust. The virtue of reciprocity – Strengthening the acceptance of the Rule of Law through peer review' in C Closa and D Kochenov (eds), *Reinforcing Rule of Law Oversight in the EU* (CUP, 2016); for an overview, see C Closa, D Kochenov and JHH Weiler, 'Reinforcing the Rule of Law oversight in the European Union' (2014) *EUI RSCAS Research Paper* 2014/25.

[5] L Pech and D Kochenov, 'Respect for the Rule of Law in the Case Law of the Court of Justice', SIEPS Report (2021); TT Koncewicz, 'The supranational Rule of Law as first principle of the European public space – On the Journey in ever closer union among the peoples of Europe in flux' (2020) 5 *Palestra* 168; P Van Elsuwege and F Grimmelprez, 'Protecting the Rule of Law in the EU legal order: A constitutional role for the Court of Justice' (2020) 16 *European Constitutional Law Review* 8; C Rizcallah and V Davio, 'L'article 19 du Traité sur l'Union européenne: sesame de l'Union de droit' (2020) 122 *Quarterly Human Rights Review* 156; D Kochenov and P Bárd, 'The last soldier standing? Courts versus politicians and the Rule of Law crisis in the new Member States of the EU' (2019) 1 *European Yearbook of Constitutional Law* 243.

[6] D Kochenov, 'Article 7 TEU: A Commentary on a much talked-about "dead" provision' (2018) 38 *Polish Yearbook of International Law* 165.

[7] Case C-64/16 *Associação Sindical dos Juízes Portugueses v Tribunal de Contas* [2018] 3 CMLR 16; Case 619/18 *Commission v Poland* [2020] 1 CMLR 6. cf. S Adam and P Van Elsuwege, 'L'exigence d'indépendance du juge, paradigm de l'Union européenne comme union de droit' (2018) 9 *Journal de droit européen* 334; L Pech and S Platon, 'Judicial independence under threat: The Court of Justice to the rescue in the *ASJP* Case' (2018) 55 *Common Market Law Review* 1836.

[8] Pech and Scheppele (n 3).

[9] Commission (n 2).

[10] ibid 2.

[11] V Reding, '*Speech: The EU and the Rule of Law – What next?*' (4 September 2013) at https://ec.europa.eu/commission/presscorner/detail/en/SPEECH_13_677.

crises – in France, Hungary and Romania – which 'quickly took a systemic dimension and revealed systemic Rule of Law problems.'[12] As she stated at that time 'the Commission has been rather successful' in dealing with those cases. Despite that optimism and the new 'pre-Article 7' mechanism introduced in 2014,[13] the situation has deteriorated significantly since 2014 and the 2019 Communication announced that it aimed 'to enrich the debate on further strengthening the Rule of Law within the Union.'[14] The Commission confirmed that there still is a problem with 'the ability of the Union to address' the Rule of Law crisis and also underlined that solving this issue is a matter of trust.[15] As the situation with the Rule of Law in the captured states deteriorated with increasing pace, the Commission's Communication offered three possible avenues for reaching possible solutions, focusing on the triad of: promotion, prevention and response.

The Commission invited stakeholders to submit their input on how to deal with the crisis of the Rule of Law in the EU. As a result, more than 60 contributions have been received (from Member States, EU institutions and bodies, international organisations and political actors, the judiciary and judicial networks, civil society organisations, academia and business associations).[16] On the one hand, the Open Society European Policy Institute underlined that the debate initiated by the Commission was not part of formal open consultations but informal ones with targeted outreach to key stakeholders.[17] On the other hand, the government of Poland expressed doubts regarding consultations and their scope suggesting that they might not bring 'desired, viable results' questioning 'whether the proposals would be legally applicable in the EU legal environment.'[18] Similar criticism can be found in the input from the government of Hungary, which stated that 'reliance on opinions of external experts and non-governmental institutions raises the question of accountability and transparency' without providing analysis if those would be correct or not. The opposite view of the European Commission's initiative was presented by Slovakia, stating that 'Such transparent and constructive approach has the potential to path the way towards proper setting of the new mechanism on the Rule of Law.'

Reactions to the Commission's consultation revealed obvious pronounced divisions between the Member States on the issue of the Rule of Law. Indeed, the Member States that provided their input to the Commission were divided into two

[12] ibid.

[13] European Commission, 'A new EU Framework to strengthen the Rule of Law' (Communication) COM (2014) 158 final; D Kochenov and L. Pech 'Monitoring and enforcement of the Rule of Law in the European Union: Rhetoric and reality' (2015) 11 *European Constitutional Law Review* 512.

[14] Commission (n 10).

[15] For a magisterial treatment of this concept in EU law, see C Rizcallah, *Le principe de confiance mutuelle en droit de l'Union européenne* (Larcier, 2020).

[16] Submissions available to the public were published at https://ec.europa.eu/info/publications/stakeholder-contributions_en.

[17] 'This appears at odds with the Commission's commitment under the Better Regulation Agenda to design EU policies and laws transparently, with evidence, and backed up by the views of citizens and stakeholders' (Open Society European Institute, 'Communication from the European Commission on further strengthening the Rule of Law within the Union: state of play and possible next steps. Contribution by the Open Society European Policy Institute' (June 2019) 15).

[18] 'Given the above, we express our doubt whether the form of a communication and an open invitation to express thoughts on the Rule of Law framework addressed to a large group of governmental and non-governmental actors will bring desired, viable results and whether the proposals would be legally applicable in the EU legal environment.' ('Poland's contribution' (17 July 2019) 1).

groups – those supporting further strengthening of the EU's response to the Rule of Law crisis (including Sweden, Finland, and the Netherlands) and those which expressed their deep scepticism (the Member States which face the on-going Article 7 TEU procedure against them, that is, Poland and Hungary). Especially the criticism expressed by the government of Hungary was of a fundamental nature – the government did not agree with the Commission's diagnosis (which was not challenged by other stakeholders) that the Rule of Law is under pressure in the EU and that this issue needs particular attention. Instead, according to Hungary, the 'Rule of Law is increasingly used as a tool of political leverage'. Instead of focusing on the national level, the Hungarian Government expressed a belief in the general need to strengthen and uphold the Rule of Law in the activities of EU institutions.[19] The opposite position was defended by the Swedish parliamentary committee which underlined that 'the broader discussion on further strengthening the Rule of Law initiated by the Commission is urgent'. Much more precise in this respect were recommendations presented by the International Commission of Jurists, which underlined that the EU institutions must enhance transparency and stakeholder participation, including in legislative proceedings and access to information.[20]

An interesting example of complete denial that any Rule of Law debate is needed was the submission of the Hungarian organisation Center for Fundamental Rights, advancing the arguments similar to those supported by the Hungarian Government. First of all, according to the Center's submission, 'the debate isn't legal in nature but political and ideological' and represents a 'clash of worldviews'. Secondly, they argued that 'sufficient safeguards for the principle of the Rule of Law were created by the Hungarian National Assembly'.[21] Thirdly, 'disregarding the national sovereignty and constitutional identities of Member States, the Commission is trying to create an EU level control over the application of the principle of the Rule of Law within the Member States.'[22] Finally, the Center pointed to the existence of 'more urgent issues' such as the migration crisis. The EU should also 'take actions regarding yellow vest movement in France, or the police abuse evident in the reaction to the Catalan independence referendum'.[23] This was, however, the only example of a submission which expressed complete denial that a debate is needed. Other stakeholders almost fully agreed that such debate in the EU is required.

The second fundamental issue which arises from the analysis of the submissions initiated by the Commission in April 2019 points to the differences regarding seemingly the most basic issue – the definition of the Rule of Law. According to the

[19] State Secretariat for EU Relations of the Prime Minister's Office, 'Position paper of the State Secretariat for EU Relations of the Prime Minister's Office, Hungary on the Consultation about the Communication of the European Commission on "Further strengthening the Rule of Law within the Union"' (28 May 2019).

[20] International Commission of Jurists, 'Submission by the International Commission of Jurists to the European Commission's Consultation on "Further Strengthening the Rule of Law Within the Union"' (June 2019) 5.

[21] Center for Fundamental Rights, 'Remarks on the Press Release on the Rule of Law circulated by the European Commission' (4 June 2019) 2.

[22] ibid.

[23] ibid 6.

Commission, the Rule of Law is 'well-defined in its core meaning'.[24] The leading scholarly accounts seem to support this view,[25] at least in part, as far as the internal definition of the concept goes.[26] The Commission usually follows the Venice Commission's main findings in this respect[27] and states that the Rule of Law includes, among others, 'principles such as legality, implying a transparent, accountable, democratic and pluralistic process for enacting laws; legal certainty; prohibiting the arbitrary exercise of executive power; effective judicial protection by independent and impartial courts, effective judicial review including respect for fundamental rights; separation of powers; and equality before the law.'[28] Probably not surprisingly, the harshest criticism of this universal definition came from a Hungarian organisation – Centre for Fundamental Rights –, which, first of all, found that the Rule of Law is a 'hard-to-define, malleable concept', which is of course true, but not entirely, given the clarity shaped by the Venice Commission, and, secondly, it found it 'worrying', when 'in the absence of a single, detailed definition it is possible to discriminate against certain Member States on the basis of the Rule of Law, considering political interests only.' According to the Hungarian Government it is national institutions that shape the content of the Rule of Law.[29] Such an approach would suggest the requirement of acceptance of different Rule of Law definitions in different Member States, which could sit uneasily, at least as far as the crucial essence of all the EU's values goes, with the wording and the spirit of Article 2 TEU.[30] The International Bar Association underlined that in the case of the Rule of Law, content of the laws matters, they must for instance protect fundamental rights. So there are of course broader versions of the definition than the one provided by the Commission. Also the International Commission of Jurists underlined that the Rule of Law is 'inextricably linked to and interdependent with protection of human rights'.[31] Narrower definitions, however, are not easily available, which is not surprising. So the Council of Europe also underlined the role of the judiciary and national human rights institutions as the main necessary condition for the Rule of Law.[32] The broadest definition, however, was provided by the European Trade Union Confederation which underlined that ensuring the Rule of Law in the EU includes enforcement of fundamental social

[24] Commission (n 2) 1.

[25] L Pech, 'The Rule of Law as a constitutional principle of the European Union' (2009) *Jean Monnet Working Paper Series* No 4/2009; L Pech and J Grogon, 'Meaning and Scope of the EU Rule of Law' (2020) RECONNECT Deliverable 7.2.

[26] L Pech, 'Promoting the Rule of Law abroad: On the EU's limited contribution to the shaping of an international understanding of the Rule of Law' in D Kochenov and F Amtenbrink (eds), *The European Union's Shaping of the International Legal Order* (CUP, 2013).

[27] Rule of Law Checklist, adopted by the Venice Commission at its 106th Plenary Session (Venice, 11–12 March 2016), CDL-AD(2016)007-e.

[28] Commission (n 2) 1.

[29] State Secretariat for EU Relations of the Prime Minister's Office (n 19).

[30] M Klamert and D Kochenov, 'Article 2' in M Kellerbauer, M Klamert, and J Tomkin (eds), *The EU Treaties and the Charter of Fundamental Rights. A Commentary* (OUP, 2019).

[31] The ICJ referred to the 'ICJ Tunis Declaration on Reinforcing the Rule of Law and Human Rights' (March 2019) available at www.icj.org/wp-content/uploads/2019/04/Universal-ICJ-The-Tunis-Declaration-Advocacy-2019-ENG.pdf.

[32] Council of Europe, 'Council of Europe's secretariat comment to the Communication from the Commission on Further strengthening the Rule of Law within the Union State of play and possible next steps' 2019.

rights. Despite all the differences regarding understanding of the Rule of Law, most of the stakeholders found that the April communication was needed due to the ongoing Rule of Law crisis, where an effective solution still has not been adopted. How broad the definition of the Rule of Law should be in the EU context was, ultimately, not an issue, given the clarity of the position adopted by the Venice Commission.

III. JULY 2019 COMMUNICATION

The July 2019 press release 'Initiative to strengthen the Rule of Law in the EU', published on the Commission's website, informed the public that the Commission 'has set out concrete actions to strengthen the Union's capacity to promote and uphold the Rule of Law'. The Communication resulting from the stakeholders' submissions underlined that it sets out 'actions for the short and medium term'.[33] The Communication's findings were supplemented with the results of a Eurobarometer survey undertaken by the Commission in all Member States, among more than 27,000 respondents. The principle of the Rule of Law was divided into 17 sub-principles which were further grouped into three areas:

1. 'Legality, legal certainty, equality before the law, separation of powers' (equality before the law, clarity and stability of law, ease in following how parliament adopts laws, lawmakers act in public interest, independent controls of law).
2. 'Prohibition of arbitrariness and penalties for corruption' (clarity of public authorities' decisions, independent review of public authorities' decisions, unbiased decisions of public authorities, making decisions in public interest, acting of corruption, codes of ethics for politicians).
3. Effective judicial protection by independent courts (access to an independent court, length or cost of court proceedings, independence of judges, the proper investigation of crimes, respect for and application of court rulings, codes of conduct of politicians).[34]

The above definition of the Rule of Law is much more detailed compared with the findings of the Venice Commission or the Commission's April 2019 Communication. The survey was further supplemented with questions about media and civil society. The Eurobarometer report shows that 89 per cent of respondents considered it important or even essential that all EU Member States respect the core EU values, including fundamental rights, the Rule of Law and democracy. However, the majority of respondents do not feel sufficiently informed about the EU's fundamental values.[35]

The July Communication follows the structure offered in the Communication published by the Commission in April 2019 and analyses the possible actions in three areas: promotion, prevention and response. Each section is summarised with conclusions divided into two groups: action which will be taken by the Commission and recommendations addressed to other institutions.

[33] Commission (n 1) 2.
[34] Rule of law, Report, Special Eurobarometer 489 (July 2019) 3-4.
[35] ibid 10.

A. Promotion

The European Commission identified two main gaps regarding the Rule of Law which need to be fulfilled within the 'promotion' part. Those include the lack of information and limited general public knowledge concerning the current challenges to the Rule of Law.[36] Numerous stakeholders referred to 'Rule of Law culture'.[37] The International Commission of Jurists presented a broad stance on this issue, arguing that 'legal and institutional safeguards for the Rule of Law amount to little without people who are committed to making their protection a reality'.[38] The European Trade Union Confederation referred to a 'Rule of Law society', which was confirmed by the Commission stating that 'the Rule of Law has a direct impact on the life of every citizen'.[39]

i. Civil Society and Media

Many of the contributions underlined a need to support (ie, financially) civil society.[40] The Communication underlined in this respect the role of the future Rights and Values programme, which needs to be accepted by the EP and Council.[41] Contributions suggested further steps such as introducing a kind of 'civil conditionality', meaning to 'link any strategy to strengthen the Rule of Law to the development of an enabling civic space in Europe'.[42] Furthermore, it was suggested to establish a 'rapid response system', allowing the detection of civic space and Rule of Law breaches. Such solutions have not been implemented, however, into the Communication. The Commission expressed its promise to 'continue to pay special attention to attempts to pressurize civil society and independent media and further support their work'.[43] The cases of Hungarian Lex-NGO[44] and Lex-CEU[45] suggest that this 'continuation' requires further improvement.[46] The former, decided in June 2020, showed that

[36] Commission (n 1) 5.

[37] Dutch Ministry of Foreign Affairs, 'Commission Communication 3 April 2019 – Rule of law, Input from Netherlands' (2 July 2019) 1; Civil Liberties Union for Europe, 'A Response to the Commission Communication on further strengthening the Rule of Law within the Union' (June 2019) 5.

[38] International Commission of Jurists (n 20).

[39] European Trade Union Confederation, 'ETUC comments on Commission Communication on "Further strengthening the Rule of Law within the Union. State of Play and possible next steps" (COM(2019) 163 final)' (24 June 2019) 1.

[40] European Humanist Federation; Civil Society Europe; Helsinki Foundation for Human Rights and Hungarian Helsinki Committee; International Commission of Jurists; Open Society European Policy Institute; Civil Liberties Union for Europe.

[41] European Commission, 'Proposal for a Regulation of the European Parliament and of the Council establishing the Rights and Values programme' (Proposal) COM (2018) 383 final/2.

[42] Civil Society Europe, 'Response to the EC Communication "Further Strengthening the Rule of Law within the Union"' (4 June 2019) 3.

[43] Commission (n 1) 6.

[44] Case C-78/18 *Commission v Hungary* [2020] ECLI:EU:C:2020:476.

[45] Case C-66/18 *Commission v Hungary* [2020] ECLI:EU:C:2020:792.

[46] 'Those civil society organisations or individuals who had conveyed their views to the EP, either in writing, in person meetings or by attending the hearings in LIBE, were frequently subjected to harassment as a result of their participation' (Helsinki Foundation for Human Rights, 'Opinion on the Communication from the Commission to the European Parliament, the European Council and the Council concerning "Further strengthening the Rule of Law within the Union. State of play and possible next steps" (COM(2019)163 final)' 4 June 2019).

the Commission definitely had not done enough to secure NGOs against negative consequences of the 'Transparency Law' adopted in Hungary. The new law, which imposed new obligations on NGOs receiving foreign funds, was found to violate obligations under Article 63 TFEU and Articles 7, 8 and 12 of the Charter of Fundamental Rights of the European Union. The Court underlined that the law in question is of such a nature as to create a 'generalized climate of mistrust vis-à-vis the associations and foundations at issue, in Hungary, and to stigmatize them.'[47] This particular case shows that 'special attention' from the Commission should involve a timely response, including application for interim measures, not only limited to diplomatic expression of 'concern',[48] especially when similar measures have been already announced by other authoritarian players.[49] The latter allows coming to the same conclusions: while the Hungarian government lost this case too, the Central European University is no longer present in Hungary as a result of the government's pressure. The case of CEU is the most worrying example of the destruction of a leading institution of higher education in full view, and with full knowledge, of the EU. The Commission's victory came too late: the school is already in Vienna and Orbán regime's obscurantism has won for now.

The same doubts apply to freedom of the media in the EU Member States. In light of the Eurobarometer survey, a wide range of media allowing for sufficient information and the expression of different opinions was important, or essential, to 87 per cent of respondents.[50] However the Commission does not discuss the most extreme cases where captured public media are platforms for domestic smear campaigns against civil society, political opposition and even against EU institutions themselves.[51]

In this context the Commission's proposed remedy is upsetting. The Communication mentions a 'yearly event on Rule of Law' for dialogue with civil society as well as a new communication strategy. The Commission thus wants everyone to speak with everyone about the Rule of Law, including national parliaments, international organisations and institutions. However, if some elections, although free, are not fair,[52] how much 'Rule of Law learning' can we expect from the dialogues between the unfairly elected 'parliaments' in the captured Member States and the real parliaments? What can we learn from the NGOs if captured Member States cut their

[47] Case C-78/18 *Commission v Hungary* [2020] ECLI:EU:C:2020:476.

[48] P Bárd, J Grogan and L Pech, 'Defending the open society against its enemies: The Court of Justice's ruling in C-78/18 *Commission v Hungary (transparency of associations)*' (*VerfBlog*, 22 June 2020) at https://verfassungsblog.de/defending-the-open-society-against-its-enemies/.

[49] 'The government is preparing an attack on NGOs in Poland' (*Ruleoflaw.pl*, 12 May 2020) at https://ruleoflaw.pl/the-government-is-preparing-an-attack-on-ngos-in-poland/; W Czuchnowski and A Kondzińska, 'Minister of Justice set to crack down on NGOs, announcing new foreign influence transparency law' (*wyborcza.pl*, 10 August 2020) at https://wyborcza.pl/7,173236,26198198,minister-of-justice-set-to-crack-down-on-ngos-announcing-new.html.

[50] Rule of law, Report (n 34) 44.

[51] A Chapman, 'Pluralism under attack: The assault on press freedom in Poland' (*Freedom House* June 2017) at https://freedomhouse.org/report/special-reports/assault-press-freedom-poland; Joint Mission to Hungary, 'Conclusions of the Joint International Press Freedom Mission to Hungary' (3 December 2019), available at https://ipi.media/wp-content/uploads/2019/12/Hungary-Conclusions-International-Mission-Final.pdf.

[52] S Walker and D Boffey, 'Hungary election: OSCE monitors deliver a damning verdict' *The Guardian* (9 April 2018) at www.theguardian.com/world/2018/apr/09/hungary-election-osce-monitors-deliver-damning-verdict.

funding streams and harass those who still dare to criticise the politicians in power?[53] The Commission seems to be willing to send a message of friendly ignorance, which could unfortunately be dangerous, given the high stakes involved.

One of the main tools allowing civil society to fulfill its functions is access to public information. Despite the fact that the need for improvement of EU institutional transparency is broadly discussed in the literature,[54] the Communication does not set any new aims in this respect. Also analysis dealing with the European judicial networks is quite general. The Commission found that those 'should be supported to further promote the Rule of Law', whereas concrete proposals were presented by the stakeholders. It was suggested that some form of judiciary representation should be recognised at the EU level.[55]

ii. The Council of Europe

The second dimension of the promotion of the Rule of Law advocated by the Commission in its 2019 Communication deals with the relationship between the European Union and the Council of Europe and its institutions (especially the Venice Commission and GRECO). Only the submission from the Hungarian Government questions the role of the findings of the Council of Europe institutions for the purpose of EU actions.[56] The recent main concerns regarding the relations between the Council of Europe and the EU dealt with the reservations expressed by the Parliamentary Assembly of the Council of Europe on possible monitoring mechanisms, which could cause the 'risks of the duplication of mechanisms and standards, fragmentation or inconsistency of applicable standards'.[57]

In addition to general reference to relations between the CoE and EU, the Commission surprisingly stated that the EU accession to the European Convention on Human Rights 'will be a strong political signal of the Union's commitment to the Rule of Law'.[58] Also numerous contributions underlined the need for such accession.[59]

[53] M Szuleka, 'First victims or last guardians? The consequences of Rule of Law backsliding for NGOs: case studies of Hungary and Poland' (2018) *CEPS Paper in Liberty and Security in Europe* No 6.

[54] A Alemanno and O Ştefan, 'Openness at the Court of Justice of the European Union: Toppling a taboo' (2014) 51 *Common Market Law Review* 97.

[55] 'Furthermore, there is a need for a formalised status within the EU, for judicial networks as representatives of the European judiciaries. The other branches of state have their own formalised EU level bodies that enable them to advise the EU Institutions. The national judiciaries of the EU do not have such a representative body.' (The General Assembly of the European Network of Councils for the Judiciary, 'The ENCJ Bratislava Manifesto. For the European Commission and European Parliament 2019 – 2024 mandate' (7 June 2019) 2.

[56] 'While objective and transparent sources like court judgements or opinions of the Venice Commission could be taken into account when assessing possible Rule of Law issues, the findings and analyses of the Council of Europe should not serve as an automatic basis for measures affecting rights and obligations stemming from EU membership' (State Secretariat for EU Relations of the Prime Minister's Office (n 19) 3).

[57] Parliamentary Assembly of the Council of Europe, 'Establishment of a European Union mechanism on democracy, the Rule of Law and fundamental rights' Resolution 2273 (2019), point 13.

[58] Commission (n 1) 7.

[59] 'In this context, the EU's accession to the European Convention on Human Rights should be pursued' ('Input of the Portuguese Government regarding the Commission Communication – Further strengthening the Rule of Law within the Union of 3 April 2019, to the European Parliament, the European Council and the Council' (25 June 2019)); 'In line with the Lisbon Treaty and Article 59 of the European Convention

This was, however, torpedoed by the Court of Justice in its infamous Opinion 2/13,[60] coming down to a bid for the purification of the absolute autonomy of the legal order of which it is the custodian, using the Rule of Law as a shield against the introduction of the high standards of human rights protection in the EU.[61] Mentioning the revamping of the Council of Europe accession process – notwithstanding the fact that the EU is obliged by the Treaties to eventually accede – is both puzzling and somewhat, if not entirely, out of place. Should the Commission formulate the constitutional capture problem clearly, there would be no need at all to spill the ink focusing on the unlikely developments that our self-minded Court does not welcome.[62] The EU's accession is of no relevance for the most burning issues facing Hungary and Poland today and the Commission could be expected to be clear on this: Rule of Law backsliding and the crisis it has caused has nothing to do with the EU's accession to the ECHR. Indirectly it was confirmed in the Council of Europe contribution, which stated that 'the expected accession of the European Union to the ECHR will reinforce the consistency of the legal obligations throughout the continent and, by subjecting the EU institutions themselves to the same obligations and same scrutiny, will reinforce EU's credibility and legitimacy in debating on Rule of Law issues and promoting common and coherent approaches based on the Rule of Law standards enshrined in the ECHR'.[63]

B. Prevention

The 'prevention' section of the Communication is dominated by the idea of new 'dedicated monitoring' of the Rule of Law related developments in Member States.[64] It eventually took the form of a Rule of Law Review Cycle, which aims to 'identify risks to the Rule of Law, develop possible solutions, and target support early on.'[65] The Cycle seems to be in line with what the European Parliament has long argued for[66] and covers a broad scope of Rule of Law issues such as law-making, effective judicial protection, the independence and impartiality of the courts, the separation of powers, and also the capacity of Member States to fight corruption, as well as media pluralism and elections. The Commission wants it to be based on existing

on Human Rights (ECHR), the EU will accede to the Convention in the future' ('Slovenia's response to the Communication on Further Strengthening the Rule of Law' 3); 'It is therefore important that the EU should accede to the European Convention on Human Rights (ECHR), as it is required to do by Article 6.2 TEU' (International Commission of Jurists).

[60] Opinion 2/13 *ECHR Accession II* [2014] ECLI:EU:C:2014:2454.

[61] D Kochenov, 'EU law without the Rule of Law. Is the veneration of autonomy worth it?' (2015) 34 *Yearbook of European Law* 74. The whole CJEU's approach to the rule of law could be described as a using the concept as a tool to claim supremacy: D Kochenov, 'Rule of Law as a Tool to Claim Supremacy' in A Bodnar and J Urbanik (eds), *Περιμένοντας τους Βαρβάρους. Law in the days of Constitutional Crisis. Studies offered to Mirosław Wyrzykowski* (CH Beck/Nomos, 2021).

[62] But see J Lindeboom, 'Why EU law claims supremacy' (2018) 38 *Oxford Journal of Legal Studies* 328.

[63] Council of Europe (n 32) 5.

[64] Commission (n 1) 9.

[65] ibid.

[66] P Bárd, S Carrera, E Guild and D Kochenov, 'An EU mechanism on democracy, the Rule of Law and fundamental rights'(2016) *CEPS Paper on Liberty and Security* No 91.

sources of information, which will be 'brought together and complemented more effectively'. Despite that the Commission announced that a network of national contact points will be established, which could serve as a 'forum for discussion' and allow for mutual exchange of information and dialogue on Rule of Law related topics. The Commission argues that the 'process of dialogue is particularly relevant for detecting potential Rule of Law issues early' and provides opportunity 'to discuss Rule of Law sensitive reforms'.[67] Furthermore, accelerated law making procedures adopted on many occasions in troublesome Member States (eg, Poland) makes such expectations naïve. Solving the problem of Rule of Law backsliding (meaning a deliberate political choice of domestic political institutions) through dialogue and cooperation is impossible, since dialogue and cooperation cannot be an answer to a calculated choice not to comply with the core principles, thus abusing the vulnerabilities of the enforcement tools available in the context of the EU legal system, while freeriding on the principle of mutual trust and reaping the economic benefits of the internal market. It is one of the reasons why the peer-review process was criticised by the stakeholders during the consultations.[68] Furthermore, conducting a broad dialogue about Rule of Law developments in Member States might be, however, challenging, if the domestic environment for discussion regarding civil society, media or academia is hostile.

There are two more problems with the regular assessment proposed by the Commission, however. First, it threatens to significantly alter the nature of EU federalism:[69] for the Commission to mingle with the essential features of the Member States outside the scope of fundamentally exceptional cases – such as Hungary and Poland today – has the potential to open Pandora's box of the re-articulation of the limits of EU action. The outcome could be ongoing violations in the powerful Member States, coupled with the increased bullying of the smallest Member States, which would have little say in the face of the Commission's pressure in a situation where the law is merely 'soft' and, consequently, the strictness of the basic rules regarding the division of powers between the EU and the Member States becomes more and more lax.[70] Secondly, the regular reporting is premised on the Member States' benevolence and their willingness to comply. Given that the starting paradigm mistakenly embraced by the Commission is entirely false, as demonstrated above, the outcomes of what the Commission proposed are highly unlikely to bring about a positive change to the EU's Rule of Law landscape, let alone solve the core Rule of Law problems on which the Commission's Communication remains silent. What they can do, however, is endanger the fragile balance of powers between the EU and the Member States in a situation where outright exceptional cases, which are absolutely

[67] Commission (n 1) 11.

[68] 'MEDEL wishes to make clear its strong opposition to a peer-to-peer review mechanism between Member States as the one that has recently been proposed' (Magistrats Européens pour la Démocratie et les Libertés, 'Contribution to the debate launched by the European Commission on "Further strengthening the Rule of Law within the Union"').

[69] R Schütze, *From Dual to Cooperative Federalism* (OUP, 2009); D Kochenov (ed), *EU Citizenship and Federalism: The Role of Rights* (CUP, 2017).

[70] O Ştefan, 'Soft law and the enforcement of EU law' in A Jakab and D Kochenov (eds), *The Enforcement of EU Law and Values* (OUP, 2017).

clear, are not referred to by name. A false paradigm cannot be placed at the core of the crucial roadmap to solve the outstanding problems, however ill-identified.

Furthermore, the stakeholders suggested that the monitoring mechanism could build upon the experience of the UN peer review mechanisms, such as the Universal Periodic Review.[71] In this respect the role of civil society cannot be limited only to the 'promotion' aspect, but needs to be secured also with respect to the 'Rule of Law review cycle'. Additionally, 'setting up structured means of input from civil society would greatly enhance transparency of the process' and 'would also contribute to protecting against possible negative consequences, such as reprisals, smear campaigns, harassment of civil society organisations or individual human rights defenders, by sending a clear message that the role of civil society is recognised and their contributions are valued by the European institutions'.[72]

In the context of its Rule of Law Communication the Commission underlined the role of the Fundamental Rights Agency, which developed the EU Fundamental Rights Information System (EFRIS) – a comprehensive database that is relevant for Rule of Law discussion. Grimheden and Toggenburg have long advocated the deeper involvement of the FRA in the management of the Rule of Law crises and it is great that the Commission is starting to take the Agency seriously in the Rule of Law context.[73] However, the Communication does not suggest that the mandate of FRA be broadened,[74] which would support the independent role of the FRA in the Rule of Law field.[75]

The main result of the Rule of Law Review Cycle is an annual Rule of Law Report[76] published by the Commission, providing synthesis of the developments and a source of information for further inter-institutional dialogue.[77] The Communication does not explain, however, how this aspect will contribute to prevention of Rule of

[71] 'The methods developed and used by the monitoring mechanisms of the United Nations human rights treaty bodies could serve as a model to build on in this respect, where there are clear rules about how those wishing to contribute information may do so, and such information is made publicly available.' (Helsinki Foundation for Human Rights (n 46); 'If a credible peer review mechanism were to be established, it could probably draw on the experience of the Universal Periodic Review (UPR), where everyone reviews everyone in order to avoid a Poland reviews Hungary type of situation. However, this would probably require a significantly higher amount of commitment and domestic resources; International Commission of Jurists – To define a clear normative basis and thematic focus for such assessments, on principles of the Rule of Law, based in EU law and on established and authoritative international standards, including those of the Council of Europe and the UN; To ensure that assessments are linked with and build on existing Council of Europe and United Nations systems and standards.' (International Bar Association, 'IBA Reflection paper on the EU Commission Communication of April 3, 2019 – Strengthening the Rule of Law within the European Union' (June 2019) 11).

[72] Helsinki Foundation for Human Rights (n 46).

[73] GN Toggenburg and J Grimheden, 'The Rule of Law and the role of fundamental rights: seven practical pointers' in Closa and Kochenov (eds), *Reinforcing Rule of Law Oversight in the EU* (n 4).

[74] J Wouters and M Ovádek, 'What political role for the EU's Fundamental Rights Agency?' (2019) *KU Leuven Working Paper* No 209.

[75] L Pech and J Grogan, 'Upholding the Rule of Law in the EU. What role for FRA?' in B Rosemary and H Entzinger (eds), *Human Rights Law and Evidence-Based Policy: The Impact of the EU Fundamental Rights Agency* (Routledge, 2019).

[76] Communication from the Commission to the European Parliament, the Council, the European Economic and Social Committee and the Committee of Regions, 2020 Rule of Law Report The rule of law situation in the European Union, COM/2020/580 final.

[77] Commission (n 1) 11.

Law backsliding,[78] whereas the Annual Rule of Law Report could be employed as a tool contributing to adoption of 'autocrat-proof EU legislation', including a suspension mechanism activated automatically when a Member State is subject to Article 7 proceedings.[79] Analysis of some contributions to the report submitted in May 2020 already shows how comprehensive the report needs to be to cover all basic Rule of Law elements. It is evident in this context that covering all of the issues presented by the stakeholders might lead to blurring the extreme cases of Rule of Law backsliding by comparing incomparable threats to the Rule of Law (ie, comparing systemic undermining checks and balances in Poland with technical obstacles to extensive length of judicial proceedings in Italy). Besides it is highly important to avoid thinking that a Rule of Law report can replace timely actions under Article 258 TFEU.

C. Response

Surprisingly one of the main features of the 'response' section seems to be minimalism: reducing response as much as possible. In light of the Commission's Communication, 'response' should be introduced 'when national Rule of Law safeguards do not seem capable of addressing threats to the Rule of Law in a Member State'.[80] Furthermore, regarding the core principles underlying EU action in terms of the Rule of Law, the Commission stated that 'the objective must not be to impose a sanction but to find a solution that protects the Rule of Law'. Interestingly, the government of Poland underlined that 'openness to dialogue must prevail over the temptation to impose sanctions or threaten with their immediate use'.[81] A completely different approach was presented by the International Bar Association, which found that 'unless or until the stakes are raised and meaningful sanctions are in place (and enforced with greater speed) infracting Member States will continue to operate with perceived impunity'.[82] That is why it should be of no surprise that 'the need for a stronger EU Rule of Law toolbox clearly emerged from'[83] the consultations initiated in April 2019, whereas the Commission still believes in the power of dialogue leading to 'swift de-escalation'.[84]

[78] For the detailed criticism regarding the Commission's Rule of law Report, see: L Pech, 'Doing more harm than good? A critical assessment of the European Commission's first Rule of Law Report', RECONNECT Blog (9 December 2020) at https://reconnect-europe.eu/blog/doing-more-harm-than-good-a-critical-assessment-of-the-european-commissions-first-rule-of-law-report/; L Ravo, '"Undrinkable Cocktails" and a Soft Bartender: A Review of the First EU Rule of Law Report', Liberties (1 October 2020) at www.liberties.eu/en/stories/eu-rule-of-law-report-2020/18889; A Mungiu-Pippidi, 'Unresolved Questions on the EU Rule of Law Report', Carnegie Europe (20 October 2020) at https://carnegieeurope.eu/2020/10/20/unresolved-questions-on-eu-rule-of-law-report-pub-82999.

[79] L Pech and D Kochenov, 'Strengthening the Rule of Law Within the European Union: Diagnoses, Recommendations, and What to Avoid' (2019) *RECONNECT Policy Brief* 13.

[80] ibid 13.

[81] 'Poland's contribution' (n 18) 3.

[82] 'Ergo, in the absence of a significant financial disincentive, the problem is unlikely to be resolved. The Article 7 procedure is, in effect, never-ending as a process. It requires unanimity, which can be hard to obtain if sympathetic Member States defend each other or have similar political priorities' (International Bar Association (n 71) 9).

[83] Commission (n 1) 2.

[84] ibid 13.

We will concentrate on three main 'response' actions provided in the Communication: 'systemic' infringement actions, the Rule of Law Framework and the Article 7 procedure.

i. Strategic Approach to Infringement Actions

The Commission underlined the role of the CJEU case law constituting a reaction to attacks on independence of the judiciary and expressed its commitment to pursue 'a strategic approach to infringement proceedings related to the Rule of Law, requesting expedited proceedings and interim measures whenever necessary',[85] especially when Rule of Law problems 'could not be solved through the national checks and balances'.[86] Let us not forget that this is – and has always been – the Commission's duty as the guardian of the Treaties and that its timid fulfilment of these duties coupled with the failure to see the full picture – like in *Commission v Hungary*,[87] has unquestionably contributed to the aggravation of the Rule of Law crisis in the European constitutional space. It is great that the Court has taken the lead and that the Commission acknowledges this and seemingly stands ready to start learning from its own mistakes. The problem, however, is that the Commission could be expected to be just as active as the Court from day one when the troubles with the constitutional capture started and this has not been the case, lending many years of largely untroubled existence to the backsliding governments busy dismantling the Rule of Law.

Despite the fact that the idea of a more systemic approach to infringement actions was analysed in the literature for years[88] and was supported by the stakeholders,[89] the recent deterioration in the field of judicial independence in Poland did not result in a timely reaction from the Commission – the request for an interim measure was submitted almost three months *after* the infringement action, regarding disciplinary regime against judges, was sent to the Court.[90] Furthermore, the latest 'muzzle law' adopted in Poland still did not result in an infringement action at the time of writing, despite political declarations,[91] including the one expressed in the Communication

[85] ibid 14.

[86] Commission (n 1) 4.

[87] Case C-286/12 *Commission v Hungary* [2013] 1 CMLR 44.

[88] See, most importantly, KL Scheppele, D Kochenov and B Grabowska-Moroz, 'EU Vlaues Are Law, after All' (2020) 39 *Yearbook of European Law* 1; KL Scheppele, 'Enforcing the basic principles of EU law through systemic infringement actions' in Closa and Kochenov (eds), *Reinforcing the Rule of Law Oversight in the EU* (n 4); A Śledzińska-Simon and P Bárd, 'The Teleos and the anatomy of the Rule of Law in EU infringement proceedings' (2019) 11 *Hague Journal on the Rule of Law* 439.

[89] 'Infringement proceedings should therefore be initiated regularly and promptly by the Commission where it identifies violations of the Rule of Law, including in cases of violation of basic principles of the Rule of Law under Article 2 TEU or the right to legal protection under Article 19.1 TEU, or where violations of Rule of Law principles affect the application of EU legislation.' (International Commission of Jurists (n 20) 13.)

[90] European Commission, 'Daily News 14 / 01/ 2020' (14 January 2020) at https://ec.europa.eu/commission/presscorner/detail/en/mex_20_56.

[91] 'Polish parliament approves judge 'muzzle law', Commission 'very concerned'' (*Euractiv*, 24 January 2020) at www.euractiv.com/section/justice-home-affairs/news/polish-parliament-approves-judge-muzzle-law-commission-very-concerned/.

that it is 'important that the EU institutions act swiftly and have a more coherent and concerted approach'.[92]

ii. The Rule of Law Framework and the Article 7 TEU Procedure

It is most regrettable that the Commission provides no critical assessment of the practices of the Rule of Law Framework or the Article 7 procedure, both boasting zero results up to now – and for very sound reasons. While the Commission awoke to the time-sensitive nature of the infringements of the values,[93] not a single word in the Communication explains why the deeply problematic Rule of Law Framework, which bought the backsliding governments so much time thanks to the Commission's own initiative, is still part of the toolbox. The Government of the Netherlands suggested, for instance, that within the Rule of Law Framework 'recommendations to Member States should be accompanied by specific action plans and technical support programmes, and linking them to specific time paths'.[94]

Setting aside diplomatic optimism[95] and criticism expressed before by the Council Legal Service,[96] the Commission should not only speed up the conduct of the Rule of Law Framework but also make it more transparent and inclusive.[97] 'Limited transparency impedes the Commission's ability to fully assess the situation in a Member State'.[98] As it was underlined by the Helsinki Foundation for Human Rights and the Hungarian Helsinki Committee, the notion of 'discussion' – a basic tool applied in the Rule of Law Framework – 'assumes that the Rule of Law can be negotiable and that it is possible to destroy the constitutional safeguards of checks and balances and then simply discuss this with the Member State'. Together with a lack of any time limits it allowed for further backsliding, which was not recognised by the Commission as a problem in its Communication. Such a dialogue 'may often benefit Rule of Law violators more than its defenders'.[99]

Also the debate on the Article 7 procedure did not result in any critical assessment in the Communication, except ensuring the role of the European Parliament in the procedure and providing *ad hoc* openness to the Council of Europe bodies.

[92] Commission (n 1) 14.

[93] M Schmid and P Bogdanowicz, 'The infringement procedure in the Rule of Law crisis: How to make effective use of Article 258 TFEU' (2018) 55 *Common Market Law Review* 1061; LW Gormley, 'Infringement proceedings' in Jakab and Kochenov (eds) (n 70).

[94] Dutch Ministry of Foreign Affairs (n 37).

[95] 'The Rule of Law Framework has proven to be a useful preliminary stage to the article 7 where important information is gathered and analyzed by the Commission, the Guardian of the Treaties. This process is useful not only to the Member State in question but also to others as it highlights concrete actions and practices giving guidance to the compliance of the Rule of Law.' ('Swedish input to the European Commission Communication on Further strengthening of the Rule of Law within the Union (COM(2019) 163 final)' (17 July 2019)).

[96] 'Rule of law framework is not compatible with the principle of conferral which governs the competences of EU institutions' (State Secretariat for EU Relations of the Prime Minister's Office (n 19)).

[97] 'The Commission did not recognise the role of non-governmental organisations, media or academia as sources of information relevant for a full and correct assessment of the situation in a Member State. Non-governmental actors are indispensable to verify the information provided by the government.' (Helsinki Foundation for Human Rights (n 46).)

[98] ibid.

[99] International Bar Association (n 71).

'Clearer procedures and timelines' recommended towards the Article 7 procedure mean, however, nothing without clear political will to decide upon clear violations of the Rule of Law by Member States. It should be worth noting not to miss the role of the procedure expressed by the Swedish government: 'One of its advantages is still the fact that the process brings light to the actual situation, which creates a pressure to comply with the breached rules. It is therefore important to continue the political dialogue within the context of article 7.'[100] Nevertheless, the consultations showed that it is difficult to avoid discussion about how Article 7 should be amended in order to improve its efficiency, meaning the probability that effective sanction will be imposed on a rogue Member State.[101]

IV. WHAT IS MISSING IN THIS PICTURE?

Communication tries to be as politically correct as possible and that is why it avoids calling a spade a spade. 'Political developments in several Member States' and 'deliberate policy choices'[102] are soft descriptions of Rule of Law backsliding – deliberate dismantling of checks and balances – applied in Hungary and Poland in order to secure a one-party system. The Commission does not introduce any differentiation between those two hard cases (where effective national redress mechanisms do not exist in practice) and typical everyday shortcomings regarding implementation of the Rule of Law principle. The Eurobarometer survey showed that 80 per cent of respondents expressed the need for some improvements regarding the Rule of Law in their countries.[103] However 'nobody's perfect'[104] shouldn't be a threshold for assessing systemic Rule of Law backsliding. The Member States that took a political choice, which is not formally available in the EU's constitutional landscape, to oppose the values of Article 2 TEU are the most important problem, not the ones which are unknowingly non-compliant and negligent.[105]

Meanwhile, contributions showed that causes of the Rule of Law crisis might be more difficult than only technical or financial shortcomings.[106] The Dutch Parliament

[100] 'Swedish input' (n 93).

[101] 'In the long term, therefore, consideration should be given to amending the TEU to reduce the scope for political influence on the Article 7 process. Such an amendment could assign the determination of a serious and persistent breach under Article 7.2 as well as the decision on sanctions under Article 7.3 to the Court of Justice, thereby providing further judicialization of the procedure. In the shorter term and within the current legal framework, the working methods of the Council should be amended to provide for greater transparency in the Article 7 process, including through increased consultation with civil society.' (International Commission of Jurists (n 20)).

[102] Commission (n 1) 5.

[103] ibid 13.

[104] A Rettman, 'Von der Leyen signals soft touch on migrants, Rule of Law' (*EUObserver*, 19 July 2019) at https://euobserver.com/news/145504.

[105] D Kochenov, 'The *acquis* and its principles: the enforcement of the "law" vs. the enforcement of "values" in the European Union' in Jakab and Kochenov (eds) (n 70).

[106] The academic literature on this important point is growing: P Blokker, 'Populist counter-constitutionalism, conservatism, and legal fundamentalism' (2019) 15 *European Constitutional Law Review* 518; Adamski (n 3); A Sajó, 'The Rule of Law as legal despotism: Concerned remarks on the use of "Rule of Law" in illiberal democracies' (2019) 11 *The Hague Journal on the Rule of Law* 371; P Blokker, 'Populist constitutionalism and meaningful popular engagement' (2018) *The Foundation for Law, Justice*

points, for instance, at a 'winner-takes-all mentality' as one of the factors which might lead to direct attacks on the checks and balances system.[107] Without dealing with such a political challenge, the need for inter-parliamentary dialogue,[108] as a suggested as part of promotion of the Rule of Law, might be a meaningless exercise. The situation in Hungary and Poland today is thus radically different from that of the Member States with troubled institutional structures, such as Greece;[109] Member States with particular electoral outcomes;[110] or Member States in principled disagreement with the EU on the functioning of some principles, as was the case with Germany and its courts pushing through the change in the EU's approach to the idea of human rights protection.[111]

Unfortunately, the Commission does not explain the nature of Rule of Law backsliding in troubled Member States. Scholars have been clear on what the key causes of the latter are: the lack of a clear will by the Member States and the inability of the EU institutions to utilise the full potential of the available legal instruments available to match the gravity of the problem. Without outlining the causes, it is difficult, of course, to expect effective solutions.

Lack of political will can be seen not only with respect to the Article 7 procedure but also can be seen during budget negotiations.[112] The Communication refers to the regulation proposal allowing the linking of EU funds and 'general deficiencies as regards to the Rule of Law in Member States',[113] as a tool which would 'avoid or remedy specific risks to the implementation of EU law or policies'.[114] On the one hand, it was suggested during the debate that conditionality 'is unlikely to produce beneficial outcomes' and might 'stimulate an instrumental, rather than a normatively driven, value-based engagement with reforms'.[115] On the other hand, the Commission does not review whether such a link between the Rule of Law requirement and access to EU funds can be established according to EU law already in force.[116]

The Communication fails to take the problem – a deeply exceptional depth of the constitutional capture in two Member States – seriously enough to place it at

and Society Policy Brief; KL Scheppele, 'The social lives of constitutions' in P Blokker and C Thornhill (eds), *Sociological Constitutionalism* (CUP, 2017).

[107] Tweede Kamer, 'Report by the Rapporteur on Rule of Law developments in the European Union' 13 March 2019.

[108] Commission (n 1) 7.

[109] M Ioannidis, 'Weak members and the enforcement of EU law' in Jakab and Kochenov (eds) (n 70).

[110] ie, FPÖ crisis in Austria leading to a reform of Article 7 TEU: K Lachmayer, 'Questioning the basic values – Austria and Jörg Haider' in Jakab and Kochenov (eds) (n 70).

[111] FC Mayer, 'Defiance by a constitutional court' in Jakab and Kochenov (eds) (n 70).

[112] E Zalan, 'EU leaders face major clash on Rule of Law budget link' (*EUObserver*, 19 February 2020) at https://euobserver.com/political/147495; J Rankin and D Boffey, 'Tensions mount between EU members ahead of budget talks' *The Guardian* (19 February 2020) at www.theguardian.com/world/2020/feb/19/tensions-mount-between-eu-members-ahead-of-budget-talks.

[113] European Commission, 'Proposal for a Regulation of the European Parliament and of the Council on the protection of the Union's budget in case of generalised deficiencies as regards the Rule of Law in the Member States' (Proposal) COM (2018) 324 final. cf M Fisicaro, 'Rule of Law conditionality in EU funds: The value of money in the crisis of European values' (2019) 4 *European Papers* 695.

[114] Commission (n 1) 15.

[115] Paul Blokker's submission, p 7.

[116] RD Kelemen and KL Scheppele, 'How to stop funding autocracy in the EU' (*VerfBlog*, 10 September 2018) at https://verfassungsblog.de/how-to-stop-funding-autocracy-in-the-eu/.

the centre of its resulting hugely befogged analysis. By failing to mention, let alone explain, what the actual core problems with the Rule of Law that the EU is facing are, the Commission has consequently left the most fundamental Rule of Law problems out of the picture, effectively disconnecting the Rule of Law Communication from the essence of the ongoing fight for the Rule of Law on the ground in the abusive Member States. It is the idea that some Member States would proactively seek to undermine the Rule of Law in order to create *de facto* one-party regimes where democracy is paralysed, and the Rule of Law is hollowed, that is missing from the Communication. Furthermore, the Commission does not provide critical analysis of the Rule of Law in the EU, which would strengthen the EU against criticism that the EU itself does not meet adequate institutional[117] and procedural requirements,[118] resulting in potentially unlawful composition of the CJEU – EU's own Court.[119]

V. CONCLUSION

It does not seem that the Communication has provided any new approach to Rule of Law 'hard cases'. The Commission absolutely failed to clarify this crucially important matter: 'what is the essence of the EU's Rule of Law problem?' the Commission's contribution seems to be punching way below the weight of that institution in terms of supplying a clear and realistic assessment of what the EU is dealing with today. It was clearly visible in the statements made by the new Commission and its President arguing that 'nobody's perfect'.[120] Belief in more dialogue constitutes an approach which will only lead to 'more time being wasted even while Rule of Law backsliding is spreading to more EU countries and endangering the very survival of the EU legal order'.[121]

[117] Kochenov (n 61).

[118] Alemanno and Ştefan (n 54).

[119] D Kochenov and G Butler, 'The Independence and Lawful Composition of the Court of Justice of the European Union: Replacement of Advocate General Sharpston and the Battle for the Integrity of the Institution' (2020) *Jean Monnet Working Paper* 2-2020 (NYU Law School).

[120] Rettman (n 102).

[121] L Pech, D Kochenov, B Grabowska-Moroz and J Grogan, 'The Commission's Rule of Law Blueprint for Action: A Missed Opportunity to Fully Confront Legal Hooliganism' (*VerfBlog*, 5 September 2019) at https://verfassungsblog.de/the-commissions-rule-of-law-blueprint-for-action-a-missed-opportunity-to-fully-confront-legal-hooliganism/.

Part Two

The People

6

The People vs Democracy? The Populist Challenge to Judicial Review

JUSTIN COLLINGS*

Democracy reads well; but it doesn't act well, like some people's plays.

Lord Summerhays in George Bernard Shaw's *Misalliance*

I. INTRODUCTION

KARLSRUHE. EIGHT JUDGES file solemnly into the courtroom and take their places, still standing, behind the bench. They stand on a wood-paneled rostrum, brilliant in their scarlet robes, their angular Renaissance hats, their ruffled white bibs. Behind them on the wall hovers Germany's federal eagle, symbol of the postwar republic – its prosperity and peace. Above the eagle looms a single word: *Bundesverfassungsgericht* (Federal Constitutional Court). These eight judges comprise one of the Court's two Senates or chambers. One of them, the panel's presiding judge, is about to announce a judgment. The announcement begins, as always, with a single, riveting phrase: *Im Namen des Volkes!* ('In the name of the People!'). True, the German justices communicate in a language that 'the People' could never reproduce. Sometimes they converse in terms the People could never understand. But they speak and write about the People's charter – Germany's postwar Constitution or 'Basic Law' (*Grundgesetz*) – and they do so, emphatically, in the People's name.

Leipzig. Thousands of demonstrators line the streets, which buzz and hum with passionate energy. The demonstrators wave a motley array of banners and signs, all of which make clear that the demonstrators are alarmed. Some signs suggest that many are angry. Their movement bears an almost implausibly portentous name – Patriotic Europeans Against the Islamization of the Occident (PEGIDA). As they march, they chant in a steady, rhythmic, incantatory refrain. It is the same refrain that resounded in these streets 30 years before, albeit under different circumstances and toward very different ends. '*Wir sind das Volk*!' they cry. 'We are the People!' Numerically, this is

* Brigham Young University.

nonsense. But symbolically, the demonstrators are in dead earnest. They, and populists like them the world over, claim to speak in the people's name. They claim to represent – indeed, they claim *to be* – the real people. They too assert their claims *im Namen des Volkes*.

At first blush, constitutional courts and populist politicians have little in common. Constitutional judges are quintessential elites – highly-educated umpires wielding technocratic expertise far from the madding crowd and (ostensibly) above the political fray. They are unelected officers shielded from many democratic and political pressures. Some defenders of constitutional judicial review believe that constitutional judges' principal *raison d'être* is to protect minority rights against majority infringement. They are, as Alexander Bickel famously put it, counter-majoritarian.[1] That is their purpose and their predicament, their problem and their point.

Populists, by contrast, are often wary of minorities, who in their view threaten to undermine the polity's identity and thwart what they term 'the People's' will. Populists rail against elites of all sorts, but they rail against constitutional judges with particular venom and vim. Judges, for their part, often reciprocate populists' distrust. Sometimes they openly return their scorn. Populists and constitutional judges are sharply divided in their outlook and upbringing, their values and aims. They often regard one another with mutual hostility and dismay.

And yet. Beneath these apparent differences and beyond their mutual mistrust, populists and constitutional courts frequently share something fundamental. Both, at times, defend their efforts through a 'thick' revisionist conception of democracy. Both are accused by their various detractors of being fundamentally antidemocratic. Both insist that their critics' objections are specious and superficial. Both respond by redefining democracy. Both claim, at bottom, to be quintessentially democratic. Both issue this response in the name of 'the People'.

Of course, the redefinition of democracy put forth by populists differs wildly from the one embraced by champions of judicial review. The underlying conceptions of 'The People' lie worlds apart. But unpacking those differences in the context of their (perhaps) ironically similar framework can be highly instructive. To do so is this chapter's basic aim. I argue that defenders of judicial review – and I count myself among their number – need to be more wary of its excesses and more open about its democratic costs. Specifically, I will suggest that redefining democracy in ways that cast judicial review as somehow more democratic than the demos is doubly dangerous: it proves the populists' point about judicial review's basic elitism, and it replicates the populists' sleight-of-hand by claiming a special prerogative to represent, and redefine, 'the People'.

II. THE POPULIST MOMENT

For the last half decade and more, populism has been described by its detractors in increasingly apocalyptic terms. A specter, one reads, is haunting more than just Europe. Populism prowls the planet. For many commentators, its daemon has already

[1] AM Bickel, *The Least Dangerous Branch: The Supreme Court at the Bar of Politics* (Yale University Press, 1962) 16 ('The root difficulty is that judicial review is a counter-majoritarian force in our system.').

been unloosed. The metaphors are menacing. Some call it an ominous 'wave',[2] others a crushing 'tsunami.'[3] At the same time, liberal democracy looks battered and weak. Its unrivaled dominance at 'the end of history'[4] belongs to the increasingly distant past.[5] The 'end of history' *is* history. Liberal democracies' economic heft has declined even as that of some autocratic nations has increased. Meanwhile, many democracies are embattled at home. Unsettling empirical research suggests that 'across North America and Western Europe, citizens really are turning away from democracy in large numbers'.[6] Some democracies face stern challenges from populist contenders. Others have already succumbed.

Perhaps the most dramatic cases are Hungary and Poland, the one-time poster children of post-communist democratic revival.[7] The populists' rise in those two lands has been attended by a concerted attack on institutions and principles of liberal democratic constitutionalism.[8] For the champions of those institutions and those principles, the results have been devastating. The attack on constitutional liberalism, in East Central Europe and elsewhere, has battered the faith of many liberal constitutionalists. Many commentators sorrowfully conclude that liberal constitutionalism is a less effective bulwark against democratic backsliding than its champions once believed.[9] '[T]he last few years', writes one of them, 'have exposed the institutional fragility of constitutional courts when they are targeted by populist forces. More broadly', this writer continues, 'we may be forced to question the capacity of the courts to protect democracy from illiberal majorities'.[10] The populists, it seems, are at the gates; the doors, it seems, are giving way.

A. What is Populism?

Among liberals, of course, there is more agreement about populism's threat than about its definition.[11] One of the most influential accounts on offer is that of

[2] See J Kurlantzick, 'The Populist Wave Will Continue' *World Politics Review* (25 February 2019).

[3] See N Barkin, 'After Trump and Brexit, Populist Tsunami Threatens European Mainstream' *Reuters* (9 November 2016).

[4] See, of course, F Fukuyama, *The End of History and the Last Man* (Free Press, 1992).

[5] 'In the span of a quarter century', write Y Mounk and R de Stefano, 'liberal democracies have gone from a position of unprecedented economic strength to a position of unprecedented economic weakness'. Y Mounk and R Stefan Foa, 'The End of the Democratic Century: Autocracy's Global Ascendance' *Foreign Affairs* (May/June 2018) 30.

[6] Y Mounk, *The People vs. Democracy: Why Our Freedom is in Danger and How to Save It* (Harvard University Press, 2018) 105. This chapter of Mounk's book summarises the findings of R de Stefano and Y Mounk, 'The Danger of Deconsolidation: The Democratic Disconnect' (2016) 27 *J. Democracy* 5.

[7] See eg I Krastev, 'Eastern Europe's Illiberal Revolution' *Foreign Affairs* (May/June 2018) 49, 49.

[8] See eg T Ginsburg and B Bugarič, 'The Assault on Postcommunist Courts' (2016) 27 *J. Democracy* 69; W Sadurski, 'How Democracy Dies (in Poland). A Case Study of Anti-Constitutional Populist Backsliding' Sydney Law School Legal Studies Research Paper, 18 January 2018.

[9] A Jakab, 'What Can Constitutional Law Do Against the Erosion of Democracy and the Rule of Law?: On the Interconnectedness of the Protection of Democracy and the Rule of Law' MPIL Research Paper Series No. 2019-15; B Bugarič, 'Central Europe's descent into autocracy: A constitutional analysis of authoritarian populism' (2019) 17 *Int'l J Const L* 597, 600; D Ziblatt and S Levitsky, *How Democracy's Die* (Crown, 2018) 130–32.

[10] Bugarič (n 9) 613.

[11] cf N Walker, 'Populism and constitutional tension' (2019) 17 *Int'l J Const L* 515, 516 ('The idea of populism is intensely fashionable, and like most intensely fashionable things, its meaning is in a constant

Jan-Werner Müller. In his elegant essay, *What is Populism?*,[12] Müller defines populism as 'a particular *moralistic imagination of politics*' that is both anti-elitist (populists bash elites as 'corrupt or in some other way morally inferior') and anti-pluralist ('populists claim that they, *and only they*, represent the people').[13] Populism, Müller maintains, 'requires a *pars pro toto* argument' with 'someone speaking in the name of the people as a whole'.[14] Populism's 'core claim' is that 'only some of the people are really the people'.[15] Its quintessence is synecdoche – the part speaks for the whole, the populist for the people.[16]

That claim, Müller insists, is moral, not empirical.[17] On his telling, populists don't claim that all the people, or even a majority of the people, support them. They claim instead that the true people support them – the authentic people, the real people, the pure people, the people not corrupted or seduced. Thus, on Müller's telling, populists dismiss electoral defeat by arguing that entrenched elites have either cheated outright by rigging the game or won an illegitimate victory by manipulating and misleading voters. Populists not only disagree with their opponents as wrongheaded; they denounce them as illegitimate. And their opponents' supporters, be they few or many, simply don't count. Only 'the People' count.

The implications of this perspective for a democracy are obvious and alarming. Power democratically won by others is, on this view, illegitimate. Power democratically won by populists is, by contrast, all-legitimating. When populists win, the People have spoken. And the People's voice covers – it might even require – a multitude of sins. Once in power, Müller notes, populists flout democratic norms and subvert democratic institutions.[18] They defy the separation of powers and scorn the rule of law. And why not? After all, anything that prevents populists giving full expression to the People's authentic will is, by the populists' logic, profoundly undemocratic. Populists see their rule as the ultimate democracy. They are, in fact, the demos. To stand in their way is to shackle the people. Any actor or institution that would do that is consummately illegitimate. To crush such illegitimacy is, for populists, the ultimate legitimacy. Such a programme, in Müller's view, is undemocratic as well as illiberal. Indeed, Müller rejects the very notion of 'illiberal democracy' as an unwitting sop to would-be tyrants. Authoritarian regimes celebrate the label,[19] and liberals should be loath to give them cause for celebration.[20]

state of evolution and contestation.'). Bugarič, following Paul Taggart, notes populism's 'chameleon-like' quality; 'it takes a variety of guises'. See Bugarič (n 9) 598–99.

[12] J-W Müller, *What is Populism?* (University of Pennsylvania Press, 2016).

[13] ibid 19–20.

[14] ibid 20.

[15] ibid 21.

[16] Other writers similarly cast populism as essentially anti-pluralist. N Urbinati, for instance, writes: 'Populism … seeks state power to implement an agenda whose main and recognizable character is hostility against liberalism and the principles of constitutional democracy, from minority rights, division of powers, and pluriparty system.' *Democracy Disfigured: Opinion, Truth, and the People* (2014).

[17] Müller (n 12) 21.

[18] ibid 41–74.

[19] As Viktor Orbán, Hungary's prime minister, has put it: 'A democracy is not necessarily liberal. Just because something is not liberal, it still can be a democracy.' Krastev (n 7) 49.

[20] See J-W Müller, 'The Problem with "Illiberal Democracy"' *Project Syndicate* (21 January 2016), at www.project-syndicate.org/commentary/the-problem-with-illiberal-democracy-by-jan-werner-mueller-2016-01?barrier=accesspaylog.

Müller's account has not, of course, gone uncontested. Robert Howse, for one, insists that 'populism can denote *any* kind of disruption of elite-directed politics in mature liberal democracies' and chides Müller and others for failing to 'recognize *equally* as populism those efforts against establishment or elite politics that are *consistent* with protecting minority rights, constitutional democracy, and pluralism'.[21] Howse celebrates such strands of populism for their powerful critique of liberal elitists, whom he censures for being more concerned with order than with liberty, and for their undue fondness for, and unjustified confidence in, judges and other technocratic elites.[22] 'Populism', Howse concludes, 'as usually and pejoratively defined to include nativism, antiliberalism, and anti-pluralism has little to do with many of today's powerful critiques of and challenges to elite liberal democratic politics'.[23] Other writers similarly define populism more expansively to include progressive and pluralist movements.[24]

At bottom, this is a tussle about terms, undergirded by very different attitudes toward liberal elites. The populists that Howse admires are, on Müller's account, 'simply not populists'.[25] Howse shoots back that this narrow and exclusive definition is 'thoroughly question-begging'.[26] The dilemma is that the broader definition lacks clarity and precision, uniting as 'populists' groups and figures that share little beyond opposition to ruling elites, whereas the narrower definition achieves clarity and precision by turning 'populism' into a swear word (or worse), a move that can't help but hurt groups who don't fit Müller's illiberal, anti-pluralist definition but who call themselves, or get called, populists.

I don't intend to pick a side in this dispute, but the populists described in this chapter are mainly the ones that Müller describes. Howse might be right that there are other populists, but Müller's populists *are* populists, even if not the only ones. As populists, they challenge constitutional judicial review – in both theory and practice – with particular intensity. And their anti-elitist invocation of 'the People' mirrors the rival, elitist invocations of 'the People' by some defenders of judicial review in ironic and unsettling ways.

In another prominent account of populism, Yascha Mounk agrees with Müller that populists are unfailingly illiberal but denies that they are invariably undemocratic.[27] Mounk warns of the conceptual confusion that stems from a common tendency to conflate democracy with liberalism. The two, indeed, have often travelled together, and their union, as noted earlier, was once consecrated as 'the end of history'.[28] But the emerging crisis of the twenty-first century, Mounk warns, is that the two have

[21] R Howse, 'Epilogue: In defense of disruptive democracy – A critique of anti-populism' (2019) 17 *Int'l J Const. L* 641, 641, 645.

[22] ibid 647–50.

[23] ibid 659.

[24] See eg C Mouffe, *For a Left Populism* (Verso, 2018); E Laclau, *On Populist Reason* (Verso, 2005).

[25] Müller (n 12) 20.

[26] Howse (n 21) 645.

[27] Y Mounk, *The People v. Democracy: Why Our Freedom is in Danger and How to Save It* (Harvard University Press, 2018) 51–52.

[28] See, of course, F Fukuyama, *The End of History and the Last Man* (Free Press, 1992).

been decoupled in some places and might become decoupled elsewhere. In Mounk's words:

> [L]iberal democracy – the unique mix of individual rights and popular rule that has long characterized most governments in North America and Western Europe – is coming apart. In its stead, two new regime forms are rising: *illiberal democracy*, or democracy without rights, and *undemocratic liberalism*, or rights without democracy.[29]

In Mounk's scheme, a democracy can be either liberal (like Canada) or illiberal (like Hungary and Poland); and an undemocratic regime can be either liberal (like the European Union) or illiberal and thus a dictatorship (like Russia).[30] His core insight is that, in its critique of the undemocratic elements of liberal regimes, populism harnesses a certain democratic energy. There is, Mounk suggests, something basically democratic about the populist challenge – even the Müllerian populist challenge – to technocratic elites. Therein lies populism's peculiar attraction.

And its peril. For in their assault on undemocratic liberalism, (Müllerian) populists attack the liberal elements alongside the undemocratic ones, thus replacing one imbalance with another[31] – substituting illiberal democracy for undemocratic liberalism. The swap is dangerous, both in its own right and because populist governments tend in practice to remain illiberal but not democratic. Populists might well come to power through free and fair elections. But they might be content to retain power without them. The populist invocation of democracy is thus fraught with peril for both liberalism and democracy.

B. Populism v Democratic Constitutionalism

Populists steer by the star of popular sovereignty, but they conceive of democracy in a particular way. (The same can be said of many elites. More anon.) They imagine political power 'as the expression of the will of a cohesive majority' – a majority understood in material rather than procedural terms.[32] To Müller, Mounk, and many other critics, populism invokes popular sovereignty and majority rule in a profoundly anti-pluralist way. As Paul Blokker puts it, 'populists situate sovereignty squarely in the nation or the people'.[33] They seek 'a return to, or a realization of, the past, that is, of a traditional order, based on 'natural' hierarchies related to ethnicity, family, and tradition.'[34] The populist pursuit, then, is for what Nadia Urbinati calls 'extreme majoritarianism':[35] populists, she says, push for a permanent majority. According to these critics, populists define democracy in identitarian rather than electoral terms. On these accounts, present majorities matter but are not synonymous

[29] Mounk (n 27) 28.
[30] ibid 36.
[31] cf Walker (n 11) 533–34.
[32] P Blokker, 'Populism as a constitutional project' (2019) 17 *Int'l J Const L* 535, 543–44.
[33] ibid 550.
[34] ibid 540.
[35] See N Urbinati, 'Populism and the Principle of Maojority' in R Kaltwasser et al (eds), *The Oxford Handbook on Populism* (OUP, 2017) 571.

with 'the People'. The latter, broader category encompasses the past. It stands for the enduring nation – its traditions and its triumphs, its valour and its values. Because elites sometimes seduce, corrupt, or deceive the masses – and because they sometimes cheat outright – elections don't always reflect the people's will. Democracy and popular sovereignty align only when the authentic people find an authentic spokesperson. Democracy works when populists win.

There is, of course, a certain 'heads-I-win-tails-you-lose' character to this conceit. But the important point is that such populists not only invoke democracy, they redefine it. That redefinition is (Müllerian) populism's defining mark.

All of this has consequences for liberal constitutionalism and for the rule of law. At least some populists downplay the constitution's status as rigid, higher law.[36] When such populists take power, their constitutional interventions are legion. They amend the Constitution frequently and dramatically.[37] They flout constitutional norms with gusto. They collapse the distinction between ordinary politics and constitutional politics. They deny that law is separate from politics or from morality. They insist that law is inseparable from its extra-legal sources – from political power or societal bonds. As Blokker summarises, 'The populist understanding of the law denies its closed, self-sufficient, and self-referential nature, and emphasizes the ultimately always already political nature of the law.'[38] Many populists also deplore liberal legalism's strong individualism, which, on their telling, erodes national unity.[39]

None of this, of course, makes populism *per se* inescapably authoritarian. Such casual equivalence is reductive.[40] Populism's relationship to constitutionalism is more complex, in part because populists in power often seek to harness the legitimacy conferred (in the eyes of outside observers) by constitutional forms, but also because populists often embrace the animating impulse of popular constitutionalism,[41] defined by Larry Kramer, one of its champions, as a belief that 'the people themselves'[42] should not only supply the constituent (or constitution-making) power but should also exercise 'active and ongoing control over the interpretation and enforcement of constitutional law.'[43] Populists assert such control with a vengeance. And they do so, unsurprisingly, at the expense of constitutional courts.

C. Populism v Constitutional Justice

Although many populists' 'critical attitude channels resentment against the constitutional *status quo ante*' across the board,[44] courts have often aroused populists' especial ire. When populist governments came to power in both Hungary and Poland,

[36] Blokker (n 32) 545.
[37] ibid 546.
[38] ibid 549.
[39] ibid 550.
[40] cf Walker (n 11) 525.
[41] ibid 527.
[42] This is the title of Kramer's prominent book. See LD Kramer, *The People Themselves: Popular Constitutionalism and Judicial Review* (OUP, 2004).
[43] LD Kramer, 'Popular Constitutionalism, Circa 2004' (2004) 92 *Calif. L. Rev.* 959, 959.
[44] Walker (n 11) 520.

they immediately made war on the constitutional court. In both countries, populist governments curtailed the Court's independence and packed it with loyalists.[45] In Hungary, after the ruling party, Fidesz, secured an impregnable two-thirds majority in Parliament, it made quick work of the constitutional court as a constraint on its rule.[46] The dismantling began when the Government changed the nomination rules so that it could nominate constitutional judges without the input of any other party. It then stripped the Court of jurisdiction in sensitive fiscal areas. Finally, it packed the Court by raising the number of justices from eight to 15. In a moment, sighs one observer, '[t]he once powerful and highly respected Court … disappeared from the political scene'.[47]

Populists pursued a parallel pattern in Poland. The ruling Law and Justice (PiS) party packed the Constitutional Tribunal with party sympathisers, altered the rules so that only a two-thirds supermajority of the Tribunal can pronounce a law unconstitutional, and injected a mandatory six-month delay between the filing of a constitutional petition and the Constitutional Tribunal's judgment.[48] The upshot, as one scholar starkly puts it, is that the Tribunal 'as a mechanism of constitutional review … ceased to exist'. In its place, 'a reliable aide of the government and parliamentary majority was born'.[49]

But populists like these don't just oppose courts as a check on what they'd like to do. They oppose them more fundamentally as a rival to their assertion of a moral monopoly on representation. Constitutional courts and populist politicians both speak in the name of the People. Populists claim to speak in the People's name exclusively. Both claims cannot be valid: the competing conceptions of the People could hardly be more different. Those competing conceptions make courts and populists inescapable rivals and implacable foes. On the populist view, there is little need for constitutional justice so long as populists are in power. The authentic people need no protection against themselves.[50]

When the European Commission began Article 7 proceedings against Poland in response to PiS's judiciary reforms, PiS defended those reforms on the ground that the judiciary had transgressed its institutional bounds and lost touch with the people. The government said the reforms were needed to redress an 'imbalance of powers' and to counteract 'the peculiar bureaucratic corporate culture which has emerged in the Polish administration of justice. Citizens', the statement continued, 'view the courts as a closed community that is very difficult to access'. They 'consider [judicial] procedures to be complex and incomprehensible'. The Government further deprecated what it called a 'cult of formalism', according to which 'it is more important that a judgement be justified on formal grounds than for it to be actually fair'.[51]

[45] B Bugarič, 'Central Europe's descent into autocracy: A constitutional analysis of authoritarian populism' (2019) 17 *Int'l J Const L* 597, 605.
[46] That majority is the result of rule-rigging. The party's share of the popular vote is much smaller.
[47] Bugarič (n 9) 606.
[48] ibid.
[49] Sadurski (n 8) 35.
[50] A Arato, 'Populism, Constitutional Courts, and Civil Society' in C Landfried, *Judicial Power: How Constitutional Courts Affect Political Transformations* (CUP, 2019) 318, 332.
[51] In Blokker (n 32) 541.

By taming the judiciary in the People's name, the government purported to bring the law closer to the people themselves. Indeed, the crux of Poland's constitutional crisis has been PiS's insistence that the Government or the Parliament, as the People's representative and spokespersons, rather than the constitutional tribunal, should have the final word on what the Constitution means.[52] It has been a clash, in other words, of rival institutional claims – between a populist variant on popular constitutionalism and the traditional credo of strong-form judicial review. It is a clash, as well, between the liberal-constitutionalist redefinition of democracy and the rival reconceptualisation of the populists.

III. CONSTITUTIONAL ANXIETIES: BACK TO BÖCKENFÖRDE AND BICKEL

Unsurprisingly, the confrontation has put defenders of constitutional liberalism on edge. The modern mood of such defenders (and, again, I am a defender) has ranged from unsettled alarm to acute despair. Populism, as a book like the present one attests, has touched a nerve. Part of the reason is obvious. An institution, constitutional judicial review, that many liberal constitutionalists cherish (and spend their lives and earn their livelihoods assessing and expounding) stands embattled in some jurisdictions, battered in others, and broken in others still. But alarm about the fate of constitutional justice specifically and constitutional liberalism more generally is also attended by deep-seated anxieties about the nature of the institutions at bay. As Neil Walker has written, perhaps 'the preoccupation [with populism] betrays a wider and more long-standing anxiety with the condition of modern constitutionalism'.[53] The anxiety stems conceptually from a pair of gauntlets thrown down more than 50 years ago by a pair of youthful titans, one in Germany and one in the US.

Ernst-Wolfgang Böckenförde was 37 years old when he first published his famous 'dictum' in 1967. 'The liberal, secular state', he wrote, 'depends upon conditions that it cannot itself guarantee'.[54] If it tried to guarantee them, it would cease to be liberal. But if it failed to guarantee them, it might not survive. That was the great dilemma – 'the great wager', as Böckenförde put it, 'undertaken for the sake of freedom'.[55] In recent years, countless commentators have highlighted the painful precariousness of the Böckenfördean conditions. As Yascha Mounk notes, 'the survival of stable democracies has always depended on the willingness of major political figures to play by the basic rules of the game'.[56] It has also depended on the readiness of voters to punish them if they don't. Both of these conditions now look fragile. Popular commitment to the democratic rule of law appears to be on the retreat. Politicians' willingness to bend or break basic rules appears to be on the offensive. 'Paradoxically', writes

[52] Blokker (n 32) 548.
[53] Walker (n 11) 529.
[54] E-W Böckenförde, 'Die Entstehung des Staates als Vorgang der Säkularisation' in *Säkularisation und Utopie. Ebehracher Studien, Ernst Forsthoff zum 65. Geburtstag* (Kohlhammer, 1967) 75, 94; for an English version, see E-W Böckenförde, 'The Rise of the State as a Process of Secularization' in M Künkler and T Stein (eds), E.W. Böckenförde, *Religion, Law, and Democracy: Selected Writings* (OUP, 2020).
[55] ibid.
[56] Mounk (n 27) 242.

Bojan Bugarič, 'constitutional democracy can play its "counter-majoritarian" role only when a majority of the people believe that it is the only game in town'.[57] In many places, it is no longer clear that most people believe this.

When Bugarič writes of constitutionalism's 'counter-majoritarian' role, he is speaking, of course, in terms made famous by Alexander Bickel. Like Böckenförde with his dictum, Bickel was 37 when he published *The Least Dangerous Branch* and articulated with imperishable precision his (or rather constitutional justice's) 'counter-majoritarian difficulty'.[58] Yes, Bickel admitted, governance in the US is complicated, and existing legislative procedures don't always or perfectly reflect the people's will. But, he insisted, 'nothing in the further complexities and perplexities of the system … can alter the essential reality that judicial review is a deviant institution in the American democracy'.[59] Indeed, by Bickel's logic, constitutional judicial review is a deviant institution in *any* democracy. Martin Shapiro puts the point with uncompromising bluntness:

> [M]any people who like democracy also like judicial review, [but] try as many of them might, it is not possible to render the two compatible. Constitutional judicial review inevitably involves a small number of unelected men and women making public policy or blocking public policy made by the people or their elected representatives. Democracy means public policy made by the people or their representatives. … [J]udicial review is always a cost to democracy, … it is public policy making by other than the demos, that is the people.[60]

Unless, that is, you reconceive the demos and redefine democracy. And this, in fact, is what many of judicial review's defenders have done and continue to do. In the face of the populist challenge to constitutional justice, some seem to be redoubling their efforts.

Those efforts seem driven, at least in part, by a pair of contrapositive fallacies: (1) because democracy is good, anything that is not democracy must be bad; and (2) because democracy is good, anything else that is good (such as judicial review) must be somehow democratic. The more democratic, the better and (*ergo*?) the better, the more democratic. The logic is loopy, but the underlying anxiety is real. Despite complacent pronouncements that the case for strong-form judicial review has already won the day,[61] there remain powerful opponents who are not populists by anyone's definition.[62] More pressingly, some who *are* populists by *everyone's* account attack constitutional courts without reprieve and justify their assault in democratic terms. In response, the effort to show that constitutional courts enrich democracy rather than displace it proceeds apace. The rest of this chapter will review and critique that effort.

[57] Bugarič (n 9) 600.

[58] Bickel (n 1) 16–17.

[59] ibid 17–18.

[60] M Shapiro, 'Judicial Power and Democracy' in Landfried (n 50) 21, 21–22.

[61] See M Kumm, 'On the Representativeness of Constitutional Courts: How to Strengthen the Legitimacy of Rights Adjudicating Courts without Undermining their Independence' in Landfried (n 50) 281, 282.

[62] See eg J Waldron, 'The Core Case against Judicial Review' (2006) 115 *Yale LJ* 1346; R Hirschl, *Towards Juristocracy: The Origins and Consequences of the New Constitutionalism* (Harvard University Press, 2004); R Bellamy, *Political Constitutionalism: A Republican Defense of the Constitutionality of Democracy* (CUP, 2007).

IV. DEFENDING JUDICIAL REVIEW BY REDEFINING DEMOCRACY

The most prominent efforts to justify judicial review by redefining democracy came in the latter part of the twentieth century from three towering figures of legal and political thought: Ronald Dworkin, John Rawls, and Jürgen Habermas, all of whom offered 'thick' accounts of democracy. Dworkin and Rawls defended representative-democracy-plus-constitutional-judicial-review as somehow more democratic than representative democracy on its own. Habermas provided the premise of a thick account but left the conclusion in favour of judicial review to his successors.

Dworkin struck first. Famously boosting constitutional courts as 'forums of principle', Dworkin argued that, in some settings, 'individual citizens may be able to exercise moral responsibilities of citizenship better when final decisions are removed from ordinary politics and assigned to courts, whose decisions are meant to turn on principle, not on the weight of numbers or the balance of political influence'.[63] Dworkin dismissed majoritarian democracy as mere '*statistical* democracy'.[64] The 'majoritarian conception of democracy' was not, for Dworkin, 'a defensible conception of what true democracy is'.[65] '[T]rue democracy', he wrote, 'is not just *statistical* democracy, in which anything a majority or a plurality wants is legitimate for that reason, but *communal* democracy, in which a majority decision is legitimate only if it is a majority within a community of equals'.[66]

True democracy. It was a telling turn of phrase. It pitted the real (communal) people against mere (statistical) democracy. *The People v Democracy*, in other words. Dworkin (and others before him) thus inverted the populists' game before they ever started playing it.

Constitutional judicial review, for Dworkin, was a *sine qua non* of true democracy. Dworkin characterised the judicial vindication of fundamental rights as a matter of principle, whereas determinations left to ordinary politics involved mere questions of policy.[67] As an arena of policy, moreover, electoral politics was beset by bids for power, seedy motives, and 'compromises that may subordinate issues of principle'.[68] Decisions by a constitutional tribunal, by contrast, could launch 'a sustained national debate … in newspapers and other media, in law schools and classrooms, in public meetings and around dinner tables'.[69] Such debates, Dworkin implied, were more republican – indeed more *democratic* – 'than almost anything the legislative process on its own is likely to produce'.[70] But beyond the quality of debates, Dworkin was unabashedly focused on outcomes. His account was relentlessly consequentialist. 'I see no alternative', he wrote, 'but to use a result-driven rather than a procedure-driven standard for deciding [institutional questions]. The best institutional structure', he concluded, 'is the one best calculated to produce the

[63] R Dworkin, *Freedom's Law: The Moral Reading of the Constitution* (OUP, 1996) 30.
[64] ibid 364.
[65] ibid 31.
[66] ibid 364.
[67] R Dworkin, *Taking Rights Seriously* (Harvard University Press, 1977) 90.
[68] Dworkin, *Freedom's Law* (n 63) 30.
[69] ibid 345.
[70] ibid.

best answers to the essentially moral question of what the democratic conditions actually are, and to secure stable compliance with those conditions'.[71] Dworkin was confident that he knew what those 'best answers' were, and that constitutional judges would reach them more often than elected officials in governments or legislatures.

John Rawls was similarly bullish on judges. Rawls, like Dworkin, looked askance at legislatures. For Rawls, as for Dworkin, a constitutional court's counter-majoritarian role was not 'straightforwardly antidemocratic'.[72] Instead, constitutional courts protected higher law 'from being eroded by the legislation of transient majorities, or more likely, by organized and well-situated narrow interests skilled at getting their way'.[73] By contrast to such legislative venality, constitutional judges were paragons of public reason. '[T]he court's role', Rawls wrote, 'is not merely defensive but to give due and continuing effect to public reason by serving as its institutional exemplar'.[74] And since public reason embodied the shared beliefs and reason of those who compose the democratic polity, what could be more democratic than public reason's 'institutional exemplar'?

Whereas Dworkin focused on outcomes and Rawls on reasons, Habermas combined the two in an emphasis on public discourse. Habermas offered what Christine Landfried has called a 'genuinely proceduralist understanding of democracy', one centered on the 'discursive level of the public debates' and on the capacity of public discourse to rationalise political power.[75] Habermas linked democratic procedures to the expectation of reasonable results.[76] Although Habermas himself was sometimes sceptical of judicial review,[77] he has inspired defences of judicial review rooted in its purported power to elevate public discourse and tame political power.[78]

Many have followed Dworkin, Rawls, and Habermas in suggesting that constitutional judicial review makes democracy more democratic. Such defences have tended to proceed in two steps – the first highlighting the democratic shortcomings of majority representation, the second extolling the democratic virtues of constitutional review.

In the first respect, many writers stress that representative democracy is not always representative. Electoral decisions, for example, are not always taken by real majorities. Fifty-two per cent of those who voted in the Brexit referendum chose leave, but only 72 per cent of eligible voters voted at all. This means that only 30 per cent of the electorate opted to leave – a momentous choice made by a decided minority. Some 62 million Americans voted for Donald Trump in 2016 – about 45 per cent of votes cast by about 58 per cent of voting-age citizens: barely over a quarter of the electorate. Turkey's president, Recep Tayyip Erdoğan, was elected in 2014 with a 52 per cent share of a 76 per cent turnout. Thus, fewer than 40 per cent of eligible voters supported the man that introduced sweeping constitutional change in 2016.[79]

[71] ibid 34.
[72] J Rawls, *Political Liberalism* (Columbia University Press, 1993) 233–34.
[73] ibid 233.
[74] ibid 235.
[75] C Landfried, 'Introduction' in Landfried (n 50) 1, 5.
[76] See J Habermas, *Between Facts and Norms* (The MIT Press, 1996) Ch 7.
[77] ibid 253–66. For an in-depth look, see MG Specter, *Habermas: An Intellectual Biography* (CUP, 2010).
[78] See eg Landfried (n 75).
[79] Many of the examples noted in this paragraph are discussed in Sabino Cassese, *La democrazia e i suoi limiti* (Mondadori, 2017) 5–6.

More fundamentally, regardless of how many voters support their accession, legislative majorities and executive authorities don't always wield power in accordance with majoritarian wishes. Legislators spend most of their time mingling with lobbyists, donors, and various social and cultural elites. As a result, they are 'increasingly insulated from the popular will'.[80] One empirical study found that congressional decision-making in the US is powerfully influenced by economic elites and narrow interests but barely touched by the views of ordinary citizens. 'When the preferences of economic elites and the stands of organized interest groups are controlled for', the authors conclude, 'the preferences of the average American appear to have only a miniscule, near-zero, statistically non-significant impact upon public policy'.[81] 'In the United States', it seems, 'the majority does *not* rule'.[82] The problem is exacerbated in other countries by the weakness of political parties. As Jan Komárek writes, 'parliaments today not only do not represent but do not govern either. Representative democracies', he maintains, 'became "hollowed" as the institutions that had mediated the relationship between the society and the state, especially political parties, have lost their significance and bec[o]me empty shells'.[83]

Such legislative shortcomings create an opportunity for constitutional courts to play a paradoxically representative role. Thus, in his influential history of the US Supreme Court and public opinion, Barry Friedman argues that because political parties are more polarised than the American people, the Supreme Court often tracks popular preferences more closely than either major party in power.[84] A similar dynamic plays out elsewhere, such as when the Canadian Supreme Court invalidated criminal sanctions for abortion in 1988 – a result, polls suggested, that 75 per cent of Canadians favoured but that elected officials couldn't or wouldn't bring to pass.[85] Because legislatures don't always express majority wishes, Luís Roberto Barroso and Aline Osorio contend that courts can play a role that is both representative and 'counter-legislative'.[86]

In a second step, champions of judicial review who take their cue from Dworkin, Rawls, and Habermas stress the deliberation-enriching and rationality-enhancing character of constitutional justice. Thus, Christine Landfried suggests that 'judicial review allows for a method of reflecting on social integration that differs from the mode of politics and, precisely because of the difference between judicial and political decision-making, increases the overall rationality of democratic governance'.[87] In Landfried's view, constitutional judicial review deepens the complexity of governance structures by offering an additional layer of deliberation based on legal methods of decision making. She is careful, however, to insist that judicial methods are not

[80] Mounk (n 27) 77.
[81] M Gilens and B Page, 'Testing Theories of American Politics: Elites, Interest Groups, and Average Citizens' (2014) 12 *Perspectives on Politics* 564.
[82] ibid 576.
[83] J Komárek, 'Rethinking constitutionalism and democracy … again?' (2019) 17 *Int'l J Const L* 992, 994.
[84] See B Friedman, *The Will of the People: How Public Opinion Has Influenced the Supreme Court and Shaped the Meaning of the Constitution* (Farrar, Straus and Giroux, 2009).
[85] L Roberto Barroso and A Osorio, 'Democracy, Political Crisis, and Constitutional Adjudication: The Leading Role of the Brazilian Supreme Court' in Landfried (n 50) 163, 178.
[86] ibid 176.
[87] Landfried (n 75) 4.

better than political ones, just different.[88] 'Constitutional courts', she concludes, 'can potentially enhance the discursive level when they listen to the arguments of persons involved in concrete cases, when they debate in judicial public hearings with representatives of politics and society about the constitutionality of specific policies, and when they interact with other courts'.[89] They can thus 'contribute to the "discursive level of public debates" (Habermas) and thereby to a more reasonable outcome of democratic politics'.[90] On Landfried's account, constitutional adjudication can be a resource for democratic governance, rather than a risk, so long as judicial decision making differs from political decision-making.[91]

Andrew Arato offers a similarly thick account of democracy. His, too, is inspired by Habermas and Rawls. Arato stresses the need for alternative conceptions of democracy, richer and more nuanced than monolithic majoritarian doctrines of popular sovereignty.[92] A democracy, he insists, 'ought not and cannot work through a single channel of representation'.[93] Drawing on the work of Pierre Rosanvallon, Arato argues that representative democracy needs to be supplemented by other democratic inputs, which Rosanvallon calls (paradoxically) 'counter-democracy'.[94] Arato advocates the 'plurality of democracy', insisting that parliamentary representation is a necessary but insufficient condition for true democracy. There are, he maintains, other avenues of representation. An extremely important avenue runs through the courts, which sometimes reflect actual majority preferences better than parliaments. For Arato, some of the most important democratic inputs come from civil society, which, in Arato's telling, is central to true democratic governance. But legislatures, he notes, aren't always receptive to civil society movements and inputs.[95] Courts, by contrast, sometimes do better. Indeed, 'one of the most important democratic channels are … the courts, which can be and are often utilized by civil society-based initiatives'.[96] 'When representation through election fails', Arato concludes, 'courts yield a second democratic channel that becomes all the more important under a populist government'.[97]

Mattias Kumm offers yet another thick account of the democratic basis for constitutional judicial review. Kumm defends judicial review as 'a forum of legally institutionalized Socratic contestation' in which the core right vindicated is the citizen's right to be offered legitimate reasons for government acts that infringe her interests.[98] On Kumm's account, the proportionality framework (which dominates constitutional adjudication virtually everywhere except in the US) forces public authorities 'into a process of reasoned engagement … that they might have

[88] ibid 5-6.
[89] ibid 6.
[90] ibid 17.
[91] ibid.
[92] Arato (n 50) 337.
[93] ibid.
[94] See P Rosanvallon, *Counter-Democracy* (CUP, 2008).
[95] See Arato (n 50).
[96] ibid 336.
[97] ibid 338.
[98] M Kumm, 'Institutionalising Socratic Contestation: The Rationalist Human Rights Paradigm, Legitimate Authority and the Point of Judicial Review' (2007) 1 *Eur JL Stud* 153, 165.

otherwise resisted'.[99] In the process, it drives unsavoury and illicit motives – such as those rooted in animus, prejudice, or unreasoned tradition – underground. Kumm's stance has a certain Rawlsian hue in its insistence that not all reasons count and its conviction that judicial review plays an indispensable role in smoking out the bad ones. Tom Hickey similarly celebrates judicial review's capacity to banish bad reasons, but he insists that this quality inheres in republican procedural values and doesn't rely at all on the belief, which Hickey ascribes to Dworkin and Rawls, that constitutional judges possess special virtue or wisdom.[100]

All these 'thick' accounts of democracy contend that 'democracy' means more than free and fair elections for a representative legislature and government. On these accounts, judicial review does not constrain democratic governance, but rather enriches it by demanding better reasons, driving better results, elevating the polity's 'discursive level', or by granting a more vivid and validating voice to 'the People', however vaguely defined.

V. CONCLUSION: WHICH 'PEOPLE' V WHICH 'DEMOCRACY'?

And therein lies the rub. For in pointing to some 'true' or 'authentic' democracy above and beyond the representative channels of electoral politics, these defenders of judicial review are implicitly (and probably unwittingly) playing at the populists' game. And they are doing so from an uncomfortably arrogant position that seems calculated to invite populist counterattacks. These 'thick' definitions of democracy conceive of the people as something transcending the formal structures of electoral democracy, whether parliamentary or presidentialist. In a way, they all pit a 'thick' imaginary of 'the People' against a 'thin' functionary of democracy. In a sense, and in that sense not unlike their populist opponents, they posit *The People v Democracy* – that is, they pit their own moralised (or proceduralised) version of 'the People' against 'democracy' of the ordinary, electoral, statistical, majoritarian sort. They play the game, to be sure, with great sophistication and finesse. But it is a dangerous game – one that perhaps has contributed to the backlash against constitutional courts now on painful display in many lands.

I contend that defending judicial review as somehow more democratic than democracy is conceptually muddled and practically dangerous. It is conceptually muddled because it mysticises 'the People' beyond the recognised rules of the political game. This is true both of those 'democratic' defences of judicial review that claim that it produces better outcomes (because of the rationalising effect of judicial discipline) and of those that assert that it fosters a richer public sphere (because of its supposedly greater sensitivity to inputs from civil society). Decisions by unelected officials can never be more democratic simply because they are better, either in their reasoning or in their result. One of the classic defences of democracy is the *faute de mieux* defence: there's no better way to decide who gets to decide. The whole point is

[99] ibid.
[100] T Hickey, 'The Republican Core of the Case for Judicial Review' (2019) 17 *Int'l J Const L* 288.

that we need democracy to decide collectively which reasons are persuasive and what results are best.

The notion that courts sometimes do a better job than legislatures of implementing the people's wishes is no less problematic. That might go a long way toward explaining why people put up with judicial power, but it doesn't make those exercises more democratic. You might be less likely to rebel against an arranged marriage if you like the spouse your parents choose. Your parents might even choose someone who suits you better than the person you might have chosen for yourself. But I don't know many democrats who, given the choice, would vote for arranged marriages – even if they were confident that their matchmakers would choose well and even if they were allowed to choose the people who chose their matchmakers. Certainly, they would not characterise the arranged marriage regime as a democratic one, or one that honoured their wishes.

Redefining democracy is practically dangerous because it invites rival redefinitions. It invites the very sort of moralised imaginaries that populists put forth and liberals regard with such dismay. The fact that many polities have embraced non-democratic institutions while maintaining that those institutions were bulwarks of 'true democracy' might well have triggered some of the backlash that has many liberals rightly alarmed.

What, then, is to be done?

'Democracy', writes Yascha Mounk, 'has nearly as many definitions as there are political thinkers'.[101] Now that constitutional lawyers have gotten in on the game, this is probably an understatement. But surely the best definition of democracy will be one that can be immediately understood by most members of the demos. A definition accessible only to sophisticated elites is sure to rouse suspicions that those elites are up to something. And so I favour a thin, 'majoritarian' definition of democracy and a defence of judicial review that openly admits its counter-majoritarian conundrum rather than defining it away or dismissing it as 'mainly bogus'.[102] '[O]ur support for judicial review', Mounk writes, 'should not blind us to its nature: the simple truth is that it takes many issues on which ordinary people have strong opinions out of political contestation.'[103] 'It's perfectly reasonable', Mounk continues,

> to think that, say, protecting sexual or religious minorities from discrimination is so important that it justifies overriding the will of the people. But if that is the case, intellectual honesty demands that we acknowledge the nature of the institution to which we are so committed: though it often sets itself against the popular will, we might then say, judicial review is justified by the fact that it protects individual rights and the rule of law.[104]

The best approach, then, is to do what constitutional courts do when they apply the far-famed proportionality test: bring all the relevant values into the open, place them together on the scales, and seek a sensible equilibrium. In this respect, it is worth recalling that whenever we describe a polity as a 'democracy' we are employing

[101] Mounk (n 27) 92.
[102] Arato (n 50) 338.
[103] Mounk (n 27) 73.
[104] ibid 73.

another form of synecdoche: we are substituting a part for the whole.[105] Democratic institutions – representative parliaments or elected governments – might compose the heart of such polities. But not every institution in such polities is or should be democratic. We needn't be taken in by our own rhetorical figures. The non-democratic institutions, such as constitutional judicial review, should be taken on their own terms and should, in those terms, be justified. What we need is a forthright explanation of why the costs to democracy are worth paying, not a subtle elaboration of why they aren't really costs to democracy at all.

Similarly, if courts are to go on adjudicating 'in the name of the people', they (and their defenders) should be clear about what this means. They should not, *à la populisme*, mystify the people as the embodiment of virtue, justice, and moral reasoning. They should make clear – as constitutional dualists from Hamilton and Marshall to Kelsen and Ackerman have always made clear – that they are speaking 'in the name of the People' in either its original, constituent capacity or in its representative, constituted capacity. When the two collide, the former prevails. But courts must be able to present that triumph convincingly as an implementation of the People's constituent will. They must persuasively show that they are enforcing in good faith an earlier exercise in popular sovereignty. That is harder to do the more creative the judges get and the further they stray from the constitutional text, history, and structure – and this without minimising the inescapable ambiguity of legal texts and the unavoidability of judicial creativity.

All of this counsels in favour of judicial caution and against constitutional adventurism. Courts would do well to regard constitutional texts as grants of judicial authority – some sweeping and clear, but many modest and vague. In the absence of a clear mandate, courts should tread carefully. This is not a call for unstinting deference and abdication; only for more of the most quintessentially judicial skills: balance and judgment. It is a call increasingly sounded by the friends of judicial review[106] – a call informed, in recent times, by sad experience. In Hungary, where the backlash against constitutional judicial review has been fierce, the Constitutional Court was unusually aggressive in its earliest years. In 1991, for instance, it invalidated 19 per cent of the statutes and 47 per cent of the decrees it reviewed.[107] Later, in a span of just five years, the Hungarian Court invalidated parliamentary inaction some 260 times.[108]

[105] See Cassese (n 79) 27.

[106] See Jakab (n 9) (warning that 'over-constitutionalization' is both dangerous and counter-productive); M Volcansek, 'Judicialization of Politics or Politicization of the Courts in New Democracies?' in Landfried (n 50) 66 ('[C]onstitutional courts that push the margins of their authority aggressively may lead to the politicization of the courts, which may, in turn, result in an erosion of judicial legitimacy, particularly in new democracies.'); M Rosenfeld, 'Judicial Politics versus Ordinary Politics: Is the Constitutional Judge Caught in the Middle?' in Landfried (n 50) 62 ('The main danger stemming from taking the constitutionalization of politics too far is the unleashing of an excessive politicization of the Constitution that tends to blur the proper boundary between ordinary and judicial politics.'); Mounk (n 27) 97 ('A system that dispenses with individual rights in order to worship at the altar of the popular will may ultimately turn against the people. Conversely, a system that dispenses with the popular will in order to protect individual rights may ultimately have to resort to increasingly blatant repression to quell dissent.'); Landfried (n 75) 16; D Grimm, 'What Exactly Is Political about Constitutional Adjudication' in Landfried (n 50) 317.

[107] See A Sajó, 'Reading the Invisible Constitution' (1995) 15 *Oxford J. L. Studies* 253.

[108] Volcansek (n 106) 70.

One needn't at all sympathise with that Court's populist eviscerators to worry that supercharged judicial aggression might, in time, pave the path toward judicial impotence.

Let me close, then, by summarising two hard truths to which friends of judicial review (myself included) would do well to attend.

The first is that it is better to balance democracy and liberal constitutionalism than to conflate them. The tension between the two is inherent, inescapable, and ineradicable. It will never go away. Trying to define it away through conceptual sleight-of-hand only makes mischief and squanders credibility. It is a logical fallacy to posit that because democracy is good everything that is good must also be democratic. Democracy is a good. It is not the only good or even the ultimate good. It is, by design, a penultimate good. Its purpose is to allow people (including the People) to identify the ultimate good for themselves. Untrammeled democracy, by contrast, is not a good. Democracy can't exist without losers, so the system should be designed with the losers in mind. A democracy should reward the winners without crushing the losers. Constitutionalism, says Bill Eskridge, exists to lower the stakes of (ordinary) politics.[109] Its purpose is to prevent any faction from capturing the state and shattering their foes. 'That, at any rate', to quote Holmes out of context, 'is the theory of our Constitution. It is an experiment, as all life is an experiment'.[110] It is an experiment in optimisation and equilibrium – a perennial balancing act between the people's capacity to act collectively and each person's right to act (and be left) alone.

The second hard truth is that we must abandon the notion that constitutional courts can right all injustices or remedy all harms – or even that they can cure all (or most) democratic shortcomings. That notion is misguided for at least three reasons: (1) it exaggerates and distorts what constitutions are meant to do, (2) it skews the balance between constitutionalism and democracy, and (3) it may trigger backlash. The proper response to the populist critique of constitutional justice is to recognise that they have half a point while insisting that it is only half a point. The proper response is to recalibrate the imbalances that constitutional justice has sometimes introduced between democracy and constitutionalism, but also to insist that the imbalances introduced by populists are often much greater and much worse. As Neil Walker observes, 'to criticize the other side for bias without being mindful of one's own bias combines caricature with a lack of self-awareness, and with a failure to appreciate that all constitutional approaches founder if they do not respect constitutionalism's precarious internal balance'.[111] Accordingly, Walker continues, 'populists can be rightly and emphatically criticized for a one-sidedness about the nature of constitutional well-being in their own critique of the one-sidedness of the "liberal establishment"'.[112]

[109] William N. Eskridge, 'Pluralism and Distrust: How Courts Can Support Democracy by Lowering the States of Politics' (2005) 114 Yale LJ 1279, 1293–94.

[110] *Abrams v. United States*, 250 U.S. 616, 631 (Holmes J dissenting).

[111] Walker (n 11) 533.

[112] ibid 533–34.

By all means, then, let us criticise the populists and, if needed, do so emphatically. But let us also realise that the proper response to a clash between 'the People' and 'democracy' is to define both terms with precision, weigh all the relevant values, and seek to optimise them in a stable equilibrium. 'The People', defined as liberal constitutionalism, and 'democracy', defined as representative government, need one another. Very likely need other things as well. But we needn't compound Böckenförde's dilemma by denying Bickel's.

7

Proceduralising the People: Deliberative Democracy, Majority Rule and the Rule of Law

SIMONE CHAMBERS*

I. INTRODUCTION

IN THIS CHAPTER, I outline a deliberative democratic reading of the relationship between the rule of law and the exercise of democratic self-government. This relationship begins with a procedural premise that there is no popular will without the rule of law. On this view then the extent to which majorities, or elite actors who claim to speak on behalf of the people, set out to dismantle the rule of law, they are dismantling the procedural conditions that give force to the claim to be exercising popular sovereignty. The critical and normative force of this position, however, depends a great deal on what one considers to be the procedural conditions that underwrite democratic self-government. If competitive elections are considered *the* democratic procedure, then only outcomes that make a direct assault on democratic elections, say by limiting the franchise, criminalising opposition parties, or cancelling elections, clearly fall a foul of the procedural rules. These are extreme cases of frontal attacks on democratic procedures. I am more interested in cases in which the outcomes of competitive elections are used to alter or weaken the rule of law (attacking the separation of powers, weakening the judiciary, strengthening the executive, and most problematic discrediting dissent and opposition as undemocratic) and send regimes in an increasingly authoritarian direction all in the name of strengthening democracy and pursuing the will of the people.[1] In these cases, procedural views of democracy that are focused on the rules of majority voting will often have to admit an inherent tension between democracy and the rule of law.

* University of California, Irvine.

[1] The cases I have in mind are, eg, Hungary, Turkey, Poland, and Venezuela. See S Chambers, 'Democracy and Constitutional Reform: Deliberative Versus Populist Constitutionalism' (2019) 45 *Philosophy and Social Criticism* 1116; KL Scheppele, 'On Being the Subject of the Rule of law' (2019) 11 *Hague Journal of the Rule of Law* 465.

On these narrow electoral views, democratic majorities are limited by, rather than constituted by, the rule of law.

In contrast to election focused views of democracy, deliberative democracy offers a more robust view of the procedures that constitute democratic self-government. In the course of this chapter, I hope to show that the robust proceduralism of deliberative democracy has a number of advantages over more minimal and formal alternatives. Why is it important to show that assaults on the rule of law are assaults on democracy and not simply assaults on liberalism? Many contemporary populist regimes thrive on and exploit the distinction between democracy and liberalism. They embrace and own labels like illiberal democracy.[2] They justify their actions by claiming to be perfecting democracy and correcting an imbalance between liberalism and democracy. To the extent that we employ conceptions of democracy that also presuppose the division between democracy and liberalism we are endorsing the framework of their justifications.

The view of democracy I outline and defend has four parts. First is a co-originality thesis that offers an argument for why one cannot separate democracy and liberalism. Second is a 'post-sovereignty' thesis in which 'the people' do not have a single identifiable unified will; rather popular sovereignty is disaggregated, exercised over time, and proceduralised in mechanisms of egalitarian inclusion. Third, this view of democracy places special emphasis on the public sphere as the locus of legitimacy rather than voting. Voting of course does not disappear and free and fair elections are a necessary part of any democratic order. But elections without the circulation of reasons, information, and justification (as well as criticism, dissent, and opposition) have significantly diminished legitimacy. The idea of 'diminished legitimacy' points to the final feature of this view: democratic legitimacy is not a dichotomous value but a continuous one. No set of democratic procedures perfectly meets the criteria of legitimacy. It is always a matter of more or less.

I begin, in the next section, with a discussion of proceduralism in democratic theory to distinguish deliberative proceduralism from majoritarian proceduralism. While the obvious difference between these two types of procedural theory is that they focus on two different procedures, deliberation, and voting, I suggest that many people misunderstand the difference between these two. Deliberation and voting are not competing methods of taking a decision because deliberation is not a decision rule and voting is not a way to decide how to vote. In democracies, most deliberation will need a vote to be decisive and, I argue, all votes need deliberation to be legitimate. Thus, in section two, I clarify the relationship between deliberation and voting and by extension consensus versus majority. With this preliminary discussion in place, I proceed to an exposition and defence of the four elements of deliberative proceduralism always keeping in the mind the goal of clarifying the place, role, and force of majorities in relation to the rule of law. At the end of the chapter, I introduce an illustration of how we might apply this framework in assessing the democratic legitimacy of referendums.

[2] V Orbán, 'Full text of Viktor Orbán's speech at Băile Tuşnad (Tusnádfürdő) of 26 July 2014' *Budapest Beacon* (26 July 2014).

I must address one final point in this introduction. What do I mean by the rule of law? This is a notoriously difficult and contested concept. I do not wish to make any strong theoretical or essentialist claims about the rule of law. Instead, I simply note how I am using the term. Following Habermas, I use the rule of law synonymously with the idea of the modern constitutional state.[3] In contrast to arbitrary, unpredictable, unstable, and despotic power, the rule of law is a rationalised legal order that is governed and structured by general, prospective, public, clear, and stable laws. 'To be governed by' implies a constitutional order of higher law that constrains ordinary law-making and the potential arbitrariness of majorities. Thus, some idea of the separation of powers and an independent judiciary with the power of judicial review is entailed by the rule of law, at least, in the way I am using the term. I also argue that dissent and opposition are essential elements in maintaining the rule of law because courts cannot do it all.

II. PROCEDURALISM AND DEMOCRATIC THEORY

Proceduralism is often contrasted to outcome-based views of democracy.[4] But here we should be careful. There are very few purely outcome-based views of democracy and most of these have been fully discredited. A pure outcome-based view holds that democratic legitimacy is entirely determined by a certain set of outcomes independent of how those outcomes were arrived at. And so we see, for example, a number of Marxist regimes claim the mantle of democratic republics not because any democratic procedures were followed but because state policy is purported to embody the democratic equality of all citizens.[5] And indeed it was this sort of outcome-based claim that inspired many early retreats into proceduralism.[6]

Within contemporary democratic theory, few people claim that democracy refers exclusively to a set of social and economic arrangements. We are all proceduralists in the sense that democracy is understood to involve, at a minimum, a set of procedures for making decisions or choosing social and economic arrangements. Thus, debates about procedure versus outcome are really debates about why we should value (or perhaps be suspicious of) this *way* of making decisions, that is, why we should value democratic *procedures* (however these are defined). For proceduralists the idea is to abstract from outcomes and look only at the intrinsic value or function of the procedure. For more outcome-based views, one values democratic procedures because they produce good outcomes; or conversely, one is suspicious of democratic procedures because they tend to (or can if not constrained) produce bad outcomes. Another way to express this distinction is through the question, do we value democratic procedures for reasons intrinsic to the procedure or for instrumental reasons?

[3] J Habermas, *Between Facts and Norms: Contributions to a Discourse Theory of Law and Democracy*, W Rheg (tr), (MIT Press, 1996).

[4] C Brettschneider, 'Balancing Procedures and Outcomes Within Democratic Theory: Core Values and Judicial Review' (2005) 53 *Political Studies* 423.

[5] A benevolent liberal dictator would be equally problematic.

[6] JA Schumpeter, *Capitalism, Socialism and Democracy* (New York, Harper Perennial, 1942).

The two most discussed instrumental views are, first, an epistemic view that values democratic procedures because they tend to arrive at the truth or, more modestly, better solutions to public policy problems than other forms of decision-making;[7] and, secondly, what I will call a Rousseauian view (but with no claim that this is based on an accurate interpretation of Rousseau) in which democratic procedures are valued because they produce a popular will.[8] Both the epistemic as well as the Rousseauian claim are rejected by proceduralists. Let me focus for a moment on the second, popular will claim and circle back on the epistemic claim.

Proceduralists in general challenge strong versions of the Rousseauian claim, especially as it is articulated in populist ideology, but they often do so on different grounds. Here I distinguish between minimalist, intrinsic, and deliberative proceduralism (which I will also call robust proceduralism). Minimalist proceduralists challenge the Rousseauian view primarily on empirical grounds. Democratic procedures, it is argued, specifically majority rule elections and plebiscites, simply cannot deliver a popular will because such a thing does not exist and aggregative procedures cannot construct it.[9] Even claims that democratic procedures facilitate responsiveness to majority preferences is challenged by the new Schumpeterians who claim there is no empirical evidence of any such relationship between procedures and outcomes in contemporary democracies.[10]

Claims that democratic procedures facilitate, channel, or produce a popular or general will are rejected and in their place we find minimalist claims that democratic procedures are a method of choosing rulers that involves a competitive struggle to get people's votes.[11] Market competition and consumer choice are considered the appropriate analogies not a supra subject named 'the people' willing the common good. Schumpeter stressed the descriptive nature of this view of democracy and this in turn spawned a great deal of empirical political science that set out to identify regimes that have competitive elections as the defining feature of democracy.[12] Some minimalists also add a normative argument that democratic procedures are to be valued because they replace violence and manage conflict.[13]

For many, minimalist proceduralism is too normatively thin to be attractive. Ironically, even though this tradition adamantly rejects populist/Rousseauian claims to produce a popular will, it has few internal defences against populist outcomes. Majorities do what they do and if populists win elections this outcome is no more or

[7] E Anderson, 'The Epistemic Dimension of Democracy' (2006) 3 *Episteme* 8; D Estlund, *Democratic Authority: A Philosophical Framework* (Princeton University Press, 2008); H Landemore, *Democratic Reason: Politics, Collective Intelligence, and the Rule of the Many* (Princeton University Press, 2013).

[8] Who holds this view? Populist politicians appear to appeal to something like this view in their rhetoric (see Chambers (n 1)) but it would be difficult to find a serious political theorist who held a crude popular will view. This is why, for example, minimalists like Achen and Bartels must refer to the 'folk theory' of democracy rather than cite any theorists. The Rousseauian view is to some extent the creation of critics of democracy. CH Achen and LM Bartels, *Democracy for Realists: Why Elections Do Not Produce Responsive Government* (Princeton University Press, 2017).

[9] Schumpeter (n 6).

[10] Achen and Bartels (n 8).

[11] Schumpeter (n 6) 269.

[12] G Mackie, "The Values of Democratic Proceduralism' (2011) 26 *Irish Political Studies* 439.

[13] A Przeworski, *Crises of Democracy* (CUP, 2019) 7; FA Hayek, *The Road to Serfdom* (University of Chicago Press, 1944) 52.

less democratic than any other outcome.[14] As Przeworski puts it, 'populist parties are not anti-democratic in the sense that they do not advocate replacing elections by some other method of selecting governments'.[15] Thus only frontal attacks on elections count as undermining democracy. As the category of 'competitive authoritarianism' suggests, even at a purely descriptive level, minimalist views of democracy seem unsatisfactory as a great deal of what might normally be considered anti-democratic behaviour is compatible with competitive elections.[16]

What I call intrinsic proceduralism offers a normatively more robust theory of democracy than minimalists. Like minimalist proceduralists, defenders of intrinsic proceduralism do not think that democratic decision-making produces substantively correct outcomes, and they are equally skeptical about ideas of the general will. But unlike minimalists, they believe that democratic procedures have significant moral value in themselves and this in turn leads to a more robust picture of the procedures themselves.[17] Rather than channelling competition, democratic procedures are understood to instantiate equality by treating each citizen fairly, with respect, or as an autonomous or free agent.

While minimalists point to the empirical fact that democratic procedures do not produce a collective will, intrinsic theorists are often motivated by a different set of concerns. They are particularly concerned with claims that democracy produces collectively good or epistemically better outcomes as they often see this as tying democratic legitimacy to contentious views of what counts as collectively good or epistemically better. As Nadia Urbinati likes to say, democracy gives citizens the right to be wrong: 'Procedures are legitimately democratic because they deliver what they are made for: to protect the freedom of its members to produce "wrong" decision'.[18] Jeremy Waldron argues that we should value democracy precisely because it involves a set of procedures that treats each with respect despite deep disagreement about ideas of the good, justice and truth.[19] Although both Urbinati and Waldron think that informed deliberation preceding votes is to be encouraged, universal franchise voting and not deliberation is the democratic procedure that embodies the value and promise of democracy.

I want to turn to deliberative democracy as a third variation on the proceduralist theme. The view departs from the first two in two significant ways. First, the procedures that constitute a democratic regime are expanded beyond free and fair elections and majority decision-making to encompass opinion and will formation as well as multiple and various institutional mechanisms through which that opinion and will impacts, determines, and shapes public policy decisions – voting being only one such mechanism. Secondly, procedures are defended both on intrinsic grounds (for example, that they embody respect for the equality of all citizens) as well as instrumental

[14] C Mudde, 'The Populist Zeitgeist' (2004) 39 *Government and Opposition* 541.

[15] Przeworski (n 13) 88.

[16] S Levitsky and AL Way 'The New Competitive Authoritarianism' (2020) 31 *Journal of Democracy* 51.

[17] MP Saffon and N Urbinati, 'Procedural Democracy, the Bulwark of Equal Liberty' (2013) 41 *Political Theory* 441; J Waldron, *Law and Disagreement* (OUP, 1999).

[18] N Urbinati, *Democracy Disfigured: Opinion, Truth, and the People* (Harvard University Press, 2014) 98.

[19] Waldron (n 17).

grounds that, if working well, they produce epistemically better outcomes than non-democratic procedures and that those outcomes are in some sense authored by citizens themselves.

III. DELIBERATION AND VOTING: CONSENSUS AND MAJORITIES

While it is true that deliberative proceduralists expand the category of democratic procedures beyond voting to include processes of opinion and will formation, it would be a mistake to think of deliberation and voting as two competing procedures of democratic decision-making. Deliberative democracy has sometimes been understood this way and as standing in opposition to aggregative democracy. What is central in the deliberative model are the reasons, justifications, and discussion that backup a decision, not simply the number of votes that support a decision. This is also sometimes thought to rest on a contrast between consensus versus majority as a decision rule. I want to suggest that the relationship between deliberative democracy and voting, on the one hand, and consensus versus majority decision rule on the other hand, has often been misunderstood.

Deliberative democracy both as a model of face-to-face practice, say in a mini public or citizens' assembly, as well as a broad paradigm to understand a full democratic system, has no problem with counting votes or with majority rule as a *decision rule*. Deliberative democracy's issue with aggregation was not an objection to voting or counting votes; it was always an objection to democratic *theory* that focused exclusively on the vote, said nothing about the opinion and will formation the preceded the vote, and invested aggregation with the full weight of democratic legitimacy. Thus, not the practice of voting but the normative weight and role of voting was the target.

Very generally, I take deliberation to mean the weighing of reasons or considerations in light of a practical decisions about what to do. Democratic deliberation involves the weighing of reasons or considerations in light of a practical decision we must take together as equals. This in turn involves certain procedural conditions that facilitate the weighing of reasons and consideration as equals. Deliberation, I want to insist, is not strictly speaking a decision rule, if by decision rule we mean how and when we stop deliberation and act on some chosen principle, policy, or practical conclusion. Deliberation is decision-oriented in that it is about taking a practical decision but it is not obviously a decision rule that dictates when a group has closure on a question and indeed many of our most important deliberations are about what rule we will choose to take various types of decisions.

Now it might be thought that consensus is the default decision rule for deliberation. The thought here is that if the essential driving force of deliberation is the persuasiveness of arguments then the natural end of this sort of activity would be when everyone was persuaded or everyone was in agreement. There is a great deal of debate within deliberative democracy theory about whether consensus is the proper end or telos of deliberation with a number of theorists abandoning the ideal.[20]

[20] S Elstub and P McLaverty, 'Introduction' in S Elstub and P McLaverty (eds), *Deliberative Democracy: Issues and Cases* (Edinburgh University Press, 2014).

But even for theorists who retain consensus as the telos of deliberation, this is understood as a regulative ideal that does not translate into either a default empirical decision rule nor a requirement that all participants take consensus as their subjective goal in real empirical encounters.[21] I have three main reasons for this claim.

First, as I have noted, the idea of a fully rational consensus is a regulative ideal. What this means is that the ideal can never be achieved in the empirical world but nevertheless we can and should use that ideal to regulate and guide our actions in this world. Thus, the regulative ideal gives us counterfactual standards against which we can evaluate better or worse practices and outcomes.[22] But how does that evaluation work exactly? We do not have access to the substance of a rationally motivated consensus. Which is to say, we do not have independent access to what people would agree to; all we have are the ideal procedural conditions that would have to be in place for us to say that the outcome is a rationally motivated consensus. Thus, the regulative ideal does not furnish us with a clear goal towards which to strive as would an ideal of substantive economic equality for example. Instead the ideal points to constructing, as best we can, the procedural conditions that would give us confidence that the outcomes approach a rationally motivated consensus among equals. These are the procedures that maximise the equal inclusion of all voices, circulation of information, and the exchange of reasons.

Our procedures will never be perfect (for example full and perfect inclusion will always be out of reach) and we as individuals will also never be perfect reasoners, thus all deliberations are in principle fallible, corrigible, and so open ended. But we do need to take decisions. And in mass democracies those decisions are often (and for good reason) taken in the form of majority voting. Although this might sound like voting is a sort of second best, a necessary evil because we cannot talk forever or as much as it would take to get a consensus, this too I think is mistaken view. Rather than seeing votes as failures to reach consensus, we should see votes as punctuating, for the purposes of action and reflection, an underlying ongoing process of democratic deliberation through which we collectively problem solve. Consensus is in principle and in practice never fully and perfectly achievable.

A second reason why consensus is not a default decision rule for real world deliberation is that for many policy questions there will be reasonable disagreement among citizens. In these circumstances, majority voting may further the goals of deliberation more than a real-world consensus decision rule. Bernard Manin argues, for example, that with majority rule we have a public record that reflects that there were other reasons and arguments that were persuasive even if they did not win the day. 'The process (majority voting) nevertheless institutionalizes the admission that there were also reasons not to desire the solution finally adopted.'[23] We often need to be reminded of the minority view. Sometimes, even if the minority view did not persuade the majority, it nevertheless contained grains of truth or partial insights. Note that this defence of a majority over a consensus decision rule is premised on

[21] M Neblo, 'Family Disputes: Diversity in Defining and Measuring Deliberation' (2007) 13 *Swiss Political Science Review* 527.

[22] ibid.

[23] B Manin, 'On Legitimacy and Political Deliberation' (1987) 15 *Political Theory* 359.

good deliberation preceding that vote. Indeed, deliberation in which the minority feels like their case was addressed and honestly considered, is one of the strongest defences of majority voting.[24]

Finally, even if we operate with the regulative ideal of a rationally motivated consensus, this does not mean that individual citizens must take the achievement of an empirical consensus as their immediate purpose or motivation for every encounter that might further deliberation. First, having consensus as the end of real-world conversations can have perverse anti-deliberative effects by, for example, motivating people to suppress their arguments or go along with the majority even if they do not fully agree. Secondly, citizens who engage in contestation and disruptive demands to be heard do not appear to be seeking consensus in any immediate sense. But from a systemic point of view we might think that they are setting out to publicise the unfair conditions of the present political dialogue. Thus, standing up and challenging a false consensus is very much part of the deliberative repertoire. We can make sense of this action because we have an intuitive grasp of what an authentic consensus might look like.

The ideal of deliberative democracy is compatible with and furthered by many different sorts of empirical decision rules even if the ideal itself points to consensus as a counterfactual telos and ideal of legitimacy. Judges, juries, legislators, and citizens are asked to vote all the time and deliberation would have little empirical impact without voting. But voting and majority rule without deliberation is, as Dewey put it, 'as foolish as its critics charge it with'.[25]

This distinction between process and decision rule can be seen very clearly in the structure and design of deliberative mini publics. There are by now countless deliberative initiatives across the world that bring citizen together in a deliberative format to discuss issues and often (but not always) take a decision or perhaps issue a joint report.[26] Voting is very common in these initiatives and can perform a variety of functions. Here are three examples. Voting can be a mechanism of deliberation itself when used as straw polls to take stock of the shifting options. There is empirical evidence that frequent votes punctuating ongoing deliberation can have a positive effect on the quality, reflectiveness, and inclusiveness of deliberation by, for example, reminding participants that there are dissenters whose concerns need to be addressed.[27]

A second function of voting is to communicate and publicise the various positions and arguments that were raised in a deliberation. The Oregon Citizens Initiative Review (CIR), created to help citizens make informed choices on state wide ballot measures, is a good example of this second function. Citizen panelists meet in a face-to-face mini public setting to hear from both sides of the issue, talk with neutral witnesses, and deliberate intensively as a full panel and in small break-out groups. At the end of the process, the group takes a vote and then writes up a one-page

[24] M Schwartzberg, *Counting the Many: The Origins and Limits of Supermajority Rule* (CUP, 2014); A Moore and K O'Doherty, 'Deliberative Voting: Clarifying Consent in a Consensus Process' (2014) 13 *Journal of Political Philosophy* 302.

[25] J Dewey, *The Public and Its Problems* (Swallow Press, 1954) 107.

[26] K Grönlund, A Bächtiger and M Setäla (eds), *Deliberative Minipublics – Involving Citizens in the Democratic Process* (ECPR Press, 2014).

[27] Moore and O'Doherty (n 24).

information sheet for voters at large which records the vote and the reasons that were raised on each side of the issue.[28] In this case it is important that all sides of the issue are presented to voters and this includes publishing the internal vote of the mini public. There is evidence that the CIR and other similar initiatives have had a positive effect on the quality (better informed voters) and inclusiveness (higher participation levels) of public referendum debates.[29] Finally, voting can be used as a closure mechanism for the group to take a decision. Can this picture of the relationship between majority voting and deliberative procedures be scaled up to the level of mass democracy? I think so.

IV. PROCEDURALISM REVISITED: CO-ORIGINALITY

Deliberative democracy endorses the view that the legitimacy of democratic outcomes, especially majoritarian outcomes, is tied to an assessment of the democratic procedures that produced the outcome. Those procedures are understood to involve more than minimal conditions to ensure competitive elections but also procedures that safeguard and enhance deliberative public opinion and will formation. Thus deliberative democracy is always procedural in some sense but is it also always purely procedural? Pure proceduralism is the view that there are no standards to evaluate the legitimacy or correctness of outcomes independent of the procedure itself. A number of deliberative democracy theorists have rejected pure proceduralism in favour of a substantive approach because, as Gutmann and Thompson point out, only by including such principles can we assert, when necessary, that 'what the majority decides, even after full deliberation, is wrong'.[30] Not only do we need substantive moral principles to be able to say when an outcome is wrong, but we also need institutions that can constrain majorities when they do wrong. This of course points to a separation of powers and an independent judiciary with the power of judicial review. Pure proceduralists respond to this criticism by asking who decides what is wrong? Where do unelected judges get the authority to limit popular will? Rights foundationalists offer arguments pointing to the pre-political origins of rights. Deliberationists tend to offer a co-originality argument often inspired by Habermas or Rawls.[31] On the co-originality view, rights and democracy are co-dependent. Habermas' version of this argument goes like this: the only plausible justification of the rights and freedoms enshrined in a Constitution is that they are the outcome of a popular democratic process; popular democratic processes only have the power to justify constitutions if they are undertaken under conditions that

[28] J Gastil and K Knobloch, *Hope for Democracy: How Citizens can Bring Reason Back into Politics* (OUP, 2020).

[29] J Suiter and T Reidy T 'Does Deliberation Help Deliver Informed Electorates: Evidence from Irish Referendum Votes' (2020) 56 *Representation* 539; Gastil and Knobloch (n 28).

[30] A Gutmann and D Thompson, 'Deliberative Democracy beyond Process' (2002) 10 *Journal of Political Philosophy* 153, 161.

[31] Habermas (n 3); C Brettschneider, *Democratic Rights: The Substance of Self-Government* (Princeton University Press, 2007); S Rummens, 'Populism as a Threat to Liberal Democracy' in CR Kaltwasser, P Taggart, P Ochoa Espejo and P Ostiguy (eds), *Oxford Handbook of Populism* (OUP, 2017); Chambers (n 1).

respect the rights and freedoms of participants, that is, under constitutions.[32] For now, I focus only on one half of this thesis: 'Popular sovereignty is (...) proceduralized in the sense that the popular will is legitimate only in so far as it is the result of a procedure of reasonable deliberation. Since private autonomy is an essential precondition of such deliberation, any outcome that does not respect individual rights has to be rejected'.[33]

The co-originality view does not merely say that elections without rights (say free speech and freedom of association) are a sham. It shifts the locus of democratic legitimacy away from elections and majority rule. Individual rights are the precondition for democratic procedures. If one thinks of democratic procedures primarily in terms of elections and voting, then the schedule of rights that can be justified this way is relatively narrow. This is a common criticism of instrumentalists like John Hart Ely[34] and Alexander Meiklejohn[35] who think of rights as necessary conditions for the equality of each citizen as a voter and law maker. Deliberative democrats begin with an ideal of deliberative opinion and will formation in which citizens exchange reasons and justifications in the process of forming their opinions and preferences regarding public issues. There are three dimensions along which this process is assessed: equality, inclusiveness, and epistemic robustness. Equality and inclusiveness begin with voting rights but move beyond the question of who gets the vote to who gets to be heard, addressed, and responded to in public discourse. With regard to the epistemic dimension, here citizens require access to dependable information not just about facts and events but also about the claims, complaints, arguments, justifications, and *cri de coeur* of their fellow citizens.

V. SELF-GOVERNMENT AND THE PEOPLE

Deliberative proceduralism not only leads away from minimalist electorally focused views of democracy but it also leads away from a Rousseauian inspired search for outcomes that embody the general or the people's will. Pluralism suggests that dissent, opposition, and difference are permanent features of all democracies and so any claim to speak for the people in a decisive unitary way will misrepresent and exclude something or someone. The fact of deep disagreement and the impossibility of a unified will have led some democratic theorists to retreat from strong claims about popular control or self-government and instead think of democracy only in terms of the equality and fairness of the process.[36] Deliberative proceduralism by contrast has not given up on the ideal of popular control and authorship. But the self of self-government is proceduralised. On this proceduralised understanding, 'the people' is 'not a collection of individuals, but a procedure of decision-making, by

[32] Habermas (n 3) 94.

[33] S Rummens, 'The Co-originality of Private and Public Autonomy' (2006) 14 *The Journal of Political Philosophy* 469.

[34] JH Ely, *Democracy and Distrust* (Harvard University Press, 1980).

[35] A Mieklejohn, *Free Speech and its Relation to Self-Government* (Harper, 1948).

[36] Waldron (n 17).

which individuals interact with each other mediated by legal institutions that channel popular demands and force representatives to adopt views and makes decisions. In the long term, these procedures can be recognised as "the Popular will" and, thus, we can eventually think of them as popular sovereignty'.[37]

The proceduralised view of the people leads to a number of conclusions. First, any decision, vote, election, or referendum is never synonymous with the people and is always fallible, corrigible, and partial. Secondly, 'the people' is always a work in progress over time. The work involved here is, on the one hand, maintaining adequate levels of the three dimensions of legitimacy: equality, inclusion, and the circulation of and access to good information as well as the undistorted views, claims, and expressed feelings of others, and on the other hand, maintaining channels of responsiveness between citizens and decision-makers. Thirdly, the assessment of whether the democratic system does a fair job in facilitating and empowering popular opinion and will formation must be assessed along multiple dimensions. Voting is essential to this process, but it would be a mistake to think that democratic authorship can be traced to a causal relationship between votes and outcomes. We want to be able to trace a connection between the considered opinions of the public (in all its plurality) to outcomes. Finally, this view places special emphasis on the structure, character, and regulation of the public sphere in determining democratic legitimacy rather than the voting booth.

VI. PUBLIC SPHERE IN A DELIBERATIVE SYSTEM

Let me begin with an idealised outline of how the public sphere might work in a healthy well-functioning democracy, always keeping in mind that this is a yard stick against which we measure real democracies. I use the term public sphere to refer to a sphere of political communication that stands between civil society and the state. Following Habermas, I understand this sphere to be 'wild', unstructured, and contain multiple forms of political communication.[38] Although individuals, groups, and institutional contributions to the wild and open communication of the public sphere may be deliberative or flow from a deliberative venue (eg, the Oregon Citizen Initiative Review I mentioned above), taken as a whole what goes on in the public sphere cannot be characterised as deliberation in any straightforward sense. Communication is highly mediated and disaggregated and ranges along a vast multi-dimensional continuum from everyday talk, to formal deliberation and includes a growing number and variety of digital platforms.

Although public problems and policy solutions are an ongoing topic of conversation throughout the public sphere, the communication is not directly tied to a decision moment in the way a face-to-face deliberation in a structured mini public or public

[37] P Ochoa Espejo, 'Populism and the Idea of the People' in Kaltwasser, Taggart, Ochoa Espejo and Ostiguy (eds) (n 31) 615.

[38] J Habermas, 'Political Communication in Media Society: Does Democracy still have an Epistemic Dimension? The Impact of Normative Theory on Empirical Research' in J Habermas, *Europe: The Faltering Project* (Polity Press, 2009) 155.

forum might be. Nevertheless, the communication is decision-oriented in the more general sense of being taken up by questions of the type 'what should we do?'. That modern liberal democratic public spheres always have this decision-oriented potential as regards communication is made evident at times of crisis and mobilisation. The murder of George Floyd at the hands of the police in May 2020, for example, and the ensuing protest movement focused the attention of millions of Americans on the question of racism and police violence. Although a systemic problem long before Floyd's brutal death, this tragedy put racism and police violence on the public deliberative agenda in the sense that 'what is to be done?' came dramatically into focus as a topic of conversation and contestation. But the public 'conversation' about what is to be done does not look like the facilitated conversations in designed settings nor does the public sphere take decisions.

Another difference between mini public deliberation and the communicative dynamics of the public sphere, is that the latter is asymmetrical in the sense that most citizens are consumers of messages rather than producers of messages. The mediators of this asymmetry, the press, social media, and other structures of communication, play an outsized role in the public sphere. We should pay as much attention to these institutions and their regulation as we do to protecting the right to vote.

Although the public sphere cannot be understood as a deliberation writ large, it can be understood as performing important functions in a deliberative system. While the public sphere does not perform a decision-making function, it performs a function of articulating and raising the problems, claims, interests, (not to mention hopes, dreams, and fears) upon and about which decisions are taken. The public sphere produces public opinion. Public opinion articulates the problems for which a democratic system seeks solutions.

Ideally, public opinion sets the broad agenda in the deliberative system. Public opinion, although reflecting the real-life concerns, interests, and problems of the public, is constituted through communication. Thus, public opinion is not an exogenous force in a democratic system but very much an endogenous force. Public opinion in the sense that I am using this term is not synonymous with surveyed attitudes about public issues. It refers instead to opinion that is produced and created via intersubjective and public processes of communication. Public and scientific publishing and discussion of survey data are part of the process through which the public sphere produces public opinion. That opinion is 'considered public opinion' to the extent that those processes trade in facts and are conducive to authentic exchanges and reflection.

Not all ideas, claims, positions, and demands raised in the public sphere can be justifiably translated into a legislative agenda and in any case all of them need clarification, articulation, and translation in order to make it onto an agenda. So the system must 'filter', to use Habermas' word, the claims and demands by putting them through a feedback loop of public scrutiny and then an ever more rigorous processes of justification.[39] As the political talk moves closer to the centre, traditional rules of deliberation and arguing become more rigorous and the conversation looks more

[39] ibid.

and more (or ideally) like a deliberation. The system as a whole is characterised by a significant epistemic division of labour.[40] The more epistemically rigorous function of arguing and deliberating over clear policy options takes place higher up the system ladder. But the content of deliberation, that is, what gets deliberated, comes out of a communicative process that filters, clarifies, and prioritises claims and narratives in the public sphere.

Democracies function properly when they respond to and act on problems, concerns and issues that confront real people in civil society. The picture of self-government to emerge from this view gives central place 'to the idea that the process of political opinion and will-formation in which citizens (actively and/or passively) participate should effectively influence and shape the laws and policies to which they are subject'.[41] Responsiveness and control are instantiated in the feedback loop between opinion and will formation in the public sphere and decision-making at the centre. Elections are one mechanism in this loop but not the only mechanism. The relationship between public opinion and responsive law-making is not a causal one where voters' actions determine policy outcomes. The relationship is re-envisioned in discursive or communicative terms as a relationship of deliberative accountability where representatives must justify their actions in terms that speak to all citizens as equal consociates.

Elections and majority rule perform three functions in the system analogous to the three functions of voting in a mini public we reviewed earlier. First, if we think of deliberatively structured opinion and will formation as an ongoing, open-ended process through which a political community publicly and collectively hashes out issues and problem solves then regular voting and elections are important moments to take stock and reflect on the direction of the conversation. Elections punctuate the ongoing underlying democratic discourse of a community. In this way, they can contribute to deliberative accountability by structuring and demanding regular justifications of platforms and policy proposals. The competitive adversarial structure of elections need not diminish the deliberative potential of these moments. We will disagree about what is the best course of action. It is important that the public gets to see and think about these disagreements (often presented in party platforms). Opposition and dissent are the catalysts of productive public debate just as they are a necessary component of legislative debate. It is not partisanship and competition per se that undermines the deliberative potential of the public sphere, it is toxic polarisation that turns disagreement into hate and exclusion. The possibility that elections can positively contribute to the circulation of reasons is severely hampered, perhaps destroyed, without strong and sensible regulation of the public sphere, especially the role of money in politics.

Elections install the winners in power, but they also record that there were losers and that they too won votes. A second function, the one that Bernard Manin stresses in his theory of deliberative democracy, is how majority rule makes the minority

[40] S Chambers, 'Balancing Epistemic Quality and Equal Participation in a Systems Approach to Deliberative Democracy' (2017) 31 *Social Epistemology* 266.

[41] C Lafont, *Democracy Without Shortcuts: A Participatory Conception of Deliberative Democracy* (OUP, 2019) 24.

visible in a way that consensus, unanimity, or super majority rules do not.[42] Whereas on an electoral focused view of democracy the important point is that next time around the minority might win the day, in a deliberative model the visibility of the minority means that those in power need to justify their actions to the minority as well. Majorities elect governments but governments govern everybody and therefore their reasons and justifications must address everybody.

Finally, voting introduces a necessary decisiveness to the process of public debate. It is a closure procedure that reflects the equal status of each citizen. In this sense it is the appropriate closure procedure for democracy. I have argued that voting without deliberation is difficult to defend. But deliberation without voting is also problematic. In a small meeting, an individual might be able to get the sense of the room after lengthy deliberation and act on that sense without a vote. And political representatives do something similar when they attend to public opinion and shape public policy accordingly. But deliberative legitimacy could not be maintained in a regime in which elites were simply attuned to the interests, concerns, and claims of citizen articulated in a public sphere and always acted on those but never had elections. This would itself undermine the very values of equality and inclusion instantiated in deliberation. Melissa Schwartzberg's defence of majority rule fits very well with the deliberative democratic view: 'if respect for the individual and independent judgment are central commitments of democracy, and if equal respect for citizens entails the presumption that citizens' judgments – again, including their judgments of their own interests – are of equal merit, then the default voting rule within democracies should be majority rule'.[43] Universal franchise is an important acknowledgement of the equal status of each individual as well as a respect for the agency of each citizen. The equality of one person one vote is an important foundation of basic political respect from which to build the more robust political equality envisioned in a deliberative system.

I have argued that the first and most important structural feature of a democratic system seen through a deliberative lens is an open and inclusive public sphere with well-functioning press and political communication. Few contemporary public spheres get high grades on any of these dimensions. All have various pathologies of exclusion, epistemic opacity and failures, and market distortions (to name just a few of the problems we face). This means that deliberative democracy theory is often a critical theory focusing on the ways that empirical and real world public spheres fail to perform their democratic function. In this critical theory, certain populist regimes have come under special scrutiny. Populists target the public sphere and the free circulation of information directly. It's not just that they do little to support public debate (a chronic problem in stable liberal democracies) it is that they actively push back against public debate and often identify the forces of the public sphere as the enemies of democracy. Here is the sharpest contrast. For deliberative democrats, opposition, criticism, dissent, counter arguments, plural points of view, challenge, are the elements and building blocks of a proceduralised popular sovereignty, for populists these are obstacles, maliciously placed in the path of the will of the people.

[42] Manin (n 23); Schwartzberg (n 24).
[43] Schwartzberg (n 24) 7.

VII. REFERENDUMS

As an illustration of the way this sort of proceduralism can furnish a framework of critical analysis, I want to take a brief look at two recent constitutional referendums. Putting constitutional questions to popular votes appears to place the rule of law at the mercy of majorities. But citizen participation in constitutional-making reform can potentially strengthen the legitimacy of the Constitution. This claim is both empirical and normative. On the empirical side there is evidence that citizen participation, especially deliberative participation at the drafting stage of constitution-making, produces citizen 'buy in' and leads to more robust democratic institutions.[44] On the normative side, citizen participation can contribute to the claim that the Constitution is the expression of 'we the people' and underpinned by the justificatory force of popular sovereignty.[45] This is the other side of the co-originality thesis that I have not been able to defend in full but is captured in Habermas' famous claim 'the rule of law cannot be had or maintained without radical democracy'.[46]

According to the view I have outlined in this chapter, the democratic legitimacy of popular decision procedures, such as referendums, should be assessed on the processes of opinion and will formation and the creation of feedback loops within an active and inclusive public sphere. This assessment of legitimacy is on a continuum. Thus, I argue that the 2015 Irish referendum has more democratic legitimacy than the Turkish referendum of 2017, not because of a higher majority threshold, but because of the deliberative scaffolding that was put in place to encourage a broad national conservation. I do not say that the Turkish referendum was illegitimate. Although there does appear to have been some voting irregularities, it is not clear that they were such as to undermine all claims to a democratic process.[47] What I suggest is that a preliminary assessment of the processes and procedures leading up to the referendum does not give us confidence (or at least, not as much confidence as we have in the Irish case) that the public sphere functioned as a credentialising force backing up the vote.

In 2012 the Irish Convention on the Constitution was established to review the existing Constitution and advise on reform.[48] The Convention had 100 members: one chair, 66 randomly selected ordinary citizens, and 33 places reserved for legislators allocated proportionate to each party's seats in Parliament. After much deliberation, consultation with civil society, and input from citizens at large, the Convention submitted 40 recommendations to the Government for consideration, several of which would require a constitutional referendum to enact. Three have subsequently

[44] TA Eisenstadt, C LeVan and T Maboudi, 'When Talk Trumps Text: The Democratizing Effects of Deliberation during Constitutional-Making, 1974–2011' (2015) 109 *American Political Science Review* 592.

[45] X Contiades and A Fotiadou, *Participatory Constitutional Change: The People as Amenders of the Constitution* (Routledge, 2018); B Ackerman, *We the People: Foundations*, Vol 1 (Harvard University Press, 1991).

[46] Habermas (n 3) xlii.

[47] N Levin, M Coker and Y Candemir, 'Inside Turkey's Irregular Referendum' *The Wall Street Journal* (25 April 2017) www.wsj.com.

[48] J Suiter, D Farrell and C Harris, 'The Irish Constitutional Convention: A Case of "High Legitimacy"?' in M Reuchamps and J Suiter (eds), *Constitutional Deliberative Democracy in Europe* (ECPR Press, 2016).

gone to a referendum, the most significant of which was the marriage equality referendum of 2015.[49] A number of scholars, as well as public intellectuals, have dubbed this process a success along with the 2018 referendum on abortion that followed a second citizens' assembly in 2016.[50] Success was measured on an evaluation of the quality of debate, inclusiveness and civility of public appeals, levels of participation especially from civil society organisations, and the post-reform satisfaction with the process including those in the minority.

The 2012–2015 constitutional process is a good illustration of how to think about proceduralised popular sovereignty in concrete terms. The process was drawn out over three years and appears to have been designed to initiate a productive public dialogue or national conversation that would not be dragged down by partisan and sectarian entrenchment and resentment. Popular opinion and will formation took place through the triangulation of three institutions mediated by an open, free, and critical public sphere: a democratically elected Parliament, a special Convention on the Constitution with a significant citizen component, and a popular referendum process. None of these institutions alone represent the definitive exercise of popular sovereignty; the people exercising democratic self-determination can be seen in a retrospective assessment of the deliberative quality, inclusiveness, and fairness of the process as whole. The mediating role of the public sphere is all important as it allowed for a national conversation over time that gave the final vote its democratic credentials.

In October 2017, Turkey went to the polls to vote on 18 amendments to the constitution. These amendments were formulated by the ruling AKP party. The thrust of the 18 amendments was to move Turkey to a presidential system and limit Parliamentary and judiciary oversight on the president. In defending the constitutional reform, a government spokesman suggested that checks on executive power are anti-democratic: 'any attempt to form an institutional control over the people's will is against democracy … the president, is elected directly by the people …. So, it would not be acceptable for the Parliament to file an interpellation motion about the actions and decisions of someone who takes his authority directly from the people'.[51] An interpolation motion is the formal request made by Parliament to the Government asking for explanation and justification of an action or policy. It is used as a device of publicity and accountability but is now apparently seen as an obstacle to democratic will.

Both the introduction of direct election as well as the expansion of presidential powers vis-à-vis Parliament was framed as enhancing citizen participation, power and sovereignty. Citizens changed the Constitution though a referendum, citizens directly elect the president, the president has fewer obstacles (checks and balances) to enacting the will of the people. On the day after the referendum, Erdoğan announced that 'this nation has realized the most democratic election, the likes of which has not

[49] The other question on the 2015 ballot was to reduce the age of candidacy for the president from 35 to 21 and then on 26 October 2018 to repeal the law against blasphemy.

[50] J Suiter, D Farrell and C Harris, '"Systematizing" Constitutional Deliberation: the 2016–18 citizens' assembly in Ireland' (2018) 34(1) *Irish Political Studies* 1; Suiter, Farrell and Harris (n 48).

[51] Quoted in B Bora, 'Turkey's constitutional reform: all you need to know' *Al-Jazeera* (17 January 2017) 5–6.

been seen in any western country'.[52] But the referendum process was not designed for maximum (let alone quality) citizen participation, but for producing an electoral mandate for an elite agenda. Not only was there no attempt to organise and initiate a national conversation about the constitutional reforms, but public debate was dominated by the Government, with active suppression of the 'No' campaign.[53] In Turkey, the 2017 referendum was intended to furnish a democratic mandate for Erdoğan's agenda. Without an inclusive participatory consultation process, however, the democratic credentials of that mandate are suspect.

VIII. CONCLUSION

In this chapter, I have outlined a deliberative democracy version of the principle 'there is no popular will without the rule of law'. This view begins with a procedural premise that the constitutional order does not constrain popular will, such an order constitutes that will. A central feature of this view is that the popular will is not synonymous with the will of the majority. Proceduralism that sees democracy instantiated in the legal structure of majority voting either has to give up on any claim that democracy is about self-government or popular control and be satisfied with the claim that democracy is a fair way to make decisions, or it must admit that democracy is about the rule of the majority and hope that the composition of that majority changes over time. Hans Kelsen, whose views have inspired a number of contemporary procedural theories, is a good example of the second limitation.[54]

Like deliberativists, Kelsen rejects a concrete understanding of the people and instead argues that 'the "People" is not, as is often naively imagined, a body or conglomeration as it were, of actual persons. Rather, it is merely a system of individual human acts regulated by the legal order'.[55] Constitutions make democracy possible because they lay out the rules and procedures through which a diverse group, characterised by deep disagreement, can govern itself without oppressing each other. But when Kelsen speaks about which rules and procedures more specifically allow for democratic collective action coordination, the proceduralised popular will turns into the majority will. 'Democracy must be parliamentary democracy, in which the ruling will of society is created by a majority of those who are elected by the majority of persons possessing political rights. As a result, political rights – and therefore freedom – are essentially reduced to the right to vote.'[56] Democracy produces a series of ruling wills that represent a set of interests and concerns, bundled and articulated in a party platform, and then supported by a majority. Nadia Urbinati explains that

[52] Quoted in Levin et al (n 47) 9.

[53] The 'No' campaign faced serious restrictions with arrests of several public figures. By some accounts, the 'Yes' campaign had 90% of the airtime during the campaign. On all press freedom indices, Turkey has been sinking. *Reporters Without Borders* ranked Turkey 157 out of 171 on press freedom for 2018, www.rsf.org.

[54] C Invernizzi Accetti and G Oskian, 'What is a Consultative Referendum? The Democratic Legitimacy of Popular Consultations' (2020) *Perspectives on Politics* 1; Saffon and Urbinati (n 17).

[55] H Kelsen, *The Essence and Value of Democracy* (Rowman & Littlefield Publishers, 2013) 36.

[56] ibid 41.

majority rule for Kelsen is defined 'within an overall temporal framework of continuity, involving the possibility of revising previously approved decisions, as well as formulating new ones'.[57] 'Revision' here suggests that regular elections over time will most likely mean, given pluralism and competition, that the ruling majority will be made up of different sets of interests. But this still equates the ruling will with the majority will.

I have tried to articulate a view that sees Constitutions as giving legal structure to a certain type of political communication rather than simply voting. This in turn means that we look at the discursive and communicative ways majorities are constructed as well as discursive and communicative ways that majorities rule. Thus, the over time analysis is not just about avoiding a permanent majority, it is also about channelling demands and creating discursive feedback loops of accountability. On this view then the minority is not left simply with the hope that they might win next time around. Minorities are made up of citizen who have the same political rights as majorities and so they deserve explanations and justification just as much as majorities. Majority outcomes can claim be a popular will to the extent that they are the product of legally instituted and political entrenched processes of equal, inclusive, and epistemically robust opinion and will formation.

[57] N Urbinati, 'Introduction' in ibid 10.

8

Elite vs People

YVES MÉNY*

THE RELATIONSHIP BETWEEN elite and people is not a new issue and one could argue that it is as old as the first manifestation of the 'political' in any civilisation. The tension between the whole, the domain of many and the part, the domain of the few, appears as soon as some individuals are excluded from the deliberations preceding decisions and when others pretend to be the only ones capable of reasoning, deciding and implementing through force or persuasion. Because, as Westerners, we tend to consider only the familiar cases of western Europe or, even worse, the single case of Athens since it is the best documented and recognised as the blueprint of our political systems, we tend to forget that democracy is not a matter only for the West, as Amythia Sen has rightly underlined. As far as we know, thanks to the increasing number of anthropological studies, most traditional cultures have combined the use of force controlled by a few (warriors, lords, king, chiefs etc …) with the necessity to build up consensus, for instance through councils or assemblies most of the time restricted to a tiny part of the population. With a few exceptions, women and children were excluded as well as the lowest social strata (from Indian untouchables to Sparta's helots). The councils, in particular in primitive groupings, were reserved to the wise men, in other words, the oldest of the village or of the city. A practice which is still alive even in the most advanced or sophisticated societies as testified by the practice of 'wise men committees' or the tradition of appointing senior persons to higher bodies such as courts, appeal bodies or independent authorities. The cover up of modernity might hide very ancestral behaviour!

Pure egalitarian societies are rare and they are more illusions than hard facts, as confirmed by observation. The present rise of populism across the world and the challenge to representative democracy is a good illustration of the utopian dream of a world without mediation or delegation, a world free of hierarchies and aristocracy whatever might be its content, meaning and actual power. It is telling that in the search for an alternative to representative democracy as we know it today, the Athenian model is often cited and taken as an example of the way to pursue in order to put in place an alternative and better model: one invokes direct democracy, referenda and popular initiatives, the deliberation and decision-making processes open

* Emeritus President, European University Institute.

to all citizens, the rejection of biased and manipulated elections and its replacement by techniques such as drawing lots. It also invokes the necessity to put under control and surveillance those in charge of executing citizens' will; or the need to shorten political terms in order to avoid clientelism, corruption, conflict of interests and the likes. These reflections and proposals for change are in line with the powerful motto launched in 1863 by Jefferson in his Gettysburg address: 'the government of the people, by the people, for the people'.

The fact that power is the prerogative of one single individual (supported in any way by a religious, military or social elite) or a restricted group of persons has, for most of mankind's history, been considered as normality rather than an anomaly. It is only in Greek cities and in particular in Athens, around the fourth and fifth century BC, that the idea that the power to govern emanates from the 'demos', from the people, brought a revolution in the traditional perspective. Its powerful and irresistible effects remained dormant for centuries, in practice for nearly 2,000 years. Even in Athens, this radical novelty would be challenged by the aristocracy/oligarchy of the time. Elitism takes its full meaning when its counterpart appears, 'the people'. A concrete social reality (the masses, the crowds, the populace) became an abstract philosophical, ideological, legal entity and scrapped the old conceptions of legitimacy. This transformation would require several revolutions and many forms of political resistance before taking place, in America and then in Europe, before expanding to the entire world. From the American and the French Revolutions at the end of the eighteenth century, the 'people' occupied the centre of the stage and will never abandon it. Tocqueville analyses this transformation in his *Démocratie en Amérique* as a 'providential' phenomenon, in other words a phenomenon whose unfolding is determined by the natural evolution of societies. Nobody or nothing can stop this deterministic and fatal evolution. Tocqueville is an aristocrat, he deplores the decline of aristocracies but he underlines that this 'tsunami' is unstoppable. And he regrets that the energies spent in vain to stop it are not better used in trying to accommodate societies and institutions to this unavoidable transformation prompted by the march towards equality:

> Le développement graduel de l'égalité des conditions est donc un fait providentiel, il en les principaux caractères: il est universel, il est durable, il échappe chaque jour à la puissance humaine; tous les évènements, comme tous les hommes, servent à son développement.[1]

Tocqueville is so convinced of this ineluctable process (and by way of consequence of the expansion of democracy) that, in his view, everything contributes to its fulfilment: the efforts to favour it as well as the attempts to combat it. The direction of history might be slowed down, stopped for a while, or circumvented here or there but there is no alternative to this millennial trend. Tocqueville does not believe in the end of history but is firmly convinced that the direction is without any doubt heading towards more equality and democracy. Stuart Mill shares the same analysis, underlying that democracy's progress cannot and should not be stopped. Today, Tocqueville's prophecy seems rather fragile and questionable: democracy is highly contested in places where it is most solidly grounded and libraries are full of books

[1] A de Tocqueville, *De la démocratie en Amérique* (Saunders and Otley, 1835) 37.

and analyses underlying the growing gap between rich and poor. However there is a difference between Tocqueville's views and present assessments. Most of the rather pessimistic forecasts about the state of democracy and the increasing differences in income are based on short or mid-term observations while Tocqueville's perspective is a very 'longue durée' vision from the first millennium to his time.

One can, however, dispute his assertion that the unavoidable rise of equality and democracy entails the disappearance of aristocracies. Tocqueville's position is actually more subtle than that. He is very conscious that every aristocracy on the decline is replaced by other forms which replace the previous hierarchies. He emphasises the fact that at every step of this long march towards equality, the differences between the aristocracy and the low classes tend to diminish: 'Le noble aura baissé dans l'échelle sociale, le roturier s'y sera élévé; l'un descend, l'autre monte; Chaque demi-siècle les rapproche, et bientôt ils vont se toucher'.[2] Indeed, it would be an illusion to believe that the emergence and the domination of the 'people' is such that it offsets the necessity for an 'aristocracy' or elite, whatever its name, composition and role. The lesson comes from afar: the much celebrated democratic regime in Athens is full of internal contradictions and first of all the fact that the so-called 'demos' (the people) was a tiny percentage of the population. Distinguished thinkers such as Moses I Finley or mythologists such as Pierre Vidal-Naquet have underlined forcefully the Athenian paradox: the beautiful deliberative democracy invented in the Greek cities was made possible only thanks to the imposition of slavery. A few thousand male citizens had the luxury to discuss and decide together while most of the 'others' (women, slaves and foreigners) were providing the manpower for the private and public economy. Democracy in the South of the US at the time of Tocqueville's observations was structurally the same.

This in-built tension between the elite and the people raises several issues: how to bring out these elites and under which conditions of legitimacy ? How much competition and turnover is needed in order to justify their power? How can democracy make use of this elitist 'fatality' and make the people and elites closer to each other to the point of 'se toucher' as Tocqueville put it? What is the impact of populist movements on the *summa divisio* elite/people?

I. THE RISE AND FALL OF ELITES: CLOSURE, CIRCULATION, INTERLOCKING

In the western world, the analysis and reflection on the elites is as old as the Greek myths. Both the *Iliad* and the *Odyssey* tell stories about the division between those who govern (the Gods and the kings, who Homer calls the 'shepherds of men') and those who are governed, that the poet calls the 'crowd', the 'mass'. The poems also evoke those who have a special place next to the governors of the world: the warriors, the old wise men, the priests. The others are barely mentioned. Later, Plato and Aristotle introduced the first concepts related to the power origin and its organisation, inaugurating a system of classification and evaluation which is still the basis

[2] ibid 36.

of our philosophical, sociological and political thinking: democracy, oligarchy, monarchy, tyranny. Much later, Montesquieu resumed a current of thought and a way of thinking which was inspirational, in particular to the American Founding Fathers. Following the American and French Revolutions, the debate has raged about the respective merits of these various regimes. Democracy was highly contested by monarchical, imperial and authoritarian regimes. From that moment, the debate about the respective role of the people and of the elites has never stopped. However, the terms of the discussion have considerably evolved over time.

The first big change was related to the legitimacy question: who is the legitimate source of power? God? The people? Then comes immediately the question of definition of 'the people' and the issue of its representation since 'the people' cannot anymore be present physically in a place where it could deliberate and decide. The feasibility issue is resolved by two tricks: a narrow definition of what constitutes the people (as in Greece, exclusion of women, foreigners and the poor); and a variety of electoral mechanisms allowing the choice of a limited number of representatives. In his recent book *Il popolo e i suoi rappresentanti*, Sabino Cassese[3] reminds us that two famous 'representatives', Tocqueville in France and De Sanctis in Italy, were elected in the first half of the nineteenth century with an extremely small number of votes (from 258 to 658, according to the election). In the UK, the 'rotten boroughs' were even worse and the scandal lasted until the 1832 Reform Act which increased the number of voters by one third (from 400,000 to 650,000). These numbers grew by successive waves under the pressure of the (male) masses or of women, but in many countries, the 'universal suffrage' has been granted only after the first post-war period for a few countries and post-1945 for the others.

Initially, most of the thinkers in Europe and in America, when favourable to this new form of legitimacy, insist that their objective is to build up a 'representative system' and a republic, not a 'democracy' in the full sense of the word, that is a system in which power is in the hands of the people. It is a position defended by the moderates in France, while the revolutionaries à la Robespierre or Danton invoke the people 'en masse et en armes' to legitimate a bloody dictatorship. In the UK, the representative principle is instrumental in allowing the survival of the monarchy while the effective power is controlled by parliamentary elites. In the US, the founding fathers play on two levels: on one hand, the power is attributed to the people ('We the People …') but simultaneously reduced by every possible means. Its capacity to act and decide is drastically limited. Power is in the hands of representatives, but even they are confined and limited by a sophisticated system of checks and balances.

One of the few who identify the unavoidable evolution from representation to democracy is Roederer in France who emphasises that elective aristocracy and representative democracy are the same.[4] While initially the irruption of the people on the stage is restricted by the right to vote or not, during the second half of the century the idea prevailed that the representatives have to be chosen for their capacity. Only those who have knowledge and experience are entitled to govern. Stuart Mill's arguments

[3] S Cassese, *Il popolo e i suoi rappresentanti* (Edizioni di Storia e Letteratura, 2019) 16.

[4] See P Rosanvallon, *Le peuple introuvable, Histoire de la représentation politique en France* (Gallimard, 1998).

in favour of the 'enlightened' find an echo on the continent, for instance in France or in Italy. Boutmy and Alfieri create in their respective countries a School capable of preparing the future 'aristocracy of merit' due to replace the old aristocracies constituted by heritage. In the UK, the same model will give birth to the London School of Economics and Politics. Not only is the 'elite' not denied legitimacy, but it is perceived as a necessity. It is at the same time interpreted, in a Tocqueville mode, as an unavoidable direction of history: old elites are thrown out and replaced by new elites more in tune with the evolution and needs of their time. This vision of governing elites recruited on the basis of their competences and capacities differs from the old elites by the origin of their legitimacy: education, merit, expertise are the new sources of power while war, religion and wealth become irrelevant (at least in theory) to justify the access to and control of power positions. Next to the elected elites will grow a technocratic one. However, these new elites will often be perceived, as a group, antagonistic to the interests of the people. New ideological movements will emerge, as diverse as the reformists embodied by the populist movements in the US at the end of the nineteenth century, or the socialist/marxist revolutionaries which consider them as a caste, as the enemies of the proletariat and servants of capitalism.

From the end of the nineteenth century, the contestation of the elite's power and the advocacy in favour of alternatives modes of government, be they populists or 'popular', triggered new visions of their formation and role. Three crucial contributions by Mosca, Pareto and Michels[5] bring a more realistic and 'sociological' approach to the issue. The question is not analysed only or mainly from a philosophical or theoretical point of view. A sociological or empirical approach is preferred. The three authors converge in recognising that everywhere, and at any time of history, the government of political systems has been in the hands of a limited part of the population, whatever name it takes. Pareto underlines that pure 'democracy' is mere wishful thinking and that elitism exists in any group, profession or organisation. It is a fact of life which cannot be denied. There is a 'superior' class and an inferior one. Mosca echoes more explicitly this assessment by stating that 'In any society – those which are underdeveloped and have barely reached the dawn of civilization as well those among the most advanced and powerful – there are two classes of people, a class which leads and another one which is led. The first class, always the less numerous, fulfills all the political functions, monopolises power and enjoys its benefits while the second, the most numerous, is led and subordinated to the first in a more or less legal, arbitrary or violent way'. Michels is even more provocative, emphasising that elitism is a universal phenomenon. Even those who criticise and denounce it are the first victims of an organisational and collective necessity. By showing that oligarchy is present even in the social democratic parties organisation, Michels insists that there is no exception to this iron rule in any institution, even those wishing or pretending to be fully democratic. These analyses are not void of normative values and preferences, but their contribution is crucial in transforming a pure ideological issue into a more scientific analysis. The purpose is not mainly to get rid of the ruling elite in the hope

[5] On this issue, see Y Mény, *Popolo ma non troppo, Il malinteso democratico* (Il Mulino, 2019) Ch 1 (forthcoming English translation, ECPR series, 2021).

that a bright future will arise, but rather to identify the rules or practices which could encourage the turnover of elites or their control for instance.

To be truthful, in addition to being realistic, these three theories define the ruling elites in a rather pessimistic way: Mosca, for instance insists upon the social features which might facilitate the constitution of elites beyond the personal qualities of the individuals: the inherited privileges of the superior class (education, networks, wealth, savoir-faire) are transmitted from one generation to the next. Over time the power of a given elite tends to consolidate and increase. It can even survive dramatic changes or revolutions, as shown by many sociological studies conducted after World War II. For instance, in spite of the fall of monarchies, the old aristocracies have kept a dominant position or at least a position much stronger that its percentage of the population in key sectors such as diplomacy or military forces. Even the communist regimes have shown that Marxism in practice does not impede the transmission of power within a narrow clique or even within the same family as in North Korea. Such observations as well as innumerable studies bringing light to the capacity to survive and thrive have contributed to weaken or demolish the benevolent myth of elites at the service of the governed. Once in power, elites, whatever is their origin, fight to keep control of power thanks in particular to the solidarity between the members of this aristocracy, 'establishment', 'caste' or 'upper class'.

The nature and composition of the elitist system varies considerably from one country to another. In some, family bonds are crucial, in particular in countries where this basic structure of sociability and solidarity is strong: in Mediterranean countries for instance or cultures influenced by religion such as Catholicism. But the preference for family is not confined within these cultural groupings. The WASP families in the US have been able to control the Presidency over time, with a few exceptions. In systems characterised by a split between ethnic/regional/religious groups, the ones which manage to get access to power might not resist the temptation 'to take it all'. Minorities subdued by the domination of the majority take their revenge by controlling some segments of power and control key positions in society. In a French society dominated by Catholics, Jews and Protestants were able to conquer eminent positions in the banking and financial sector as it is the case in Asia for the Chinese community, for the Indians in Eastern Africa or the Lebanese in Western Africa. Solidarity, secrecy and strategies of survival are crucial components of this fight for power and influence, often associated with wealth and key positions. The Francophone were the dominant elite for more than one century in Belgium while in the Netherlands, the co-existence of different – and often conflictual – social and religious groups was guaranteed by political agreements securing a fair distribution of power and minimising political conflicts. Two successive issues come up once one of these limited groups has taken over: the first one is the monolithic or pluralistic character of these influential elites. The elite in a given system may be both fragmented and pluralistic and as such does not jeopardise, for instance, the democratic character of society or regime. The massive inquiry by Robert Dahl in the city of Newhaven concludes that, indeed, the city was run by a local elite but that there was not a single dominant group controlling the various centres of power and influence. Autonomous and diversified elites were fighting each other or managed segments of local power without being able to control the whole apparatus and economic/social/ideological fabric of the city. The situation is different when local or national elites have conquered such a monopolistic grip on the economy and politics of a territory that its permanence looks like eternity! There are a few communes in France, for instance, where the main owner of the land, an aristocratic family, has been at the helm of the small community since the Revolution without any interruption. It is a rather marginal case, but more powerful examples can be observed in North Korea, in Latin America, in India (the Gandhi family), in Pakistan (the Butho family) etc. Such is the consolidation of these narrow elites that assassination becomes the privileged instrument to put an end to their domination.

Fortunately, it is less the case in modern democracies where elites are not drawn from a few families. The elitist phenomenon, however, persists within narrow groups once they have succeeded in transforming positions acquired on the basis of merit into unassailable strongholds. For this to happen, elites need two instruments: control of access and time. One can observe this strategy at work in particular in the areas which require expertise, education and a certain number of informal, non-written attributes such as language, accent, clothing or membership of 'old-boy networks'. These powerful groupings being in a position of power have a huge capacity to resist change and challenges as demonstrated by the persistence of public schools and Oxbridge networks in the UK, 'énarchie' in France or Spanish techno-structure. Since the post-war period, they have consolidated their capacity to remain at the top of power structures in spite of the many criticisms about their closure, their interlocking character and their biased policy choices. Thanks to their capacity to organise themselves (through formal associations or membership in clubs which matter or informal linkages), to lobby the politicians, to navigate between private and public sectors and to develop conscious strategies of group combined with individualistic interests, they manage to overcome the recurrent phases of criticism and challenges to their privileged positions. They even have a crucial advantage over the political representatives: they do not need to face elections and run the risk of being defeated. In the famous novel by Lampedusa (*The Guepard*), the prince Salina explains that 'Everything must change in order to remain the same'. The capacity of elites to adapt, to adjust and to control access is the condition of their survival.

For the political elites which cannot escape periodical elections, the stakes are higher. Over time, ad hoc strategies to secure their positions have been developed: for instance, the insurance to get a safe constituency where the chances of being defeated are closed to zero thanks to the sociological composition of the electorate or to the sophistication of gerrymandering practices (a national sport in the US!); the manipulation of electoral systems in order to get the preferred results has become an art in Italy (fortunately, there are often some unexpected results since the voters enjoy fooling those who tried to trap them!); in France the 'cumul des mandats' up to its recent drastic limitations was playing the same office. The tacit agreement between parties to preserve their power has grown over time. The collapse of membership has been compensated by the support provided by public institutions and the financial resources collected through dubious means replaced by public funding which insures a privileged access to those already in place. Katz and Mair emphasised this 'cartelisation'[6]

[6] RS Katz and P Mair, 'Changing Models of Party Organisation and Party Democracy: The Emergence of the Cartel Party in Party Politics' (1995) 1 *Party Politics* 5–28.

process of the dominant political parties aiming at protecting their oligopoly, overcoming their political differences and keeping the outsiders at a distance. The British and American cases are the most striking examples of collaboration between the two main parties in order to maintain their duopoly, but complicity between dominant parties is observable nearly everywhere.

Oligarchy is an iron law of organisations as Mosca and Michels have emphasised. But there is also another iron law applicable to oligarchies/aristocracies/elites: their survival is conditioned by their capacity to open up their narrow group to new generations, social strata and newcomers. Elites which closed themselves into self-service organisations are condemned to die and disappear. The process is usually slow (brutal in the case of revolution or war) but the end-destination is beyond any doubt. The slow decay of the Venice ruling elites did not survive Bonaparte's blow; the French aristocracy in 1789 was powerless in the face of the popular tide. And the old Russian or Chinese elites were swept away by their respective Revolutions. Sometimes the old elite manages to survive at the price of U-turns or radical changes when the country offers few alternatives to the ruling elites. It is often the case of bureaucracies since it is impossible to fully eradicate the administrative elites of the past regime (as it happened after World War II in France or in Italy) while political purge was more extreme (but not complete) in Germany after the collapse of the Nazi regime in 1945 and of the communist East-German regime in 1989.

If elitism is not a mere social or political choice but a hard fact that historians as well as political scientists or sociologists have observed, that law has organised and consolidated, that ideology has legitimised and strengthened, one might wonder what space remains to the people which has become the unique source of political legitimacy, not only in democracies but in authoritarian regimes as well (the exceptions are few, since even dictators pretend to govern in the name of the people).

II. RECONCILING SOVEREIGNTY OF THE PEOPLE AND GOVERNMENT OF THE ELITE: A MATTER OF CONVENTIONS

At first sight, invoking the people as a supreme source of legitimacy while being confronted with the inevitability of governing elites is a quasi-insurmountable paradox. Many thinkers have tried to face this dilemma and offer interpretations and solutions.

The first group is a rather eclectic one but concurs with the fact that there is no middle of the road solution. Some, like Rousseau, affirm that sovereignty is inalienable, absolute and indivisible. Any other solution puts the people in chains. This radical statement implies either a kind of utopian form of government by a people involved in constant deliberation and decision-making processes or an embodiment by an ill-defined sovereign such as that suggested by Thomas Hobbes. It is why Rousseau has often been considered as the intellectual father of totalitarian regimes.

Another radical alternative was suggested 200 years later by Schumpeter who attributes to the people a single role: the choice of representatives. Like Rousseau, but in a different manner, he is convinced that, once that duty is accomplished, the power of the people is void up to the next election. Rousseau was condemning it,

Schumpeter observes it as a plain fact and accepts it in the name of realism as well as efficiency.

Both interpretations are obviously very frustrating since the people has at best, a very limited say in political affairs – and it is a negation of the democratic ideal – or is deprived effectively of its powers in the name of a 'volonté générale' as difficult to identify than to translate into democratic institutions and policies. A true fallacy.

In reaction and opposition to these extreme views, many thinkers, political actors and policy-makers have tried to conceive and propagate intermediate interpretations over time and space. The most pragmatic have been for a long time the British who never placed the sovereignty in the people but who, through contorted but efficient transformations, maintained the sovereign monarch and transferred his/her prerogatives to the Parliament. Up to the recent use of 'consultative'(!) referenda, the people was not the sovereign. Brexit, from this point of view, has constituted a frontal shock between an old conception and a new one, while never dissipating the fog hiding the contradictions and conflicts between these antagonistic views. Actually, the Fifth Republic in its article 4, creates the same confusing melting of two diverse theories by stating that 'La souveraineté nationale appartient au peuple qui l'exerce par l'intermédiaire de ses représentants et du référendum'. The art of reconciling the opposites.

A. The 'Sovereignty of the People' Convention

The 'people' is at the core of the democratic construction. It has appeared as the only credible alternative to a power deriving from divinity, and the only possibility to provide legitimacy to republican governments. For the first time in history, the American and French Revolutions relied upon a concept which has become, step by step, the universal point of reference with very few theocratic remaining exceptions. However, this ostensibly undisputed principle is not as easy to implement in practice. In the line of Rousseau's philosophy, the people is 'one' and its sovereignty 'indivisible'. It is an abstract concept which can never be embodied: it is impossible to physically gather the 'people' which is never capable to express itself unanimously and whose members' diversity is as great as the number of individuals which compose it. The sociological reality is at odds with the philosophical and legal proclamation. The irony is that at the time of this philosophical revolution, the reality was very far from the ideal proclaimed in the new constitutions. The American fundamental law may well have started with the famous and celebrated 'We the People …' but the actual people was male, excluded slaves, and the new Federal Constitution was adopted in Philadelphia by violating the mandate that the members of the convention had received from their respective states. The similar discrepancy could also be observed in France, where the Paris revolutionaries applied the same restrictions and 'terrorised' the country 'in the name of the people'. Later on, Lincoln strengthened the illusion by coining a slogan as beautiful as it was illusory; a magnificent slogan which suffers from a major defect: who constitutes the 'people' and how to ensure that it is capable to choose, decide and control? It is the resolution of this dilemma that justifies the second convention as the basis of the democratic construction.

B. The 'Representative Principle' Convention

This principle is not by itself related to democracy. It has been used politically in England from the Middle Ages and as a legal instrument in many other countries as well. However, its prodigious extension derives from the incapacity to recreate the idealised Greek democracy in modern large polities. Since 'the people' cannot be assembled, its representation by selected representatives would become the solution to the stalemate induced by the concrete implementation of direct democracy. From the nineteenth century onwards, the representative principle would become the core of the democratic development. It has many political and practical implications: the organisation of elections, the possibility (or not) to set up political associations (parties), the relationship between the elected delegates and the government etc. However, this radical and novel reliance upon 'people's sovereignty' failed to apply in practice. Actually, not every member of the people is entitled to vote and to contribute to the choice of representatives. And once elected, the delegate is not subject to an imperative mandate. As advocated by Edmond Burke, the delegate is free to decide according to his reason, reflection and choice, according to what he thinks is best and not according to the preferences of his electors. The 'principal' (the people), becomes the 'agent' and the agent (the delegate) becomes the principal. The representative principle convention is so crucial that it will become the key feature and the standard of what democracy is about: no democracy without representation. During the unfolding of the democratic construction, the principle has never been seriously challenged as principle, with few exceptions. Most of the criticisms and calls for improvement have focused on the (mal)functioning of its implementation: from restricted voting to universal suffrage; from male monopoly to sex equality; from rotten boroughs or gerrymandering to better designed constituencies; from party cartelisation to open competition; from narrow elite's recruitment to better sociological representation. The main restriction to the representative principle has come from the admission that some functions would be better fulfilled by independent 'experts', for instance, in matters such as justice or economic regulation. However, the magnitude of this technocratic expansion and its related critique by 'pure democracy' ideologues, has greatly varied over time and space.

C. The 'Majority Principle' Convention

Today, the 'majority principle' is the most diffused and widely accepted principle among democracies. According to this convention, 'the first past the post' or 'the winner takes it all'. The winner may win by a large margin, or just by one vote and it does not make, politically or legally, a difference. However, the Anglo-American tradition mitigated the radicalism of this approach, by introducing another convention; the principle of moderation and of respect of the rights of the minority. James Madison, for instance was fearful of what he labelled 'the tyranny of the majority'. On the contrary, the French tradition is a long story of majority domination and abuse inspired by Jacobin culture, whose latest radical manifestation was expressed in 1981 by a deputy of the left shouting to the opposition: 'You are legally wrong because you belong to the political minority'.

This democratic construction has been torn between two different and opposite directions. On one hand, it ensured that a country could be governed by a stable and undisputed majority. In that spirit, a whole set of rules and experiences have been tried in order to secure that objective (ie, electoral systems, constituencies, party discipline, parliamentary regulations etc). On the other hand, the Madison warning has contributed to fostering the creation of checks and balances, the protection of the rights of the minority, the invention of fairer electoral systems (proportional representation) and parliamentary safeguards in order to avoid the excesses of the majority. In some cases, there is even a deliberate will, in particular, in fragmented societies, to prevent a single party from obtaining and exercising power alone (ie, Netherlands, Israel). It has been successful in avoiding the control of power by a single party, but has favoured the cartelisation of party coalitions (ie, Austria, Nordic countries). Given the various limitations or biases brought about by electoral rules and the increasingly high levels of voting abstention, it is quite common that the 'majority of the people' does not represent more than one-third of the electorate. The majority rules, in spite of the dominant convention, become harder to legitimise and make acceptable policies and decisions imposed by a de facto minority.

D. The Citizen/Nationality Convention

The democratisation process has evolved together with the construction of the Nation-State and in many cases it is difficult to decipher which development comes first. The two phenomena are actually intimately related and intertwined. Nations, as well as democracy, have a key concept in common – citizenship. The members and (supposedly) founders of the nation are its citizens, and democracy is based as well upon the will of these same citizens. It's a lasting legacy of Athens' democracy based on a narrow concept of autochtony and citizenship. However, this process of mutual reinforcement has not been linear. For instance, the US excluded slaves and after the Secession War, a de facto discrimination and legal segregation endured up to the 1960s. In the UK, British citizens were formally first and foremost, 'subjects of the Crown' while Irish citizens resident in the UK were entitled to vote. In a few countries (ie, Netherlands), foreign residents can participate in the local elections, an exception applicable to European citizens residing in one of the 27 EU Member States. These peculiarities are interesting cases, but the cast iron rule applicable to all the countries using elections in order to determine the selection of political elites, is that only citizens of a given nation can participate in the choice of their representatives. In practice, long-term foreign residents can benefit fully from every right granted to citizens except one: the participation in national political bodies identified with democratic regimes.

This convention (broken, to my knowledge only by the French Constitution of the Year I/also known as the 'Montagnard' Constitution of 1793, but never implemented in practice), is both inclusive (everybody is citizen) and exclusive (only nationals can belong to the Republic body). The consequences of this binary choice in the course of the nineteenth century have been rather dramatic. It has exacerbated nationalism, contributed to the emergence of the minorities issue, permitted the secession of parts of composite states, accelerated the breaking up of empires and, even more importantly, trapped the democratic idea and ideals within the borders of the nation-state. Two centuries after the twin American and French Revolutions which, little by little, made democracy feasible by linking it to the representative principle, thinkers and policy-makers are trapped in a new impasse: the 'impossibility' to conceive of democratisation beyond the Nation-State. In spite of the interesting attempts to infuse democracy in a regional body such as the European Union, democracy seems stuck at the national level and many argue that democracy is possible only within the Nation-State, in the same way that in the eighteenth century, democracy was considered a system fit only for small polities (ie, local communities) only.

To sum up, democracies are structured by principles which determine their institutions, as well as their functioning. However, they can be challenged since, in actual fact, they are founded on social and political conventions. As long as these conventions are accepted (and in particular the 'representation' convention), democracy, as we know it, can work properly. It does not mean that these conventions cannot evolve and adapt, as testified by the changing meaning of 'people', 'nation', 'majority', and 'representation' over time or according to the vagaries of each culture. They can also be complemented by additional conventions, which are less stringent or not 'universally' accepted: for instance the intensity and diversity of the checks and balances, or the liberal components which limit the power of the majority. There are also possible divergences on the meaning of the 'rule of law' principle, or opposing views about the extent of the welfare state (very limited and not universal in the US, very generous and inclusive in the Nordic countries, for instance). But beyond these variations, the four conventions we have listed are considered as the necessary foundations of any democratic system.

It is precisely these foundations which are challenged in various ways, by the many diverse populist movements, which have emerged again in the US and mushroomed in Europe, as well as in other regions. They usually avoid challenging democracy per se, but instead contest or interpret the 'conventions' that everybody considered as the sacred tables of the divine law, in a different way. One can indeed disagree totally with these new interpretations, but one has to recognise that this exercise of revision and contestation is perfectly legitimate. The democratic creeds are based on conventions, they are not self-evident truths. They are social and political constructs whose strength derives from their historical and political efficiency, but certainly do not preclude the possibility to envisage and construct alternatives. After all, the resilience of democracy is intimately related to its capacity to integrate and digest elements foreign to the idea of democracy stricto sensu, but which have become part and parcel of what we habitually define as 'democratic'. We have forgotten their origins and their contradictions: from the fundamental rights to the role of experts, from the role of constitutional courts, to the checks and balances, all these key ingredients of democratic systems, are actually vivid contradictions of the idea that 'le peuple est roi'.

III. THE PEOPLE AGAINST THE ELITE: THE POPULIST CHALLENGE

Populism is a movement born in the US at the end of the nineteenth century at a time of radical and sweeping economic, technological and social changes. It was the time of the so-called first globalisation, in other words, the incredible expansion of trade, commerce and exchanges favoured by revolutions in the means of communication (steam engines, telephone) and transportation (train networks, transatlantic transport, Suez and Panama canals etc). It was also a time of both an extraordinary growth and development and of concentration of wealth. The big cities as we still know them today (London, Paris, Vienna, New York, Chicago) were shaped during the 50 years preceding World War I. In parallel, lower strata of capitalist societies were suffering from exploitation and poverty in Europe, pushing millions of people to emigrate to the Eldorado of the time, the US. Many of these features seem to have been replicated over the past 30–40 years.

However, during the first globalisation three or four empires were dominating the world and democracy was the exception. In Europe, 'democracy' (in a rather limited and narrow form) was a privilege of a few countries, mainly the UK and France, each in its own way and tradition while the US was embodying the single case of democratic regime beyond Europe. It was an ambitious aspiration affirmed both by the 1787 Constitution as well as by the successive Presidents and in particular Lincoln after its victory over the southern slavery states. His advocacy of the power of the people was not forgotten 20 years after his Gettysburg address and his speech became the rally point of all those dissatisfied with the growing inequalities and the domination of politics by corrupted capitalist elites. Contrary to what happened in many authoritarian regimes, dissatisfaction did not manifest itself through a revolutionary mobilisation. The anger and the protest were directed against the failures and the drawbacks of both the market and the state. The contestation of capitalism and democracy was not aiming at getting rid of this 'couple' but to correct their most salient defects and attempt to build up a fairer and more egalitarian system. The main objective was to give back power to the people and to put aside elites accused of betraying the mandate they had received from the people. 'Oust the chacals out' was the word of the day. The American populists had a plain and simple answer to the contradictions between people and elites: to give back full power to the people and get rid of the old political elite.

On the basis of this proclamation, the populists position themselves vis-à-vis the democratic creeds/conventions and put forward many radical proposals, many of which were adopted later on, in spite of being unable to win national and presidential elections. The populist programmes of today do not differ that much from that early blueprint.

A. A Common Reference Point and Diverging Interpretations: the People

As stated by Margaret Canovan,[7] if populism has an ideology, it is 'the ideology of the people'. Indeed, the 'people' is at the core of the populist claims. Left and right populist movements claim to speak for the people, to be 'the' people betrayed by the elites. They also share with democratic elites the reference to 'the people' as a unique

[7] M Canovan, *Populism* (Harcourt Brace Jovanovitch, 1981).

source of legitimacy. However, a marked divergence stems from the way 'people' is defined. In classical democratic theory, 'the people' is an abstract concept, embracing all the members of the nation, independently of race, age, gender or social position. This theoretical inclusiveness (which leaves aside only the foreigners), does not exclude actual distinctions based on selection (ie, choice of representatives) or expertise/knowledge (ie, delegation of powers to the competent knowledgeable persons). These elites act on the basis of a direct delegation by the voters (who might be actually a minority) or by a sub-delegation of the representatives to experts. All are supposed to work 'for' the people on the basis of these delegations, which contribute to make 'democracy' feasible and manageable. Democracy, as we know it, is based on mediation, and as stated by Schumpeter, the only power of the people is to choose, and possibly sanction or reward the representatives, on the occasion of the next election.

Consequently, society is divided into two strata: one which holds the ultimate power of choice and sanction, but cannot do anything between two electoral consultations; and an elitist group, which directly or indirectly controls and detains power in every segment of society, in particular, at a political level. It is a vertical structure divided between the top and the bottom. The populists – all populists without exception – reject this vertical division and introduce a holistic perspective: 'the people' means everybody in society, but excludes the elites, which are rejected as corrupt, incompetent or self-interested. The 'people' according to this vision, is the 'real people', the people of the street, the people of the bar, the people who are denied a say, the sovereign whose power has been hijacked for the profit and benefit of the few. The populist programme is to bring back those marginalised and excluded, to make the people's voice heard. This implies a major use of direct democracy, in order to make sure that those in power execute the 'will of the people'.

A recent example has been offered by the Italian 5 Stars Movement (M5S) after the March 2018 elections. The Movement became the first Italian party and received more than 30 per cent of the votes. After several weeks of discussions and bargaining, M5S concluded a 'contratto di governo' with the Lega, and decided to submit the project to the approval of their party members. Indeed, M5S has extensively used electronic means of communication as a modern and effective way to put direct democracy in to practice. The activists of M5S were asked to approve or not the political deal. Over 40,000 M5S members expressed a vote on the so-called 'Rousseau' electronic platform and the vast majority approved the deal. The contrast could not be greater: on the one hand, more than 10 million voters had voted for choosing 'their' representatives, and on the other hand, a direct consultation of the Movement's activists had triggered the participation of a few thousand registered members. The irony of this situation revealed a contradiction between discourse and plain reality: the Movement had, in a very short period of time, brought to light the emergence of a new elite, in spite of all the populist rhetoric. The Movement could march to power with the blessing of 40,000 activists: a new 'elite' was born!

In spite of their fierce criticism of the representative system, populists, in most democracies, can obtain access to power, only by using the representative parliamentary mechanisms already in place. In other words, before having the possibility to introduce institutional changes to rebuild democracy as the populists see fit, they have to swallow the representative pill. However, the populist movements have been more successful in forcing the traditional political forces to take up part of their political agenda and accept the reforms they have advocated: it was the case in the last years of the nineteenth century in America, or presently in many European countries where the populists have pushed for the use of referenda. Even when they have been successful enough in their promotion of an unmediated democracy, they are faced with an even bigger challenge: how to transform the theoretical and undisputable supremacy of the people into workable mechanisms involving the whole people? As there is no feasible and realistic solution even in times of revolutionary technology, the way out is often found in the worst possible manner: pretending that one man is 'the' voice of the people, the true and sole interpreter of the people's will and aspirations. The populists dislike the 'representatives' but, at the end, put themselves in the hands of a single individual. The 'people' is embodied in one single person, a leader who pretends, and may be recognised indeed by the masses, as the one who speaks best for themselves. This solution is obviously a fallacy. First of all, because it pushes the essence of representation to the absurd: 'the people' is not represented in its diversity by hundreds of representatives, but by a single individual! Secondly, because this monopoly of representation is a slippery slope: the 'masters' become followers of a leader, who is, more often than not, tempted by authoritarianism. The people's movements become the subordinate mass party, at the disposal of the leader with no limits, and no checks and balances. The 'rule of the majority' might rapidly become the undisputed and authoritarian iron rule of a single person, as both history and present developments testify. An hobbesian nightmare.

When acceding to power, the populist movements face two major risks: the first one is to succumb to the illusions of full and constant participation of the masses, as well as to the illusory charms of spontaneity. The risk is that the unanimity against the old elites may quickly transform itself into deep divisions along interest lines. Conflicts may soon become more acute and move from the assembly to the streets. The second risk is the illusion that citizens are available for constant participation and involvement. Actually, the majority of citizens are not ready to sacrifice the limited free time available for their private and family duties to the benefit of public involvement. As shown by Albert Hirschman,[8] civic participation is neither constant nor linear. They are cycles and alternation between private and public mobilisation and participation. By necessity, the exercise of power has to be delegated (or taken over) by new 'elites'. In the end, populism might be nothing more than a radical 'sweeping operation' of elite change, which is normally observed at times of revolution or post-war periods. The 'dégagisme', has no real programme, ideology or philosophy. It is best encapsulated by the People's Party slogan in the final years of the nineteenth century 'Throw the jackals out' or by the Poujade's slogan in the 1950s in France, 'Sortez les sortants' (Oust the incumbents!) Nothing less, nothing more ?

[8] A Hirschman, *Shifting Involvements: Private Interests and Public Action* (Princeton University Press, 1982).

B. The Paradoxical Impact of Populism on Democracy

Democracy, as we know it today, is a mixed bag, a 'bricolage'[9] resulting both from historical adaptations and from a succession of 'trial and error' processes. Far from being the simplistic 'government of the people, for the people, by the people' which remains an ideal rather than a full set of rules and institutions, democratic regimes are complex systems which have integrated many components and features from different origins, some of which were even initially conceived as impediments to the power of the crowd. They have also borrowed instruments born in different contexts or conceived as direct expressions of the popular will. There is not a universal blueprint or rules to follow, beyond a limited number of principles that each country has adapted, according to its own needs and creeds. In the successive phase, the 'good practices' observed in one country or set of countries, might be borrowed and imported by others, with necessary adjustments.

For the time being, and contrary to what the People's party managed to get in many American states, the populist parties in Europe have not been in a position to impose their institutional preferences. They have only been able to distort the existing instruments, such as in Hungary, for instance. As they are most of the time part of a coalition, it is difficult to impose their preferences on reluctant partners, unless they manage to get a full majority. But in many countries they have succeeded in substituting themselves, at least for a part, to the old dominating elites. The most spectacular case is represented by Italy where newcomers have swept out most of the elites who dominated the Peninsula's political life since World War II. Sabino Cassese talks of 'una svolta', a U-turn.[10]

Any mediation is perceived as a potential for treason: central bankers, courts and judges, as well as the European Commission, become the favourite target of the populists. Independent bodies are subject to the same criticism. Pluralistic views are rejected for the benefit of a pure and cohesive social body. From Turkey to Poland, Hungary to Israël, and America to Venezuela, the many forms of populism join together in attempting to erase the rules or institutions, which limit the aspirations of the people (or rather of the leader who expresses them).

In spite of fighting both elites and representation in the name of the 'sovereign people', the populists have been largely unsuccessful in putting down the basic principles of existing democracies. First, because, in most cases, they do not have full control of the majority in Parliament, and have to be associated with other parties in a coalition government. And more importantly, because in practice, there is no real viable alternative to the efficient principle of representation. 'Governing by the people' does not last more than a few days of excitement, and usually ends in authoritarian, or despotic governments

But the type of solutions they propose or apply when in power, do not provide a blueprint for the future. Bluntly said, it is a politics of regression.[11]

[9] Mény (n 5) 43.
[10] Cassese (n 3).
[11] H Geilselberger (ed), *The Great Regression* (Polity Press, 2017).

9

The Double Fiction of the People

CESARE PINELLI*

I. SOVEREIGNTY AND THE PEOPLE

IN THE CONSTITUTIONS as well as in theoretical discourses, the concept of the people is closely intertwined with that of sovereignty. And both pertain, together with democracy, representation, citizenship, and the rule of law, to the family of 'essentially contested concepts'.[1]

Sovereignty is a concept deeply rooted in the rise of the modern state in Europe, and has been used since then in a range of versions going from omnipotence of the sovereign power's holder, thus conceived as a never-ending source of constitutional legitimacy, to a mere synthesis of the constitutionally established authorities. Whenever structured in these terms, debates prioritise the venerable category of sovereignty over that of the people, which is thus likely to be reduced to a mere successor of the sovereign state.

A different perspective is afforded by inquiring into how 'the people' as such is presented and discussed, departing from the issue of whether it corresponds to a natural entity, or it pertains to the artificial concepts inhabiting constitutional theory. For the purposes of this contribution, such issue goes back to the controversy between Carl Schmitt and Hans Kelsen, each one reproaching the other for relying upon a fictitious people, and will be later re-shaped with the emergence of a conception of the Constitution's legitimacy based on the presumption of the people's values correspondence with constitutional principles. Such conception, it is contended, should function as a term of reference for giving an account of the current malaise of constitutional democracy, to the extent that it involves the people's relationship with the Constitution. It is against such background that the reappearance of the fictitious claim of the people as a natural entity needs to be viewed, with the related question of whether it should be considered a cause, or instead a symptom, of the democracy's malaise. A response, it is argued, would usefully orient the recent debate on the populist surge, which runs the risk of being affected by a 'Babelian confusion of voices'.[2]

* University of Rome Sapienza.

[1] WB Gallie, 'Essentially contested concepts' (1956) 56 *Proceedings of the Aristotelian Society* 167–98.

[2] Editorial, 'What is Populism? Who is the Populist?' (2018) 5(2) *Democratic Theory* VI.

II. SCHMITT'S PEOPLE AS 'A POLITICAL UNITY' AND THE IDENTITY PRINCIPLE

The notion of the people as a fictitious entity had already emerged a century ago, in the controversy that opposed Carl Schmitt to Hans Kelsen on the relationship between democracy and liberal individualism. For both the universal (male) suffrage was reached due to a common struggle of democracy and liberal individualism against royal absolutism, and the main reference of democratic theory was Jean-Jacques Rousseau. However, they interpreted even these common elements in opposite ways.

For Schmitt, the crisis of parliamentarism 'springs from the consequences of modern mass democracy and in the final analysis from the contradiction of a liberal individualism burdened by moral pathos and a democratic sentiment governed essentially by political ideals. A century of historical alliance and common struggle against royal absolutism has obscured the awareness of this contradiction'.[3]

Elsewhere he speaks of the state's 'two opposing formative principles', namely that of 'identity (specifically, the self-identity of then existing people as a political unity, if, by virtue of its own political consciousness and national will, it has the capacity to distinguish friend and enemy)', and that of 'representation, through which the government represents the political unity'.[4]

Implementation of the former 'signifies the tendency toward the minimum of government and personal leadership. As this principle is realised to an ever-greater degree, the resolution of political affairs occurs ever more "of itself" thanks to a maximum of naturally given or historically achieved homogeneity. That is the ideal condition of a democracy, as *Rousseau* presupposes it in the "Contrat social"'. To the contrary, 'a maximum degree of representation would mean a maximum amount of government. So long as it is genuinely at hand, it could get by with a minimum of homogeneity of the people and could form a political unity out of national, confessional, or diverse class-based human groups. The danger of this condition is that the subject of the political unity, the people, is ignored and the state, which is never anything other than a people in the condition of political unity, loses its substance. That would then be a state without people, a res populi without a populus'.[5]

Vis-à-vis that dilemma, Schmitt takes clearly the position for 'the self-identity of the genuinely present people, which is not a type of representation. What is meant by the word "identity" is the existential quality of the political unity of the people in contrast to any normative, schematic, or fictional types of equality. [....] Under this presupposition, it is thoroughly correct when *Rousseau* states that what the people will is always good. Such a principle is correct not on the basis of a norm. It is correct because a people's existence is based on its homogeneity'.[6]

Not only does Schmitt use the theory of the *pouvoir constituant* for asserting that competencies constitutionally assigned to the people, such as elections and instances

[3] C Schmitt, *The Crisis of Parliamentary Democracy. Preface to the Second Edition* (1926) (The MIT Press, 2000) 72.

[4] C Schmitt, *Constitutional Theory* (1928) (Duke University Press, 2008) 247–48.

[5] ibid.

[6] ibid 264–65.

of voting, do not exhaust its existence 'as an entity that is directly and genuinely *present*, not mediated by previously defined normative systems, validations, and fictions',[7] he also discredits the representation principle as being founded on a fiction. Even with the imperative mandate, that would eliminate the representative character of the popular assembly, 'voting would be continuous, but not by the people as a unity. It is also revealed here that the people cannot be represented, as *Rousseau* rightly emphasised. The people are either entirely present and engaged or generally not involved, and in this case the people are not represented. Instead, the political unity as a whole is. The idea of representation contradicts the democratic principle of self-identity of the people present as a political unity'.[8]

How could, then, this 'political unity' express itself? 'The natural form of the direct expression of a people's will' is for Schmitt 'the assembled multitude's declaration of their consent or their disapproval, the *acclamation*. In modern, large states, the acclamation, which is a natural and necessary life expression of every people, has changed its external form. In these states, it expresses itself as "public opinion"'.[9] Although the latter 'arises and exists in an "unorganized" form', with the inherent danger 'that invisible and irresponsible social powers direct public opinion and the will of the people', the answer 'lies in the essential presupposition of every democracy. The danger is not great as long as there is a substantive democratic homogeneity among the people, and as long as the people have political consciousness that can distinguish between friend and enemy. If the substantive prerequisites of democracy are displaced, no organization or statutory norm serves as a remedy'.[10]

Schmitt's notion of the people as a 'political unity' remains legally indeterminate, namely irreducible to the people's qua electorate, whereas it contains a maximum degree of political determination, being referred to a homogeneous collectivity expressing itself through acclamation.

The notion's legal indeterminacy, with the emergence of an autonomous political sphere, has deeply attracted various schools of thought, going from Italian post-marxism during the 1980s to American post-modernism in the following decade. The 'Schmittian renaissance'[11] tends, however, to obliterate the inescapable connection of Schmitt's demystification of representative democracy with his insistence on concepts such as 'the natural form of the direct expression of the people's will', 'substantial homogeneity', or 'identity', whose reality is just taken for granted.

Furthermore, the very mechanism through which such a people expresses its own will, acclamation, should not escape the objection which Schmitt raises to the majority principle, namely that 'The substantive decision is often already rendered by the manner of posing the question.'[12] The same occurs with acclamation, with the effect that the identity of the governor with the governed cannot be achieved. Here Schmitt hides power through a further fiction. Unsurprisingly, the theory of identity hosted in

[7] ibid 271.
[8] ibid 289.
[9] ibid 131.
[10] ibid 274–75.
[11] On which see WEScheuerman, *Carl Schmitt. The End of Law* (Rowman & Littlefield, 1999).
[12] Schmitt (n 4) 304.

Constitutional Theory will lay the basis for a sequence of works aimed at legitimising 'the concrete constitutional situation of the present day' on the eve of the Nazi regime's establishment.[13]

III. THE DOUBLE FICTION OF THE PEOPLE IN THE KELSENIAN CONCEPTION OF DEMOCRACY

Kelsen's view resembles that of Schmitt on the ground that 'The battle, which was waged against autocracy at the end of the eighteenth and at the beginning of the nineteenth centuries, was essentially a battle for parliamentarism. A Constitution would give parliament decisive influence in government and put an end to the dictatorship of the absolute monarch and the privileges of the estates.'[14] However, contrary to Schmitt he adds that, when parliamentarism 'has achieved complete and absolute dominance, as is the case today, [....] the decision regarding parliamentarism is at the same time a decision regarding democracy'.[15] And the former 'means government by a collegial organ democratically elected by the People based on universal, equal suffrage and the principle of the majority'.[16]

The question of how could the majority principle be reconciled with universal suffrage was thus for Kelsen crucial both for democracy and for parliamentarism. Although considering Rousseau 'possibly the most important theorist of democracy',[17] he criticised his famous warning that the English people is free only when it elects the MPs, with the consequent advocacy of direct democracy:

> Even if the ruling will of the state is formulated by direct popular vote, however, the individual is free only at the moment he casts his vote, and even then only if he votes with the majority, not if he belongs to the overruled minority. Thus, the democratic principle of freedom appears to demand that the possibility of being overruled be minimized: a qualified majority and possibly even unanimity are required as guarantees for individual freedom. Given that practical politics are defined by conflicts of interest, however, such guarantees are so implausible that even a radical apostle of freedom like Rousseau requires unanimity only for the original contract that initially creates the state.[....] This consequence clearly reveals the incompatibility that exists between the idea of individual freedom and the idea of social order. Such an order, by its very nature, is possible only if its validity is objective, i.e., ultimately independent of the will of those subject to that order.[18]

Given the contrast 'between the idea of individual freedom and the idea of social order', an absolute majority represents for Kelsen 'the relatively greatest approximation to the idea of freedom'.[19] As he adds bluntly, 'social reality *is* rule and leadership. [....] In this regard, democracy is characterised not by the fact that the

[13] On this see D Grimm, 'The Concept of Constitution in Historical Perspective' (1990) in *Constitutionalism. Past, Present, and Future* (OUP, 2016) 122.

[14] H Kelsen, *The Essence and Value of Democracy* (1929 2nd edn) (Rowman & Littlefield, 2013) 30.

[15] ibid 31.

[16] ibid 32.

[17] ibid 5.

[18] ibid.

[19] ibid 6.

ruling will is the will of the People, but rather that a broad segment of the subjects, that the largest possible number of the community's members, participates in government. Even this participation, however, is generally limited to a certain stage of the process (commonly referred to as the legislative sphere) and consists only in the creation of the legislative organ'.[20]

What really differentiates democracy from autocracy, he argues, 'is not the lack, but the abundance of leaders', who are selected through election,[21] while autocracy 'covers up the most important problem in politics with a mystical-religious veil, which conceals the birth of the divine hero from the profane masses. In truth, this means that the answer to the question of who should become leader and how they should do so is left to the arbitrariness of force'.[22]

Under democratic regimes, he contends, the idea of freedom is instead 'transformed from a rejection of leadership into the idea that leadership should be open to everyone', and 'the demagogic assumption that all citizens are equally capable of performing any particular political function' is turned into 'the mere possibility that all citizens can be made capable of performing these functions'.[23] On the other hand, 'there is nothing more problematic than this unity which goes by the name, the People. Sociologically, it is riddled with national, religious, and economic differences and thus represents more a bundle of groups than a coherent, homogeneous mass. Here, one can speak of unity only in a normative sense. As a consensus of thoughts, feelings, and wills and as a solidarity of interests, the unity of the People is an ethical-political postulate. National or state ideology asserts the reality of this postulate by way of a common, no longer questioned, fiction'.[24]

Kelsen's assumption of the fictitious concept of 'the people' is twofold, be it viewed through the lens of the identity principle, to borrow the Schmittian categorisation, or through those of the representation principle. Not only 'the people' is for him affected by national, religious and economic differences that only legally can be reduced to unity. He is also convinced of 'the glaring fiction inherent in the theory already articulated in the French Assembly of 1789 – that parliament by its very nature is nothing more than a representative of the People, whose will alone is given expression in parliamentary acts –'.[25]

Furthermore, 'various apologists for the idea of popular sovereignty' presuppose for him 'that the People, and only the People, are in possession of the truth and have insight into what is good. [....] Even Rousseau is not far from doing so, when he justifies the binding nature of majority decisions, that is, the authority of the majority, on the basis that the minority has erred regarding the true content of the *volonté générale*. But everyone suspects that the defenders of democracy are making use of an argument here, which is foreign to the very nature of democracy. That which was able to demand popular acceptance due to a single leader's charisma cannot be

[20] ibid 83.
[21] ibid 91.
[22] ibid 94.
[23] ibid 95.
[24] ibid 16.
[25] ibid 33.

transferred to the many of the anonymous mass, to the average citizen: the claim of a highly personal relationship to the Absolute or to God, as whose messenger, instrument, or son the autocrat appears'.[26]

Here Kelsen's criticism of popular sovereignty shifts from the sociological consideration of the people as 'a bundle of groups' to the epistemic assumption 'that only relative truths and values are accessible to human cognition and that, consequently, every truth and every value must – just as the human individual who finds them – be prepared to abdicate its position and make room for others'.[27] But both arguments aim at defending democracy, if conceived as a regime that

> offers every political conviction the opportunity to express itself and to compete openly for the affections of the populace. That is why the dialectical process in both the popular assembly and parliament, which is based on speech and counterspeech and paves the way for the creation of norms, has been identified – not incorrectly – as being democratic. The rule of the majority, which is so characteristic of democracy, distinguishes itself from all other forms of rule in that it not only by its very nature presupposes, but actually recognizes and protects – by way of basic rights and freedoms and the principle of proportionality – an opposition, i.e., the minority. The stronger the minority, however, the more the politics in a democracy become politics of compromise. Similarly, there is nothing more characteristic of the relativistic worldview than the tendency to seek a balance between two opposing standpoints, neither of which can by itself be adopted fully, without reservation, and in complete negation of the other.[28]

Far from reflecting nostalgia for the oligarchical regimes of the nineteenth century, the Kelsenian theory of democracy aimed at coping with the challenges which the contextual rise of universal suffrage and of party politics posed to continental Europe's regimes. Although the fate of the Weimar Republic brought scholars to depict it as merely 'formalistic', if not as tending to legitimise whichever regime, for others it was 'contempt of actual democracies, sometimes couched in terms of the defence of the "real" democratic ideals', that contributed to the inter-war rise of dictatorships, while Kelsen's theory defended 'the viability of a realistically interpreted democratic ideal in a hostile world'.[29]

Born in the midst of a conflict between *Weltanshauungen*, the Schmitt v Kelsen controversy might appear a century later outdated for a number of reasons. And yet, their opposite approaches to 'the people' are likely to resonate in the reflections on contemporary democracies, concerning what still remains the most unmanageable concept among those generally used by constitutionalists.

IV. CONSTITUTIONAL DEMOCRACIES: COMMON ELEMENTS

Continental Europe's post-totalitarian countries, including those that established a democratic system with the fall of the communist regime, experimented with a new

[26] ibid 102.
[27] ibid 103.
[28] ibid.
[29] E Lagerspetz, 'Kelsen on Democracy and Majority Decision' (2017) *Archiv für Rechts-und Sozialphilosophie* 20.

stage of their constitutional experience. The principle of popular sovereignty was there re-shaped due to recognition of social and cultural pluralism, to the strengthening of the rule of law mechanisms, and to the admission of certain limits to national sovereignty for the pursuit of international security and peace.

For some, these elements compose a conception of constitutionalism that 'views the fundamental tenets of constitutional law as expressing universal, liberal, Enlightenment principles, whose authority is superior to that of all national politics, including national democratic politics', allowing 'constitutional law, interpreted by unelected judges, to countermand all governmental actions, including laws enacted by democratically elected legislators.'[30] To the contrary, 'American, or democratic, national constitutionalism' holds 'that a nation's constitution ought to be made through that nation's democratic process, because the business of the constitution is to express the polity's most basic legal and political commitments. These commitments will include fundamental rights that majorities are not free to violate, but the counter-majoritarian rights are not therefore anti-democratic. [....] Over time, from this perspective, constitutional law is supposed to evolve and grow in a fashion that continues to express national interpretations and reinterpretations of the polity's fundamental commitments'.[31]

Such opinion underestimates both the common elements affecting constitutional democracies worldwide beyond cultural cleavages, and the challenges which they currently share.

A 'problematic relationship' between 'two constitutional premises – the government of the people by the people and the government of the people by laws –'[32] is discernible not only in the US, but also in Europe and elsewhere, as far as constitutional democracy is held as a form of government combining principles and institutions corresponding to different modes of legitimacy, namely popular election of the political representatives and the rule of law in the sophisticated version available with the introduction of constitutional justice. Settlements of the power's structural divide are there made dependent on how power should be exerted in compliance with democratic constitutions that recognise the rights of citizens outside the realm of politics, and in the meanwhile give citizens the chance to maintain the legitimacy of such a realm through the exertion of their own political rights. The spheres of democracy and of the rule of law are therefore structurally divided in terms of power to the extent that such division is reputed to be instrumental to the exertion of citizens' fundamental rights, the political ones included.

Conflicts might of course arise between these principles and institutions, some of which even reveal an internal ambivalence: the majority principle can be viewed either as the main expression of political power or as the product of democratic compromise, to the extent that it presupposes an opposition. In that event, various kinds of adjustments are, though, constitutionally provided, that are open themselves to diverse interpretations, hence providing a flexibility that has proved to give

[30] J Rubenfeld, 'The Two World Orders' in G Nolte (ed), *European and US Constitutionalism* (Council of Europe Publishing, 2005) 236–37.

[31] ibid.

[32] F Michelman, 'Law's Republic' (1988) 97 *The Yale Law Journal* 1493.

constitutional democracies the opportunity of absorbing even strong tensions, if these do not challenge the very system's premises.

V. THE POPULIST CHALLENGE

While challenging constitutional democracy from within, populist parties fall into the latter hypothesis. Their appeals to 'the people' seemingly rely on the principle of popular sovereignty at the expenses of the rule of law and of respect for political or cultural minorities. And, once in power, they follow a winner-take-all approach, paying lip service to the majority principle.

Hence derive 'constitutional retrogressions' such as dismantlements of inter-branch checks, perpetrated inter alia in Poland and Hungary through court-packing operations and modifications of the competences or of the financial independence of constitutional courts. These provoke an erosion of the rule of law notwithstanding the observance of formal legality.[33] In the same direction goes the increasing use of constitutional amendment or replacement aimed at making 'a state significantly less democratic than it was before', namely a regime with 'a relative absence of accountability and a lack of rights protection'.[34]

Constitutional retrogression is deemed as consisting in 'a simultaneous decay in three institutional predicates of democracy: the quality of elections, speech and associational rights, and the rule of law'.[35] More subtle threats to democracy emerge here than those posed by totalitarianism, since at least formally free elections continue to be held. It is this feature that qualifies these regimes as 'hybrid', or as standing in-between constitutional democracy and the totalitarian state. Fundamental rights may therefore be seriously restricted, independence may be jeopardised for the judiciary and non-majoritarian authorities, but elections are taken, whatever their democratic quality might be: 'These regimes generally satisfy international actors in that they are sufficiently democratic to avoid sanctions and other consequences – elections are held, and they are not mere shams. There is enough electoral competition for opposition forces to compete and occasionally win. But at the same time, the deck is systematically stacked against those trying to unseat incumbents through a variety of means'.[36]

But why do constitutional democracies appear helpless vis-à-vis the populist surge?

It should first be noted that populist parties or movements are not, nor should they be, legally contrasted. Even in Germany, whose Basic Law allows the Federal Constitutional Court to declare the dissolution of any political party that seeks to undermine or abolish the free and democratic order or to endanger its existence (Article 21 BL), the court refrained from adopting such a measure against such an

[33] GA Tóth, 'Constitutional Markers of Authoritarianism' (2018) *Hague Journal on the Rule of Law* 17.
[34] D Landau, 'Abusive Constitutionalism' (2013) 47(189) *University of California, Davis* 195 and 200 respectively.
[35] A Huq and T Ginsburg, 'How to Lose a Constitutional Democracy' (2018) 65 *UCLA L.Rev. 78* 117.
[36] Landau (n 34) 199.

ultranationalist party as the NPD,[37] thus declining 'to provide further fodder for the populists' familiar narrative that the establishment systematically suppresses the voice of "the people"'.[38] As affirmed by the FCC's President, reactions to the populist challenge should derive primarily from the political process itself.[39]

Nor does Article 7 TEU provide restrictions of the populist governments' conduct as such, being referred to the existence of systemic violations by a Member State of the 'common values' enumerated in Article 2 TEU, including 'the rule of law and respect for human rights'. On the other hand, its enforcement mechanisms rest ultimately in the hands of national governments as represented in the European Council. Their current inertia should be blamed vis-à-vis what has been called 'the purposeful destruction of the rule of law inside EU member states'.[40] At any rate, it is due to political reasons, rather than legal.

The idea that responses to populism should come from politics itself reflects a core principle such as pluralism, which constitutional democracies could not renounce without betraying themselves. It is respect for pluralism, together with the rule of law, that impedes whichever degeneration of majoritarianism into the winner-take-all rule, thus rendering inter alia unpredictable the electoral outcome. To the contrary, populist regimes deny in practice the reversibility of political power, with the majority in charge willing to rest in power by all means: pluralism is there variously obstructed because it might hamper such possibility, not because it contrasts with an ideological tribute to the people's will. Respect for pluralism engenders thus a structural asymmetry in terms of power, that gives populists a competitive advantage on their adversaries.

However, absence of legal reactions against populist parties or governments does not tell us enough about why constitutional democracies appear helpless vis-à-vis the challenge that is thus at stake. To this end, an inquiry is needed into how the people are conceived in these democracies, and then into whether such conception can interpret the social transformations we are assisting with. Both issues will drive us far beyond that of populism.

VI. THE PEOPLE'S VALUES AS A KEY FACTOR OF THE CONSTITUTION'S LEGITIMACY

According to Neil MacCormick, popular sovereignty 'does not imply or presuppose the existence internal to the state of any constitutional or political organ enjoying either legal or political sovereignty in the internal sense. Indeed, it is the absence of any such organ – king, president, or Parliament, or whatever – that forces us to identify the people as the ultimate possessor of the sovereignty of their state. This does

[37] Federal Constitutional Court, 17 January 2017, *Neue Juristische Wochenschrift* 611, on which see L Schuldt, 'Mixed Signals of Europeanization: Revisiting the NPD Decision in Light of the European Court of Human Rights' Jurisprudence' (2018) *German Law Journal* 810, 817.

[38] A Pirang, 'Renaissance of Militant Democracy?' (27 March 2917), see www.lawfareblog.com.

[39] A Voßkuhle, 'Demokratie und Populism' (2018) *Der Staat* 120, 134.

[40] J-W Müller, 'Reflections on Europe's "Rule of Law Crises"' in PF Kjaer and N Olson (eds), *Critical Theories of Crisis in Europe. From Weimar to the Euro* (Rowman & Littlefield, 2016) 162.

not mean that there is an entity "the people" that has an existence distinct from or prior to their constitution. On the contrary, they count as "a people" by virtue of the constitution that makes them so'.[41]

In a similar vein, Pierre Rosanvallon assumes that democracy is founded on a fiction both because it shapes the people as an artificial body, and because it requires universal rules for governing society, thus presupposing a permanent indeterminacy of the concrete people.[42]

Far from presupposing the people as a substantial homogeneous entity, democratic constitutions are here believed as constructing the people as holder of sovereignty. Such account leaves thus the Schmittian theory of identity outside the perimeter of the people's constitutional concept. But do these constitutions incorporate the Kelsenian assumption, somewhat echoed by MacCormick, of the people as a mere fiction, corresponding to a bundle of groups whose definition as a whole solely depends on the Constitution?

Under democratic constitutions, the people compose a community sharing something more than the procedures that make it an electorate. It also shares a certain set of values that are constitutionally translated into principles. It is the presumption that the translation corresponds to the people's credence – or 'the expectation' that people have about the laws under which they live – that confers legitimacy to the constitution.[43] 'It is the very purpose of our Constitution', wrote Justice Brennan, 'to declare certain values transcendent, beyond the reach of temporary political majorities'.[44] These values transcend thus the political majorities of the moment, without being considered metaphysical, or morally indisputable, truths; on the contrary, they may count as evaluations of the common interest, provided that they are projected beyond mere political contingencies.

Accordingly, the people are presumed sovereign on the ground that they are provided with the choice of repudiating the values they shared when the Constitution was formulated. It is the very Constitution's endurance that depends on that choice. Whenever constitutional principles fail to reflect the people's utmost cherished values, the Constitution ceases as well to exert its function of ensuring the stability of a certain legal order.

The Constitution's relationship with the people is thus grounded on a conventionalist premise, namely the translation of popularly perceived values into constitutional principles. While remaining free, whichever choice of the people regarding their further adherence to those values is thus provided with a term of reference. In this sense, sovereignty can no more be intended as omnipotence even with respect to the people's ultimate power of denying the constitutional principles' congruence with their own present values.

[41] N MacCormick, *Questioning Sovereignty. Law, State, and Nation in the European Commonwealth* (OUP, 1999) 131.

[42] P Rosanvallon, *Le peuple introuvable. Histoire de la représentation politique en France* (Gallimard, 1998) 22 ff.

[43] J Habermas, *Between Facts and Norms: Contributions to a Discourse Theory of Law and Democracy* (MIT Press, 1996) 447.

[44] WJ Brennan, 'The Constitution of the United States: Contemporary Ratification' (1986) 27 *S.Tex. L. Rev.* 436.

On the other hand, democratic constitutions presuppose such a possibility, having abandoned the pretention of possessing time, be they the Lycurgus's eternal constitution or the opposite claim reflecting a revolutionary epoch, that each generation should master its own future. The amending procedures may demonstrate this point, as well as the poor predictive capacity of constitutional principles. It should rather be noted that, while structuring the interplay of the authorities that are variously enabled to pursue these principles, democratic constitutions rely on time. Memories of the constitutional past are thus differentiated, and transformative virtues and self-correction among citizens are correspondently enhanced, with a view to preparing the future.[45]

Constitutions exert thereby an integrative together with a normative function, although different accounts may of course be afforded of the relationship between these functions. For some, 'A written constitution's normative force depends ultimately on whether it works to recall a people to itself over time: a means by which a people re-collects itself and its fundamental commitments.'[46] For others, 'A constitution will have an integrative effect if it embodies a society's fundamental value system and aspirations, if a society perceives that its constitution reflects precisely those values with which it identifies and that are the source of its specific character.'[47] Therefore, 'a constitution can confer identity only as long as the system it has established is perceived as being a "good" one. If the society living under this system does not see the system as good, it will reject the very constitution that gives the system a binding character and protects it with its instruments of power. In this case the constitution no longer contributes to a society's integration and in the end fails even in fulfilling its legal function. This was the fate of the Weimar constitution'.[48]

Contrary to Kelsen, for whom it was nonsensical, a notion of the people's identity is thus suggested in contemporary constitutionalism. It runs, however, in the opposite direction of the Schmittian identity principle.

VII. IDENTITY AS SAMENESS AND IDENTITY AS SELFHOOD

Relying on Paul Ricoeur's key distinction between an *idem* identity, as the identity of something that is always the same which never changes, and an *ipse* identity as sameness across and through change,[49] Michel Rosenfeld assumes that self-identity 'can either connote sameness or selfhood' even while 'conceived as belonging to a collective self'.[50] Being a social construct regarding what each community thinks of itself, a people's identity may vary according to whether it ascribes to the people

[45] Y Hasebe and C Pinelli, 'Constitutions' in M Tushnet, T Fleiner and C Saunders (eds), *Routledge Handbook of Constitutional Law* (Routledge, 2013) 18.

[46] J Rubenfeld, *Freedom and Time. A Theory of Constitutional Self-Government* (Yale University Press, 2001) 177.

[47] Grimm (n 13) 148.

[48] Grimm (n 13) 149.

[49] P Ricoeur, *Soi-même comme un autre* (Seuil, 1990).

[50] M Rosenfeld, 'Constitutional Identity' in M Rosenfeld and A Sajó (eds), *The Oxford Handbook of Comparative Constitutional Law* (OUP, 2013) 757.

the pretention of looking the same through different generations, or the possibility of recognising its own distinct self from all other selves despite the changes which occurred to it through different generations. A choice for the latter seems reflected in the assertion that the place and function of constitutional identity, as distinguished from the national, 'is determined by the need for dialectical mediation of existing, evolving, and projected conflicts and tensions between identity – or, more precisely, identities – and differences that shape the dealings between self and the other within the relevant polity committed to constitutional rule and favourably disposed toward the aims of constitutionalism'.[51]

Unlike Schmitt's notion of identity as homogeneity, which requires the people's sameness, democratic constitutions not only presuppose, but even to a certain extent promote, a notion of people's identity in the sense of selfhood. Their conception of time should be connected at this respect with the recognition of social, political, and religious pluralism, whose intrinsic dynamic both structures and enhances changes of opinions, habits, and beliefs within the people over time. The scope of the Constitution's integrative function should be considered coextensive with that dynamic, provided that 'difference as a structural principle of democracy requires consensus about fundamental values and procedures. Where fundamental consensus is lacking, difference turns into violence and destruction'.[52] The Constitution's stability is thus believed to depend on the flexibility of its formulation, as well as occurring with the balance between majoritarian democracy and the rule of law.

A partially different perspective emerges from the opinion that democratic politics depends on the invocation of a 'We' whose boundaries 'are not drawn once and for all, its identity is never fixed, the self of self-legislation remains to be formed by and in the legislation it gives itself. The legal institutionalisation of the sensitivity for this dialectic can be found in constitutional democracy's insistence on both majority rule and rights of minorities'. The latter, in particular, provides minorities with 'the opportunity to defer any fixation of the identity of the people'.[53]

A collective self as identified *through* diversities emerging among the people should not be confused with a collective self as identified *with* those diversities. The former hypothesis presupposes self-reflexivity, which is possible as far as a distinct self can ultimately be distinguished from all the other selves. This possibility, as already mentioned, is ensured from a common adherence to the Constitution's fundamental values, not just to its procedures.

The hypothesis of a collective self as merely identified with diversities denies the possibility of self-reflection. It results from post-modernist accounts of pluralism as a never-ending flux of different experiences, contrary to a contemporary constitutionalism depicted as intrinsically embedded in the statist tradition.[54] Such accounts

[51] ibid 761.

[52] A von Brünneck, 'Comment: Difference and Democracy from the Constitutional Law Perspective' in K Rabe and A Sattler (eds), *Difference and Democracy. Exploring Potentials in Europe and Beyond* (Campus, 2011) 80.

[53] L Corrias, 'Populism in a Constitutional Key: Constituent Power, Popular Sovereignty and Constitutional Identity' (2016) 12 *EuConst* 24.

[54] See N Krisch, *Beyond Constitutionalism. The Pluralist Structure of Postnational Law* (OUP, 2010) and J Tully, *Strange Multiplicity: Constitutionalism in an Age of Diversity* (CUP, 1995).

are at best inaccurate, neglecting the clear distance separating that constitutionalism from the monistic structure affecting the traditional state on the European continent. Hence derives a 'false opposition' that impedes an understanding of 'the subject(s) of both the plurality of legal norms at stake and the plurality of corresponding constitutional constraints. It is not a matter of choosing the one over the many or *vice versa*, but of explaining who the many are and how they ought to relate in the absence of ultimate authority of the constituted orders'.[55]

VIII. THE ROLE OF HABITS IN ENSURING CONSTITUTIONAL LEGITIMACY

The Constitution's relationship with the people is differently suggested by András Sajó. For him, constitutions 'single out and privilege moral concerns and values and turn them into habits: a rule or a principle will be respected and emotionally endorsed as convention, without raising the issue of moral appropriateness'.[56] He makes dependent people's acquiescence on

> a strong status quo bias: the world is believed to be just, and any given arrangement that does not make one's life chances worse off is fundamentally acceptable, irrespective of the nature of the arrangement. What really matters (even for a Rousseauist theory) is that the public sentiment emotionally echoes what is expressed in the constitution and some fundamental laws, and thus authorship is not a must. Moreover, over time, people are born into the constitutional culture. They will find the constitutional arrangement as granted and given, a kind of "natural order" without which order cannot exist for everyday life, even if increasing multiculturalism challenges these assumptions.[57]

Habits do work for ensuring law's efficacy in general. However, do they suffice for ensuring as well the legitimacy of principles and rules aimed at governing law, as those contained in the Constitution, or something else is needed? The question needs to be posed further, since the assumption that people acquiesce to a kind of 'natural order', corresponding to 'moral concerns and values' which constitutions 'single out and privilege', is referred to constitutions, be it democratic or autocratic. In such an account, the Constitution's open texture, which is typical of the former, 'may accommodate new, emotionally shaped cognitive frames which enable emerging intuitions to prevail',[58] but does not seem to play a role in maintaining the Constitution's legitimacy. Nor does recognition of pluralism, whose function should consist in paving the way to different habits, thus constantly putting into question the idea of a 'natural order'.

Significantly, while giving great importance to habits, Tocqueville observed that democracy motivates citizens to obey the law, 'for as the minority may shortly rally the majority to its principles, it is interested in professing that respect for the decrees of the legislator which it may soon have occasion to claim for its own. However irksome an enactment may be, the citizen of the United States complies with it,

[55] S Besson, 'The Truth about Legal Pluralism' (2012) 8 *EuConst* 358–59, reviewing Krisch (n 54).
[56] A Sajó, *Constitutional Sentiments* (Yale University Press, 2011) 114.
[57] ibid.
[58] ibid 76, making the example of stem cell research.

not only because it is the work of the majority, but because it originates in his own authority, and he regards it as a contract to which he is himself a party'.[59] A law, he added, 'is observed because it is a self-imposed evil in the first place, and an evil of transient duration in the second'.[60]

The opinion that for the founding fathers 'the greatest menace to freedom is an inert people; that public discussion is a duty; and that this should be a fundamental principle of American government'[61] might even appear an 'attractive tale'.[62] It is exactly an inert or conformist people though that is evoked from the assumption that what ultimately counts for ensuring a democratic constitution's legitimacy is popular acquiescence to a 'natural order'.

Sajó notes however that 'The construction of public sentiments is never-ending, and there is no guarantee that the individual liberty-enhancing arrangement cherished in constitutional sentiments will not be replaced by a communitarian system of a sort where love or hatred, inclusion or exclusion will be the norm, where duties are not bound by rights and self-determination, and choices are replaced by an all-encompassing welfarism of do-good.'[63]

The hypothesis sheds light on the following events as the people's tendency to privilege securitarian measures against the 'others', or neglect of self-determination. While using the category of public sentiments, these reveal a dominance of fear, irrespective of whether it has been provoked, or at least fuelled, by populist parties. Which constitutional consequences have at any rate been followed?

IX. THE WANING OF A LONG-SIGHTED PERSPECTIVE OF POLITICS

The abovementioned constitutional retrogression reflects inter alia a quest for securitarian measures, but constitutional texts are generally spared from being revised. Even the 2011 Hungarian Constitution, the sole one to be enacted under a populist regime in Europe, pays lip service to the ECHR, although thus contradicting the ethno-nationalist version of identity which it foreshadows.[64] Populist regimes, we have seen, circumvent, rather than abolish, the rule of law, and exhibit a formal acceptance of the representation principle.

These elements put into question the current assumption that makes dependent the Constitution's legitimacy on the people's adherence to a set of values as translated into constitutional principles, which only the emergence of alternative values among the people could deny. It is as if popular commitment to constitutional democracy could vanish without being substituted with the belief in alternative values.

[59] A de Tocqueville, *Democracy in America* (1840) (The Pennsylvania State University, 2002) 275.

[60] ibid 276. On this see S Holmes, 'Tocqueville and democracy' in D Copp, J Hampton and JH Roemer (eds), *The Idea of Democracy* (CUP, 1993) 29 ff.

[61] *Whitney v California*, 274 U.S. 357, 375 (1927) (Justice Brandeis concurring).

[62] Sajó (n 56) 127.

[63] ibid 86.

[64] See inter alia ALPap, 'Who Are "We the People"? Biases and Preferences in the Hungarian Fundamental Law' in Z Szente, F Mandák and Z Fejes (eds), *Challenges and Pitfalls in the Recent Hungarian Constitutional Development. Discussing the New Fundamental Law of Hungary* (L'Harmattan, 2015) 55 ff.

The hypothesis requires further exploration. Long-term changes deserve attention in this respect, such as the crisis of representative democracy and the advent of a new communicative system.

The former is itself a multi-faceted issue, including distrust for democratic politics, the crisis of the political accountability mechanism, and the emergence of a new criticism of the representation principle. These phenomena are hugely discussed in current literature, although not always with the awareness that the crisis of democratic politics was similarly caught decades ago. In particular, Otto Kircheimer's well-known formula of the 'catch-all party'[65] reflected a broader picture comprehending reduction of politics already to individual personalities, the waning of political opposition, disconnection of party leaders from the mass population and depoliticisation of the latter.[66] Even the crisis of parliament as the archetypical democratically legitimised institution was certified some time ago: 'During the rise of constitutional government since the eighteenth century, much has been placed in the ability of democratically elected parliaments to deliver a form of government that meets the high hopes placed in them. Today, there is a wide consensus that these hopes have not been sufficiently fulfilled. There is a commonly held notion that parliaments are too weak, that they lack constitutional authority or that the heyday of parliamentary control is behind us.'[67]

According to these accounts, the crisis of representative democracy not only persists, but it can also be interpreted as creating the premises for changing popular perception of common values, to the extent that these require a temporal perspective.

The point is that representative democracy encapsulates a specific notion of time. Citizen-voters choose their own representatives for a mandate usually lasting five years, without being entitled to recall them in the meantime, but having the chance of evaluating their conduct through the ballot box at the next election. Citizen-voters are thus, in principle, able to hold representatives, and decision-makers more generally, to account. The whole cycle of representative democracy and political life is intended to realise the principle of political accountability. The rule that electors are prevented from recalling their chosen representatives during the five-year mandate is therefore not to be seen simply as a limitation, but also as an opportunity for evaluating how representatives have converted their own interpretation of the electors' interests into concrete policies.

Party failings, reduction of politics to individual personalities, and, on the other hand, increasing complexity of government, do play a role in putting such a mechanism at risk. Furthermore, most citizens judge politicians from afar and experience politics as spectators, and combine 'a substantial level of cynicism about politics with occasional outbursts of moral indignation as to its failings and frustrations'.[68]

[65] O Kircheimer, 'The Transformation of Western European Party Systems' in J LaPalombara and M Weiner (eds), *Political Parties and Political Development* (Princeton University Press, 1966) 177–200.

[66] A Krouwel, 'Otto Kircheimer and the Catch-All Party' (2003) *West European Politics* 31 ff.

[67] AW Bradley, KS Ziegler and D Baranger, *Constitutionalism and the Role of Parliaments* (Hart, 2007) 1.

[68] C Hay, G Stoker and A Williamson, *Revitalising politics: have we lost the plot?* (Hansard Society, 5–6 November 2008) 16.

What annihilates political accountability is, however, the fact that public debates are disconnected from a reasoned confrontation between programmes or policies concerning the future of the country, and needing time to take shape and then to be evaluated by the voters. Those debates are today structured in terms of individual events, and through a series of fleeting media-driven perceptions.[69] Unsurprisingly, representatives tend to construct a successful image before the electors, irrespective of what it means in political terms. Relieved from the burden of being evaluated according to their policies, and instead obsessed with daily opinion polls, they concentrate on instantiating the electors' current preferences, rather than their interests over the life of a legislature.[70]

The good reasons for a long-sighted perspective of politics are thus denied,[71] with the effect that the crisis of political representation differs radically from those that periodically characterised its bicentennial life. As it has been noted,

> [t]he question has always been posed in terms not of *why*, but of who and how? Whom shall we entrust to represent us? How do we ensure that they remain true to their mission? How do we protect ourselves from those who lead or govern? This has for two hundred years or so been the stock in trade of thinking about politics […] But what is becoming clearer is that the growing alienation from representative practices and processes is moving us beyond the 'who' and 'how' questions towards the 'why'.[72]

The emergence of the 'why question' challenges definitively the twofold idea that political representation requires a distance between the representative and the represented, and that it consists in a partial, and therefore political, interpretation of the will of the people, that needs to be confronted in parliament with further political interpretations.

Significantly, the rise of populism corresponds to the emergence of the 'why question' among the electors. While traditional parties adapt themselves to the media-driven scenario of politics, populists claim to mirror the people's will, as if they were per se alien to give an interpretation of it. What populists deny is 'any kind of pluralism or social division: in the populist imagination there is *only* the people on the one hand and, on the other hand, the illegitimate intruders into our politics'.[73] Accordingly, they abhor political debates: their truth must directly reach the electors eventually, after having attacked the morality of their adversaries, but not through discussion with them. Justice Holmes's metaphor of a 'free marketplace of ideas' from which truth would emerge appears here to be a relic of the past.

X. THE NEW COMMUNICATIVE SYSTEM AND 'THE ETERNAL PRESENT'

Unlike a mediated form of politics, which deprived a populist leader of the means to make the people identify with him, in the age of social media 'politicians find

[69] But see already JM Guéhenno, *La fin de la démocratie* (Flammarion, 1993).

[70] Y Mény and Y Surel, *Par le peuple, pour le peuple* (Fayard, 2000) 75 ff.

[71] G Hermet, *Les populismes dans le monde. Une histoire sociologique. XIXe-XXe siècle* (Fayard, 2001) 50.

[72] S Tormey, *The End of Representative Politics* (Polity, 2015) 58.

[73] J-W Müller, '"The people must be extracted from within the people": Reflections on Populism' (2014) *Constellations* 11, 13.

the missing direct link with the people through the Internet', where they can bond together by a simple finger touch, and politics is 'more or less demystified and become transparent'.[74] Online decision-making processes, it might be added, are for the moment provided with scarce democratic credentials, thus posing further the question of how can 'the function of democratic learning embedded in the multi-stage process of constitutional governance' deal with 'the pervasive simultaneity of political communications', with the following 'instantaneous decision-making style, displacing the stepwise and deliberative political tempo that is critical to norm translation and internalization in constitutional governance'.[75]

Populists are thus provided with unknown opportunities for imposing their style of politics as well as for shaping the political agenda. Hence a competitive advantage, that should be added to the already mentioned asymmetry between respect for pluralism characterising constitutional democracies, and the tendency of populist governments to obstruct plurality of voices, projects, and memories.

The impact of the new communicative system on democracy goes, however, far beyond the populist rise.

A century ago, Schmitt predicted 'that one day through ingenious discoveries, every single person, without leaving his apartment, could continuously express his opinions on political questions through an apparatus and that all these opinions would automatically be registered by a central office, where one would only need to read them off. That would not be an especially intensive democracy, but it would provide a proof of the fact that the state and the public were fully privatized'.[76]

Opinions on political questions flow today continuously on the web and social media, which shape public opinion to an extent going far beyond Schmitt's ingenious prediction. First and foremost, individual political opinions and further individual data are at the disposal of 'giant firms' that are reputed to be 'so dominant in their markets and so close to governments that they break most of the rules of what economists understand by the free market'.[77] The advent of the new communicative system, no less than the global financial market, engenders a dramatic shift in the realm of power from democratically elected authorities to private companies, which attempts of regulation appear for the moment inadequate to deal with.

It has been observed that 'While worrying incessantly about the menace of populism, elitist liberal democrats don't see large concentrations of private power in the hands, for example, of Big Tech (Google, Facebook) or Big Finance as threats to freedom, or as narrowing or even manipulating human choices.'[78] Shouldn't the remark involve though populist governments as well, or are these prone to contrast large concentrations of private power in the people's name? Global corporations have little to be worried about regarding both the reciprocally fierce adversaries of the moment. It is those committed to constitutional democracy's principles that should be worried about unchecked global powers, and gather their efforts for finding measures aimed at limiting the latter.

[74] M-SKuo, 'Against instantaneous democracy' (2019) 17 *I•CON* 560.
[75] ibid 564 and 567 respectively.
[76] Schmitt (n 4) 274.
[77] C Crouch, *The Strange Non-Death of Neo-Liberism* (Polity, 2011) 75.
[78] R Howse, 'Epilogue: in defense of disruptive democracy – A critique of anti-populism' (2019) *I•CON* 649.

The new communicative system conforms meanwhile common imagination to immediate concerns or impulses, contracting both the sense of the past and that of the future. It should be recalled that 'Our freedom is temporally extended. A people must have law from the past, and it must project law into the future, to be self-governing. We can achieve liberty only by engaging ourselves in a project of self-government that spans time.'[79] The so called 'eternal present' is thus likely to annihilate freedom, through which value-ridden dimensions of human experience can be both perceived and mutually exchanged.

A further symptom of the increasing irrelevance of values among the people should thus be added to the emergence of the 'why should we be represented?' question. Here lies the kernel of democracy's malaise, that has to do with a deep transformation affecting cognitive learning processes, and therefore the whole dimension of our living together. A cognitive challenge is thus posed to constitutionalism. How could it be apprehended is a question that goes beyond the purposes of this contribution. What should at any rate be taken into account is that 'By continuing to attribute to persons, interests, powers or systems the agency and responsibility of crises [....], there can be no entry into the new dimension of intelligibility and non-intelligibility imposed by the irruption of the "world" at the boundaries of social communication and its non-mediated contact with it.'[80]

XI. IS THE DOUBLE FICTION OF THE PEOPLE REAPPEARING?

The hypothesis of a popular remoteness from values questions the assumption relating the Constitution's legitimacy to the presumption of peoples' adhesion to constitutionally embedded values. At the same time, current developments show that the Constitution's normative function can formally survive the extinction of the integrative. Democracy's malaise exonerates populists from the burden of erecting a new building. They can just erode the substance of a democratic constitution's principles, and exploit its rules and procedures until the sole vestige of free election remains of it.

Do fictions play a role in such a process, and if so, which role do they play? At first sight, the populist claim of acting in the people's name revives the Schmittian divide between friend and enemy, namely between 'we the people' and 'the others', that nurtures his idea of an authentic people contrasting the fiction of representation.[81] On the other hand, under populist regimes, free elections are held in formal compliance with the representation principle and the majority rule.

The double fiction of the people resulting from the Kelsen/Schmitt controversy, we have seen, amounted to an intractable dilemma between liberal democracy and totalitarianism. The populist claim of acting in the people's name exhibits a pale resemblance to that supported by Schmitt. The imaginary homogeneous people

[79] Rubenfeld (n 46) 177.

[80] J Clam, 'What is a Crisis?' in PF Kjaer, G Teubner and A Febbrajo (eds), *The Financial Crisis in Constitutional Perspective. The Dark Side of Functional Differentation* (Hart, 2011) 215.

[81] B Stanley, 'The thin ideology of populism' (2008) 13(1) *Journal of Political Ideologies* 103.

as suggested by populists reflects their 'thin ideology',[82] that mirrors the virtual world running parallel to the real in our time far better than the desiccated political legacies of their adversaries. Such world's fictions clearly differ from that hidden behind previous appeals to the people's will as well as from the artificial concepts of constitutionalism.

In practice, populist appeals to the people can therefore coexist with a representation principle that has lost its ultimate function of ensuring competition between political views of the people's interest. The same occurs with the majority rule, that no more presupposes, as in the Kelsenian account, respect for minorities, nor requires external control through rule of law mechanisms, and can thus be deceptively reduced to a winner-take-all rule.

XII. ELITE'S DETACHMENT FROM THE PEOPLE AND PEOPLE'S DETACHMENT FROM THE CONSTITUTION

A double fiction of the people is now envisageable. Compared to that ignited during the Weimar tragedy, it reflects a modest landscape, where both the populists' substantialist claim of acting in the name of the people and their formal, and instrumental, tribute to democracy's rules depend on, and at the same time fuel, a seemingly harmless disconnection of the real people from the Constitution.

Some suggest instead an opposition between 'populists' and 'anti-populists', or 'elitist liberal democrats', as reflecting 'radically different conceptions of how democracy should operate in the contemporary Western European political landscape – both valid, but very much at odds with one another'.[83] Reference is made to the balance between the 'democratic' and the 'liberal' pillar of constitutional democracies, which each camp argues has been tipped too far in one or in the opposite direction.[84]

Such perspective is centred on the political conflict of the moment, and corresponds fairly to the dichotomy 'people v elite' which populists have imposed at the centre stage of the political and even of the academic debate. The issue is thus neglected of how the people's attitude toward the Constitution has evolved in times of democratic malaise. The elite's detachment from the people should appear prima facie less relevant, and worrying, than the risk of people's detachment from the Constitution. While the latter is likely to be suggested, the hypothesis that it depends on a waning of long-sighted approaches, blurring as such whichever constitutional vision, needs further reflection, with the related question of how the cognitive challenge will be addressed that the communicative system poses to constitutional democracies.

[82] ibid 106.
[83] B Moffitt, 'The Populism/Anti-Populism Divide in Western Europe' (2018) 5(2) *Democratic Theory* 2.
[84] ibid 9.

10

Stronger Together? Populist (and Non-Populist) Politics of Peoplehood

JAN-WERNER MÜLLER*

DOES EVERY POLITY have a politics of the people? In one sense, yes. Every political unit needs some account of who belongs and who does not, or, put differently, which people are in this together and why. Of course, day-to-day politics rarely revolves around these fundamental questions, though it seems plausible to think that controversy around them has become more pronounced in recent years. The reasons usually cited are the increasing number of refugees and immigrants in a number of countries (countries, one should say, to which people who have the luxury of writing and speaking about theories of peoplehood would pay attention). Less obviously, there are anxieties about supposed demographic decline and the shifting ethnic composition of the demos due to differences in birth rates among various ethnic groups (both of which have fired the imagination of right-wing populists eager to stoke fears of a 'great replacement' of current populations).[1] In any case, evidence concerning sentiments of 'togetherness' in today's democracies can certainly sound alarming: for instance, 35 per cent of people in France say they have *nothing* in common with their fellow citizens; while a right-wing agitator like the late American talk radio host Rush Limbaugh exclaims on his nationally syndicated show: 'I see more and more people asking what in the world do we have in common with the people who live in, say, New York?'[2]

For a long time, the Nation-State – and associated ideologies of ethnic or cultural nationalism – has been the default option for providing some sort of account of 'who are the people'. But nationalism is now also regularly associated with what has widely been described as 'the rise of populism' around the globe. There's no doubt that

* Princeton University. This chapter partially draws on ideas first developed in my *What is Populism?* (Penguin, 2017) and *Democracy Rules* (Penguin, 2021) titles. I am grateful to Cas Mudde and Annie Stilz for comments on an earlier version of the latter parts of this text.

[1] See for instance I Krastev, 'The Fear of Shrinking Numbers' (2020) 31 *Journal of Democracy* 66–74 and E Kaufmann, *Whiteshift: Populism, Immigration, and the Future of White Majorities* (Abrams Books, 2019). For important normative contributions to the debate: D Miller, *Strangers in our Midst: The Political Philosophy of Immigration* (Harvard University Press, 2016) and P Bou-Habib, 'The Case for Replacement Migration' (2019) 29 *Journal of Political Philosophy* 67–86.

[2] J Fourquet, *L'archipel français: Naissance d'une nation multiple et divisée* (Paris, 2019).

populist leaders put basic questions of who truly belongs to the people into play. In the process, they engage in what I will call in this chapter a highly *exclusionary* form of identity politics.[3] This populist strategy threatens fundamental features of the rule of law, equality before the law in particular. As I'll explain further below, such threats are not an accidental by-product of the populist politics of peoplehood; rather, they are always part of the programme.

In this chapter, I shall first propose an understanding of populism centred on the idea that populists claim uniquely to represent the 'real' or authentic people (as opposed to the conventional wisdom that anyone who dares to criticise elites is already a populist). I also explain why this notion of a monopoly of representing the people is so damaging to democracy and the rule of law. Subsequently, I point to some underlying reasons as to why populism might resonate so strongly in our era (without, I hope falling into the trap of thinking that there must be a *single* macro-cause – globalisation, migration etc – that explains a phenomenon that can be found in many parts of the globe). I suggest that in a number of countries we might be witnessing what I'll call a *double secession* from ordinary democratic politics and, ultimately, the social contract itself: a secession of those at the very top of society and those at the very bottom (the reasons behind the two secession are of course very different; moreover, these secessions often remain largely invisible).

I then propose an alternative to a populist politics of peoplehood that neither collapses into cultural nationalism nor rejects the legitimacy of borders; it is based on norms, but it does not exclude the contestation of the precise shape of these norms within the rules of the democratic game (some have sometimes called such a position *constitutional patriotism*).[4] I am not suggesting that such an account can magically defeat populist forces. But I insist that having answers to basic questions about belonging is an urgent desideratum for, broadly speaking, liberals, who, all too often, have not taken populism seriously as a normative proposition of sorts and thus lack an adequate normative response to populist challenges.[5]

I. THE POPULIST POLITICS OF PEOPLEHOOD

It is frequently asserted that scholars and journalists (not to speak of politicians and 'ordinary citizens') simply can't agree on what populism is. I would respectfully differ. Many social scientists and political theorists have in fact converged on what can broadly be called an ideational approach.[6] They might differ on the extent to which populism should be classified as an ideology; but they do reject notions according to which populism is a matter of particular electoral support (as in: 'only frightened

[3] Which is not to say that all so-called identity politics is exclusionary, let alone detrimental for democracy.

[4] Myself, for instance: *Constitutional Patriotism* (Princeton University Press, 2007). The original formulations were offered by Dolf Sternberger and Jürgen Habermas.

[5] See also C Rovira Kaltwasser, 'The Responses of Populism to Dahl's Democratic Dilemmas' (2014) 62 *Political Studies* 470–87.

[6] C Mudde and C Rovira Kaltwasser, 'Studying Populism in Comparative Perspective: Reflections on the Contemporary and Future Research Agenda' (2018) 51 *Comparative Political Studies* 1667–93.

lower-middle class people vote for populists'); they also refuse the idea that populism is a question of quality – or, rather, lack thereof – when it comes to policy (that is, the still widespread view, especially among economists, that populists are characterised by having very simplistic understandings of the world or necessarily make irresponsible, or outright demagogic, election promises).

It is misleading, then, to equate populism with 'criticism of elites' or 'anti-establishment attitudes'. While such an equation has become conventional wisdom, it is actually based on a rather peculiar thought. After all, any old civics textbook would instruct us that keeping an eye on the powerful is a sign of good democratic citizenship; yet nowadays we are told incessantly that precisely such a stance is populist (and, by implication, according to many observers, dangerous for democracy and the rule of law). Now, it is true that populists, when in opposition, criticise sitting governments (and, usually, also other parties). But, above all, they also do something else (and that's crucial): in one way or another, they claim that they, *and only they*, represent what they often refer to as the 'real people' or also the 'silent majority'.

At first sight, this might not sound particularly nefarious; it does not immediately amount to, let's say, racism or a fanatical hatred of the European Union, or, for that matter, a principled opposition to the notion of the rule of law. And yet this claim to a monopoly has two for liberal democracy (and particularly the rule of law and ideals of equal political inclusion) detrimental consequences. Rather obviously, populists then also assert that all other contenders for office are fundamentally illegitimate. This is never just a matter of disputes about policy, or even about values, which, after all, are completely normal and, ideally, even productive in a democratic polity.[7] Rather, populists assert that their rivals are simply corrupt, fail to serve the interests of the people on account of their bad, or let's say 'crooked,' character, etc etc. More insidiously, populists also claim that those who do not agree with their ultimately symbolic construction of the people (and hence usually do not support the populists politically) might not properly belong to the people in the first place. After all, the suggestion that there is a 'real people' implies that there are some who are not quite real – folks who just pretend to belong, who might actually undermine the polity in some form, or who at best are second-rate citizens.[8]

Such a message that only some truly belong to the people systematically undermines the standing of certain citizens. Obvious examples are minorities (whose standing might already be vulnerable for one reason or another) and recent immigrants who

[7] Of course, we can debate what 'productive' (which has become a cliché in this context) really means. Two suggestions: conflicts can be clarified (an epistemic benefit) and be processed such that compromise becomes more plausible (a political benefit, as more citizens might identify with a legislative outcome); lastly, there is the well-known argument deriving from Machiavelli's *Discorsi* that conflict – as long as groups recognise themselves as legitimate partners to a conflict – actually has an integrating function. See AO Hirschman, 'Social Conflicts as Pillars of Democratic Market Society' (1994) 22 *Political Theory* 203–18.

[8] This symbolic message (which has very real consequences though) can usefully be compared to Sandra Day O'Connor's endorsement test developed in *Lynch v Donnelly*: 'Endorsement sends a message to nonadherents that they are outsiders, not full members of the political community, and an accompanying message to adherents that they are insiders, favored members of the political community.' As so often, treating people as inferior and excluding them can then produce the very evidence which appears to prove that unequal treatment is justified.

are suspected of not being truly loyal to the polity. Think of Narendra Modi's policy of creating a register of genuine citizens; ostensibly, this is about identifying illegal immigrants; but especially in combination with new refugee policies which effectively discriminate against Muslims, its actual message is abundantly clear to Hindu nationalists; the latter understand perfectly well that the package is meant to affirm the real, that is, Hindu people, and put fear into one particular minority, namely Muslims.

In short, where populists come to power, one consequence of this exclusionary stance can also be that such citizens no longer enjoy full equality before the law (or even protection of the law at all):[9] they are treated differently in conspicuous ways, perhaps not necessarily by judges in court, but in many ordinary encounters with bureaucrats who have understood perfectly well what is expected from the very top.[10] That is not even to mention the unleashing of hate on streets and squares. There is significant evidence, for instance, that Trump rallies are associated with a local increase in assaults.[11] The concept of 'trickle-down aggression' – coined by the philosopher Kate Manne – captures the dynamic well.

Note how this exclusionary stance is not exactly the same as nationalism, if we understand the latter to mean that every cultural nation is entitled to its own state, and that the imperative of preserving the nation has independent moral weight.[12] To be sure, all populists need to provide some content for their notion of 'the people'; and it is hardly an accident that right-wing populists have so often reached for an ethnically defined understanding of the nation to do so (or opted for outright nativism). But, in principle, one can be a populist for whom the definition of the people is primarily political or ideological (think of Hugo Chávez's notion of Bolivarian socialism for the twenty-first century); what matters in this case is that those who disagree with the supposedly uniquely authentic representative of the people are declared illegitimate and quite possibly put *hors la loi*.

II. WEAKER TOGETHER, STRONGER APART?

'Brexit and Trump' are commonly mentioned together to illustrate the rise, or sheer political power, of populism. One curious fact has rarely been remarked upon: the campaigns which supported Hillary Clinton and Remain had very similar-sounding slogans – which spectacularly failed to resonate with large parts of the electorate: 'Stronger Together' and 'Stronger in Europe'. Evidently, a significant number of

[9] Think of the violent Hindu nationalists tolerated (and sometimes clearly incited) by the Modi government in India.

[10] For some examples of what Trump's populism has meant on the ground, see D Matthews, 'Donald Trump, the family separation crisis, and the triumph of cruelty' (*Vox*, 19 June 2018), available at www.vox.com/2017/1/28/14425354/donald-trump-cruelty and S Harp, 'I'm a Journalist but I Didn't Fully Realize the Terrible Power of U.S. Border Officials Until They Violated My Rights and Privacy' (*The Intercept*, 22 June 2019), available at https://theintercept.com/2019/06/22/cbp-border-searches-journalists/ and AC Thompson, 'Inside the Secret Border Patrol Facebook Group Where Agents Joke About Migrant Deaths and Post Sexist Memes' *Pro Publica*, available at www.propublica.org/article/secret-border-patrol-facebook-group-agents-joke-about-migrant-deaths-post-sexist-memes.

[11] L Diamond, *Ill Winds: Saving Democracy from Russian Rage, Chinese Ambition, and American Complacency* (Penguin, 2019) 106.

[12] D Miller, *On Nationality* (OUP, 1995).

citizens felt that they might be stronger, or in some other sense better off, by actually separating.

I don't want to make too much of this coincidence; slogans don't decide outcomes. But I think it gives us a clue that what 'together' means today has been put profoundly into question. Just *why* are we in this together, many people might be asking, and what exactly do I have to do with the fate of these *other* people. Obviously we are not in this together because all our identities and interest fully align – if that were the case, we certainly would not need democracy, which, after all, offers an institutional machinery peacefully to process conflicts (primarily over interests, but, arguably, also about identities).[13] And also not because we necessarily share one overarching substantive ideology – as sociological realists like Niklas Luhmann often pointed out sardonically, such pre-modern notions of all-encompassing social integration (or contemporary communitarian kitsch) hardly seem appropriate for modern, complex, and highly differentiated societies.[14]

And yet it can be argued that something has changed recently such that the question of the people is more in play than previously in the post-war era. I call this phenomenon the 'double secession'.

The first secession, to put it bluntly, is that of the most privileged. They are nowadays often lumped together under the category of 'liberal cosmopolitan elites', an invective thrown around by populist leaders, but also a term employed by a growing number of pundits and social scientists. This designation is somewhat misleading in at least two respects: first, while it is true that these elites are very mobile (at least potentially, if not always in fact), they are not necessarily cosmopolitan or liberal in any strong normative sense – if, by cosmopolitan we don't mean folks with the highest frequent flyer status, but those committed to the idea that all humans stand in the same moral relation to each other (or, put simply, that, ultimately, borders have no real normative significance). While prominent members of various elites – including globally recognisable stars – make a show of international charity work, one would search in vain for advocates of what in political philosophy might possibly be called genuine global justice. And it is worth remembering that, in the 1990s and early 2000s, globalisation was also usually justified not with its *globally* beneficial effects, but with the benefits it would bestow on national constituencies (that in fact that it wasn't a boon for everyone – that some won, and some lost – is another story).

'Mobility' is often more a matter of options, rather than a day-to-day reality. Sociologists have demonstrated that in many Western countries, economic and administrative elites still follow education and career paths that are distinctly national.[15] At the same time – and this is crucial – they appear to be able to retreat from any real dependence on the rest of society (I say 'appear' because they of course still rely on police, half-way usable roads, etc). Not every one of them might literally live in a

[13] A Przeworksi, *Crises of Democracy* (CUP, 2019).

[14] For Durkheim, this would have been the mechanical solidarity based on fully shared norms, or *solidarité par similitude*.

[15] For this argument about functional elites and their self-reproduction in national self-reproduction, see for instance Michael Hartmann's work, such as *Die Abgehobenen: Wie die Eliten die Demokratie gefähren* (Campus, 2018).

gated community, but the underlying trends of 'self-sorting' and homogenisation of life-worlds are clear. After all, with a globalisation of supply chains, workers do not have to be in the same polity; with 'free trade' regimes, consumers do not have to be in the same polity; and, with the shift away from mass armies, one also does not depend on one's fellow citizens to serve as soldiers.[16]

An openly avowed (though also quite cartoonish) version of this secession of the economically powerful is provided by Silicon Valley billionaire Peter Thiel. Thiel self-identifies as libertarian (and ended up not only as an adviser to Donald Trump but as one of the figures trying to adorn Trumpism with actual ideas). In a programmatic statement, he writes that 'in our time, the great task for libertarians is to find an escape from politics in all its forms – from the totalitarian and fundamentalist catastrophes to the unthinking demos that guides so-called "social democracy"'.[17] He is putting his hope into 'some sort of new and hitherto untried process that leads us to some undiscovered country'. Since, alas, there appear to be very few 'undiscovered countries', Thiel is betting on 'cyberspace', 'outer space', and 'seasteading' (as in 'settling the oceans').

Thiel's dismissive remarks about the demos provoked strong reactions – in particular, his sentence that 'since 1920, the vast increase in welfare beneficiaries and the extension of the franchise to women – two constituencies that are notoriously tough for libertarians – have rendered the notion of "capitalist democracy" into an oxymoron'. He later clarified that he did not advocate disenfranchising citizens. Indeed, the whole point of his thinking was that the demos had to be written off as simply hopeless; the best one could do was to seek distance from it. This attitude may as well be called secession. It is often not nearly as visible (let alone justified with more or less philosophical-sounding techno-cliches as in Thiel's case). But it is happening.[18] The sordid reality that corresponds to Thiel's pining for undiscovered countries are transnational accounting tricks with stateless entities. As two distinguished economists observe:

> ... US firms have in 2016 ... booked more than 20 % of their non-US profits in 'stateless entities' – shell companies that are incorporated nowhere, and nowhere taxed. In effect, they have found a way to make $ 100 billion in profits on what is essentially another planet.[19]

These kinds of secessions are not undertaken by actual 'citizens of nowhere' (nor does the money really end up nowhere); nor does any of this have anything to do with cultural cosmopolitanism, even if right-wing populist leaders, ever ready to wage culture wars, portray things that way. But the latter's critique does contain a kernel of truth: some citizens in effect take themselves out of anything recognisable as a half-way decent social contract. To be sure, none of this is entirely new: the Abbé Sieyes, writing about French aristocrats, already observed that 'the privileged actually come

[16] Or, put differently, are seeing a decline in Durkheimian organic solidarity. I am grateful to Ivan Krastev for stimulating thoughts in this context.

[17] See his 'The Education of a Libertarian' at www.cato-unbound.org/2009/04/13/peter-thiel/education-libertarian.

[18] See also P Osnos, 'Doomsday Prep for the Super-Rich' (*The New Yorker*, 30 January 2017).

[19] E Saez and G Zucman, *The Triumph of Injustice: How the Rich Dodge Taxes and How to Make Them Pay* (Norton, 2019) 77–78.

to see themselves as another species of man'. They eventually discovered that they were not (just as much as some today will eventually discover that that there are no undiscovered countries).

The other secession is less visible. It might appear to resemble the *secessio plebis* in the Roman Republic, when the plebs literally left the city, in effect organising a kind of general strike to bring about major political change. But, actually, it's nothing like it. I refer to the fact that an increasing number of citizens at the lower end of the income spectrum (to put it very neutrally) no longer vote or in any recognisable form participate politically. Of course, I do not suggest that this de facto self-separation is based on a conscious programme in the way Thiel's space (or spaced-out) fantasies are; there is no 'undiscovered country' for them; there's only the land of deprivation and quiet despair, which can be as much inside people's mind as it is on maps of what is sometimes euphemistically called 'disadvantaged communities'.[20] As is well known, such a largely invisible secession also becomes self-reinforcing: political parties, for the most part, have no reason to care for those who don't care to vote; this in turn strengthens the impression of the poor (to the extent they can pay attention at all) that there's nothing in it for them, when it comes to politics. The end result is declining and specifically also ever more *distorted* participation. Claus Offe sums up the logic at work:

> … as people are conditioned to 'waste' their rights and political resources, and as competing political elites and political parties come to understand that parts of the electorate are less likely than others to make use of their political resources, those elites will concentrate their platforms, campaigns and mobilization strategies upon those segments of the citizenry who actually 'count' and neglect others, launching a negative and exclusionary learning cycle of mutual alienation between elites and underprivileged citizens.[21]

How does all this relate to populism? Like all political parties, they offer what Pierre Bourdieu once called a 'vision of divisions', which is to say, they offer an interpretation of society's major political fault lines – and then seek to mobilise citizens accordingly.

[20] Wolfgang Merkel has coined the term 'two-thirds society' for this phenomenon – the bottom third has effectively disappeared from political life completely. See also B Teinturier, *'Plus rien à faire, plus rien à foutre'*: *La vraie crise de la démocratie* (Robert Laffont, 2017). For empirical evidence, see A Schäfer and H Schwender, '"Don't play if you can't win": does economic inequality undermine political equality?' (2019) 11 *European Political Science Review* 395–413. They conclude starkly, 'Moving from the most egalitarian to the most unequal countries depresses turnout – all else being equal – by 7 to 15 percentage points (depending on the exact model), which is comparable in magnitude to the effect of compulsory voting. Within Germany, where institutional variables do not differ, relatively deprived regions have significantly lower levels of turnout. Finally, we find that turnout declines for all income groups in unequal countries but particularly strongly for low-income groups. Our findings, therefore, unambiguously support the relative power approach – the rational abstention approach – that expects inequality to have a negative impact on political engagement. Our analyses show that in more unequal countries, fewer people turn out and vote. The idea that inequality mobilizes the poor to greater political activism because "more is at stake" clearly does not have any empirical grounding.'

[21] C Offe, 'Participatory Inequality in the Austerity State: A Supply-Side Approach' in A Schäfer and W Streeck (eds), *Politics in the Age of Austerity* (Polity, 2013) 196–218; here 203. Thomas Piketty adds that we should not assume that those who secede/abstain are by default racists; as Piketty puts is, 'if the less advantaged truly supported anti-immigrant movements, their turnout should be at a peak today. The fact that it is very low clearly shows that many less advantaged voters are not satisfied with the choices presented to them'. *Capital and Ideology*, tr A Goldhammer (Harvard University Press, 2020) 754.

That is by no means in and of itself dangerous or somehow illegitimate. Democracy, after all, is about division, not abut consensus, or about what General Mattis, Donald Trump's ill-fated Secretary of Defense called 'fundamental friendliness' (which, lamenting the lack of 'political unity' in his country, he was sorely missing in the second decade of the twenty-first century).[22] The promise of democracy is not that we shall all agree, and it does not require that we must exhibit 'uniformity of principles and habits', as Alexander Hamilton had it; rather, it is the guarantee that we have a fair chance of fighting for our side politically and then can live with the outcome of the struggle, because we will have another chance in a future election (and the rule of law is of course crucial in containing conflicts). Hence it is not enough simply to complain that populists are divisive.[23]

Both right-wing and left-wing populists are not always wrong when they make claims that get at something like the secession of the powerful. But they are wrong to reduce all conflicts to questions of belonging or to deem disagreement with them as automatically illegitimate (those who disagree must be traitors). That is the reason why genuine left-wing populists (which is to say: actors who claim a monopoly of representing the people) are also prone to bend the rule of law; there is no reason to protect the rights of their opponents, once the latter have been deemed not to deserve a place in the political game at all.[24]

More particularly, right-wing populists (who, as said before, are for the most part committed nationalists today) effectively engage in a form of culture war centred not so much on 'bringing people together' but, rather, on conjuring up something like a secession of the supposedly 'real people'. Yet, since the real people can hardly secede from their own homeland, the actual logic is one of expelling all those from the polity (at the very least symbolically) who do not truly belong to the people.[25] In effect, these will hardly be the most powerful; rather, it is usually already vulnerable minorities who will be harassed and have their rights denied. In effect, populism of this kind often amounts to nothing else than a systematic defence of an ethno-state, with the twist that actual majorities feel like victims under attack, or at the very least form communities of shared outrage.[26]

Populism is not uniquely responsible for polarisation, but it is important to understand that, in one sense, its key strategy simply *is* polarisation. After all, it seeks to divide polities into homogeneous groups and then insinuates that some groups do not truly belong at all or are fundamentally illegitimate. Instead of being characterised by cross-cutting identities and interests, the political world is simplified and rendered as

[22] D Filins, 'James Mattis, a Warrior in Washington' (*The New Yorker*, 29 May 2017).

[23] Of course, non-populists are also often confronted with the accusation of 'divisiveness'. The accusation – and the accompanying call for 'civility' – seems to aim at keeping certain conflicts out of the political game, rather than improving the rules of the game as such.

[24] Think of the way the de facto ruler of Poland, Jarosław Kaczyński, charges an independent judiciary with 'legal impossibilism'.

[25] Though the notion that the real people might also need to retreat does exist: Austria's right-wing populist party, the Freedom Party, owned a pretty small inn (*Pension Enzian*); there they hid gold with the argument that one day they might need a refuge, in case a European civil war broke out. I am grateful to Isolde Charim for mentioning this bizarre inner secession scenario to me.

[26] Krastev (n 1) and C Fieschi, *Populocracy: The Tyranny of Authenticity and the Rise of Populism* (agenda, 2019) 162.

a picture of one central cleavage, quite possibly one that is of existential importance (along the lines of 'if the wrong side wins, we shall perish').[27] Disquiet about what I called the double secession is channelled by right-wing populists into collective fear or even a basic moral panic that 'the country is being taken away from us' (when in fact both those at the top and those at the bottom are taking themselves out of the country – though, as I've by now said ad nauseam, for different reasons).[28]

Under such conditions of a perceived existential threat, citizens might be more willing to condone breaches of democratic principles and the rule of law (and it might be easier for politicians to portray judges as 'enemies of the people').[29] Political groupings are brought together not by what John Stuart Mill called 'common sympathies', but by what political scientists refer to as 'negative identity' – opposition to political actors deemed traitors or disloyal minorities, rather than a shared political project.[30] Populists seek to deepen a central division in society, simplify it into a matter of are-you-for-or-against-the-leader and thus raise the price their supporters have to pay for actually putting democracy and the rule of law above their partisan interests (as they perceive them in light of populist agitation).[31]

Let me add three further observations about populists in power. Evidently, they claim that victory at the ballot box translates into everyone having to accept now that they, *and only they*, represent the will of the people. Never mind that they often did not reach an actual majority (let alone a supermajority): the BJP, for instance, won a mere 37 per cent of the vote in the elections in India in 2019, but, as a result of the first-past-the-post system, received a majority in Parliament (a similar outcome can be observed in Poland in 2015, where the Law and Justice Party, on the basis of 37 per cent of the vote share (19 per cent of eligible voters) gained a majority in the Seijm and took this as a mandate to dismantle the rule of law). In Hungary, Viktor Orbán declared the 2010 election, in which his party received a majority of the votes and a super-majority in parliament, a 'revolution the ballot box' – construing a comprehensive mandate for constitutional as well as far-reaching social and political changes, even though a new Constitution had not been part of the election manifesto.

Secondly, at least a number of right-wing populists have engaged in a strategy of what can only be called bait-and-switch. They initially present themselves as if they sought to reverse the double secessions, but in fact end up loosening constraints on economic elite activity further, while distracting the downtrodden with Kulturkampf

[27] A nuanced account of such dynamics is provided in L Mason, *Uncivil Agreement: How Politics Became Our Identity* (University of Chicago Press, 2018).

[28] The former chair of the right-wing populist Alternative for Germany once claimed that 'we need the fearful to move majorities'. L Jacobsen, 'Im Bund mit den Ängstlichen' (*Zeit online*), available at www.zeit.de/politik/deutschland/2015-11/alternative-fuer-deutschland-parteitag-frauke-petry-hannover.

[29] For a wonderfully succinct reminder as to why they are not: Geert Corstens, *Understanding the Rule of Law*, trans. Annette Mils (Hart, 2017).

[30] I am grateful to Cristóbal Rovira Kaltwasser for pressing this point. There is not a significant literature on 'negative partisanship', especially in the US.

[31] MW Svolik, 'Polarization versus Democracy' (2019) 30 *Journal of Democracy* 20–32. As Svolik puts it, 'the political acumen of Chávez, Orbán, or Erdoğan lay in their ability to draw political battle lines along societal cleavages that were only simmering when these leaders were first elected. Once they succeeded, elections confronted their supporters with the choice between their partisan interests on the one hand and democratic principles on the other'.

(or further exclude them from politics altogether, through raising the barriers to political participation).[32] Some, by encouraging critics of the Government to emigrate and by enfranchising co-ethnics residing abroad, even come close to bringing about the very homogeneous people in whose name they had always already been speaking (put differently, the populist 'people' becomes a self-fulfilling prophecy). Hungary is an obvious example of this; Orbán appears to have found a way to implement Bertolt Brecht's ironic injunction in his poem *The Solution* that, if the people have disappointed the Government somehow, the Government should elect another people.[33]

III. TOWARDS A NON-POPULIST ACCOUNT OF THE PEOPLE

Does all this mean that 'people talk' is inherently dangerous, perhaps somehow automatically illiberal, or even as such bound to be exclusionary? The answer is no. In fact, it would be peculiar if one sought to dispense with people talk in a democracy entirely. For instance, what would one think of a professional politician who, when asked about her vision of the people, could only reply that she had no idea, but could discuss some great technical fixes for the recent local sewage problems (or, like Dutch liberal Mark Rutte, answered that 'vision is like an elephant that obstructs one's sight')?

Politics as a profession includes the duty to have given some thought to what constitutes the people – there is nothing strange about that. What marks the difference between the populist and the non-populist politician, is that the former treats 'the people' as effectively a fallible proposition, a vision, or a hypothesis, so to speak, that can be disproven (at least temporarily) at the ballot box.[34] By contrast, the populist politician not only always already knows the uniquely correct answer to the query 'who are the people' – they also treat that answer as if it were a given, indisputable fact. It is an assertion, in other words, that cannot truly be rejected at the ballot box; if it is, then there must have been fraud, corruption, etc. Thus, populists do not claim to *form* the will of the people, as, broadly speaking, democratic politicians would do; rather, they pretend that they are just *finding* it.[35]

[32] Efforts at voter suppression by the Republican Party in the US are the most obvious example. Think of Paul Weyrich, one of the founders of the conservative movement avowing openly: 'I don't want everybody to vote. Elections are not won by a majority of people. As a matter of fact our leverage in the elections quite candidly goes up as the voting populace goes down.' Quoted in A Lichtman, *The Embattled Vote in America* (Harvard University Press, 2018) 248.

[33] *Nach dem Aufstand des 17. Juni Ließ der Sekretär des Schriftstellerverbands In der Stalinallee Flugblätter verteilen Auf denen zu lesen war, daß das Volk Das Vertrauen der Regierung verscherzt habe Und es nur durch verdoppelte Arbeit zurückerobern könne. Wäre es da Nicht doch einfacher, die Regierung Löste das Volk auf und Wählte ein anderes?*

[34] To be sure, confirmation of a vision at the ballot box does not mean carte blanche – the implementation of a vision is constrained by leaving open the possibility of the present minority gaining office and re-shaping the conception of the people yet again.

[35] The contrast between forming and finding was first suggested by Ernst Fraenkel. Note, for instance, Narendra Modi claiming: 'I am merely the medium' and 'it is the people whose voice is resonating'. S Khilnani, 'The idea of India says persuade not dictate' (*Times of India*, 15 August 2017), at http://timesofindia.indiatimes.com/india/the-idea-of-india-says-persuade-not-dictate/articleshow/60063019.cms. Carl Schmitt's position is interestingly ambiguous here; witness his observation in *Crisis of Parliamentary*

Of course, this difference, significant as it is, does not exhaust the question of what makes for a non-populist conception of the people. As I said at the beginning, one ought to have such a conception, while bearing in mind that 'peoplehood' is only one aspect of democratic politics, and probably; and, in most circumstances, hardly the most important one.

Debates around this issue have been caught between two extremes: on the one hand, the notion that a correct normative theory would dictate the shape of political boundaries; on the other, the view that, precisely because such theorising amounts ipso facto to an undemocratic imposition, one should leave the question of the people entirely to contestation (even quite an unruly one); from this angle, any criteria of togetherness look like an illegitimate way to cut off genuine democratic struggle over boundaries.[36]

Normative theorists would be right in saying that such a throwing up of one's arms in the face of more or less democratic contestation leaves one speechless in the event of certain outcomes (for instance, populist politicians systematically disempowering or even disenfranchising minorities); while advocates of contestation no doubt have a point in casting doubt on the notion of a uniquely correct normative answer; an answer, that is, which would leave the demos with no other role than gratefully accepting the right plan handed down by political philosophers.[37] Then again, they often implicitly assume that contestation means inclusion; and it's unclear what they can say if it actually leads to a shrinking demos (or, put more bluntly, the de facto political exclusion of various minorities).[38]

Both answers, then, are unsatisfactory. Perhaps that's because the question is badly posed. We're not looking at a globe populated by humans and asking what would be the correct way of dividing them into discrete peoples; we'd be searching in vain for an Archimedean point from which to do this.[39] I suggest we embark on a different route and, to do so, first take a wider view of the political landscape we are trying to traverse. What we are really interested in is not just 'the people' in the abstract, but the people as a *democratic* people. Of course, that's presuming a lot. In particular, it presumes that a distinct group is committed to realising a way of life according to principles of equality and freedom; it presumes a collective will to share one another's political fate, as John Rawls once put it.[40] Furthermore – and

Democracy: 'The will of the people is of course always identical with the will of the people, whether a decision comes from the yes or no of millions of voting papers, or from a single individual who has the will of the people even without a ballot, or from the people acclaiming in some way. Everything depends on how the will of the people is formed.'

[36] The dilemma is nicely laid out in J White and L Ypi, 'The Politics of Peoplehood' (2015) *Political Theory* 439–65.

[37] Note that, contrary to a common image of populists as unruly and norm-breaking, they in a certain way actually belong on the first side of the dilemma: the norm is that the people are those who the populists, as unique representatives of the people, say the people are.

[38] It seems rather insufficient to say, where such exclusionary measures dominate, 'they usefully alert us to the pressing need to promote counter-perspectives and act as a provocation to do so'. See White and Ypi (n 36) 456.

[39] A Stilz, *Territorial Sovereignty: A Philosophical Exploration* (OUP, 2019).

[40] As Josh Ober has pointed out, a group seeking the benefits of social cooperation without a master is rare, but hardly unknown; it's not absurd to assume a group is seeking non-tyranny, though, as Ober concedes, it may well be that 'things have happened in the past (good, bad, just unjust)'. See his *Demopolis*

presuming even more – a joint intention to live according to such principles has to translate into an imperative to maintain an institutional machinery – a state, for shorthand – which enforces such a joint commitment and which, ideally, is subject to the rule of law.[41]

One may well object that what needed to be proven has now just been presumed. But this very rough sketch of a democratic people does not prescribe a specific answer in the endless conflict over boundaries; it just limits possible contestation in three not so trivial ways:

First, a distinctly democratic people cannot expel or disenfranchise citizens (that is, exclude them against their will); for such a measure would blatantly deny their status as free and equal members of the polity. Denying those who seek expulsion or disenfranchisement their wishes is not a violation of democratic principles or the rule of law, as such citizens fail to subscribe to the collective democratic project in the first place; less obviously, no particular effort to justify policies is owed to them, since they do not accept the shared framework of the polity at all.[42] Denying the standing of other citizens is outside what we may as well call a *hard border* of democratic conflict.

Secondly, in struggles over boundaries, one cannot simply assert a supposedly self-evident pre-political conception of the people. That is what defenders of a particular ethnic conception of the nation tend to do (who do not necessarily have to be populists assuming that the popular will just somehow needs to be *revealed* by the leader).[43] The problem is not that a position which seeks to restrict immigration (or to coerce new arrivals to assimilate to a dominant culture) is as such outside democratic debate; at issue is not the substance of this view, but the way it is being asserted: it actually tries to put peoplehood beyond political conflict altogether by pretending that it is naturally given. As the legal theorist Christoph Möllers has pointed out, 'where there is final certainty about the concept of the people, democracy has ended'.[44]

Thirdly: some hold that democracy requires the justification of all decisions which end up coercing others. Borders affect not just those inside them, but also subject those who are kept out by them; hence the latter must be part of the decision-making process.[45] The conclusion is that, ultimately, from the point of view of a consistent democrat, the demos must be nothing less than global. The same conclusion appears to follow if one adopts a somewhat weaker criterion and argues that virtually all decisions in a democratic state – whether coercing others directly or not – have effects on

(CUP, 2016) 37–8. In that sense, Carl Schmitt was not so wrong when he wrote that 'democracy presupposes a people whose members are similar to one another and who have the will to political existence'. The problematic notion is obviously that of 'similarity', which proved expandable for Schmitt, up to the point of racial homogeneity.

[41] Stilz (n 39) 98.

[42] ibid and J Quong, 'The Rights of Unreasonable Citizens' (2004) 12 *Journal of Political Philosophy* 314–35. Quong argues persuasively that citizens who fundamentally reject the notion that the polity is composed of free and equal citizens are excluded from the constituency of justification; that does not mean that their basic rights have to be denied as such, though it can mean that their freedom to form parties has to be restricted.

[43] F Wolkenstein, 'Populism, liberal democracy and the ethics of peoplehood' (2019) 18 *European Journal of Political Theory* 330–48.

[44] C Möllers, *Das Grundgesetz: Geschichte und Inhalt* (CH Beck, 2019) 103.

[45] A Abizadeh, 'Democratic theory and border coercion: No right unilaterally to control your own borders' (2008) 36 *Political Theory* 37–65.

non-citizens; and since all affected by a decision should have a say in it, we once more end up with a call for something like world democracy.

A conventional response to this position is that one simply can't conceive a political machinery that would allow a global demos to determine a collective will (let alone consistently implement universally binding decisions) – without turning into some kind of tyranny. Another would deny that giving a say to all affected by a decision is the correct take on democracy; after all, it is also not true that, within a polity, citizens not affected by a policy are officially excluded from debating and deciding. Yet another objection would emphasise that there are very different and yet legitimate ways of implementing the principles of freedom and equality; peoples disagree about the particulars even of basic political rights; everyone might have their own reasons for disagreeing, but these could all be perfectly good ones – grounded, for instance, in diverging historical experiences, diverging value commitments that touch on basic rights (but don't uniquely determine them), diverging views of the empirical effects basic rights might have on different people, etc, etc.

The 'it's gotta be global' view achieves the opposite of what the defenders of an ethnic perspective want: it expands the people to the absolute maximum (and, to be consistent: aliens would also have to be included in debates over whether they could be excluded from Earth). But on one level the two apparent extremes have something in common: they stop a democratic conflict over peoplehood in its tracks; the size of the people is given; forms of togetherness are no longer enacted, evolving, fought over, and reshaped over time.[46]

These points do not translate into saying that borders should never be changed, or that any process at the end of which a demos has apparently shrunk is automatically illegitimate, or has to involve violations of the rule of law. Think of a permanently alienated cultural minority which cannot express itself because a dominant group instrumentalises the state to promote its own culture at the expense of all others; such a situation may be grounds for actual legal secession – which would leave a diminished demos behind (though even with separations and secessions among democratic peoples, there is no such thing as a right to expel).

Questions of immigration and democratic citizenship will continue to be contested; the point is that there are many, but not infinite, ways of contesting them in polities committed to principles of equality and freedom, as well as the rule of law. What does 'contestation' mean concretely, then? In theory, single citizens can make a new beginning as to how we think about these questions; but the reality is that contestation is undertaken by groups – be it parties, trade unions, even media. As Judith Shklar once observed, in a piece tellingly entitled 'Let Us Not Be Hypocritical': 'a people is not just a political entity, as was once hoped. Parties, organised campaigns, and leaders make up the reality'.[47] That reality can look better or worse. Parties and

[46] I am not suggesting a moral equivalence between the two views; there remains much to be said for a conception of peoplehood that, in light of a commitment to reciprocity, is sensitive to externalities. Wolkenstein mentions the campaign for Scottish independence as an example of actors who tried to justify their aims to both insiders and the most relevant outsiders (the rest of the UK, and the EU). See Wolkenstein (n 43) 343–44.

[47] Quoted in A Przeworski, *Democracy and the Limits of Self-Government* (CUP, 2010) 27. This is really just another way of saying that a political people isn't actually an 'entity' at all, but an ongoing pluralistic

media – the intermediary institutions considered crucial for making representative democracy function properly ever since the nineteenth century – structure conflicts, including conflicts about peoplehood. While a systematic reassessment of their role under twenty-first century circumstances is beyond the scope of this chapter, let me at least say that an important task for them is to respond to the double secession discussed further above.

This also brings us back to the rule of law. The rule of law is indispensable in securing private autonomy. But it also maintains the conditions of public autonomy, that is, democratic debate, the formation of intermediary powers (based on rights to free speech and free association), and, ultimately, of course, free and fair elections; this, in turn, is crucial for the continuous enactment of peoplehood and its public justification.[48] Hence, extending Möllers' thought, one might say that those who seek to achieve final certainty about the people are also likely to be done with democracy and the rule of law. The latter, by making basic democratic rights such as freedom of speech and freedom of association robust, also enables re-opening the question of the people.

This also means that the double secession is not best addressed by somehow constructing 'majority cultural rights', as some theorists have claimed.[49] It is best tackled by, first, reaffirming joint intentions about core political principles ('constitutional essentials', in Rawls terminology), and, real mobilisation to keep the powerful in and to get the downtrodden back into the democratic game.[50] For such efforts, basic democratic rights are essential; and they must be secured by an effective rule of law. This, finally, also underlines that a discussion of populism and peoplehood does not have to end with playing liberalism and the rule of law off against democracy.[51] We need to have it all, so to speak.

process: J Habermas, 'Constitutional Democracy: An Uncertain Union of Paradoxical Principles?' (2001) 29 *Political Theory* 766–81.

[48] J Habermas, *Between Facts and Norms*, tr William Rehg (MIT Press, 1996). Note what I am not saying: I am not asserting that basic political rights do not belong to democracy, but instead to the rule of law; rather, I am claiming that freedom of political speech and association belong to democracy, while an independent judiciary committed to equality before the law is essential in making these rights and protecting them. On this point, see also J Ober, *Demopolis: Democracy Before Liberalism in Theory and Practice* (CUP, 2017).

[49] For instance, L Orgad, *The Cultural Defense of Nations: A Liberal Theory of Majority Rights* (OUP, 2015). It is telling that, in the end, Orgad himself actually defends 'constitutional identity' (which one might as well re-describe as constitutional patriotism) and no substantive account for a majority to use the state to protect, or promote, majority culture.

[50] For concrete suggestions in this context (which apply in the US and beyond), see BI Page and M Gilens, *Democracy in America? What Has Gone Wrong and What We Can Do about It* (University of Chicago Press, 2017).

[51] For an example of such a misguided conceptual and normative splitting, see Y Mounk, *The People vs. Democracy* (Harvard University Press, 2018); for crucial counter-arguments, see Ober (n 48).

11

Does Illiberal Democracy Exist?

GÁBOR HALMAI*

Modern liberalism has become obsolete

Vladimir Putin

I. ILLIBERAL THEORIES

ILLIBERALISM CAN BE understood as a critical reaction to liberalism. The subjects of illiberal criticism are both liberal theories and liberal societies. As Stephen Holmes argues, illiberals or anti-liberals are unwilling to examine liberal theories and liberal societies separately, because they assume that liberal societies perfectly embody liberal ideas, therefore the failing of liberal societies follows directly from the inadequacy of liberal principles.[1] This chapter will discuss the current state of play of both illiberal theories and illiberal societies in East Central Europe.

Illiberal critics of liberalism also portray and demonise liberalism as a single coherent phenomenon. However, conservative liberals have little in common with social democratic ones, nor neo-liberals with classical ones.[2] As Ralf Dahrendorf has rightly pointed out, Friedrich von Hayek and Karl Popper may well both be seen as liberal thinkers, but their views are quite different from each other.[3]

While discussing illiberalism the focus of this chapter will be institutional. From this perspective the main object of illiberal critique is liberal democracy, which in my view is not merely a limit on the public power of the majority, but also presupposes rule of law, checks and balances, and guaranteed fundamental rights. This means that there is no democracy without liberalism, and there also cannot be liberal rights without democracy.[4] In this respect, there is no such a thing as an 'illiberal or

* Professor and Chair of Comparative Constitutional Law, European University Institute, Florence, Italy, gabor.halmai@eui.eu.

[1] See S Holmes, *The Anatomy of Antiliberalism* (Harvard University Press, 1993) XIV.

[2] See J Zielonka, *Counter-Revolution* (OUP, 2018) 20.

[3] R Dahrendorf, *Reflections on the Revolution in Europe* (Times Books, 1990) 25–26.

[4] cf J Habermas, 'Über den internen Zusammenhang von Rechtsstaat und Demokratie' in *Zum Begriff der Verfassung. Die Ordnung der Politischen*, ed, (U. Preuss, Fischer, 1994) 83–94. English version: J Habermas, 'Rule of Law and Democracy' (1995) 3 *European Journal of Philosophy*. Also Juan José Linz

anti-liberal democracy'.[5] Those who perceive democracy as liberal by definition claim that illiberalism is inherently hostile to values associated with constitutionalism, as an institutional aspect of liberal democracy: separation of powers, constraints on the will of the majority, human rights, and protections for minorities. Therefore, the also oxymonoric 'illiberal' or 'populist' constitutionalism[6] is necessarily authoritarian in character.[7]

Distinct from illiberal theories, the second part of the chapter discusses three main relations of illiberal societies: the social, the economic and the political. Among other things, I want to figure out whether the backsliding of liberalism in East-Central Europe is a proof or consequence of failure of liberal ideas.

A. Autocratic Leaders' Rhetoric

In a speech delivered on 26 July 2014, before an ethnic Hungarian audience in the neighbouring Romania, Prime Minister Viktor Orbán proclaimed his intention to turn Hungary into a state that 'will undertake the odium of expressing that in character it is not of liberal nature'. He added:

> We have abandoned liberal methods and principles of organizing society, as well as the liberal way to look at the world. … Today, the stars of international analyses are Singapore, China, India, Turkey, Russia … and if we think back on what we did in the last four years, and what we are going to do in the following four years, then it really can be interpreted from this angle. We are … parting ways with Western European dogmas, making ourselves independent from them … If we look at civil organizations in Hungary, … we have to deal

and Alfred Stepan assert that if governments, even being freely elected violate the right of individuals and minorities, their regimes are not democracies. See JJ Linz and A Stepan, 'Toward Consolidated Democracies' (1996) 7(2) *Journal of Democracy* 14, 15. Similarly, János Kis claims that there is no such thing as nonliberal democracy, or non-democratic liberalism. See J Kis, 'Demokráciából autokráciába. A rendszertipológia és az átmenet dinamikája' [From Democracy to Autocracy. The System-typology and the Dynamics of the Transition] (2019) 1 *Politikatudományi Szemle* 45–74. Those critics, which argue that liberalism as a 300-year-old concept predates liberal democracy, forget that not only democracy but also liberalism presupposes general and equal suffrage.

[5] J-W Müller, 'The Problem with "Illiberal Democracy"' *Project Syndicate* (21 January 2016).

[6] For instance, Paul Blokker considers 'populist constitutionalism' as an alternative, conservative understanding of constitutional order, which, among other things, is a reaction to injustices resulting from liberal democratic politics, to unbalanced emphasis on formalistic liberal institutions, rights, and norms, and an aggressive institutionalisation of a liberal understanding of law in the post-1989 transformation. See P Blokker, 'Populist Constitutionalism' in C de la Torre (ed), *Routledge Handbook of Global Populism* (Routledge, 2018); P Blokker, 'Populism As a Constitutional Project' (2019) 17(2) *ICON*. Using Isaiah Berlin's terminology on 'false populism' I argue somewhere else that this 'authoritarian populist constitutionalism' is only a rhetoric, and not a real populist appeal to the 'people'. See G Halmai, 'Populism, Authoritarianism and Constitutionalism' (2019) 20(3) *German Law Journal*.

[7] Following Juan José Linz's classical categories authoritarianism is in between democratic and totalitarian political systems. See JJ Linz, *Totalitarian and Authoritarian Regimes* (Lynne Rienner, 2000). Writing about Franco's Spain, Linz has already outlined the following four main characteristics of authoritarianism: limited, not responsible political pluralism, without elaborate and guiding ideology, without political mobilisation, and with formally ill-defined, but quite predictable limits of power. See JJ Linz, 'An Authoritarian Regime: the Case of Spain' in E Allard and Y Littunen (eds), *Cleavages, Ideologies and Party Systems* (Helsinki, 1970). Regarding the constitutional markers of authoritarianism as a pretence of democracy, such as the lack of procedural rights, institutional guarantees and public discourse, see G Attila Tóth, 'Constitutional Markers of Authoritarianism' (2018) 11(2) *Hague Journal on the Rule of Law*.

with paid political activists here ... [T]hey would like to exercise influence ... on Hungarian public life. It is vital, therefore, that if we would like to reorganize our nation state instead of it being a liberal state, that we should make it clear, that these are not civilians ... opposing us, but political activists attempting to promote foreign interests ... This is about the ongoing reorganization of the Hungarian state. Contrary to the liberal state organization logic of the past twenty years, this is a state organization originating in national interests.[8]

Four years later at the same venue Orbán again expressed his support for illiberal democracy, adding that he considers Christian democracy as illiberal as well:

There is an alternative to liberal democracy: it is called Christian democracy ... Let us confidently declare that Christian democracy is not liberal. Liberal democracy is liberal, while Christian democracy is, by definition, not liberal: it is, if you like, illiberal.[9]

In June 2019, after Fidesz was suspended from the centre-right party family, EPP set up a special committee to examine the Fidesz party's adherence to democratic standards. One of the questions the members of the committee, former Austrian Chancellor Wolfgang Schüssel, former European Council President Herman Van Rompuy and former European Parliament President Hans-Gert Pöttering addressed to Viktor Orbán was: 'Please explain what you mean by the expression "illiberal state"?' The Fidesz chairman and Hungarian Prime Minster's response was:

We are Christian democrats and we are differing nowadays at least in three aspects from the liberals: The first one is the conviction that family is fundamental, and family is based on one man and one woman. We believe that this needs to be protected, which the liberals deny. Secondly, while the cultural life of every country is diverse, a Leitculture, a cultural tradition is present everywhere. In Hungary this is Christian culture. We respect other cultures, but our own has a prominent role for us, and it is our responsibility to preserve it. Liberals refuse this concept. The third aspect is that liberal democrats are everywhere pro-immigration while we are against immigration. So whether one admits it or not: Christian democrats are illiberals by definition.[10]

In a conversation with the French philosopher, Bernard-Henry Lévy Orbán identified liberalism with totalitarianism, and illiberalism with true democracy:

Liberalism gave rise to political correctness – that is, to a form of totalitarianism, which is the opposite of democracy. That's why I believe that illiberalism restores true freedom, true democracy.[11]

In July 2019 in the yearly Băile Tuşnad/Tusnádfürdő Free University camp Orbán admitted that 'illiberalism' carries a negative connotation, and therefore he changed the terminology calling illiberalism 'Christian liberty', which according to him is 'a genuine model of a theory of state, a unique Christian democratic state'. He made it clear, however, that 'Christian liberty does not mean individual liberty, because

[8] See V Orbán, 'Speech at Băile Tuşnad (Tusnádfürdő) of 26 July 2014' *Budapest Beacon* (29 July 2014).

[9] See Prime Minister Viktor Orbán's Speech at the 28th Bálványos Summer Open University and Student Camp, 28 July 2018. Tusnádfürdő (Băile Tuşnad).

[10] The leaked letter has been published by Politico at www.politico.eu/article/viktor-orban-rejects-epp-concerns-rule-of-law/.

[11] B-H Lévy, 'How an Anti-totalitarian Militant Discovered Ultranationalism. After 30 years, I spoke with Viktor Orbán again' *The Atlantic* (13 May 2019).

individual freedoms can never encroach on the interests of the community. There is indeed a majority that must be respected, that is the foundation of democracy.'[12]

In a speech, delivered in mid-September 2019 at the 12th congress of the Association of Christian Intelligentsia he said that 'Christian liberty' is superior to the individual liberty – defined by John Stuart Mill in his *On Liberty* – which can only be infringed upon if the exercise of one's liberty harms others. Christian liberty, by contrast, holds that we ought to treat others as we want to be treated.[13] 'The teachings of "Christian liberty"' – he added – 'maintain that the world is divided into nations'. As opposed to liberal liberty, which is based on individual accomplishments, the followers of 'Christian liberty' acknowledge only those accomplishments that also serve the common good. While liberals are convinced that liberal democracies will eventually join together to form a world government a la Immanuel Kant in the name of liberal internationalism, Christian liberty by contrast considers 'nations to be as free and sovereign as individuals are, and therefore they cannot be forced under the laws of global governance'.

In the system of 'Christian liberty' Hungary has a special place:

> We shouldn't be afraid to declare that Hungary is a city built on a hill, which, as is well known, cannot be hidden. Let's embrace this mission, let's create for ourselves and show to the world what a true, deep, and superior life can be built on the ideal of Christian liberty. Perhaps this lifeline will be the one toward which the confused, lost, and misguided Europe will stretch its hand. Perhaps they will also see the beauty of man's work serving his own good, the good of his country, and the glory of God.[14]

Another new element of the speech is where Orbán puts 'Christian liberty' at the centre of the 'Christian democratic state', 'a new and authentic model of state and political theory', which has been reached in the last 30 years by two big steps. The first has been the liberal democratic transition in 1989, while the second, more important one is the national or Christian regime change in 2010.

Regarding the new constitutional order, introduced by the 2011 Fundamental Law of Hungary, Orbán admitted that his party did not aim to produce a liberal constitution. He said:

> In Europe the trend is for every constitution to be liberal, this is not one. Liberal constitutions are based on the freedom of the individual and subdue welfare and the

[12] See www.miniszterelnok.hu/yes-to-democracy-no-to-liberalism/. As Yale law and history professor, Samuel Moyn pointed out President Trump had also begun to nudge the political culture in the same direction. He quoted Sohrab Ahmari, a conservative journalist, who approvingly explained Trump's policy as re-ordering the common good and ultimately the Highest Good,'that is, the Christian God' – Moyn argues. See S Moyn, 'We Are in An Anti-Liberal Moment. Liberals Need Better Answers' *The Washington Post* (21 June 2019).

[13] See www.miniszterelnok.hu/orban-viktor-beszede-a-kereszteny-ertelmisegiek--szovetsegenek-kesz-xii-kongresszusan/. This time the webpage of the Prime Minister, besides the original Hungarian text of the speech, contains no English, but only a German language translation: www.miniszterelnok.hu/viktor-orbans-rede-auf-dem-kongress-des-verbandes-der-christlichen-intellektuellen-kereszteny-ertelmisegiek-szovetsege-kesz.

[14] As Éva S Balogh points out this passage is taken from the Gospel of Matthew, (5:13-15), without identifying it. See ÉS Balogh, 'Orbán, the New Jesus Delivers His Sermon on the Mount' *Hungarian Spectrum* (15 September 2019).

> interest of the community to this goal. When we created the constitution, we posed questions to the people. The first question was the following: what would you like; should the constitution regulate the rights of the individual and create other rules in accordance with this principle or should it create a balance between the rights and duties of the individual. According to my recollection more than 80% of the people responded by saying that they wanted to live in a world, where freedom existed, but where welfare and the interest of the community could not be neglected and that these need to be balanced in the constitution. I received an order and mandate for this. For this reason the Hungarian constitution is a constitution of balance, and not a side-leaning constitution, which is the fashion in Europe, as there are plenty of problems there.[15]

Orbán also refused separation of powers, checks and balances as concepts alien to his illiberal constitutional system: 'Checks and balances is a U.S. invention that for some reason of intellectual mediocrity Europe decided to adopt and use in European politics'.[16]

B. The Ideology of 'Illiberal Democrats'

The ideological foundation of Orbán's illiberalism can be found in the works of his two court ideologues, the sociologist and former liberal MP, Gyula Tellér and András Lánczi, a political scientist. It is easy to prove that Orbán in his 2014 speech on 'illiberal democracy' recited a study of Tellér published earlier on that year, that Orbán assigned as compulsory reading for all his ministers.[17] Tellér claims that the 'system of regime-change' has failed because the liberal constitution did not commit the government to protect national interests, therefore the new 'national system' has to strengthen national sovereignty, and with it the freedom of degree of government activity. This, Tellér argues, is necessary against the moral command of the liberal rule of law regime, according to which 'everything is allowed, what does not harm others' liberty'.

Lánczi's anti-liberal concept can be found in his book *Political Realism and Wisdom*, which was published in English in 2015, as well as in an article published in 2018, after Fidesz' third consecutive electoral victory.[18] Lánczi's critique is an outright rejection of liberalism as a utopian ideology, which is – similar to communism – incompatible with democracy.

Similarly to Orbán, the at that time Prime Minister Beata Szydło (with Kaczyński, ruling from behind the scenes as he holds no official post), described the actions of the PiS Government dismantling the independence of the Constitutional Tribunal and

[15] See 'A Tavares jelentés egy baloldali akció' (The Tavares report is a leftist action), Interview with PM Viktor Orbán in the Hungarian Public Radio, Kossuth Rádió, 5 July 2013.

[16] Interview with Bloomberg News, 14 December 2014.

[17] See G Tellér, 'Született-e Orbán-rendszer 2010 és 2014 között?' (Was an Orbán System Born between 2010 and 2014?) *Nagyvilág* (March 2014).

[18] See A Lánczi, 'The Renewed Social Contract–Hungary's Elections' 2018 IX(3) *Hungarian Review*. For a detailed analysis of Lánczi's arguments see KL Scheppele, *The Opportunism of Populists and the Defense of Constitutional Liberalism* (2019) 20 *German Law Journal* 3.

the ordinary courts as a blitz to install an illiberal state. In mid-September 2016 at a conference in the Polish town of Krynica, Orbán and Kaczyński proclaimed a 'cultural counter-revolution' aimed at turning the European Union into an illiberal project. A week later at the Bratislava EU summit, the prime ministers of the Visegrád four countries demanded a structural change of the EU in favour of the nation states.[19] Witold Waszczykowski, Poland's minister of foreign affairs, expressing his own and his governing PiS party's anti-liberalism went as far as to mock liberalism as 'a world made up of cyclists and vegetarians, who only use renewable energy and fight all form of religion'.[20]

Ryszard Legutko, the main ideologue of PiS, similarly to his Hungarian counterpart, Lánczi, also likens liberal democracy with communism, both being fuelled by the ideas of modernisation and progress.[21] Both Lánczi and Legutko assert together with other anti-liberals with one voice that liberalism and communism, or for that matter its ideology, Marxism are secretly allied and share a common ancestry that they are two offshoots of an Enlightenment tradition.[22] Legutko also accuses liberalism's aim to root out all forms of inequality, and asserts that human right, as legal norms that promote equality become 'arbitrary claims, ideologically motivated, made by various political groups in blatant disregard of the common good'.[23]

This critique of liberalism goes back to the concept of *Volksgemeinschaft* (national community), or *völkisches Recht*, one of the core principles of National Socialist law, which can be characterised negatively by rejection of the individualistic, normative concept of the people (*Volk*) as the sum of nationals of the state, as presented in the 1918 Weimar Constitution.[24] *Volksgemeinschaft* together with the *Führerprinzip*, the other main principle of National Socialist Weltanschauung aim to overcome individualism, hence it means strong anti-liberalism. Due to Carl Schmitt's well-known flirts

[19] Slawomir Sierakowski even speaks about an 'illiberal international'. See S Sierakowski, 'The Polish Threat to Europe' *Project Syndicate* (19 January 2016).

[20] 'Haben die Polen einen Vogel', *Bild* (3 January 2016).

[21] See R Legutko, *The Demon in Democracy: Totalitarian Temptations in Free Societies* (Encounter Books, 2016) 2–9.

[22] This anti-liberal political theory is present outside East-Central Europe as well. For instance Patrick Deneen's book, *Why Liberalism Failed* (2018) is directed at the left in the US targeting both contemporary progressivism and 'classical liberalism' of conservatives. See also the Israeli political theorist Yoram Hazony, whose book *The Virtue of Nationalism* (2018) also criticises those conservatives who defend liberal democracy. As Marc Plattner convincingly argues, the common goal of all these thinkers is to conflate liberal democracy with contemporary progressivism and thus to suggest that conservatives should have no interest in supporting or defending liberal democracy. See M Plattner, 'Illiberal Democracy and the Struggle on the Right' (2019) 30(1) *Journal of Democracy* 16–17.

[23] Legutko (n 21) 135. In a recent article, Paul Blokker characterises both Legutko and Lánczi as conservative intellectuals who have provided ideas for the conservative populist project, and important contributions to rethinking/re-imagining constitutional democracy in the contemporary European context. See P Blokker, 'Populist Counter-Constitutionalism, Conservatism, and Legal Fundamentalism' (2019) 15(3) *European Constitutional Law*.

[24] Regarding the role of *Volksgemeinschaft* in National Socialist law, see O Lepsius, 'The Problem of Perceptions of National Socialist Law or: Was There A Constitutional Theory of National Socialism?' in C Joerges and NS Ghaleigh (eds), *Draker Legacies of Law in Europe. The Shadow of National Socialism and Fascism over Europe and its Legal Traditions* (Hart, 2003) 19–41.

with National Socialism it is not surprising that the critical stance of the new illiberals towards liberal constitutionalism is also related to a Schmittian understanding of the Constitution, and to his critique of liberal constitutionalism and its conception of the rule of law.[25] The Constitution in Schmitt's view is an expression of 'the substantial homogeneity of the identity and the will of the people', and guarantee of the state's existence, and ultimately any constitutional arrangement is grounded in, or originates from, an arbitrary act of political power. The absolute authority of the political will of the people overrides all constitutional requirements, which according to Schmitt are signs of depoliticisation tendencies caused by liberal democracies. This is the reason that he elaborated on *The concept of the Political*[26] (*Das Politisches*) based on the distinction between friend and enemy, which is precisely the opposite of liberal neutrality.[27]

In other words, in Schmitt's view the basis of the Constitution is 'a political decision concerning the type and form of its own being', made by the people as a 'political unity', based on their own free will. This political 'remains alongside and above the constitution'.[28] Schmitt also portrays the people as an existential reality as opposed to the mere liberal representation of voters in Parliament, holding therefore that Mussolini was a genuine incarnation of democracy. Schmitt goes so far as to claim the incompatibility of liberalism and democracy, and argues that plebiscitary democracy[29] based on the homogeneity of the nation is the only true form of democracy. But Schmitt is talking about these intermittent plebiscites as a tool to tap the resource of consent by the governed within a 'qualitative' and strong totalitarian state, the authority of which rests on the military and the bureaucracy, and which

[25] As Heiner Bielefeld demonstrates Carl Schmitt systematically undermines the liberal principle of the rule of law. See H Bielefeld, 'Deconstruction of the Rule of Law. Carl Schmitt's Philosophy of the Political' (1996) 82 *Archiv für Rechts- und Sozialphilosophy* 379–96.

[26] C Schmitt, *The Concept of the Political* (University of Chicago Press, 2007).

[27] See H Bielefeld, 'Carl Schmitt's Critique of Liberalism: Systematic Reconstruction and Countercriticism' (1997) X(1) *Canadian Journal of Law and Jurisprudence* 67.

[28] See C Schmitt, *Constitutional Theory* (Duke University Press, 2008) 125–26. This idea is also shared by a part of the French constitutional doctrine, influenced by Rousseau's general will. This is the reason that the representatives of this doctrine hold that during a constitutional transition a referendum is sufficient to legitimate a new constitution. See the French Constitutional Council's approval of De Gaulle's 1962 amendment to the 1958 Constitution, ignoring the Constitution's amendment provisions.

[29] The Hungarian political scientist, András Körösényi, implementing the Weberian concept describes the Orbán regime as a 'plebiscitary leader democracy', where the activity of the leader (or Führer? – GH) is posteriorly approved by the people, but since this approval can be withdrawn this is still a democratic system. See A Körösényi, 'Weber és az Orbán-rezsim: plebiszciter vezéremokrácia Magyarországon' (Weber and the Orbán-regime: Plebisciter Leader Democracy in Hungary) (2017) 4 *Politikatudományi Szemle* 7–28. In a more recent interview however, Körösényi admitted that the for the withdrawal of approval currently a miracle is needed. See 'Csak a csoda segít' (Only the Miracle Helps), hvg, (20 June 2019). In contrast, Wojciech Sadurski using Guillermon O'Donnell's 'delegative democracy' concept characterises the Polish system after 2015 as a 'plebiscitary autocracy', in which the electorate approves of governmental disregard of the constitution. See W Sadurski, *Poland's Constitutional Breakdown* (OUP, 2019) 242–43. Similarly, Juan José Linz, to avoid confusion, proposes the addition of adjectives to 'authoritarianism' rather than to 'democracy' for such regimes: eg 'electoral authoritarianism'. Also, Larry Diamond refers to 'electoral authoritarianism' in hybrid regimes. See L Diamond, 'Thinking About Hybrid Regimes' (2002) 13(2) *Journal of Democracy* 21, 24.

cannot accept the existence of political opposition.[30] In other words the strong state cannot be liberal.[31]

As Mattias Kumm argues, Carl Schmitt's interpretation of democracy, inspired by Rousseau, and used by authoritarian populist nationalists, like Viktor Orbán as 'illiberal democracy', becomes an anti-constitutional topos.[32] Consequently, I equate constitutionalism with liberal democratic constitutionalism.[33] This does not mean, however, that constitutions cannot be illiberal or authoritarian. Therefore, it is legitimate to talk about constitutions in authoritarian regimes, as Tom Ginsburg and Alberto Simpler do in their book,[34] but I do not agree with the use of the term 'authoritarian constitutionalism'[35] or 'constitutional authoritarianism'.[36] Besides the

[30] See C Schmitt, *Legalität and Legitimität* (Duncker & Humblot, 2012) n 51, at 93–94. Quoted by A Somek, 'Authoritarian Constitutionalism: Austrian Constitutional Doctrine 1933–1938 and Its Legacy' in C Joerges and NS Ghaleigh (eds), *Darker Legacies of Law in Europe: The Shadow of National Socialism and Fascism over Europe and its Legal Traditions* (Hart, 2003) 375.

[31] Regarding the revival of Carl Schmitt in the Hungarian political and constitutional theory see A Antal, 'The Rebirth of the Political – A Schmittian Moment in Hungary' Transcript of the lecture given at the Constitutional systems in Middle Europe. The cycle of meetings about political ideas of Tadeusz Mazowiecki organised by Polska Fundacja im. Roberta Schumana on 6 November 2017, Warsaw. Also Z Balázs, 'Political Theory in Hungary After the Regime Change' (2014) 7(1) *International Political Anthropology* 5–26.

[32] M Kumm, 'Demokratie als verfassungsfeindlicher Topos' *Verfassungsblog* (6 September 2017).

[33] In contrast, others also regard other models of constitutionalism, in which the government, although committed to acting under a constitution, is not committed to pursuing liberal democratic values. See for instance M Tushnet, 'Varieties of Constitutionalism' (2016) 14(1) *ICON*. On 11 October 2019 Tushnet posted the following message to his Facebook page: 'My lecture today was on "Varieties of Constitutionalism" and argued that a thin version of constitutionalism requires only (1) that there be some entrenched provisions, (2) that there be some mechanism for resolving disputes about what the law is that is oriented solely to making decision according to law, and (3) that the regime receive popular consent to the regime as a whole measured over some reasonable period of time. (Lots of complexities elided here.) The first subtext, which almost surfaced in the discussion afterwards, is that the Chinese leadership doesn't really have to fear constitutionalism as such (as it seems to do), if the very thin version I outlined counts as constitutionalism (which I think it does). The second subtext is that, if the idea of thin constitutionalism were accepted the way would be open for discussions about whether thin constitutionalism should be thickened (discussions that are harder to have if the idea of constitutionalism is ruled off the table from the outset)'. Similarly, Gila Stopler defines the state of the current Israeli constitutional system as 'semi-liberal constitutionalism'. cf G Stopler, 'Constitutional Capture in Israel' (2017) *I•CON*.

[34] T Ginsburg and A Simpser, *Constitutions in Authoritarian Regimes* (CUP, 2014).

[35] See for instance Somek (n 30); Turkuler Isiksel, 'Between Text and Context: Turkey's Tradition of Authoritarian Constitutionalism' (2013) 11 *Int'l J. Const. Law.* 702; M Tushnet, 'Authoritarian Constitutionalism' (2015) 100 *Cornell Law Review* 391. Somek deals with Austria before the Anschluss, Isiksel with Turkey, while Tushnet tries to generally pluralise the normative understanding of nonliberal constitutionalism, differentiating between an absolutist, a mere rule-of-law, and an authoritarian form of constitutionalism, Singapore being the main example of the latter. Most of the chapters in H Alviar Garcia and G Frankenberg (eds), *Authoritarian Constitutionalism. Comparative Analysis and Critique* (Edward Elgar, 2019) – as the editors' preface states, 'challenge the notion of a single "proper sense" of constitutionalism that is coexistensive with and exhausted by the discrete elements of the liberal paradigm'. In the introductory chapter, Günter Frankenberg argues that 'liberal orthodoxy treats authoritarian constitutionalism not just as a contested concept, but as a mere travesty or deceitful rendition of the rules and principles, values and institutions of what is innocently referred to as "Westerm constitutionalism"'. See G Frankenberg, 'Authoritarian Constitutionalism: Coming to Terms with Modernity's Nightmares' in Garcia and Frankenberg (eds) (ibid) 7.

[36] S Levitsky and LA Way, 'The Rise of Competitive Authoritarianism' (2002) 13 *Journal of Democracy* 51.

constitutions in the communist countries, both current theocratic and communitarian constitutions are considered as illiberal.[37] Theocratic constitutions, in contrast to modern constitutionalism, reject secular authority.[38] In communitarian constitutions, like the ones in South Korea, Singapore and Taiwan, the well-being of the nation, the community and society receive utilitarian priority rather than the individual freedom, which is the principle of liberalism. But in these illiberal polities, there is no constitutionalism, their constitutions – using Pablo Castillo-Ortiz's term – are 'de-normativised'.[39] In other words, in my view 'illiberal constitutionalism' is an oxymoron.

Besides illiberal constitutionalism there are also attempts to legitimate 'nonliberal constitutionalism' as a subtype of constitutionalism. Graham Walker uses the term for constitutionalist structures, 'wherever people value some aspects of communal identity more than autonomy of individual choice'.[40] Walker's main example for the nonliberal, rather local than universal values is the multicultural grant of group rights to native peoples and the distinct society of Québec, but he also mentions the state of Israel, which fails its noncitizen residents in many regrettable ways, as well as the tribal life of the native American nations in the US. The common characteristic of all these approaches is 'to indict the notion of individual autonomy rights as a form of naïve and homogenizing universalism, and to unmask the ethnic and moral "neutrality" of the liberal state as a covert form of coercion'.[41] Walker builds up his concept using Charles Howard McIlwain's understanding of constitutionalism in his 1940 book.[42] According to McIlwain the limitation of government by law is not necessarily liberal, because the rights of individuals are not centralised, and there is no need for a public authority to be a neutral arbiter among competing value systems. Among the more contemporary thinkers, Walker relies on Stanley Fish's scepticism about individual rights of all kinds. In his notorious articles from 1987[43] and 1992[44] respectively, Fish argues that because liberalism conceives its rational principles precisely as supranational and nonpartisan, 'one can only conclude, and conclude nonparadoxically, that liberalism doesn't exist'. According to Walker, nonliberal constitutionalism historically was anticipated in some features of Republican Rome or of medieval Europe, or in the millet system of the Ottoman Empire, while in more recent history in Canada before the 1982 Charter of Rights and Freedoms. He also considers the evolving multiculturalist/tolerationist American university campus practices as an

[37] L-A Thio, 'Constitutionalism in Illiberal Polities', in M Rosenfeld and A Sajó (eds), *Oxford Handbook of Comparative Constitutional Law* (OUP, 2012) 133. Contrary to my understanding, Thio also talks about 'constitutionalism' in illiberal polities.

[38] There are two subcategories distinguished here: The Iranian subcategory, where Islam is granted an authoritative central role within the bounds of a constitution; and the Saudi Arabian subcategory, where Islam is present, without the formal authority of modern constitutionalism.

[39] See P Castillo-Ortiz, 'The Illiberal Abuse of Constitutional Courts in Europe' (2019) 15 *European Constitutional Law Review* 48–72 at 67.

[40] G Walker, *The Idea of Nonliberal Constitutionalism* (1997) 39 *Ethnicity and Group Rights* 154–84 at 155.

[41] ibid 157.

[42] CH McIlwain, *Constitutionalism, Ancient and Modern* (Cornell University Press, 1940).

[43] S Fish, 'Liberalism Doesn't Exist' (1987) *Duke Law Journal*.

[44] S Fish, 'There's No Such Thing as Free Speech and It's a Good Thing, Too' (1992) 17(1) *Boston Review*.

embryonic version of nonliberal constitutionalism, and 'politically correct' thinkers who promote such policies as hostile to the notion of 'individual rights'.[45]

The problem with Walker's concept is that he conflates constitutionalism with constitution. While the latter indeed predates the enlightenment, the former, together with liberalism, does not.[46] The 'constitution' as the configuration of public order defined by Aristotle or Cicero did not require the notion of individual rights, while modern constitutionalism does.[47] For instance Montesquieu in *The Spirit of Laws* argues that the constitutional system based on the separation of power is necessary for securing political liberty and preventing the emergence of 'tyrannical laws' and 'execution of laws in a tyrannical manner'.[48] This means that 'fettered power', which, according to Walker is the essence of constitutionalism, presupposes guaranteed individual rights. The same applies to definitions of constitutionalism, emphasising 'limited government'. For instance Giovanni Sartori defines constitutionalism as 'a fundamental law, or a fundamental set of principles, and a correlative institutional arrangement, which would restrict arbitrary power and ensure "limited government"'.[49] Also, András Sajó and Renáta Uitz describe constitutionalism as a liberal political philosophy that is concerned with limiting government.[50] But the main aim of limiting government is to guarantee individual rights. In other words, modern constitutionalism is by definition liberal. Not only the anti- or illiberal version, but also the nonliberal one is oxymonoric.

II. ILLIBERAL SOCIETIES

A. Social Relations

Historically, in the East-Central European countries, there were only some unexpected moments of quick flourishing of liberalism and liberal democracy followed

[45] As we have seen earlier, Hungarian PM Viktor Orbán opposes 'political correctness' as a liberal concept. See his interview with Bernard-Henry Lévy in n 11.

[46] 'Classic liberalism' in its 19th century European sense means individual liberty and free market. See A Sajó and R Uitz, *The Constitution of Freedom: An Introduction to Legal Constitutionalism* (OUP, 2017) 13.

[47] Carl J Friedrich, one of the authors Walker refers to, in the later editions of his famous text on *Constitutional Government and Democracy* emphasises that the single function of constitutionalism is safeguarding each person in the exercise of 'individual rights'. See CJ Friedrich, *Constitutional Governance and Democracy: Theory and Practice in Europe and America,* 4th edn (Blaisdell, 1968) 24, 7. Walter Murphy, another author, quoted by Walker after the democratic transition in Eastern Europe, has also talked about 'protecting individual liberty' as the ultimate civic purpose of constitutionalism. cf WF Murphy, 'Constitutions, Constitutionalism and Democracy' in D Greenberg, SN Katz, MB Oliviero and SD Wheatley (eds), *Constitutionalism and Democracy: Transitions in the Contemporary World* (OUP, 1993).

[48] Montesquieu, *The Spirit of the Laws*, (transl and eds AM Cohler, BC Miller, HS Stone) (CUP, 1999) Book XI, Ch 6 at 157. (Quoted by Gábor Attila Tóth, 'Constitutional Markers of Authoritarianism' (2018) *Hague Journal on the Rule of Law*).

[49] See G Sartori, 'Constitutionalism: A Preliminary Discussion' (1962) 56 *The American Political Science Review* 855.

[50] Sajó and Uitz (n 46) 13.

by an equally quick delegitimisation of it. For instance shortly after 1945, till the communist parties took over, and also after 1989, when liberal democracy again seemed to be the 'end of history'.[51] Otherwise, in the national history of the Central and Eastern European countries, authoritarianism, such as the pre-1939 authoritarian Hungarian or Polish politics, played a much more important role in the transformation.[52] Maybe the only exception was the independent Czechoslovakia established after World War I, led by its first President Tomáš Garrigue Masaryk.[53]

As mentioned earlier, modernisation is the main enemy of illiberal theory. As surveys on the links between modernisation and democracy show, the society's historic and religious heritage leaves a lasting imprint.[54] According to these surveys, the public of formerly agrarian societies, like many of the East Central European ones, emphasise religion, national pride, obedience, and respect for authority, while the public of industrial societies emphasise secularism, cosmopolitanism, autonomy, and rationality.[55] Even modernisation's changes are not irreversible: economic collapse can reverse them, as happened during the early 1990s in most former communist states. These findings were confirmed by another international comparative study conducted by researchers of Jacobs University in Bremen and published by the German Bertelsmann Foundation.[56] According to the study, which examined 34 countries in the EU and the OECD, countries in East Central Europe have had a low level of social cohesion ever since the post-communist transformation, Hungary is ranked at 27th, between Poland and Slovakia. Social cohesion is defined as the special quality with which members of a community live and work together.

Even though the transition to democracy in East Central Europe was driven by the fact that a large share of the population gave high priority to freedom itself, people expected the new states to produce speedy economic growth, with which the country could attain the living standards of West preferably overnight, without painful reforms. In other words, one can argue that the average people in these countries

[51] See B Trencsényi, M Kopeček, L Gabrijelčič, M Falina, M Baár and M Janowski, *A History of Modern Political Thought in East Central Europe: Volume II: Negotiating Modernity in the 'Short Twentieth Century' and Beyond, Part I: 1918–1968* (OUP, 2018).

[52] See S Avineri, 'Two Decades After the Fall: Between Utopian Hopes and the Burdens of History' *Dissent* (30 September 2009).

[53] When the preamble of the 1992 Czech Constitution incorporated the principle of a civic nation 'in the spirit of the inviolable values of human dignity and freedom as the home of equal and free citizens', it was a hint to Masaryk's belief in the universal validity and critical power of democracy and liberty elaborated in his study on *The Czech Question*. See J Přibáň, *The Defence of Constitutionalism. The Czech Question in Post-national Europe* (University of Chicago Press, 2017) 115–16.

[54] See R Inglehart and C Welzel, 'Changing Mass Priorities: The Link between Modernization and Democracy' (2010) 8(2) *Perspectives on Politics* 551–67.

[55] ibid 553. This is one of the reasons for Czechia's less religious society. Christian Welzel in his more recent book argues that fading existential pressures open people's minds, making them prioritise freedom over security, autonomy over authority, diversity over uniformity and creativity over discipline, tolerance and solidarity over discrimination and hostility against out-groups. On the other hand, persistent existential pressures keep peoples' minds closed, in which case they emphasise the opposite priorities. This is the utility ladder of freedom. C Welzel, *Freedom Rising. Human Empowerment and the Quest for Emancipation* (CUP, 2013).

[56] D Schiefer, J van der Noll, J Delhey and K Boehnke, *Cohesion Radar: Measuring Cohesiveness* (Bertelsmann Foundation, 2013).

pursued the West in 1989–90, though not so much in terms of the Western political and constitutional system, but rather in terms of the living standards of the West. Claus Offe predicted the possible backsliding effect of the economic changes and decline in living standards, saying that this could undermine the legitimacy of democratic institutions and turn back the process of democratisation.[57] This failure, together with the emergence of an economically and politically independent bourgeoisie, the accumulation of wealth by some former members of the communist nomenclature, unresolved issues in dealing with the communist past, the lack of retributive justice against perpetrators of grave human rights violations, a mild vetting procedure, and lack of restitution of the confiscated properties, were reasons for disappointment. Again, Czechia has been different both regarding the bourgeoisie and the harsher transitional justice measures.

Trying to explain the attitudes of voters to support populist authoritarian pursuit of illiberal leaders, such as Orbán or Kaczyński, Ronald Inglehart and Pippa Norris suggest that it would be a mistake to attribute the rise of authoritarian populism directly to economic inequality alone, as psychological factors seem to play an even more important role. Older and less educated people tend to support populist parties and leaders that defend traditional cultural values and emphasise nationalistic and xenophobia appeals, rejecting outsiders, and upholding old-fashioned gender roles.[58] Similarly, Will Wilkinson argues that urbanisation is a process that divides society in cultural values. While it creates thriving, multicultural, high-density areas where socially liberal values predominate, it also leaves behind rural areas and smaller urban centres that are increasingly uniform in terms of rather illiberal values.[59]

B. Economic Relations

Paradoxically, politically illiberal leaders, like Viktor Orbán of Hungary, use (neo) liberal economic policy to support their autocratic (constitutional) agenda.[60] As many argue, referring to Karl Polányi's influential book, *The Great Repression*, that the resistance to social democracy through authoritarianism in the name of economic liberalism prepared the ground for Fascism, and can lead to autocracy again.[61]

Other, mostly left-wing populists react to the unfulfilled promise of social-rights constitutionalism, based on TH Marshall's concept of social rights being continuous to civil and political rights, which turned out to be a lie in most of East Central European countries' constitutional practice.[62] As Samuel Moyn argues, a commitment

[57] cf C Offe, *Designing Institutions for East European Transitions* (Institut für Höhere Studies, 1994) 15.

[58] R Inglehart and P Norris, *Cultural Backlash, Trump, Brexit, and Authoritarian Populism* (CUP, 2019).

[59] W Wilkinson, *The Density Divide: Urbanization, Polarization, and Populist Backlash* (Research Paper of the Niskanen Center, June 2018).

[60] This phenomenon is named by Michael Wilkinson as authoritarian liberalism. See MA Wilkinson, 'Authoritarian Liberalism aa Authoritarian Constitutionalism' in H Alviar and G Frankenberg (eds), *Authoritarian Constitutionalism* (Edward Elgar, 2019).

[61] See Wilkinson, ibid, and also B Bugaric, 'The Two Faces of Populism: Between Authoritarian and Democratic Populism' (2019) 20(3) *German Law Journal*.

[62] Andrew Arato and Jean Cohen, analysing the normative theory of left populist Ernesto Laclau and Chantal Mouffe respectively, go even further by claiming that left populism also cannot avoid the

to material equality disappeared, in its place market fundamentalism has emerged as the dominant force of national and global economics.[63]

The new illiberal system of 'national cooperation' in Hungary has left behind the vulnerable members of society, homeless people and refugees, and tries to diminish or cut the solidary actions of the members of the Hungarian society. In this respect Orbán's right-wing authoritarian populism even differs from the policy of other right-wing populists, such as the French National Front or Austria's Freedom Party, who – similarly to Orbán – mobilise their supporters with exclusion through immigration policy, but as opposed to the Hungarian PM, they often also emphasise inclusion through social rights and economic security.[64]

The packed Hungarian Constitutional Court rubberstamps the government's neoliberal economic policy, changing its predecessor's practice, which in the mid-1990s was willing to strike down austerity measures for the protection of social rights closely tying them to the protection of equal human dignity. Although social solidarity was an underdeveloped societal practice from the beginning of the democratic transition for several reasons, the at that time Constitutional Court strongly committed itself to the protection of human dignity and in this way guaranteed a higher profile for social (solidarity) rights, especially in the case of social care based on neediness.

As a contrast, in the 'non-solidary' system of the Hungarian Fundamental Law of 2011 social security does not appear as a fundamental right, but merely as something the state 'shall strive' for, which is a step backward in comparison with the 1989 Constitution. Social insurance is not a constitutional institution any more, and the provisions of the Fundamental Law do not guarantee equal dignity and the former level of property protection. The recent case law of the Constitutional Court reaffirms the initial concerns, the dignity of social solidarity got lost in the illiberal backsliding of the past 10 years.

C. Political Relations

The expansion of political illiberalism in East Central Europe through the introduction of a new illiberal constitutional regime went the furthest in Hungary and Poland. In the case of the former it was through a brand new constitution enacted in 2010, or through legislative changes that ignore the valid liberal constitution, as has been the case in Poland since 2015. Ironically, both countries are still members of the European Union, a value community based on the principles of liberal democracy.

authoritarianism inherent in the strategy and logic of populism despite the inclusionary and democratising projects of the left movements it attaches to and despite the democratic socialist rhetoric of left populist leaders and their organic intellectuals. See A Arato, 'Political Theology and Populism' (2013) 80(1) *Social Research* and JL Cohen, 'What's Wrong with the Normative Theory (and the Actual Practice) of Left Populism?' (2019) 26(3) *Constellations*. In my view it is certainly true for Latin American populists from Peron through Morales, Correa, till Chavez and Maduro, but not necessarily for European left populist parties, such as Podemes, Five Star and Syriza. The last two did not even show serious authoritarian pursuits while in power.

[63] S Moyn, *Not Enough. Human Rights in an Unequal World* (Harvard University Press, 2018).

[64] See A Weale, *The Will of the People. A Modern Myth* (Polity, 2018) 40–42.

i. Hungary

In 2010 Orbán's Fidesz party returned to power with the absolute majority of the votes, and due to the inherited disproportional election system that gained a two-third majority of the seats, which made it possible for them to enact a new, 'illiberal' constitution. This constitution, entitled the Fundamental Law of Hungary was passed by Parliament on 18 April 2011. The Fundamental Law breaks with a distinguishing feature of constitutions of rule-of-law states, namely, that they comprise the methods of exercising public authority and the limitations on such authority on the one hand and the guarantees of the enforcement of fundamental rights on the other.

In December 2011 the Parliament enacted a controversial election law with its gerrymandered electoral districts, making the electoral system even more disproportional, by increasing the proportion of single-member constituency mandates, eliminating the second round, introducing a relative majority system instead of the absolute majority, and introducing 'winner-compensation', which favoured the governing party. With this rigged electoral system Fidesz both in 2014 and 2018 was able to renew its two-thirds majority with less than a majority of the popular vote. Beyond the change of the electoral law Fidesz made the playing field even more uneven by dismantling free media, and threatening civil society.[65]

On 11 March 2013, the Hungarian Parliament added the Fourth Amendment to the country's 2011 constitution, re-enacting a number of controversial provisions that had been annulled by the Constitutional Court. The most alarming change concerning the Constitutional Court was the decision to annul all Court decisions prior to when the Fundamental Law entered into force. At one level, this would have made sense, but the Constitutional Court had already worked out a sensible new rule for the constitutional transition by deciding that in those cases where the language of the old and new constitutions was substantially the same, the opinions of the prior Court would still be valid and could still be applied. In cases in which the new constitution was substantially different from the old one, the previous decisions would no longer be used. Constitutional rights are key provisions that are the same in the old and new constitutions – which means that, practically speaking, the Fourth Amendment annuls primarily the cases that defined and protected constitutional rights and harmonised domestic rights protections to comply with European human rights law. With the removal of these fundamental Constitutional Court decisions, the government undermined legal security with respect to the protection of constitutional rights in Hungary. This regime is not merely illiberal, in not respecting human dignity, minorities' and individual's rights, the rule of law, and separation of power, but it is not democratic either, because the outcome of the elections are not uncertain anymore.[66] It can be considered as a 'pseudo-democracy'.[67]

[65] Steven Levitsky and Lucan Way argued: 'Clearly, Hungary is not a democracy. But understanding why requires a nuanced understanding of the line between democracy and autocracy … Orbán's Hungary is a prime example of a competitive autocracy with an uneven playing field'. S Levitsky and L Way, 'How autocrats can rig the game and damage democracy' *The Washington Post* (4 January 2019).

[66] The OSCE election observers were very critical of both the 2014 and 2018 elections, noting that 'overlap between state and ruling party resources', as well as opaque campaign finance, media bias, and 'intimidating and xenophobic rhetoric' also hampered voters' ability to make informed choices. See www.osce.org/odihr/elections/hungary.

[67] 'The test of a democracy is not whether the economy is growing, employment is rising, or more couples are marrying, but whether people can choose and replace their leaders in free and fair elections.

ii. Poland

Poland's 1989 negotiated democratic transition preceded Hungary's, but it followed Hungary's constitutional backsliding after the Law and Justice Party (known as PiS), led by Jarosław Kaczyński, regained parliamentary elections in October 2015, after two years of rather unsuccessful governing between 2005 and 2007. PiS returned to power with a vengeance, committed to reshaping the entire constitutional system in order to create a 'new and virtuous Fourth Republic'.[68] This meant a systemic and relentless annihilation of all independent powers that could check the will of the ultimate leader. In that respect, his role model is Viktor Orbán.[69] In 2011, PiS published a long document, authored largely by Kaczyński himself, on the party's and its leader's vision of the state. The main proposition of this paper is very similar to the one that Orbán described in a speech in 2009: a well-ordered Poland should have a 'centre of political direction', which would enforce the true national interest. This illiberal counter-revolution of both Orbán and Kaczyński is based on a communist rejection of checks and balances, as well as constitutionally entrenched rights.[70]

Unlike FIDESZ in 2011, PiS lacks the constitution-making or amending two-thirds majority in the Polish Parliament. Therefore, it started to act by simply disregarding the liberal democratic Constitution of 1997. The first victim was the Constitutional Tribunal, which already in 2007 had struck down important elements of PiS' legislative agenda, including limits on the privacy of public officials to be screened and freedom of speech and assembly.[71] In Orbán's playbook, which is seemingly followed by Kaczyński, the other major target has been the media, the civil service and the ordinary courts. As opposed to Hungary, for the dismantlement of liberal democratic institutions PiS does not really needed a new constitution because what they have been doing since the autumn of 2015 is already a de facto change to the Constitution through sub-constitutional laws. Wojciech Sadurski calls this a constitutional breakdown resulting in an authoritarian regime.[72]

This is the test that Hungary's political system now fails. When Viktor Orbán and his Fidesz party returned to power in 2010 with a parliamentary supermajority, they set about destroying the constitutional pillars of liberal democracy … By the 2014 elections, Orbán had rigged the system. Yes, multiparty elections continued, but his systematic degradation of constitutional checks and balances so tilted the playing field that he was able to renew his two-thirds majority in parliament with less than a majority of the popular vote (and did so again in 2018) … Orbán has transformed Hungary into not an illiberal democracy but a pseudo-democracy'. See L Diamond, 'How Democratic Is Hungary?' *Foreign Affairs* (September/October 2019).

[68] Kaczyński's conspiracy theory that liberal intellectuals had become allies to former communists led to a final split of the opposition movement Solidarity. The new government parties both in Hungary and Poland rejected '1989' for the same reasons: namely, absence of radicalism of the democratic transition, and for the alleged liberation of the communist elites. See I Krastev, 'Walesa, Gorbatchev and Freedom's End' *The New York Times* (14 March 2016).

[69] As early as 2011 Kaczyński announced he wanted to create 'Budapest in Warsaw. cf J-W Müller, 'The Problem with Poland, *The New York Review of Books* (11 February 2016).

[70] Wojciech Sadurski, professor of constitutional law, who was the Kaczyński brothers' fellow student at the University of Warsaw in the 1970s, says that this vision bears a striking resemblance to the writings of Stanislaw Ehrlich, their joint ex-Marxist professor. See W Sadurski, 'What Make Kaczyński Tick?' (2016) *I•CON*.

[71] About the battle for the Constitutional Tribunal see TT Koncewicz, 'Polish Constitutional Drama: Of Courts, Democracy, Constitutional Shenanigans and Constitutional Self-Defense' (2015) *I•CON*.

[72] See W Sadurski, *Poland's Constitutional Breakdown* (OUP, 2019). Professor Sadurski's harsh criticism of the democratic backsliding both PiS and the Polish government initiated several court procedures

III. CONCLUSION

In the first part of this chapter, I tried to answer the question, whether there is a genuine constitutional theory of 'illiberal constitutionalism'? I argued that the constitutional concept, which rejects liberalism as a constitutive precondition of democracy, cannot be in compliance with the traditional idea of liberal democratic constitutionalism. This concept has nothing to do with any majoritarian constitutional model based on the separation of power, or with political constitutionalism, or any kind of weak judicial review, and it misuses the concept of constitutional identity.

The second part of the chapter investigated the social, economic and political relations of illiberal societies. Regarding the first issue I found that there has been a very weak historical tradition of liberalism and modernisation in the East-Central European societies, and also the main driving force of the transition to liberal democracy was to reach the living standard of the West. The lack of success to achieve this goal, together with the accumulation of wealth by some former members of the communist nomenclature, and the failures of redistributive justice efforts were the reasons for disappointment also in the liberal democratic pursuits. Regarding the economic relations, the rise of economic inequality and the decline of social security and solidarity has paradoxically also been caused by the neoliberal economic policy of some of the illiberal political forces. These political actors have changed the entire political and constitutional structure into an illiberal system, mostly not based on their ideological conviction, but rather for the sake of building up and keeping an unrestrained power.

One of the reasons of the illiberal turn has been that there was a lack of consensus about liberal democratic values at the time of the transition. In the beginning of the democratic transitions in these new democracies, preference was given to general economic effectiveness over mass civic and political engagement.[73] The satisfaction of basic economic needs was so important for both ordinary people and the new political elites that constitutions did not really make a difference.[74] Between 1989 and 2004, all political forces accepted a certain minimalistic version of a 'liberal consensus', understood as a set of rules and laws rather than values, according to which NATO and EU accession were the main political goals. But as soon as the main political goals were achieved, the liberal consensus died,[75] and full democratic consolidation was never achieved.[76]

against him. See Oepn Letter in Support of Wojciech Sadurski, *Verfassungsblog* (6 May 2019) at https://verfassungsblog.de/stand-with-wojciech-sadurski-his-freedom-of-expression-is-yours/.

[73] Dorothee Bohle and Béla Greskovits state that East Central European democracies had a 'hollow core' at their inception. See D Bohle and B Greskokovits, *Capitalist Diversity on Europe's Periphery* (Cornell University Press, 2012).

[74] See UK Preuss, *Constitutional Revolution. The Link Between Constitutionalism and Progress* (Humanities Press. 1993) 3.

[75] See I Krastev, 'Is East-Central Europe Backsliding? The Strange Death of the Liberal Consensus' (2007) 18 *Journal of Democracy* 56–63.

[76] J Dawson and S Hanley, 'What's Wrong with East-Central Europe? The Fading Mirage of the Liberal Consensus', (2016) 7 *Journal of Democracy* 20–34.

An initial failure of the 1989 constitutional changes – namely the disproportional election systems – also contributed to the electoral victories of Fidesz in Hungary and PiS in Poland, the illiberal autocratic forces. In the case of Fidesz 53 per cent vote share resulted in 68 per cent in 2010 and even less than the majority of the votes again into two-thirds of the seats in Parliament both in 2014 and 2018. This made Fidesz able to change the entire constitutional system after its electoral success in 2010. PiS in 2015 got 51 per cent of the seats in the Sejm for 37.6 per cent of the votes, and again the majority of seats for 43.6 per cent of the votes in 2019. With their absolute majority they were able to enact laws – after packing the Constitutional Tribunal, even unconstitutional ones – without any need to consult with their parliamentary opposition.

According to some authors, the prospects for liberal constitutional democracy in the newly independent states of Central and Eastern Europe following the 1989–90 transition were diminished by a technocratic, judicial control of politics, which blunted the development of civic constitutionalism, civil society, and participatory democratic government as necessary counterpoints to the technocratic machinery of legal constitutionalism.[77] Adherents to this viewpoint argue that the legalistic form of constitutionalism (or legal constitutionalism), while consistent with the purpose of creating the structure of the state and setting boundaries between the state and citizens, jeopardised the development of participatory democracy.[78] In other words, legal constitutionalism fell short, reducing the Constitution to an elite instrument, especially in countries with weak civil societies and weak political party systems that undermine a robust constitutional democracy based on the idea of civic self-government.[79]

One can raise the hypothetical question whether earlier and more inclusive or participatory constitution-making processes could have ensured the durability of democratic institutions. Indeed, there was no early constitution making, and the amendment processes that happened instead were not participatory. Neither Poland nor Hungary enacted a new constitution right after the democratic transitions of 1989. Instead, in both countries as a result of the Round Table negotiations, between the representatives of the authoritarian communist regime and their democratic opposition, the illegitimate legislature was put in the position of enacting modifications to the old Stalinist constitutions. This was done based on the elite agreement without any consultation with the people. In the case of Poland, the 1952 Constitution was slightly modified in April 1989, while in Hungary the 1949 Constitution was comprehensively amended in October 1989. This was called by Andrew Arato 'post-sovereign' constitution-making.[80] It is true that in Poland, the democratically elected

[77] See this argument in P Blokker, *New Democracies in Crises? A Comparative Constitutional Study of the Czech Republic, Hungary, Poland, Romania and Slovakia*, (Routledge, 2013). Also Wojciech Sadurski argued that legal constitutionalism might have a 'negative effect' on new democracies and might lead to the perpetuation of the problem of both weak political parties and civil society. See W Sadurski, 'Transitional Constitutionalism: Simplistic and Fancy Theories' in A Czarnota, M Krygier and W Sadurski (eds), *Rethinking the Rule of Law After Communism* (CEU Press, 2005) 9–24.

[78] See R Albert, 'Counterconstitutionalism' (2008) 31(1) *Dalhousie Law Journal* 4.

[79] cf Sadurski (n 77) 23.

[80] A Arato, 'Post-Sovereign Constitution-Making in Hungary: After Success, Partial Failure, and Now What?' (2010) 26 *South African Journal of Human Rights*.

Parliament enacted the so-called Small Constitution in 1992, but it only changed some elements of the state organisation, without the ambition of becoming the final closing act of the democratic transition. The new constitution was only enacted in 1997, again without participatory process, like a referendum. In Hungary, a similar new constitution-making effort failed in 1996, and even though the content of the 1989 comprehensive amendment fulfilled the requirements of a liberal democratic constitution, its heading had 1949 in it. With that Fidesz, after its electoral victory in 2010, could claim the need to enact a new constitution of the democratic transition and it had all the votes to enact what it wanted. But this was not a liberal democratic constitution anymore.

One can only speculate whether an earlier and more participatory constitution-making process would have been a guarantee against backsliding. There is nothing to suggest that an earlier and more participatory constitution-making process would have prevented the populist turn. As the Polish example proves, even the existence of a liberal democratic constitution does not constitute an obstacle against backlash. In my view, those proponents of participatory constitutionalism who argue that with participation backsliding it would not necessarily have happened, do not sufficiently take into account the rise of populism and the lack of civic interest in constitutional matters, due to poor constitutional culture.[81]

So far, the liberal elite seems to be unable to protect the liberal democratic ideals, which certainly indicates that the special historical circumstances require a longer period of time to build up a liberal democratic political and constitutional culture. But the democratic backsliding is not a proof of the failure of liberal democracy altogether,[82] as illiberal leaders and their court ideologists want people to believe.

[81] See similarly the critical reviews on Blokker's book (n 77) by Jiri Priban and Bogusia Puchalska in ICONnect. 'Book Review/Response: Paul Blokker, Jiri Priban and Bogusia Puchalska on Civic Constitutionalism' *Int'l J. Const. L. Blog* (10 September 2013).

[82] In their book, Ivan Krastev and Stephen Holmes argue that the fact that liberal democracy had no alternative in 1989, and East Central European countries had to imitate the Western model, contributed to the success of illiberalism in the region. See I Krastev and S Holmes, *The Light that Failed: A Reckoning* (Allen Lane, 2019). In my view, there was both a rightist nationalistic and a leftist democratic socialist alternative during the post-communist transition, and copying the West could only be harmful if there would have been equally promising scenarios available. After all, the imitation of liberal democracy in Germany after World War II and in Spain, Portugal and Greece did not result in illiberal regimes.

12

Majority Rule, Democracy and Populism: Theoretical Considerations

WOJCIECH SADURSKI*

THE WORLDWIDE GROWTH of populism around the world – from Poland to the Philippines, from Hungary to the US – has triggered the development of an influential idea that populism is a majoritarian corrective to what is an increasingly non-majoritarian model of democracy, with a number of 'counter-majoritarian' devices built into it, such as the powers of courts and tribunals, of regulatory agencies and central banks, or supranational norm-producing institutions not accountable to the majority of a given polity. Under this perspective, populism is a desired and desirable majoritarian-democratic modification of excessively non-democratic liberalism. As Cas Mudde put it succinctly, 'In essence, the populist surge is an illiberal democratic response to decades of undemocratic liberal policies'.[1]

But how democratic is majority rule itself? The question may be seen as silly: after all, democracy *is* majority rule. Certainly it is so with certain constraints and limitations built into it – for instance for the sake of the protection of constitutional principles not subject to everyday amendment by a simple majority – but these constraints and limitations *modify* the scope of the application of majority rule rather than *undermine* it in its very essence. Whatever else democracy means, the argument goes, it must begin with the recognition of majority will as determinative of the policies the government pursues. Take majority rule away from the centre of political life and you dismantle the very essence of democracy.

This is, in many respects, true. One cannot conceive of democracy simpliciter without the centrality of majority rule to it. But, as this short chapter will argue, the relationship between democracy and majority rule is more complex than such a simple proclamation might suggest. Majority rule, as a moral and political principle, is not self-justifying: it requires some good moral, principled justifications, and these justifications must resonate with those for democracy itself. In other words, we value majority rule *for some reasons*, and not as an inherently valuable idea,

* Challis Professor of Jurisprudence at the University of Sydney; Professor in the University of Warsaw.

[1] C Mudde, 'Europe's Populist Surge' (2016) 95 *Foreign Affairs* 25, 30.

and these reasons must be the same as that which we value in a democracy. The resonance between the *rationales* that can be provided for majority rule on the one hand and for democracy on the other is key to understanding the deep connection between majority rule and democracy. And an excavation of those deeper reasons both for the moral-political ideal of majority rule and for the political model of democracy must be sensitive to the fact that if a reason provided for the former (majority rule) is weak or questionable, it cannot figure in the justification for the latter (democracy) as allegedly supporting a connection between both concepts. And it is likely that some supports provided for populism rely precisely on such bogus grounds for majority rule. This at least will be the conclusion of this chapter.

The chapter will proceed in the following way. First, I will reflect upon the best rationales for the majority rule, and will eliminate some obviously non-persuasive rationales (such as efficiency, simplicity, and intuitive judgments). Secondly, I will argue that the strongest and the most persuasive rationale for majority rule relies upon the ideal of the political equality of all citizens, and that the best understanding of an ideal of political equality (supporting that of democracy) appeals to equality of political opportunity. Thirdly, I will argue that equality of political opportunity has some important institutional implications both at the stage of political deliberation and at the stage of actual collective decision-making. Fourthly, I will conclude that contemporary populism, with its unconstrained majority rule, plebiscitary model of politics, and 'winner takes all' blueprint, offends against the major institutional implications of equality of political opportunity, and thus departs from, rather than enshrines, a model of democracy based on certain morally attractive rationales for the majority principle itself.

I. RATIONALES FOR MAJORITY RULE: THREE NON-STARTERS

Let me first consider briefly, and equally briefly dismiss, the weakest of the arguments for majority rule, namely that it is so intuitively correct that it should be taken as self-evident. Indeed in today's practice, a great number of intuitively plausible procedures involve decisions by a majority: the laws passed by parliaments, the verdicts laid down by courts in panels composed of more than one judge, the election of a new pope by the conclave of cardinals, the regulations adopted by clubs and associations, the decision of faculty committees on controversial issues, as well as the informal decisions between friends as to where to dine together tonight.

But it is enough to make this argument explicit to see how tenuous it is because we may, almost instantly, produce a number of counter-examples, that is, the contexts in which majority rule is *not* adopted, not even intuitively or prima facie. In such contexts, postulating majority rule would sound inappropriate, for instance when unanimity is required (as in many jury systems or in some voluntary organisations practicing blackballing in the admission of new members) and, conversely, there are contexts in which only one person, or a few persons, are in a privileged position to make the decisions for the group: consider some of the decisions in a family, in the army, or in a church structure. In particular, in those circumstances where the rightness of the decision relies significantly upon the ascertainment of some empirical facts, relying on majority rule seems almost perverse. Consider the issue of establishing the criminal guilt of a particular public figure, such as in the once-notorious criminal trial of OJ Simpson in the US. It seemed that much of the general public held strong views about his guilt or otherwise, but to subject the verdict of the court to a national referendum would seem too absurd to seriously contemplate. For every instance in which we can claim that majority rule *intuitively* makes sense as a good collective decision-making procedure, we may counter it with an example where, equally intuitively, such a procedure would be nonsensical or grossly unfair. So no, majority rule cannot benefit from its alleged self-evident status. Or to put it more precisely: whoever claims that majority rule (as they do for so many other moral or political ideals) is 'self-evident' simply is unwilling or unable to produce any reasonable arguments for it.

In the same category as the argument that it is self-evident is the argument (produced here arguendo only as I am unaware of anyone making a serious claim for this rationale) that majority rule displays a certain elegant simplicity and thus is easy to apply in practice. Without more, it is simply not true that majority rule is 'simpler' to operationalise than, for example, the principle of one person's rule or that of unanimity. Finally, consider the third argument, namely that of efficiency. It *may* be thought that one of the main advantages of majority rule is that a decision supported by a majority will be likely to enjoy greater compliance in society than the minority-backed decision (or a single person's decision) simply because there will be a larger number of those who substantively agree with the decision (having voted for it or for the representatives who enacted that decision) than those that oppose it. To be sure, 'efficiency' so understood (through the prism of a probability of compliance) would be even higher in cases of unanimity, but then we know that finding actual consensus for politically salient and difficult decisions is impossible so a requirement of unanimity would in fact give even a very small minority a power of veto over collective decisions, which is anathema to majority rule.

But the efficiency-based argument for majority rule is implausible for a number of reasons. First, there are many, much more effective methods of ensuring compliance: for instance, by establishing mass terror and cruel penalties for non-compliance. Surely, efficiency does not render these methods legitimate in any way. Secondly, it is question-begging to suggest that those who support a given rule at the stage of contemplating it, that is, ex ante, are particularly likely to comply with it once it is in force, that is, ex post. Perhaps they are or perhaps they are not: it seems to be a merely contingent and context-sensitive proposition, much too weak upon which to hang such a momentous principle as that of majority rule.

II. THREE CONCEPTIONS OF POLITICAL EQUALITY

As these three putative rationalisations turn out to be non-starters, we have to search elsewhere. Fortunately, it is not too mysterious or controversial to claim that majority rule enforces an ideal of the *political equality* of citizens. Jeremy Waldron put it well by saying that majority rule 'attempts to give each individual's view the greatest weight possible … compatible with an equal weight for the views of each of the others'.[2] Waldron adds, 'the method of majority decision also accords maximum decisiveness to each member, subject only to the constrain of equality. In this sense, majority-decision presents itself as a *fair* method of decision-making ….'[3] Even a cursory reflection suggests that a correlative of the idea that every person should count equally (in her votes, choices, preferences, etc) is the idea that the majority should prevail. Any other decision-making rule seems to grant more weight to some people rather than others.

But the relationship between majority rule and equality is far from obvious. Consider this simple example, meant to reduce ad absurdum the very principle of majority rule: 'imagine you, me, and a third person in the same room. Two of us decide that you should give your life to serve us. Is our decision legitimate, do you have an obligation to obey simply because we were a majority within the room? … On the face of it, you can claim that our decision "enslaves" you and denies you "equal status" with us'.[4] But this example, provided by Robert A Burt, shows that the decisions taken by the majority may lead to drastically inegalitarian results. This is clear and banal: the majority can exploit, oppress, and even enslave a minority. But this does not show that the majority rule itself does not presuppose *some* egalitarian moral principles. So the true question is what kind of equality is sufficiently attractive and at the same time so plausibly connected to majority rule that it can be seen to underlie the very ideal of democracy?

A good way to proceed is by drawing some distinctions between (what may be called) different currencies of equality in a political context; in other terms, different answers to the question: equality of *what*? In this regard, Ronald Dworkin's distinction between equality of impact and that of influence is most helpful. The difference is that while the impact a person makes is defined as 'the difference he can make, just on his own, by voting for or choosing one decision rather than another', the person's influence is defined as 'the difference he can make not just on his own but also by leading or inducing others to believe or vote or choose as he does'.[5] When applied to the considerations of political equality, impact is not a useful category, claims Dworkin. In vertical relations (as between the citizens and officials) 'equality of impact' is just unthinkable (how can an ordinary citizen have an equal impact to that of the President?), while in the horizontal dimension (as between different citizens) it is not ambitious enough because it cannot account, for instance, for the importance of freedom of speech, of political associations, etc in contributing to political equality. This would seem to leave 'equality of influence' as the only attractive interpretation of political equality. Not so, warns Dworkin: to try to bring about equality of influence (in the sense just defined) would offend against a great number of important features of a liberal-democratic society. We would need to equalise not only those sources of influence which most of us consider to be illegitimate (such as unequal financial means), but also those which are perfectly legitimate sources

[2] J Waldron, *The Dignity of Legislation* (CUP, 1999) 148.
[3] ibid 148, emphasis in original.
[4] Robert A Burt, *The Constitution in Conflict* (Harvard University Press, 1992) 27–28.
[5] R Dworkin, *Sovereign Virtue* (Harvard University Press, 2000) 191.

of unequal influence, and which are based on the fact that 'some people are more politically motivated or trained or charismatic than others'.[6] If we tried to equalise some of the sources of *these* inequalities (that in turn lead to unequal influence), it 'would conflict with other egalitarian goals'[7] and, more generally, it would be 'incompatible, even in principle, with other attractive aspects of an egalitarian society'.[8]

My own solution to this unwholesome dilemma is to postulate a third conception, building upon the inadequacies of equality of political influence and of impact: the ideal of equality of *political opportunity* – an ideal which Dworkin fails to consider, and yet which seems to be particularly well suited to addressing the specific concerns raised by him. Let us recall the main reason why he urges us to reject the ideal of equality of influence: it is because the ideal is unable to discriminate between different sources of political inequality, some of which may be legitimate and others not. The ideal of equality of opportunity simpliciter (ie, not only with regard to *political* opportunities) can be presented, in a somewhat stylised manner, as occupying a space halfway between a purely formal equality of opportunity and the equality of effect, where the distinguishing criterion concerns the grounds of access to the means of satisfying the conditions regulating the distribution of a particular good. When only few such grounds matter for our judgment of equality of opportunity being satisfied (and they are thin and easily satisfiable; for instance, a citizenship in a given state) then we call (often disparagingly) such an ideal a purely 'formal' equality of opportunity because it is unacceptably blind towards the many grounds of unequal access that we know are significant. If, on the other hand, all possible grounds of unequal access count for a judgment of equality of opportunity, then such an ideal effectively collapses into equality of outcome, because any unequal outcome is taken to be a sufficient symptom that inequality of access was at play. An ideal of genuine equality of opportunity must be thicker than formal majority rule (because it must be sensitive to a large number of factors which makes access for some of us more difficult due to the conditions required in a distribution of desired goods), but at the same time stop short of collapsing into equality of outcome because it must acknowledge that some causes of unequal outcomes are (or at least, may be) legitimate.

If equality of opportunity is viewed in this way, then it resonates with the argument leading Dworkin to reject the ideal of equality of influence (in the Dworkinian strict sense of 'influence' contrasted to 'impact', as already mentioned). Indeed, one of the main reasons for rejecting this ideal is that some of the imaginable ways of equalising political influence would lead to highly unattractive results. The manner in which Dworkin depicts the ways that these results would be unattractive evokes the perversity of some ways of equalising the factor of qualification under the equality of opportunity analysis. For instance, one way of rendering influence more equally distributed would be by limiting the resources that people can freely spend on the means of politically influencing others. In a less inegalitarian society

[6] ibid 196.
[7] ibid.
[8] ibid 198.

than our societies are, this would be contrary to the value of equality, Dworkin says, because it would 'prevent some people from tailoring their resources to fit the lives they wanted though leaving others, who had less interest in politics, free to do so'.[9] To translate this scenario into the language of equality of opportunity, such a result would plainly and obviously offend against equality of opportunity because it would equalise the outcomes conditioned by inequalities that can be traced fully to choice-sensitive factors.

I have elaborated on the model of equality of political opportunity, in some detail, elsewhere.[10] I will not rehearse the argument here. All I want to assert is rather modest and, hopefully, uncontroversial: that equality of political opportunity is an attractive and plausible interpretation of political equality; not that it is *the* interpretation. Under this assumption, we may now say that our task is to see whether equality of political opportunity is congruent with majority rule. And, theoretically, there are three possible answers to this question: (1) that there is no such congruence at all; (2) that there is an automatic and simple congruence (whereby implementing the majority rule procedure always gives effect to equality of political opportunity); and (3) that the majority rule procedure gives effect to political opportunities but only under some conditions and constraints. It is position (3) that I am going to advocate for, and in the process, specify the conditions and constraints that must be adopted if majority rule is going to promote rather than frustrate the ideal of equality of political opportunity.

III. EQUALITY OF POLITICAL OPPORTUNITY AND MAJORITY RULE

How is the principle of equal political opportunity related to majority rule? The relationship is only indirect. Equal political opportunity applies quite obviously to the *deliberation* stage of the political process. It is with respect to this stage that the concept of equal influence, as articulated by Dworkin, was generated in the first place (and indeed, it was *defined* in terms that are only relevant to the deliberation stage), and the ideal of equal political opportunity enters the stage as a remedy to the defects that the ideal of equal influence had. But it is worth asking: an opportunity *to* what sort of deliberation should be equalised, under the principle of equal political opportunity? From an individual point of view, the purpose of deliberation is, it would seem, two-fold: first, it is to acquire the best ideas and information for oneself; second, to affect the views of other people. Equal political opportunity is, obviously, mainly concerned with the second function of deliberation because it is the second function which is relevant to political *influence*. What can equal opportunities, with regard to this function, be the opportunities *to*? I suggest that the object of the opportunities (that is, the benefit which the opportunities are targeted towards) is located somewhere half-way along the spectrum between being able to communicate one's views and being able to actually convince the audience to one's views. The former good is too weak: a mere ability to communicate is too thin a good for people wanting to attain it, without more. The latter good, an ability to convince one's audience

[9] ibid 197, fn omitted.
[10] See W Sadurski, *Equality and Legitimacy* (OUP, 2008) 77–91.

to one's own views, is too strong to lend itself for equalisation. The likelihood of convincing the audience is largely dependent upon the audience's *prior* views, which belongs to the category of factors outside of the speaker's control and are not the subject of 'equalisation' in the equal-opportunity discourse. This is due to the various causes of disagreement between people that can neither be explained by a lesser rationality of some people than others, nor by the fact that those different views are merely rationalisations of people's narrow interests, which themselves are different. John Rawls labelled these reasons 'the burdens of judgment'.[11] In Rawls's view, those causes include the fact that the evidence bearing on a case is often conflicting and complex; there may be disagreement about the weight of different kinds of considerations that are relevant; concepts are often vague, indeterminate, and subject to hard cases; our experiences are different and these differences affect the way we assess evidence, etc. Even assuming that listeners are fully receptive to the speakers' arguments, a number of decisive factors of the effectiveness of persuasion are, and should remain, outside the powers of speakers.

So if the ability to communicate one's views is too weak, and the ability to convince one's audience is too strong, to constitute the object of political opportunity, what is a plausible in-between these two extremes? It can probably be characterised as the ability to effectively get one's own political message across to the audience one wants to reach. Anything less is an insignificant good; anything more is implausible because it engages the factors which are, and should remain, outside the control of a person making such a communication. But it is quite plausible to claim that equal political opportunity in the deliberation stage of collective decision-making should mean equality of opportunity to reach one's desired audience, to get one's message across, to be heard. Elsewhere, I have argued at some length about the attractiveness of the ideal of an 'equal opportunity to be heard' as a plausible and meaningful interpretation of equalising expressive opportunities.[12] I will not summarise my conclusions here, beyond stating that the ideal of equality of opportunity seems to effectively capture the various policies aimed at equalising access to the media of political communication because '(1) being heard by one's audience is an important social good which many people seek, and (2) we may legitimately and meaningfully aim to reduce the impact of those factors which are outside the speaker's control and affect his or her access to the means of effective speech'.[13]

So much for equal political opportunity at the stage of political deliberation. When it comes to the stage of actually making a decision, we obviously do not need to find an interpretation of the good of political *influence*: by voting (either in elections or referenda or in parliament) we do not try to *influence* anyone but we actually take the decision. It is too late to talk about influence here, and thus also about political opportunities to affect decisions. Majority rule is therefore an institutional embodiment of what Dworkin called 'equal impact': the weight that a person's vote has (taken on its own) in collective decision-making. But there is an indirect connection between equal impact and equal political opportunity which parallels the connection

[11] J Rawls, *Political Liberalism* (Columbia University Press, 1993) 54–58.
[12] W Sadurski, *Freedom of Speech and Its Limits* (Kluwer, 1999) 73–98.
[13] ibid 85.

between voting and deliberation. If there was no vote at the end of the road (for instance, if the decision was to be taken by a benevolent dictator who would tolerate all sorts of deliberations but did not care about them one bit when taking decisions, or if the decisions were taken by lottery), then deliberation would be meaningless. It could, and perhaps would, still go on, but the motivations that people would have to participate in first-order deliberation (about the decisions to take), as opposed to second-order deliberation (about how to change the decision-making process) would be nil. So equality at the output stage of the system radiates upon the importance of equality at the input stage, so to speak. There should be a degree of continuity in the egalitarian credentials of all stages of the process, if equality is our true reason for settling upon majority rule.

It is important to be clear about this connection. It is not my argument that if we violate the principle of equality of political opportunity at the deliberation stage then the effect of equality of impact at the stage of decision-taking (in the institutional form of majority rule) is in some way damaged or compromised. It is rather the case that the adoption of majority rule at the final stage reveals the sincerity of our intention to give effect to the principle of equality in the political process, and therefore the integrity of this intention demands that we try to respect it at earlier stages of the process as well, especially since these earlier deliberative stages inform the substance of the decision itself.

IV. POLITICAL EQUALITY, MAJORITY RULE, AND POPULISM

This has been a roundabout way of arguing that the connection between democracy and majority rule is mediated by the principle of equality (a particular conception of it: equality of political opportunity), but if that is the case, then certain institutional conditions are necessary for equality of political opportunity to occur, both at the deliberation stage and at the stage of decision-making. I cannot embark on a detailed account of what such institutional conditions might be like because it would call for an extended blueprint of an institutional theory of democracy – a much too ambitious task for this short chapter. But one can sketch such a design. At the deliberation stage, we need to have institutions in place which assure true freedom of expression, of assembly, of association, etc. These rights and freedoms are necessary for deliberation to be truly authentic, unconstrained, and unaffected (or at least not affected too dramatically) by the disparities in resources of social power. Not just the absence of censorship or prior restraint (in other words, not just the Hyde Park model of freedom of speech), but also forms of equalising access to public media may be considered as essential. There should also be precautions against the various forms of silencing dissident, unpopular, or minoritarian points of view. If some people are too harassed or intimidated to make their viewpoints known in public, deliberation is reduced, and so is equality of political opportunities. There should also be, occasionally, protections for anonymity in order to shield members of unpopular minorities against reprisals, social punishments, and opprobrium. There needs to be a culture of openness and toleration, under which expressions of new and unusual ideas are not instantly met with anger and intolerance.

In turn, at the decision-making stage, the institutional structures of equality of political opportunity should assure proper consideration of various proposed options and variants of the final decision, the possibility for unconstrained persuasion of the unconvinced and the undecided, room for compromise and 'splitting the difference', patience in respecting the rule of '*audiatur et altera pars*'. There should be room for consultation, various audits and statements by experts, social learning from the 'best practices', etc. All this can be implemented in deliberative legislatures. As Jeremy Waldron observes, 'simplicity and haste are the obverse of responsible legislative decision-making, precluding, as they do, the time and space for thought and speech – and, within the realm of speech, for successive rounds of proposal, reply, amendment, and reconsideration that genuine engagement with legislative issues requires'.[14] Representative democracy, at its best, offers scope and opportunities for representatives of the people to listen carefully to each other, and allows them to be convinced by an argument employed by their adversaries. Waldron beautifully describes this process as 'a way of transforming impulse and sentiment into judgment, by and for the sake of the interplay of representative with constituent, constituent with party, representative with representative, representative with party, party with party, and citizen with citizens generally ….'.[15] Reflection and careful deliberation are the cornerstones of the representative model; as Cass Sunstein puts it, reconstructing the views expounded in the Federalist Papers, 'Representatives would have the time and temperament to engage in a process of reflection. … [They] would be free to engage in the process of discussion and debate from which the common good would emerge'.[16]

As one can see, both at the stage of deliberation and decision-making, modern populists do not act in accordance with the template just sketched. Populists' regimes are impatient with freedom of speech for minorities, in particular unpopular and stigmatised minorities. And at the stage of decision-making, they dislike slow, patient deliberation in parliaments, preferring a 'winner takes all', plebiscitary model of politics, under which the leader (usually, a charismatic leader) obtains a carte blanche for the period of his or her parliamentary or presidential term. As Nadia Urbinati put it well, populists in power favour 'a politics of partial inclusion that justifies a discriminatory use of state power against the minority'.[17] Hence, the antipathy of modern populists to the separation and dispersion of powers that is seen as a constraint upon the political will of a homogeneous community; which it, naturally, is.

Contemporary populism comes in different shapes and sizes, and I have recently offered a rather detailed account of one particular version of a populist model of politics: being that practised in Poland after 2015.[18] But for all their differences and local eccentricities, all populisms have this common denominator: they abhor pluralism, minority rights, and constitutional constraints upon simple majority rule.

[14] J Waldron, *Political Political Theory* (Harvard University Press, 2016) 141, endnote omitted.

[15] ibid 142.

[16] CR Sunstein, 'Lessons from the American Founding' in CR Sunstein (ed), *Can It Happen Here? Authoritarianism in America* (HarperCollins, 2018) 57, 69.

[17] N Urbinati, 'Populism and the Principle of Majority' in C Rovira Kaltwasser, P Taggart, P Ochoa-Espejo and P Ostiguy (eds), *The Oxford Handbook of Populism* (OUP, 2017) 571, 586.

[18] W Sadurski, *Poland's Constitutional Breakdown* (OUP, 2019).

In these ways, they fail to implement equality of political opportunity which, as I had argued earlier in this chapter, infuses the procedure of majority rule with moral attractiveness and renders it meaningful. So if equality of political opportunity is the true rationale for majority rule-based democracy, populism is the opposite of democracy, so understood.

13

The Role of New Technologies in Deliberative Democracy

JOSÉ LUIS MARTÍ*

I. INTRODUCTION

IN 1962, WHILE the war in Vietnam was getting worse and student movements all around Europe and the US started to mobilise and fight for civil and social rights, freedom and democracy, Douglas Englebart, an engineer working in the mythical Stanford Research Institute (SRI) at Menlo Park, and better known later on for being the inventor of the mouse, wrote a seminal report for a complete new way of understanding the role of the nascent digital technology: 'Augmenting Human Intellect: A Conceptual Framework'.

The whole world was in those years immersed in a time of change. New social movements of protest, new political and philosophical ideas of radical democracy, feminism, and decolonisation, new artistic and cultural trends (such as the new jazz, rock and roll, a new way of understanding cinema, the irruption of television, etc), were emerging and spreading all around the planet. The real cultural globalisation started back then. But it was, above all else, the development of computerisation and digital technology which had the biggest transformative potential. It was an optimal time for dreams and unabridged imagination, two words that were omnipresent in politics and culture (just think of Martin Luther King and John Lennon). Everyone wanted to live in a better world. And it is not surprising that in that context the pioneers of digital technology were seeking exactly the same thing: how to change the world for the better. Englebart thought of his Research Report as the 'public debut of a dream'. As he stated in the abstract:

> This is an initial summary report of a project taking new and systematic approach to improving the intellectual effectiveness of the individual human being. A detailed conceptual framework explores the nature of the system composed of the individual and the tools, concepts, and methods that match his basic capabilities to his problems. One of the tools that shows the greatest immediate promise is the computer when it can be harnessed for direct online assistance integrated with new concepts and methods'.[1]

* Pompeu Fabra University.

[1] D Englebart, 'Augmenting Human Intellect: A Conceptual Framework', Report of the Stanford Research Institute (1962) ii.

Almost 60 years later, it is time to get back to Englebart's dream. New technologies have proven to have a great potential for being destructive of democracy and freedom. This is true. But they have also proven Englebart right. They have an enormous capacity to strengthen human intellect, both at the individual and collective level. And this is the exact key role that new technologies should have in our societies, not to mention in a deliberative democracy. Their central role must be that of augmenting human individual and collective intelligence to strengthen the quality and legitimacy of democracy and protect us from democracy's oldest enemy: domination.

In this chapter I will review the exact ways in which new technologies can play that role. As I will show, technologies are essential to protect us from the dangers they create themselves. The idea that new technologies in general, and AI in particular, is compromising our privacy and basic freedoms and may kill democracy is gaining visibility.[2] However, and let me be very clear on this, there is no way back from the digital revolution. Digital technologies are unavoidable. They are simply too good to give them away. On the other hand, the dangers they reinforce or reinvigorate always existed. Technology is certainly instrumental, for instance, to more sophisticated forms of domination. But domination is not new at all. And digital technologies are also instrumental to the cure of that malaise. The conclusion I suggest, however, is not that we need good applications of technology to fight against its wicked applications in order, so to speak, to remain in the same place. That would be enough as a justification. But my purpose in this chapter is not, so to speak, *defensive* of democracy and freedom. On the contrary, I am convinced that Englebart was fundamentally right in identifying digital technology as key to *augmenting our intelligence* and our capacity to deal with the many and complex challenges that are threatening our world today, and ultimately to strengthening democracy and making progress in our dreams of having a better world. Digital technologies have the potential for allowing democracy to take a big leap forward.

In the next section, I present the idea of deliberative democracy and explain why it is so important for us. I also mention some of the main threats against democracy which are leading some people to claim that democracy is in crisis. In section III, I briefly elaborate on the idea of collective intelligence and its importance

[2] H Rheingold, *Smart Mobs. The Next Social Revolution* (Basic Books, 2002); H Rheingold, *Net Smart. How to Thrive Online* (The MIT Press, 2012); J Lanier, *Who owns the Future?* (Simon & Shuster, 2013); J Lanier, *Ten Arguments for Deleting Your Social Media Accounts Right Now* (Henry Holt and Co, 2018); N Bostrom, *Superintelligence. Paths, Dangers, Strategies* (OUP, 2014); Z Tufekci, *Twitter and Tear Gas* (Yale University Press, 2017); D Helbing et al, (2017) 'Will Democracy Survive Big Data and Artificial Intelligence?' (2017) *Scientific American*; J Bartlett *The People vs. Tech. How the Internet is Killing Democracy (and how we save it)* (Random House, 2018); P Nemitz, 'Constitutional democracy and technology in the age of AI' (2018) *Phil. Trans. R. Soc. A.* 376; L Floridi et al, 'AI 4 People's Ethical Framework for a Good AI Society: Opportunities, Risks, Principles, and Recommendations' (2018) 28 *Minds and Machines* 689–707; F Pasquale, 'A Rule of Persons, Not Machines: The Limits of Legal Automation' (2019) 87(1) *George Washington Law Review* 1–55; C Álvarez Pereira, 'Digital for Life? The Blind Spots and Its Reframing for Desirable Futures', *IEEE 18th International Conference on Cognitive Informatics and Cognitive Computing*, manuscript (2019); D Innerarity, *Una teoría de la democracia compleja. Gobernar en el siglo XXI* (Galaxia Gutenberg, 2020); C Veliz, *Privacy Is Power. Why and How You Should Take Back Control of Your Data* (Transworld, 2020); F Pasquale, *New Laws of Robotics* (The Belknap Press of Harvard University Press, 2020).

to democracy. Finally, in section IV I review the major negative impacts that digital technologies are having on democracy, especially regarding the factors of its crisis, but I also provide several examples of how new technologies may strengthen the quality of our democracies and our governance.

II. DELIBERATIVE DEMOCRACY AND POLITICAL LEGITIMACY

Deliberative democracy is the ideal of democracy according to which legislative and governmental decisions in particular, and public decisions in general – with only a few exceptions – in order to be politically legitimate, should be taken as a result of a process of an ongoing public deliberation in which citizens must have been able to participate, directly or indirectly, as free and equals, arguing for their preferred solutions with the aim of, in Habermas' famous dictum, convincing others 'by the force of the better argument, and not by the argument of force'.[3] Under ideal conditions, we might assume, such public deliberative process should be conducive to large political consensus based on public reasons.[4] And, insofar as certain (not necessarily ideal) conditions are granted, some of which I come back to in the next section, these deliberation-based agreements and decisions may have epistemic value.[5]

However, this ideal of deliberative consensus based on public reasons, correctly understood, does not imply neither that actual political pluralism is bad or a sign of a failure,[6] nor that self-interest, or political strategic behaviour, or social protest and resistance, or concern for underlying imbalances of power, should be all ruled out or have no place in our democracies.[7] This ideal establishes a normative aspiration and provides a scalar standard that is very useful to assess actual institutions, processes and decisions from the point of view of democratic legitimacy.

[3] J Habermas, [1992] *Between Facts and Norms* (The MIT Press, 1996); see also C Nino, *The Constitution of Deliberative Democracy* (Yale University Press, 1996); A Gutmann and D Thompson, *Democracy and Disagreement* (Harvard University Press, 1996); J Bohman and W Rehg (eds), *Deliberative Democracy. Essays on Reason and Politics* (The MIT Press, 1997); J Elster (ed), *Deliberative Democracy* (CUP, 1998); J Cohen, 'Deliberation and Democratic Legitimacy' in A Hamlin and P Pettit (eds), *The Good Polity* (Blackwell, 1998) 17–34; J Fishkin and P Laslett (eds), *Debating Deliberative Institutions* (Blackwell, 1999); S Besson and J Luis Martí (eds), *Deliberative Democracy and Its Discontents* (Ashgate, 2006); JL Martí, *La república deliberativa. Una teoría de la democracia* (Marcial Pons, 2006); JL Martí, 'The Epistemic Conception of Deliberative Democracy Defended' in S Besson and JL Martí (eds), *Deliberative Democracy and Its Discontents* (Ashgate, 2006) 27–56; J Mansbridge et al, 'The place of self-interest and the role of power in deliberative democracy' (2010) 18(1) *Journal of Political Philosophy* 64–100; J Mansbridge and J Parkinson, *Deliberative Systems* (CUP, 2012); C Lafont, *Democracy Without Shortcuts: A Participatory Conception of Deliberative Democracy* (OUP, 2020).

[4] J Rawls, 'The Idea of Public Reason Revisited' (1997) 64(3) *The University of Chicago Law Review* 765–807; JL Martí, 'Pluralism and consensus in deliberative democracy' (2017) 20(5) *Critical Review of International Social and Political Philosophy* 556–79; Lafont (n 3).

[5] Nino (n 3); Martí, *La república deliberativa* (n 3); D Estlund, *Democratic Authority. A Philosophical Framework* (Princeton University Press, 2007); H Landemore, *Democratic Reason. Politics, Collective Intelligence and the Rule of the Many* (Princeton University Press, 2013).

[6] Martí (n 4).

[7] Mansbridge et al (n 3); JL Martí, 'The Right to Protest and Contestation in a Deliberative Democracy' in Martin Belov (ed), *Peace, Discontent, and Constitutional Law: Challenges to Constitutional Order and Democracy* (Routledge, 2021).

The expression 'deliberative democracy', as Jon Elster rightly put it, has two components: the democratic part, which requires full, direct or indirect, inclusion of all affected capable adults in public decision-making; and the deliberative part, which requires such decision-making process to start giving everyone the possibility to exchange reasons and arguments in favour or against certain positions and engage in a process of reciprocal argumentation with the aim of convincing others, and a disposition to be convinced by those others if they show better arguments.[8] It would be a mistake to presume that an indirect citizen engagement, one that comes mediatised through political representation, is necessarily worse or a second-best in terms of the ideal of full inclusion regarding any direct form of engagement, such as a plebiscitary government run by permanent referenda. For the same reason, it would be a mistake to presume that, in real conditions, any departure from idealised forms of impartial argumentation and rational debate, such as some varieties of self-interested mobilisation or social protest, would be equally wrong or a second best. Social protest and even some exercises of civil disobedience might actually pay an excellent service to the ideal of deliberative democracy, since they may be the most adequate form of stating some demands and criticising social and political injustice. They should actually have a central role in any well-functioning deliberative democracy.[9]

What the ideal of deliberative democracy centrally requires from our real-life political systems is the introduction of fully inclusive and quality deliberative processes in our public institutional decision-making, particularly in our legislatures,[10] as much as the existence of a healthy non-institutional public sphere in which an ongoing, unrestricted, open, quality public deliberation should take place.[11] Moreover, as Habermas develops in his view of the Two-Track Model, these institutional and non-institutional, or formal and informal, realms of deliberative democratic politics should have an adequate articulation so that democratic representatives and public officials, on the one hand, and ordinary citizens, on the other, may engage in turn in some deliberative relationship. Asking citizens to review what their representatives do every four years in the elections, and cast their votes, as a way of approving or refusing their performance, is not enough. Generalised, effective, and fluid mechanisms of engagement and deliberation between ordinary citizens and politicians and officials are also needed in order to ensure that formal deliberations taking place within the institutional system, both intra- and inter-institutions,[12] are really representative of people's interests and views.

As contemporary republicans also committed to the ideal of deliberative democracy like Philip Pettit have clearly shown, democratic political legitimacy requires the existence of sufficiently widespread and effective mechanisms of public contestation and popular control through which the people can exert their ultimate

[8] Elster (n 3); see also Habermas (n 3); Gutmann and Thompson (n 3).

[9] Martí (n 7).

[10] J Bessette, *The Mild Voice of Reason: Deliberative Democracy and American National Government* (The University of Chicago Press, 1994).

[11] J Habermas, [1962] *The Structural Transformations of the Public Sphere* (The MIT Press, 1989); Habermas (n 3).

[12] JK Tulis, 'Deliberation Between Institutions' in Fishkin and Laslett (eds) (n 3) 200–11.

sovereign power over what their representatives decide and do. Democracy does not require, not even ideally, that everyone take part in every public decision-making.[13] There is nothing wrong in the delegation of power to certain individuals and institutions, which is not only desperately needed in our big-scale and increasingly complex democracies, but also a good articulation of our overall interests, not all of which are strictly political. But the political representation that emerges from such delegation in order to be democratic and legitimate must always ensure that the law, and by extension public decisions in general, falls under the ultimate control of the people, so that such law can be deemed to protect the people's interests and views and be expressed on the people's terms.[14] Only then can we properly say that our democratic institutional representative system realises the ideal of self-government to a sufficient degree. Hence, the importance of public contestation and protest, and the crucial role that social movements and civil associations such as NGOs and other kinds of public watchdogs play, is absolutely central. There must be institutional mechanisms of public deliberation, participation and engagement, as the Habermasian Two-Track Model requires, but also a healthy and vivid public life able and always ready to react, contesting and protesting public decisions when injustice arises.[15]

This theory of deliberative democracy, in its republican form or in any other variant, is the dominant view today in democratic theory, even if, of course, there is much discussion about how to finely understand it, especially on the details. But, insofar as democratic legitimacy is concerned, the ideal of deliberative democracy is largely regarded as the correct one. It is important to understand here the crucial distinction, nowadays almost unanimously accepted by all political philosophers, between justice and legitimacy.[16] There are different ways to draw such distinction, but let me use what I take to be the clearest and most economic one, even at the price of being over-simplistic, which is also largely compatible with most of the different understandings: legitimacy and justice are, simply put, the two realms of normative political philosophy that aspire to answer two different normative questions, respectively.

Justice aspires to answer the question of what is the correct thing to decide and do for political institutions in a particular situation or as an instance of general lawmaking. In order to know whether a decision or law is just, we need to revise its content, its substance, and assess it against a certain substantive standard. Such a substantive standard must be provided by a particular theory of justice. Different

[13] P Pettit, *Republicanism. A Theory of Freedom and Government* (CUP, 1997); P Pettit, *On The People's Terms. A Republican Theory and Model of Democracy* (CUP, 2012).

[14] Pettit *On The People's Terms* ibid.

[15] ibid.

[16] For a clear and compelling drawing of such distinction, see Pettit (ibid) Ch 1; see also T Christiano, 'Democracy' *Stanford Encyclopedia of Philosophy* (2006) at https://plato.stanford.edu/entries/democracy/; T Christiano, *The Constitution of Equality* (OUP, 2008); T Christiano, 'Authority' *Stanford Encyclopedia of Philosophy* (2012) at https://plato.stanford.edu/entries/authority/; JL Martí, 'Democratic Legitimacy and the Sources of International Law' in S Besson and J d'Aspremont (eds), *The Oxford Handbook on the Sources of International Law* (OUP, 2017) 724–45; S Besson and J Luis Martí (eds), 'Legitimate Actors of International Lawmaking. Towards a Theory of International Democratic Representation' (2018) 9(3) *Jurisprudence* 504–40.

theories of justice may overlap and therefore agree on their assessment of a particular decision or law, but no assessment is possible unless you presuppose at least one particular theory of justice. As it happens, however, theories of justice endorsed by different people usually differ in their evaluations of concrete decisions or laws, and this is because they provide different, sometimes very different, substantive standards for the evaluation. And this fact, the fact of deep and pervasive disagreement about the preferred theory of justice, is actually the first of the two main reasons why the question that legitimacy is concerned with is of the highest importance.[17]

Legitimacy aspires to answer the question of who (and how) should make the public decisions and laws, perceived as a, at least partially, content-independent question. Thus, regardless of the content of such decisions and laws – with perhaps some exceptions – we may ask whether the person or institution who made them had the right to do so and whether they used the right mechanism and followed the right procedure. In a world characterised by such pervasive disagreements about justice, it turns out to be of the utmost importance that we can at least agree on who should be given the right to rule and under what circumstances such person or institution may legitimately exert such a right, in a way that is mostly independent of our respective and differing substantive theories of justice. Thus, the theory of legitimacy aspires to provide such a mostly content-independent[18] normative standard that allows us to assess whether a particular decision or law was made by the right person or institution following the right procedure and in the right circumstances.

Previously I said that the pervasive fact that we deeply disagree about what justice requires gives us a reason to care about political legitimacy. We cannot be indifferent to who makes public decisions and how, since depending on who that person is, they will make decisions that we may regard as just or unjust. The second reason is that, independently of the justice or injustice of public decisions, we should not be indifferent to who (and how) makes public decisions, that is, decisions that apply to us all and that, in one way or another, are taken in our name. This is because we care about being able to run an autonomous life, both at the individual and collective level. We all have this experience at the individual level. No matter how right others' paternalistic decisions over our lives may be, we give value to the fact of being able to make our own decisions, including the capacity of making our own mistakes, in what regards the way we run our lives, especially when third parties are not involved. The same applies to the collective level, with the additional feature that in that area third-party affectation is always the case, unless unanimous agreement is obtained. No matter how right others' paternalistic decisions might be over our public life, over our living together, we give value to the fact of being able to collectively make our

[17] Marti, 'Democratic Legitimacy and the Sources of International Law' (n 16); Besson and Marti (n 16).

[18] In the text I say that a legitimacy standard must be 'mostly content-independent', or that such standard must allow us to assess particular decisions and laws regardless their content with 'perhaps some exceptions'. The reason for these caveats is that some political philosophers argue that legitimacy requires some very basic substantive justice as a precondition. Thus, an authority that makes a decision that grossly violates human rights, such as committing a genocide, can hardly be regarded as a legitimate authority, or at least such a decision should not be considered legitimate. Not everybody agrees on this, however. But I do not need to take sides in this chapter, and thus I prefer to leave this point open.

own decisions, including the capacity of making our own collective mistakes. This is, finally, nothing other than the idea of self-government, which we in modern times connect to the idea of democracy. As I discuss in the next section, such an idea of self-government must be also connected with the increasingly important notion of collective intelligence.

It is important to notice, however, that democracy in general, and not only this particular deliberative understanding of it, is in crisis in our present world.[19] Several factors are threatening the future of democracies, some of which are being stimulated by the emergence of digital technologies. Let me simply mention the most important ones. First of all, democracy, as a form of self-government, can only survive insofar as citizens believe in it and trust in the democratic institutions that support it. But we are living in times of a significant breach in social and political trust as well as of a decline in the levels of support for democracy as the best political regime.[20] In the eyes of many scholars and ordinary citizens the representative bridge between representative bodies and political parties and the citizenry is broken. This is why many speak about a crisis of representation, rather than a crisis of democracy. Another major problem that is connected with the latter, perhaps it even derives from it, is the emergence of populism all around the world.[21] Let me be very clear: populism is not a form of democracy. It has nothing to do with direct or participatory democracy or with empowering the people. It is actually the opposite of that. Populism today is, and has always been in our history, just a strategy of some elite to manipulate the people and use it to throw away the ruling elite. Such populist elite has never intended to empower the people, but to empower itself and remain in power as long as possible. This is true of Perón, and Berlusconi, and LePen, and Salvini, and Trump, and Bolsonaro, and any other commonly accepted example of populism.

Still an additional threat to democracy, which also connects to the former two, is that of fake news and polarisation. This phenomenon is occurring in every democracy and is quickly eroding our common forums and spaces of plural deliberation in the informal public sphere. This is one of the factors of democratic crisis that is more closely related to the emergence of digital technologies. A fourth major concern for modern democracies is the mismatch between the most important challenges and dangers that our political systems must face, such as climate change, global health – including the fight against the pandemics – nuclear security, global inequalities and injustice, among others, the protection of human rights, and the political resources that nation states may mobilise. We are in need of more effective global political solutions, whether they come either from brand new global democratic institutions or from qualitatively better forms of global cooperation among democratic states. Finally, and as I discuss in greater detail in the last section, we are living with

[19] Y Mounk, *The People vs. Democracy. Why Our Freedom Is in Danger and How To Save It* (Harvard University Press, 2018); S Levitsky and D Ziblatt *Hoe Democracies Die* (Crown, 2018); A Przeworski, *The Crises of Democracy* (Harvard University Press, 2019).

[20] RS Foa, and Y Mounk, 'The Danger of Deconsolidation: The Democratic Disconnect' (2016) 27(3) *Journal of Democracy* 5–17.

[21] J-W Müller, *What is Populism?* (University of Pennsylvania Press, 2016).

unprecedented levels of global concentration of power in authoritarian regimes, like China and Russia, and in a few private corporations, like Google, Amazon, Facebook or Apple.

To conclude this section, let me summarise it by saying that deliberative democracy is the dominant conception of political legitimacy today, and that it requires, at least ideally, that public decisions and laws should be made as a result of a process of an ongoing public deliberation in which citizens must have been able to participate, directly or indirectly, as free and equals, arguing for their preferred solutions with the aim of convincing each other and achieving some general reason-based consensus. This ideal comes with a series of very important implications for our institutional design as well as for the way in which our democratic life in the public sphere is run, many of which I have tried to outline in this section. But it also faces important major threats on a more practical level that will probably require deep transformations in our democratic systems to deal effectively with them. Like many other scholars, I am convinced that the idea of collective intelligence that is presupposed by the notion of self-government should be the main source of energy for guiding such much needed transformations.

III. DEMOCRACY AND COLLECTIVE INTELLIGENCE (CI)

The idea of collective intelligence is far from being new. The Ancient Greeks were already familiar with it. Aristotle is credited for having explicitly defended the thesis of 'the wisdom of crowds' in his *Politics*,[22] although the same view was also defended by Demosthenes, Democritus, Protagoras, and Thucydides, among many others.[23] Many philosophers and social scientists across history, like Machiavelli, Spinoza, Condorcet, Rousseau, John Stuart Mill, Dewey, Hayek, Rawls, and Habermas, have been aware of the power of collective intelligence (CI). Despite this idea's long history, however, we still know very little about how CI works. More research about how groups of people can decide and act intelligently is needed. Fortunately, in the last few years we have seen an explosion in the literature on this topic.[24] We can actually

[22] Aristotle [1981] (4th century BC) *Politics* (Penguin); see also JL Martí, 'Aristóteles y la sabiduría de la multitud' (2018) 8 *Teoria Politica* 139–66.

[23] J Ober, *Mass and Elite in Democratic Athens* (Princeton University Press, 1989).

[24] See for instance P Levy, *L'Intelligence Collective: Pour Une Anthropologie du Cyberspace* (Editions La Decouverte, 1994); Rheingold, *Smart Mobs. The Next Social Revolution* (n 2); Rheingold, *Net Smart. How to Thrive Online* (n 2); J Surowiecki, *The Wisdom of Crowds* (Little Brown, 2004); L Hong and S Page, 'Groups of Diverse Problem Solvers Can Outperform Groups of High-Ability Problem Solvers' (2004) 101(46) *Proceedings of the National Academy of Sciences of United States* 16385–89; C Sunstein, *Infotopia: How Many Minds Produce Knowledge* (OUP, 2006); S Page, *The difference. How the Power of Diversity Creates Better Groups, Firms, Schools* (Princeton University Press, 2007); B Noveck, *Wikigovernment. How Technology Can Make Governments Better, Democracy Stronger and Citizens More Powerful* (Brookings Institution, 2009); B Noveck, *Smart Citizens, Smarter State* (Harvard University Press, 2015); Landemore (n 5); T Malone and MS Bernstein (eds), *Handbook of Collective Intelligence* (MIT Press, 2015); G Mulgan, *Big Mind. How Collective Intelligence Can Change Our World* (Princeton University Press, 2018); T Malone, *Superminds. The Surprising Power of People and Computers Thinking Together* (Little Brown, 2018).

say that CI has emerged as a new entire field of interdisciplinary research, where philosophers, mathematicians, social scientists, biologists, and computer scientists collaborate to try to understand under what exact circumstances groups of individuals may develop and exercise their cognitive capacities.[25]

As it happens with most social concepts, especially at the early stages of our study of them, the concept of CI is controversial and diverse definitions have been provided. All of them agree that CI refers to a certain general capacity of groups that, based on certain cognitive components, allows them to make collective decisions and take collective action that may be regarded as rational or non-arbitrary. As Howard Rheingold emphasised, this capacity generally emerges from certain conditions of coordination, cooperation, and collaboration.[26] In addition to that, as we will see in the next section, and as Englebart made clear from the very beginning, CI may be largely strengthened or augmented by the use of new technologies.

Some definitions of CI are very broad, such as the one popularised by some of the seminal works in this area by Thomas Malone: collective intelligence is just the result of 'groups of individuals acting collectively in ways that *seem* intelligent'.[27] Intelligence, for Malone, must be understood as 'the ability to solve problems well' and it seems obvious that groups can have that too.[28] If a group meets certain basic conditions that allow it to have such ability, at least apparently, they become a 'supermind'.[29] By using such a minimalist and broad understanding, Malone intends to keep neutral regarding the controversial technical notion of intelligence and the very rich philosophical disputes around the idea of collective action and group agency.

Others endorse more precise definitions. Mulgan, for instance, defines collective intelligence as 'any kind of large-scale intelligence that involves collectives choosing to be, think, and act together', so for him, CI 'is in two senses a concept about choice: *who* we choose to be and *how* we choose to act'.[30] Interestingly, this act of choice may be conscious or unconscious. As the literature of social choice emphasised from the 1950s onwards, 'some mechanisms allow individual choices to be aggregated in a socially useful way without requiring any conscious collaboration or shared identity'.[31] This connects with a quite generalised assumption in the literature: namely, groups of individuals may develop CI even if all their members are unaware of it. But most scholars of CI share the further assumption that certain specific kinds of groups governed by certain specific kinds of rules and systems, and under some specific conditions that foster collaboration, may generate higher forms of CI, especially when they make use of the new technologies to create some combination of humans and machines.

[25] Malone and Bernstein (n 24) 1–13.

[26] Rheingold, *Smart Mobs. The Next Social Revolution* (n 2); Rheingold, *Net Smart. How to Thrive Online* (n 2); see also Noveck, *Wikigovernment* (n 24); Noveck, *Smart Citizens, Smarter State* (n 24) and Mulgan (n 24) for more developed analyses of how these collaborations may emerge.

[27] Malone and Bernstein (n 24) 1; see also Malone, *Superminds* (n 24) 20.

[28] Malone, *Superminds* (n 24) 8.

[29] ibid 20.

[30] Mulgan (n 24) 14–15.

[31] ibid 15–16.

These are what Mulgan refers to as 'hybrid assemblies',[32] or what Rheingold calls 'virtual communities',[33] or what Benkler simply calls 'networks'.[34]

When we speak about CI we are attributing to groups of individuals a feature that is normally attributed to some individuals. It is important to notice that, even if we attribute some elements or some degrees of intelligence to certain kinds of non-human animals, the highest forms of individual animal intelligence that we know are exclusive of humans, and more specifically of human beings that develop their conditions of living an autonomous life, that is, of living their lives under cognitively informed, structured free choices or judgements, some of them of a second order kind.[35] There are many and diverse conditions of autonomy, but they certainly include some level of training or education, some basic wellbeing, and some basic conditions of dignity and self-respect. Thus, even if groups may definitely *seem* to have some kind of collective intelligence, as Malone rightly points out, it is far from obvious that they *really* have it, at least in the same sense that human autonomous individuals do. This is why the first relevant question turns to be under what conditions or requirements groups may really develop some level of intelligence.

In my view, the idea of CI presupposes, first of all, some form of group or collective agency, some form of common mind, as some authors have called it, which is certainly thicker than Malone's minimalist definitional requirements. Philosophers have been discussing for more than 30 years now about how such an idea of group agency might be understood.[36] And we do not need to take sides for any of the views advanced by them in particular. But all of them include some basic conditions regarding the rules that explicitly or implicitly govern the group and allow it to count as having a collective will, as well as being able to make decisions and act collectively. These would be, for instance, rules designating *who* is allowed to make decisions in the name of the group and *how*, that is, under what conditions, or through which procedure, individual preferences might be aggregated into social or collective ones. And other rules that determine under what condition certain features may be attributed to the whole group (as when we talk of collective actions, or collective intentions, or group responsibility). As I say, all these different types of rules might be just implicit, in which case the existence of certain cultural norms of coordination, cooperation and collaboration and certain participatory attitudes distributed within the group become crucial, as Rheingold rightly notes.[37] The idea of group agency is very complex from a

[32] ibid 27–30 and Ch 18.

[33] Rheingold, *Smart Mobs. The Next Social Revolution* (n 2) and Rheingold, *Net Smart. How to Thrive Online* (n 2) Chs 4 and 5.

[34] Y Benkler, *The Wealth of Networks: How Social Production Transforms Markets and Freedom* (Yale University Press, 2006); Y Benkler, *The Penguin and the Leviathan. How Cooperation Triumphs Over Self-Interest* (Crown Business, 2011).

[35] On the idea of second order decisions, see C Sunstein and E Ullman-Margalit, 'Second Order Decisions' (1998) *John M. Olin Program in Law and Economics Working Paper 57*.

[36] See, for instance, P Pettit, *The Common Mind. An Essay on Psychology, Society and Politics* (OUP, 1993); C List, and P Pettit *Group Agency* (OUP, 2011); AS Roth, 'Shared Agency' *Stanford Encyclopedia of Philosophy* (2017) at https://plato.stanford.edu/entries/shared-agency/.

[37] Rheingold, *Smart Mobs. The Next Social Revolution* (n 2) and Rheingold, *Net Smart. How to Thrive Online* (n 2).

philosophical point of view. It is sufficient for us now to say that what exact kinds of rules are needed in order to have a group agency remains an open question.

Even if we still do not know much about the specific conditions in which groups may develop their shared agency and their CI, and therefore decide and act more autonomously maximising the ability to make the correct choices, it is clear that this notion of CI is intrinsically linked to the ideal of deliberative democracy and self-government that I described in the previous section. In other words, if we want our democracies not only to be minimally legitimate, but also decide and act intelligently, that is, make better decisions and laws, enact better policies, and, ultimately, govern themselves better, we must achieve a better comprehension of how CI works, which includes a question about under what epistemic conditions groups as large as political communities can make those intelligent choices.[38] What is more, if the factors that lead some people to speak about the crisis of democracy and the crisis of representation that were summarised at the end of the last section are taken into consideration, it is even more important that we care more about the specific ways in which CI might be empowered.

And it is true that we do not know enough in this area and much more interdisciplinary research is needed. But we know quite a lot after 25 centuries of thinking about 'the wisdom of crowds'. Let me summarise some of the things we know, which will be of much help for my assessment of the role that technologies may play in strengthening deliberative democracy and augmenting our CI in the next section.

First of all, we know that groups may have the ability to make right decisions under the right conditions. This is so because of several factors. Let me group all these factors under three categories, which I will refer to as three different powers of CI. The first and most basic power may be called the power of aggregation – it has also been called 'the miracle of aggregation' – which is the one we know better. As Aristotle already famously noticed,

> the many, who are not as individuals excellent men, nevertheless can, when they have come together, be better than the few best people, not individually but collectively, just as feasts to which many contribute are better than feasts provided at one person's expense.[39]

A group of people, especially a large one, may outperform, in solving certain kinds of problems or making certain kinds of decisions, any individual or even a subset of the best members of such group. There are different factors that explain this phenomenon. One is the so-called 'law of the big numbers', or Bernoulli's Theorem, after the Swiss mathematician who developed the first complete mathematical proof, in *Ars Conjectandi* (1713), of an insight previously given by Gerolamo Cardano in the sixteenth century. The idea behind such law or theorem is very simple. The expected value of something (for instance of tossing a coin or making a prediction) is much

[38] Nino (n 3); Martí, *La república deliberativa* (n 3); Martí, 'The Epistemic Conception of Deliberative Democracy Defended' (n 3); Estlund (n 5); Noveck, *Wikigovernment* (n 24); Noveck, *Smart Citizens, Smarter State* (n 24); Landemore (n 5); S Linares, *Democracia participativa epistémica* (Marcial Pons, 2017); Lafont (n 3).

[39] Aristotle (n 22) Book III, 1281a–1281b.

more accurate, the larger the number of iterations we introduce. Getting heads when tossing a coin has an expected value of 50 per cent. And the more times you toss the coin the more likely it is that you get heads 50 per cent of the time. When we apply this to predictions or to decisions, what happens is that some people may have very mistaken views, but, insofar as you have a group of people whose members are on average sufficiently knowledgeable, gross mistakes will tend to be marginal and neutralise each other, while the group will tend to make decisions that will be more likely to be correct.

Another parallel mechanism that fuels the power of aggregation is what Condorcet identified as the Jury Theorem. If you have a group of people, like a jury, deciding on whether a suspect is guilty or innocent, which is a binary question, and the individual competence of the group members is superior to 0.5, which means they have individually more than a 50 per cent chance of getting the right answer, and their votes are sincere and independent from each other, then the larger the group is the higher the probability that it makes a correct decision. Condorcet's Jury Theorem (CJT) has been validated from a mathematical point of view, even if it remains controversial to what extent it can be applicable to real world circumstances and whether its conditions really obtain.[40] For many modern political philosophers, like John Rawls, the CJT provides an argument in favour of very big groups of decision-makers, and therefore of big democratic majorities.

Finally, we find more recent attempts to explain the power of aggregation that derive it not only from how big the groups of decision-makers are, but also from how diverse or plural they are. This is the case, for instance, of Lu Hong and Scott Page's several theorems, such as the Diversity Trumps Ability Theorem, according to which a group of problem solvers randomly selected and who are sufficiently large and diverse will outperform in the ability of solving problems any subgroup of the most capable among them.[41] Even if these theorems, similarly to what happens with the CJT, only work under some specific conditions, such conditions seem to be less practically demanding than those of the CJT. Diversity is the key, and it is usually associated with the size of the group in the sense that large groups, especially if they are randomly selected, tend to be more diverse than smaller ones. These theorems have been revised and analysed in their application to democratic politics by Helene Landemore.[42]

What is important is that all these variants of the power of aggregation work on the basis of the mere addition of knowledge, preferences, or judgement, regardless of whether there is any specific interaction between the members of the group. The second power of CI, instead, derives from a very specific form of social interaction: namely, deliberation.[43] For many scholars in a long tradition that traces back

[40] Martí, 'The Epistemic Conception of Deliberative Democracy Defended' (n 3) 185–93; Martí (n 22); Landemore (n 5) 147–56; and Linares (n 38) 141–50.

[41] Hong and Page (n 24) and Page (n 24).

[42] Landemore (n 5).

[43] Habermas (n 3); Nino (n 3); Martí, 'The Epistemic Conception of Deliberative Democracy Defended' (n 3); Martí (n 22); Landemore (n 5); Linares (n 38); Lafont (n 3).

to Aristotle as well, deliberating before making a collective decision increases the probability of making a correct one, basically because it minimises the probability of error. Why is it so? There are several mechanisms that explain it. First of all, there is an information pooling effect. No single individual has access to all relevant information. Experts may have some technical knowledge that may be very relevant to make a particular decision, but ordinary citizens may also have had personal experiences regarding the topic to be decided or may have seen others having such experiences in ways that might be relevant to consider as well. Even experts may have individual access only to a fragment of the whole truth. Relevant knowledge and information tend to be dispersed across the society.[44] Giving the chance to decision-makers to pool all that information and knowledge before making the decision strengthens their individual and collective capacity to make the correct one. This pooling effect seems to have a clear aggregative dimension. In the end, the size and diversity of the group, again, may be key to strengthening the effect. But the pooling effect only happens if people have the chance to communicate with each other publicly, and it gets more robust when the group members are given also the opportunity to weigh and deliberate the different facts and viewpoints that emerge from this initial pooling.[45]

In addition to this information pooling effect, deliberation helps the decision-makers to refine their respective positions, since they first, must think carefully on their views and find the most compelling way to argue for them, and secondly, they may be helped by others to detect logical mistakes or other weaknesses in their reasoning by going through a deliberative process. Thus, deliberation may strengthen individual judgements and facilitate mutual and collective learning in a way that may strengthen the collective ability to make the correct decisions. Finally, and as a result of the latter, deliberation allows some people to change their minds and views, when they are exposed to others' arguments and ideas, that is, in the face of better reasons, and this in turn may lead the group to larger and more solid (more reason-based) consensuses or agreements, which correlate again with the group's ability to make correct decisions.[46]

There is a third power of groups that strengthens their CI and that emerges over time only when aggregation and deliberation have already taken place and reiterated their practice: this is what some people refer to as the power of collaboration and collective learning. When groups of people have a sustained practice of aggregating their views and deliberating together about them, they learn to trust each other in a different, particular way and to collaborate in a deeper form for mutual benefit.[47] They may organise themselves in more horizontal, networked, open structures and develop deeper ties based on trust and the common good, which are the basis for the highest levels of CI.

[44] Noveck, *Smart Citizens, Smarter State* (n 24).

[45] Martí, 'The Epistemic Conception of Deliberative Democracy Defended' (n 3); Martí (n 22).

[46] Martí, 'The Epistemic Conception of Deliberative Democracy Defended' (n 3); Martí (n 4); Martí (n 22).

[47] Benkler, *The Penguin and the Leviathan* (n 34); Rheingold, *Net Smart. How to Thrive Online* (n 2); Noveck, *Smart Citizens, Smarter State* (n 24).

In addition to these three powers, scholars such as Geoff Mulgan have made important contributions to our understanding of the organising principles of CI. Mulgan identifies five such principles:[48]

(1) The autonomous commons in the intelligence system, which relates to 'how much the elements of intelligence are allowed free rein, and not subordinated too easily to ego, hierarchy, assumption or ownership', and this in turns requires 'a dialectical approach to intelligence'.
(2) The balanced use of the capabilities or elements of intelligence, one that is suited to the tasks at hand. Mulgan identifies nine elements of CI: A live model of the world, observation, focus, memory, empathy, motor coordination, creativity, judgement and wisdom.
(3) The capacity to focus, that is, of 'attending to what really matters and not being distracted', which in turn has a diverse granularity in the sense that such focus needs to be tuned to the different scales at which it might be applicable.
(4) The group's capacity to be reflexive and recursive, that is, the ability to self-analyse, learn and adapt or change to improve.
(5) The capacity to integrate for action, that is, the ability to take coordinated action even in complex situations.

All these five 'principles' or 'elements' are susceptible to being strengthened, even if we need to do more research on the exact ways in which this is so.

Finally, there are several dimensions of CI that are critical to the possibility of sustaining and, if possible, strengthening such intelligence, to which scholars have paid due attention. On the one hand, there is the set of rules and procedures that make it possible, first, but also strengthen the group's ability to act together and make collective decisions, and this has been specifically studied by the philosophical literature on group agency.[49] On the other hand, there is the infrastructure, the resources, and other background conditions that may help groups to develop and increase their CI, and this has been studied more carefully by the experts on networks and collective or social minds.[50] In addition to that, there exist factors of identity and collective consciousness that may lead CI to its highest levels.[51] And, finally, there is the study of how new technologies may decisively contribute to strengthen or augment CI and bring it to totally unprecedented levels.[52] It is precisely to this last dimension that I turn in the next section.

In sum, CI remains an underdeveloped field of interdisciplinary research, despite its centrality in the way we conceive democracy, and how democracies should work

[48] Mulgan (n 24) 65–69.

[49] Pettit, *The Common Mind. An Essay on Psychology, Society and Politics* (n 36); List and Pettit (n 36); Roth (n 36).

[50] M Minsky, *The Society of Mind* (Simon & Schuster, 1987); Rheingold, *Smart Mobs. The Next Social Revolution* (n 2) and Rheingold, *Net Smart. How to Thrive Online* (n 2); Benkler, *The Wealth of Networks* (n 34); Benkler, *The Penguin and the Leviathan* (n 34); Malone and Bernstein (n 24); Malone, *Superminds* (n 24); Mulgan (n 24).

[51] Rheingold, *Net Smart. How to Thrive Online* (n 2); Mulgan (n 24).

[52] Englebart (n 1); Minsky (n 50); Rheingold, *Smart Mobs. The Next Social Revolution* (n 2) and Rheingold, *Net Smart. How to Thrive Online* (n 2); Noveck, *Wikigovernment* (n 24); Noveck, *Smart Citizens, Smarter State* (n 24); Malone, *Superminds* (n 24); Mulgan (n 24).

to be entirely legitimate and deal with the new factors of crisis mentioned in the previous section. However, I hope this outline may be enough to help us in the analysis of how new technologies may serve the values of deliberative democracy in the present world and in our immediate future.

IV. NEW TECHNOLOGIES AND DELIBERATIVE DEMOCRACY

After presenting what deliberative democracy is, and having summarised what we currently know about collective intelligence as the main factor of self-government in the context of a deliberative democracy, let me finally turn to the role the new technologies can play in the current world in regards to such deliberative democracy. And let me start by summarising some of the negative impacts that the current digital revolution is having on democratic politics in general. I am convinced that, all things considered, digital technologies will bring very positive transformations from which we will all benefit. But it is obvious that they have also negative consequences, some of which we are already noticing and which are well known by everyone. I will focus on five of such main threats or concerns.

First of all, new technologies have created an unprecedented threat on our privacy and civil and political liberties. Governments, as we learned through the NSA scandal after Edward Snowden's leak, as well as private companies, may spy on us and have access to large amounts of private and personal data in a way that may be incompatible with freedom and democracy.[53] Non-democratic regimes, such as China and Russia, are using technology, from AI and facial recognition to Internet censorship, invigilation and bots-led manipulation, to run unprecedented large programmes of social control, extending the domination they exert over their citizens to almost all levels of social and personal life. But the NSA scandal teaches us that democratic governments may exert this kind of monitoring and control as well. Even worse, private companies, such as Google, may have access to large amounts of information about everyone's life, including non-customers of the company, which means that they may enjoy high levels of power over many people.

Secondly, the Facebook and Cambridge Analytica scandal showed us how access to such large amounts of data may allow some people to manipulate the public, and more specifically, the people's political behaviour and preferences. Democracies will no longer be the same after the 2016 US Presidential Election. AI vested with big data analysis algorithms and machine learning technology inspired by behavioural science have proven to be effective in influencing people's judgements and emotions in ways that such people may be unaware of, just as subliminal advertisements could do in the past – which was actually the reason they were banned. New technologies in general may distort democratic politics and make possible new forms of political manipulation and domination from which we need to defend ourselves.

[53] Lanier, *Who owns the Future?* (n 2); Lanier, *Ten Arguments* (n 2); Tufekci (n 2); Bartlett (n 2); Veliz (n 2).

Thirdly, social media and networks are also playing a negative role in the functioning of democratic politics, and more particularly on public debate and the public sphere. Group polarisation, echo chambers, hyper-partisanship, misinformation, the spread of fake news, the rise of populism, all these phenomena already existed before the digital revolution, but social media platforms such as Facebook, Twitter, and Instagram have specially contributed to intensify all of them up to a very dangerous point for democracy.[54] Furthermore, there is no doubt that all these forms of disinformation are particularly damaging for the deliberative ideal of democracy described.[55]

Fourthly, the rise of new technologies has allowed an unprecedented global concentration of power. If we focus on AI, for instance, only a few governments and private corporations have sufficiently developed research to keep AI under their control. We are talking mostly about China, Russia, Google, Facebook, Apple, Amazon, and Microsoft, none of which has the general interest or the global common good high in their priorities. Regarding the tech private corporations now, the problem is not only that they are big, wealthy and powerful. The problem is that they are globally powerful to such extent that no government on Earth is able to bridle them and control what they do. Take the case of Apple and the tax scandal in Ireland at which even the European Commission was unable to discipline the company. Or take the case of Facebook and the US Congress. If we see democracy as the most legitimate form of government that was born to protect freedom and avoid public and private domination, these new super-powerful actors should be all subjected to the jurisdiction of a democratic global government able to impose some rules and duties and defend the people's rights. But there is no such thing yet.

Fifth, and finally, the current world, global and largely digital, is characterised by a growing complexity. The big challenges we face at a global level, from peace and security maintenance to climate change, and from socioeconomic growing inequalities to global health and the Covid-19 crisis, are all interrelated in a complex way. And technology is also contributing to make things even more complex. It is not only that technology itself is becoming too sophisticated for most ordinary non-techy people. In some cases, it is hard to understand even for experts themselves. Take the example of algorithms combined with machine learning that evolve in ways that make selections that even the computer scientists who initially coded those algorithms are no longer able to understand.[56] The existence of technical issues or domains is not new in the history of democracy. Ordinary citizens and politicians have often needed the help of experts in order to deal with some issues. Think of the examples of monetary

[54] LW Bennett and A Segerberg *The Logic of Connective Action. Digital Media and the Personalization of Contentious Politics* (CUP, 2013); Omidyar Group (2017) 'Is Social Media a Threat to Democracy', working paper, at www.omidyargroup.com/pov/2017/10/09/social_media_and_democracy/; Tufekci (n 2); Y Benkler, R Faris and H Roberts, *Network Propaganda: Manipulation, Disinformation, and Radicalization in American Politics* (OUP, 2018); Lanier, *Ten Arguments* (n 2); Bartlett (n 2); Veliz (n 2).

[55] S Chambers, 'Truth, Deliberative Democracy, and the Virtues of Accuracy: Is Fake News Destroying the Public Sphere?' *Political Studies* (2020), published online; S McKey, and C Tenove, 'Disinformation as a Threat to Deliberative Democracy' (2020) *Political Research Quarterly*, published online.

[56] Tufekci (n 2).

policy, investment policy, the health system, or the legal and judicial system. Technology is a new source of complexity, and one particularly hard to tackle from the point of view of deliberative democracy and CI.[57] If democracy requires ultimate effective popular control, as I argued in section II, we need the people to understand, first, how the object they are trying to have control over works. In depending on how AI for instance evolves, that might prove to be plainly impossible.[58]

These are five well-known major threats or negative impacts of technology for the future of our societies and democratic politics. But new technologies have a much more positive role to play in defending and strengthening deliberative democracy. In fact, as I said at the beginning of this chapter, digital technologies might be decisive in strengthening and augmenting individual and collective intelligence, which in turn might be the only possibility for humankind to face effectively major global challenges. Let me explore the most basic ways it may do so.

First of all, new technologies are also called information and communication technologies (ICTs). This is so because they are wonderful to help us solve one historical problem: the economy of information. Having access to relevant information and granting it to everyone has always been critical for democracy, but it has also been very costly. Such relevant information, as I said before, is usually dispersed across society. Sometimes it is very difficult to make it emerge, since those who have access to valuable information will have incentives to keep it for themselves, hidden from the eyes of others. Even the information that lies in the hands of the government or the administration has been traditionally unshared or remained hidden behind closed doors. New digital technologies, however, make full disclosure and total transparency possible for the first time at a very low cost.[59] And it is very important to notice that this mass of information may flow in both directions. On the one hand, governments may be more open and transparent than ever at no cost or very little cost. On the other, such governments may have access to invaluable information and data coming from their citizens, ranging from feedback, complaints, or suggestions and inputs of any kind, to automatic screening of citizens' preferences and judgements on very diverse issues.[60] Think for instance on what governments and administrations can do by using sentiment analysis techniques, which allow them to screen the social media platforms and anticipate the public's opinions or reactions regarding any particular issue or policy.[61] Or think on the data sharing movement, which attempts to convince people to share their day-to-day data with the administration to help it improve its services and policies in a number of ways. It is obvious that this data sharing may

[57] Innerarity (n 2).

[58] Bostrom (n 2).

[59] A Fung, M Graham and D Weil, *Full Disclosure. The Perils and Promise of Full Disclosure* (CUP, 2007).

[60] Noveck, *Wikigovernment* (n 24); Noveck, *Smart Citizens, Smarter State* (n 24).

[61] B Noveck, 'CrowdLaw: Collective Intelligence and Lawmaking' (2018) 40(2) *Analyse & Kritik* 359–80; D Sharma, M Sabharwal, V Goyal and M Vij, 'Sentiment Analysis Techniques for Social Media Data: A Review' in A Luhach, J Kosa, R Poonia, XZ Gao and D Singh (eds), *First International Conference on Sustainable Technologies for Computational Intelligence. Advances in Intelligent Systems and Computing*, vol 1045 (Springer, 2020).

come with associated risks of social control and privacy violations, but there are ethical ways to treat such data as a common good, very distant from the use private corporations are currently making of it, and subject to strict regulations, protecting the citizens' anonymity at the same time.

These are just two examples of the impressive technologies of big data analysis that relate, in turn, to machine learning and AI algorithms that may be an invaluable support to lawmaking and policymaking. As it happens, the most promising developments will probably come from the combination of different technologies and techniques, and they may have a great impact in fostering the power of aggregation that lies behind CI, and ultimately behind all forms of democratic decision-making. ICTs are not only good in allowing information to flow in all directions, but they are also amazing in aggregating really large amounts of information. Officials and public decision-makers are now able to process unprecedented amounts of relevant information that can significantly strengthen their ability to make correct decisions, that is, their CI.

This power of aggregation gets boosted also in respect to voting procedures. Electronic voting has been a reality for decades now,[62] making it possible to scale up democracy to, again, unprecedented levels. The security of e-voting systems has improved very significantly since the earliest experiments were done in the 1960s. And Blockchain technology is the last innovation that allows governments or private organisations to attain the highest levels of security ever known.[63] Several organisations, for instance, have already developed Blockchain-secured electronic voting systems in which citizens or customers may vote through their mobile phones very easily in seconds. Take the examples of the Votem platform (www.votem.com), or the Polys initiative from the Kaspersky Lab (www.polys.me). But think also on the Democracy Earth initiative (www.democracy.earth) that has been working for years in creating a global voting system that might potentially allow every human being on earth with an Internet connection to vote in a secured voting process. The potentiality of new technologies to aggregate people's preferences at a global scale also opens new opportunities to think on global democracy and articulate better responses to the global and complex issues that I mentioned above.

But new technologies are not only wonderful to fuel the power of aggregation. They can also pay great service to the power of deliberation. At a very basic level, ICTs are, again, communication technologies that allow people very far away from each other to communicate at no cost or very little cost. Citizens may now engage in political debate and public deliberation with other people all around the world. Many scholars have emphasised the importance that such a fact will have in what has been called the deterritorialisation of politics and democracy.[64] This would be a radical shift. Democratic politics has always been territorial in the sense that the scope

[62] D Gritzalis, 'Principles and Requirements for a Secure E-Voting System' (2002) 21(6) *Computers and Security* 539–56.

[63] A Ben Ayed, 'A Conceptual Secure Blockchain-Based Electronic Voting System' (2017) 9(3) *International Journal of Network Security and Its Applications*.

[64] Benkler, *The Wealth of Networks* (n 34); Rheingold, *Net Smart. How to Thrive Online* (n 2); M Castells, *Networks of Outrage and Hope* (Polity Press, 2012).

and the limits it had were defined by the limits of the territory where the relevant political community was based, either the polis or city, the region, the country, or even the transnational community. New technologies, however, have the potential to dynamite this dimension. If we need to decide whether to impose significant restrictions on car traffic in the city of Barcelona, why exclude from this debate citizens living in other cities nearby, or in other cities in Spain, or anywhere in the world? Any person might potentially have a relevant insight, a brilliant and innovative idea, or a personal relevant experience that she might want to share with the others to the benefit of collective deliberation and better decision-making. In the analogical world there was a physical limit to the kind of conversation that democratic politics presupposed. But in a digital world there is no such limit anymore.

This brings me to a second point concerning the power of deliberation. The traditional view says that deliberation is only genuine and fruitful if it happens between relatively small numbers of people. We all have the experience of sitting in a room with 50 other people for a meeting and having very little chance to talk or no chance at all. As a university professor I can say that the most fruitful academic debates or seminars with students happen between no more than 10 people around a table. Here the obstacle is not only physical, understood as spatial, but a structural difficulty to scale up genuine deliberation, a free exchange of arguments and counterarguments, to numbers of participants that go beyond 10. But what initially appears to be a difficulty, may easily become an opportunity. The literature on online deliberation has grown enormously in the last 15 years.[65] We now know more and more about how deliberation might be structured in online systems in a way that not only makes it possible for large amounts of people to deliberate in a genuine way, but actually maximises the quality of argumentation as well.

If you think carefully on it, it is easy to see why. Space and time are significant limitations in face-to-face deliberation. First of all, it is hard to find adequate spaces for large numbers of people to meet and deliberate. Secondly, and more importantly, if you try to have a sequential deliberation in a plenary assembly with many people, it may be impossible to give them all the chance to participate, and the meeting will inevitable turn boring, loose and unproductive after a few hours. But the online world does not suffer from spatial or time constraints. You may start a deliberation on an online platform in a forum-like structure and thousands of citizens may participate asynchronically, read and benefit from what others have said and also make their own large or tiny contribution. It all depends on how the design is done, on how deliberation is structured.[66] All it requires is the understanding that online deliberation

[65] T Davies and SP Gangadharan, *Online Deliberation: Design, Research, and Practice* (CSLI Publications, 2009); YM, Baek, M Wojcieszak and MX Delli Carpini, 'Online versus face-to-face deliberation: Who? Why? What? With what effects?' (2012) 14(3) *New Media & Society* 363–83; WB Towne and JD Herbsleb, 'Design Consideration of Online Deliberations Systems' (2012) 9(1) *Journal of Information Technology & Politics* 97–115; W Zhang, X Cao and MN Tran, 'The Structural Features and the Deliberative Quality of Online Discussions' (2012) 30(1) *Telematics and Informatics* 74–86; D Frierss and C Eilders, 'A Systematic Review to Online Deliberation Research' (2015) 7(3) *Policy and Internet* 319–39; L Cervone, *Digital Technologies for Deliberative Democracies. Models and Applications for Continuous Civic Engagement* (manuscript, Thesis submitted at the University of Bolonia, 2017).

[66] Davies and Gangadharan (n 65); Baek, Wojcieszak and Delli Carpini (n 65); Towne and Herbsleb (n 65); Zhang, Cao and Tran (n 65).

has its own rules and properties. It may be as genuine as small group face-to-face deliberation, but it simply achieves its results in a different form. There exist several successful examples of how to organise quite good online political deliberation, such as the online platform Better Reykjavik[67] in Iceland, designed by the Citizens Foundation, or the Platform Decidim[68] in Barcelona. The most important shift when you turn online is that deliberation must be regarded as ongoing and very long-term, and also that contributions might come in very different forms and qualities: sometimes in the form of long, well-grounded written interventions, other times in the form of very short, but decisive and highly influential comments.

We need to learn more, however, about how to maximise the quality of online deliberation and do it in a way that remains compatible with really large numbers of participants. Would it be possible to organise a long-term deliberation with one million people? Or with the 47 million Spanish citizens? Or with the population of the whole planet? The most important challenge is to discover better ways to structure argumentation in a way that machine learning and AI may help us to identify who is making similar arguments in separate discussions and which arguments gather more support and emerge as stronger than others. And there are currently several efforts being done in this direction by several research groups in the world.[69] If you could organise thousands of smaller, first level online discussions, and then use digital technology to scale up those conversations to second-level, wider ones, identifying quickly the kind of arguments and counterarguments that emerge similarly at both levels, you might then easily escalate this model to a number of levels, and therefore reach a potentially quasi-infinite number of participants. The spectacular progress that AI is making in recent years in the area of natural language analysis allows us to predict that this will be possible very soon. And the next challenge will be then to find out which are the optimal conditions at which such hyper-deliberation may take advantage of dispersed knowledge, distinct talents, different points of views and creativity, etc; in one word, of CI.

These comparative advantages of online deliberation are not a panacea. We still face huge difficulties in avoiding group polarisation, fake news and debate manipulation through social media platforms, such as Facebook and Twitter. The most recent development is that the companies who own these platforms seem to be, for the first time, interested in improving the quality of the debate that they host, and avoid fake news and other forms of infoxication. Achieving a good quality of deliberation under controlled conditions in a well-designed public platform does not avoid the threats and interferences that privately controlled communications may introduce in the informal public sphere. But people will not stop using the existing technologies to communicate with each other from one corner of the planet to another. In fact, we are just at the beginning of a whole new era that will be characterised and structured

[67] https://reykjavik.is/en/better-reykjavik-0.

[68] https://www.decidim.barcelona/?locale=es.

[69] See, for instance, T Krauthoff, C Meter, M Baurmann, G Betz and M Mauber, 'D-BAS. A Dialogue Based Online Argumentation System', in S Modgil, K Budynska, and J Lawrence (eds), *Computational Models of Argument. Proceedings of COMMA 2018* (IOS Press, 2018) 325–26.

over such technologies. What we need is to learn more and faster about how digital technologies may work in favour of CI and not in detriment of it.[70] And, ideally, we should not leave that research in the hands of the few owners of the biggest social networks in the world, because, as I said, they have already accumulated too much power.

Finally, the area that remains more underexplored is the contribution that new technologies may make to foster the power of collaboration. The early visionaries of a hybrid CI, a collective intelligence that gets augmented and strengthened by the use of digital technologies, as in Douglas Englebart's dream, always thought that technology has the potential to incentivise human collaboration, disrupting the deepest overarching principle of our capitalist, modern societies – namely, self-interested individualism – and helping humans to find much better articulations for mutual cooperation under the structure of powerful, horizontal social networks.[71] And it is true that we already have some real examples that show that they might have been right all this time. Perhaps the stellar one is Wikipedia. But we are still making a very slow progress in understanding the real underlying principles that may extend the success of Wikipedia to all other areas of social and political life. Technologies themselves are developing as we discuss this, so it is difficult to discover all their real potential, while we still do not know where they will lead us. It is vital that we continue doing research on this idea of hybrid or tech-enabled CI.[72]

Let me conclude by mentioning a very promising new approach and methodology that is specifically oriented to do that, to research on how new technologies may help public authorities of any kind to make better laws or public decisions taking advantage of tech-empowered collective intelligence: this is the basic idea of CrowdLaw.[73] CrowdLaw is emerging as a new global movement of scholars, democratic theorists, public innovators, lawyers, etc, all committed to the aim of strengthening the quality of lawmaking and public decision-making, and at the same time its legitimacy, by using new technologies that can empower CI, under the assumption that, as we saw in the last section, relevant knowledge and adequate talents and skills are dispersed in our societies, and when adequately organised, they can decisively help us to improve our governance.

In conclusion, deliberative democracy is suffering many pressures today, many of which originate or become aggravated by the emergence of digital technologies. Some people even talk about a global crisis of democracy. And it is true that many people feel disengaged and very distant from democratic politics. But the truth is that

[70] Rheingold, *Net Smart. How to Thrive Online* (n 2).

[71] Englebart (n 1); Minsky (n 50); Rheingold, *Smart Mobs. The Next Social Revolution* (n 2) and Rheingold, *Net Smart. How to Thrive Online* (n 2); Benkler, *The Wealth of Networks* (n 34); Benkler, *The Penguin and the Leviathan* (n 34).

[72] Noveck, *Smart Citizens, Smarter State* (n 24); Malone and Bernstein (n 24); Malone, *Superminds* (n 24); Mulgan (n 24); P De Filippi and A Wright, *Blockchain and the Law. The Rule of Code* (Harvard University Press, 2018).

[73] https://crowd.law; Noveck, *Smart Citizens, Smarter State* (n 24); Noveck (n 61); V Alsina and J Luis Martí, 'The Birth of the CrowdLaw Movement: Tech-Based Participation, Legitimacy, and the Quality of Lawmaking' (2018) 40(2) *Analyse & Kritik* 337–58.

such technologies will not disappear, and they are not the only cause of this eventual crisis. On the contrary. We face too many and too complex existential threats today that are on an unprecedented scale. If anything can save the deliberative democratic legitimacy of our systems, that is precisely a wise use of digital technology. It is only that we need to know it better and develop it in the right direction. And yet, digital technologies must play not only a defensive role of democracy, as we know it, but also a transformative, creative one that help us to make democracy evolve into something new and better. It is time for humble learning and growth. All together now.

Part Three

Democracy and its Enemies

14

Is Democracy Still the Worst Form of Government Except All Others?

GIANFRANCO PASQUINO*

I. INTRODUCTION

'MANY FORMS OF Government have been tried, and will be tried in this world of sin and woe. No one pretends that democracy is perfect or all-wise. Indeed it has been said that democracy is the worst form of Government except for all those other forms that have been tried from time to time ….' Winston Churchill's long, duly elaborate sentence, pronounced 11 November 1947, has been and continues to be widely quoted, especially by those who want to praise democracy without being criticised. It is my opinion that this sentence should be more correctly interpreted as a sober English understatement of true appreciation for democracy. I am confident that Churchill himself would agree with my rephrasing the assessment, mind you, it was not his own assessment, he was reporting. Hence, he would probably state that certainly democracy has drawbacks and shortcomings. Nevertheless, it is the form of government that up to this day has clearly demonstrated it is able to function better than any known alternative. To be even more precise: all the alternatives that have been tried so far, and they are many, have proved to be worse than democracy, than existing democracies. In fact, it is interesting to remark that nobody among the many contemporary critics of democracy has gone so far as to propose a full-blown alternative. At the most, some improvements have been suggested to be introduced into the existing democratic frameworks, the most elaborate ones being the different forms of 'deliberative democracy'.[1] The only

* Alma Mater Studiorum Bologna. Gianfranco Pasquino is Emeritus Professor of Political Science at the University of Bologna. Former President of the Italian Society of Political Science (2010–2013), he is fellow of the Accademia dei Lincei. Co-editor of *The Oxford Handbook of Italian Politics* (2015), his most recent book is *Italian Democracy. How It Works* (2020).

[1] JS Fishkin, *Democracy When the People Are Thinking. Revitalizing our Politics Through Public Deliberation* (OUP, 2019); A Floridia, *From Participation to Deliberation: A Critical Genealogy of Deliberative Democracy* (ECPR Press, 2017).

exception that has been somewhat praised is represented by (the type of) populism suggested by some scholars[2] and practised by some political leaders (most recently, to the full, by Hugo Chavez in Venezuela).

It may be interesting to stress that many Western intellectuals, professors of law and political science, columnists, mass media operators and, of course, politicians frequently criticise their respective democratic regimes as well as, often, the very idea of democracy. At the same time, all over the world the opponents of non-democratic regimes courageously and obstinately carry out their dangerous struggle against non-democratic regimes exactly in the name of Western democracy. It is the democracy(ies) they have seen at work while being in exile in Paris or London, while working in some European countries, while studying at Oxford or Harvard, while watching CNN. Perhaps, one can remark that those 'democratic' opponents in non-democratic regimes are fighting in the name of the democratic *ideal*, while most of the problems identified by Western and non-Western critics concern the *reality* of existing democracies, their functioning, their performance, their capability to meet the citizens' expectations, to keep their promises.[3] The distinction between democracy as an ideal and really existing democracies (made most precisely and convincingly by Sartori in 1987)[4] must be kept in mind in order to avoid all kinds of analytical confusions. Is there a *crisis of* democracy as an ideal or are there *problems in* the working of really existing democracies? Would Winston Churchill suggest searching for a form of government transcending democracy or would he pragmatically point at all possible improvements to existing democracies (even those not in the Anglo-Saxon mould)?

In this chapter, I will first deal with the most difficult task of defining 'what is a democracy'. Then, on the basis of the definition I will attempt to classify the existing political regimes and to assess how many of them can be considered democracies and whether there have been significant negative developments in recent times. Next, I will explore whether the expression 'crisis of democracy' is justified especially in the light of the appearance of the populist challenge. Claiming that populism is not the only challenger because religious fundamentalism must be taken into consideration, my analysis will disentangle what is a *crisis* of the democratic ideal and what are the *problems* in the functioning of really existing democracies. Then I will turn to the thorny issue of the kind of damages that the populists may produce to the body of democracy. In the end, what one may want to call the litmus test is represented by the evaluation of democracy on the part of the 'democratic' citizens themselves. Even though the citizens may not necessarily be the best judges, because often they are carried away by circumstances and emotions, their opinions (must) carry a lot of weight. In a democracy it is up to them to decide how bad (or how good) is democracy as a form of government. It is also up to them to say whether more than 70 years after Churchill's statement, other forms of government may seem to be more appealing and are considered less bad than the democracy(ies) that are known.

[2] E Laclau, *On Populist Reason* (Verso, 2005); C Mouffe, *For a Left Populism* (Verso, 2019).
[3] N Bobbio, *The Future of Democracy* (Polity, 1987).
[4] G Sartori, *Theory of Democracy Revisited* (Chatham House Publishers, 1987), 2 vols.

II. DEMOCRACY, DEMOCRACIES, ADJECTIVES

An acceptable definition of democracy is required before proceeding to assess the strength and quality of contemporary democracies and them being the least objectionable of all forms of government. Rivers of words have been spilled upon a variety of definitions,[5] but a working definition is absolutely indispensable. Otherwise, scholars and analysts run the risk, some of them knowingly and deliberately, but no less guilty, of constructing a democratic straw man and to attribute to him all the shortcomings and diseases of a failing democracy. On the contrary, in order to see which democracies are being eroded, are in decline or have 'died' it is indispensable to define with some precision what is to be considered a democracy in the twenty-first century. There are plenty of confused, misleading, often manipulated definitions of what is a democracy. In many instances, some adjectives are added, such as, for instance, 'popular', 'guided', 'socialist', that thwart the true meaning and content of democracy (this is not the case of Collier and Levitsky in 1997 whose adjectives contribute to a better understanding of the variety of existing democracies) and make any analysis devoid of meaning and substance.[6]

To start with, scholars are, or ought to be, aware that resorting to the etymology, democracy as 'power of the people', is necessary, but insufficient. Rightly, we have all learned that both power and people require many specifications. To make a very long story short, most specifications have been formulated through time and most scholars have come to the conclusion that a regime may be considered democratic when it contains two composite elements: a cluster of rights and a set of institutional mechanisms and structures.[7] Without, on the one hand, civil and political rights and, on the other, free and fair elections, separation of powers, checks and balances and political accountability, no regime can be defined as democratic. Then, of course, all democratic regimes can be classified with reference to the way they respect, protect and promote civil and political rights, to the integrity of their electoral rules and procedures, to the existence of the rule of law, to the working of their institutions. Indeed, the issue of the quality of democracy deserves our attention both when dealing with specific political systems and in comparative perspective.[8]

Many analysts are willing to stress that for a democracy to come into being and to exist, regular elections must be held. While, of course, one can bluntly and correctly maintain: 'no elections no democracy', the opposite 'elections hence democracy' is not necessarily true. For a variety of reasons, in many authoritarian regimes elections have been held in the past[9] and even today some non-democratic regimes hold

[5] See G Sartori, *Democrazia e definizioni* (Il Mulino, 1957); G Sartori, *Democratic Theory* (Wayne University Press, 1962).

[6] D Collier and S Levitsky, 'Democracy with Adjectives: Conceptual Innovation in Comparative Research' (1997) 3 *World Politics* 430–51.

[7] Here, I deliberately avoid the issue of the socio-economic requisites of democracy. The analyses by Lipset (1994) and Huntington (1991) are both illuminating.

[8] For a preliminary attempt, see L Diamond and L Morlino, (eds), *Assessing the Quality of Democracy* (The Johns Hopkins University Press, 2005).

[9] G Hermet, A Rouquié and J Linz, *Des élections pas comme les autres* (Presses de la Fondation Nationale des Sciences Politiques, 1978); G Hermet, R Rose and A Rouquié (eds), *Elections Without Choice* (Palgrave, 1978).

elections. However, those elections are essentially neither free nor fair,[10] and their most important goal is definitely not that of transforming the regime into a democracy, but of acquiring some international legitimacy (and of obliging the opponents to come into the daylight to be apprehended and made harmless).

On my part, I strongly resist the temptation to call these regimes 'electoral democracies'.[11] Where elections are neither free nor fair and have no chances of leading to the replacement of those in office by a team of those in the opposition, one cannot speak of democracy, not even of an electoral democracy. Still, non-democratic elections can be looked at in two different ways. On one hand, they are a homage to a revered democratic practice performed in order expediently to meet some international standards (in some cases, successfully). On the other hand, though far from certainty,[12] the electoral process, electoral campaigns and electoral mobilisations may all be learning experiences. They may teach something about how to run political activities. They may stimulate the interest of all the citizens and may contribute to the weakening and discarding of a non-democratic regime.

Democracy as an ideal combines freedom with equality and puts the emphasis on political participation. Different degrees and combinations of freedom, equality and political participation give birth to different types of really existing democracies. From time to time, some scholars[13] emphasise that democracy as an ideal requires the existence of citizens who are highly informed and knowledgeable, have equal possibilities of affecting political decisions, are willing and capable of participating at any point in time and, some would add, nourish strong feelings of efficacy. None of these conditions is ever fully attained. Indeed, the ideal democracy is bound to remain a (distant) ideal because 'ideal' citizens simply do not exist or, in any case, are always a tiny minority. In practice, in a really existing democracy all citizens are free to decide how much energy and time they are willing to put into the acquisition of political knowledge. They are free to decide whether, when and how much they want to participate. The(ir) feelings of efficacy depend on too many uncontrollable factors, none of which has a place in the definition of democracy. By way of comparison, non-democracies do not want their citizens to be informed and knowledgeable. Indeed, they suppress and/or manipulate all kinds of information. Often, they either prevent the citizens from participating or oblige them to participate, that is, non-democratic regimes forcibly mobilise their citizens (subjects). For what is known of contemporary non-democratic regimes,[14] it would be almost impossible to find citizens who show feelings of efficacy to the understandable exception of those close to the rulers. Those who criticise democracy point to the very paradoxical situation in which the power

[10] A Schedler (ed), *Electoral Authoritarianism. The Dynamics of Unfree Competition* (Lynne Rienner, 2006).

[11] LF Diamond, *Developing Democracy. Toward Consolidation* (The Johns Hopkins University Press, 1999).

[12] Schedler (n 10).

[13] Recently CH Achen and LM Bartels, *Democracy for Realists: Why Elections Do Not Produce Responsive Government* (Princeton University Press, 2016).

[14] S Levitsky and L Way, *Competitive Authoritarianism. Hybrid Regimes After the Cold War* (CUP, 2012).

to elect the representatives and the decision-makers is exercised by poorly informed citizens whose political participation is volatile and whose sense of efficacy is quite limited, who will not be in a position to evaluate the performance of those in office and to enforce accountability. It is a poor consolation to say that in any case democratic citizens fare better than citizens/subjects in non-democratic countries and that they have the possibility of improving on all counts. A democratic regime populated by alienated and apathetic citizens is bound not to last.

A. Identifying and Measuring Democracies

Equipped with the two clusters of elements containing the rights of the individuals and the mechanisms and structures of the political system, it is now possible to proceed to the identification of the various political regimes and to their classification. Several organisations have proceeded to this type of exercise, for instance, Freedom House and, more recently, V-Dem. Because of the clarity and simplicity of the criteria utilised (that would have pleased Churchill), I have decided to rely on the data collected and presented by the Economist Intelligence Unit that are being used to elaborate a Democracy Index. Five components concur with the definition of the Democracy Index: (1) electoral process and pluralism; (2) civil liberties; (3) the functioning of government; (4) political participation; and (5) political culture. On this basis, *The Economist* has codified four types of political systems: full democracies, flawed democracies, hybrid regimes, and authoritarian regimes as follows:

Full democracies are nations where civil liberties and fundamental political freedoms are not only respected but also reinforced by a political culture conducive to the thriving of democratic principles. These nations have a valid system of governmental checks and balances, an independent judiciary whose decisions are enforced, governments that function adequately, and diverse and independent media. These nations have only limited problems in democratic functioning.

Flawed democracies are nations where elections are fair and free and basic civil liberties are honoured but may have issues (eg, media freedom infringement and minor suppression of political opposition and critics). These nations have significant faults in other democratic aspects, including underdeveloped political culture, low levels of participation in politics, and issues in the functioning of governance.

Hybrid regimes are nations with regular electoral frauds preventing them from being fair and free democracies. These nations commonly have governments that apply pressure on political opposition, non-independent judiciaries, widespread corruption, harassment and pressure placed on the media, anaemic rule of law, and more pronounced faults than flawed democracies in the realms of underdeveloped political culture, low levels of participation in politics, and issues in the functioning of governance.

Authoritarian regimes are nations where political pluralism has vanished or is extremely limited. These nations are often absolute monarchies or dictatorships. They may have some conventional institutions of democracy but with meagre significance, infringements and abuses of civil liberties are commonplace, elections (if they take place) are not fair and free, the media is often state-owned or controlled by groups associated with the ruling regime, the judiciary is not independent, and there are omnipresent censorship and suppression of governmental criticism.

The following table gives the number and percentage of countries and the percentage of the world population for each regime type in 2018.

Table 1 Full democracies, flawed democracies, hybrid regimes, authoritarian regimes

Type of regime	Score (s)	Number of countries	Percentage of countries	Percentage of world population
Full democracies	$8 < s$	20	12.0	4.5
Flawed democracies	$6 < s \leq 8$	55	32.9	43.2
Hybrid regimes	$4 < s \leq 6$	39	23.4	16.7
Authoritarian regimes	$s \leq 4$	53	31.7	35.6

Source: *The Economist* Intelligence Unit website. EIU Democracy Index (1 March 2020).

This table usefully photographs the situation in 2018. It may be interesting to (re)visit the 'waves' through which political systems have acquired the status of democratic regimes. In his important overview, Huntington[15] indicated that the number of democratic regimes, combining full democracies with flawed democracies, was 29 in 1922, 12 in 1942, 36 in 1962, 30 in 1973 and 58 in 1990. According to several sources (here I rely on the data of the PEW Research Center published in December 2017): 96 out of 167 countries with populations of at least 500,000 (67 per cent) were democracies of some kind. That is, the worst form of government except all the others has shown a significant expansive capability. However, if one abandons the perspective of the *longue durée* and focuses the attention on the past 30 years, the picture that appears suggests a slightly less positive interpretation. According to the data presented in the 2019 Report of Freedom House (Table 2), with the revealing title *Democracy in Retreat*, negative changes have been relatively limited.

Table 2 Free, Partly Free, Not Free Countries from 1988 to 2018

	1988	1998	2008	2018
Free	35.8	45.5	46.1	44.1
Partly free	26.7	28.3	32.2	30.3
Not free	37.6	26.2	21.8	25.6

Source: Adapted from the 2019 Report of Freedom in the World, p 2.

Table 2 suggests several considerations concerning the 'fluctuations' of democratic regimes, but it can certainly not be interpreted as irrefutable evidence of the existence of a major 'crisis'. Moreover, as I have already said, but I want to repeat, in order to understand the current state of contemporary democracies and their undeniable problems, one has to take a long view. I will make two points. The

[15] SP Huntington, *The Third Wave. Democratization in the late Twentieth Century* (University of Oklahoma Press, 1991) 26.

first one is that the word 'crisis' has been associated with democracy almost from the very beginning of its existence. Leaving aside the breakdown of some democracies in the 1920s and 1930s, whose causes have been admirably analysed in the essays collected by Juan Linz and Alfred Stepan,[16] in the 1970s what attracted the scholarly and political attention was the so-called crisis of governability.[17] Ungovernability was interpreted fundamentally as a disequilibrium between the overload of political and socio-economic demands and the decision-makers' battery of instruments and capabilities.[18] No wonder that, in a few cases, the analysts have raised the issue of the need to reform the representative assemblies and the governmental institutions. In the late 1990s citizens' disaffection constituted the essential problem[19] and the abnormal fluctuations in the performance of many democracies[20] acquired visibility and elicited debates and conflicts. All these factors: overload, limited capabilities, disaffection and poor performance appeared to be responsible for the malfunctioning of democratic regimes. In the last decade, following the post-2008 economic recession, the populist challenge has come to the fore. It has been analysed in a great number of books of highly uneven quality.[21] To anticipate what will be my more reasoned assessment, populism affects the working of some specific democratic regimes. It attempts to distort the mechanisms and the structures of the political systems. It also poses a serious threat to the existence of a liberal-democracy. However, so far no democracy has fallen prey to a populist party/movement. What remains to be seen is whether and how much populism is successful in the erosion of the democratic framework in an irreversible way.

The second point that appears clearly to the scholars who take the long view is that, nonetheless, democracy has shown its capability to extend itself through time and space. Many an authoritarian regime has come and gone while most of the really existing democracies once they have acquired their status have been quite successful, few exceptions and few changes aside, in retaining it. Though himself largely inclined lucidly to see more problems than opportunities, more negative factors than bright futures, Huntington did paint an overall positive trend for democracy. His approach was grounded in the identification of waves pushing several political systems in the democratic corral. In 1984 he asked himself a highly significant question: 'Will more countries become democratic?'.[22] Persuasively argued, at that time his answer was 'all things considered, probably no'. Then, 1989 brought in the third

[16] J Linz and A Stepan (eds), *The Breakdown of Democratic Regimes* (The Johns Hopkins University Press, 1978).

[17] M Crozier, SP Huntington and J Watanuki, *The Crisis of Democracy. Report on the Governability of Democracies to the Trilateral Commission* (New York University Press, 1975).

[18] R Rose (ed), *Challenge to Governance. Studies in Overloaded Polities* (Sage, 1980).

[19] SJ Pharr and RD Putnam, (eds), *Disaffected Democracies. What's Troubling the Trilateral Countries* (Princeton University Press, 2000).

[20] RD Putnam (ed), *Democracies in Flux. The Evolution of Social Capital in Contemporary Society* (OUP, 2002).

[21] The best ones being J-W Müller, *What is Populism?* (University of Pennsylvania Press, 2016); Y Mény, *Popolo ma non troppo. Il malinteso democratico* (Il Mulino, 2019); and the collection of essays by Kriesi and Pappas: H Kriesi and TS Pappas, *European populism in the shadow of the great recession* (ECPR Press, 2015).

[22] SP Huntington, 'Will More Countries Become Democratic?' (1984) 2 *Political Science Quarterly* 193–218.

wave of democratisation.[23] What is notable in Huntington's interpretation is his capability to identify, analyse, and explain the reverse waves that led to de-democratisation or, simply, to the fall of some newly arrived democracies. At the end of his major comparative study, he did not deny the possibility of a 'third reverse wave',[24] but he considered it highly hypothetical.

However, Huntington provided a list of what he called the 'potential causes of a third reverse wave': (1) systemic failures of democratic regimes to operate effectively could undermine their legitimacy; (2) 'a general international economic collapse on the 1929–30 model could undermine the legitimacy of democracy in many countries'; (3) 'a shift to authoritarianism by any democratic or democratizing great power could trigger similar snowballing actions in other countries'; (4) 'the shift to dictatorship by several newly democratic countries because they lacked many of the usual preconditions for democracy could possibly undermine democracy in other countries where those preconditions were strong': reverse snowballing; (5) if a nondemocratic state greatly developed its power and began to expand beyond its borders, this too could stimulate authoritarian movements in other countries'.[25] All these factors retain their potential to affect not only the functioning, but also the transformation and the life itself of (some) contemporary democracies. Huntington[26] has gone farther in identifying five possible forms of authoritarianism where and whether some democratic regimes fail: (a) authoritarian nationalism; (b) religious fundamentalism; (c) oligarchic authoritarianism; (d) populist dictatorship; and (e) communal dictatorship. Of course, each of these potential outcomes deserves special attention. But, in the light of the contemporary challenges addressed against existing democratic regimes, one must stress that 30 years ago Huntington foresaw that populism and religious fundamentalism had to be given the utmost consideration.

III. BACKSLIDING, EROSION, ALTERNATIVES

At this point, it is necessary to discover and distinguish two analytical perspectives both dealing with the foreseeable future of democratic regimes. First, there are those who maintain that really existing democracies are undergoing a process of backsliding and erosion that show the potential of leading to their demise and death. Secondly, there are those who stress that what is challenged is democracy as an ideal and that the alternatives are already here and available. Having defined democracy as a cluster of rights and a set of rules and institutions, it becomes possible and relatively easy to identify where the erosion and the backsliding may in fact take place. I know of no better starting point than the report on Hungary drafted by the Dutch EuroMP Judith Sargentini, elected by the Greens, member of the Committee on Civil

[23] Huntington (n 15).
[24] ibid 290–94.
[25] ibid 292–93.
[26] ibid 293–94.

Liberties, Justice and Home Affairs, approved by the European Parliament, 4 July 2018. The European Parliament stated its concern with the policies of the Hungarian Government led by Prime Minister Viktor Orbán in the following areas (I quote):

(1) the functioning of the constitutional and electoral system;
(2) the independence of the judiciary and of other institutions and the rights of judges;
(3) corruption and conflicts of interest;
(4) privacy and data protection;
(5) freedom of expression;
(6) academic freedom;
(7) freedom of religion;
(8) freedom of association;
(9) the right to equal treatment;
(10) the rights of persons belonging to minorities, including Roma and Jews, and protection against hateful statements against such minorities;
(11) the fundamental rights of migrants, asylum seekers and refugees;
(12) economic and social rights.

In this appropriately dense report, one can find an extended catalogue of the many elements that contribute to the identification of a political system as democratic and, conversely, whose disappearance and/or absence signal that I (not alone) have called backsliding and erosion of the democratic nature and quality of a political system. Having won and won again, repeatedly, elections whose fairness has not been decisively ascertained,[27] the Hungarian Prime Minister Viktor Orbán has reacted by stating clear and loud that, indeed, Hungary is an illiberal democracy.[28] The question is 'should one define democratic a regime in which civil and political rights are not respected and enforced, but violated at the pleasure of the, albeit elected, ruler(s)?' My answer is negative and goes as far as to maintain that the erosion of those rights means the erosion by bits and pieces of democracy itself. The loss or deprivation of those rights is a long step towards the demise and death of democracy.

How exactly have real democracies died or run the risk of dying? Taking into serious account the international context, which is by far not favourable to the survival, in several cases, of the young democracies existing in the 1920s and 1930s, the European democracies whose breakdown was studied in the essays collected by Linz and Stepan,[29] did not die of more or less natural causes. They were killed and

[27] There has been an unfortunate tendency to 'observe' the electoral process only few weeks before the vote then focusing on the casting and the counting of votes. In several instance infringements and frauds affecting the vote take place well in advance of the day of voting. Some good literature has been published recently (see P Norris, *Why Electoral Integrity Matters* (CUP, 2014)).

[28] Not surprisingly, the President of Russia, by no means a democracy, Vladimir Putin has not only indirectly sided with Prime Minister Orbán. In fact, Putin went even further bluntly stating as a matter of fact that 'the liberal idea has become obsolete', offering the explanation that 'it has come into conflict with the interests of the overwhelming majority of the population'. Worth reporting is the sharp reply by Donald Tusk, former Prime Minister of Poland, at the time President of the Council of Ministers of the European Union: 'what I find really obsolete is authoritarianism, personality cults and the rule of oligarchs'. Together, Putin and Tusk provide a good catalogue of the enemies of democracy: (illiberal) populists, authoritarians, single ruler, oligarchs. Interview published in the *Financial Times* (27 June 2019).

[29] See n 16.

the murderers have been identified. More precisely, what I am saying, contrary to many unsubstantiated beliefs, is that it was not the institutional arrangement of those democracies that doomed them to death. They were not impotent democracies, unable to decide. The non-democrats, without whose support the anti-democrats could have not won, were embedded within the democratic institutions. Indeed, it was their betrayal of those institutions that decisively opened the path to the collapse of the democratic regime. Attempting to provide a satisfactory explanation of the shifts from democratic to authoritarian political systems, Huntington[30] states that 'apart from those produced by foreign actors, transitions from democracy to authoritarianism were almost always produced by those in power or close to power in the democratic system'.[31]

In a way, in several cases it was the behaviour of the powerholders, not only of the political leaders, but also of the entrepreneurs and of the opinion leaders that opened the way to the enemies of democracy. Their criticisms of the politicians often lead to the formation of 'technocratic', non-political governments. It is true that in very few cases, confined in time and space, the governments of contemporary democracies have been made of non-political, non-partisan experts,[32] but the simple existence of those governments constitutes a challenge to democracy from two points of view. On the one hand, governments made of unelected technocrats shatter the principle of the sovereignty of the people that ought to be manifested and translated through free elections. On the other hand, the existence of unelected technocrats at the helm of a political system calls into question the possibility of implementing what probably is the most important democratic principle: accountability. More precisely, the technocrats are never asked to justify, explain, accept responsibility for what they have done, not done, poorly done. And, of course, they rarely feel obliged to do so because they have no popular constituency empowered to evaluate their performance and to block or renew their 'mandate' to govern.

It is probably too early to enquire whether the behaviour of some political protagonists, especially populist leaders, has caused severe and permanent institutional wounds to the democratic frameworks. More precisely, once in office or when challenging the establishment and the rules of the democratic game, have the populists affected not only the dynamics of democratic regimes, but also their very mechanisms and structures?[33] For the time being, one is allowed to state that the challenges coming

[30] Huntington (n 15) 291.

[31] Huntington (n 15) 316 is fully consistent with his belief that elites are responsible for the construction of democratic regimes: 'economic development makes democracy possible; political leadership makes it real'. By saying so, he revises the justly famous set of generalisations formulated by Lipset (see SM Lipset, 'The Social Requisites of Democracy Revisited' (1994) 1 *American Sociological Review* 1–18).

[32] G Pasquino and M Valbruzzi, 'Non-partisan governments Italian-style: decision-making and accountability' (2012) 5 *Journal of Modern Italian Studies* 612–29; D McDonnell and M Valbruzzi, 'Defining and classifying technocrat-led and technocratic governments' (2014) 4 *European Journal of Political Research* 654–71; G Pastorella, 'Technocratic Governments in Europe: Getting the Critique Right' (2016) 4 *Political Studies* 948–65.

[33] In order to defend democracy some leaders may feel temporarily obliged to restrict civil liberties, to limit political activities, to abridge the freedom of the press, to declare the state of emergency and to keep it for a long time, to concentrate power in the executive branch or leader.

from the (religious) fundamentalists[34] have been more serious than those launched by the populists. It is true that, both the fundamentalists and the populists, claim one way or another that democracy has failed and that they are capable of constructing a better form of government. But the fundamentalists challenge not only democracy as the rule by the people, but the very autonomy of politics. In 'their' political system what is acceptable and allowed or unacceptable and forbidden is defined by the fundamentalists and is said to descend from religious principles interpreted by religious authorities. The fundamentalists put an end to politics as it has been known and practised, not without obstacles, since Machiavelli, preventing and outlawing all types of democratic competition.

To be sure, the populist challenge does aim at the heart of democracy. There is always a streak of populism in really existing democracies. Up to recent times I would have written 'to the exception of the UK', but not a few British scholars have expounded serious criticism and worries concerning the way the Brexit issue has been dealt with by the Prime Ministers. All democracies recognise that the people are the owner of sovereignty and that political power can be legitimately obtained only through pre-established rules and procedures that are activated by the people. Here one finds the first major cleavage separating the populists from the (liberal-) democrats. The former believe that there should be no intermediation between the people and the ruler(s) chosen by the people. The latter believe that the power of the people must be exercised according to the laws and within the limits inscribed into the Constitution (I have paraphrased article 1 comma 2 of the Italian Constitution). There is a second major difference between the populists and the (liberal-)democrats. The populists' dogma is that the leader, who has been entrusted with power by the people, knows of no institutional check. The populist view is that executive power should not be hampered either by the legislative or by the judicial power. On the contrary, the liberal-democrats hold that no institution is superior to the others, that all institutions somewhat share power and accountability and that all citizens are the repository of fundamental and inalienable rights.

For the populists, the votes are the trump (sic). Voting is the activity through which a direct relationship is established between the leader and the people. All forms of pluralism, but, especially, political pluralism, must recede and, in any case, since they may be divisive, are not to be tolerated. In the 'theory' and practice of populism the dividing line is not between the majority and the minorities. It is drawn between the leader sustained by his people and the enemies of the people (the establishment, the bankers, the intellectuals, the journalists, the technocrats, the scientists, and,

[34] The plural is necessary because practically all religions have their own fundamentalists. See the excellent comparative analysis by GA Almond, SR Appleby and E Sivan, *Strong Religion: The Rise of Fundamentalisms around the World* (The University of Chicago Press, 2011). F Fukuyama in *The End of History and the Last Man* (The Free Press, 1992) almost totally underestimated religious fundamentalism as a challenge to the victorious liberal-democracies. On the contrary, Huntington (see SP Huntington, *The Clash of Civilizations and the Making of a New World Order* (Simon and Schuster, 1996)) considered religious beliefs a fundamental component of each and every civilisation.

of course, the Jews) against whom exclusion and repression are appropriate, often inevitable, measures.[35] In all contemporary democracies the populists have gained some or a lot of ground without ever winning the absolute majority neither of votes nor of seats. In a few instances, it may be more appropriate to say that some political leaders who, through generally speaking legitimate electoral procedures, have obtained the power to govern, have transformed themselves once in office. Only then, in order to wield and retain political power, they have resorted to a populist style in rhetoric and governmental actions: witness the experiences of Viktor Orbán and Donald Trump.[36]

While, of course, the identification of the leaders who are populist is important, here we are more interested in understanding whether the populists can in fact improve the working of their democratic regime or whether (and how) the populists introduce 'deplorable' and irreversible changes in those regimes. Insofar as they fire the judges and pack the judiciary, subjugate the mass media, purge the universities, and subvert the political discourse, the populists do distort democracy, debase its quality and may affect the working of the political system for a long time to come. Some of these distortions are in the making in a handful of countries,[37] but it is too early to reach a reliable assessment. Before even attempting to find which distortions (and how important) have been introduced in those political systems where the populists are especially strong, it may be interesting to look at the opinions and the assessments of the citizens themselves concerning their political systems and their satisfaction with the working of their respective democracies. Contemporary scholars and political analysts are quite fortunate because a wealth of reliable data is easily available. The next section is devoted to showing and interpreting those data.

A. The Functioning of Democracy(ies)

Once it has been ascertained that a country is a democracy, the next step is to evaluate its functioning. Above, previously, I have made use of data provided by some organisations assessing the quality of democracy with reference to acceptable

[35] I am much indebted to Müller's (n 21) short and sharp analysis. See also N Urbinati, *Democracy Disfigured: Opinion, Truth, and the People* (Harvard University Press, 2014) and the collection of essay edited by Kriesi and Pappas (n 21).

[36] P Norris and R Inglehart, *Cultural Backlash. Trump, Brexit, and Authoritarian Populism* (CUP, 2019). On Trump see the article by RC Lieberman, S Mettler, PB Pepinsky, KM Roberts and R Valelly, 'The Trump Presidency and American Democracy: A Historical and Comparative Analysis' (2019) 2 *Perspectives on Politics* 470–79.

[37] Hungary and Poland are usually considered a poignant example of populist distortions, but it is remarkable that quite a number of US political scientists have expressed their scholarly fears and concern for what Trump has been doing (S Levitsky and D Ziblatt, *How Democracies Die. What History Reveals About Our Future* (Penguin Random House, 2019); Y Mounk, *The People vs. Democracy: Why Our Freedom Is in Danger and How to Save It* (Harvard University Press, 2018) 9 and several articles in the March and September 2019 issues of the journal *Perspectives on Politics*).

uniform criteria. In what follows I will rely on the opinions of the citizens themselves offering as wide a spectrum as possible. I will start by looking to some Latin American countries that have been democratic since the 1990s. Then I will focus on two continents, Africa and Asia, where many non-democratic situations and regimes still exist. Finally, I will deal with the Member States of the European Union.

When it comes to democratic situations, experiences, evolutions, Latin America has always been a troubled continent and has offered plenty of examples of non-democratic outcomes. Starting in the 1990s all Latin American countries seemed to have constructed and preserved a democratic regime. After more or less 10–15 years of democratic life, the evolution of the degree of satisfaction with the functioning of democracy in the Latin American continent has, to say the least, not been positive.

In all the countries I have chosen, with the exception of Chile, Table 3 shows that in the period between 2006 and 2018 there has been a decline. In some cases, such as Venezuela, Argentina, Brazil, the decline has been quite steep. Let me highlight the case of Venezuela, where Chavez' populist rule was considered highly satisfactory from a democratic perspective in 2006, while in 2018 his successor Maduro's rule has sunk the Venezuelans' satisfaction with democracy well below the Latin American average. The four/five million Venezuelans who have left their country in the past few years are a living testimony and a clear evidence of the disintegration of Venezuelan democracy. However, all this being said, when it comes to the alternatives, in 2018 48 per cent of the Latin Americans said that democracy is preferable, while 15 per cent wished for authoritarianism (28 per cent being 'indifferent'). Curiously, the LatinoBarometro has also inquired about the degree of agreement with the Churchillian statement: democracy having problems, but still being the less worse form of government. In 2006 74 per cent of the respondents agreed; in 2018 the percentage, though still high, has declined to 65.[38]

Table 3 Degree of satisfaction (much + somewhat) with the functioning of democracy in selected Latin American countries

	Argentina	Bolivia	Brazil	Chile	Uruguay	Venezuela	Latin America
2006	50.1	39	36.3	42.1	55.9	57.1	39.7
2018	27.1	26.2	8.7	42.2	46.8	11.8	24.4

Source: LatinoBarometro selected years.

A somewhat different story is told by the surveys conducted in Africa. Table 4 shows that almost half of the African respondents are fairly and very satisfied with democracy.

[38] Source: 2018 LatinoBarometro, p 15 and p 31.

Table 4 Satisfaction with democracy

	2005–2006	2016–2018
My country is not a democracy	1.6	1.4
Not at all satisfied	14.6	18.6
Not very satisfied	21.5	25.9
Fairly satisfied	28	34.1
Very satisfied	18	15.6
Don't know	16.2	4.5

Question: Overall, how satisfied are you with the way democracy works in [your country]?
Source: www.afrobarometer.org/.

Secondly, a growing percentage of respondents, that in 2018 became a large majority, declare they disapprove and strongly disapprove the two most frequent alternatives to democracy in their countries, that is one party rule (Table 5) and military governments (Table 6).

Table 5 One party rule is preferable to democracy

	2005–2006	2016–2018
Strongly disapprove	42.6	50.2
Disapprove	27.7	21.8
Neither approve nor disapprove	5.1	2.3
Approve	12.4	12.5
Strongly approve	8.6	10.4
Don't know	3.5	2.8

Question: There are many ways to govern a country. Would you disapprove or approve of the following alternatives? Only one political party is allowed to stand for election and hold office.
Source: www.afrobarometer.org/.

Table 6 Army rule is preferable to democracy

	2005–2006	2016–2018
Strongly disapprove	45.5	52.3
Disapprove	27.1	21.6
Neither approve nor disapprove	7.6	3.6
Approve	10.4	12.1
Strongly approve	5.2	7.2
Don't know	4.1	3.2

Question: There are many ways to govern a country. Would you disapprove or approve of the following alternatives? The army comes in to govern the country.
Source: www.afrobarometer.org/.

Though (or perhaps, exactly because) they are mostly living in non-democratic regimes, sizable, and, what is perhaps even more important, growing majorities of African respondents are saying that they consider two widely experimented alternatives to democracy worse forms of government.

When it comes to several Asian countries, again the percentage of respondents who are fairly and very satisfied with democracy is extremely and surprisingly high (Table 7).[39]

Table 7 Satisfaction with democracy in selected Asian countries

	2005–2008		2014–2016	
	%	Valid %	%	Valid %
Not at all satisfied	4	4.4	4.6	4.98
Not very satisfied	18.6	20.7	24.6	26.5
Fairly satisfied	52.3	58.3	53.7	58.1
Very satisfied	14.8	16.5	9.6	10.4
Can't choose	8.2		6.2	
Declines to answer	2.2		1	
Don't under-stand the question			3	

Question: On the whole, how satisfied or dissatisfied are you with the way democracy works in your country? The percentages refer to Cambodia, China, Indonesia, Mongolia, Philippines, Singapore, Taiwan, Thailand, Vietnam

Source: www.asianbarometer.org/data.

As a logical consequence, very high majorities, over 70 per cent, reject all authoritarian solutions: a strong leader, one-party rule and military governments. In all likelihood, many of those respondents are familiar with authoritarianism because at one time or another, all of those authoritarian solutions have been implemented in their countries. Even today, in Asia some authoritarian regimes are alive and, so to speak, thrive.

[39] Several of the countries surveyed, notably Cambodia, China, and Vietnam, are most certainly not democracies. Therefore, one can legitimately interpret the answers of the respondents not as an evaluation, but, which is even more important for our analytical purposes, as a wish.

Table 8 Approval and disapproval of authoritarian tendencies in selected Asian countries

	We'd get rid of parliament and elections and have a strong leader		Only one party should be allowed		The army should come to govern	
	Valid % (2005–08)	Valid % (2014–16)	Valid % (2005–08)	Valid % (2014–16)	Valid % (2005–08)	Valid % (2014–16)
Strongly approve	6.3	8.4	7.6	7	4.5	5.6
Approve	15	19.7	15.8	23.3	16	18.3
Disapprove	52.7	43.9	46.1	38.3	50.1	39.8
Strongly disapprove	26	27.8	30.5	31.3	29.5	36.3
			The question was not asked to 33% of the 15,452 respondents			

Questions: There are many ways to govern a country. Would you disapprove or approve of the following alternatives? For each statement, would you say you strongly approve, approve, disapprove, or strongly disapprove?
We should get rid of parliament and elections and have a strong leader decide things.
Only one political party is allowed to stand for election and hold office.
The army (military) should come in to govern the country.
Source: www.asianbarometer.org/data.

Summing up, the survey data clearly indicate that significant majorities of African and Asian respondents undoubtedly believe that democracy is a better form of government than any authoritarian alternative. I would put it this way: according to them any and all authoritarian forms of government are worse than any type of, even if unknown, democracy.

It is time to turn to the data regarding the status of democracy among several Member States of the European Union (the worst form of supranational quasi federalist organisation except all others …). In Table 9 I have ranked all the Member States with respect to the degree of their citizens' satisfaction with the working of democracy in their respective countries.

Table 9 Degree of satisfaction of Europeans with the way democracy works in their country

	Very	Fairly	Not satisfied	Not at all satisfied	Total satisfied
Europe at 28	9	46	30	12	55
Denmark	41	50	7	1	91
Luxembourg	24	61	10	2	85
Holland	22	60	14	3	82
Sweden	20	60	14	5	80

(continued)

Table 9 *(Continued)*

	Very	Fairly	Not satisfied	Not at all satisfied	Total satisfied
Eire	22	58	14	4	80
Finland	13	65	17	4	78
Austria	20	57	18	4	77
Belgium	7	63	22	8	70
Portugal	3	61	31	4	64
Malta	13	50	21	12	63
Poland	9	50	24	10	59
UK	10	49	25	7	59
Czech Republic	6	53	33	6	59
Estonia	5	50	31	7	55
Hungary	13	42	26	18	55
Latvia	6	49	29	13	55
France	6	48	29	14	54
Croatia	3	38	36	22	41
Cyprus	5	34	45	16	39
Slovenia	2	37	47	13	39
Bulgaria	6	32	29	27	38
Italy	5	32	40	20	37
Lithuania	3	34	45	15	37
Spain	5	32	43	19	37
Slovakia	4	31	42	22	35
Romania	2	30	47	19	32
Greece	3	25	49	23	28

Source: The data presented in Table 9 must be read jointly with those of Figure 1 that show an interesting development. In all the countries surveyed to the revealing exception of the UK, the satisfaction with democracy has gone up from 2015 to 2019: a rather encouraging trend.

Overall, more than half (55 per cent) European citizens declare that they are very and fairly satisfied. These data, that contradict the opinion of many scholars, are significant in themselves, but a couple of additional considerations are required. First, in the two Eastern European countries, Poland and Hungary, whose top office holders show more than a modest dose of populism, the citizens are (nonetheless?) quite satisfied with the working of their democracy. Secondly, somewhat surprisingly the British citizens' evaluation of their democracy is on par with that of Polish and Czech citizens. On the whole, the data concerning the European Union Member States seem to indicate that, though 'crisis' is certainly not the most appropriate word to be used, there exists among the European citizens a not negligible degree of dissatisfaction with the working of their national democracy. With the exception of the UK, citizens' satisfaction with their national democracy in 2019 was higher than in 2015 as Figure 1 clearly shows.

Figure 1 Satisfaction with national democracy

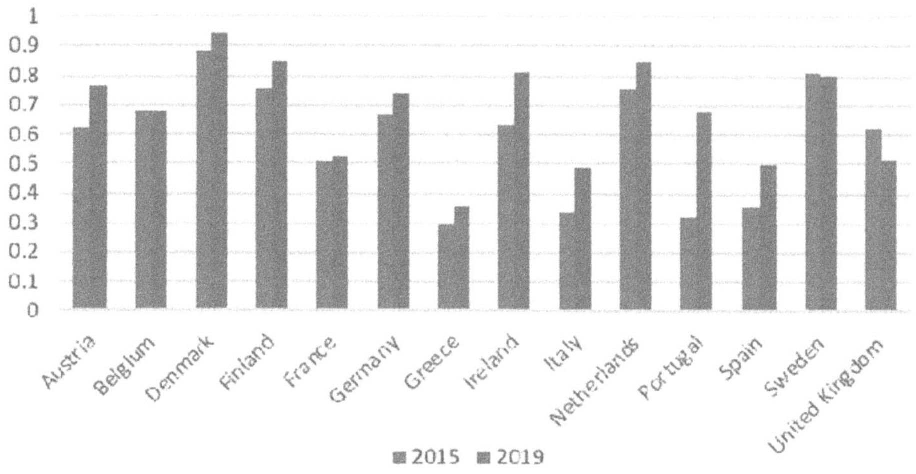

Source: adapted from Eurobarometer Survey 89.2. March 2017–April 2018. *Democracy on the Move*, p. 39.

IV. CONCLUSION

There continue to be many good reasons to believe that Churchill's assessment of democracy as the worst form of government except all the others deserves still to resonate. The available evidence provides a lot of food for thought. I will summarise what can be learned propounding three major ascertainable points. First, on the one hand, all the available data collected by a variety of specialised organisations converge in estimating that the number of democratic regimes has increased even in recent times. The second consideration is more general. Most scholars and practitioners are well (perhaps, too) aware that all over the world democratic regimes are being challenged in a more serious way than at any time in the post-war period. In the Western world democracy has long been taken for granted and considered (almost) unassailable. The recent challenges in well-established democracies have caused surprise and preoccupations because they were substantially unexpected. In fact, both disaffection with democracy as such and dissatisfaction with really existing democratic regimes have increased. Figure 2 suggests that there has been an overall preoccupying trend that makes it imperative to monitor all types of negative changes.

Figure 2 Countries with net declines in aggregate score have outnumbered those with gains for each of the past 12 years

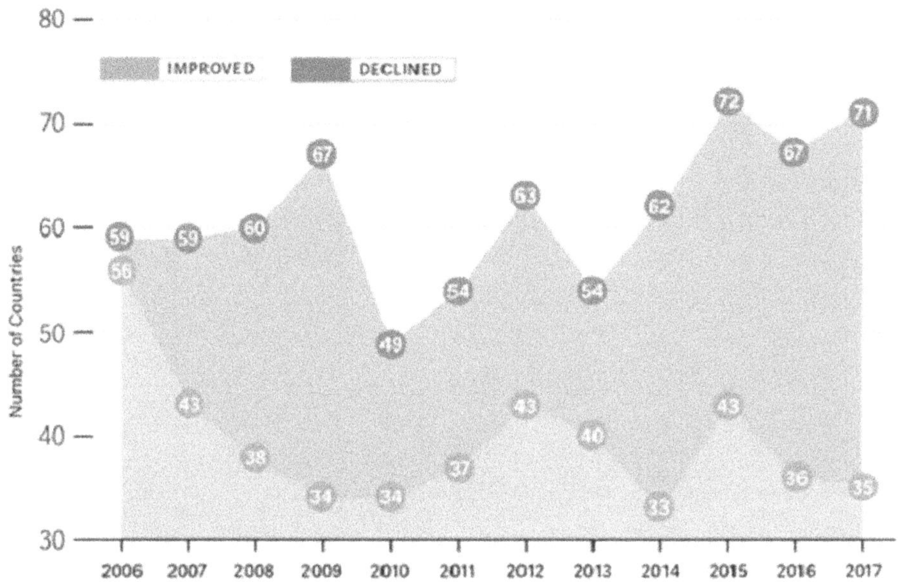

Source: Democracy in decline, www.freedomintheworld.org.

Thirdly, it is important to emphasise that no Western democracy has so far succumbed to the populists, but some democratic regimes have indeed been shaken and remain under vicious attacks. Nevertheless, all things considered, taking a leaf from Mark Twain's book of witty sentences, one can safely conclude that all reports of the death of democracy are greatly exaggerated. So far (Western, universal) democracy, as millions of men and women who are day by day fighting to achieve it and to make it work, has exhibited strength and resilience. It remains a 'work in progress', endowed with mechanisms and structures capable of learning and reforming itself, widely appreciated because it has proven to be not just the 'worst form of government except all others'. Confidently, one can conclude that in fact democracy is perceived and remains by far a better form of government than any existing alternative.

* I gratefully acknowledge the help and suggestions given to me by Riccardo Pelizzo.

15

The Old-Fashioned (or Out of Fashion?) Prohibition on the Imperative Mandate

BENEDETTA BARBISAN*

I. THE OLD-FASHIONED PROHIBITION ON THE IMPERATIVE MANDATE

THE IMPERATIVE MANDATE surfaced as part and parcel of medieval usages. When in Castile and Leon the right of assembling the Cortes belonged to the king who notified in advance the time and place of the meeting and also its purposes with a letter of convocation, representatives of the municipalities could be instructed on how to act and cast their vote, and which grievances to present. Whenever there was great doubt on how to deliberate, the deputy's duty was to ask for a suspension, get back to his *concejo* and receive directions. As long as meetings were not fixed and letters of convocation detailed the nature of the issues at stake, making a decision in advance and imposing it by the *concejo* upon their chosen representatives was easy, and all the deputy later owed his *concejo* was a complete account of the proceedings to absolve himself of any responsibility. Only when, at the end of the thirteenth century, those meetings became regular especially in Aragon and Catalonia, were the letters of convocation less and less specific on the matters of the meetings and the king started desiring the municipalities to entrust their deputies with a broader and more general power.[1] That was the beginning of the end of the imperative mandate.[2]

* University of Macerata.

[1] AM Holden, 'The Imperative Mandate in the Spanish Cortes of the Middle Ages' (1980) 24 *Am. Pol. Sc. Rev.* 886.

[2] In the Late Middle Ages, it became customary across Europe that the king made decisions with the consensus of the kingdom's representatives. These assemblies, called Cortes in the Iberian peninsula, were variously named: Parliament in England, in France and the Netherlands Estates general, in Poland and the Empire Diet. With the flourishing of cities, these bodies were gradually integrated with the representatives from the urban bourgeoise citizenry, part of which could not attend all the meetings, with the result of urban oligarchies appointing a number of representatives in their place. For the Parliament of Westminster, this phenomenon started in the late 13th century, whereas in France it was in 1302 that Philip IV the Fair summoned the representatives from the cities to assure supremacy over the authority of the Pope Boniface VIII (see B Aguilera-Barchet, *A History of Western Public Law. Between Nation and State* (Springer, 2015) 190–97).

The imperative mandate has been at odds with most countries in the world since when the idea of *popular sovereignty* gave way to *national sovereignty*, proclaimed in the *Declaration universelle des droits de l'homme et du citoyen* (article 3: 'The principle of any sovereignty lies primarily in the nation'), echoed in the 1791 French Constitution at Title II, Section 3, article 7 ('The representatives elected in the departments shall not be representatives of a particular department, but of the entire nation, and no mandate may be given them') and replicated in the 1812 Constitution of Cádiz,[3] the 1822 Portuguese Constitution[4] and in the 1831 Belgian Constitution.[5]

Popular sovereignty was grounded on the notion that representation was alienation: as Jean Jacques Rousseau famously argued in 1762 in his *Du contrat social*, '(b)eing nothing less than the exercise of the general will, sovereignty can never be alienated. [...] Sovereignty, for the same reason as makes it inalienable, cannot be represented; it lies essentially in the general will, and will does not admit of representation: it is either the same, or other; there is no intermediate possibility. The deputies of the people, therefore, are not and cannot be its representatives: they are merely its stewards, and can carry through no definitive acts. Every law the people has not ratified in person is null and void – is, in fact, not a law'.

National sovereignty, on the contrary, entailed the idea that there was no service to the common good without representatives' independence from their electors, as Edmund Burke explained in 1774 when he addressed his *Speech to the Electors of Bristol*, where he conjured 'the happiness and glory of a Representative, to live in the strictest union, the closest correspondence, and the most unreserved communication with his constituents. Their wishes ought to have great weight with him; their opinion high respect; their business unremitted attention. It is his duty to sacrifice his repose, his pleasures, his satisfactions, to theirs; and, above all, ever, and in all cases, to prefer their interest to his own. But, his unbiassed opinion, his mature judgement, his enlightened conscience, he ought not to sacrifice to you; to any man, or to any sett of men living. [...] Your Representative owes you, not his industry only, but his judgement; and he betrays, instead of serving you, if he sacrifices it to your opinion'.

Constitutions forbid imperative mandate through plain and simple prohibitions,[6] by mentioning representation in the name of the Nation[7] or the interests of the people[8] or finally referring to the representatives' conscience.[9] Major departures from this well-established practice occurred in the twentieth century under communist

[3] 'The Cortes is the junction of all the deputies who represent the nation' (art 27).

[4] 'Sovereignty lies essentially with the Nation. It may not therefore be exercised save by its lawfully elected representatives' (art 32).

[5] 'The members of the two houses represent the nation and not simply the province or the subdivision which may have elected them' (art 32).

[6] The 1958 Constitution of France, art 27, the 1978 Constitution of Spain, art 67(2), the 2010 Constitution of Croatia, art 75, the 1991 Constitution of Romania, art 69(2), the 1992 Constitution of Mali, art 64, the 2010 Constitution of Senegal, art 64(1), the Rules of Procedure of the EU Parliament, Rule 2.

[7] The 1948 Constitution of Italy, art 67, the 1831 Constitution of Belgium, art 25, the 1997 Constitution of Poland, art 104, the 2016 Constitution of Côte d'Ivoire, art 96(1), the 1991 Constitution of Bulgaria, art 67(1), the 1982 Constitution of Turkey, art 7.

[8] The 1991 Constitution of Romania, art 69(1), the 1949 German Basic Law, art 38(1).

[9] The 1953 Constitution of Denmark, art 56, the 1949 German Basic Law, art 38(1).

regimes, where deputies exerted powers issuing from the sovereignty of the people,[10] were guided by the electors' interests,[11] responded to the populace by reporting periodically on their work[12] and could be removed by the electorate[13] in case of betrayal.

In spite of its infrequency, in December 2007 the Council for Democratic Elections of the European Commission for Democracy Through Law (the Venice Commission) recommended the imperative mandate as a possible area of study.[14] The appointed rapporteur, the Spanish representative Carlos Closa Montero, presented a preliminary overview,[15] remarking that this interest 'on a notion which is widely unaccepted in democracies is not alien to the fact that certain countries have used the institution to try to deal with a specific problem (crossing the floor, party defection, party switching)'.[16] The 1996 Constitution of Ukraine, for instance, stated that 'members of the Verkhovna Rada are bound to remain members of the parliamentary faction or bloc in which they were elected' (article 81). Ukrainian parliamentary life had been witnessing a growing custom of switching parties, which the legislative promptly reacted to in 2001 by proposing a constitutional amendment to terminate the deputies' mandate in lack of a connection with their nominating party. The Venice Commission expressed severe criticism of this proposal, arguing that it would weaken the Verkhovna Rada by interfering with an independent mandate of the representatives, no longer in a position to freely follow their convictions, but the reform was, however, passed in 2004.

Anti-defection measures are recurrent in nascent democracies rather than in established ones,[17] so the *party administered mandate* enforced in Ukraine can be traced also in the 1996 Constitution of South Africa, at article 47(3) ('A person loses membership of the National Assembly if she ceases to be a member of the party that nominated her as a member of the Assembly') and in the 1949 Constitution of India, at article 102(2) ('A person shall be disqualified for being a member of either House of Parliament if he is so disqualified under the Tenth Schedule'[18]).

[10] The 1949 Constitution of Hungary, art 10(2).

[11] The 1971 Constitution of Bulgaria, art 86(1), the 1968 Constitution of DDR, art 56.

[12] The 1965 Constitution of Romania, art 60, the 1936 USSR Constitution, art 142, the 1952 Constitution of Poland, art 87.

[13] The 1960 Constitution of Czechoslovakia, art 39(2), the 1936 USSR Constitution, art 142.

[14] 23rd Meeting of the Council for Democratic Elections, *Meeting Report* (Venice, 13 December 2007) 3, available at www.venice.coe.int/webforms/documents/default.aspx?pdffile=CDL-EL-PV(2007)004-e.

[15] Adopted by the Council for Democratic Elections on 14 March 2009 and by the Venice Commission on 12–13 June 2009.

[16] C Closa Monteiro, *Report on the Imperative Mandate* 2, available at www.venice.coe.int/webforms/documents/?pdf=CDL-EL(2008)031-e.

[17] See M Goeke and C Hartmann, 'The Regulation of Party Switching in Africa' (2011) 29 *J. Cont. African Studies* 263; K Janda, *Adopting Party Law, in Political Parties and Democracy in Theoretical and Practice Perspective*, National Democracy Institute for International Affairs, Washington D. (2005) and K Janda, *Laws Against Party Switching, Defecting or Floor-Crossing in National Parliaments*, The Legal Regulation of Political Parties, Working Paper no 2 (August 2009). There are only six countries that mandate legislators to vote according to party diktat: Bangladesh, Guyana, India, Pakistan, Sierra Leone and Zimbabwe.

[18] In 1985, the government led by Rajiv Gandhi passed an anti-defection law through the 52nd constitutional amendment, known as the Tenth Schedule to the Indian Constitution, with the purpose of addressing the problem of representatives disobeying their party's decisions in critical times or shifting allegiance in favour of a different group from the one that had nominated them. The idea behind this law

Another institution related to the imperative mandate is the *recall*:[19] in Europe, for example, the 2004 Constitution of Belarus generically provides that deputies' seats may be vacated 'as determined by the law' (article 72). The *Electoral Code of the Republic of Belarus* specifies at article 129 that a deputy who has not 'justified the trust of the voters' or failed 'to execute the deputy's duties as stipulated by law' may be recalled on the initiative of no less than 20 per cent of his constituents.

Under far more unambiguous terms, the institution of recall has recently been introduced in the UK with the Recall of MPs Act 2015, under which an MP becomes subject to a recall petition process if she is convicted of an offence and ordered to be imprisoned or detained, if the House of Commons orders her suspension from the service for a length of time or if she is convicted for providing false or misleading information of allowances claims. The recall petition process is set in motion by the Speaker of the House and then sent to the constituency of the MP to allow voters to sign for recall within the next six weeks. The petition is successful when at least 10 per cent of the eligible electors have signed it. As of today, the recall petition process has been approved in three cases.

But it is in the US that the recall heavily surged at the start of the twentieth century: despite Edmund Randolph's Virginia Plan to adopt it for the members of the first house of legislative elected by the people, the Constitutional Convention in Philadelphia eventually failed to encompass it in the US Constitution and the recall went into eclipse for a century. It reappeared in the 1892 and 1896 platforms of the Socialist-Labour Party and the Populist Party under the label of imperative mandate. Its first codification happened with the approval of the 1903 Los Angeles Charter, which rapidly spread in other 25 California localities: at the time, California politics was dominated by the railroad industry and its biggest conglomerate, the Southern Pacific Railroad,[20] like other states, was under the yoke of oil companies. The national fight to introduce the recall aspired to clean up the moral and political health of the country, returning the power to the people against corrupt influences. The then President of the US, the Progressive champion Theodore Roosevelt, eased the nationwide blossoming of direct democracy – comprising the first primary elections, the popular initiative, the referendum and, in fact, the recall – which peaked with the XVIIth Amendment that made the US Senate elective and the XIXth that legalised women's suffrage. Today, the recall is in use in 19 US states,[21] where it is

was to strengthen political stability by curbing party switching fuelled by the lure of pecuniary gains and by reaffirming political parties' role through a bond of loyalty between the deputies and the organisation that arranged for their electoral expenses and under whose manifesto candidates fought for their election (see R Sinha and P Kaur, *Anti-Defection Law: Intent and Impact*, PRS Legislative Research (New Delhi, 2019)). Article 2 of the Tenth Schedule provides that any member of the House shall be disqualified '(a) if he has voluntarily given up his membership of such political party; or (b) if he votes or abstains from voting in such House contrary to any direction issued by the political party to which he belongs or by any person or authority authorised by it in this behalf, without obtaining, in either case, the prior permission of such political party, person or authority and such voting or abstention has not been condoned by such political party, person or authority within fifteen days from the date of such voting or abstention'.

[19] The 1945 Constitution of Indonesia, art 2213; the 2019 Constitution of Cuba, art 113.

[20] J Spivak, 'California's Recall: Adoption of the 'Grand Bounce' for Elected Officials' (2004) 82 *California History* 20.

[21] They are: Alaska, Arizona, Colorado, Georgia, Idaho, Illinois, Kansas, Louisiana, Michigan, Minnesota, Montana, Nevada, New Jersey, North Dakota, Oregon, Rhode Island, Washington and Wisconsin.

possible to remove officials from their elective seats in the legislative, executive and judicial power.

Closa Montero's report made a point in discerning between the *stricto sensu* definition of imperative mandate on one side and formulas related to the imperative mandate like the recall and the party administered mandate on the other: that these two notions may be kept separated and distinguished is actually not entirely intelligible and not even practised on a large scale, but can be detected, for example, in the 1990 Constitution of Namibia, which establishes at article 45 a strict prohibition on the imperative mandate ('The members of the National Assembly shall be representative of all the people and shall be guided by the objective of the Constitution, public interest and their conscience') and at article 48(1) letter b that, if a political party informs the Speaker of the National Assembly that some deputy no longer belongs to the party that nominated her, such member shall vacate her seat. But, even though the aim pursued by this kind of measure (ie, preventing deputies crossing the floor or the 'sale' of mandates to the top payer) was sympathetically contemplated, the Venice Commission eventually reaffirmed that 'the basic constitutional principle which prohibits imperative mandate or any other form of politically depriving representatives of their mandates must prevail as a cornerstone of European democratic constitutionalism'.[22]

Those brought to the fore by the usage of recall and the party administered mandate are problems variably concerning the stability of the government in power, the integrity of the electoral process, the parliaments' capacity to address effectively the needs of the country, the deputies' moral fabric – more generally, the relationship between the people and their representatives in the attempt to put off betrayals of the fundamental trust based on which voters elected the deputy to power. In reality, imperative mandate (and the institutions related thereof) prevent representatives from balancing public interest, the constituency interest and the party affiliation according to their conscience, deter their ability to check on the government and call it accountable when they are asked instead to comply with their party's discipline of voting, breach the accountability chain between electors and elected because of the party's interference, with few party leaders unilaterally taking major decisions in lieu of the larger body of legislators.

Nonetheless, imperative mandate not only appears more progressive and democratic to those vouching for a more responsive, trustworthy and accountable action of representatives towards the electorate, but it is today on the radar of those political movements determined to purge representatation from its ugliest distortions, bridge the cleavage between constituents and elected, and finally place the people – anything but a neutral political definition, 'one of the grounds for the bitterest human animosity and vicious behaviours'[23] – at the heart of politics again.

[22] European Commission for Democracy Through Law (Venice Commission), *Report on the Imperative Mandate and Similar Practices* 14, available at www.venice.coe.int/webforms/documents/default.aspx?pdffile=CDL-AD(2009)027-e.

[23] C Rovira Kaltwasser, 'The Responses of Populism to Dahl's Democratic Dilemmas' (2014) 62 *Political Studies* 470, 474.

The Italian Five-Star movement, for instance, asked its representative elected to power in the 2018 elections to sign a contract obliging them to pay 250,000 euros should they violate the movement's code of conduct. Podemos in Spain put forward the idea of a daily control of their representatives' work and the right to recall, while the Grüne in Germany talked of an imperative mandate binding its deputies at the Bundestag. Since 'through populist movements the population seeks to occupy the stage and not just be a mass of silent, atomised spectators [...], (p)opulists' claim to the imperative mandate can be understood as a symptom of a lack of confidence in both the representatives and the establishment, a sign of the dissatisfaction of a huge part of the population with a kind of democracy in which those in power are increasingly distant from the government and which has essentially become a complicated mechanism of procedures'.[24] In other words, imperative mandate is the call for a rejuvenated, genuine democracy in the context of the crisis of representative politics.

Yet, looking at the millenary development of representative government, these problems seem to have materialised at some other time in history. Five issues somehow affecting the relationship between electors and elected – by no means unprecedented, the distance of their first insurgence notwithstanding – are debated today, but were also disputed before, at some point during this long evolution. They are: alternation to power, that is, the principle of *rotation* in office; the special morality and intellect of deputies, that is, the *superiority* of representatives over voters; the *ambiguity* of election as a mixed institution, combining aristocratic and democratic elements; the power of parliaments to tackle and sort out the questions people care about, that is, the notion of *discussion* within a representative assembly; and, lastly but no less importantly, the hiatus between the government of the people and the *wishes* of the electorate.

All these matters hint, one way or another, at the distance and dissatisfaction mentioned above, because of which populist movements claim the imperative mandate to stand out as the ultimate remedy to the abuses and alterations lamented in the crisis of representative politics. But has the imperative mandate the actual power to amend the current disfunctions? Is it truly the right call to overcome the issues arisen and mend the broken political connection between constituents and deputies? To assess if the imperative mandate can keep the promises populists pledge, we are to investigate whether this institution proves to be the appropriate toolbox for this set of problems – the alternation in office, the mixed nature of elections, the alleged superiority of the elected, the debate in a representative assembly, and the juxtaposition between the government of the elected and the wishes of the people – that shall be discussed in the next section.

II. IS THE PROHIBITION ON THE IMPERATIVE MANDATE OUT OF FASHION?

In its political and institutional narrative, populism embraces a manichean distinction between a morally pure, fully unified people against elites that are deemed

[24] M Tomba, 'Who's Afraid of the Imperative Mandate?' (2018) 1 *Critical Times* 108, 109 and 114.

corrupt or morally inferior.[25] Subsequently, representation cannot be but elitist and representatives members of the evil establishment. Those elected to power, in other words, take advantage of their privileges to ascend to their offices, use their position only to foster the interests of their inner circle against the 'real' people and struggle to perpetuate their grip on power.

Rotation in office and selection of the governing elites have existed as salient questions since Ancient Greece, where they used to be cardinal features of the political culture. At the time, Athenians had established a connection between democracy and sortition: as, for the most part, the functions of governors and governed could not be performed at the same time, it was essential to enable every citizen to occupy the two positions alternately: 'democratic freedom consisted not in obeying only oneself but in obeying today someone in whose place one would be tomorrow'.[26] In this system, citizens spontaneously entered the pool of those to be lotted and were then drawn through purpose-built machines called *kleroteria*.

In that era, lot appeared the most effective method to grant alternation, limiting the electorate's freedom of choice being the only absolute guarantee for a compulsory rotation. In his *Politics*, Aristotle maintained that democracy arises from the idea that those who are equal in any respect are equal absolutely and, on the grounds that they are all equal, they claim equal participation in everything. Also Herodotus in his *The Histories* praised the *isonomia* (equality of law and political rights), according to which offices were allotted by sortition, power was held accountable and deliberation took place in public. In sum, allocating public offices by lot was considered *democratic* vis-à-vis election, believed to be *oligarchic*.

In contemporary participatory theories aiming at breaking with *oligarchic* democracy and replacing it with a more profound democracy in favour of the 'true' people, fairness in alternation to power may be thought to be advanced through imperative mandate: if lot turned out beneficial to achieve good government according to a certain idea of distributive justice of functions, imperative mandate could offer a certain proximity between the decisions taken by the governors and the views of the governed affected by those decisions and an implicit idea of fungibility in the course of time. In this sense, the imperative mandate would function as an instrument of equalisation between governed and government and hence as a premise to their alternation to power.

Still, this idea moves from the assumption that the people are always willing and capable to hold office and to overcome the possible limits and imbalances for true participation. But what if the people have neither the *will* nor the *skill* to partake in politics? Citizens can in fact be *apathetic*, as somehow reflected in the low or decreasing turnout in institutions designed for participation, which may be due to a set of causes.

First, the *negative trade-off* between the high cost of participation and the low outcomes extracted:[27] fighting for a cause is less and less a political parties' job, now

[25] See J-W Müller, *What Is Populism?* ()University of Pennsylvania Press, 2016) and C Mudde and C Rovira Kaltwasser, *Populism. A Very Short Introduction* (OUP, 2017).

[26] B Manin, *The Principles of Representative Government* (CUP, 1997) 28.

[27] F Pereira da Silva, 'Debating New Democratic Experiences of Andean Governments on Their Own Terms' (2015) 29 *Socialism and Democracy* 41, 43.

superseded by the most diverse NGOs and private collective actors in the public sphere, which have shifted from activism to advocacy. This transformation signals a tendency to practice *speaking for* instead of *engaging with*, which in turn frames engagement with constituents in terms of *contract to represent* motivated by the logic of success.[28] In light of this phenomenon, known as the *NGOization of politics*, it appears more convenient for the classic electorate to delegate groups of interest to voice their needs and to struggle for them (thanks to the process by means of which nongovernmental institutions are colonised by governmental ways of doing business[29]) instead of participating directly in politics through the worn out procedures of the traditional representative democracy. In this vein, for many politics has changed the tune and has become a matter of personal issues, local injustices, campaigns that representative institutions are not as equipped to respond to as courts[30] in the face of which NGOs file their stakeholders' petitions.

Secondly, the *antipolitical culture* by reason of which 'contemporary political disaffection is not [...] a story of the decline of civic virtue, nor is it a story of political apathy – it is one of disenchantment, even hatred, of politics and politicians'.[31] What counts even more is that many of us may still vote and celebrate the deliberation day as a festivity of democracy, but in reality we no longer believe in representation. Our societies have moved from collective identities to a complex mix of single identities and post-identities so that people think of themselves as *unrepresentable*.[32]

Such plurality of identities with its unrepresentability leads straight to the third cause, that is, the *atomisation of societies*, which is twofold: to begin with, every group entertains the idea that its own identity is inaccessible to those that cannot share their same experience. In the German language, there exists a distinction between 'experience' (*Erfahrung*) and 'lived experience' (*Erlebnis*): *Erfahrung* refers to experiences that can be shared, like two people observing chemical experiments in two different laboratories. With *Erlebnis*, on the contrary, it is meant the subjective perception of experience, which cannot necessarily be partaken.[33]

But also single individuals feel their histories separated from those of others and their situations too specific to be comprehended by others: (h)ence societies today increasingly understand themselves in terms of minorities. A minority is no longer merely 'the smaller number'. It has become one of a series of diffracted expressions of the social totality. Society nowadays manifests itself as a long litany of minority conditions. 'People' has become the plural of minority'.[34]

[28] S Lang, *NGOs, Civil Society, and the Public Sphere* (CUP, 2021) 91–92.

[29] Harwood Institute for Public Innovation, *The Organization – First Approach*, Bethesda MD (Harwood Institute, 2009) 21.

[30] See B Barbisan, 'Flashes in the Pan or Constitutional Metamorphoses? Courts Like Medieval Parliaments in the Crisis of Representative Politics' (2018) 5 *EJCL* 213.

[31] C Hay and G Stoker, 'Rivitalising Politics: Have We Lost the Plot?' (2009) 45 *Representation* 225. See also C Pinelli, 'The Populist Challenge to Constitutional Democracy' (2011) 7 *Eur. Const. L. Rev.* 5.

[32] S Tormey, *The End of Representative Politics* (Polity Press, 2015) 82.

[33] F Fukuyama, *Identity: The Demand for Dignity and the Politics of Resentment* (Profile Books, 2018) 1625–34.

[34] P Rosanvallon, *Democratic Legitimacy: Impartiality, Reflexivity, Proximity* (Princeton University Press, 2011) 4.

Moreover, present-day uncertainty due to the unfastening of labour ties is such a powerful individualising force that individuals 'simply do not sum up into a "common cause" […] Troubles may be similar, but unlike the common interest of yore they do not form a "totality which is greater than the sum of its parts" […]'. The sole advantage the company of other sufferers may bring is to reassure each one that fighting the troubles alone is what all the others do daily – so reinvigorating the flagging resolve to go on doing just that: fighting alone.[35]

On a different account, citizens can be *equal only in theory* as to their education, communication, time availability, economic conditions, social status and therefore lack the abilities to participate in politics. It is nothing more than a pure *abstraction*, then, to think that every member of society is ready and apt to take part in a more direct democracy, for there are divides in contemporary states that the imperative mandate cannot heal to make direct democracy work. For instance, the platform used by the Five-Star Movement, called *Rousseau*, to poll their affiliates about the most contentious matters on the political agenda and to endorse the candidates aspiring to run for elective seats requires an internet connection and to be digitally literate, which cannot be universally taken for granted, especially among the elderly or those residing in rural areas. But even analogic means of political participation can prove unaccessible to those that are ill-equipped as to analytical attitudes, critical thinking, leisure time to reflect, ability to acknowledge and express one's own grievances, etc.[36]

The world of pure direct democracy and imperative mandate labours under the misapprehension that citizens are always self-sufficient in determining their political drive with the only result that, in the process of administering their political sovereignty, citizens somehow unfit to share political equality are pushed to the margins and end up inhabiting an isolated dimension. As paradoxical as it may sound, imperative mandate that aims at making citizens all alike under a perfect political equality including, inter alia, alternation to office is actually successful only in opening the social crevices wide and rendering the weakest weaker.

The Most Serene Republic of Venice practised sortition until its fall in 1797, when the new representative governments in the US and France were leaving sortition behind once and for all – and apparently with no debate[37] – as a method of

[35] Z Bauman, *The Individualized Society* (Polity Press, 2001) 831–39.

[36] K Grönlund and H Wass, *Finnish National Election Study (FNES) 2015*, Finnish Social Science Data Archive (2016) available at http://urn.fi/urn:nbn:fi:fsd:T-FSD3067 charted the political participation, political attitudes, party allegiance, candidate and party choice, and voting behaviour of Finns. The study showed that, while the lack of involvement in politics is generally taken as a symptom of apathy and indifference, political participation is a multifaceted concept, a mixture of resources, motivation, mobilisation and institutional conditions, and can actually reflect social inequalities. Emphasising the role of motivational factors easily leads to *responsibilisation* of the individual. Instead, non-voters or 'passive voters' are not necessarily citizens that do not want to go to the ballots or suffer from a solidarity deficit. Such 'empathy-gap' perspective denies the association between various kinds of societal inequalities and participation. Sometimes people do not take part in politics simply because they cannot for lack of adequate resources (see also Democratic Audit UK, *The Empathy Gap: understanding Why Some People Don't Vote* (6 October 2016), available at www.democraticaudit.com/2016/10/06/the-empathy-gap-understanding-why-some-people-dont-vote/#_edn1).

[37] C Schmitt, *Verfassungslehre* (Duncker & Humblot, 1928) § 19 noted that, in spite of its success in guaranteeing an identity between rulers and ruled, lot had become impracticable in large modern states.

appointing governors.[38] The real turning point happened when the legitimisation of authority came to be perceived as stemming from the consent of those over whom it would be exercised, when the political equality at centre stage was the right to consent to power and no longer an equal chance to hold office.[39]

Electing rulers instead of lotting them brings along two more critical aspects in the relationship between the people and the establishment: a *principle of distinction*[40] that characterises the status of the elected and that conveys the idea of elections as a *mixed institution* of aristocratic and democratic features. Is the imperative mandate desirable and effective to respond to these criticalities?

When medieval tradition and modern natural rights theories converged to shift from lot to election – that is, when the quest for equality in the allocation of offices gave way to conferring political legitimacy to those functions through the consent and will of the people – a *principle of distinction* came into being referring to the contrast between the electors' status and that of their representatives. In different European countries and in the US, various measures were put into force to assure a higher social standing of the elected,[41] introducing an aristocratic or oligarchic flavour to representation, reinforced by the same dynamics of choice and cognitive constraints in the electorate that led the voters to trust representatives they perceived noticeable, different from their contestants, and somehow different from themselves. Candidates with qualities too similar to their voters' would end up indistinguishable and less successful. As James Madison aired in *The Federalist* 57, '(t)he aim of every political constitution is, or ought to be, first to obtain for rulers men who possess most wisdom to discern, and most virtue to pursue, the common good of the society, and in the next place, to take the most effectual precautions for keeping them virtuous whilst they continue to hold their public trust. The elective mode of obtaining rulers is the characteristic policy of republican government'.

[38] J Harrington, *The Prerogative of Popular Government* in JGA Pocock, *The Political Works of Jams Harrington* (CUP, 2010) 486.

[39] Manin (n 26) 92.

[40] ibid 94.

[41] The selective process of election was generally conditioned by the tendency of voters to turn to the most prominent figures in their social context and the exorbitant cost of electoral campaigning affordable only for very few. However, single policies corroborated this natural divide. In England, eg, the Qualification Act was passed in 1710 requiring a property qualification for MPs higher than that imposed to vote (£600 per annum for knights and £300 for burgesses): intended to foster the independence from the Crown and to avert corruption, no attempt was made to repeal the Act and both Whigs and Tories ended up agreeing to it (see P Langford, 'Property and "Virtual Representation" in Eighteenth-Century England' (1988) 31 *The Historical Journal* 83). In France, in 1789 the hegemonic grasp of Fayettists on the Revolution manoeuvred the Constituent Assembly to decree that election was open only to candidates owning land and paying taxes of at least one *marc d'argent* (corresponding to 54 days' labour, whereas voters were required to be able to pay a three days' labour tax). This act provoked little criticism with the major exception of Robespierre who, despite his strong opposition, was defeated and the *marc d'argent* policy reiterated the year after (in this regard, see G Kates, 'From Liberalism to Radicalism: Tom Paine's Rights of Man' in B Kuklick (ed), *Thomas Paine* (Routledge, 2018) and M Crook, 'The Rights of Man and the Right to Vote: The Franchise Question During the French Revolution' in GM Schwab and JR Jeanneney (eds), *The French Revolution of 1789 and Its Impact* (Greenwood, 1995). In the US, the only reason why the 1787 Constitution did not embrace any property requirements was due to the insormountable dissent among the drafters on a uniform threshold in both the northern and southern states. But, along the debate for the ratification, Anti-Federalists recurrently objected that the too wide a distance between elected and electors prevented any social likeness between the two sides.

The coexistence in election of a 'natural aristocracy' of representatives, on one hand, and a tentative degree of proximity between the electorate and the elected, on the other, casts a light on its appearance as a *mixed institution*, in analogy with the notion of a mixed constitution. Still, unlike the mixed constitution, which comprised a number of elements easy to deconstruct, in the case of election '(i)ts two properties are so tightly interwoven that they cannot possibly be separated from each other. […] the egalitarian and inegalitarian properties being the two sides of a single, indissoluble operation, the elective procedure may be perceived either as wholly democratic or as wholly aristocratic, depending on which way it is looked at'.[42]

Rousseau did not reject elections per se but, echoing Montesquieu's argument, objected to its aristocratic nature. Yet, more importantly than using elections or not, in *Considérations sur le gouvernement de Pologne*, written in 1772, he abandoned the radical denial of representation expressed in the *Du contrat social* and approved instead a form of non-deliberative delegated democracy, different from a representative (deliberative) democracy. To him, representation was a contract and, like any contract, could be of alienation – when sovereignty ultimately residing in each individual citizen is shifted to others – or of delegation, when representatives carry the burden of examining and sorting problems out, but do not have the last word on which legislation eventually to pass. In other terms, delegation was a form of direct decision by other means, whereas representation implied a reallocation of political will.

In his theoretical duel with Emmanuel Sieyès over the role of primary assemblies – that is, local meetings for direct citizen involvement, where neighbours prepared instructions (*cahiers de doléance*) intended to bind the deputies at the Estates-General – Rousseau in the *Du contrat social* stated that the meanest citizen was 'as sacred and inviolable as that of the first magistrate; for in the presence of the person represented, representatives no longer exist'. From the antagonistic camp, Sieyès believed that primary assemblies were not called to exercise the *pouvoir constituant*, but they were the bearers of the *pouvoir commettant*, generating genuine representatives instead of simple vote carriers.[43] Sieyès based his vision on the idea of *nation*, an abstract entity with a will of its own that deputies were charged with identifying, whilst Rousseau conceived the political community as a collection of separate individuals.

Rousseau's theory of delegation intended to create a public space where citizens could relate in reciprocity and equality, each being both a sovereign and a subject. To this scope, when he wrote about delegates voting in the assembly, 'this "c'est ne pas voter" but "c'est opiner" […]: first, the delegates do not make authoritative decisions; and second, they exercise only the faculty of judgment, not the will. […] Whenever they are given the power to make decisions, deputies are no longer deputies but representatives *or*, in Rousseau's reasoning, sovereigns'.[44]

[42] Manin (n 26) 155–56.

[43] J Colón-Ríos, 'Constituent Power, Primary Assemblies, and the Imperative Mandate' in H Lerner and D Landau (eds), *Elgar Handbook of Comparative Constitution-Making* (Edward Elgar, 2019) 98.

[44] N Urbinati, 'Rousseau on the Risks of Representing the Sovereign' (2012) 53 *Politische Vierteljahresschrift* 646, 657.

The crucial distinction here is between *constituēre* and *alienare*: deputies' job is to propose, discuss, draft the laws, but never to ultimately authorise them. '(T)hey opine but do not want'.[45] As a result, to make people count and possess their political sovereignty, delegates exercise *judgement* and voters express *authorisation*. But only the former involves a process of getting together, assessing issues and positions, forming opinions and debating, aggregating preferences – in a word, growth and mutual learning, which are a prerogative only of the very few acting as delegates. Conversely, authorisation leaves the people with the political *will*, which certainly touches the process with the holy oil of their sovereignty, but with a minimal degree of participation – what is required to rubber-stamp the entire operation. It is not only the *vertical* participation that is missing here – that is a more integrated connection between the site of the judgement and that of the authorisation – but a *horizontal* mode that would ignite a form of osmosis within the number of citizens owning the ultimate political will. Regrettably, this model allows the elite to strengthen their unity through speech and reflection, while the citizens are asked only to say 'yes' or 'no'.[46]

But this dichotomy does no more than allow to sneak in the back the principle of distinction that was thrown out of the front door. The twisted logics behind this division of labour is that the superiority of the people in the name of their political sovereignty asks for representatives entrusted with judgement only, which in turn requires knowledge, experience, maturity and expertise. Eventually, the supremacy of the constituents and their political will over their deputies limited to opine ends up re-establishing the pre-eminence of skilful, gifted, seasoned representatives over the sovereign people with their imperative but nonetheless inane holy oil.

This is the sort of division of labour that lies at the core of the imperative mandate, which revolves around a *proprietary* notion of political sovereignty. Still, the cost of political sovereignty is the isolation of each from the others, leading to an atomised personal development, in total detachment, supposedly self-sufficiently but, more pragmatically, in solitude. Embracing the concept of political sovereignty as a *property* belonging to the people with no intermediaries but only mere executioners of the judgement, imperative mandate privatises representation, breaks the links that keep together the members of the political community and leaves each at the mercy of her own – whether resourceful or not – will and skill.

In the twentieth century, especially its second half, the political marginalisation of groups and individuals and their unorganised advocacy were surmounted through the action of various established intermediate bodies, with political parties on top of it. Political parties have been omitted from this discourse on representation and imperative mandate so far because of the ambivalent role they tend to play in the relationship between elected and electors that imperative mandate would aspire to improve: if, on one hand, political parties should lose grip on their deputies to allow a more fluent, sympathetic alliance between rulers and ruled, on the other hand they are the only actors that can impose a discipline on deputies to guarantee their perfect

[45] ibid 647.
[46] ibid 661.

compliance with the instructions of the electorate. This is the typical ambivalence that leaps out every time more accountability of representatives to their constituents is promised, for political parties serve the not negligible purpose of sanctioning deputies or reporting them to the authorities in charge of penalisation when they contravene the electorate's wishes. Imperative mandate, then, makes political parties necessary, if not indispensable, for the answerability of politicians to the people. And in fact, the examples of institutions related to imperative mandate we have examined above all fatally contradict that political parties are destined to recede under imperative mandate.

It is against an individualistic state that endows citizens with individual subjective rights that Hans Kelsen argued the *non-individualistic essence of political parties* with their 'strong collectivizing tendency'.[47] He was in the company of other jurists of the epoch ascribed along the same line of thought, but it is doubtless that in the 1920s, when Kelsen wrote *Vom Weser und Wert dem Democratie*, the mainstream doctrine, in particular under the Weimar Republic, was highly critical of political parties, to say the least, as epitomised by Carl Schmitt and his *Der Hüter der Verfassung*. Schmitt believed in the importance of identifying the neutral state with one, solid, general will of the people, crystallised in the father-figure institution of the President of the Republic, the only one empowered to summarise and protect that univocal, homogeneous voice. Political parties threatened that unity, fragmented it in a variety of political addresses and petitions detrimental to the common good. To him, political parties parcelled out the *total* 'in that every organized social power-complex, from the choir and the sports club to the association of armed self-defence, aims to realise *totality*, as far as possible, *within itself and for itself*'.[48]

Kelsen, on the contrary, was firmly persuaded that isolated individuals had little weight in political life unless they associated with others to share the same affinities and purposes. In his view, democracy could exist only if between the state and the individual arose collective groups, each representing an orientation common to its members: a political party. To him, democracy necessarily was a party state.

But political pluralism brings along conflict within representative assemblies, at least according to Rousseau and Schmitt that, mutatis mutandis, both postulated the notion of the general will of a unified community put at risk when a plethora of different parties, each perched on its own idea of *totality*, compete to move on their agenda at the expense of the others. Kelsen rebuffed their fiction and pierced the veil of the objective interest of the state: discussions in parliaments were the signal of democratic vibrancy. After all, the idea of representation positing the equality of wills in a collective body had always been associated with the trial of discussion. 'Debate acts as a screen or filter, whatever the origin of bills may be. But this is enough to secure an essential effect on decision-making: no measure can be adopted unless a majority deems it *justified* after argumentative scrutiny. Representative government

[47] H Kelsen, *Essence and Value of Democracy* (Rowman & Littlefield, 2013) 42, n 8.

[48] C Schmitt, *The Guardian of the Constitution* (1931), as translated in L Vinx, *The Guardian of the Constitution: Hans Kelsen and Carl Schmitt on the Limits of Constitutional Law* (CUP, 2015) 137 (italics added).

is not a system in which everything must originate in debate, but in which everything has to be justified in debate'.[49]

And, after passing the trial of discussion, in order to deliberate, representation may very likely need to converge towards a common point that, far from being unanimous, stands as the outcome made possible by striking a *compromise* among some of the opinions raised in the debate. In Kelsen's view, illustrated in 1925 in his *Allgemeine Staatslehre*, compromise favoured that which bind over that which divided those who were to be brought together; compromise meant to get along, and social integration was only possible through compromise. 'No harmonious society with a spontaneous reconciliation of interests exists, neither the regulation of divergent interests nor social integration can be achieved except by negotiation, which is always provisional'.[50]

Kelsen was so confident of the pivotal role to be attributed to political parties that suggested borrowing several elements of the imperative mandate to secure their contribution to a healthy democracy: according to his doctrine, in fact, voters should control their representatives by means of the recall that political parties could activate in case of major deviations of the deputies from the party's programme. What counts here is not the evident discrepancy between the strong accent put on compromise as an essential component of good government and such emphasis on certain features of the imperative mandate – which compromise can be actually drawn within the boundaries of imperative mandate? – but the importance Kelsen acknowledged to political parties to surmount the isolation of individuals and convey their ideas for an efficient political action. In other words, it was only the intermediation of parties that could liberate the electorate from the irrelevance they were condemned to should they remain disconnected from the others, sovereign but alone. In Kelsen's doctrine, it is only political parties that can treat the malaise of political solitude attached to citizens in reason of their political sovereignty.

The argument has now come full circle insofar as imperative mandate serves the purpose, inter alia, of removing all intermediaries – political parties first and foremost – to reconnect constituents and deputies, but political parties serve in turn the purpose of imposing the discipline that makes that direct connection possible.

III. CONCLUSIONS

Imperative mandate and the institutions related thereof are believed to invigorate the relationship between constituents and their representatives, correcting the distortions that affect alternation to power, the aristocratic nature of elections and the oligarchy of deputies, the debate in assemblies – in sum, all that is needed to secure the proximity, if not identity, of the delegates' decisions to the people's wishes.

[49] Manin (n 26) 191.

[50] S Baume, 'Rehabilitating Political Parties: An Examination of the Writings of Hans Kelsen' (2018) 28 *Intellectual History Review* 425, 433.

From the arguments exposed above, what conversely emerges is the imperative mandate's overall failure to overcome these problems and bridge the distance between the populace and the establishment. If imperative mandate involves an equivalence across the two sides of representation and an interchange to power, it should be taken into account that citizens might be either apathetic or inadequate to partake in political life, and the imperative mandate per se cannot provide the recommended toolbox to run for elective seats and operate them. To circumvent the elitist trait of elections, a division of political labour could be introduced, distinguishing the judgement attributed to representatives and the will resting in the hands of the electorate alone. Still, Rousseau's idea of political sovereignty generates the twofold effect of depriving citizens of the real learning process employed in political decision-making and subsequently of keeping each separate from the rest of the community. This *proprietarian* notion of political sovereignty is counterbalanced by the conspicuous cost of isolating individuals and forcing them to count on their personal resources only, if they have any. Sovereignty as *property* paves the way to political detachment and insignificance.

But, if delegates are charged with judgment, their job requires discerning qualities that end up reinstating the principle of distinction that, as the typical privilege of any elite, imperative mandate is supposed to fight. And even political parties, viewed as the villain of the story, are those intermediate bodies that the imperative mandate is supposed to evict from the political scenario to unburden the relationship of ruled with rulers. However, individuals left to their forces alone carry little weight, so they do necessitate parties, even if only for dictating the discipline deputies should comply with under the imperative mandate's rule.

To the fiction of a general, univocal will of the people and the scepticism coeval jurists opposed to political pluralism and its fragmentation, Hans Kelsen retorted that democracy flourishes through discussion and political compromises. Compromise not only means keeping at bay the overarching power of majorities with political moderation – that is, with the margin that separates the quantity behind a majority and the quality of its decision-making. Compromise is the fiercest denial of any *proprietarian* impulse of representation, deliberation being the encounter of diverse political options and identities that debate and rule assuming that nobody shall prevail in force of the binding, exclusive sovereignty they serve. Representation is not arm wrestling, the survival of the fittest or the law of the strongest. Representation hinges on the force of arguments and, when Rousseau stressed that delegates opine but do not want, he did not imply it should be a mere game of strength. Modern representative governments repudiate imperative mandate because no individual is entitled to impose her will on that of others, regardless of her social distinction or affluence and especially regardless of her constituents' dignity, intellect or will.

The prohibition on the imperative mandate was elaborated in the same age of the first recognition of individual rights and freedoms in the *Déclaration universelle des droits de l'homme*, that is the time when Europeans ran up against the dilemma of how to provide the source of community in a new constitutional order that accentuated the rights of the individual. How was it possible to reconcile the self-directed individual with the idea of a common welfare?[51] It is in this regard that the *trial of discussion* first and the subsequent disposition to strike a *compromise* are conducive to the aim of interweaving the numerous, adversarial claims springing from society in a deliberation hopefully pursuing a greater good.

But this method of deliberation, based on trial of discussion and compromise, makes sense only when the greater good *is* the target political actors strive for and the electorate regards as paramount, when the forces that draw us together as a community win over those that keep us apart as single individuals. Imperative mandate, though, is claimed also when citizens embarking on politics are in search for *empathy* from their representatives, an attitude radically excluding the method of deliberation based on trial of discussion and compromise.

This will certainly sound like an outlandish statement. After all, empathy is a byword for altruism and hailed as an essential virtue – when you empathise with others, you are more likely to leave your selfishness behind and assist them. During his presidential campaign, Barack Obama used to refer to an 'empathy deficit' affecting the world,[52] and it has also been suggested that the notion of evil be conceptualised as an 'empathy erosion'.[53] Nothing seems as likely as empathy to boost the performance of a good politics aspiring to achieve the common good.

But empathy – what Adam Smith called 'sympathy' in his *The Theory of Moral Sentiments* (1759), meaning a process by which experiencing the world as others do or at least as we think they do – is not only the sort of imagination upon which justice, democracy and ethics are contingent. In the comprehension of others that it kindles, empathy is a capricious emotion, biased and parochial.[54] What in fact makes us familiarise, get closer and react before others is hardly far from what we think right, good, commendable, which in representative politics does not necessarily correspond to the optimum.

Empathic concern is the tendency to experience sympathy or compassion for another person who is in distress. Empathic concern is operated by an other-oriented emotion that motivates individuals to take action in favour of those in pain. Yet, empathy is never neutral, as even those who are more likely to feel empathy for others are decidedly unlikely to find a common ground towards opposite powerful identities. In other words, individuals are more prone to experience empathic concern in the face of ingroup members rather than outgroup members. As a consequence, this partisan favouritism, in the face of which highly empathic subjects display greater partisan bias in the censorship of ideas and feelings of schadenfreude, fuels negative attitudes

[51] L Hunt, *Inventing Human Rights. A History* (WW Norton & Co, 2008) 64.

[52] 'You know, there's a lot of talk in this country about the federal deficit. But I think we should talk more about our empathy deficit – the ability to put ourselves in someone else's shoes; to see the world through the eyes of those who are different from us – the child who's hungry, the steelworker who's been laid-off, the family who lost the entire life they built together when the storm came to town. When you think like this – when you choose to broaden your ambit of concern and empathize with the plight of others, whether they are close friends or distant strangers – it becomes harder not to act; harder not to help' (B Obama, *Commencement Address*, Xavier University, New Orleans LA, 11 August 2006).

[53] S Baron-Cohen, *The Science of Evil. On Empathy and the Origins of Cruelty* (Basic Books, 2011).

[54] P Bloom, *Against Empathy. The Case for Rational Compassion* (Harper Collins, 2016).

towards the outparty. In sum, empathy tends to exacerbate *political polarisation* rather than alleviate the harm against others: '(g)iven their increased outgroup antipathy, those high in empathic concern may also be *less willing to entertain policy proposals from opponents* whom they disproportionately blame (relative to copartisans) for social ills. These patterns may contribute to *decreased willingness to compromise with the opposing party* and more negative attitudes toward bipartisanship'.[55]

There is another dark side of empathy, so to speak, in representative politics, that is when citizens want their deputies to look exactly like them and to make every effort as to execute what the electorate *stricto sensu* wishes. This form of empathy, dangerously close to self-absorption, responds to a *narcissistic* push, by reason of which the voter, driven by a repressed rage and fantasies of power, in an outburst of grandiose self-aggrandisement uses her representatives as instruments of gratification until their shortcomings disappoint her. According to this form of narcissism, even social justice is dramatically reduced to mere personal psychological issues[56] – paraphrasing an old essay,[57] a 'me' politics.

Both these facets of empathy in politics incorporate a disposition that gives energy to the temptation of *privatising representation*, which imperative mandate would gladly accommodate. Let us be clear: there is nothing bad in wanting another kind of politics, one that involves the people more directly. But insofar as politics revolves around selecting our representatives on the basis of their character or personal success, it will be hardly surprising that elections come to resemble a beauty contest with candidates running for seats like beauty pageants.[58] If a new relationship between ruled and rulers is in order, some attention should be paid to the qualities of the latter and necessarily to the insuppressible role of intermediate bodies in this regard, otherwise the only possible outcome is an unfaltering shortfall between what is promised and what is delivered.

In the end, the problem that makes imperative mandate incompatible with European democratic constitutionalism, as the Venice Commission noted, has nothing to do with its medieval roots or the fragmentation of sovereignty in a plurality of powers that contradicts the 'obsession' of democratic constitutionalism with unity[59] or its democratic excess, that modern constitutionalism would seek to tame.[60] The trouble is that imperative mandate cares for the neglect the people experience because of the inefficiencies of their representative government only to treat it with a different type of neglect – when citizens are left alone in the process of developing their political wisdom, isolated in an atomised society, where representation is reduced to a *property* paradigm.

[55] EN Simas, S Clifford and JH Kirkland, 'How Empathic Concern Fuels Political Polarization' (2020) 114 *Am. Pol. Sc. Rev.* 258, 267 (italics added).

[56] C Lasch, *The Culture of Nascissism. American Life in an Age of Diminishing Expectations* (WW Norton, 1991).

[57] T Wolfe, 'The 'Me' Decade and the Third Great Awakening' *New York Magazine* (23 August 1976).

[58] Tormey (n 32) 45.

[59] Tomba (n 24) 114.

[60] ibid 115.

16

Party Fatigue in European Democracies

PIERO IGNAZI*

I. INTRODUCTION

IN HIS LANDMARK *Parties and Party Systems*[1] Giovanni Sartori warned that to ensure the democratic standing of a political system, democracy should reign in inter-party competition rather than in intra-party life. He pointed out the systemic importance of competition, and discarded intra-party dynamics. This 'realist' approach, in line with the bitter considerations of Robert Michels[2] against an oligarchic drive in the German Social Democratic Party (and, *in extenso*, also in the other parties), deems political parties a locus of inescapable conflict, and inevitable power struggles. Indeed, the story of political parties since their inception is interwoven with disputes among different components, usually demonised with the despised term of faction. Ideological and programmatic visions have represented the visible and 'noble' part of clashes undergone in the party's arena; however, under that veil, ferocious power struggles have been acted out. The idea that power was something negative and even 'dirty' reflects the romanticist ideal fought for general goodwill. The mid-nineteenth-century *epopée* for national independence all over Europe, carried mainly by Mazzini's preachings, left its mark on political organisations' conduct. A sort of Weberian *Wertrationalität*, founded on high and noble aspirations detached from petty ambitions, impinged on the nascent parties of the late nineteenth century. This vision of political activity left its imprint on political parties, and created an inner contradiction between the ideals of: (i) general and disinterested action to be displayed in the open field of the political system, and (ii) the reality of intra-party power struggles between different factions. This contradiction has been further nurtured by a superseding imperative which ontologically affects political parties: a drive for harmony and unity, or, put another way, an obligation to comply with a holistic and monist vision. Any conflict with society and, a fortiori, the polity, had to be eradicated in, and for, the 'good society'.[3]

* University of Bologna and Sciences Po Paris.

[1] G Sartori, *Parties and Party Systems* (CUP, 1976).

[2] R Michels, *Political Parties, A Sociological Study of the Oligarchical Tendencies of Modern Democracy* (Rand McNally [1911], 1962).

[3] N Urbinati *Democracy Disfigured* (Harvard University Press, 2014).

Conflict was bad not only *within* political parties but also in society at large. Parties thus had to overcome two barriers: one in the *political system as a whole*, the acceptance of the party per se; and one *inside the party itself*, the acceptance of intra-party divisions. These two difficulties have different impacts on the democratic system. We concur with Sartori[4] that the system dimension is much more important for democracy. Acknowledging that political representation and governmental decisions should pass through the parties represents a watershed in the achievement of full democracy. However, as will be discussed infra, the intra-party dimension affects system dynamics – it is not confined to the sphere of any single party. In fact, it would be quite implausible to suggest that what occurs within the party has no influence on the political system. In essence, this is linked to the homeostatic property of each complex organisation or aggregate, where every component tends to get along, and harmonise its organisational forms, means, and ends. A sort of echo, or contagion effect, reverberates into and across the system; therefore, a party operating in a democratic system is driven to adapt itself to the rules of the system.

The examples of this process in post-war Europe are quite telling. The communist and neo-fascist parties, respectively moulded on the *Führerprinzip* and the Leninist and democratic centralist model in the first post-World War II decades, gradually abandoned those organisational principles and moved towards the acceptance of more traditional and 'democratic' intra-party modalities. This does not imply an automatic and strict relationship between micro (intra-party dimension) and macro (system dimension): undemocratic parties still survive in democratic systems (and vice versa, an occurrence which raises another set of questions). At the same time a relationship between what is considered a pillar of the 'chain of delegation'[5] and rewarded as such in almost all democratic constitutions[6] and the logics of the system cannot be ignored.

In this chapter, the evolution of the two dimensions of the party's standing – in the political system and in its internal dynamics – will be treated sequentially, starting with the former.

II. THE LONG JOURNEY TO PARTY LEGITIMACY

A. The Rejection of the Party Per Se

Let's start from the roots. The etymology of party comes from the Latin verb *partire* meaning to divide; the derived noun *pars* means part. All Western languages, including Russian (but not other Slavic idioms) have that root. The genetic code of party thus contains the germs of partiality and division. As a consequence, the acceptance of party entails the acknowledgement of the feasibility of difference and opposition,

[4] Sartori (n 1).

[5] K Strom, W Muller and T Bergman, 'Challenges to Party Democracy' in K Strom, W Muller and T Bergman (eds), *Delegation and Accountability in Parliamentary Democracies* (OUP, 2003) 651–704.

[6] I van Biezen, 'State Intervention in Party Politics, The Public Funding and Regulation of Political Parties' (2008) 16(3) *European Review* 337–53.

of division and conflict. This means the political party is 'something' that infringes and goes counter to the principles that Western civilisation has always considered desirable in society and in polity: union and harmony, consensus and agreement, concord and cohesion. These elements were rated – and still are, to a large extent – the supreme values of human relations in all its forms.[7] Where division and strife emerge, every evil would prevail. This descent into the turmoil of social and political life is connected with the unleashing of different interests and passions. If these drives are not kept under control, political and social fabrics break down. Only unity can avoid this danger.

This holist and monist vision has for centuries moulded almost any theorisation of politics. From ancient Greece to medieval theological and secular speculations, from *raison d'état* and absolutism to modern statecraftism and nationalism, Western civilisation has always longed for unity, and despised whatever could infringe on such valuable *bonum commune*. The political party, for long misinterpreted under the guise of faction, was the enemy *par excellence*, the demon which destroys the holistic frame and brings conflict and destruction. As Nancy Rosenblum[8] wrote, the anti-party tradition nurtured by a holist conception 'insists that political society should be a unity and that divisions are morally unwholesome and politically fatal. The formulations are familiar: an organic body, an indivisible nation or people, unitary royal or popular sovereignty, a general will that cannot err, one determinable common good'.

Disorder, friction and striving for change are all inescapable by-products of a partisan presence. No political thinker until the late eighteenth century ever imagined arguing in favour of division. What could be acquired was tolerance, at best. Even when differences of opinion were described as plausible, they had to be compounded into a single aim. The contradiction between acknowledging difference and pledging unity is well illustrated by Montesquieu:

> what is spoken of as union of the political body is in fact something very ambiguous, the true one is a union of harmony, following which all the parts, albeit seemingly opposed to each other, concur to the common good, just like some dissonances in music concur to the overall harmony.[9]

Montesquieu was anticipated by a millennial-old, infinite set of references on the same line, the famous Menenius Agrippa apologue. Confronted by a plebeian revolt against the *optimates*, Agrippa argued that each component of society was indispensable for society's effective working, precisely as all organs are necessary and complementary for the survival and proper functioning of the body. Many others agreed with this assessment. Cicero, for example, following Agrippa's organic metaphor, asserted that only harmony among the parts sets the conditions for the best government. Whatever deepens a disagreement and organises the different parts in a reciprocal fight should be expelled, because it threatens the commonwealth and the very existence of the *res publica*.

[7] N Rosenblum, *On the Side of Angels, An Appreciation of Parties and Partisanship*. (Princeton University Press, 2008); J White and L Ypi, *The Meaning of Partisanship* (OUP, 2016).
[8] Rosenblum (n 7) 26.
[9] Montesquieu, 1999 [1734], Ch IX 'Considerations'.

This concept has lasted for a long time, as Montesquieu's citation highlights – not even the American and French revolutions modified this anti-pluralist attitude. In France, the initial explosion of free speech and political mobilisation, including a massive enlargement of the franchise, went hand in hand with a suspicion of any kind of political organisation: on the one hand, they resembled too closely a reframing of the *ancien régime*'s *corps intermediares*, and on the other hand they risked dividing the unity of the nation, something prized above all else by revolutionaries. In America, political parties profited from a different context and a slower and differentiated pace of enfranchisement. Contrary to their French counterparts, the American revolutionaries did not need to reverse the pre-existing political practices that local communities and the colonies had already adopted many decades earlier. They could rely on what they had already set. They were extraneous to the furore against the old regime.

Nevertheless, the Founding Fathers 'despised the very idea of political parties'.[10] Madison, in particular, considered that a community crossed by different parties becomes 'much more disposed to vex and oppress each other than to cooperate for the common good'.[11] A contradiction was there, however: parties/factions were considered dangerous for the well-being of the nation, while, at the same time, individual freedom and competitive elections pushed towards the installation of party politics. In the end, the competition between federalists and republicans convinced Madison to embrace the idea of a political organisation to gain a majority in Congress so that, 'by about the Third or Fourth Congress, then, political parties had come into existence'.[12] In sum, the American experience, and more particularly Madison thoughts, suggest that the harmful danger of the 'violence of factions' *could be reduced to a minimum only in the context of a state erected on the basis of the 'republican principle'* (popular government, separation of powers, and federalism). On the contrary, the French experience, although inspired by the principles of the Enlightenment, kept at a distance, and finally forbade after 1794, the presence of any political organisation. The holist principle of the unity of the nation disbanded the liberal and pluralist premises of the Revolution. France would long have ambivalent relations with any form of political organisation: on the one hand it was invoked as an element of freedom and contestation of power; on the other hand it was seen as a factor of division and thus enfeeblement of the state and the nation. In sum, the 'recreation of One People' was at the centre of concerns, and it would remain so for a long time.

Virtually no one would deny that divisions spring from anything other than petty, sectorial or vested interests, and are thus harmful to the common good, regardless of whatever political organisation should concur is a general, 'principled' ideal, be it the nation or the state, class or race. When the ideology/mythology of the *Tiers état*, first, and the proletariat, later, emerged, they were total and absolute principles: nothing

[10] JH Aldrich, *Why Parties?* (Chicago University Press, 1995) 93.

[11] J Madison, 'Federalist No. 10' in A Hamilton, J Madison, and J Jay, *The Federalist Papers*, (ed Jacob E Cooke) (Wesleyan University Press J, 1787).

[12] Aldrich (n 10) 81.

could obstruct the deployment of the general will under class divisions – this became even worse when race supplanted class as the principle for uniformity.

The American and French revolutions offered an opportunity to implement the ideas of toleration and freedom that had been developing since the previous century. Sartori is once more unequivocal when he claimed that '(p)arties came to be accepted (…) with the realization that diversity and dissent are not necessarily incompatible with, or disruptive of, political order. In this ideal sense parties are correlative to, and dependent upon, the *Weltanschauung* of liberalism'.[13] However, that intellectual critical juncture represented a necessary condition, not a sufficient one. The acceptance of opposition was accepted in principle but not in practice. Any opposition had to follow the narrow track designed by the established power. Parliament was the only locus of politics: there, 'wise men' met to decide by deliberation. Any infringement on the activity of those noble spirits, devoted to the nation's interest only, was harmful. Passions excited by unscrupulous 'politicians', already excoriated by Jonathan Swift's sarcasm in *Gulliver's Travels, A Voyage to Brobdingnag*, might overwhelm the rationality of the liberal–notable parliament.

B. The Rejection of the Organised Party and of its 'Intrusion' into Parliament

The fear that passions – a sort of synonym for faction – could destroy the political order triggered hostility towards parties all through the liberal nineteenth century. That fear and that hostility were precisely ignited by the irruption in the public sphere *and into the institutions* of new actors – either socialists, radicals or Catholics – all extraneous to the traditional elites, although largely run by members of the elite classes. Incoming parties could no longer profit from the condescending consideration of being 'honourable connections', in the footsteps of Burke's approach, because they were not composed of a few 'wise men'. Rather, they rather represented those 'bold men',[14] that is, a sort of political parvenus 'that take the lead to which others are entitled and […] soon come to power not natural to them' (ibid). What the English writer foresaw at the end of the eighteenth century was actually to come a century later.

Liberal thought did not display its potential for pluralism, nor did it allow for full liberalisation and democratisation. In fact, male enfranchisement and the entry of mass parties were not hailed as a fundamental passage towards a more equalitarian system: on the contrary, they were seen as the triumph of the machine and the tyranny of numbers, demagogy and petty personal interests. The room gained by the political party even in the representative institutions, troubled the old elites and a large part of the liberal-conservative intelligentsia because the new parties' representatives were considered nothing else than mere '*politicien*'. With the advent of parties, parliament was no longer guided by the 'internal necessities' of legislative activity, but rather by

[13] Sartori (n 1) 13.

[14] EC Black, *The Association: British Extraparliamentary Political Organization,1769–1793* (Harvard University Press, 1963) 10.

the 'external bond of the popular will'; therefore, the party had, in a way, 'replaced representation with mandate'.[15]

Throughout the nineteenth and twentieth centuries, anti-partyism was intertwined with the question of representation. On the one hand, parties represented sectarian interests which were at odds with the realisation of the general will embodied by the state or the nation. On the other hand, mass parties undermined the possibility of representing the true interests of the people, because the 'party-machine' drove out the best and wisest people and favoured the ambitious and unscrupulous '*politicien*'.

This criticism was expressed with much vigour by Mosei Ostrogorski: he reproached the American import of the political machine, exemplified by the Birmingham caucus which reduced MPs to 'simple puppets on the parliamentary stage'.[16] Ostrogorski envisaged mortal danger for the liberal representative system in the arrival of new parties and, especially, in their structuring as caucuses and machines. In this way politics was degraded because any 'party boss plays with wants and appetites, with credulity and vanity'.[17] The traditional individual system of representation, where rationality and deliberation were the standard practice, would be flooded away by the masses brought into the political sphere by the party machines. According to Ostrogorski, the party emerging from the Birmingham election had no restraint in exciting the masses, and raising emotions over rationality to its own advantage, as it had to gain the vote from a much larger electorate than in the past. Moreover, in order to win in these new, 'competitive' elections the party had to command full and blind obedience from their members, who were obliged to follow the leadership with no possibility of displaying free will and calm judgement. The new party adopted a Caesaristic and autocratic structure where bosses imposed total submission and followers lost their individuality, becoming just numbers or *masse de manoeuvre*.

The anti-party criticism of the turn of the century was of a different kind compared to the past. Political conflict and pluralism were no longer the 'enemy' *par excellence*: the political party was there, a reality difficult to avoid, as was the process of enfranchisement. The idea of opposition and of organisation of dissent had finally broken the glass ceiling. Some pockets of resistance had remained here and there, but party politics and 'the' party had become a reality. The target of the liberal-conservative elites was the negative effect of party dominance on institutions. Their argument relied on the axiom that the extension of individual rights and universal male suffrage, as well as the development of political organisations *linked to the popular will rather than to the whim of the government*, would have favoured the triumph of passion over reason, of sheer numbers over careful deliberation, and thus of demagogy over republican virtues.

This new version of anti-partyism did not prevent its complete legitimation: in the twentieth century it became, *in theory and practice*, the pillar of all political systems: democratic, of course, and even non-democratic.

[15] G Quagliariello, *La politica senza partiti, Ostrogorski e l'organizzazione della politica tra Ottocento e Novecento* (Laterza, 1993) 126.

[16] M Ostrogorski, *Democracy and the Organization of Political Parties* (Haskell House [1902], 1970) 609.

[17] ibid 403.

C. The Final Legitimation in Theory and Praxis

The final breakthrough of parties into the arena of 'legitimate politics' is indebted to a new theorising on their role outside and inside parliament. A powerful intellectual movement, ranging from the public law schools in Italy, Germany and France, and including Max Weber, recognised that a collective body arisen from society rather than from parliament *had the right to inspire government and control parliamentary activity*. In essence, representation had moved from individual to collective: in this way the political party was the indispensable instrument to grant representation.

Two most prominent and internationally renowned scholars, first Max Weber and later Hans Kelsen, stringently argued in favour of the legitimacy of party politics.[18] Indeed, they finally vindicated any intellectual resistance. In a nutshell, for Weber (see especially *Politik als Beruf*)[19] parties are essential to democracy because the competition which connotes electoral democracy can be enforced only by them, since they are the vehicles for a *legitimate* representation of the popular will. Parties are the 'necessary' instruments for political activity, and parliament has to abide by their role: its activity should be directed and governed by parliamentary party groups. Weber's acknowledgement of the political conflict as inevitable and positive, and of the central role of parties in mastering this conflict for the fair working of institutions, dismissed any nostalgia for statecraftism in the German cultural space (including Italy).

Along the same lines, and displaying even more rigour, Hans Kelsen offered a very convincing argumentation not only of the legitimacy but also of the indispensability of parties as '(m)odern democracy virtually rests on political parties'. In fact, he considered party pluralism synonymous to democracy. Thus, modern democracy should be a *Parteienstaat* and all 'efforts (…) to discredit political parties (…) constituted an ideologically veiled resistance to the realization of democracy'.[20] This implied that the masses represented by the parties had become the true source of democratic legitimacy.

With Kelsen the ideological and intellectual resistance to pluralism on the one hand, and to (legitimate) party politics on the other, was finally removed. The political party has attained a central role in political systems, and *it will never abandon such a position, despite criticism and deficiencies.*

It is quite ironic that once parties had achieved full legitimacy they were disbanded in some countries, namely in Russia, Italy and later Germany. And it is even more puzzling that such eradication occurred *without writing off the 'idea' of party*. On the contrary, in the interwar totalitarian regimes the party acquired the highest status ever attained. The sole party remaining after the elimination of all the other parties became the alpha and omega of politics – nothing could stand above or outside it. The regime implanted in these countries was based on one-party rule and the legitimacy of the state rested with the party and its leader.

[18] I Bryan, P Langford and J McGarry Bryan (eds), *The reconstruction of the juridico-political: Affinity and divergence in Hans Kelsen and Max Weber* (Routledge, 2015).
[19] M Weber, *Political Writings* (ed and tr P Lassman and R Speirs) (CUP [1919], 1994).
[20] H Kelsen, *The Essence and Value of Democracy* (Rowman and Littlefield [1929], 2013) 39–40.

Pluralism was rejected, but, paradoxically, not the instrument which had implemented it. The inner contradiction of the totalitarian party is that the part became the totality.[21] To put it even more provocatively, this passage was a step in favour of the party. In fact, previously, nineteenth-century liberal-conservative regimes *were not founded on any party*.[22] Rather, they were founded on established elites who sent their representatives to parliament, with no consideration for any formal or structured organisation (with the exception of Great Britain). The novelty of the totalitarian regimes is that the basis of their rule was party-based. The idea that this new instrument was the centre of mass politics was not enfeebled by the eradication of pluralism. Parties in the plural were banned and thus the monist and holistic tradition had returned with a vengeance: however, the party had achieved the pinnacle of power as it ran, managed and controlled every sphere of society and government.

In Italy and Germany this experience left profound traces in post-war party politics. Parties of the pre-totalitarian era not only recaptured their structures but implemented them with a thrust designed to embed them in society, or at least their respective *classe guardée*. The model of the party of total integration shifted to one of social integration.[23] This was particularly clear in Italy[24] where fascist saturation through the sacralisation of politics was such that, after the war, both Catholics and communists resumed many organisational features of the National Fascist Party (PNF) model; they went as far as fostering an 'explicit reworking – and sometimes imitation – of the fascist party in a series of initiatives in the welfare, leisure and cultural dimension'.[25] On a similar line, Juan Linz[26] suggested that the evolution of the Christian Democratic Union (CDU) in Germany highlighted an 'unwanted legacy of fascism' even if with a peculiar meaning: in fact, Linz was referring to Adenauer's project to embrace all social constituencies, rather than building a penetrating and capillary organisation, which the CDU was not to implement until the 1970s.[27]

Mass parties inherited the hegemonic project of their totalitarian predecessors, in the sense that they pointed at pervasively controlling society and the state apparatus: the macroscopic difference was that the political environment was completely different. However, every party tried to master each sector of society. In a way, this is not so alien to the consociational model[28] which might be interpreted as a 'totalitarian' hold on a certain portion of society: a sort of *cuius regio, eius religio* applied to the plural, segmented society.

[21] M Gregorio, *Parte Totale. Le dottrine costituzionali del partito politico in Italia tra Ottocento e Novecento* (Giuffrè, 2013).

[22] D Ziblatt, *Conservative Political Parties and the Birth of Modern Democracy in Europe* (CUP, 2017).

[23] S Neumann, 'Toward a Comparative Study of Political Parties' in S Neumann (ed), *Modern Political Parties, Approaches to Comparative Politics* (University of Chicago Press, 1956).

[24] L Morlino, 'Is There Another Side to Fascist Legacy?' in S Larsen (ed), *Modern Europe after Fascism* (Columbia University Press, 1998) 662–96; R Chiarini and L Germano, 'Le eredità del passato autoritario nella democratizzazione italiana' in PG Grilli di Cortona and O Lanza (eds), *Tra vecchio e nuovo regime, il peso del passato nella costruzione della democrazia* (Il Mulino, 2011) 41–78.

[25] A Ventrone, *La cittadinanza repubblicana* (Il Mulino, 1996) 119.

[26] ibid 28–9.

[27] E-C Hornig, 'The Genetic Origin of the CDU and its Developmental Path to a Catch-All Party' (2003) 22(1–2) *German Politics* 82–96.

[28] A Lijphart, ' Typologies of democratic systems' (1968) 1(1) *Comparative political studies* 3–44.

III. PRESENT DISCONTENT: ROOTS AND EVOLUTION

After World War II, the political party enjoyed a unique moment in terms of consent and confidence: it was rewarded as the herald of a new/renewed period of freedom. Just as mass parties in the 1920s were welcomed by millions of people because they represented the first means for entering the political realm, similarly, in the post-war years, parties represented in the eyes of public opinion the means through which democracy would be recast. The return to, or the conquest of, democracy after the war was linked to multi-partyism: the presence of parties (in the plural) embodied the end of autocratic, oppressive one-party rule. Democracy was invoked by all parties[29] irrespective of their actual ideological leaning, as in the case of the Italian Communist Party (PCI) and the French Communist Party (PCF)[30] and it was seen as inextricably intertwined with multi-partyism. Party (in the singular) could have been of whatever species, granted that many parties existed on an equal footing: without them no democratic and free politics were conceivable.

Parties were granted the 'bonus' of being the carrier of a new and confident epoch after the gloomy years of dictatorships and war. The political party acquired the aura of an unavoidable tool for implementing a truly open and plural society. Thoughtfully, Schattschneider,[31] although active in a country not affected by any interruption of democratic and multi-party regime such as in the US, wrote in the early 1940s his famous statement that 'modern democracy is unthinkable save in terms of the parties'. In sum, that was the 'golden age' of parties.[32]

However, parties have wasted that aura. A precise turning-point in the organisational and attitudinal-affective decline of parties cannot be defined. But a sign of fatigue emerged in 1968, with the youth revolt throughout Europe. Indeed, parties eschewed that event/obstacle. They maintained their hold on the societal sphere and institutions; better, they even reinforced their position through neo-corporatist arrangements, but that could not last indefinitely. The crisis finally arrived; by the end of the twentieth century parties experienced a dramatic collapse in terms of membership, attachment, confidence and trust.

The organisational features of parties have changed in recent times. The data on membership reveals a consistent decline in the long term.[33] Some parties in some years experienced a revamping in membership[34] as the recent case of the Labour Party

[29] M Conway, 'The Rise and Fall of Western Europe's Democratic Age, 1945–1973' (2004) 13(1) *Contemporary European History* 67–88; M Conway, 'Democracy in Western Europe after 1945' in J Kurunmäki, J Nevers, and H Te Velde (eds), *Democracy in Modern Europe, A Conceptual History*, Vol 5 (Berghahn Books, 2018) 231–56.

[30] P Corduwener, *The Problem of Democracy in Postwar Europe: Political Actors and the Formation of the Postwar Model of Democracy in France, West Germany and Italy* (Routledge, 2017).

[31] EE Schattschneider, *Party Government* (Rinehart, 1942) 1.

[32] R Katz and P Mair, 'Changing Models of Party Organization and Party Democracy: The Emergence of the Cartel Party' (1995) 1(1) *Party Politics* 5–28.

[33] I van Biezen and T Poguntke, 'The Decline of Membership-Based Politics' (2014) 20(2) *Party Politics* 205–16; E van Haute and A Gauja (eds), *Party Members and Activists* (Routledge, 2015).

[34] AK Kölln, 'Party membership in Europe, Testing party-level explanations of decline' (2016) 22(4) *Party Politics* 465–77.

under Jeremy Corbyn's leadership in the late 2010s reveals.[35] However, the general trend is a descending one. The import of this feature goes beyond the mere organisational difficulties it may raise – it touches on the actual identity of the political party. The party was set up in order to gather people (thus a collective entity) to achieve some goal (for a collective purpose). Means and aim were/are both collective. If the party is deprived of these features it loses its identity; in particular, if its collective feature, assured by hopefully large membership, wanes, it becomes a sort of 'club of politicians', self-referential, ambitious and exploitative. This is a devastating image that has been developing throughout democracies, although Clarke at al[36] demonstrate that this situation is not completely alien to previous periods, especially in the UK.

Another level of analysis on the party perception concerns the affective relationship that voters have vis-à-vis the party. This relationship has been classified as 'party identification', a concept originally proposed by the Michigan school as 'the sense of personal attachment which the individual feels towards the [party] of his choice'.[37] Party identification could thus be considered an affective, psychological (positive) relationship between the individual and the party.[38] At any rate, where party identification is taken as an indicator of the party's favourable reception in the mass public, the relinquishing of this relationship is unquestionable. In almost every advanced OECD country there is 'overwhelming evidence of a glacial erosion of partisan identification in the electorate (…) which has reduced the proportion of habitual loyalists in the electorate who support their party come rain or shine'.[39] The electorate has become detached from political parties either in sheer numbers and/or in their strength of party identification.

Finally, if we consider the classical question of confidence in political parties surveyed in many countries and in the European Union, the deterioration appears to have begun many decades before.[40] The youth riots of 1968 offered the first sign of uneasiness in the face of traditional political parties. However, the unrest was managed by the mainstream parties and no radical innovations were introduced in any political party. Indeed, the demands and dissent of demonstrators and protestors were too radical and extreme to be received by traditional political actors. That young constituency 'wanted the impossible', as someone wrote on the walls of the Sorbonne in Paris, the epicentre of the cross-national movement. The mainstream parties had

[35] L Audickas, N Dempsey and P Loft, 'Membership of UK political parties' (Commons Briefing papers, SN05125, 2019) at https://researchbriefings.parliament.uk/ResearchBriefing/Summary/SN05125.

[36] N Clarke, W Jennings, J Moss and G Stoker, *The Good Politician. Folk Theories, Political Interaction, and the Rise of Anti-Politics* (CUP, 2018).

[37] A Campbell, PE Converse, WE Miller and DE Stokes, *The American Voter* (University of Chicago Press, 1960) 88–9.

[38] F Berglund, S Holmberg, H Schmitt, and J Thomassen, 'Party identification and party choice' in J Thomassen (ed), *The European Voter* (OUP, 2005) 106.

[39] P Norris, *Democratic Phoenix: Reinventing Political Activism* (CUP, 2002) 104; J Pharr and R Putnam, *Disaffected Democracies, What's Troubling the Trilateral Countries?* (Princeton University Press, 2000) 16; Strom, Muller and Bergman (n 5) 656.

[40] RJ Dalton, 'Political Support in Advanced Industrial Democracies' in P Norris (ed), *Critical Citizens, Global Support for Democratic Government* (OUP, 1999) 63–65; A Krouwel, *Party Transformations in European Democracies* (SUNY, 2012) 98–99.

to keep things going, solicited, inter alia, by the spectre of the 'rising expectations' evoked by the Trilateral Commission.[41] The answer to that social and political effervescence was a neo-corporatist solution and it proved effective in the short term as the oil shocks were mastered by Western economies without further social upheaval. But in the medium term it produced a backlash when creeping dissatisfaction for that solution found the opportunity to finally emerge.

The 1980s undoubtedly represented a critical juncture in this process. The processes mentioned above – decline in membership, party identification and confidence – accelerated during that decade, and, on a different account, party systems changed their composition with the entry of two new political families that took hold – the Greens and the populist extreme right – even if they did not attain significant electoral results. In the face of this critical setting, mainstream parties instead turned their attention to keeping hold firmly of the reins of power by igniting a process of encroachment into the state.

Today, parties are responsible for their present fate because they have signed a sort of Faustian pact: they have given away their soul in exchange for a longer life. Speaking plainly, parties 'entered' the state to benefit ruthlessly from its financial and material resources, thus abandoning any link with society, including party members. Acting like this, parties have been caught in a 'legitimacy trap': the acquisition and accumulation of more resources and more power has been paid for with less trust and, ultimately, less legitimacy.

Parties are challenged now because they are solidly implanted at the centre of the political system: they have become part of the state. This condition is the basis of both their strengths and their weaknesses. Strength is provided by the spoils parties obtain from the state thanks to either an encompassing partyness of government, and a pervasive patronage; weakness is caused by their loss of legitimacy as representatives of the people's needs and demands.

A cursory look at the development of party budgets and the distribution of the various entries (mainly public funds, membership fees and donations) provides empirical validity to this tendency.[42] Moreover, according to Kolln[43] '[p]arties respond[ed] to declining membership size by employing more staff, increasing their headquarters expenses, and relying more heavily on state funding'. This means that parties' elites compensated the membership shrinking with a concentration of resources in the central headquarters at the expense of the local units and their activities. The mobilising capacity at the grass roots level was considered somewhat irrelevant. Politics had to run from the centre by the leader and through mass media. Personalisation of politics, however, needed even more resources than before because of the communication and advertising costs. Parties' financial needs were largely covered by state funds and the parties' wellbeing only recently after the Great Recession (and in only a few countries), has been curtailed.

[41] M Crozier, S Huntington and J Watanuki, *The Crisis of Democracy, Report on the Governability of Democracies to the Trilateral Commission.* (New York University Press, 1975).

[42] P Ignazi, *Party and democracy. The Uneven Road to Party Democracy* (OUP, 2017).

[43] AK Kölln, *Party decline and response, the effects of membership decline on party organisations in Western Europe, 1960–2010* (Leiden PhD Dissertation, 2014) 200.

The parties' prosperous income did upset public opinion in many countries: a recent survey in Europe shows that 71 per cent think that 'it is wrong to fund political parties by means of public money'. This percentage spans from a low of 55 per cent in Sweden to a high of 83 per cent in Spain.[44] Beyond the fact, at the same time, 46 per cent of the same sample is concerned with the influence that lobbies and vested interest could have on political parties in the absence of public financing, the general malaise vis-à-vis state support is unquestionable.

This attitude is further exacerbated by the political representative's profile in terms of her/his personal income, fringe-benefits linked to her/his role and lifestyle, even more than malpractice or corruption. It's precisely the politician's image that offers the more visible, and more problematic, expression of the parties' opulence and distance from the everyday life of the mass public.

A. Politicians' Image

Direct attention on politicians might well act to mutually reinforce mistrust between parties and politicians. Political parties rather than politicians have long been the object of confidence or rejection, although the latter have not always been immune from negative considerations, from the days of the Roman Senate (criticised angrily by Cato), to British MPs (in the excoriating satire of Jonathan Swift). A closer look at the role of politicians suggests that even in the golden age of parties, before the recent steep development in personalisation of politics, political leaders played a crucial role in the relationship with the electorate and party membership. Also, in proportional representation systems, people often said that they voted for a specific party leader rather than for the party label. Indeed, prominent leaders have at times fascinated the general electorate and gained significant attention. More recently the diffusion of new forms of media, first television, and more recently social media, have inflamed a greater personalisation of politics. Otto Kirchheimer[45] already foresaw the effect of television on party politics either inside the party, or in the political system at large. A leader's appeal through television enlarged his/her autonomy vis-à-vis the other members of the party elite and, a fortiori, the membership. Privileged leaders' access to the media gave them a resource – communication – that enabled them to distance internal competitors; at the same time this increased the distance between the rank and file and local leaders who would/could never profit from that resource. This process created conditions for an increase in the remoteness of politicians, and inevitably of political parties. As the perception of politicians distant from ordinary citizens was transferred to the political party, a mutually reinforcing sentiment of distrust among the citizenry was in operation.

Beyond the technological innovations that brought politicians onto TV channels, another important change has affected their role and perceptions of it. In all European countries the state has introduced forms of public subsidies to political parties,

[44] Ipsos Online Panel 2017. Courtesy of Nando Pagnoncelli, Ipsos Italy.

[45] O Kirchheimer, 'The Transformation of the Western European Party Systems' in J LaPalombara and M Weiner (eds), *Political Parties and Political Development* (Princeton University Press, 1966).

and in some cases, directly to candidates. An incomparable swathe of money has arrived to fund political parties. As advanced above, parties have become enormously richer in comparison to the first post-war decades. But this is only one side of the coin. What is even more remarkable is the increase in the salary of members of parliament. Almost everywhere in Europe, MPs receive more, many times more, than the average salary in their country.[46] The rationale for this generosity is well known: it centres on the importance of the job function, and the necessity of lowering the risk of MPs being attracted by vested interests, lobbies and other sources of temptation from fulfilling their political duties. Beyond any evaluation of the validity of these motivations, what is at stake here is the impact of this affluence on public opinion. As Peter Mair[47] argued many years ago, the high salary and, above all, the fringe benefits linked to representative and governmental functions are seen as an indebted privilege. Recent research by Pedersen and Pedersen[48] assesses that the attitude towards politicians' pay is quite negative even in a country such as Denmark, where politics and parties are not as badly valued as in other countries. In addition, the negative view seems so established that people do not change their critical attitude towards politicians even if a reduction in their salaries is implemented.

The abundant flow of money and the seizure of many positions in state-controlled bodies have enacted a barely inevitable 'corrupting effect'. It is no surprise that a 2017 international survey shows that 'people in the Netherlands (56 per cent), Germany (59 per cent), the UK (61 per cent) and France (65 per cent), *do not believe that most political leaders are honest*. Furthermore, most believe that politicians *do not live in the same world as normal citizens* – that they do not understand the everyday issues and problems ordinary people experience'.[49] More specifically, an Ipsos-Mori[50] survey on British citizens found that 'most MPs put their own interests first' (62 per cent), 'most MPs use their power for their own personal gain' (68 per cent) and 'most MPs make a lot of money by using public office improperly' (68 per cent). British MPs provide a telling example of the (positive) financial impact of serving in parliament. A comparison between Conservative and Labour MPs suggests in fact that their activity in parliament 'almost doubled the wealth of candidates of the Conservative Party, but had no appreciable effect for Labour candidates'.[51]

Contrary to the sceptical view on politicians' pay, the economic value of the parliamentary office finds surprisingly positive consideration in some economists' analyses. For example, Messner and Polborn write that:

> Potential candidates for political office will be influenced in their decision whether to enter the competition – as in any other profession (*sic!*) – by financial considerations. The wage

[46] K Mause, 'Self-Serving Legislators? An Analysis of the Salary-Setting Institutions of 27 EU Parliaments' (2014) 25(2) *Constitutional Political Economy* 154–76, 158.

[47] P Mair, 'Political parties, popular legitimacy and public privilege' (1995) 18(3) *West European Politics* 40–57.

[48] RT Pedersen and LH Pedersen, 'Citizen Attitudes on Politicians' Pay: Trust Issues Are Not Solved by Delegation' (2019) *Political Studies*, at https://doi.org/10.1177/0032321719850073.

[49] Kantar, *Les Européens et le populisme Regards croisés France, Allemagne, Royaume-Uni et Pays-Bas* (Kantar public, 2017) 4 (emphasis added).

[50] Ipsos Mori, *Expenses Poll for the BBC* (2009).

[51] AC Eggers and J Hainmueller, 'MPs for sale? Returns to office in postwar British politics' (2009) 103(4) *American Political Science Review* 513–33, 351.

> and/or other benefits of the office will have an effect on the set of candidates who are willing to run for office, and hence possibly on the person of the elected official and the policy outcome.[52]

Even more, other economists have addressed the question of (what they unfortunately define as) the 'quality of politicians', by controlling their earnings before and after their parliamentary office: if their salary was higher after they finished their terms, they were good politicians (sic!). This approach views representatives as politicians that exploit their role for personal private gain, not for general well-being: the decision to enter politics is the perspective of personal financial gain, rather than for what Max Weber called '*Beruf*'. Indeed, any ingenuous consideration of politicians as missionaries should be discarded. However, the mass public in advanced democracies is, increasingly, negatively affected by the high status of politicians and by the perception that they care for her/himself – or at best her/his own party – and not for the citizenry at large. This analysis/view eschews any other consideration on the question of sleaze, malpractice and corruption. The devastating effect on the Italian public and on the party system itself of the 'Tangentopoli' affair, discovered by the Clean Hands investigation in the early 1990s, is a case in point. Other corruption scandals have produced political earthquakes in more recent years in less established democracies (eg, Slovakia, Romania). The demand for politicians to behave properly, honestly and decently is mounting everywhere, even when citizens themselves do not abide scrupulously by the rules.

Corruption is a pathology of representatives' behaviour. What is at the centre here is rather the physiology, that is, the standard practice of MPs' activity. Thus, beyond any pathological/criminal element of political practice, the present furore directed against politicians should be framed in a physiological pattern: it is precisely the politician's standard activity, or better, their present status, that harms the political body.

Politicians are rated negatively for how much they gain, how they behave, and (last *and* the least) how they work.[53] This latter function is not rated so important as long as electorate demands are channelled somewhat accurately and effectively, and congruent policy outcomes are produced.[54] In this context recent research has offered a quite surprising positive view in terms of congruence: voters judge and evaluate this aspect but it does not influence their affective relationship with politics, parties and politicians. European and, more generally, Western public opinion requires different behaviour by politicians, well beyond the minimal requirement of honesty: they desire the return of a sense of belonging and identity binding them and politicians. The sort of representative they require is 'the good politician', as spelled out in the title of the masterful research by Clark et al,[55] the folk image of party and politician is very demanding as all virtues are demanded, but fulfilling the role is very demanding in itself.

[52] M Messner and MK Polborn, 'Paying Politicians' (2004) 88(12) *Journal of Public Economics* 2423–45, 2423 (emphasis added).

[53] Clarke (n 36).

[54] K Heidar and B Wauters, 'Representativeness of parties Old problems, new in challenges' in K Heidar and B Wauters (eds), *Do Parties Still Represent? An Analysis of the Representativeness of Political Parties in Western Democracies* (Routledge, 2019).

[55] Clarke (n 36).

B. Attempts at Renewal

Transformations undertaken by the parties themselves since the 1990s started a process of alienation from the public, even before a general disenchantment began to take hold. Whereas public opinion longed for a renewed militancy and passion totally disinterested in terms of individual benefits (think of the romanticist enthusiasm for the students' revolt of 1968 and the collective movements), parties followed another route: they emphasised features such as hyper-personalisation[56] managerial management,[57] interpenetration with the state and financial means,[58] reliance on new media communication[59] and demise of the party on the ground.[60] All these changes modified internal party dynamics and logics; even more so, they changed external perceptions of the party too.

Parties have enforced some intra-party innovations to counteract membership demobilisation, the most practised of which has been the introduction of direct democracy procedures for the selection of leaders and candidates.[61] Indeed, in a number of European and extra-European countries, parties moved away from established modalities of the internal selection of party leadership and candidates towards ampler opportunities for direct participation; such involvement includes also decision-making on some relevant issues, as in the case of the French Socialist Party on the EU Constitution issue in 2005, or the German Social Democratic Party (SPD) on entering the Große Koalition in different moments.

In principle, the opportunity to play a role in the intra-party chain of decision-making provides the membership with more salience, and more centrality. However, one could question whether this is the main route to a proper 'democratisation' of political parties.[62] More specifically, it should be questioned if such an 'openness': (i) implies an effective significance to members' empowerment; (ii) is the best way to revitalise the linkage between party and society; and ultimately (iii) whether it really 'democratises' parties.

The openness looks like Alice in the Wonderland's mirror: the impossible is possible. What appeared a democratisation of political parties turned out to be a dispossession of functions – and power – by the intermediate vertical and horizontal party strata, that is, the activists and middle-level elites.

The passage towards more openness and inclusion cannot be seen naively as inspired by the sole drive of enlarging participation and democratising the internal

[56] T Poguntke and P Webb (eds), *The Presidentialization of Politics* (OUP, 2005).

[57] R Katz and P Mair, *Democracy and the Cartelization of Political Parties* (OUP, 2018).

[58] Ignazi (n 42).

[59] DL Swenson and P Mancini, *Politics, Media, and Modern Democracy* (Greenwood Publishing Group, 1996).

[60] van Biezen and Poguntke (n 33).

[61] W Cross, G Rahat, O Kenig and S Pruysers (eds), *The Promise and Challenge of Party Primary Elections: A Comparative Perspective* (McGill-Queen's University, 2016).

[62] K Carty, 'Are political parties meant to be democratic?' in W Cross and R Katz (eds), *The Challenges of Intra-Party Democracy* (OUP, 2013) 11–26; P Ignazi, 'The four knights of intra-party democracy: A rescue for party delegitimation' (2020) 26(1) *Party Politics* 9–20; F Wolkenstein, 'A Deliberative Model of Intra-Party Democracy' (2016) 24(3) *Journal of Political Philosophy* 297–320.

life of the party. One aspect usually left out is that the members' empowerment may be motivated by internal pressures and power conflicts. In this occurrence intra-party dynamics may spring from two different sources: from the desire of the leadership to write off any constraint from other party actors; or from competing minority factions intending to show the leadership's lack of consensus in the rank and file.

In both cases, either when leadership wants to reaffirm itself or when a competing 'dominant coalition' wants to get power and overthrow the leadership, the membership is 'employed' as a *masse de manoeuvre* to be thrown against the contenders. The former occurrence – the leadership seeking to re-affirm itself by, for instance, soliciting a plebiscitary confirmation – appears more frequent today.

Richard Katz and Peter Mair, in many of their writings, both jointly and separately, have repeatedly warned of the risk of marginalising militants and middle-level elites by empowering the membership only.[63] Calling the membership up (and, a fortiori, the sympathisers) directly bypasses party structures and middle-level elites. As a consequence, these intermediary components, traditionally considered the effective backbone of the party for their role as an aggregative clearing-house of bottom-up flows of demands, are now at pains to regain their function. In sum, the openness and inclusion of the membership play against them. A series of cases study from Italy,[64] Norway[65] France[66] and Germany[67] confirm the displacement and even mistreatment of this peculiar strata.

The idea that direct democracy was the master way to democratise and revitalise parties reveals a negative consideration of the traditional multi-stage internal decision-making process, that is, delegate democracy. This preference has a clear rationale: it has been motivated by deep-seated frustration and disappointment for intra-party oligarchic practices, already criticised since Robert Michels' analysis.[68] However, Michels' criticism could be taken not only as a whip against the deficits of internal democracy. Indeed, the German scholar was also quite a realist on the illusory and manipulative character of direct democracy and membership (apparent) empowerment: 'the weight of an oligarchy is rarely felt when the rights of the masses are codified and *when each member may in abstract participate in power*'.[69] Moreover, Michels also provided a warning against the Bonapartist drive in party

[63] F Faucher, 'New Forms of Political Participation. Changing Demands or Changing Opportunities to Participate in Political Parties?' (2015) 13(4) *Comparative European Politics* 405–29. A Gauja, 'The Individualisation of Party Politics: The Impact of Changing Internal Decision-Making Processes on Policy Development and Citizen Engagement' (2015) 17(1) *The British Journal of Politics and International Relations* 89–105. Ignazi (n 62).

[64] P Ignazi and E Pizzimenti, 'The reins of intra-party power in the Italian political parties (1990–2011)' (2014) 44(3) *Rivista Italiana di Scienza Politica* 223–45; P Ignazi and P Bordandini, *I muscoli del partito* (Il Mulino, 2018).

[65] N Aylott and N Bolin, 'Managed Intra-Party Democracy: Precursory Delegation and Party Leader Selection' (2017) 23(1) *Party Politics* 55–65.

[66] R Lefebvre, 'Des partis en apesanteur sociale?' in I Martinache and F Sawicki (eds), *La fin des partis?* (La Vie des Idèes-Puf, 2019); F Sawicki, 'La présidetianlisation de République a-t-elle eu raison des partis politiques?' in I Martinache, and F Sawicki (eds), *La fin de partis politiques*? (La Vie des Idèes-Puf, 2009).

[67] K Detterbeck, *Multi-Level Party Politics in Western Europe* (Palgrave Macmillan, 2012).

[68] Michels (n 2).

[69] ibid 216, emphasis added.

dynamics because of a leader's direct investiture. In such an occurrence 'there is not a single leader who fails to think and to act [...], and to say *Le Parti, c'est moi*'.[70]

In this way the appeal to the members eclipses the principle of delegated democracy inside and, inevitably, outside the party. This passage implies a downgrading of the delegated representative modality and, correspondingly, a fostering of a plebiscitary approach to politics.[71]

The organisational changes surveyed above have not met their goals. On the contrary, they have produced unsatisfactory outcomes. The members themselves appear unhappy with their empowerment. A massive survey on party members in different countries assesses that '(d)espite being granted more rights in some decision-making processes, members' attitudes towards the functioning of their party and intra-party democracy' are far from being unanimously positive.[72]

In conclusion, membership still shrinks and demobilises, leaders go their own way, confidence plummets and, on a different account, anti-democratic forces gain momentum. Even '[i]nformal forms of party affiliation [...] can function as a buffer, but they will not change the trend towards an increasing alienation from the party system'.[73]

The rise of challenger parties raises some (and even many) concerns, as in most cases the plebiscitary drive is becoming visible more and more decisively. Democracy itself is under threat because the development towards plebiscitarian practices in intra-party dynamics has had an effect on the external environment too, favouring a populist surge.[74] The parties' efforts to regain confidence has proved fruitless, up to this point. Is there any way out of this deadlock?

IV. CONCLUSIONS

The negative reception parties have attained today reveals, while disguised, some traces of the hostility and disdain that for so long accompanied the idea itself of division, partition and thus 'party'. The advocacy of unity and homogeneity is being revamped these days under the guise of populism and sovranism. The idea of a homogeneous undivided community at national or subnational level has taken hold in many countries. Beneath the xenophobic and nationalist policies which represent the visible surface only, lies a hostility to pluralism and, inevitably, to parties. There is no contraction if these policies are purported by political parties: it's the old story of

[70] ibid 221, emphasis in original.

[71] B von dem Berge and T Poguntke, 'Varieties of Intra-Party Democracy: Conceptualization and Index Construction' in S Scarrow, P Webb and T Poguntke (eds), *Organizing Political Parties: Representation, Participation and Power* (OUP, 2107) 151.

[72] Gauja and van Haute (n 33) 191.

[73] L Hooghe and AK Kölln, 'Types of party affiliation and the multi-speed party: What kind of party support is functionally equivalent to party membership?' (2018) *Party Politics*, at https://journals.sagepub.com/doi/10.1177/1354068818794220, 9.

[74] L Bardi, S, Bartolini and A Treschel, 'Responsive and Responsible? The Role of Parties in Twenty-First Century Politics' (2014) 37(2) *West European Politics* 249.

totalitarian parties that practised democratic institutions until they no longer needed them. The diffusion and enforcement of a negative attitude towards party politics in general and 'politicians' in particular by an 'anti-party party'[75] is consistent with the aim of such a party: to delegitimise all the others and present itself as the sole alternative because it would be the only one capable of overcoming any division and fissure in society and the polity, thus fulfilling an agonising unity and harmony.

The conundrum is that the populist attack, and the de-legitimation of parties, have been favoured by the mainstream parties themselves. Following Katz and Mair's seminal interpretations,[76] parties are *state-centred* organisations: they moved towards the state and implanted themselves at the centre. On the one hand they are still at the core of the process of formation of every public policy, although regulatory independent agencies and supranational entities directly or indirectly intervene in the policy-making process. On the other hand they avail themselves of, and benefit from, state-linked resources such as public subsidies, patronage, and clientelism for their activities. In this way, following the first pattern, they have become, even more so than in the past, unavoidable junctures of public life; and following the latter pattern, parties have acquired an unprecedented amount of resources that make them strong, wealthy, and pervasive. In sum, they are at the centre of every state activity.

A defence of party politics should contemplate a plea for abandoning the parties' state-centred status and reviving the linkage with civil society. Such an aim is quite crucial because the parties' deterioration harms the democratic system itself: 'as parties fail, so too fails popular democracy', Peter Mair wrote.[77] The mounting populist and plebiscitary wave suggests how pervasive is the crisis and how dramatic the challenge. But there is no way out of political parties. All the alternatives advanced by advocates of citizens' direct initiatives may flank and integrate partisan activity, *but they are no substitute for it*. Parties are 'necessary evils'.[78] It is hard to put them 'on the side of the angels'.[79] However, the recovery of their legitimacy is an utmost necessity to counteract the mounting plebiscitary and populist wave. Democracy would be inconceivable without parties, as long as we acknowledge the importance, centrality, and legitimacy of regulated political conflict.

New and newly organised parties, more intra-party deliberative arenas, and a larger room for, hopefully more carefully designed, direct democracy means, might revive party and politicians' image among the mass public. Parties such as the Movimento 5 Stelle in Italy, Podemos in Spain and La République en Marche in France, have offered a new, internet-based, internal structuring, and, at the same time, they have collected a large electoral consent. Their example may fade away in few

[75] P Ignazi, 'The crisis of parties and the rise of new political parties' (1996) 2(4) *Party Politics* 549–66; R Katz, 'The Internal Life of Parties' in KR Luther and F Müller-Rommel (eds), *Political Parties in the New Europe* (OUP, 2002).

[76] R Katz and P Mair (eds), *How Parties Organize: Change and Adaptation in Party Organizations in Western Democracies* (Sage, 1994); Katz and Mair (n 32).

[77] P Mair, *Ruling the Void: the Hollowing of Western Democracy* (Verso, 2013) 13.

[78] R Dalton and S Weldon, 'Public Images of Political Parties, A Necessary Evil?' (2005) 28(5) *West European Politics* 931–51.

[79] Rosenblum (n 7).

years, or offer a guideline for the renewal in traditional parties. However, beyond any organisational innovation, in order to recapture the public consent a more sober and more 'in touch' political personnel is needed. If representatives do not change their lifestyle and their approach towards the mass public (and keep their hands off any financial temptations …) parties will not recover.

17

Market Power and Democracy

ANTONIO CUCINOTTA*

DEMOCRACY IS A historical phenomenon, subject to change and evolution; and the economic structures of societies are also intrinsically variable and evolutionary; in this sense, the coexistence and relationship between capitalism and democracy cannot always be understood by means of immutable legal and political formulas, but they must rather be continually rethought in the light of the most important shifts in production relationships and changes carried out by science and technology. In Orwell's *1984* televisions equipped with cameras control the life of community members, spying on all forms of behaviour, 24 hours a day: any possibility of privacy is thus cancelled to standardise conducts to the ideology of the dominant party. The Orwellian dystopia is an indictment of the claims of totalitarian regimes to bend reality to the goals they set, which materialises the socio political nightmares of the twentieth century that the technology of the beginning of the third millennium, although in a deeply changed historical context, makes it operationally possible at an extreme level which had been unthinkable before then. A serious threat to the (global) economic order emerges today, it being based on an asymmetric control of information between the users of the networks and the firms that dominate them; we entered the age, as it has been called, of 'surveillance capitalism':[1] a challenge for the economic and political order which the democracies themselves do not seem adequately prepared to face.

The digital platforms introduced by the 'new economy' have enormously increased the possibilities of human contact and interchange between persons and groups. It has been called 'the most participatory and accessible communications' medium that humanity had ever known' (to quote the language of the judicial review of the 1996 Communication Decency Act, which was the US Congress' statute, promptly declared constitutionally illegitimate by the courts, aimed to limit and control internet communications in a misguided attempt to protect minors from inappropriate materials). Today, our chances to interact with other human beings are unpredictably

* University of Messina.

[1] S Zuboff, *The Age of Surveillance Capitalism: The Fight for a Human Future at the New Frontier of Power* (Profile Books Ltd, 2019).

increased, disclosing possibilities to the life of the new century not yet fully explored. In this innovative context, however, it is not improper to recall the insights of Karl Polanyi who, decades ago, defined as 'great transformation' the becoming a commodity of land, money and labour: a phenomenon at the origin of the capitalistic form of production, which is intrinsically historical and contingent since it can take on different features, not necessarily all sustainable from a constitutional and democratic point of view. What we are experiencing in our times is a new 'great transformation': our political opinions, sexual orientations, judgements and preferences about people, things and places, even the images that capture moments of personal relationships, are becoming valuable information used for transactions on the markets. In other words, the new 'great transformation' of the digital age turns information and experience in general that make up our personality into goods, so as to control them commercially through large telematic platforms mostly without our consent, or with a consent expressed only formally and often unknowingly.

The 'great transformation' of the digital age of 'surveillance' requires new categories of thought to grasp the contemporary dynamics of capitalist relationships and understand not only how the markets work, but how they are formed and evolve as well, especially to perfect legal rules aimed at the protection of public interest. A prominent feature of digital markets is that services offered by big companies are often free, and therefore strongly appreciated by users, whose enormous demand gives relevant market power to digital firms: access to the Google search engine, for example, is free; access to Facebook is free (as it is to the subsidiary WhatsApp); shipping charges and the search for online shopping are almost free.

Still, as economists explain, 'there is no free lunch'; 'free' services offered by digital economy companies are only apparent; the goods actually transacted on these markets are the data of network users that can be collected, stored and used in a wide variety of ways, giving a special character to market power in the digital era. To this scenario we have to add relevant scale returns of the digital big firms: production costs, indeed, decrease more than proportionally with the number of users reached, and network externalities make technologies and services increasingly cheaper depending on the number of users involved.

Hence, digital age markets impose a particular consideration on an asset still pivotal in mass market of consumer goods: information and its processing for commercial purposes through advertising. It's a key feature of contemporary economies which social sciences are often not properly structured to grasp, while it deeply modifies people's lifestyles, establishing new behaviours and mass habits, and giving powers never seen before to the few companies that control the supply.

These characteristics of digital era markets had already emerged, at the end of the last century, with the US Microsoft antitrust case, when the monopoly of personal computer operating systems was strictly scrutinised for attempt to monopolise the internet browsers market. Microsoft then won the 'browsers' war by eliminating the 'first mover' 'Netscape' from the market and by offering its product 'Explorer' for free together with the monopolised operating system ('Windows').

It is evident how this case provided a textbook example of those theoretical and practical problems brought about by the high technology markets: the internet Microsoft browser was sold for free through a 'tie-in' with the monopolised operating system (the 'tying product' Windows). The two markets were affected by significant network externalities, since the value of both products was increasing along with the number of users. There was also a problem of 'path dependence', that is: strong market dependence on initial conditions, an occurrence that could actually prevent the prevalence of the best product in the market. And the problem of Microsoft conduct was primarily strategic, since Microsoft thought that the free sale of the browser Explorer could protect its monopoly from the threat that internet browsers would technologically replace operating systems.

The antitrust action of the Department of Justice did not prevent Microsoft, though sentenced in court, from winning the 'browsers war'. New technologies, in cases like this, along with the size of digital market businesses and the unpredictability of technological innovations, raise a serious problem for democratic systems: is antitrust law really the most powerful and appropriate weapon that legal systems can activate to protect the values of democracy in the economic field? Are the categories through which we scientifically 'think' the functioning of the economic system adequate to understand the 'new economy'? In the era of global markets is not a uniform response to the challenges of concentrated economic power required? And is not this response problematic if we consider the distance within the dominant values in the legal systems of the various continents?

Orwellian dystopia ultimately recalls Polanyi's assertion: the capitalistic form of production, indeed, can transform almost any aspect of individual and social life into a commodity. Still it proceeds according to its own rules which are not all easily malleable by public hand. However, as it has been written, 'capitalism without competition is not capitalism'.[2] For the classics of economic thought, Adam Smith *in primis*, not only efficiency but also fairness of social relationships, as structured by capitalist form of production, depend on the fact that the competitive conditions of the markets are maintained, even coercively, and consequently an excessive concentration of economic power is discouraged.

This, however, is not an easy-to-achieve public policy objective: according to the common experience of antitrust, in fact, especially in the mass market of consumer goods, the complexity of the rules that support competition is self-evident. To make these rules more flexible an adequate critical awareness of the nature of competition is needed. And here the true 'paradox' of antitrust lies, since competition is a practical problem relatively easy to understand for the layman, but which implies theoretical questions rather difficult to deal with for scientific thought. This difficulty which economic analysis places on the legal thought depends on the fact that, as noted by Hayek, 'the tautological method which is appropriate and indispensable for the analysis of individual action seems to have been illegitimately extended to problems in which we have to deal with a social process in which the decision of many individuals influence one another and necessarily succeed one another in time'.[3]

[2] J Tepper and D Hearn, *The Myth of Capitalism. Monopolies and the Death of Competition* (John Wiley & Sons, 2019) XV.

[3] FA Hayek, *'The Meaning of Competition'*, in FA Hayek, *Individualism and Economic Order* (University of Chicago Press, [1948] 1980) 93.

If we wanted to synthesize in a few words the theoretical difficulties underlying the antitrust analysis we should oppose static equilibrium analysis of the neoclassical theory to the most recent versions of the (Austrian school) approach to the 'market process'. The latter is better equipped to grasp the primary good valorised by competition; that is: information, its circulation, and the capacity of competitive markets, much more than monopolistic ones, to drive the actors' choices on the basis of the more efficient 'exploitation' of available data. The market process, indeed, actually 'creates' value exploiting the information disseminated among the various economic operators. And it is precisely by keeping 'open' and pluralistic markets that antitrust makes economic action more efficient, as shown by the performances of large companies in the digital era, mainly due to the control of information through advertising, which creates in an extraordinarily fast time an enormous market power, but also provides significant benefits to the public of users.

The problem is that neoclassical equilibrium analysis is 'static', since it omits to consider the dynamic process of interaction between economic decisions, because it mainly proceeds on the assumption of 'perfect information' for market agents, and therefore it fails to grasp the main benefit that 'open' and 'pluralistic' or, in other words, 'competitive' markets ensure to the public of consumers. That is, increasing the opportunities for economic agents, through the acquisition of information, to make complete economic calculations, thus orienting production and consumption decisions toward the greatest possible efficiency. The 'pure' equilibrium analysis, assuming perfect information, presupposes this efficiency already achieved, and thus it cannot grasp the main virtue of competitive markets: *id est*, the possibility to allow a complete and efficient calculation of the costs of economic decisions, which tend to approximate the minimum ones and therefore the best allocation of resources (if significant market power is absent).

The neoclassical perspective does not create an irreconcilable conflict between antitrust doctrines founded on the economic analysis and the so called 'non-economic goals' of antitrust, which would affect antitrust extending its objectives beyond 'consumer welfare's protection'. Instead, the 'pro market' doctrines popularised in the last decades of the last century by the 'Chicago school' won a majority of the US Supreme Court in cases like *Sylvania*[4] (vertical restraints), *Ligget*[5] (predatory pricing), *Kodak*[6] (aftermarket for repair parts, *dissenting opinion*) and *Leegin*[7] (resale price maintenance) although they are based on 'an oversimplified economics that often rests on unfounded or disproven assumption'.[8]

The 'perfect competition' model, indeed, with its restrictive assumptions, has pervaded the neoclassical economic analysis, and most of questionable 'laissez faire' doctrines in antitrust are based on the oversimplifications that derive from this model. Starting with the hyperrationality of homo oeconomicus, that generates a style and

[4] *Continental Television v GTE Sylvania*, 433 U.S. 36 (1977).
[5] *Brooke Group Ltd v Brown and Williamson Tobacco Corp.*, 509 U.S. 209 (1993).
[6] *Eastman Kodak Co v Image Technical Services Inc.*, 504 U.S. 451 (1992).
[7] *Leegin Creative Leather Products v PSKS Inc.*, 551 U.S. 877 (2007).
[8] T Wu, *The Curse of Bigness. Antitrust in the New Gilded Age* (Columbia Global Reports, 2018) 91.

an analysis model in which, as Hayek pointed out[9] 'it seems that that skeleton in our cupboard, the "economic man", whom we have exorcised with prayer and fasting, has returned through the back door in the form of quasi-omniscient individual'.[10] And it is precisely the relationship between economic decisions and agents' knowledge that makes the models of neoclassical theory problematic and often fallacious in their reception in the legal analysis, not only in antitrust.

To grasp the crucial theoretical problem of the sophisticated law and economics antitrust doctrines, we should note that in all economic systems whose institutions are oriented toward efficiency, this latter depends on a virtuous conjunction of cooperation and conflict among economic agents. That is, a combination of the advantages of cooperation among several actors (which take shape mainly in the firms), with those of conflict, or rivalry, among several decision-making units (which take shape in competitive markets). It is precisely the mix of these advantages that neoclassical models fail to properly evaluate virtually even by eliminating it: since this mixture of hierarchies and contracts is based on an intrinsically dynamic process which involves the interactions among the decisions of a multitude of operators. It is a process not necessarily competitive because it can be affected by the firms' market power. In fact, the 'static' equilibrium models are able to represent only the theoretic extreme outcomes of this process in the form of a 'perfect market', where no agent has market power. But this approach does not show how the maximum efficiency results described by the perfect market model are or should be in practice achieved: although it is clear that the efficiency of economic performance is the main benefit of competition, and therefore of the dispersed market power.

Indeed, in the case of the firm, the contribution of inputs and individual workers is centrally organised through a hierarchical system of 'commands' allowing the benefits of cooperation between agents engaged in distinct tasks and duties to be exploited. In the case of markets, instead, decentralised decisions become efficient precisely because the conflict, 'the rivalry game' among several separate decision-making units, ensures that the best or cheapest solution may prevail, mainly thanks to the fact that the (competitive) price system carries out the information on which the correct individual economic calculation is based.

Observing the raw facts of economic life, Ronald Coase asked a central question to the 'Law and Economics' researches, wondering why firms exist; that is, why economic activities are not completely decentralised in the markets. The answer is that the same price system tendentially regulates this option between hierarchy and contract: the production, in fact, is organised in firms where 'transaction costs' in the markets are higher than the costs of the same activities controlled by organisations.

If the specific advantage of competitive 'conflict' against hierarchical 'cooperation' depends on the competitive pricing system which regulates economic decisions

[9] FA Hayek, 'Economics and Knowledge' in Hayek (n 3) 46.

[10] It is true that the oversimplified assumptions of the '*homo* oeconomicus' have been largely challenged by the 'behavioral economics' whose insights the recent antitrust literature has widely incorporated; cf A Tor, 'Understanding Behavioral Antitrust' (2014) 92 *Tex. L. Rev.* 573; A Reeves and M Stucke, 'Behavioral Antitrust' (2011) 86 *Ind. L. J.* 1527; M Stucke, 'Behavioral Economists at the Gate: Antitrust in the Twenty-First Century' (2007) 38 *Loy. U. L. J.* 513.

in the markets, through 'pluralistic' rivalry between various offers (and demands) of goods and services, this mechanism, however, may be deliberately suppressed by the same firms, when they find it more convenient to cooperate with each other rather than to compete for the control of scarce resources.

Hence, the antitrust central issue is to prevent the public benefit of conflict between the firms (together with the general interest in an efficient allocation of resources) from being replaced by the private advantage of anticompetitive cooperation. If the anticompetitive conducts, indeed, increase the incomes of the operators involved, at the same time they neutralise the benefits of market rivalry that allow us to constantly improve goods and services and to contain their costs, thus achieving a pre-eminent public interest.

So, the disadvantage for society as a system of exclusive control of resources is that the monopolist is protected against the possibility that other operators may jeopardise his position of strength. Antitrust therefore aims to protect the general interest threatened by a form of private cooperation among firms when this last intends to exclude beneficial effects of competitive rivalry in open and pluralistic economies. On this foundation, antitrust is the interface of democracy in the economic field which preserves the dispersion of economic power and activates specific protections whenever private economic power threatens the general interest.

Competition, then, demands 'rules' and so do markets in order to function properly: rules like those protecting 'property rights' and regulating civil liability, as well as institutions limiting excessive economic power. A power that, in contemporary global markets, has expanded to levels never known before, also because of the political and judicial evolution of the antitrust approach. In a capitalist, democratic society like the US, it has been written, a shared 'understanding' of antitrust must be consolidated: 'the antitrust rules employed from the 1940s to 1970s were, on the whole, consistent with this political bargain. The Chicago oriented reforms pushed the rules so that they approached the noninterventionist edge of the permissible spectrum. In retrospect, that is why we have seen the development of substantial and widening market power'.[11]

For a full appreciation of contemporary markets, especially those founded on the private control of relevant information, a change of theoretical perspective is necessary: like that determined by the interplay, not yet fully explored, between the 'neoaustrian' and 'neoinstitutionalist' schools of thought. The latter, in particular, have tried to explain the advantages of cooperation in the firm over exchange on the markets. However, the 'transaction costs' for this purpose theoretically developed by Coase are nothing more than 'selling costs' in the sense of Chamberlin. Hence, a category of 'costs' thought to draw attention to the monopolistic element of price formation in real markets. The transaction costs, indeed, correspond to resources employed in market operations to collect relevant information on goods and their prices, identify counterparties, run negotiations, enter into agreements, monitor implementation and so on. Chamberlin has placed at the centre of his researches

[11] J Baker, *The Antitrust Paradigm. Restoring a Competitive Economy* (Harvard University Press, 2019) 40–42.

the costs 'to sell' or, in other words, to 'create' a market. That is: costs that increase demand for those who produce or otherwise offer products or services of any kind, as distinct from production costs. The typical 'selling cost' is advertising (a dimension of the functioning of mass markets absolutely essential to understand the new 'great transformation' of digital economies). Advertising 'creates' a market: in the sense that, enhancing demand, it facilitates exchange of goods and services, just like Coase's 'transaction costs' permit to enter into contracts once the relevant information has been obtained. Hence, 'selling costs' are a special case of 'transaction costs'.

The costs to 'create markets', in Coase and in Chamberlin, are therefore related to the acquisition and circulation of the relevant information in market negotiations. For this reason they cannot be grasped by 'pure' or 'perfect' competition models, since the latter are built on the assumption of the agents' perfect information. However, drawing attention to the 'imperfect' information means trying to understand the monopolistic element of prices formation in real markets: the asymmetry of knowledge among market agents involves almost always market power, that is: power on prices. If this power is a priori excluded by the perfect competition model (largely abused in the analysis of 'the Chicago oriented reformers'), antitrust analysis misses an essential part of economic explanations for competition issues: issues such as why firms exist and acquire a certain size, how the choice between contract and firm is completed by professional agents, and the reasons for the extension of markets. Coase and Chamberlin converge in emphasising the limit of orthodox neoclassical tradition, incapable of framing these questions, insofar as it assumes 'perfect' knowledge.

These costs of private bargaining are quite obvious in mass consumer markets, where manufacturing firms must reach final consumers, provide them with product information, persuade them in the choice between goods of different brands, signing contracts to provide pre- and post-sale assistance, etc. These markets are, of course, imperfectly competitive – as attested by the ubiquitous diffusion of 'branded' products – and therefore the nature of the perfectly competitive model, in which the market has no costs because at the current price a firm can sell as much as it likes, cannot be applied to them.

And it is precisely the nature of trade in mass markets of consumer goods that has been completely altered by the 'third' industrial revolution: considering the power of the 'giants' of the digital era, there is even less substantial 'reciprocity' of market exchange. Digital platforms hold an extraordinary market power thanks to the information that they are able to collect and control, enabling an unprecedented 'profiling' for marketing purposes of network users: a power which has profoundly altered the 'selling costs' of consumer goods, redefining the characteristics of advertising channels that influence the purchasing preferences and decisions of consumers, by reducing transaction costs with direct benefit for users. However, partly thanks to increasing economies and returns of scale, the giants of the digital age have acquired enormous power over trade and prices, profoundly modifying the market behaviour, the activities of mass media (all largely subsidized by advertising) and in general remodeling the ways in which knowledge is disseminated in contemporary social systems, including even the way in which political consensus is formed.

The combination of these factors which increase the firms' market power makes competition law, especially the antitrust, an essential part of the 'rules of the games' of economic systems on which political consensus is founded, particularly in democracies, mainly because it restricts private power on markets. After all, antitrust has become an essential part of the legal rules that facilitate the functioning of markets in autocratic political systems as well (like China or the Gulf countries): and this legal transplant testifies that the anti-monopoly rules, born in the context of the western legal tradition, have spread across all legal systems because they serve primarily to increase market efficiency, which, in fact, largely depends on the full operation of competition.

Competition is, in fact, the force that not only determines the order of the markets, distinguishing it from the production of public goods, but also that makes it 'desirable' as socially efficient, because in the spontaneous order of competitive markets, agents reach their planned goals at the lowest cost (provided there is no monopolistic control of resources). This is because competition consists of all the actions through which an agent strives to achieve what another agent strives to achieve at the same time. In this common, profane sense of rivalry race that rewards the best action, competition is a spontaneous regulator mechanism of 'economies', which compares them by making the best decisions prevail, mainly through the price system. The 'best' economic decisions are those that achieve the goals pursued at the lowest costs, or that guarantee the highest quality of goods and services offered, correcting the agents' mispredictions and incorrect expectations.

Punishing the wrong expectations and rewarding the correct ones, making the most convenient or best quality offers prevail, as such judged by those who demand them, the market order produces socially desirable results through the socialisation of the benefit of exchange, which increases the capacity for exploitation and control of resources by private agents, and the privatisation of its costs. In competitive markets, indeed, all participate in the increase of wealth made possible by the trade system, which expands the opportunities available, while the losses fall on the agents who are wrong to plan the use of resources and that, therefore, lose opportunities to increase their own welfare and may be excluded from the market.

The antitrust in itself, therefore, does not contrast the great dimension of firms in relation to the market (which may also depend on the superior efficiency of 'monopolists', as it often happens with the 'giants' of the digital age); rather, it aims to protect the general interest threatened by private cooperation among firms, commercial restrictions and abuses (including the misuse of digital information) as soon as these phenomena tend to exclude the beneficial effects of competitive rivalry in open and pluralistic economies. In this sense, the rules protecting competition safeguard a mechanism and a procedure which have a universal significance in human societies. To prove that, it is enough to consider the importance of those 'rules' governing, and making possible, recreational activities and sports, including the agonistic and professional ones. (It is not by chance that the 'game theory' is a sophisticated instrument to understand the competitive strategy of firms.)

The same, debated, concept of 'homo oeconomicus', which summarises the rational behaviour of market agents especially in the neoclassical tradition of economic science, was justified by the analogy with the idea of natural selection in evolutionary biology: in the sense that on markets, as in the environments where the animal species live, only those agents who best exploit their computing capabilities prevail. But evolution through competition, rivalry between individuals and groups, is at the base of a large series of phenomena affecting the foundations of the human consortium: as in the case of scientific research, just to introduce another example, whose results depend on 'competition' between research programmes, among which those who more fully explain the phenomena investigated prevail. Moreover religions, arts, culture develop and evolve themselves also thanks to the selective and coping skills of competition, which include not only conflict but also imitation and the consequent diffusion of the most successful models.

So, it is quite natural to introduce a parallelism between the majority method, which is at the root of modern democracies, and competition in economic field, which determines who has the power to decide in economic systems as well. Competition, in this sense, avoids evil effects resulting from the concentration of economic power in the hands of a few people: a circumstance that can affect the economic decisions of the multitudes and delete fairness ensured by the 'competitive' method. The antitrust, from this point of view, can be legitimately considered the 'interface' of democracy in the economic field: it aims to prevent that a few influential decision-makers, with relevant price power, distort 'competitive' resource allocation, the only one able to create a fair correspondence between the decisions of those who produce and offer goods and services and the decisions of those who request them. So described, anti-monopoly law, against today's exponential growth of big firms' power in global markets, is part of that 'rule of law' which protects the rights of all against the economic distortion attributable to the power of the few.

As it was well written, 'competition matters because it prevents unjust inequality, rather than the transfer of wealth form consumer or supplier to the monopolist. If there is no competition, consumers and workers have less freedom to choose. Competition creates clear price signals in markets, driving supply and demand. It promotes efficiency. Competition creates more choices, more innovation, economic development and growth, and a stronger democracy by dispersing economic power. It promotes individual initiative and freedom. Competition is the essence of capitalism, yet it is dying'.[12] This 'agony' is an emergency of our time, which requires the regulatory models of antitrust to be harmonised and made consistent in different areas of the world, encouraging their convergence and making the global principles of economic governance more uniform.

[12] Tepper and Hearn (n 2).

18

Economic Crisis and Liberal Democracies

MORENO BERTOLDI AND MICHELE SALVATI*

I. INTRODUCTION

THE PURPOSE OF our chapter is adding historical evidence to a point that concerns economists as much as lawyers, historians, sociologists, political scientists and philosophers, the main contributors to this volume. We are convinced that the present political difficulties of liberal-democratic regimes, and the ensuing contrast between democracy and the rule of law, basically have to do with an internal weakness or ambiguity of liberalism itself, when this worldview is confronted with the choices that democratic governments and their electorates are facing in the context of a fast process of economic globalisation and revolutionary technological change.

What we call 'internal weakness/ambiguity' of liberalism – since the early nineteenth century the dominant worldview in the countries going through the experience of the industrial revolution[1] – mainly refers to one of the fundamental freedoms that liberalism proclaims: the freedom of individuals endowed with the necessary economic resources – capitalists, as they were later called – of organising production through free markets for labour and commodities. But does such a freedom also imply as a necessary consequence that the state, the supreme political authority of a community and the holder of the legitimate power of using means of coercion, should limit its role to simply enforcing the web of private contracts that a market organisation of production entails? And should the state stick to these limits even when the reaction of its citizens threatens other crucial values of liberalism, in particular when a conflict appears between democracy and the rule of law?

These questions are at the centre of a long controversy that periodically resurfaces when a free market economy – capitalism, hereafter – goes through a phase

* European Commission and University of Milan respectively.

[1] The literature on liberalism as the dominant worldview of modernity is immense. We give a single recent reference that, besides providing a large survey of the previous literature, is very close to our views: E Fawcett, *Liberalism: The Life of an Idea* (Princeton University Press, 2016). It is Fawcett's focus on politics and policies, on the varieties of national experiences, and his understanding of the basic (but ambiguous) message of liberalism that makes his book an ideal complement to our chapter.

that imposes material hardships and/or a worsening of living conditions onto a large section of the population. This controversy predates universal suffrage democracy, the full recognition of political rights, and the fusion of democracy with liberalism that prevailed after World War II in most economically advanced countries. And the answers to the questions mentioned above have always been essentially two, if we restrict our analysis to scholars and politicians of liberal-democratic persuasion. The first answer was and is that the state should interfere as little as possible in the functioning of a capitalist economy and endorse – better, promote – whatever organisation of the economy is resulting from the free choices of economic agents. The second answer was and is that the state has the duty to interfere in order to prevent not only the sufferings of many of its citizens, but a possible collapse of liberalism itself. Even before universal suffrage democracy, citizens could give origins to 'counter-movements'[2] attacking not only a dogmatic and inflexible version of individual economic liberty – our 'first answer' – but the very core of a liberal worldview.

It is impossible to summarise the wealth of arguments that were (and are) deployed by both sides of the controversy. We mentioned Karl Polanyi, whose book remains one of the best guides for understanding liberalism and capitalism: after reading it, it is very difficult to hold the view that capitalism is a spontaneous and 'natural' order of society. It is instead a political construction originally forced upon society by the liberal elites that held political power between the eighteenth and nineteenth centuries in England, and were influenced by the great political philosophers of the previous century. Adam Smith, however, was a liberal philosopher and the main founder of political economy as a separate field of study, but his political ideas can hardly be reconciled with the first answer to the problem of properly defining economic freedom.[3] Our second key reference is a contemporary of Polanyi, John Maynard Keynes: his *General Theory*, which revolutionised economic theory and policy in the mid-twentieth century, is inspired by a political vision that falls neatly into the second answer.[4]

Polanyi and Keynes: these are our main guides both in the following descriptive economic account and in the theoretical and normative considerations that we will draw from it. Keynes died in 1946, soon after the end of the war; Polanyi in 1964, without leaving any sustained analysis of the first post-war years in the light of his book, published 20 years earlier. Since we don't want to participate in the deceptive game of 'what–they-would–have-said-now', Polanyi and Keynes remain a powerful inspirational guide in the back of our minds, but the analysis and the normative

[2] Polanyi sees the expansion of capitalism worldwide as a 'double movement' of attempts to submit the entire society to a capitalist logic and of societal reactions against them ('countermovements'). These reactions could remain within the framework of a liberal polity (eg, the rise of unionism and of reformist social-democratic parties) or, in extreme cases (Fascism and Communism) could move outside it, subverting the basic institutions and eliminating the individual rights of liberalism. See K Polanyi, *The Great Transformation* (Ferrar &Rinehart, Inc, 1944). A recent, important appraisal of Polanyi's book is F Block and M Somers, *The Power of Market Fundamentalism: Karl Polanyi's Critique* (Harvard University Press, 2014).

[3] E Rothshield, *Economic Sentiments: Adam Smith, Condorcet and the Enlightenment* (Harvard University Press, 2001).

[4] JM Keynes, *The General Theory of Employment, Interest and Money* (Macmillan, 1936).

judgements that follow in the 70 and more years after the end of World War II and on the perspectives that liberal states are facing today are due to our understanding of what happened in economically Advanced Liberal Democracies (ALDs) in such a long period.

In section II we start with the phase of 'embedded liberalism' from the end of World War II to the early 1980s, briefly rehearse the economic and political reasons of its crisis, and end with the rise of 'neo-liberalism' and the Great Recession of 2007–08. We define this first phase as one of 'embedded liberalism'[5] instead of 'regulated capitalism', as is usual, because in ALDs capitalism is always regulated by the state, surely so at the national level and, in its most successful phases, also at the international one. The difference among our 'phases' basically depends on the vision that prevails in the relevant political authorities (states/international community) and shapes the 'regulation' adopted: whether it is one that tries to make compatible a liberal polity and a capitalist economy with the welfare of the large majority of society through an explicit 'interference' in the market system; or one based on the idea that self-regulating markets will automatically reach those aims and any interference would be damaging. This said, we often follow the usual definitions, talking of regulated capitalism as a synonym of embedded liberalism and of de-regulation as the policy that dismantled the rules that made liberalism socially embedded and substituted them with new ones more favourable to the neo-liberal view that became dominant after the Reagan-Thatcher era.[6]

Section III extends the analysis of the neoliberal phase to what happened after the Great Recession of 2007–08, exploring the macroeconomic policies adopted by the main ALDs and some of their political consequences, populism in particular. Section IV tackles the key question of this chapter: why a satisfactory social embedment of liberalism was possible in the post-World War II phase but proved so difficult in the following, neo-liberal one. Our answer refers to three sets of causal factors – international; domestic and structural-economic; political, cultural and cognitive – that were present in the first phase and absent or weak in the second one. The short section V briefly hints at the possibility of finding new factors of embedment that may substitute or reinforce those present in the first phase but eroded by neo-liberalism, globalisation and technical progress in the second one. Only new or renewed sources of embedment will allow democracy to go again hand in hand with liberalism and the rule of law.

This chapter was completed in December 2019. At the time of the final editing – September 2020 – the world was just recovering from of the deepest and sharpest recessions ever experienced by a capitalist economy, as a consequence of the epidemic

[5] JG Ruggie, 'International regimes, transactions, and change: embedded liberalism in the postwar economic order' (1982) 36(2) *International Organization* 379.

[6] Embedded liberalism and neo-liberalism are definitions that follow from the two answers that can be given to the question of what is meant by 'economic freedom'. But also remaining within the wide field of a liberal worldview there is a great variety of embedded liberalisms and neo-liberalisms that can be envisaged, stretching from extreme market fundamentalism (on the right) to a quasi-socialist reshaping of society (on the left). Since we survey actual historical experiences our gamut is more narrow, due to the weight of forces of continuity and path-dependence.

of Covid-19. So we found it necessary to add a few pages (section VI) in order to analyse this recession in the context of the conceptual framework of our chapter.

II. THE CRISIS OF POST-WAR 'EMBEDDED LIBERALISM' AND THE RISE OF NEOLIBERALISM

The Great Depression undermined the *gold standard* and the *laissez faire* paradigm that was its corollary. In its aftermath, most economists and policymakers realised that only regulated capitalism, supported by counter-cyclical fiscal and monetary policies, was a viable response to the economic collapse that the global economy was facing. However, in the 1930s, with the meltdown of the gold standard and the global economic order it entailed, each country proceeded in its own way towards regulated capitalism. It is worth noting that regulated capitalism was not necessarily a synonym for democracy. On the contrary, many of the countries that converted to regulated capitalism in the aftermath of the Great Depression were authoritarian or totalitarian regimes. Still, the 1930s also gave rise to the first forms of what will become known as embedded liberalism, that is, democratic countries where markets, which before the Great Depression operated disconnected from society, were embedded in it through regulations, a welfare state and macro-economic policies aimed at reaching a full employment. This was the case of the US under FDR's New Deal or the Scandinavian countries, where social-democratic parties rose to power.

It was only after World War II, with the defeat of the Axis, that regulated capitalism and democracy started to coincide, at least in Western advanced countries. Moreover, the lessons of the 1930s led the new hegemonic power – the US – to create a new international order, based on fixed but adjustable exchange rates, a gradual reduction of the barriers to trade and a set of international institutions that would help make the order stable.

The withdrawal of the Soviet Union and its satellites from the new global order in the second half of the 1940s paradoxically had the effect of strengthening it. US isolationist positions dissipated when the Soviet threat over Western Europe and Japan became evident. As a result, the US became the 'benevolent hegemon' of the Western World and, through the Marshall Plan, provided massive economic aid for the recovery of the shattered economies of Western Europe. While the US did not refrain from interfering in the domestic political affairs of some Western European democracies, in general it favoured soft power interventions to more muscular actions.

Moreover, the Soviet challenge, with its narrative claiming the empowerment of workers, equality and the end of exploitation, led social actors and policymakers in Western liberal democracies to look for durable and mutually advantageous compromises. These compromises took different forms, depending on the specificity of the institutions of a country, the structure of the economy (size of companies, degree of external openness, international specialisation), the degree of unionisation, and the nature of industrial relations (conflictual versus cooperative). It is, however, remarkable that, despite their diversity, these new forms of embedded liberalism all delivered for almost 30 years (*les trentes glorieuses*) strong growth, full employment, and relatively low inflation. Income and wealth inequalities declined.[7] Spurred by education, a more egalitarian social structure and full employment, Western liberal democracies experienced upward social mobility on a scale never seen before. Last but not least, international trade became again a significant growth engine as tariffs were gradually cut through a series of trade rounds. Still, capital controls remained in place, keeping wage competition and the expansion of finance in check.

Strong economic growth and the related rapid rise in household disposable income increased the support for democratic regimes in general and mainstream political parties, while the influence of communist parties, with the exception of Italy and France, receded significantly. Economic dynamism and democratic political regimes created a self-reinforcing virtuous circle. Kalecki's prediction that capitalism and full employment were incompatible seemed disproved: embedded liberalism was the formula that squared the circle.[8]

However, at the end of the 1960s the symbiotic relationship between regulated capitalism and democratic regimes started to show signs of strain. At an international level, the Bretton Woods system of fixed but adjustable exchange rates came under pressure and collapsed in 1971. At a domestic level, in many countries radical student protest spread to large segments of the working classes, triggering distributional conflicts that were exacerbated by oil shocks, a decline in productivity growth and an acceleration of inflation.[9] Governments in advanced economies struggled to run the economy at full employment while keeping inflation under control. The push in some countries by trade unions and left and centre-left parties to move the balance further in favour of labour and the bid to gain power in the workplace ultimately failed. *Le government de la gauche* in France (1981–83), instead of rewriting the labour-capital compromise (in favour of labour), ended up in closing the Fordist era of regulated capitalism.

High inflation, lower growth and social unrest led to the rise in the US and the UK of a new, more radical, brand of conservatism. The neo-liberal revolution carried out by Margaret Thatcher in the UK and Ronald Reagan in the US translated into a significant de-regulation of the economy, privatisations, and the weakening of the unions.[10] Macro-economic policy was not any longer aimed at ensuring full employment, but at slashing inflation. Full employment could occasionally occur in the mature expansionary phase of the business cycle, but it would be the exception rather than the rule. In the 1980s the neo-liberal paradigm won the day, as inflation declined while growth picked up supported by the animal spirits of capitalists who saw the balance of power switching to their advantage, as well as by expansionary fiscal policies (through tax cuts and military spending). One by one, governments in

[7] See T Picketty, *Le capital au XXI siècle* (Seuil, 2013).

[8] M Kalecki, 'Political Aspects of Full Employment' in *Political Quarterly*, vol 14 (Wiley-Blackwell, 1943).

[9] See on this P Armstrong, A Glyn and J Harrison, *Capitalism Since 1945* (OUP, 1991) and A Glyn, *Capitalism Unleashed* (OUP, 2006).

[10] See C Johnson, *The Grand Experiment: Mrs. Thatcher's Economy and How It Spread* (West View Press, 1993) and M Feldstein (ed), *American Economic Policy in the 1980s* (NBER, The University of Chicago, 1994).

advanced countries, including on the centre-left, converted to its core assumptions, although many of them kept institutional frameworks that avoided a full convergence to 'liberal market economies'.[11] The neo-liberal consensus also led to the lifting of capital controls, as they were considered an obstacle to the effective allocation of capital. Free movement of capitals now disciplined the macroeconomic policy of a country, pressuring it to introduce structural reforms that could attract foreign capital. The margins of manoeuvre of national governments shrunk significantly, making of Margaret Thatcher's TINA ('There Is No Alternative') a self-fulfilling prophecy.

The 1980s were also the period of the opening up of China and the change of emerging markets' stance vis-à-vis foreign capital inflows gave rise to a worldwide phase of globalisation. The dissipation of the risk that large emerging countries would nationalise private capital, as well as the growing competition among them to attract foreign capital through deregulation and privatisation, opened the floodgates: capital started to flow downhill, from advanced economies to Emerging Market Economies (EMEs) and developing countries. The so-called 'Washington consensus', that is, a set of policy prescriptions applicable almost to every advanced and emerging economy, created a fundamental imbalance by making the world safe for capital,[12] and in so doing dis-embed once again economic liberalism from democracy. As a result, income and wealth inequalities in advanced economies started to rise rapidly.[13]

At the time such developments were not considered a major shortcoming. After having defeated fascism through World War II, capitalism and liberal democracy had overcome the last major possible alternative system: communism. As Francis Fukuyama put it in his famous 1989 article on 'The End of History?':[14] 'what we may be witnessing is not just the end of the Cold War, or the passing of a particular period of post-war history, but the end of history as such: that is, the end point of mankind's ideological evolution and the universalization of Western liberal democracy as the final form of human government'. For Fukuyama, the fall of the Soviet bloc represented 'the unabashed victory of economic and political liberalism'. Contrary to Polanyi, Fukuyama did not see any contradiction or tension between economic liberalism and political liberalism. They reinforced each other, with positive spillovers also on international relations: the death of the communist ideology implied 'the growing "Common Marketisation" of international relations, and the diminution of the likelihood of large-scale conflict between states'.

The end of the Soviet bloc coincided with a period of growth and prosperity in Europe, which accelerated the process of unification that had started in 1959. The single currency project received a boost with the fall of the Berlin Wall, as a single

[11] R Hall and D Soskice (eds), *Varieties of Capitalism. The Institutional Foundations of Comparative Advantage* (OUP, 2001).

[12] See Q Slobodian, *Globalists: The End of Empire and the Birth of Neoliberalism* (Harvard University Press, 2018) and S Wertheim, *A World Safe for Capital – How Neoliberalism Shaped the International System*, Foreign Affairs, May/June (Council on Foreign Relations, 2019).

[13] See T Piketty, *Le capital au XXI siècle* (Seuil, 2013) and B Milanovic, *Global Inequality. A New Approach for the Age of Globalization* (The Belknap Press of Harvard University Press, 2016).

[14] F Fukuyama, *The End of History?*, *The National Interest* n 16 (Center for the NatInterest, 1989).

currency and a common monetary policy were seen by many European leaders as instruments to anchor Germany to the European Union. The integration process seemed unstoppable, and mainstream parties supported it.

If the 1980s were the years of the neoliberal revolution and the political dominance of conservative parties, the 1990s saw the revival of centre-left parties on both sides of the Atlantic. In the 1980s these parties had been successfully labeled by their right wing opponents as the parties of the past. Conservatives had become the party of change and dynamism, while democrats and social democrats were stuck in the preservation of an economic system that in the 1970s had generated just stagflation and unemployment. However, centre-left parties experienced a drastic change of leadership in the last decade of the century. The traditional left, favouring a strong presence of the state in the economy, expanded welfare programmes (sometime unsustainable), and Keynesian fiscal policies lost ground. The new, younger generation of leaders (Clinton in the US, Blair in the UK, Schroeder in Germany) did not feel encumbered by the past. They were ready to embrace the new neo-liberal paradigm, while bending it to allow for a fairer distribution of the gains from globalisation and the more efficient allocation of resources. They, and not the conservatives, were the leaders of modernity and change.

The new centre-left leaders succeeded in bringing on their side high-middle class professional figures generated by the new economy. They also promoted a significant economic, social and environmental modernisation of advanced countries. Some of their welfare reforms helped lower unemployment (Germany) or support low-income working households (the US). However, their policies failed on three accounts: (1) they were unable to significantly mitigate the costs of globalisation. Societies became increasingly divided between winners and losers. The discontent among the latter was growing, although initially it failed to find political representation; (2) they underestimated the systemic risks that increasingly deregulated financial markets represented for the economy. Forgetting inter alia Polanyi's and Minsky's warnings that self-regulating financial capitalism was a utopia,[15] centre-left leaders went along with the dominant paradigm, and sometimes the liberation of the financial Prometheus happened under their watch; and (3) in the EU, they did not act to review the macroeconomic tools at their disposal, in particular the fiscal one, to strengthen government's ability to respond to a downturn.

The centre-left political supremacy did not last long. By the mid-2000s, with the exception of the UK, conservatives had returned to power in all major advanced economies. In the US, the Bush Administration introduced massive tax cuts and pushed further financial deregulation. This led to an unsustainable debt-led growth model that will be epitomised by the rise and fall of subprime loans. In the European Union, now mostly under the watch of centre-right governments, on the surface things seemed to move in the right direction, with relatively strong growth and declining unemployment. However, under the surface, important imbalances were developing both in the surplus and the deficit countries of the Euro area. Mainstream political parties

[15] K Polanyi, *The Great Transformation* and H Minsky, *Stabilizing an Unstable Economy* (Yale University Press, 1986).

continued to dominate the political scene, while populist movements remained at the fringe of the political system.

All this happened while the process of globalisation continued unabated, with even fewer policy efforts to compensate the losers. Global supply chains developed rapidly, while massive financial flows moved almost seamlessly around the world. Global capitalism and, with it, the end of history seemed destined to prevail.

III. THE GREAT RECESSION AND ITS IMPACT ON LIBERAL DEMOCRACIES

The collapse of Lehmann Brothers in September 2008, and the downward spiral it triggered came as a shock. On the one hand, policymakers thought they had in their toolbox all the instruments needed to avoid a major financial crisis; on the other hand, a repetition of the Great Depression was in itself unconceivable. Was it not conventional wisdom among mainstream economists and policymakers that financial markets had become self-equilibrating and therefore possible deviations from equilibrium would be only temporary and rapidly reabsorbed?

The crisis that could not have happened triggered an enormous credibility loss for mainstream policymakers, as well as the economic profession. Facing a major economic disaster, economic policy authorities scrambled to find effective solutions to a crisis that for months mimicked a collapse similar to the Great Depression of the 1930s. Neoliberal policy prescriptions were abandoned and Keynesianism was taken off the shelves and implemented. Differently from the 1930s, in 2008–09 policymakers acted decisively: central banks brought interest rates to zero, private banks had to raise capital (if need be by accepting the injection of public money), governments introduced impressive fiscal stimulus packages. Through the G20, the policy response was coordinated at an international level. By the second half of 2009 the global economy had already started to recover. However, the crisis was systemic, and the recovery did not produce a strong economic rebound. Growth remained sluggish and sub-par. In the meantime, millions of people lost their jobs (and many of them also their houses), wealth losses were huge, and the banking sector remained impaired.

Against this backdrop, resentment against the world of finance and policymakers became widespread.[16] The management of financial institutions was accused of having put their greedy interests ahead of financial stability, while policymakers were held responsible for not having acted in time to prevent the crisis. Moreover, because of the bail out of the banking sector with public money, they were suspected to be complicit with the financial world.

Globalisation too came heavily under fire. While globalisation criticism predates the global financial crisis, the Great Recession worked as a catalyst for globalisation discontents. As the neoliberal paradigm crumbled (and with it the TINA assumption), some of the outcomes of globalisation, in particular its impact on employment and on the distribution of income and wealth, came under scrutiny. These developments

[16] M Funke, M Schularick and C Trebesch (2015), *Politics in the Slump: Polarization and Extremism after Financial Crises* (European Commission, 2015).

triggered two separate reactions. From the globalisation critics on the left came the request that future trade deals should contain much stronger labour and environmental standards, the interests of multinational companies and international finance should be curbed, and manufacturing jobs at home should be protected. Part of the right instead moved away from free trade in favour of bilateral managed trade, the protection of national productions through tariffs and non-tariffs barriers, as well as the closure of the borders to foreign workers.

The US was the first country to experience a populist backlash in the aftermath of the Great Recession. In 2009–10 President Obama passed three major pieces of legislation: a large stimulus package to counter the economic recession, the Affordable Care Act (Obamacare), and a major financial reform (the Dodd-Frank Act). However, he had to make compromises to keep everybody on board in his camp, as Republicans refused to cooperate. As a result, all three pieces of legislation did not go far enough and some Democratic constituencies, disgruntled by rising inequalities and insufficient political and economic changes, moved to the left and asked for more radical reforms. Over the years these constituencies would become increasingly influential in the Democratic Party, mounting a serious challenge to the more moderate leadership that controls it. However, the major beneficiary of the Great Recession in the US was the populist right. High unemployment, racial tensions, illegal immigration, a skyrocketing fiscal deficit, and an effective grassroots campaign against Obamacare, presented as the anteroom of socialism, favoured the rise of radical conservatives, who gathered around the Tea Party. After the successful mid-term elections of 2010, these conservatives emerged as the strongest and most combative faction inside the party. The inability of the Republican leadership to bring under control the Tea Party insurgency created a fertile ground for the rise of candidate Trump in the 2016 elections.

In Europe initially the dissatisfaction for the way the crisis was dealt with did not translate into an immediate surge of populist parties. Parties in government were often defeated when elections were held, but they were replaced by mainstream parties in the opposition. In the end, the policy response had been relatively effective: growth turned positive in the second half of 2009, unemployment rose, but in general less than in the US, and fiscal deficits were also lower.

However, the European policy response had three major flaws. The first one related to the fact that many policymakers remained anchored to the neoliberal theoretical framework and fiscal orthodoxy.[17] As a result, countries like Germany and the Netherlands were pushing for rapid fiscal consolidation across the board well before the Greek crisis. Such developments had quite ominous consequences for the aggregate fiscal stance of the Euro area. When the sovereign debt crisis struck, the Euro area fiscal policy became strongly pro-cyclical and made the recession significantly worse. On the monetary side, one would have to wait for Mario Draghi's 'whatever it takes' in July 2012 before the ECB fully acted as (conditional) lender of last resort, leading to a significant reduction in the spreads. The second major flaw was the inability

[17] For a critique of the neoclassical theoretical framework and fiscal orthodoxy, see P Krugman, *End This Depression Now!* (WW Norton and Company, 2012), M Blyth, *Austerity. The History of a Dangerous Idea* (OUP, 2013) and A Tooze, *Crashed: How a Decade of Financial Crises Changed the World* (Viking, 2018).

of acting decisively on banks, recapitalising them and restoring the impaired credit channel. While the US intervened swiftly, Europe was slow to react. The outcome was a severe tightening of financial conditions in the countries affected by the sovereign debt crisis. Last but not least, the EMU construction was not built to withstand a major systemic shock and authorities had to scramble to fix it while the crisis was unfolding. The architectural flaws, in particular the lack of effective instruments to support countries facing severe difficulties, led to very suboptimal outcomes.

These flaws led to a double dip of the Euro area economy, with many of its members facing years of austerity, high unemployment rates, and declining real wages. The length and depth of the recession, which was unprecedented in post-war Western Europe, undermined the support for mainstream parties on the centre-left and the centre-right.

The mainstream parties on the centre-left found themselves in a particularly vulnerable position as the 'modernisation' of social democracies in the 1990s led them to embrace large parts of the neoliberal paradigm. In the aftermath of the Great Recession this paradigm was not holding any longer. However, abandoning it in favour of 'old' Keynesian policies, was highly controversial as it would have meant reneging the 'modernising' approach of the last 20 years. Therefore, staying on the course, even with a flawed paradigm, appeared to many centre-left parties as the least-worst option. This led social-democratic parties in Northern Europe to abandon the European perspective and focus on the narrow interest of their respective countries and constituencies. In doing so, they were trapped in the conservative ordoliberal narrative and became hardly distinguishable from the mainstream parties of the centre-right. In France and the Mediterranean countries the situation was even more uncomfortable. Most centre-left leaders realised that austerity would have led their countries to a prolonged deep recession, but they did not have room for manoeuvre to carry out more expansionary fiscal policies. Therefore, *obtorto collo*, they had to go along with austerity policies. The discrepancy between the (quasi) Keynesian rhetoric and the austerity practice led to a major loss of credibility. Even centre-left administrations that stretched European fiscal flexibility to the limits did not succeed in convincing voters that the 'narrow path'[18] was the right strategy to follow. At the dawn of the new decade the mainstream centre-left parties find themselves in a dismal state. They have lost large chunks of their traditional working-class electorate, which has often shifted to populist movements both on the left and on the right. More importantly, they have been unable to develop a new narrative, torn as they are between a reformed neo-liberal paradigm and more radical, but still quite magmatic new approaches.

Conservative parties have fared better during the crisis and its aftermath, even if over time their position has also weakened significantly. The Northern conservative parties were able to get their way in shaping the economic policy of Europe, profiting from the fact that their countries were not under market pressure and they had a flawed, but coherent ordoliberal narrative to sell both to the European authorities and their national constituencies. While for the general public this narrative had moral

[18] PC Padoan, *Il sentiero stretto … e oltre* (Il Mulino, 2019).

connotations (prudent savers of the North versus deficit-prone spendthrifts of the South), it appealed to European policymakers as it promised the return to economic stability through confidence effects, while respecting the fiscal rules. Moreover, German conservatives were flexible enough to show pragmatism each time the Euro area was on the brink of a breakdown, as it would have been extremely damaging for their economy. Against this backdrop, Northern conservatives electorally performed quite well, at least until the migration crisis started in 2015. Conservatives in Southern European countries and France faced instead the same problems that were plaguing the centre-left mainstream parties in the South of Europe. As a result, when in government, they had also to implement austerity measures that sapped their popularity. Finally, mainstream UK conservatives, who were in favour of remaining in the EU, underestimated the support for the leave option, fuelled by growing inequalities, a rejection of immigration from other European countries, economic insecurity and an outdated sense of national pride. The withdrawal referendum did not go as expected, and this drifted the party towards the populist right.

Initially the sovereign debt crisis seemed to benefit more the populist left (or movements that, like the Five Star Movement in Italy, had economic policy platforms close to those of the radical left) than the ethno-nationalist/sovereignist right. This was because what propelled populist movements in the aftermath of the Great Recession was a combination of opposition to austerity policies and rejection of globalisation (topics on which the populist left had a quite strong narrative), without an identity/ethno-nationalist component.

However, the populist right was also on the rise. After the electoral victories in Hungary (2010) and Poland (2015), right wing sovereignists were able to have a major breakthrough in Western Europe in 2016 when they won the EU withdrawal referendum in the UK. The biggest upset came however from the US on 8 November 2016, when to almost everybody's surprise Donald Trump was elected president on an anti-immigration, ethno-nationalist, and protectionist platform. According to him, the US had been on the decline for the last 30 years because its elites had put their interests ahead of the interests of the country and in so doing allowed for unfavourable trade deals and massive illegal immigration flows. Therefore, to address inequalities and regain prosperity, the country did not need to pursue redistribution policies or open up further the economy, but rather to pursue supply-side policies (tax cuts, deregulation) that, together with the withdrawal from unfavourable international agreements (eg, the Paris Agreement on climate change), would have boosted domestic economic growth and employment. It did not matter that these policies would increase inequalities inside the US and favour US elites, as far as they would bring some benefits also for the low middle-class and people living in rural areas, and the costs of the policies pursued could be shifted outside the US or on migrants, and/or the urban and suburban high-middle class. During his years in power, President Trump has remained faithful to this narrative and acted accordingly. In doing so, he has become the reference point for many right-wing populists around the world, who also call for economic nationalism and anti-immigration policies.

In continental Europe, the time for the sovereignist/ethno-nationalist parties came in the second half of the decade, due to the large immigration inflows from Syria and Africa. These flows allowed them to link identity issues with the economic discontent lingering below the surface. European nationalist and xenophobic parties immediately embraced in their political platforms key elements of the programmes that led Brexiteers and President Trump to victory. Initially the revised political formula seemed to prove politically successful: far right ethno-nationalist anti-EU parties rose to double digit levels in many European countries. More importantly, Italy became a populist political laboratory: the Five Star Movement and the Lega created an unprecedented populist coalition with the aim of overhauling the Italian political system and to force the acceptance of their policies over the European institutions. Still, confronted with the harsh realities of government, right wing populists suffered major setbacks: for instance, the political and economic chaos created by Brexit has led most of populist parties in continental Europe to tone down their anti-EU rhetoric and reconsider their pledge to leave the Euro. In Italy the coalition between two different brands of populism collapsed after one year, undermined by deep political divisions and a stagnating economy. Despite a good score in the European elections of 2019, they were not able to avoid mainstream parties retaining a strong majority in the European Parliament.

There is no doubt that in the last decade many of the pillars on which liberal democracies in advanced economies were laying on have been eroded. The global liberal order is crumbling as the 'benevolent hegemon' that shaped it has decided to leverage its strength and rely much more on unilateralist policies. Stable political systems relying on the alternation in government of mainstream centre-left and centre-right parties are now in tatters, while in many countries Polanyian countermovements are in full swing. In the US populist issues will be at the centre of the presidential electoral campaign. In some countries (eg, France) a new dualism, between a centrist pro-European party and a right-wing populist anti-EU party has emerged. In other countries, grand coalitions had to be formed. Even where the traditional centre-right/centre-left dialectic is still at work, parliamentary majorities have become smaller and more unstable. All this would not have happened in the absence of the catalyst represented by the Great Recession and the economic and financial turmoil that ensued.

IV. THE ROLE OF ECONOMIC FACTORS IN EXPLAINING POPULISM IN ADVANCED LIBERAL DEMOCRACIES

In the previous two sections we surveyed the main macroeconomic policies pursued by the ALDs during the phases of embedded liberalism and of neo-liberalism and described some of their political consequences. In this section we will better define the basic characters of these two phases and try to show why the first one met with an extraordinary success, both from an economic point of view and from that of stabilising conditions of liberal democracy. The number of countries and the amount of world population, however, were much smaller than in the following neo-liberal phase, the one that unified the world under the rule of 'Capitalism, Alone'.[19] Taking

[19] B Milanovic, *Capitalism, Alone* (The Belknap Press of Harvard University Press, 2019).

into account the much larger scale on which economic development has been spreading, many elements of this phase can also be seen as extraordinary achievements. But most of the countries involved were not, nor they are now, liberal democracies. And in the countries that had experienced the previous phase of embedded liberalism the situation has worsened, both from the point of view of economic growth and from that of supporting conditions of liberal democracy. So, it is to the ALDs that we will continue to restrict our attention.

Many of the chapters of this book are devoted to the synthesis of democratic and liberal principles which prevailed in our ALDs after World War II and to the threats it is now facing. Here we would like to underline the characters that made such a synthesis democratically sustainable, that is, the conditions of 'social embedment' in which a liberal democracy was functioning in that period. The conclusions we reached in our survey are essentially two. The first one, roughly stated, is that a liberal-democratic synthesis can work smoothly if the citizens are in a large majority satisfied with the social and economic situation they live in. In other words, if the 'output' of liberal-democratic governments largely coincides with the requirements of society. The second conclusion is that such an output is possible but very difficult to achieve in a capitalist economy, especially so in a globalised economy undergoing a phase of revolutionary technological change, as both developments shift the balance of power in favour of capital. The golden age in which liberal democracy went hand in hand with a satisfactory responsiveness of governments to the demands of society was due to exceptional circumstances that do not prevail any longer.

Let's consider our first conclusion, the one relating to the consensus to liberal-democratic governments when they meet deeply felt social demands. Most citizens do not care about the reasons why this happens: these reasons may well have to do with a favourable international situation for which a national government cannot claim any merit. But since democracy is a national affair, it is probable that the satisfaction of the citizens will translate into electoral consensus for the government. In the case where social demands are not met, for whatever reasons, the blame would fall on national governments, and citizens would be led to enquire whether 'democracy' is working properly. The answer of populist movements is negative, because a representative liberal democracy is far away from the ideal of 'government by the people' of Lincoln's Gettysburg Address (government of, by and for the people).[20] An important point follows from this: the origins of discontent are normally due to the worsening of social and economic conditions and to the fact that they are allowed to persist, for which national governments may (or may not) bear any responsibility. However, the quality of national governments and of representative liberal-democratic institutions are issues that populist movements would inevitably raise in both cases. In other words: even if the causes of discontent are located in the 'output' side, the

[20] On the ambiguous concept of people we refer to Y Meny, *Imparfaites démocracies. Frustrations populaires et vagues populistes* (Presses de Sciences Po, 2019) especially chapter 2. The same author and JW Mueller, *What is Populism* (University of Pennsylvania Press, 2016) are our main references on the immense literature on populism. For democracy and its inevitable conflict between reality and ideal we stick to the classic book by G Sartori, *The Theory of Democracy Revisited* (Chatham House Publishers, 1987).

search for remedies will involve the 'input' level of democracy, pretending to give 'the people' – an imagined, unitary community – a real possibility of expressing its will.[21] And a 'populist democracy' – this is its unsustainable claim – would then solve the problems of discontent against which the people is reacting.

Let's now move to our second conclusion. Both the possibility and the difficulty of making capitalism compatible with a liberal democracy – in other words, of 'embedding' liberalism in society – are the subject of a vast literature, ranging from those who deny that such a possibility exists in a capitalist society to those who admit it, but subjecting capitalism to reforms of various intensity.[22] The evidence that an embedded liberalism may exist is given, however, by the simple fact that it has existed in the long period of the *trente glorieuses*; and that such an embedment may prove difficult can be inferred from the entire history of capitalism, including the phase we are living in. So, our next step is that of identifying the main factors that made the embedment possible after World War II and then showing why all of them have been eroded in the following phase of neo-liberalism. In our outrageously short analysis, they are reduced to three kinds of interlinked factors: international, structural/economic, and political/cultural/cognitive.

The first factor refers to the existence of a country whose economic and military hegemony was unchallengeable in the Western world after World War II. Moreover, the US was led by an elite devoted not only to the creation and maintenance of a liberal-democratic polity in most of the advanced countries under its influence,[23] but also to fostering those economic and social conditions that make liberal democracy possible and enduring, that is, conditions of embedment: the seminal paper of JG Ruggie[24] was the first to refer to this factor in the literature on international relations.

The second factor refers to the political, cultural and cognitive conditions that induced the elites of the two major Anglo-Saxon powers to embrace an embedded version of liberalism. It was a generation of leaders who had the memories of World War I, of the Great Depression, of the rise of communism and fascism still fresh in their minds. But how to react to the causes that had made international political conflict so disruptive and the spread of popular discontent so dangerous in (and for) liberal democracies? A powerful hegemon in international relations was not a sufficient condition: the hegemon had also to induce all countries under its influence to adopt policies able to make capitalism compatible with full employment and the satisfaction of the most pressing demands of their citizens. This is why the Keynesian revolution was so important: not only did it offer the theoretical tools necessary to design the appropriate economic policies, but it contributed to create a cultural climate favourable to their adoption just in the Anglo-Saxon centre of the liberal world and among liberal economists. And Keynes was in a unique position to do so.

[21] On the expressions of 'input' and 'output' as a shorthand for the two main sources of legitimacy of a democracy see FW Scharpf, *Governing in Europe: Effective and Democratic?* (OUP, 1998).

[22] For a good survey of the incompatibility thesis, common in the radical Left, see the Introduction of Streeck in W Streek, *How Will Capitalism End?* (Verso, 2016). The author is an important scholar whose former liberal persuasion was not tarred by major doubts.

[23] The situation was different in Third World countries, where containing communism and/or economic interests took priority over liberal-democratic principles.

[24] Ruggie (n 5).

Our last factor, certainly not the least one, refers to the structural/economic conditions prevailing in the single countries of the 'free world'. Most of the countries to which the phase of embedded liberalism applied had institutionally strong states and advanced economies: the disruptions caused by the war were rapidly overcome. They were all on the verge of a technological and organisational revolution that only the US had begun to experience before the war – Fordism – but they had the capacity to fully exploit it after the war.[25] The social and economic properties of this revolution were very favourable to a political project of embedded liberalism. A very fast growth of income and productivity, a strong labour demand for semi-skilled workers, wages growing in line with productivity – together with the pledge to full employment by all the parties that held government responsibility and with the growth of labour Unions – and, last but not least, a relatively homogeneous population[26] were the conditions that made the expansion of welfare states both a universal political demand and an economically feasible one. With very high GDP growth, a strong increase in private consumption could go hand in hand with an increase in the public expenditures, that is, with a vast enlargement and deepening of the institutions of the Welfare State.

If we turn to the situation prevailing now, the first thing to notice is that all the factors that made embedment possible after World War II have been eroded in the following phase of neo-liberalism. A caveat is required, however. All ALDs share a common experience of embedment which has shaped lasting expectations and have built institutions of welfare that are very popular and hard to uproot. But the trends heading to change are unmistakable.

At the international level the hegemony of the US as a champion of embedded liberalism is a thing of the past (at least for now, although much will depend on the outcome of the 2020 US presidential elections). The US is still the most powerful nation of the world and (a fortiori) of the liberal world, but the economic, cultural and political conditions that led to the embedment strategy it pursued after World War II are increasingly threatened both by internal and by international developments. It is true that the heydays of neo-liberalism and deregulation are gone with the financial crisis and the Great Recession, but no realistic alternative has been developed in their place. The forces making for inequality – globalisation, financialisation and ICT revolution – remain unchecked under Trump's presidency: while his unilateralist and neo-mercantilist strategy has been a *chef d'oeuvre* of populist policy, if pursued consistently it will risk a serious trade war and a world recession. If one considers the problems for which a close cooperation of all the most important countries would be essential – first of all that of climate change – the risk of a Hobbesian world shouldn't be undervalued.

[25] On Fordism and its crucial role in creating an original growth regime, see the analyses developed by the French Regulation School, in particular R Boyer, *La Théorie de la régulation: fondements et développements* (La Decouverte, 2015) and B Coriat, *L'atelier et le chronomètre. Essai sur le taylorisme, le fordisme et la production de masse* (Christian Burgeois, 1979).

[26] The exception was the US. Racial discrimination was a crucial factor in impeding a universal health insurance and in making the US health sector very expensive and less accessible. On the complex relation between share of immigrants and support for welfare state in Europe, see A Alesina, E Mulard and H Rapoport, 'Immigration and Preferences for Redistribution in Europe' at https://scholar.harvard.edu/files/alesina/files/paper_immig_redis_080219correct.pdf.

A possible alternative – a collective hegemonic power including large regional unions with a common currency – has been tested in Europe with the creation of the Euro. The political conditions seemed to be very favourable, since this area includes most of the countries that that had shared the experience of embedded liberalism. However, the difficulties not only of creating a political Union, but even of completing the more modest design of the Economic and Monetary Union, has contributed to serious growth divergences and endless quarrels among Eurozone members. As a way of building a benign collective hegemon, this route doesn't seem likely to provide an alternative any time soon. Together with immigration, Euro area policymakers' inability to avoid a double dip after the Great Recession is the reason why populist movements are able to depict the European Union as a cumbersome transmission belt of the trends prevailing in the international economy and 'going alone' as a better alternative. Summing up on this point: a single or collective hegemon, able to rule over an immense variety of heterogeneous states according to a benign institutional design, would face difficulties belonging to an order of magnitude much greater than those faced by the US after World War II.

Moving now to the structural-economic situation that most ALDs have to face at the domestic level, we have already mentioned the difference between the social consequences of Fordism – the technological and organisational revolution that characterised the phase of embedded liberalism – with those prevailing after the political victory of neo-liberalism. Domestic deregulation and free capital movements in search of profit opportunities around the world, together with a slow-down of the rate of growth of advanced and mature economies, began to undermine since the early 1980s the post-war social compromise: the 'great moderation' of wage growth, the rise of unemployment and precarious employment in the industrial sectors facing an increasing competition of low-wage countries started to change the distribution of income in favour of capital and to increase personal income and wealth inequality. This was a first step, however: on top of it, as globalisation advanced, the ALDs began to feel the consequences of the ICT revolution and of the great expansion and sophistication of the financial industry, both requiring a highly trained workforce and both susceptible of monopolistic behaviour. Pre-tax personal earning differentials experienced a fast increase that tax-averse fiscal systems were unwilling (or simply unable) to restrain: the case of the US remains extreme, but also in the ALDs with a deeper experience of embedment and of social-democratic governments disposable income inequality has been growing, although at a much slower pace.[27]

Always with regard to the structural-economic situation, another crucial difference between the present period and the post-war period of embedded liberalism is that globalisation, financialisation and the ICT revolution, while they have strengthened the bargaining position of the rich and the wealthy, have not translated (yet?) into a return to productivity growth levels similar (or even close) to those of the *trente glorieuses*.[28] As a result, the possibility that ALDs will continue to face low aggregate

[27] I Saez and G Zucman, *The Triumph of Injustice* (WW Norton, 2019).

[28] On productivity slowdown in advanced economies see RJ Gordon, *The Rise and Fall of American Growth* (Princeton University Press, 2016) and A Posen and J Zettlemeyer, *Facing up to Low Productivity Growth* (Peterson Institute for International Economics, 2019).

productivity growth in the years to come cannot be excluded and is even likely. Low productivity growth and the fact that, after the tax reforms of the neo-liberal era, productivity gains are disproportionally appropriated by the richest segments of the population,[29] have two important consequences: (1) they make the distributional conflicts more difficult to solve; and (2) they put a strain on the solvency of the welfare state. Embedding liberalism in a situation of low productivity growth is objectively difficult, as it is almost inevitable that a new social compromise would imply some losses for the highest income groups of a country (instead of minor gains, as it was the case during the period of embedded liberalism of the twentieth century). However, as these groups maintain a very strong negotiating position (unions are weak, there is not an existential threat on the horizon, after the long neo-liberal era taxation remains unpopular, etc), their interest for such a compromise remains quite limited.

Briefly we turn to the political/cultural/cognitive factor. Both at the international level and at the domestic one the situation is much more complex and confused than it was just after World War II. At the international level, capitalism has won the world game and the national powers competing for hegemony are now all capitalist countries with different shades of democracy, or not democratic at all. As we have just seen, obtaining an agreement on a common architecture of international economic and financial relations seems an impossible task, given the great differences of degrees of development, interests and national cultures among the players. If it is true that the illusion of self-adjusting markets has suffered a hard blow by the recession of 2007–08, the neo-liberal consensus is still strong and an alternative policy as neat and cogent as Keynes offered at the eve of the war hasn't yet appeared. Probably we should not expect that a cultural breakthrough should come from a new *General Theory* or from a Grand Design conceived by an economist of genius: given the importance of political and international factors, only the convergence of efforts in all social science and in many countries could produce a large consensus on a more progressive set of policies. Economics is moving in this direction. Unconventional monetary policy is no longer 'unconventional'. Fiscal policy has become again a legitimate instrument of economic policy and, unthinkable until few years ago, central bankers call for its activation. Environmental economics is expanding at a very rapid pace and sustainable finance is now embraced by many financial institutions, The statement (by Nobel Prize Robert Lucas) that 'nothing [is] as poisonous' for sound economics as 'to focus on questions of distribution'[30] is now widely rejected by the profession and the issues of fair taxation, the elimination of tax evasion, tax loopholes and tax havens is becoming a top priority in government agendas. So, reasons of hope that sooner or later a cultural breakthrough may happen are not to be excluded.

All in all, our analysis does not point to the conclusion that the ALDs will face in the foreseeable future an irresistible race to the bottom. Short of a dramatic economic

[29] See in particular, H Boushey, *Unbound – How Inequality Constricts Our Economy and what We Can Do about It* (Harvard University Press, 2019); Milanovic (n 19); and Saez and Zucman (n 27).

[30] R Lucas, *The Industrial Revolution: Past and Future* (2003 Annual Report of the Federal Reserve Bank of Minneapolis, 2004) 5–20.

crisis, world demand for highly sophisticated products and services will remain strong, both in the ICT sector and in many others, and mature economies are in a good position to cater for it. The advantages of co-location and co-specificity, of a highly trained and educated workforce, make it difficult that entire clusters of innovative industry and services may be transferred in low wage countries.[31] But will the growth of nationally rooted (or, better, regionally or city rooted) advanced sectors provide sufficient economic resources for feeding a process of socially inclusive growth at the national level? Democracy, elections and social movements are political forces mainly operating at this level, where politics has to also take into account the demands of a vast hinterland of regions and people left behind. The relatively uniform pay and work conditions that prevailed during the Fordist era, both a cause and a consequence of the strength of labour unions, are not going to come back. Industrial and service workers are now ranging between the highly skilled and educated workforce of the advanced sectors and a long tail of unemployed or precariously employed citizens (and immigrants) at the bottom of the income distribution: in between there are a large mass employed in public or private sectors with very diverse conditions of employment, income and social mobility.

All these international and domestic developments seem to play in favour of populist and ethno-nationalist movements and parties. As we recalled at the beginning of this chapter, regulated capitalism is not a synonym for liberal democracy. What illiberal parties try to do at the current juncture, in particular on the right, is to reduce the disconnect between markets and society by preserving and even strengthening some non-market dimensions of the economic system. However, two crucial pre-conditions apply to this strengthening: (1) only the citizens of the country (preferably belonging to the same ethnicity/race) should benefit from the welfare state (which is electorally rewarding in periods of real or perceived economic difficulties); and (2) the economic system remains 'safe for capital' (unions remain weak, if there is re-distribution is from the (liberal-democratic) cities to the (ethno-nationalistic) periphery and not necessarily from the richest to the poorest; and the asymmetry of power in favour of capital that prevailed during the neo-liberal era is not put in discussion (the illiberal parties and movements present themselves as pro-business)). Against this backdrop, in recent times illiberal/nationalistic governments in advanced economies have fared quite well, from a (short-term) economic viewpoint: the US economy, boosted by massive tax cuts (favouring mostly corporations and the wealthy) and the increase of federal spending, is in a situation of full employment, while countries like Poland and Hungary are among the fastest growing in the European Union. While for these two last countries there is certainly a catch-up effect, they do not seem to be penalised by foreign investors for their rejection of liberal democracy and its rules.

Reverting to our Polanyian categories a conclusion seems to follow: if more effective policies of embedment are not found, there will be ample room for social discontent and counter-movements. In these conditions a danger for the institutions of a liberal polity will always be present.

[31] See T Iversen and D Soskice, *Democracy and Prosperity* (Princeton University Press, 2019).

V. CONCLUSIONS

In light of what has been happening in liberal democracies since the global financial crisis, in the previous section we advanced a rather pessimistic outlook about the possibility of returning to a phase of embedded liberalism of the same kind and intensity of that the ALDs experienced in the 30 years after World War II: despite the crisis of neo-liberalism, globalisation and technology seem to toll a death bell for the possibility of including a large majority of their working age population in conditions of decent employment and promoting realistic perspectives of social mobility. So, the question is: is there some possibility of embedding liberalism even in economic and social conditions that seem at first sight so unfavourable?

If a liberal-democratic government aims at a 'narrow version' of embedment – that of obtaining an electoral majority for a policy that pursues the objective of economic growth in this phase of full globalisation and technical change – T Iversen and D Soskice[32] seem to justify a more optimistic outlook. Despite the increase of populist, anti-liberal, movements, liberal governments in the advanced countries have managed until now to prevail in democratic elections and probably will in the future. They will prevail if they succeed in ensuring that median incomes will grow at least at the same pace of the whole economy, even if a gaping gulf were widening between the extremes of the personal income distribution: this is the thesis of our authors. Moreover, the Great Recession is now more than 10 years old, and its negative impact is fading: the return to a more 'normal' situation should either weaken the populist movements or lead them to converge to the mainstream. If this 'optimistic' outlook was to be realised, this would mean that Rodrik's trilemma[33] – that it is impossible to obtain together full globalisation, national policy autonomy and democracy, and one of these goals must be abandoned – portrays too dramatic a situation. True: many democratic policy choices would be incompatible with full globalisation and the countries that tried to follow them would pay a very high price. But what if the policy requirements of globalisation are pursued by an independent state and democratically accepted by its citizens? Both democracy and national independence conditions would be satisfied and with them also the requirements of globalisation, especially if the liberal world, our ALDs, were able to agree on an international design aimed at softening some of its most damaging characters.

No doubt many advanced countries will try to follow such a 'narrow version' of embedment and probably some of them will succeed: those which are already complying with the requirements of globalisation and technical progress and are led by politicians resolute and competent enough to find ways to compensate the losers and channel their discontent towards non-populist arrangements. But some won't: a few southern-European countries belonging now to the Eurozone – Italy in particular – are possible candidates for such a destiny. This is the reason why we are sceptical

[32] ibid.

[33] D Rodrik, *The Globalisation Paradox – Democracy and the Future of the World Economy* (WW Norton, 2013).

about the narrow version of embedment that these authors are proposing: something more powerful should be found to assuage the resentment of the citizens. If the winter of discontent is mainly fuelled by the perception of injustice of the status quo and by the policies that liberal states are now following, it is the solid evidence on which such a perception is based that should be contrasted by a project of embedment suited to the present conditions.

Branko Milanovich[34] gives a good summary of the unjustified inequalities of our societies, mainly (but not only) referring to the US: the extreme polarisation of the personal distribution of income and wealth and its self-perpetuating character; the role of different educational trajectories for the rich and the poor; the slow-down of upward social mobility; the influence of wealth on politics; the popular reaction to immigration; an increasing corruption, just to mention some of the ills analysed by the author. In all, a society more similar to a plutocratic oligarchy than to a democracy. Many of the European ALDs are far from such a dismal kind of 'democracy': but if the most advanced nation among the liberal ones, the former hegemon of the 'free world', is embracing this model there is something to worry about from the very viewpoint of liberalism.

Remedies compatible with a liberal polity and a capitalist economy for the ills we mentioned are possible in principle. These remedies, however, would raise intense distributional conflict, take a long time to produce favourable effects (… but democracy is notoriously short-sighted) and would lack the simplicity and unifying character of the embedment policies of the post-war period: it is hard to tell whether an embedment strategy seriously inspired by a vision of equality of opportunity could reconcile the citizen with a liberal elite. And who has tried to give such a strategy a more radical bent, like Thomas Piketty, has produced a blueprint of reforms[35] that can be criticised both from the point of view of economic and financial feasibility and from that of its political consequences.[36]

Reconciling democracy (with its necessary embedment), a liberal polity and capitalism in conditions of globalisation and revolutionary technological change will prove a hard job. The liberal world is far from the situation prevailing in the inter-war period. Were the present situation to worsen, however, one of its effects is already looming ahead. Some countries – hopefully many, those where the institutions of liberal democracy are more solidly rooted and where economic and institutional conditions are more favourable – will resist the tendency towards illiberal democracy or worse, just as a few countries resisted the rise of fascism, communism and authoritarianism after World War I. It is impossible to predict what will happen to the others. And to the world at large.

[Milan, 15 December 2019]

[34] Milanovic (n 19).

[35] T Piketty, *Capital et idéologie* (Seuil, 2019).

[36] For a critique of Piketty's policy proposals see J Piasni-Ferry, *Thomas Piketty New Book: Impressive Research, Problematic Solutions* (Peterson Institute for International Economics, Blog, 19 September 2019) at www.piie.com/blogs/realtime-economic-issues-watch/thomas-pikettys-new-book-impressive-research-problematic.

VI. ADDENDUM: THE COVID-19 CRISIS AND ITS POSSIBLE IMPACT ON LIBERAL DEMOCRACIES

The chapter was completed in December 2019. Since then Covid-19 has spread around the world triggering the sharpest and deepest recession in the history of capitalism. Its duration has been much shorter than other major crises. At the time of the writing of this Addendum (September 2020) a rapid recovery is already taking place. If it will not be jeopardised by a new wave of the virus, most ADL will return to 2019 GDP levels between 2021 and 2022. However, even in this relatively benign scenario, hundreds of millions of people around the world will have lost their jobs, millions of firms went or will go out of business, and, because of the massive policy response to keep the economy afloat, public debt will rise dramatically.

At the beginning of our chapter we explained how exceptional circumstances led to the rise and success of embedded liberalism in advanced capitalist countries. These circumstances were the loss of political legitimacy of capitalism both in its laissez-faire form (because it led to the Great Depression) and its more authoritarian form (as it led to Nazism and Fascism); the need of a new consensus among the liberal-democratic parties sustaining a market economy; and, last but not least, the ideological challenge coming from the Soviet Union and the communist movement.

At the time, these exceptional circumstances pointed in the direction of the creation of forms embedded liberalism. If a bit of counterfactual and speculative history is allowed, only a return to isolationist policies by the US or the victory of Republican Senator Robert Taft in the 1948 US presidential elections could have led to different outcomes: that is, the 'Finlandisation' of Europe by the Soviet Union or the roll back of the New Deal and the return to a laissez-faire world economy respectively. However, the US did not disengage, while Senator Taft was defeated by John Dewey, a moderate Republican, in the Republican primaries. In turn, Dewey lost against Truman in the presidential race, and embedded liberalism *cum* the Cold War got its way.

Now, with the Covid-19 crisis, exceptional circumstances are back, although they are very different from those that prevailed at the end of World War II. This time around they do not point towards a single, most likely outcome. What it is clear is that they accelerate dramatically the long-standing tensions between capitalism and liberal democracies, which in our conclusions above we expected would unfold in relatively slow motion.

On the one hand, the Covid-19 crisis is making a strong case for a return to updated forms of embedded liberalism: as the Editorial Board of the *Financial Times* pointed out, 'beyond defeating the disease, the great test all countries will soon face is whether current feelings of common purpose will shape society after the crisis. As western leaders learnt in the Great Depression, and after the second world war, to demand collective sacrifice you must offer a social contract that benefits everyone'. Countries with a strong public health sector and wide social safety nets are performing much better than countries where the public health sector has been neglected in favour of the private sector and social safety nets are much weaker. The US, with its self-described best health system in the world and most flexible economy among major advanced economies, has shown complete unpreparedness in addressing the Covid-19 crisis and its unemployment rate is skyrocketing: in just a few weeks it has moved from record lows to Great Depression levels. Countries like Germany and France, instead, despite delays and mistakes, are seeing lower mortality rates and much less dramatic spikes in unemployment. Moreover, as South Korea and Taiwan – two of the most vibrant democracies in East Asia – show, an effective government can contain the virus and keep the economy running by using exclusively democratic instruments.

However, on the other hand, ethno-nationalist illiberal democracies as well as authoritarian regimes, also see their position strengthened.[37] With panic spreading, citizens are more ready to devolve part of their rights to the government in exchange for safety. In addition, illiberal democracies and authoritarian regimes can be perceived by citizens facing a worsening of their economic conditions as less encumbered in taking swift decisions in difficult times. Therefore, illiberal or authoritarian leaders can take the opportunity to advocate for themselves emergency powers for an unlimited amount of time, as has happened in Orban's Hungary, or make acceptable the use of Artificial Intelligence instruments that in future may limit even more the freedom of speech and dissent of citizens (as is the case in China).

As for the Global Financial Crisis, this time again we expect that economic developments will play a critical role in determining how liberal democracies in advanced economies will exit the crisis and be reshaped by it. For the time being (September 2020) the economic front looks relatively quiet, as massive policy support has been provided. However, difficult choices will have to be made with regard to how to prioritise between reducing unemployment, enhancing economic growth, ensuring debt sustainability, tackling growing inequalities, providing health security, addressing climate challenges, just to mention few crucial issues. As pointed out correctly by Adam Tooze, 'If the response by business and households to the unprecedented coronavirus shock is a flight to safety, it will compound the forces of stagnation. If the public response to the debts accumulated by the crisis is austerity, that will make matters worse. It makes sense to call instead for a more active, more visionary government to lead the way out of the crisis. But the question, of course, is what form that will take and which political forces will control it'.[38] Against this background, should the US move further away from international cooperation in favour of America first and/or should European leaders choose to repeat the mistakes of the past, showing little solidarity and putting the short-term interests of their countries ahead of those of the European Union, the risk of a significant narrowing of the quality and the number of liberal democracies will become real.

Moving forward, we see three possible post-Covid-19 scenarios for liberal democracies. The first one, most likely to materialise if President Trump prevails in the US November presidential elections and European leaders, after having opted for solidarity and putting in place a major Recovery Plan at EU level, reverse course and tighten too early the macroeconomic policy stance, leads to few nation-based 'narrow versions of embedded liberalism' (as we called them in our conclusions). In such a

[37] PC Baker, 'We can't go back to normal: how will coronavirus change the world?' *The Guardian* (4 April 2020).

[38] A Tooze, 'The Normal Economy is Never Coming Back', *Foreign Policy* (The Slate Group LLC, 2020).

scenario, the great powers (US, China, India, Russia to a certain extent) will create their spheres of influence, while globalisation is rolled back because of growing geostrategic rivalries. While some European democracies would not come out unscathed by the depth and brutality of the crisis, drifting towards forms of illiberal democracy, most of them would preserve liberal-democratic regimes. However, they would be isles surrounded by rising ethno-nationalistic illiberal democracies (with the US becoming a hybrid form, combining liberal democratic features alongside more illiberal ones, which have already manifested themselves during the Trump presidency) and authoritarian regimes. The role these narrow versions of embedded liberalism would play at an international level would be increasingly irrelevant, as they would have undermined the foundations of the European Union and therefore its possibility to leverage their collective strength.

In a second scenario, the exceptional circumstances generated by the Covid-19 crisis could provide an acceleration leading to the return to updated forms of embedded liberalism. Should former Vice-President Joe Biden prevail in the November presidential elections, he is likely to pursue a liberal-progressive agenda, which would aim at achieving a more inclusive and less unequal US society. He would also provide new momentum to international cooperation and coordination, as it was the case during the Obama presidency. The exceptional circumstances of the Covid-19 crisis could also lead European leaders to realise not only that new forms of embedded liberalism are able to provide better solutions than the old neoliberal/ordoliberal recipes in a world characterised by radical uncertainty, large imbalances and growing social unrest. The EU Recovery Plan goes in this direction and is potentially a game changer. These developments would make it possible, in Adam Tooze's words, to come out with 'more active and more visionary' policies to lead the way out of the crisis. In such a scenario, the US and the European Union, in alliance with democracies in East Asia and emerging market economies, would be able to make liberal democracies attractive again not only to their citizens, but also to the rest of the world.[39]

There is also a third, much direr scenario, that could be a consequence of the following factors: (a) before the Covid-19 crisis the global economy had just started to finally overcome the legacy of the global financial crisis. Still, important structural weaknesses remained, and the pandemic has exacerbated some of them; (b) in recent years the cooperation spirit that had characterised the aftermath of the global financial crisis has been undermined by some of the major players: the US and China *in primis*. The risk here is that, after an initial powerful policy response, each major country will go its own way, irrespective of the common good, definitively destabilising the global economy; (c) inside different countries short-sighted ruling classes could prevail, unable to understand that they have to offer a new social contract and reduce inequalities. In this case overstretched public finances, high private debt,

[39] This seems to be a top priority for the President Joe Biden, who has committed to organise during his first year in office 'a global Summit for Democracy to renew the spirit and shared purpose of the nations of the free world. It will bring together the world's democracies to strengthen our democratic institutions, honestly confront nations that are backsliding, and forge a common agenda' (Biden (2020)).

persisting high unemployment, and a significant loss of revenue for the middle class could determine a situation where social structures become unstable and unreliable, leading to a social collapse.[40] These combined factors could lead to a situation where, as pointed out by Wolfgang Streek, 'the social order of capitalism would then issue, not in another order, but in disorder or entropy – in a historical epoch of uncertain duration when, in the words of Antonio Gramsci, "the old is dying but the new cannot be born", ushering in "an interregnum in which pathological phenomena of the most diverse sort come into existence" – in a society devoid of reasonably coherent and minimally stable institutions capable of normalizing the lives of its members and protecting them from accidents and monstrosities of all sorts'.[41]

Although we consider the interregnum a tail risk scenario, it cannot be entirely be ruled out as the fault lines at international level and within societies are rapidly widening. The hope for those who still consider liberal democracy, with all its ills and shortcomings, the most preferable political regime is that in the end some variant of the second scenario will prevail. Still, as we complete this chapter, it seems to us that this is not a foregone conclusion and the first scenario has also significant chances of materialising. In this respect, the outcome of the US elections and its spillovers on the European Union and globally will be crucial. As for the purpose that mainly concerns this book – the control and reduction of the potential conflict between democracy and rule of law – our orders of preference and probability are the same as those we share as economists.

* The views are those of the authors and they do not reflect those of the institution to which one of them belongs.

[Milan, 10 September 2020]

[40] B Milanovic, *The Real Pandemic Danger is Social Collapse*, Foreign Affairs, March/April (Council on Foreign Relations, 2020).

[41] Streek (n 22) 36.

19

Social Identities, Borders and Majorities

GIAN PRIMO CELLA*

to Alessandro Pizzorno

I. SOCIAL IDENTITIES

THE TERM 'IDENTITY', with all its freight of uncertainties and ambiguities, appears on the scene not only in the social sciences but also in the language of everyday life, whenever individual subjects or social formations are involved in moments of transition or transformation – when, to both subjects and observers, the condition that is being left is clearer than the condition that is being aspired towards. It is no coincidence that the term is typically used to describe the construction of youthful personalities, the more or less tormented departure from the phase of adolescence, or to represent the transformation of the female condition, with the related search for meanings and images. At first glance, 'identity' may seem to belong more to the field of psychology than to that of the social sciences: later on, however, it will be possible to discover, with a number of reservations suitably taken into account, its relevance to the world of sociology.

The current phase in all post-industrial societies – those, in other words, that have actually moved on out of the twentieth century (the real century of industry) – is characterised by the blurring of the more traditional and established forms of social belonging, the return of individual and collective subjects with expectations and aspirations that are almost pre-industrial in nature. The inadequacy of the most established sources of classification and distinction; the relentless spread of instruments of communication that transform the character and structure of social relations; the expansion of those processes of globalisation that appear, meanwhile, to nullify many sources of distinction (and therefore of identity creation): these are all factors that are at the origin of social relations with aims that are in the end defensive and protective. This is the scenario in which the term *identity* – individual or collective – reappears, although the distinction between these two intimately linked adjectives

* University of Milan.

is an extremely uncertain one. The reference to collective identities will always be related to the emergence of individual identities, in an intertwining of subjective and objective elements that both constitutes the value of the concept of identity and also the origin of the ambiguity that surrounds its use. In the history of Western political thought, the most illustrious (and famous) antecedent – not so much of identity as of the ends for which it is used – can be traced to the Marx-Hegelian distinction between *Klasse an sich* and *Klasse für sich*, a distinction which, it must be admitted, has not always proved fruitful in terms of sociological research. In this case, 'for itself', an explicit sign of identity and of 'awareness', constituted the necessary condition for class action, and for the overcoming of all opposition between the individual and the collective. But, in contemporary scenarios, the weakening of the class structure and the absence of a revolutionary political party makes the reference to this venerable distinction a problematic one.

However, even this classical representation reveals a large number of the meanings that can be attributed to the term *identity* – a term that represents multiple processes, not all of which are made explicit in the crowded literature on the subject: not only the process of formation of individual identities, but also the moment of finding one's identity (in a condition, a movement, a group), and, finally, the process of identification, which, to performative ends, is conducted external to individuals or groups. To take this multiplicity of processes into account, illuminating support is provided by the theory of identity developed at various times by Alessandro Pizzorno,[1] at least starting from his 1970s research regarding trade union struggles in various European contexts. This revealed the existence of two types of action (and of strike): those with contractual objectives and those for recognition (of a new subject or of new demands or claims). It is to Pizzorno that we owe the return of the concept of identity to the fields of social theory and sociological research, through the rediscovery of the Simmelian concept of 'sociality' (*Vergesellschaftung*) and of the Hegelian argument regarding the theme of recognition. The dimension of sociality makes it possible to discover the formation of identities through the relationship with others (or, in the micro-social context, with the other), while the aspect of recognition becomes essential in terms of understanding and explaining the formation of collective identities.

Pizzorno[2] also reminds us that perhaps the simplest, and certainly the most common, method for the affirmation of identity is that of recognition by opposition, as a consequence of the definition of borders – sometimes material borders (such as territorial boundaries), but in many cases borders of a metaphorical kind (as in most of the distinctions between social groups). Distinction based on metaphorical borders can sometimes be uncertain, and identity formation is led to move in the

[1] In the autumn of 2019, a few months after his death, a conference was held in Milan at the Feltrinelli Foundation and the University of Milan to reflect on Pizzorno's work, in particular on the relationship between identity and collective action, with important contributions from S Berger, M Calise, C Crouch, D Della Porta, P Schmitter, L Sciolla, S Tarrow, C Trigilia and S Veca. The discussions at this conference will be kept in mind during this essay.

[2] A Pizzorno, *Il velo della diversità. Studi su razionalità e riconoscimento* (Feltrinelli, 2007).

direction of a search for material boundaries. A current example can be found in the typical tendency of many populist movements to bolster their call to the people (the boundary between the latter and the elites never having been more unstable) with an implicit or explicit evocation of national boundaries (observed in slogans such as 'America first', 'Italians First' etc).

These, then, are the theoretical premises of this chapter, the development of which will follow the following pattern: the role of borders in the formation of social identities; the call to the people with the related search for identity transferred towards national borders; the effects of these calls on the application of the majoritarian principle and the paradoxes that emerge as a consequence, from the rise of the 'fictitious community' to the affirmation of the 'fictitious individual'.

II. BORDERS AS DISTINCTION

Distinction by contrast is the form that corresponds most closely to borders and the processes of definition that these make possible. Thus, the easiest way to define identity is through recognition by opposition.[3] Borders, which most of the time only require a sign that can be transformed into a symbol, become non-renounceable in the construction of identities – those identities that can in some way be related to territories, whether a state, a nation, a region, an ethnic-cultural group or a community. None of these identities can be imagined if they are not related to distinction from others, where a connection with a spatial dimension is always involved, a territory defined by borders.

There is no surprise, then, in the fact that border scholars have, in a more or less conscious way, readopted almost Schmitt-like tones in order to describe these tasks of distinction by opposition, or rather by contrast, for the purpose of attributing meaning in the construction of identity. Such tones are justified above all by the effects of boundaries of state origin, as was shown in a famous piece of research[4] on the definition (in the seventeenth century) of the Franco-Spanish border in the Pyrenean region of Cerdanya. In this case, national identity is interpreted as a continuous and socially constructed process of definition of 'friend' and 'enemy', in a logic of extension of the process of boundary maintenance, between a 'we' and a 'them' within local communities, devoid of any significant objective differences. It is as if the identities in formation were always in search of a spatial dimension, in some cases explicit (material boundaries), in other cases implicit and indirect, as in the recent examples of the Arab or Islamic 'springs' (2010–12), identified by the Cairo or Istanbul squares that became recurring locations for demonstrations and conflict. This is the process that Loredana Sciolla[5] has interpreted as a 'locative aspect' of identity

[3] I developed these topics in more detail in Cella, *Tracciare confini. Realtà e metafore della distinzione* (Il Mulino, 2006).

[4] P Sahlins, *Boundaries. The Making of France and Spain in the Pyrenees* (University of California Press, 1989).

[5] L Sciolla, 'Identità personale e collettiva' in *Enciclopedia delle Scienze sociali*, vol IV (Istituto della Enciclopedia italiana, 1994) 500.

and political geographers like Herb and Kaplan have described with the concept of 'nesting', proposing a definition of national identities as 'bounded communities of exclusion and opposition'.[6] We know how this dimension or, better, the search for this dimension, has been compromised in recent decades by the extension of globalisation processes and the erosion of boundaries between social affiliations (from those of an economic category to those of a religious nature, at least for non-Islamic cultures). The erosion of traditional (real and metaphorical) boundaries urges the formation of collective identities towards the search for new boundaries. And a large part of the identity formation that we are witnessing in the contemporary world is based around this search.

If we return to the social experience of the border, or to what appears to be a practical anticipation of distinction,[7] certain borders could well be described as *hard* (as those who crossed the Iron Curtain in the years of the Cold War will know) while others are metaphorical; however, these definitions are not, in certain respects, of great importance. The symbolic scope is present in both versions of the distinction and the effectiveness of the second depends on the ambiguous significance related to the experience of the first. It is certainly wise to pay heed to the invitation of border scholars not to allow the metaphorical or metonymic use of the term 'borders' to prevail.[8] In these cases, an instrumental use of the term might be discerned, aimed above all at reinforcing discourse regarding identity or social formation otherwise lacking in consistency. And yet it should be remembered that borders, even those made manifest by walls or physical barriers, always carry an additional metaphorical significance, evident in particular in the ideological or mythological definitions of so-called 'natural borders'. Indeed, as shown by examples of classic anthropological research, such as that on an Andalusian village by Julian Pitt-Rivers,[9] members of communities can perceive and 'see' borders beyond their material appearance.

Systems of inequality, too, presuppose borders, institutionalised in whole or in part, just as the nature and aims of political representation depend on the closures or limitations deriving from external (state) and internal (local-regional) borders. The expression of interests and the methods of composition of the conflicts arising from this expression are in turn related to the mechanisms for the definition and redefinition of borders. Borders can alter the character and orientation of political protest and demand. This is precisely what happens in the spread of localist protest – protest, in other words, deriving from a particular territory, expressed through identities, real or imagined, linked to the territory itself, and which tends in more or less explicit ways to redefine the borders. The most significant implication linked to the spread of this protest regards the transformation of interests and related conflicts. It should be remembered that pressure of a localised kind with related requests for the redefinition of borders, or of the political-administrative attributions related to them (as in

[6] GH Herb and DH Kaplan, *Nested Identities. Nationalism, Territory, and Scale* (Rowman & Littlefield, 1999) 15.

[7] The mandatory reference here is P Bourdieu, *La Distinction* (Minuit, 1979).

[8] H Donnan and TM Wilson, *Borders: Frontiers of Identity, Nation and State* (Berg, 1999) 16.

[9] J Pitt-Rivers, *The People of the Sierra* (Criterion Books, 1954).

the demands for autonomy of Italy's *Lega Nord*), are always ambivalent in nature. On the one hand, they indicate the search for new identities, on the other, they indicate the fragmentation (or blurring) of traditional identities. Localism can also have devastating effects on political conflict in liberal-democratic structures, transforming problems previously faced with the logic and practice of functional or pluralistic representation into political conflict (subject to the majoritarian principle). This kind of representation is expressed through networks of organised groups and proceeds through agreement or compromise, always requiring the survival of all the parties involved (ie, the various minorities), according to the logic of unanimously-taken decisions.

Localism, and, even more so, secessionism, with related collective identities, allowing the creation of a population (or, better, of a 'people'), or even of a 'group', on a defined and carved-out territory, with a supposed supra-individual unity, will determinedly pursue majority decisions, with the associated implicit possibility of silencing (or overwhelming) minorities. It remains to be explored what this process means for our usual way of considering liberal-democratic structures with connected pluralistic systems of relationships or, if you wish, for polyarchies, in the classic interpretation offered by Robert Dahl.[10] It is to this theme that the most significant part of the vast and alluvial literature on populism that has come into being over the past two decades has been dedicated.[11] The relationship between localism and processes of globalisation is only apparently a paradoxical one and reveals the dynamics that translate into contexts of a glocal kind (a banal neologism, a mix between global and local, but effective in the idea it provides). These are the dynamics that can justify the maintenance, if not the proliferation, of borders in contexts that are globalised and relentlessly criss-crossed by tech-giant promoted networks, disclosing the operation of an unexpected trade-off between the dissolution of external, and the increase of internal, borders. While the latter are more permeable than the former, they are no less involved in strategies of closure or usurpation, and of transformation in the allocation of public goods.

III. PEOPLE AND NATIONAL IDENTITY

It is at this point, if the issue of spatial limits or the (somewhat uncertain) borders of the 'people', and of their equally uncertain corresponding identity, is to be dealt with, that the problem arises of the relationship between the nation and the people themselves. These are terms that are often employed as interchangeable in everyday language (in their ability to evoke), if not as synonyms, when they are not, in more sophisticated language, employed in the context of a people-nation hendiadys. Nowadays, with the current wave of populism, it appears that the people are subsuming the nation within

[10] See, of the many theoretical contributions, the famous R Dahl, *A Preface to Democratic Theory*, expanded edition, (1st edn 1956) (The University of Chicago Press, 2006).

[11] For a survey of this literature, see C Rovira Kaltwasser, et al (eds) *The Oxford Handbook of Populism* (OUP, 2017).

themselves, something also due to a resistance to making use of a term ('nation') that is both exacting and challenging – one that carries unpleasant connotations, and is too likely, at least as a perception, to translate into a kind of nationalism that western political cultures find difficult to manage. Within these cultures, when the nation is considered as a source of identity, it must always be remembered how far this is from the 'patriotic' connotations that it was able to assume in other dramatic periods. We are a long way from the *Pro patria mori* of which Kantorowicz spoke, referring to the famous letter written by the archbishop of Malines for Christmas 1914 (the first Christmas of Germany's occupation of Belgium) in which he exalted the redemptive value of sacrificing one's life in defence of the homeland.[12] This, despite the fact that, in the last few decades, in the Balkans and in Russian-influenced Eastern Europe, there have been versions of nationalism willing to take offensive steps, starting from declared, sometimes instrumental, defensive motives. Similarly, not so long ago, there were the times of the independence struggles, marked by strong identitary traits, and the related terrorist atrocities, of Ireland and the Basque Country. There have also, in recent times, been tragic examples of the 'nationalistic' tendencies of many Islamic religious cultures. With these warnings, in an age of populism and sovereignism, the problem of the relationship between 'the people' and 'national identity' is one that deserves to be taken up again. Insecurity deriving from the economic crisis can also be translated into cultural characteristics, with the nation always ready to take possession of, and redeploy, them, once again, as PA Taguieff observes when he speaks of *insécuritasion identitaire.*[13]

Bernard Yack[14] considered the problem in an essay that starts from the idea of both concepts belonging to the category of 'imagined communities', as proposed in a famous book by Benedict Anderson.[15] He adds an important clarification with regard to the discourse of individual and collective identities: 'the people' would present an image of a community 'over space', while 'the nation' would qualify as a community 'over time'. In both cases, the use of the exacting term 'community' would signal a search for internal unity, in a homogeneity that was at least partial. However, if 'the nation' offered a bridge to overcome divisions between generations, the bridge offered by 'the people' could close the gap between individuals and between groups with the aim of controlling state authority.[16] 'The people' would always exist, also sociologically, continues Yack with a certain excess of realism, available if anything to be invoked (or invented) at particular moments; 'the nation' would be the result of the long work of history, of the sedimentation of memories and symbols. This distinction explains why, although we are often willing to refer to 'nation building', we rarely talk about 'people building'. Recourse to the concept of community implies a moral foundation which, according to Yack, in many respects brings 'the people' closer to 'the

[12] The reference is to an essay that originally appeared in 'American Historical Review' in 1955, now available in EH Kantorowicz, *I misteri dello Stato* (Marietti 1820, 2005) 67–97.

[13] PA Taguieff, *La revanche du nationalisme* (Presses Universitaires de France, 2015) 70.

[14] B Yack, 'Popular Sovereignty and Nationalism' (2001) 4 *Political Theory* 517–36.

[15] B Anderson, *Imagined Communities* (Verso, 1991).

[16] Yack (n 14) 520–21.

nation'. Neither one nor the other could live, become galvanised, with recourse to simple images of group belonging. It is in this context that it is appropriate to resort to the concept of identity, with its related requirements for recognition.

The dichotomous interpretation (*space-time*) is certainly an effective one, but not wholly convincing. Both categories, people and nation, are always in search of a spatial delimitation across borders capable of providing the *distinction* necessary for their existence and their recognition. 'The people' are never invoked, identified or mobilised in reference to *all* peoples, except in the passionate, but ill-fated, appeals of Giuseppe Mazzini. Nowadays, in the exhortations of populist movements, the people, and popular identity, are almost always presented without explicit adjectives, this being a requirement of representation according to the *logics of equivalence*,[17] but with an implicit adjective that functions as a predicate, in reference to national affiliations. Popular identity has never been, and would never be, successful in proclaiming and acting as a subject without a spatial and territorial designation. The most significant historical example, one still well-remembered today, involves the 'Jewish people' (there has rarely been talk of a Jewish nation), which, through the Zionist movement, achieved international political prominence in 1917 when the Balfour declaration *recognised* the principle of a 'national home for the Jewish people' in Palestine. With reference to another famous case, it is a recognition that is still lacking in the history of the Kurdish people.

For nations, always presented as distinct from one other, if not from all the others, and sometimes *against* the others, the search for borders is equally decisive. This is subject to the development of the territorialisation of politics, an excellent example of which can be found in the process of invention of the nation as the foundation of the legitimacy of the republican state that Emmanuel Joseph Sieyès developed in his *Que'est-ce que le tiers état?* (1788).[18] The abbé Sieyès proposes a hendiadys, *nation-state*, which is concomitant with that of *nation-people*, even though it is from this that it develops. It represents a part, albeit a large part (the Third Estate, personified as *le Tiers*), for the whole thing, 'une nation complète'. It is a position that, with the affirmation that 'la nation existe avant tout, elle est l'origine de tout', today's scholars of nationalism could classify as 'primordialist'. Identities would be discovered, not built.

If we return to the processes of building collective identities, we can see how the logics of equivalence proposed by Laclau operate in both concepts (people and nation) while in both cases responding to different categories of questions originating from the individual subjects involved. Where 'the people' are concerned, questions in the field of political representation will tend to prevail, while with 'the nation' those aimed at recognition will be expressed. In the case of the people, the 'antagonistic frontier' is built inwards; in the case of the nation, outwards. Borders, a term here

[17] I refer here to the effective distinction proposed by E Laclau, *On Populist Reason* (Verso, 2005) between two logics of social construction: the *logics of difference* and the *logics of equivalence*. In the former, particularities and differences are accentuated; in the latter, equivalences are focused on, creating an 'antagonistic frontier', such as that between people and elites.

[18] EJ Sieyès, *Qu'est-ce que le tiers-état?* (Champs classiques, 1988).

more appropriate than 'frontier', serve in both cases to strengthen internal unity and to be recognised from the outside. In the case of the people, however, they assume a metaphorical dimension more than anything else (you will never be able to trace a border line between the people and the elites); in the case of the nation, they can expand to occupy a dimension that is more disturbingly real. This is sometimes the result of divisive lines that are wholly imagined, such as those that enjoy the appellation of natural borders – which often do not divide and distinguish at all. The definition 'natural' is established in treaties between institutionalised representatives and therefore has very little of the natural in it. In certain historical moments, these borders represent nothing more than the expansionist and aggressive will of the state – a border line, in other words, that the state would like to reach, even through violent means, as in the case of the Nazi *Lebensraum*.

Of course, 'imagined' though they are, 'the people' and 'the nation' are identities that acquire concreteness and opportunities for affirmation through mutual reinforcement: the people can identify themselves in a space, acquiring the practice of 'where to look' and 'where *not* to look' (as in the case of the dramatic events of migration); the nation will find itself included within the institutional process of the formation of popular sovereignty. But how do individual subjects recognise the matter of 'where', how do they learn to imagine it, how are they invited (or forced) not to forget it? *Banal* questions of this kind are provided with answers by Michael Billig in a book on 'banal nationalism', which appeared more than two decades ago and is still extremely topical today.[19] It has the gift of being highly explanatory in a sector that, over packed with evocative imagery, is often devoid of concrete social actors.

To answer these questions, Billig makes use of a linguistic tool that, while not particularly well remembered, is employed in essays regarding language and politics: deixis. This is a procedure that consists in demonstrating not only the identity of the speaking subject, but also the location of the utterances in time or space, through demonstrative pronouns and adjectives, and adverbs of time and place. Events involving people and nation are scattered with these deictic elements, aimed at representing and *recognising* the people in that particular territory (and in that territory only) or that nation (and not others) in an international context, or that nation-people in the context of a particular form of evocation or mobilisation (also in electoral terms). The elements are extremely simple and expressed through short, compact words: 'the', 'this', 'here', 'we', 'always', 'never', etc.

Here is how, very *banally*, 'the people' join 'the nation' through reference to territory, confirming their own identity. Degeneration and exploitation with aggressive intentions will always be possible, but it is through these 'daily' argumentative mechanisms that the relationship between people and nation is founded. In this process, something that will also be very important is the performative power of those who, more or less legitimised, will be willing to attribute popular identity to an aggregate of subjects extracted from a wider social reality, in some cases aided by reference to a national territory. It is something that comes close to a real 'performative magic'

[19] M Billig, *Banal Nationalism* (Sage, 1995).

aimed at constituting not only the collective subject-actor but also the group that, through this subject, aspires to be represented. It is what Bourdieu calls a 'théorie de la représentation unifiante', moving between Hobbes, linguists such as Benveniste and philosophers of ordinary language (like Austin or later Wittgenstein): 'la multitude des individus isolés accède au statut de personne morale lorsqu'elle trouve dans la représentation unitaire de sa diversité que lui donne son représentant l'image constitutive de son unité; autrement dit, elle se constitue comme unité en se reconnaissant dans la représentation unique'.[20] In terms similar to those of Pizzorno, we might say that it is a matter of identifying with the outcome of a power of identification.

It is not difficult to understand how unity (of the people) is fostered by uniqueness (of the nation). The 'we' of the people is made more effective by external recognition, facilitated by real or metaphorical borders, by *our* specificity or, better yet, by *our* uniqueness. It is for this reason that disputes regarding names – 'name wars', even – are scattered through all matters involving nation-people affirmation. Some are very widespread, such as those regarding the preferences to be agreed upon in relation to names deriving from different national languages spoken in the same city or geographical location – the centuries-old story of Südtirol – *Alto Adige* being an example. Others are rarer, and more dramatic, such as disputes over the appropriation of a name of a region or a territory. One case, still not wholly resolved, involves quarrel between the Republic of Macedonia (ex-Republic of Yugoslavia) and the Greek government over the use of the name of the classic region. In such cases, while external borders are not directly at risk, certain consequences are – in other words, the recourse to the name of the nation for the appeal, mobilisation, and exploitation of popular identity in electoral contests.

IV. COLLECTIVE IDENTITIES AND THE MAJORITARIAN PRINCIPLE

Perhaps the most significant consequence of the evocation of the people as a source of identity, whether or not reinforced by national identity, regards the called-for overcoming (not always implicit), if not the downright negation, of the divisions, differences and specificities that have permeated modern society since its inception. The process of 'people building', or the step that follows on from its evocation and naming, is based on this negation, and the chances of affirming the process will be greater the more the constitution of the people as a unitary collective entity is made possible, with the result, however, that political choices proceed as if this constitution were plausible and imminent. The unitary subject, even if the result of the invention or fiction, is a necessary condition for the application of the principle and rules of majority voting, at least in historical contexts in which the phase marked by a more or less orderly search for unanimity has come to an end, with the related veto powers in the possession of individual or collective actors.[21]

[20] P Bourdieu, *Langage et pouvoir symbolique* (Fayard, 2001) 267.

[21] Regarding these matters, see the classic text by E Ruffini, *La ragione dei più* (Il Mulino, 1977) and the more recent collective work edited by S Novak and J Elster, *Majority Decisions* (CUP, 2014).

In fact, the recourse to the principle and rules of majority voting is closely related to the affirmation (real or fictitious) of collective subjects (with corresponding identities), whether these are parliamentary assemblies, 'corporations', councils of voters (as in the Holy Roman Empire), or groups of individuals with aspirations towards social or cultural homogeneity, *limited* by effective boundary lines. Taking into account the fact that individuals or groups who have to surrender to the decision find it difficult to accept the principle, political theory has identified the source of majoritarian expression not in individuals but in the collective subject. It is not individuals who express themselves, but the collective subject.

This is the trait that is discovered by returning through history to those moments when the adoption of the principle could certainly not be taken for granted, having as it did to compete with other principles (and rules). These ranged from unanimity, to *sanioritas* (the wisest or most knowledgeable), to *senioritas* (the oldest), and even to the drawing of lots. It is a trait that confirmed the weakness of individualistic arguments in explaining the majority vote, once those crude and brutal arguments relating to the 'the greater the number, the greater the strength' were set aside. The step forward, theoretically and politically, was accomplished when the origin of willingness was identified not in individuals, but in the body, in the *collegium*, in the 'corporation' – in the unitary collective subject, in other words. This led to the exclusion of the principle for those matters (especially religious issues) which generated irremediable fractures in the unitarity of the subject. These characteristics are closely connected to one another: the impossibility of justifying and legitimising the majority principle on an individualistic basis entails the need for the unitary collegium, but this becomes impractical or inadvisable when the cleavages and conflicts cannot be reconstituted, or when partisan social aggregations (social classes, groups, associations, but also *states* in the *ancien régime*) placed unitarity in jeopardy.

It is this interconnection that gives rise to the often neglected relevance of the majority principle to the thinking of social and political theory – a relevance that emerges even more clearly when we consider, as in the case of popular identity, the spatial delimitations that accompany the definition, or redefinition, of collective subjects. The contemporary vicissitudes of localist, or in any case territorial, demands, and of the related manipulations of borders, are here to prove it. The recognition of the people as a unitary collective subject will always be problematic, especially in times in which the commingling of the spiritual and the secular sphere, with the relative metaphor of the *corpus mysticum*, at the origin of all representations of fictitious people, is so attenuated, sometimes vanishing utterly.

The unitarity of the subject, real or presumed, is made possible by unitary representation through the leader and by the achievement of appropriate spatial boundaries, sometimes with related aspirations-demands regarding 'living space' or 'natural borders', as occurred in the first decades of the twentieth century. In these cases, the people and the nation can reinforce themselves in terms of political expression and in their opportunities for recognition, albeit always with the former's greater dependence on internal borders and the latter's on external ones. In both situations, borders contribute to reinforcing the name of the people, with the identification of 'the other' to which the people are in opposition. Internally, while the distinction with the elites is uncertain, the external borders contribute to giving the people a name, as Francisco Panizza observed in the introduction to a collective book that brings together important pieces regarding issues of populism from the radical or 'left' perspective: 'we can only name the people by naming its other'.[22]

This is what always happens with localist movements, albeit with ambitions or political demands of varying intensity (from administrative autonomy to federalist claims to complete secession). It is a matter of the search for, or the discovery of, or perhaps the invention of, territorial areas in which, through the construction of a unitary collective subject, the majority choice or decision acquires a foundation or legitimacy. This is in opposition to other forms of regulating interests or preferences, whether constitutional or contractual (typical of pluralist structures), which require not only recognition but also the survival of all the parties involved and their interests. In these cases, it is precisely the formation of collective identities that compels individuals to interpret their interests in a different, alternative way. This is what happened with Brexit and the subsequent political elections in December 2019. The 'unitary' street protests of 'the people' in Barcelona, in the autumn of 2017, and then over the following two years, with their expectations and demands for majority decisions for independence, show the extraordinary, and disturbing, possibilities of the overwhelming (or negation) of the distinctiveness and flexibility of one of the richest, most advanced, variegated societies in post-industrial Europe. This also involves the circumvention and violation of constitutional rights which, it should not be forgotten, are in the main rights *against* majorities, as Norberto Bobbio observed, making use of Dworkin's terminology, in an interesting piece of work that is perhaps forgotten today.[23]

In the same essay, Bobbio focused on the limits (and rules) of the majority principle: the *limits of validity* (the absolute or relative nature of the principle); the *limits of application* (the exclusion of various matters from the principle); and the *limits of effectiveness* (those that concern both the breach of conditions of equality and the irreversible nature of many majority decisions).

The limits of validity are the most relevant to the formation of new collective identities. In the case of absolute validity, the principle should apply in every case, even when the content of the decision could be the abolition of the principle itself. It would be paradoxical for the theory of democracy, but the issue is less obvious than it may seem, and in order to address it Bobbio introduces the term 'rule', recognising that 'the rule of the majority cannot have absolute validity because the true, essential nature of a principle is to prohibit its own negation'.[24] The tension between principle and rule is found, but this must assume the status of a 'rule of the game', accepted unanimously (à la Rousseau) by all the participants in the game. Whether it is a decision or an election, it is a status that in certain contexts, such as the Federal Republic of Germany, takes the form of explicit protection of the constitutional characteristics, with the loss of the rights of participation for the 'anti-system' forces.

[22] F Panizza (ed), *Populism and the Mirror of Democracy* (Verso, 2005) 6.

[23] N Bobbio, 'La regola di maggioranza: limiti e aporie' in N Bobbio et al, *Democrazia, maggioranza e minoranze* (Il Mulino, 1981) 55.

[24] ibid 53.

The territorial aspect limits the validity of the principle: if the game cannot be reversed, it could always be abandoned. This is why those who protect the game (whether guaranteeing authority or constitution) are led to render difficult, if not impossible, secessions decided by majority – secessions that could cancel the right of the unitary collective subject (the original state structure) to express itself, by a majority, on the maintenance of the unity of the subject itself. This is one of the basic limits that rule of law places on the formation and mobilisation of collective identities.

One good example of these limits is the recent (but long-historied) tension between Catalonia's demands for independence and the constitutional refusal expressed by the central government of Madrid. As has been said, the definitions or redefinitions of borders do not adapt well to majority decisions, helping to limit the validity of the majority principle, especially where the limits are constitutionally sanctioned, as in the case of article 5 of Italy's republican constitution. The implementation in 2014 of the referendum in Scotland regarding secession from the UK (later rejected) was possible precisely due to the non-existence (or uncertain nature) of a single written constitution sanctioning the limits of the pragmatic and traditional majoritarian 'Westminster model' parliamentary structure. And, for the same reasons – the failure to explicate the limits to majoritarian solutions – the UK's exit from the European Union through Brexit was not prevented. If anything, the application of majoritarian rules is a consequence of the redefinition of borders, with tension and conflict as regards the construction and affirmation of new collective subjects. Against this background, it is possible to evaluate the nature of that 'right to self-determination' which, historically, from Woodrow Wilson's proclamations at the end of the Great War onwards, has generated more, sometimes tragic, problems, than it has helped solve. It is the definition of borders, internal first of all, and then external in the search for recognition, which establishes and justifies the claims for the application of a law, which almost never finds constitutional legitimacy.

Borders, especially when they are proposed, lived with and proclaimed in tandem with 'popular sovereignty', make the creation of *the others* possible – those who oppose these demands, but also those who would have to submit to, or suffer because of, the declamation of 'nationalism'. It is the territory that renders the law applicable, with majority principle and rules as a consequence. It is this nature, so easily infected by violence, that gives rise to the problematic character of the 'right to self-determination' – a character that has been acknowledged in recent times by certain political theorists who have paid careful attention to the moral foundations of national identities. One of these theorists is Bernard Yack, who explicitly entitles a chapter of his latest book *What's Wrong with National Rights to Self-Determination*. This is a problematic matter which should not come as a surprise within social structures where there is widespread willingness (which creates identity) to transform claims into rights – or, in other words, as Yack says, to treat questions about 'the *right* thing to do' in the same way as questions about 'to have a *right* to do it'.[25]

[25] B Yack, *Nationalism and the Moral Psychology of Community* (The University of Chicago Press, 2012) 235.

The Catalan issue reveals the different roles played by borders in terms of people and national identities. The latter are projected towards external borders and find a sense of distinction in them. International recognition is, as a consequence, decisive, as is shown by what happened in the Balkans at the end of the twentieth century, first with the disruptive case of Slovenia and then the subsequent, more tragic events in Kosovo. The different attitude towards the European Union is also significant. The Catalan protest demonstrates that the same international treaties that populist and sovereignist movements oppose – believed as they are to be at the origin of the violations of people's rights to the expression of their majority aspirations (especially through referendums)[26] – can instead represent a resource to be employed in order to reinforce and, above all, recognise, national identity. Similar dynamics are likely to be seen in Scotland, following the UK's Brexit referendum result and the subsequent political elections in December 2019. The nation-people, squeezed between external and internal borders, especially in the era of global markets, will be seen to vacillate between these contradictory attitudes at an international level.

Both collective identities – one linked to the recourse to the people and one centred on the nation – defined by their external borders, tend to weaken, if not negate, the identities connected to other social affiliations. There has been talk of a 'negation' of pluralism by the populist movements that have appeared on the scene in recent decades. With regard to this observation, the opinion of many scholars who have dedicated themselves to the topic is unanimous, albeit varied. Christa Deiwics[27] recalls how the continuous recourse of populists to majority voting poses a danger for the government of pluralist democracies, essentially a 'government by minorities', which can encompass various ethnic, economic and socio-cultural groups. JW Müller argues that the *pars pro toto* argument (typical of populists) not only entails anti-elitist attitudes, but also leads to anti-pluralist ambitions, an expression of the uniqueness of the people's representation and the related hostility towards various forms of social intermediation (such as NGOs or trade unions).[28] Outside identitarian disputes, it must be said that this aversion is accompanied by a manifest impatience with independent authorities, a form of regulation and control that is certainly anomalous with respect to the logic of majoritarian democracy, but compatible with pluralist structures.

Identification of people with nation will define the process that will lead with greater determination to a unity capable of silencing all partisan identities and

[26] Rovira Kaltwasser recently highlighted this trait in an essay dedicated to the response of populist parties and movements to Dahl's two democratic dilemmas (the definition of the people and the limits of self-government): 'Given the populist nature of these parties, they defend the majority principle at any cost' ('The Responses of Populism to Dahl's Democratic Dilemmas' (2014) 62 *Political Studies* 482). On the same theme, also N Urbinati: 'Populism in power is a majoritarianist regime' ('Populism and the principle of majority' in *The Oxford handbook of Populism* (n 11) 586.

[27] C Deiwics, 'Populism', *Living Reviews in Democracy* (Center for Comparative and International Studies Zurich, 2009) 3.

[28] Not all movements or parties to classed as 'populist' show such impatience with the intermediation of large associations. See the Latin American experience of the 1930s and 1940s, where populist parties relied on strong unions (with the related strong identitary mobilisation) and state intervention. See RB Collier and D Collier's wide-ranging reconstruction, *Shaping the Political Arena* (Princeton University Press, 1991).

belongings. It is not a new identification (or concern) and it can, should one so wish, be traced back to Rousseau's words in his *Discours sur l'Économie Politique* of 1755, with its warning against deviations resulting from 'particular societies': 'la volonté de ces sociétés particulieres a toûjours deux relations; pour les membres de l'association, c'est une volonté générale; pour la grande société, c'est une volonté particuliere, qui très-souvent se trouve droite au premier égard, et vicieuse au second'.[29] Only by silencing particular interests, which increase the closer we get to partisan societies, can we achieve the general will, not only as the most just objective but also as the voice of the people: 'la voix du peuple est en effet la voix de Dieu'. This is the inspiration behind the radical anti-pluralism of the French Revolution, described by Pierre Rosanvallon,[30] which focuses in particular on Sieyès' aspiration to re-establish the unity of the people (a single people) in the nation, starting from a regenerating assimilation of all individuals. It is the triumph of the logics of equivalence, which nation building makes possible, its well-defined external borders keeping internal borders under control, drastically reducing their influence.

V. IDENTITIES: PARADOXES AND FICTIONS. CONCLUSIONS.

At this point, let us look at certain theoretical arguments to account for the reappearance of the word 'people' and national identities in contemporary political-social scenarios, with the related uncertainties this implies for pluralist democracy. The following, and conclusive, step might then be taken to explain the social and institutional conditions that make this reappearance possible and plausible today. A *vaste programme*, certainly, and one that can only be touched upon here: one that also, however, immediately reveals certain obstacles in the way. The first of these is to register a certain reluctance shown by those in the political sector to make explicit use of the term 'people' as a signifier (and identity source). It is, instead, often replaced by expressions with ethnic-cultural overtones, which above all involve a spatial dimension defined by borders that are sometimes brutally material in form (the building of walls) and, at other times, more indirect and mediated, but with not dissimilar effects (prohibiting the acceptance of migrants). In relation to identity, it is as if collective identity was not buttressed by the coherent transformation of individual identities. Which individual actor is *representative* of the people of the twenty-first century? National support – if not yet nationalist, at least sovereignist – is rediscovered in uncertainty. The performative efficacy of the statements of political leaders is not cancelled out, more concealed though it might be.

In some respects, these dynamics can be represented by the opposition between population (without identity) and people (identity source) that Michel Foucault spoke of in his reflections on the microphysics of power.[31] It is an extremely important and recurring contrast in French affairs, and with it we are, for example, able to account

[29] JJ Rousseau, *Œuvres complètes*, Tome III (Gallimard, 1966) 246.

[30] P Rosanvallon, *Le peuple introuvable* (Gallimard, 1998).

[31] See the lessons held at the Collège de France in 1977/78 in M Foucault, *Sécurité, Territoire, Population* (Gallimard-Ehess, 2004).

almost perfectly for the disorder – insurrection, one might almost say – of the *gilets jaunes* on Parisian streets (and elsewhere) in 2018–19. It is a contrast that certainly seems particularly suitable to describe popular insurgencies, whether rebellious or revolutionary, and yet its application to situations that are not wholly related to the dynamics of social movements can also prove effective. And this is precisely due to its ability to describe the exhortation, the evocation, the manifestation of the people that act on the willingness of individuals belonging to a population to 'withdraw from' or 'elude' the dominant rules of social coexistence or, one might say, of sociality.

This willingness can be facilitated (eg, referring to national identity), even perhaps created, but there is no doubt that it is fuelled by permissive social conditions. These are the conditions that need to be considered if answers are to be provided to the question of 'why today' – conditions that can be interpreted as being influenced by at least three types of paradox. There should be no surprise at the use of the term paradox, appropriate as it is to indicate situations in which the relationships or social characters described (or imagined) derive from premises which are then negated by consideration of actual reality. Paradoxes generate, against common opinions, conditions of uncertainty or indeterminacy, so that the structures of sociality are exposed to the influence of fictions or inventions. The perfect model of the paradox in social theory remains the example relating to the dynamics of collective action: the individual parts of a large entirety might all be interested in achieving a collective goal (a public good), but if they act on the basis of individual rationality it is likely that the goal will not be achieved – confirming the triumph of 'free rider' logic.

The first paradox, that of the 'individualist', identifies the widespread diffusion – which for many years has appeared unstoppable – of individualist topics in the social sciences and also in everyday language: something that has taken place at precisely the moment when the dominant forces in culture and economic-social relations are collective actors and subjects (think of the web tech-giants) that certainly have little of the individual about them. Corporate actors, as James Coleman would have said, while seeming to enhance and amplify the possibilities of individual choice, in fact direct, guide and force this choice, contributing to frustrate the structures of the social, economic, professional, commercial and cultural relationships in which modernity's individual subjects continue to collocate themselves. These actors deploy the enhanced instruments and artifices of the digital world to propose and support a new type of individualism founded on the basis of singularities, impervious to the values that contributed to creating the structures of pluralist society, and as such manipulable by the collective actors themselves.[32]

The second paradox, that of the 'community', is in only apparent contrast to the first. It describes a true situation of 'collective narcissism' (gliding over the oxymoron), where individuals focused almost exclusively on themselves and on the reproduction of their own image or profile are, however, permanently connected through the web and the various social networks that provide many of the virtual community's

[32] Regarding this irruption of 'singularities', especially in the new middle classes, see the fine contribution by German sociologist A Reckwitz, *Die Gesellschaft der Singularitäten: zum Strukturwandel der Moderne* (Suhrkamp, 2017).

resources, sometimes originating real, unstable and insecure communities, with corresponding collective identities. But, as Mauro Calise has pointed out, *connectivity* is a very different kettle of fish from *connectedness*.[33] This paradox also presents a *global* aspect, which, especially in the more neglected or deteriorated areas of industrial societies, inspires a sort of closure in local (and national) communities. The intention being to exclude other ethnic-cultural groups, it is a closure practised by individuals shaped through influences and pleas deriving from the web, sometimes, with specious reference to tradition and to refuge in the safe warmth of the *völkish*, not wholly alien to degeneration into violence. Following the arguments proposed in this essay on the non-renounceable role of borders in terms of distinction and recognition, we might, if we do not reject the idea of a neologism, redefine this paradox with the use of the adjective 'borderly'. Many authors in recent years have noted, at least implicitly, such a paradox in operation, the most lucid being Pierre-André Taguieff: 'Contrairement a une idée reçue reprise sans examen critique dans la communauté savante elle même, la diffusion mondiale des valeurs individualistes et l'accéleration de la mondialisation n'ont nullement mis fin à la demande d'identification nationale'.[34]

The third paradox employs the momentous adjective 'egalitarian', describing a situation in which the widespread perception of the structure of socio-economic inequalities is deformed by opposition to indeterminate elites; by opposition to others; by the confused expansion of orbits of comparison; and by the disappearance of traditional circles of reference: those that in some way might allow an effective correspondence between aspects of inequality and reactions towards them. In considering this particular paradox, it might be suggested that, rather than a reaction to economic and social inequalities, the origin of today's populist movements lies in fact in an inadequate (and illusory) perception of their structure. It is a perception that leads to the neglect or erasure of inequalities within the 'people' themselves in order to accentuate external inequalities (in relation to the elites, or to *the others*, on the other side of the border). This paradox can seem incomprehensible or without foundation if one does not consider the fact that, in sociological research, it has always been difficult (if not impossible) to explain actions and mobilisations on the basis of the extent of the discrepancies or inequalities in status, rights, incomes and opportunities. The vast literature of recent years, mainly from (often illustrious) economists, has unfortunately not taken into account these characteristics of the relationship between the macro (the structure of inequalities) and the micro (individual reactions to this structure). The reflections of a typical representative of English reformist culture have been neglected or ignored: in his book more than half a century ago Walter G Runciman[35] stated that dissatisfaction with the system of privileges and rewards in a given society was never attributable in strict proportion to the degree of effective inequality suffered by its various members. To explain the relationship between inequality and identity fuelled by populism, it will also

[33] At the conference in honour of Alessandro Pizzorno mentioned previously. See also M Calise and F Musella, *Il principe digitale* (Laterza, 2019).

[34] Taguieff (n 13) 303.

[35] WG Runciman, *Relative Deprivation and Social Justice* (Routledge, 1966).

be necessary to take this paradox into account – an unexpected one, perhaps, for political observers and operators, but well known in social theory at its best.

These paradoxes lead to social groupings which, although not alien to individualist or *singularist* traces, can turn out to be willing to be represented through the empty signifier of the 'people', activating the corresponding identity. Social affiliation becomes indeterminate or unstable. The political populism on offer nowadays, constantly stimulated by majoritarian ambitions in tandem with pleas to reinforce or redefine internal or external boundaries, acts precisely on this trait. Social paradoxes turn out to be particularly fertile in terms of enabling inventions and fictions useful to 'people building' and its affirmation as an empty signifier, suitable to put forward as a source of identity. Fictions, above all: where inventions are concerned, there seems to be a theological element, necessary to a large extent, towards which virtually no widespread sensitivity seems to exist, at least in Western cultures. The figures of Rousseau, despite the almost blasphemous use of his name by an Italian populist movement, and indeed of Sieyès himself, would find only a faint echo today.

The *individualist* paradox makes it possible to represent social groupings *as if* they were made up of free individuals willing (and able) to react towards any form of abuse and corrupt authority. The *community* paradox, through the mediation of borders, enables the representation of social groups *as if* they were galvanised by strong community ties (almost *Blut und Boden* in sentiment) – ties that are threatened by aberrant foreign agents breaking through internally (immigration) or looming externally (the requirements of global markets and the demands of international economic/financial authorities). The *egalitarian* paradox makes it possible to influence subjects that oppose the elites (not always clearly defined), *as if* the structure of inequality in which these very subjects are inserted is irrelevant. Overall, if we go back to Laclau's concepts, the paradoxes seem to impede the 'logics of difference' and favour the 'logics of equivalence'. The way forward for 'the people' as an identity would seem to be open.

The paradoxes, in other respects, indicate a situation in which a series of elements – the blurring of traditional social affiliations; the decline of large associations of functional interests (typical of the Taylor-Fordist era); the disappearance of the culture of work; the crumbling of political ideologies that were widespread during the last two centuries; and the inexorable increase in secularisation processes – render the procedures and logics that characterised the pluralism of democratic societies, with their forms of representation, both political and otherwise, impracticable, or indistinguishable. It was a development that had already been prepared by that technocratically-laced monism of the *pensée unique* that had become so diffuse in the decades of the neo-liberal surge.

The same process, involving the difficulties or infeasibility of the 'logics of difference', was also apparent in the decades preceding the French Revolution and has been reconstructed in exemplary style by Rosanvallon in his *Le peuple introuvable*. It is a book that merits the greatest attention from those who are today shocked and surprised by the reappearance of 'the people' and 'popular identity' in contemporary political discourse. Of course, the 'bodies' of the societies of the *ancien régime* are not the social groups (with related associative belonging) that have established modern pluralist structures, even though more than one theorist of pluralism has turned to them to discover the dynamics and logic of the representation of interests and relations with state apparatus.[36] However, it is undeniable that the disappearance or gradual evanescence of 'bodies' and 'states' forces the processes of social representation, undertaken by leaders (intellectuals or politicians) endowed with 'authority' and social recognition, to search for foundations of representation that are not based on simple aggregations of individuals. It was a search that was also undertaken in the twentieth century at the end of the era of liberal individualism, protected by restricted electoral suffrage. Pluralism, with related 'logics of difference', provided the way to carry out this search with significant success – something also true in the French case, albeit with delays and contradictions due to the residual individualism of the Revolution. When pluralist representation finds itself in difficulty, the ground is formed on which calling on the people and their majoritarian ambitions becomes more diffuse. The conditions of this manoeuvre's success today are influenced, as we have just seen, by a series of social paradoxes that are perhaps unexpected and certainly misunderstood.

To assess the difficulties or malaise of the associations of representation of the groups and of pluralist democracy itself, however, it is not sufficient to consider social and economic transformations and their effects on the relationship models between groups and their interests, as in industrial relations. It becomes necessary to consider the political context in which these difficulties appear and are expressed and nourished – a context marked in all major experiences by evocation of the 'people' and by subsequent attempts to activate the related identities, with the connected negation of the divisions and differences that permeate the structures of the main western societies. The political process of 'people building', the step successive to its evocation, is based precisely on this negation and the chances of affirming the process will be greater the more the formation of the people as a unitary collective subject, in opposition to the elites, takes shape. The unitary subject, or the corresponding fiction, proves to be a necessary element for the application of, or demand for, the principle and rules of majority voting – something that is also true in the case of a referendum. The unitarity of the subject, whether real or presumed, is made possible by the unitary representation of the leader and by the search for appropriate spatial delimitations and for distinctions across borders. Examples of these include ideas of the 'America first' type and the recurring practices, implicit or explicit, of 'welfare chauvinism'. Identity feeds not only on anti-elitist exhortations, but also on anti-pluralist demands and ambitions. These are the expressions of the uniqueness of the representation of the people and of the demands for recognition, sometimes under the disturbing shadow of unexpected versions of national identity. We should know by now what the stakes are for the structures of pluralist democracy.

[36] With regard to this, see the fundamental reconstruction by D Runciman, *Pluralism and the Personality of the State* (CUP, 2005).

Part Four

Elected and Non-Elected

20

The Role of Judges in a Representative Democracy

LORD MANCE*

The topic suggested reminds me of David Foster Wallace's fable of the fish:

> Two young fish are swimming along and they happen to meet an older fish swimming the other way, who nods at them and says 'Morning, boys. How's the water?' And the two young fish swim on for a bit, and then eventually one of them looks over at the other and goes 'What the hell is water?'

As judges, we react intuitively to cases, though Daniel Kahnemann's book *Thinking, Fast and Slow* warns us of the dangers of over-reliance on intuition. We also spend much time deliberating slowly about lawyers' submissions and past caselaw. But, consciously or unconsciously, we all have some form of judicial philosophy, some way in which we approach our role as *judges in a representative democracy*.

In a UK context, representative democracy reminds us ineluctably of Edward Burke, the advocate of Parliamentary independence of thought. But, more than 200 years after Burke and Wilberforce, the reality in Westminster model democracies is that the executive has a strong control over the legislature. Parliament in the seventeenth century prevailed over the Crown, but the modern reality (Brexit apart during 2019) is that the Executive normally rules through Parliament. At the same time, we have seen increased state intervention in everyday life, greater awareness of individual rights and less deferential attitudes to authority. All this has affected judicial activity and public expectations of the judiciary.

The judiciary is the third pillar of the state. In identifying and applying the common law, it is a primary actor. In giving effect to legislation it is more than an agent of the legislature. Rather it is a junior partner, mediating by interpretation between the legislator and society. This is however no small role: anyone who reads the caselaw developed under, say, the Marine Insurance Act 1906 or the Proceeds of Crime Act 2002 will see its significance; likewise, no continental code can be understood or applied without reference to extensive caselaw to be found in substantial commentaries.

* UK Supreme Court.

More fundamentally, the judiciary stands as a counter-weight to the other two pillars, the legislature and the executive. Each needs the other, even if they are sometimes in healthy tension. The judiciary ensures that the pillars stay within their spheres and act in accordance with the law. Greater executive activity has given this role greater prominence. The judiciary also stands for certain values. In most countries of the world, many of these values are prominently expressed in a constitution, with a fundamental rights chapter. That, famously, does not apply to the UK itself. But it applies to the many common law countries where the Head of State was once or still is the Queen. They received what are called Westminster style constitutions, because they were modelled on what were believed to be the conventions underpinning the success of the UK's unwritten constitution.

Representative democracy contrasts with Athenian style direct democracy, or rule by referenda. Referenda can have unpredictable effects. The outcome of the UK's most recent experience in 2016, the third in 50 years, was not widely predicted, and some have suggested that it may have contributed to President Trump's election as President of the US. During the ensuing years, it also led to two landmark decisions of the UK Supreme Court: *R (Miller) v Secretary of State for Exiting the EU*[1] and *R (Miller) v The Prime Minister* and *Cherry v Advocate General for Scotland*.[2] In the first *Miller* case, the Supreme Court had to consider, among other points, whether the referendum vote to leave the European Union confirmed that the Executive could, by use of the royal prerogative, give notice to leave the European Union, without the prior sanction of a Parliamentary statute. The legislation providing for the referendum did not state the consequence of a Leave or a Remain vote. The Court held, by a majority of 8 to 3, that it remained for the UK Parliament to decide by statute whether the UK should leave the European Union. The contrary proposition would have meant that the Executive by a foreign policy decision could fundamentally change the internal law of the UK – a matter which the Supreme Court held that it was for Parliament, not the Executive, to decide. However, the Supreme Court also held that Parliament in this context meant the UK Parliament. The devolved legislatures (for Scotland, Northern Ireland and Wales) had no legal right to a direct role or veto. That part of the Supreme Court's decision, legally correct though it was, has of course been used as ammunition in the devolved Scottish government's quest for a further Scottish independent referendum.

The second *Miller* case arose, because in 2019 – at an important stage in the then hotly debated issue whether Brexit could and would go ahead – the new Prime Minister, Mr Boris Johnson, advised the Queen, and the Queen in Her Privy Council agreed, to prorogue Parliament. A short prorogation measured in days, to end one Parliamentary session and commence another with a Queen's speech setting out the Government's programme, would have been usual. But the prorogation announced was for the unusually long period of some five weeks, and no reason was given for that. Parliament was duly advised by the Lords Commissioners that the Queen in Council had decided that it should be prorogued and treated itself accordingly.

[1] [2017] UKSC 5.
[2] [2019] UKSC 41.

All accepted that the Queen had no discretion to disregard such advice, but the Prime Ministers' decision and all that flowed from it were successfully challenged in the Supreme Court. In a Parliamentary democracy, it could not be open to the Executive to dispense with Parliament for whatever period it decided, without any, let alone any good, reason. To hold the contrary would have been to reverse the constitutional settlement decided in favour of Parliament against the King in the seventeenth century. The Supreme Court thus held that the validity of the Prime Minister's advice was justiciable, the advice was held unlawful, as being beyond his powers, and the Queen in Council's decision to prorogue Parliament was likewise unlawful. The Lords Commissioner in announcing the decision to prorogue were acting without any legal basis – it was as if they had attended Parliament bearing a blank piece of paper. Parliament had not (validly) been prorogued, and it was recalled, and continued to act, as if it had never been.

Issues like those in both *Miller* cases show courts protecting the very essence of democracy. Not surprisingly, each decision was followed by some complaints that judges were claiming a role beyond their proper competence, coupled with general suggestions that there ought to be greater control (? by politicians) over judicial appointments. It is therefore worth reminding ourselves briefly of some essential pre-conditions to effective judicial activity: part institutional, part personal.

Institutionally, there must be a due separation of powers. The judiciary must be able to operate independently of the other two branches: see the widely accepted Bangalore Principle of Judicial Conduct endorsed by the United Nation's Economic and Social Council as ECOSOC 2006/23. Its independence should be guaranteed at the highest constitutional or legal level: see Opinion No 1 (2001) of the Council of Europe's Consultative Council of European Judges ('CCJE'), para 14.[3] This principle has been held to underlie Westminster model constitutions, in a series of remarkable cases from all over the Commonwealth: *Liyanage v The Queen;*[4] *Hinds v The Queen;*[5] *Ahnee v DPP of Mauritius;*[6] *R (Anderson) v Secretary of State for the Home Department;*[7] *DPP of Jamaica v Mollinson*[8] and *The State v Khoyratty.*[9] It was described in them as 'a characteristic feature of democracies', 'based on the rule of law'.

Separation of powers means security of tenure, normally until a defined retirement age.[10] Security also means freedom from significant disciplinary sanctions save after a judicial process for good cause, appropriate facilities, adequate guaranteed remuneration, and control over core judicial activities, such as listing and deployment. In some

[3] The CCJE's Opinions are available on the Council of Europe's website, and examine many different aspects of the judicial role.

[4] [1967] 1 AC 259.

[5] [1977] AC 196.

[6] [1999] 2 AC 294.

[7] [2002] UKHL 46; [2003] 1 AC 837.

[8] [2003] UKPC 6; [2003] 2 AC 411.

[9] [2006] UKPC 13.

[10] Though ad hoc extension or re-engagement at a time when all judicial ambition is spent exemplifies why this is not an absolute rule.

systems, judges also have their own budget and greater control over courts and their management, despite the administrative burden. Promotion at least should also be on objective, non-political grounds. Some countries operate politically based systems for initial, and some even for appellate, appointments. That can work, as the examples of both Germany and Switzerland illustrate, but experience over recent decades in the US counsels it as a model to avoid. Inevitably, some of these pre-conditions can only be fulfilled with the cooperation of the legislature and/or executive: where else, for example, is a budget to come from?

Individually, a judge must also be both honest and incorruptible and independent of the parties and issues before him.

A more basic pre-condition for the effective exercise of the judicial role is acceptance by society at large and mutual institutional understanding, indeed dialogue – even if sometimes rather tense – with the other pillars of the state. The common law only established itself by taking account of the needs, attitudes and values of the communities and individuals it serves. The other side of the coin is that all three pillars of the state need to be sensitive to and respect each other's roles. In 1788, Alexander Hamilton predicted in Federalist paper No 78, that the Judiciary would be the weakest of the three branches of the proposed US government, because it would have 'no influence over either the sword or the purse, … It may truly be said to have neither FORCE nor WILL, but merely judgment'. That is true, but, if put into effect, the state would no longer function under the rule of law. The probably apocryphal statement of President Andrew Jackson about Chief Justice Marshall's decision in *Worcester v Georgia* 1832: 'He has made his decision. Now let him enforce it!' is a recipe for the end of the judicial role and indeed of democracy. When alive, Jackson is reported as saying 'I was born for the storm, and calm doesn't suit me'. Photo shoots have shown that President Trump moved a portrait of Andrew Jackson into the Oval Office.

However that may be, a better model for the co-existence of the three pillars is found in Lord Hope's attractive dictum in *R (Jackson) v Attorney General*;[11]

> In the field of constitutional law the delicate balance between the various institutions whose sound and lasting quality Dicey at p 3 likened to the work of bees when constructing a honeycomb is maintained to a large degree by the mutual respect which each institution has for the other. In *Pickin v British Railways Board* [1974] AC 765, 788A–B Lord Reid observed that for a century or more both Parliament and the courts have been careful to act so as not to cause conflict between them. This is as much a prescription for the future as it was for the past.

In *Vriend v Alberta*,[12] where the Canadian Supreme Court held refusal to employ a homosexual to be contrary to the Charter, Justice Iacobucci described the inter-relationship as a dialogue, with a positively democratic element:

> 136 In carrying out their duties, courts are not to second-guess legislatures and the executives; they are not to make value judgments on what they regard as the proper policy choice; this is for the other branches. …

[11] [2005] UKHL 56; [2006] 1 AC 262 at [25].
[12] [1998] 1 SCR 493.

> 139. To my mind, a great value of judicial review and this dialogue among the branches is that each of the branches is made somewhat accountable to the other. The work of the legislature is reviewed by the courts and the work of the court in its decisions can be reacted to by the legislature in the passing of new legislation (or even overarching laws under s. 33 of the Charter). This dialogue between and accountability of each of the branches have the effect of enhancing the democratic process, not denying it.

How then is the judicial role to be defined? In *R (Anderson) v Secretary of State for the Home Department*,[13] Lord Steyn quoted from Windeyer J[14] who had said:

> The concept seems to me to defy, perhaps it were better to say transcend, purely abstract conceptual analysis. It inevitably attracts consideration of predominant characteristics and also invites comparison with the historic functions and processes of courts of law.
>
> Nevertheless it has long been settled in Australia that the power to determine responsibility for a crime, and punishment for its commission, is a function which belongs exclusively to the courts: …

Thus, in *Liyanage*, the legislature usurped the judicial role, when it legislated ad hominem to change procedure and redefine criminal offences to assist the prosecution of individuals allegedly involved in an attempted coup d'état. In *Hinds*, it did so, when it transferred judicial power to a New Gun Court, the majority of whose members did not qualify as judges under the Constitution. In *Khoyratty* the JCPC upheld the Mauritius Court of Appeal's decision that, since the grant or refusal of bail is an essentially judicial function, a constitutional amendment removing any right to bail pending trial in terrorism or serious drugs cases (which could mean for years) was not merely contrary to the separation of powers, but so antithetical to the concept of democracy as to infringe the most deeply entrenched provision of the Constitution of Mauritius, section 1, providing that Mauritius shall be a sovereign democratic state.

If the legislature must not impinge on the judicial sphere, one may say that judges should avoid law-making and should stick to identifying and applying the law. And this is certainly an important general distinction. Law-making is essentially political, while identifying and applying the law is the role of the courts. Judicial decisions may have political implications, but that does not make them political. They are decided on legal argument and bases. The Supreme Court was were at pains to draw attention to this in both *Miller* cases, and it is critical that it should be appreciated.

But it will already be clear – from what I have already said about the judges' responsibility for the common law and for the interpretation of statute law – that applying the law is not an exercise in logic or mathematics. Indeed, *pace* Oliver Wendell Holmes, who said: 'The life of the law has not been logic; it has been experience',[15] the life of the law is not just past experience, it is often closely related to an assessment of the future consequences of what will be decided.

For a long time, judges down-played the implications of their role. Indeed, in the interests of legal certainty or perhaps for fear of undermining their authority, they

[13] [2002] UKHL 46; [2003] 1 AC 837, 890–891 at [50].

[14] In *R v Trade Practices Tribunal, Ex p Tasmanian Breweries Pty Ltd* [1970] HCA 8; (1970) 123 CLR 361, 394.

[15] The Common Law (1881) 1.

denied it. According to what is called the 'declaratory' view of the common law, in its most traditional guise, the common law never changed. The judges merely revealed it from time to time. In the eighteenth century, Sir William Blackstone, first Vinerian Professor of English law in Oxford, and later a colleague of Lord Mansfield on the bench, argued that the legal system and common law were fundamentally Saxon achievements.[16]

Continental thinking saw the judicial role in similar terms and devised codes accordingly. Montesquieu saw the judge as 'La bouche de la loi' – the mouthpiece of the law. Article 5 of Napoleon's Code civil, enacted against a background of abusive misuse of power by pre-Revolutionary judges and still in force, went so far as to pronounce: 'Il est défendu aux juges de prononcer par voie de disposition générale et réglementaire sur les causes qui leur sont soumises'. It is perhaps responsible for the laconic reasoning of the Cour de cassation to this day.

The declaratory theory was still alive in 1892, when Lord Esher MR, later Viscount Esher, subscribed to a similar view to Blackstone's, saying in *Willis & Co v Baddeley*:[17]

> This is not a case, as has been suggested, of what is sometimes called judge-made law. There is, in fact, no such thing as judge-made law, for the judges do not make the law, though they frequently have to apply existing law to circumstances as to which it has not been authoritatively laid down that such law is applicable.

Put in these extreme terms, the declaratory theory, with its natural law overtones, was a useful protective device. It avoided questions about the legitimacy of judges to develop the law. The modern press encourages us to think about such questions. It asks who these unelected judges are, but does not always consider whether we might be worse off if judges were elected, or how the common law would have developed to meet modern needs without judicial activity.

It is nearly 50 years since Lord Reid openly acknowledged extra-judicially that it was a fairy tale to suggest that judges do not make the common law. A notice in the exhibition space in the home of the UK Supreme Court and Judicial Committee of the Privy Council home in Parliament Square is, I think, appropriately open about the position:

> [Judges] will consider the implications of [a] decision, and will ensure that it is consistent with the general purpose and scheme of the law or principle .... Concerned ...
>
> Judging is thus not a science, but a discipline. The good judge is loyal to well-established approaches and methods of reasoning. But she or he may in the last analysis have to exercise an important judgment as to the relevant weight of different and sometimes competing considerations, in deciding in which sense to state or restate the legal position.

This is not to say that the declaratory theory has no continuing use. It is a way in which we explain why a development in the law or an over-ruling of a prior authority affects the case in which it occurs *and* all other cases, past or present – rather

[16] The Commentaries, Book 4, Ch 33, 404–404, credit King Alfred with new-modelling the constitution 'to rebuild it on a plan that should endure for ages, dispersing justice to every part of the nation which wise institution has been preserved for near a thousand years unchanged, from Alfred's to the present time'.

[17] [1892] 2 QB 324, 326.

than having purely prospective effect as a change for the future. In that respect, the theory amounts to a pragmatic acknowledgement of the possibility of judicial error or second thoughts. The law is occasionally prone to that risk, like any other human institution.

If judging is a discipline, not a science, what are the disciplinary controls? The exhibition notice mentions loyalty to well-established approaches and methods. These are epitomised by the common law use of precedent and analogy. They help ensure consistency, the hallmark of any system of law or equitable adjudication. But it can also have dangers. In the US, when oil and gas started to attract litigation, courts initially invoked the rule of capture, which applied to wild animals. They soon found this an unhelpful analogy. David Hume in *An Enquiry concerning Human Understanding* accurately described experiences which many of us, I suspect, have had:

> If direct laws and precedents be wanting, imperfect and indirect ones are brought in aid; and the controverted case is ranged under them by analogical reasoning and comparisons, and similitudes, and correspondencies, which are often more fanciful than real.

Judge Richard A Posner in *The Problems of Jurisprudence*,[18] p 83, has noted that a proliferation of precedents may be a warning, rather than an encouragement. They may show that the rule to which the precedents relate has proved an irritant – producing a blister, rather than a pearl.

What then where there is no direct precedent and no helpful analogy? As even Lord Esher accepted, judges have often to consider what or whether a common law rule applies to a particular, perhaps novel situation. The common law tends to develop incrementally and cautiously, to that extent perhaps even experimentally in a scientific way. The process has been attractively compared by Professor Ronald Dworkin[19] with the production of a chain novel by a series of different novelists, each adding a chapter, with the task of achieving as much overall coherence as possible and, one might add, with the final chapters perhaps providing some generalised key to all that preceded.

The process is particularly evident in the field of tort. *Hedley Byrne v Heller & Partners*,[20] which upset university finalists by appearing on 28 May 1963 just before their final exams when the writer was at Oxford, drew on prior authority to identify a general principle of liability for negligent misrepresentation causing financial loss in contexts of proximity akin to contract, where one party had to the knowledge of the other justifiably relied on the other's representation. But sometimes the law is too quick. *Anns v Merton LBC*[21] generalised the liability of local authorities towards owners of houses suffering from the effects of negligence by local authority building works inspectors performing their statutory duty. Within a few years the principle was found to operate in an unsatisfactorily haphazard way, and was overruled in *Murphy*

[18] (Harvard University Press, 1990).
[19] In *Law's Empire* (Belknap Press, owned by Harvard University Press, 1986).
[20] [1964] AC.
[21] [1978] AC 728.

v Brentwood DC.[22] A recent attempt to resuscitate it by reliance on the state's duty to respect and protect private life was rejected in *Gresty v Knowsley DC*.[23]

The exhibition notice in the UK Supreme Court also mentions the judicial role in assessing the weight of different considerations, when deciding how to state or restate the law. Two other UK Supreme Court cases evidence this process. In *Willers v Joyce*,[24] the Court restated the law of illegality, moving away from Lord Mansfield's inflexible rule that no-one can rely on illegality, with the result that loss lies where it falls. In *Patel v Mirza*,[25] the Supreme Court accepted a general right to claim damages for malicious pursuit of a civil action: in each, the Court might even be said to have trod boldly, rather than incrementally, but the reader may wish to discount that comment, as it comes from a writer who was one of those dissenting in each case.

In a series of cases, the UK Supreme Court has reminded counsel not to forget the common law or to treat it as beyond the age of child-bearing: *R (Guardian Newspaper)*;[26] *Osborn v Parole Board*;[27] *HS2*;[28] and *Kennedy v The Charity Commission*.[29] With the domestication of fundamental rights under the Human Rights Act, the Supreme Court found that issues or supposed issues were being pursued under the European Convention on Human Rights (the ECHR), which were or could have been covered by the common law. In the same vein, the Privy Council has emphasised that, where there are common law remedies, for example in contract or tort, it is inappropriate, and unhelpful, to try to dress the claims up as constitutional issues. In other countries, such as Germany, the courts seem to have managed to maintain a greater focus on their own domestically enacted protective rights, or to assimilate those with the Convention rights.

Even in areas as apparently clinical as contractual interpretation, the judge's role is never purely mechanical.[30] The judge's role is to give effect to the parties' intentions, derived from the words used in the light of the terms of the contract as a whole and the surrounding circumstances known or taken to have been known by the parties when they made the contract – excepting (for pragmatic reasons) evidence of contractual negotiations or of subjective declarations of intention. The result has been, subject to that one important exception, 'to assimilate the way in which such documents are interpreted by judges to the commonsense principles by which any serious utterance would be interpreted in ordinary life': *Investors Compensation Scheme v West Bromwich Building Society*.[31] Some academics think that recent Supreme Court and Privy Council case law shows a continuing tension between literalist and purposive

[22] [1991] 1 AC 398.
[23] [2012] EWHC 29 (Admin).
[24] [2016] UKSC 33 & 34.
[25] [2016] UKSC 42.
[26] [2012] EWCA Civ 420; [2013] QB 68 at [88].
[27] [2013] UKSC 61.
[28] [2014] UKSC 3.
[29] [2014] UKSC 20.
[30] There was a time when a series of 'rules' of interpretation aimed at making it so. But now: 'Almost all the old intellectual baggage of "legal" interpretation has been discarded': *Investors Compensation Scheme v West Bromwich Building Society* [1997] UKHL 28, [1998] 1WLR 896.
[31] See n 30.

or consequentialist interpretation of contractual language. Since judges on both sides of this case law insist that there is nothing between them in principle, it is a matter of impression whether any difference exists in the actual decisions they reach. However, I add, having recently attended a conference in this area with German lawyers, that the common law is probably still at the textualist end of a range compared with other European systems. Common lawyers tend to believe that an examination of the text, set in the context of the surrounding circumstances, is likely to be a fruitful starting point for the discovery of the parties' objective intent and meaning.

If judges have a certain freedom in relation to the common law, since it is after all their creation, what of the judicial role in relation to written or statute law? It is here that the judicial role is most sensitive. The common law legislator often speaks in very detailed terms, but still there are situations overlooked or ambiguity. The courts have inevitably to decide whether and if so how the gap can be filled or the ambiguity resolved. As with contractual interpretation, so here too courts have traditionally relied on technical rules of textual construction, some still useful. But today their approach parallels in an elevated way that of contractual interpretation. We examine the words used in the context of the scheme as a whole and against the background of whatever is identified as the 'mischief' which the statute set out to address. A purposive construction is increasingly supported by reference to general principles which it is presumed that the legislature will have intended to observe. There is, for example, a presumption against any intention to legislate with extra-territorial effect; a presumption against penalisation of any activity by doubtful words; and, most importantly, a conception of fundamental common law rights – for example the right to liberty, the right to free speech, the right not to incriminate oneself and the right to legal professional privilege in respect of one's communications with a legal adviser.

In *R v Secretary of State for the Home Department ex Parte Simms (AP)* Lord Hoffmann said:

> Fundamental rights cannot be overridden by general or ambiguous words. This is because there is too great a risk that the full implications of their unqualified meaning may have passed unnoticed in the democratic process. In the absence of express language or necessary implication to the contrary, the courts therefore presume that even the most general words were intended to be subject to the basic rights of the individual.

The majority in the first *Miller* case relied on this principle when concluding that Parliament, when it signed the UK up to EU law and law-making processes by the European Communities Act 1972, cannot have intended to leave it to the executive to sign the UK out at any stage without Parliamentary blessing.

Ex p Simms was decided in the UK context, where Parliament is sovereign. Since October 2000, this principle has a statutory homologue, since UK courts are obliged to interpret legislation as far as possible consistently with the ECHR. But the principle in *ex p Simms* still represents a first port of call, often enabling the courts to avoid inconsistency with fundamental principles, whether or not located in a constitution.

This brings me to a core and sometimes controversial role of judges in a representative democracy: that is, in relation to public and constitutional law issues. In countries with a written constitution, a step change in judicial approach is usually evident, when a question arises about the interpretation and application of the constitution.

The Judicial Committee of the Privy Council, which serves as the constitutional court of many countries with written constitutions identified this step change in *Matadeen v Pointu*,[32] as follows:

> .... constitutions are not construed like commercial documents. This is because every utterance must be construed in its proper context, taking into account the historical background and the purpose for which the utterance was made. The context and purpose of a commercial contract is very different from that of a constitution. The background of a constitution is an attempt, at a particular moment in history, to lay down an enduring scheme of government in accordance with certain moral and political values. Interpretation must take these purposes into account. Furthermore, the concepts used in a constitution are often very different from those used in commercial documents. They may expressly state moral and political principles to which the judges are required to give effect in accordance with their own conscientiously held views of what such principles entail. It is however a mistake to suppose that these considerations release judges from the task of interpreting the statutory language and enable them to give free rein to whatever they consider should have been the moral and political views of the framers of the constitution. What the interpretation of commercial documents and constitutions have in common is that in each case the court is concerned with the meaning of the language which has been used. As Kentridge A.J. said in giving the judgment of the South African Constitutional Court in *State v. Zuma* [1995] (4) B.C.L.R. 401, 412:
>
> 'If the language used by the lawgiver is ignored in favour of a general resort to 'values' the result is not interpretation but divination.'

In a constitution, society expresses its commitment to enduring principles of which judges are to be the future guardians, whatever may from time to time be the vicissitudes of majoritarian or political opinion. It is easy to protect the interests of the majority or the popular. But, as Justice Iacobucci observed in *Vriend v Alberta*, 'The concept of democracy is broader than the notion of majority rule, fundamental as that may be'. Where the law matters is when it protects the legitimate interests of unpopular minorities, including those strongly suspected of committing or intending very serious misdeeds. Those interests include due process and freedom from punishment without a finding of guilt. Thus, when it comes to the fight against terrorism, as the former Chief Justice of Israel, Aron Barak, said: 'Sometimes, democracy fights with one hand tied behind its back. Nonetheless, it has the upper hand'.[33]

Although the UK has no formal written constitution, it has however an (increasing) number of important constitutional instruments. These start with the seminal provisions of Magna Carta, now understood as enshrining core elements of the rule of law:

> No Freeman shall be taken or imprisoned, or be disseised of his Freehold, or Liberties, or free Customs, or be outlawed, or exiled, or any other wise destroyed; nor will We not pass upon him, nor condemn him, but by lawful judgment of his Peers, or by the Law of the land. We will sell to no man, we will not deny or defer to any man either Justice or Right. (article XXIX in the 1297 version of Magna Carta)

[32] [1998] UKPC 9.
[33] *Public Committee against Torture v Israel*, 26 May 1999, HC 5100/94.53(4) PD 817, 845.

Other quasi-constitutional instruments include the Petition of Right 1128, the Bill of Rights (or in Scotland Act Claim of Right) 1689, the Act of Settlement 1701, The Act of Union 1707, the European Communities Act 1972, the Human Rights Act 1998, devolution legislation (the Scotland Act 1998, Northern Ireland Act 19998, the Wales Acts 2014 and 2017) and the Constitutional Reform Act 2005: see *R (HS2 Action Alliance Limited) v The Secretary of State for Transport*.[34] The courts have developed a distinction between such measures and 'ordinary' statutes, which may mean that all or some of the former are incapable of repeal save by express words or even, in the case of the European Communities Act, that they lie outside the scope of the power delegated by Parliament to the European Union (while the UK was a member of the European Union): see the *HS2 Alliance* case, paras 207–08.

At a more day-to-day level, there has taken place a remarkable modernisation and systematisation by the courts over the last half century of the power of judicial review. This does not (outside the area of European Union law, during the UK's membership of the European Union) embrace the power recognised in the US by *Marbury v Madison*[35] to strike down primary legislation as constitutionally impermissible. But it does embrace a scheme whereby both subordinate legislative and executive action are open to review on grounds of legality, procedural fairness and rationality.

Generally expressed powers, whether they be statutory or prerogative, must therefore be exercised only within their proper limits and for the purposes for which they were created: the second *Miller* decision derived the proper limits of the prerogative power to prorogue from the consideration that such a power could not have

> the effect of frustrating or preventing, without reasonable justification, the ability of Parliament to carry out its constitutional functions as a legislature and as the body responsible for the supervision of the executive. [second *Miller* case, para 50]

Decision-makers must observe due process, acting fairly and reasonably. Expectations about procedural steps such as consultation, and, more controversially, expectations about substantive rights may have to be respected: see most recently *United Policyholders Group v Attorney General of Trinidad and Tobago*.[36]

Courts also review decision-making for its substantive reasonableness. Traditionally this has been only in a diluted, *Wednesbury* sense,[37] that censures decision-making which no reasonable decision-maker could have reached. But increasingly it has been recognised that the intensity of review may increase, depending on the nature of the interests at stake and their suitability for judicial review. The emergence of fundamental rights chapters, charters or conventions has also introduced the concept of proportionality, which the common law has started to pick up in allied areas: see for example *Kennedy v The Charity Commission*.[38] On the other hand, courts have

[34] [2014] UKSC 3, para 207.
[35] 5 US (1 Cranch) 127 (1803).
[36] [2016] UKPC 17.
[37] The name comes from the case of *Associated Picture Houses Ltd v Wednesbury Corp* [1948] 1 KB 223, where the principle was described.
[38] [2014] UKSC 20.

recognised that they are not and should not act as primary decision-makers. To repeat Justice Jacobucci's words: 'In carrying out their duties, courts are not to second-guess legislatures and the executives.' Judicial activity depends on the context. On issues of liberty, freedom of movement, speech or religion, courts can claim a special expertise. On issues about the use of public resources or economic judgment, the elected legislature or executive is better placed.

But in none of these cases, is it legitimate for the executive to submit that it is undemocratic for the courts to become involved. In *A (FC) v Secretary of State*,[39] a case about the potentially indefinite detention of aliens suspected of terrorism, the Attorney General submitted that, just as it was for Parliament and the executive to assess the threat facing the nation, so it was for those bodies and not the courts to judge the response necessary to protect the security of the public, since this called for an exercise of political and not judicial judgment.

Rejecting this submission, Lord Bingham said:

> I do not in particular accept the distinction which he [the Attorney General] drew between democratic institutions and the courts. It is of course true that the judges in this country are not elected and are not answerable to Parliament. It is also of course true … that Parliament, the executive and the courts have different functions. But the function of independent judges charged to interpret and apply the law is universally recognised as a cardinal feature of the modern democratic state, a cornerstone of the rule of law itself. The Attorney General is fully entitled to insist on the proper limits of judicial authority, but he is wrong to stigmatise judicial decision-making as in some way undemocratic.

History often repeats itself. A similar battle recently unfolded before the 9th Circuit Court of Appeals in *Washington and Minnesota v Trump*.[40] The judgment recites that

> The Government contends that the district court lacked authority to enjoin enforcement of the Executive Order because the President has 'unreviewable authority to suspend the admission of any class of aliens.' The Government does not merely argue that courts owe substantial deference to the immigration and national security policy determinations of the political branches – an uncontroversial principle that is well-grounded in our jurisprudence … Instead, the Government has taken the position that the President's decisions about immigration policy, particularly when motivated by national security concerns, are unreviewable, even if those actions potentially contravene constitutional rights and protections. The Government indeed asserts that it violates separation of powers for the judiciary to entertain a constitutional challenge to executive actions such as this one. There is no precedent to support this claimed unreviewability, which runs contrary to the fundamental structure of our constitutional democracy.
>
> Within our system, it is the role of the judiciary to interpret the law, a duty that will sometimes require the '[r]esolution of litigation challenging the constitutional authority of one of the three branches.' … We are mindful that deference to the political branches is particularly appropriate with respect to national security and foreign affairs, given the relative institutional capacity, informational access, and expertise of the courts.

[39] [2004] UKHL 56.
[40] (No. 17-35105), decided 9 February 2017.

There are a few issues, mostly involving the royal prerogative, usually in the field of armed conflict or treaty making, which current authority identifies as non-justiciable, that is as requiring judicial abstention. The UK Supreme Court examined them recently in the field of international activity in *Rahmatullah (No 2) v Ministry of Defence*[41] and *Belhaj v Straw*.[42] But they are rare indeed, and can be put aside in the present discussion. In the second *Miller* case, the Prime Minister and Advocate General for Scotland invoked domestic non-justiciability. They did so firstly, and as already recounted unsuccessfully, in relation to the Prime Minister's advice to the Queen. But they also relied on the statutory immunity from judicial scrutiny provided by article 9 of the Bill of Rights 1689 (another inherited feature of the seventeenth century's constitutional battles). Article 9 provides that

> The Freedome of Speech and Debates or Proceedings in Parlyament ought not to be impeached or questioned in any Court or Place out of Parlyament.

So, it was argued, the Supreme Court had no power or right to adjudicate upon the suggested invalidity of the prorogation. The Supreme Court in response pointed out that the aim of article 9 was to protect debates and decisions of Parliament – the 'core or essential business of Parliament'. The prorogation in contrast was nothing of the sort: it was the act of the Executive imposed on Parliament from outside, not something on which Members of Parliament could or did speak or vote. Rather than represent the core or essential business of Parliament, 'it brings that core or essential business of Parliament to an end'. It was for the Court to construe the ambit of article 9, and, as a matter of statutory construction, article 9 was no bar to a decision that the prorogation was invalid and ineffective.

Judges in a representational democracy are not therefore ciphers or agents of past history or of the current legislature. Even in states like the UK without a written constitution, they have a significant role in defining the practical impact of what the legislator decides.

Against the background, it is natural that attention should focus on the judges: who they are, with what attitudes and values they approach their work, and whether and, if so, how they are accountable to those they serve and whose interests are affected by their decisions. It is perhaps equally unsurprising, though a little depressing, that the manifesto with which the Conservative Party under which Prime Minister Johnson won a resounding electoral victory in December 2019 should state that 'After Brexit we also need to look at the broader aspects of our constitution: the relationship between the Government, Parliament and the courts; the functioning of the Royal Prerogative; …[43] In our first year we will set up a Constitution, Democracy & Rights

[41] [2017] UKSC 1 (Crown act of state).

[42] [2017] UKSC 3 (foreign act of state).

[43] The full text from this point reads: 'the role of the House of Lords; and access to justice for ordinary people. The ability of our security services to defend us against terrorism and organised crime is critical. We will update the Human Rights Act and administrative law to ensure that there is a proper balance between the rights of individuals, our vital national security and effective government. We will ensure that judicial review is available to protect the rights of the individuals against an overbearing state, while ensuring that it is not abused to conduct politics by another means or to create needless delays. In our first year

Commission that will examine these issues in depth, and come up with proposals to restore trust in our institutions and in how our democracy operates'. It would be sad if any element of this manifesto proposal were attributable to resentment at the loss of either or both of the *Miller* cases.

As to who we are, a judicial appointments system needs to have the confidence of society generally, as well as ensuring a judiciary of appropriate quality and with an appropriate cross-section of skills. This is one of the pre-conditions to the effective exercise of the judicial role, but this is not the place to go further into it. Various approaches exist, all with pros and cons. The important thing is that it should be essentially non-political. The example of US federal judicial appointments is one to avoid. Happily, there is no hint (no overt hint, in any event) in the Conservative Party manifesto of a few recent suggestions that there should be greater political involvement in UK judicial appointments.

The attitudes and values with which judges approach their work is, on the other hand, central to the judicial role. I have already mentioned some controls on judicial excess or exuberance: loyalty, precedent and methodology. Judiciaries usually also develop an internal collegiality. This aids cohesive jurisprudence, but should never degenerate into cliqueness or arrogance,[44] or unwillingness to give effect to the judicial oath sworn by each individual judge to administer justice without fear or favour, affection or ill-will.

What enables the judiciary, what gives the judiciary the right, to identify and apply any particular set of attitudes or values, especially if the values selected may conflict with what a majority of the population might think or wish? In countries with a written constitution, the constitution serves as a deliberately crafted social contract, democratically introduced to entrench values immune from ephemeral or insensitive majoritarian opinion.[45]

But even that is only a complete answer if the Constitution leaves no room for doubt, choice or change. The originalist approach to interpretation adopted by the late Justice Scalia might have it so. One may however be sceptical whether even the originalists really avoid value-free judgments. Was the US Supreme Court value-free in *District of Columbia v Heller*,[46] when it held that the possession of handguns, but

we will set up a Constitution, Democracy & Rights Commission that will examine these issues in depth, and come up with proposals to restore trust in our institutions and in how our democracy operates'.

[44] Our Victorian forebears do not seem to have been immune to the latter failing. On Queen Victoria's Diamond Jubilee, the judges of the Royal Courts of Justice gathered to consider their loyal address. The draft began: 'Your Majesty, Conscious as we are of our manifold failings ….' To which one elderly response was: 'Well, for my part, I am not quite sure about that'. To which that great lawyer, Bowen LJ, quick as a flash proposed the final version: 'Your Majesty, Conscious as we are of each other's failings ….'.

[45] Justice Iacobucci put this powerfully in *Vriend v Alberta*: '134 … our Charter's introduction and the consequential remedial role of the courts were choices of the Canadian people through their elected representatives as part of a redefinition of our democracy. Our constitutional design was refashioned to state that henceforth the legislatures and executive must perform their roles in conformity with the newly conferred constitutional rights and freedoms. That the courts were the trustees of these rights insofar as disputes arose concerning their interpretation was a necessary part of this new design. 135. So courts in their trustee or arbiter role must perforce scrutinize the work of the legislature and executive not in the name of the courts, but in the interests of the new social contract that was democratically chosen.'

[46] 554 US 57 (2007).

not it seems machine guns, was within the Second Amendment provisions that: 'A well regulated militia, being necessary to the security of a free state, the right of the people to keep and bear arms, shall not be infringed'? However that may be, originalism is not I think a prominent feature of constitutional interpretation outside the US.

What then are the values to which judges should aim to give effect in interpreting and applying either a written constitution or any other law? The matter was well put by Dickson CJ in *R v Oakes* at p 136:[47]

> The Court must be guided by the values and principles essential to a free and democratic society which I believe to embody, to name but a few, respect for the inherent dignity of the human person, commitment to social justice and equality, accommodation of a wide variety of beliefs, respect for cultural and group identity, and faith in social and political institutions which enhance the participation of individuals and groups in society.

The former Chief Justice of Israel, Aaron Barak, spoke to similar effect in *The Judge in a Democracy* (2006). He underlined the importance of the judicial role not just in relation to the other pillars of the state, but also in embedding the concept of the rule of law in society generally, in ensuring what the CCJE has called 'social peace'. The book engages closely with the judicial role, faced with issues of violence and national security. Barak is at pains to answer concerns that his approach confers on the judge too prominent a status or that 'democracy is too important to be left to the protection of judges who are not elected or otherwise accountable to the people' (see p 88).[48]

None of this of course fully answers the question how judges identify 'the values and principles essential to a free and democratic society' to which Dickson CJ referred, if these do not appear in a written constitution, or, still more pertinently, how judges decide what weight to give to such values and principles as do appear or as they do identify. Loyal though we are by inclination and training to the law, we are each of us different in our make-up and individual personalities, and in difficult cases this may evidence itself. Not long ago, Professor Rachel Cahill-O'Callaghan of Cardiff University won the Society of Legal Scholars Best Paper Prize for a paper entitled 'Reframing the judicial diversity debate: personal values and tacit diversity', analysing the position as the highest UK level and concluding that 'despite the lack of explicit diversity, there is an element of tacit diversity in the Supreme Court, which is reflected in judicial decisions'. The interesting thing here is that diversity was being examined implicitly on the basis that it may be a good thing, as it is generally and rightly accepted to be in the outward composition of courts and other bodies in a diverse society. A degree of diversity at the stage when an appellate court is discussing a decision internally can clearly help to ensure that all viewpoints are taken into

[47] [1986] 1 S.C.R. 103.

[48] Barak's book was welcomed by distinguished commentators, including Lord Pannick, noting in the *Times* that 'Barak points out that tension between the courts and other branches of government is natural and it is desirable. If the courts' decisions were always welcomed by the executive, judges would not be doing their job properly. Barak's thesis is … of fundamental importance.' Barak's moderation did not however prevent his thesis being panned by the US Judge Robert Bork. His highly polemical review under the title 'Barak's Rule' is worth reading for the light it throws on US originalist thinking, which Bork sees – I would suggest, fallaciously – as the *vade mecum* to 'preserving a democratic order – the rule of law rather than the rule of judges'.

account. Diversity to the point where different constitutions of the same appellate court may reach different decisions is more problematic.[49]

There is probably no complete answer to the questions I have been discussing. We live in an imperfect world, in a universe which we can never fully comprehend. None of us will ever be, or meet, Ronald Dworkin's Judge Hercules, whose intellectual muscles enabled him to identify the true weight that any particular factor merited and so to discern the best of all conceivable solutions to any problem that came before him (or her). But without judges there would be no administration of justice or rule of law at all. And this brings me to the final aspect of the judicial role which I wish to underline, our duty to account, so far as we can, for our stewardship of the law.

Independence and accountability are, as one Canadian commentator put it, 'rather testy friends'.[50] Judges cannot be directly or personally accountable like agents or contractors for mistakes or faults in their judicial decision-making.[51] But ensuring as much accountability as possible is an important part of the judicial role. This in turn links with Chief Justice Barak's theme about inculcating law into society, and ensures that, despite any unanswered conundra, all elements of society will continue to coexist under the rule of law.

First, the primary remedy for erroneous decisions is that there should be an appropriately accessible and speedy appeal process, unless, of course, one finds oneself in the unfortunate position of thinking that a final court of appeal, like the Privy Council, has got something wrong.

Secondly, in order to account to the parties, and to enable them to assess whether to appeal where appropriate, our judgments must address the issues, they must explain to the parties why we have come to the conclusions we have on fact and law. They must cut to the chase, focusing on and analysing the points that matter, and not engaging in wide-ranging and unnecessary recitation or discourse, whether of fact or law.

[49] Two recent cases illustrate how the differing weight placed on different considerations may lead to overt differences in judicial conclusions: (i) In *Arorangi Timberland Ltd v Minister of the Cook Island* [2016] UKPC 32, where the issue was whether the JCPC should hold that a particular state pension fund provision was unduly discriminatory against immigrant workers, and there was a difference of opinion about the weight to be given to the local jurisdiction's choice of scheme. (ii) In *Nicklinson v Ministry of Justice* [2012] UKSC 39, where the Supreme Court had to consider whether the blanket criminalisation of assisting suicide was justifiable under the ECHR, in a case of locked in syndrome. We all agreed that under the Strasbourg court's jurisprudence the question fell within the UK's margin of appreciation, and was for the UK to decide. Five Justices (Lord Neuberger, Lady Hale, Lord Mance, Lord Kerr and Lord Wilson) held that the Court had constitutional authority to make a declaration that the general prohibition on assisted suicide in section 2 was incompatible with article 8. Of those five, Lord Neuberger, Lord Mance and Lord Wilson would not grant a declaration of incompatibility in these proceedings, but Lady Hale and Lord Kerr would have done so. Four Justices, Lord Clarke, Lord Sumption, Lord Reed and Lord Hughes, concluded that the question whether the current law on assisting suicide is compatible with article 8 involved a consideration of issues which Parliament was inherently better qualified than the courts to assess, and that under present circumstances the courts should respect Parliament's assessment.

[50] P Hughes, 'Judicial Independence: Contemporary Pressures and Appropriate Responses' (2001) 80 *Can Bar Rev* 181, 184.

[51] The state may be made responsible for judicial failings, without recourse against the judge. A judge who commits an offence under the general law, such as corruption, would of course be liable to prosecution like any other citizen: see below.

At the appellate level, the common law has a freedom which not all systems enjoy, by permitting both concurring and dissenting judgments. They can contribute not only to the clarity of the analysis, but also to the law's future development as well as to its acceptability in the eyes of the parties and wider society. In courts which insist on single style judgments, fruitful internal discussions may well take place in private and lead to changes of position and compromises. Common law judges should also encourage such discussions, one should not dissent on every little point. There is an aphorism that a dissent should only to be written when one's natural indolence is outweighed by one's indignation at the folly that one's colleagues are about to perpetrate. Be that as it may be, the freedom to speak out, when really necessary, seems to me an additional and immensely beneficial bonus enjoyed by common law courts.

Thirdly, we must also aim at – and succeed in – avoiding delay. Delay, at any level of a court system, kills memory and destroys touch, it makes the ultimate task of deciding and writing judgments much more difficult: see *Tex Services Ltd v Shibani Knitting Co*.[52]

Fourthly, we must remember that there may be persons other than the parties who may be concerned in or affected by our decisions and reasons. They may be third parties. They may be society at large or the executive or legislature. Our decision may constitute an important precedent or guide. It must be framed accordingly to be clear, understandable and usable. We must also expect and accept that our judgments will occasionally arouse controversy. The Privy Council once famously remarked that 'Justice is not a cloistered virtue; she must be allowed to suffer the scrutiny and respect, even though outspoken, the comments of ordinary men': *Ambard v Attorney General of Trinidad and Tobago*.[53] We might choose different language today, judges must expect to put up with a great deal of vigorous criticism, not just from 'ordinary men', but hostile commentators or highly skilled legal experts. But courts should certainly be as cautious about deploying counter-measures such as supposed contempt of court as the Privy Council was warning in *Ambard*.

Fifthly, court procedures should be transparent and accessible. The UK Supreme Court and the Judicial Committee of the Privy Council have been at pains to make their procedures transparent and accessible – by welcoming visitors to our courtrooms (yearly attendance is approaching 100,000), by web-casting hearings, so that they can be watched across the world, by press releases, by short oral explanations of our reasons on YouTube and by the services of an effective press office, which has developed the most excellent liaison with the media. In addition, we receive members of other judiciaries, as well as school and university groups, with whom a Justice will frequently meet or have lunch.

Sixthly, judges nowadays regularly attend conferences and speak publicly on legal and sometimes other themes, without of course addressing current or in any controversial way past cases.

Finally, on the sad occasions when this is necessary, if judges misconduct themselves in connection with their judicial office, they may expect to be disciplined. We

[52] [2016] UKPC 31.
[53] [1936] AC 322.

have in the UK formally established, judicially-based processes for this. Judges are of course no more immune than any ordinary citizen in the UK if they commit an offence under the general law, such as corruption.

All this contributes to mutual understanding and 'social peace'. But social peace is a two-sided affair. Ultimately our societies depend on shared bonds and mutual understanding. From time to time, voices do speak in terms which are not helpful to the rule of law. When Prime Minister, Mr Cameron reacted to a European Court of Human Rights' decisions that at least some convicted prisoners should have the vote, by saying that they made him physically sick and that he would clip the wings of the court. The *Mail Online* reacted to the High Court's judgment in *Miller* (later upheld in the Supreme Court) by putting a picture of the three High Court judges on its front page with the caption *Enemies of the People*, and referring, deplorably as well as wholly irrelevantly, to the publicly acknowledged homosexuality of one of them. Happily, by 24 January 2017 when we gave our judgment, things had calmed down. The furthest the *Daily Mail* then went was a photo of the three dissentients captioned *Champions of the People*, which was even quite witty!

There will always be disagreement about individual decisions. The writer does not, however, share the apparent view of a former colleague and recent Reith lecturer[54] that law has subsumed within its realm too much of the essential decision-making that politicians should undertake, still less that this can be attributed to judicial hyperactivity. Occasional disagreements about individual decisions of one power or another are not only inevitable, but healthy in a thriving democracy. But an underlying culture of mutual understanding and sympathy between the different powers of the state is critical to the rule of law. And suggestions that this can no longer exist in the UK, and that drastic action is called for, carry the risk that they may be self-fulfilling. The rule of law must rest on a similar level of general acceptance to that which Professor Herbert Hart QC identified as grounding the concept of law itself;[55] and we should all work together to promote, not to undermine, this.

[54] Lord Sumption giving The BBC Reith Lectures: www.bbc.co.uk/programmes/b00729d9.
[55] *The Concept of Law* (Clarendon Law Series, 2d, 1997).

21

Closely Observed Judges, or the Great Comeback of Authoritarianism in Poland

MAŁGORZATA GERSDORF,* MATEUSZ PILICH **

Iam vero illud stultissimum, existimare omnia iusta esse quae scita sint in populorum institutis aut legibus.

Etiamne si quae leges sint tyrannorum?

Cicero, *De legibus (On the Laws)*, I, 42[1]

I. INTRODUCTION

IN 2009, AN Australian-born English political scientist John Keane published his monument work entitled *The Life and Death of Democracy*.[2] Though it is by no means a prophetic book, as the eminent author basically collected and took his readers through the world's political history, many of his insights may surprise with its relevance and timeliness. Asking a question whether the world's democracies 'have a rosy future', Professor Keane warns against being overly optimistic about the endless prosperity: '... the history of democracy is still being made as the world's clock ticks, as each sunrise gives way to each new sunset'.[3]

* University of Warsaw.

** University of Warsaw.

Abbreviations index: CT–Constitutional Tribunal (*Trybunał Konstytucyjny*), Dz.U.–Journal of Laws (*Dziennik Ustaw*); OSNC – *Orzecznictwo Sądu Najwyższego. Izba Cywilna* [Supreme Court Reports. Civil Chamber], OSNK – *Orzecznictwo Sądu Najwyższego. Izba Karna* [Supreme Court Reports. Criminal Chamber], SAC – Supreme Administrative Court (*Naczelny Sąd Administracyjny*), SC – Supreme Court (*Sąd Najwyższy*); OTK – *Orzecznictwo Trybunału Konstytucyjnego* [Constitutional Tribunal Reports].

[1] 'But truly the most foolish thing is to think that everything is just that has been approved in the institutions or laws of peoples. And if those laws are from tyrants?', translated by D Fott, (Cornell University Press 2014), www.nlnrac.org/classical/cicero/documents/de-legibus.

[2] J Keane, *The Life and Death of Democracy* (Simon & Schuster, 2009) (cited in a Kindle edition, without page numbering).

[3] See ibid, *Introduction*.

Obviously, democracy – just as economy does, for instance – lives and dies in the rhythm of cycles. It undergoes crises. It changes its nature and manifests itself in different forms, sometimes detrimental to the people, now elevated to the rank of a collective sovereign endowed with the supreme power. It tends to go down. It may sound like a slogan to repeat after Alexander Hamilton that there is nothing more erroneous but to say that democracy is perfect: 'The ancient democracies in which the people themselves deliberated never possessed one good feature of government. Their very character was tyranny; their figure deformity.'[4] The people, too, can be the worst kind of a tyrant, unless the law with its Constitution-founded system of the checks and balances imposes a constraint on the common will. No need to say that the judiciary plays the critical role here.

After a steady growth throughout the second half of the twentieth century, which resulted in circa 37 per cent of the world population living in democratic states, the most successful era for the sovereignty of the people seems to come to an end. Far from the political insight as they are, jurists have to ask questions about the reasons and consequences of the current state of things. Addressing it within the framework of the present paper, we would like to focus solely on one specific case: Poland – one of the first countries of the former Eastern Bloc that underwent a peaceful 'velvet' revolution in 1989, as a result of which it transformed its system from authoritarian to democratic.

Over the last 25 years of relative political stability, Poland has created an impression worldwide that it as a country became a true 'consolidated' democracy. The state of affairs did not change even as a result of a temporary seizure of power in 2005–07 by an episodic right-populist coalition. The legal situation in Poland since 2015 – with the takeover of power by the radical-right coalition of the 'Allied Right' (*Zjednoczona Prawica*) under the leadership of the 'Law and Justice' party[5] – brought a complete turnover. In spite of being at any time by far lower than the constitutional majority, the ruling camp has treated its electoral win as a *carte blanche* for radical changes, not necessarily within the framework of the constitutional authorisation. Due to the natural limits of the present study, they could not be outlined in detail; still, it is enough to point out to readers that since 2015, the Polish Constitution and the state system have not changed in terms of the supreme law of the land, but public authorities, including the judiciary, have been hollowed out internally: this was primarily due to the court-packing at the highest levels of power and the deepening ideologisation of legal life, which is the work of the network of the captured state organs, organisations affiliated with the Law and Justice camp and the machine of social media. They all constitute an organised system of pressure on judges. Both the Polish Constitutional Court and the National Council of the

[4] A Hamilton, *The works of Alexander Hamilton; compris. his corresp. and his polit. and official writings, excl. of the federalist, civil and military*, ed by John C Hamilton, vol 2 (John F Trow,1850) 440.

[5] In the 2015 parliamentary election, the governing coalition 'United Right' obtained 235 out of 460 seats in the lower house (*Sejm*), supported by 37.58% of the voters (with voting participation slightly exceeding 50% of the whole voters' population). In the Senate, the respective numbers of seats won by the coalition equaled to 61 out of 100. It is worth noticing that the last 2019 election brought no change in terms of the number of seats in the lower house (in spite of the increase of the social support in absolute numbers), and still the number of Senators representing the governing parties in the upper house dropped to 48; cf https://parlament2015.pkw.gov.pl/; https://sejmsenat2019.pkw.gov.pl/sejmsenat2019/.

Judiciary have already become façade institutions and no longer play their usual role. The same fate will surely await the entire judicial system in a not too long period of time.

Although still classified as a country with a consolidated democratic system,[6] The Republic of Poland is undergoing deeply unfavourable transformations from the point of view of the future of democracy in the country and beyond.[7] Periodical analyses of the state of compliance with fundamental rights and freedoms by leading non-governmental organisations of the Western world show a gradual but uninterrupted tendency to limit fundamental rights and freedoms as well as the independence and impartiality of the courts. For the sake of giving an example, the report presented in 2018 by the American think-tank Freedom House shows a significant decrease in the degree of democratic governance mechanisms,[8] as well as the rapid decline in the index of independence of the judges and the judiciary. The overall assessment of the different factors of the assessment is shown in the table below:

Table 1 Nations in Transit Ratings and Averaged Scores: Poland © *Freedom House*

NIT Edition	2009	2010	2011	2012	2013	2014	2015	2016	2017	2018
National Democratic Governance	3.25	3.25	2.75	2.50	2.50	2.50	2.50	2.75	3.25	4.00
Electoral Process	2.00	1.75	1.50	1.25	1.25	1.25	1.50	1.50	1.50	1.50
Civil Society	1.50	1.50	1.50	1.50	1.50	1.50	1.50	1.50	1.75	2.00
Independent Media	2.00	2.25	2.25	2.25	2.50	2.50	2.50	2.75	3.00	3.00
Local Democratic Governance	2.00	1.75	1.75	1.75	1.75	1.50	1.50	1.50	1.75	2.00
Judicial Framework and Independence	2.25	2.50	2.50	2.50	2.50	2.50	2.50	2.75	3.25	4.25
Corruption	2.75	3.25	3.25	3.25	3.25	3.50	3.50	3.50	3.50	3.50
Democracy Score	2.25	2.32	2.21	2.14	2.18	2.18	2.21	2.32	2.57	2.89

Source: Freedom House.

[6] For a closer outlook of the general Polish position, see Freedom House, 'Democracy in Retreat: Freedom in the World 2019. Poland' at https://freedomhouse.org/country/poland/freedom-world/2019.

[7] Over the decade 2009–18: a decrease from 3.25 to 4.00 on a scale of 1 to 7 points, where 1 means a democratic regime, whereas 7 stands for an undemocratic one; see Freedom House, 'Nations in Transit 2018: Poland' at https://freedomhouse.org/sites/default/files/NiT2018_Poland_0.pdf.

[8] Over the decade 2009–18: a decrease from 3.25 to 4.00 on a scale of 1 to 7 points, where 1 means a democratic regime, whereas 7 stands for an undemocratic one. Basically, Poland is still classified as 'consolidated democracy'; Freedom House, *Nations in Transit 2018* (ibid).

In another report from the same organisation (2019) it was emphasised that despite the generally positive assessment of the fairness of the trial, a particularly high potential for influencing the course of proceedings and the politicisation of the judicial system results from the personal merger of the functions of the Minister of Justice and the Prosecutor General, which had effected in 2016. The authors of the report are also concerned about the scope of powers of special services to monitor the communication activity of citizens, including access to metadata and supervision of the movement of foreigners without the prior consent of the court (assessment of 3/4 points).[9] Mainly for these reasons in the category of the rule of law, Poland – albeit still qualified as a 'free country' – received from Freedom House an average partial rating of 11/16 points: relatively, the lowest in the whole survey.

Freedom House's rating is not isolated. As for various aspects of the changes introduced, it has been repeatedly confirmed in official positions and opinions of competent international organisations.[10] A deep regression in the field of the rule of law in Poland has been found, among others in the statement of third party interveners: Amnesty International and the International Commission of Jurists, lodged before the European Court of Human Rights in the case of *Jan Grzęda v Poland* (application no. 43572/18),[11] as well as in numerous scientific publications that have appeared in the last few years. No need to reiterate that in several recent judgments of the Court of Justice of the European Union, the most important aspects of the anti-constitutional populist backsliding taken against the EU law background have been summarised.[12]

The example of Poland compared to other countries of the Eastern Central Europe that are happening to undergo systemic crises is specific because, first, judges – for some material reasons that will be explained later on – were from the outset in the eye of the political storm; secondly, the evolution of the Polish case shows a radical and quite common disagreement and resistance of the lawyers' circles against the destruction of the structures of the democratic state ruled by law. Significantly, the voice of protest comes from within the Polish judiciary – it is the voice of the judges themselves, and mainly of common courts, being under the greatest pressure aimed at subordinating them completely to political authorities. It basically is due to

[9] Freedom House, *Poland*, s F2 (n 6).

[10] See, among others, Venice Commission, *Opinion on the draft act amending the act on the National Council of the Judiciary, on the draft act amending the act on the Supreme Court, proposed by the President of Poland, and on the act on the organization of ordinary courts adopted by the Venice Commission at its 113th Plenary Session (8–9 December 2017) – Opinion No. 904/2017*, at www.venice.coe.int/webforms/documents/default.aspx?pdffile=CDL-AD(2017)031-e; *Report of the UN Special Rapporteur on the independence of judges and lawyers on his mission to Poland*, A/HRC/38/38/Add.1, at http://doc.rmf.pl/rmf_fm/store/UN_REPORT.pdf; Proposal for a Council Decision on the determination of a clear risk of a serious breach by the Republic of Poland of the rule of law, COM (2017)835 final, 2017/0360 (NLE), at https://eur-lex.europa.eu/legal-content/EN/TXT/?uri=CELEX%3A52017PC0835.

[11] Amnesty International & International Commission of Jurists, *Written submissions on behalf of the Interveners*, at www.amnesty.org/download/Documents/EUR3714922019ENGLISH.PDF.

[12] cf CJEU judgments: of 25 July 2018, Case C-216/18 PPU *LM* [2019] 1 CMLR 18; Case C-619/18 *European Commission v Poland* [2020] 1 CMLR 6; Joined Cases C-585/18, C-624/18 and C-625/18 *AK v Krajowa Rada Sadownictwa* [2020] 2 CMLR 10; C-824/18 *AB and others v Krajowa Rada Sadownictwa (Nomination des juges à la Cour suprême – Recours)* http://curia.europa.eu/juris/documents.jsf?num=C-824/18.

the activity of judges' associations, which currently have several thousand members (approximately 40 per cent of the total number of judges),[13] that the aforesaid protests are noticeable not only in the country but also abroad.[14] It can be considered as a quite unique situation in the region, in which the activities of judges to defend the rule of law relatively rarely took on a massive character.[15]

Historically, one may be tempted to say that, in general, authoritarian inspired political actions rarely induce lawyers to contest them (and in any case this attitude characterises individuals rather than the entire environment). The probable reasons are twofold.

First, courts constitute a comfortable façade of normality, leaving a space for citizenry to easily adapt themselves to changes that adversely affect rights and freedoms of individuals when the institutional appearance of the status quo is maintained. Achieving these goals becomes in turn more difficult when the judiciary is undergoing profound transformation.[16] Even in countries that do not quite respect

[13] The exact statistics in this respect are not known; there are four main judicial associations as regards the common courts: Polish Judges' Association 'Iustitia' (*Stowarzyszenie Sędziów Polskich 'Iustitia'*, reporting circa 3,500 members), Judges' Association 'Themis' (*Stowarzyszenie Sędziów 'Themis'*, no data available), as well as three 'specialised' organisations: Association of Family Judges in Poland (*Stowarzyszenie Sędziów Rodzinnych w Polsce*, circa 260 members), Family Judges' Association 'Pro Familia' (*Stowarzyszenie Sędziów Rodzinnych 'Pro Familia'*, no data available), and the National Association of Administrative Courts' Judges (*Ogólnopolskie Stowarzyszenie Sędziów Sądów Administracyjnych*, no data available).

[14] Reports on the attitudes of Polish judges and public prosecutors towards the subjection of the judiciary to the executive are quite numerous, see eg AI, *Poland: Free Courts, Free People. Judges Standing for Their Independence* at www.amnesty.org/en/documents/eur37/0418/2019/en/, London: Amnesty International 2019; AI, *Poland 2019: The State of the Judiciary*, London: Amnesty International 2019, at www.amnesty.org/download/Documents/EUR3714032019ENGLISH.PDF; J Kościerzyński (ed), *Justice under pressure – repressions as a means of attempting to take control over the judiciary and the prosecution in Poland. Years 2015–2019*, Warsaw: Polish Judges' Association 'Iustitia' – 'Lex Super Omnia' Association of Prosecutors 2020 at www.iustitia.pl/images/pliki/raport2020/Raport_EN.pdf.

[15] As for instance in Hungary, where the protests of judges against the governmental interventions had been relatively weak, at least until open conflicts began between the newly established – and controlled by the parliamentary majority – National Judicial Office (*Országos Bírósági Hivatal Elnöke*, OBH) and an old National Judicial Council (*Országos Bírósági Tanacs*, OBT), the latter being one of the basic institutions of the judicial self-government. One of the most spectacular events was the stepping down by 5 members and 12 substitute members of the Council (OBT), which had (allegedly) been forced by the OBH and court presidents subject to it. Moreover, the mission undertaken by the European Association of Judges (EAJ) in April 2019 established other worrying facts, such as for instance drastic cut-off of public financing assigned to the Association of Hungarian Judges (*Magyar Bírói Egyesület*, MABIE). It seems quite interesting to note, however, that unlike in Poland, Hungarian judges have not been positioned by the government as a political enemy, hence reasons for wide-spread protests might so far have been perceived as questionable; cf S Gass, G Reissner, and G Woratsch, *Subcommittee of the EAJ Working Group on the Situation in Member Associations: Report on the fact-finding mission of the EAJ to Hungary*, 03/05/2019 at www.iaj-uim.org/iuw/wp-content/uploads/2019/05/Report-on-the-fact-finding-mission-of-a-delegation-of-the-EAJ-to-Hungary.pdf. The state of affairs in Bulgaria, which resembles that of Poland in terms of governmental verbal reactions to the manifestations of the judges' independence, looks even worse. Still, the Bulgarian judiciary as the whole remains silent; see *Report from the Commission to the European Parliament and the Council on Progress in Bulgaria under the Cooperation and Verification Mechanism*, 22.10.2019, COM(2019) 498 final; R Vassileva, 'Is Bulgaria's Rule of Law about to Die under the European Commission's Nose? The Country's Highest-Ranking Judge Fears So' at https://doi.org/10.17176/20190517-144144-0; S Stoychev, 'This is how Bulgarian Judicial Independence Ends … Not with a Bang but a Whimper: New Reforms Labelled as Implementation of EU Recommendations Endanger Judicial Independence in Bulgaria' at https://doi.org/10.17176/20190603-235634-0.

[16] HP Graver, *Judges Against Justice. On Judges When the Rule of Law is Under Attack* (Springer, 2015) 35.

the Western pattern of the rule of law, everyday social life is generally governed by some legal regime. Admittedly, authoritarian rulers do not respect the law as a regulator of political life; this, however, does not prevent average individuals from functioning according to legal provisions.[17]

Secondly, the judges usually are not revolutionaries and they do not rise up against authoritarianism. They are aware of their insecure position in the political system as well as their weakness vis-à-vis the executive, which inclines them to apply only a subtle pressure for political reform at the margins of political life.[18] By the way, such an approach appears to be beneficial for them. On the one hand, personal changes in the judiciary are rare, and if they do occur, it is by court-packing rather than by replacing existing judicial officers with completely new persons.[19] On the other hand, the quasi-natural judicial self-restraint is often motivated by the fear that an open demonstrating of one's beliefs and opinions may be qualified as contrary to the lawyers' ethos of the State service and thus be subject to disciplinary accountability.

Such attitudes are of course also noticeable in Poland, but they do not set the tone of public debate; the prevailing belief is that when facing the situation of a drastic threat to the rule of law, every lawyer – even a judge – has not only the right but also the duty to speak.

Why is the phenomenon of Polish resistance among lawyers so important? In our opinion, this is because the indifference of judges to the authoritarian agenda of legislative and executive authorities is contrary to the Constitution. The judiciary also holds a mandate from the people and cannot be indifferent to a violation of the fundamental law as an expression of the supreme will of the sovereign. Moreover, under specific circumstances – namely, when judges are facing overtly illegal actions against their independence, necessary in order to keep the fair trial guarantees – resistance to political pressures turns out to be the only way out. Such examples have not been uncommon in the recent history.[20] The true independence of the judiciary does not seem to constitute a significant value for authoritarian political formations: at best, it is a temporary state of things, and at worst – a fig leaf obscuring the emerging 'prerogative state'.[21] In the regimes moving from liberal democracy to electoral

[17] This is an essential conclusion of a well-known theory of the 'dual state' (*Der Doppelstaat*) worked out by Ernst Fraenkel. Far from the brutality and atrocities of the Third Reich, today's 'illiberal democracies' lean towards this dual mode of functioning, which makes this intellectual model fit for them; cf E Fraenkel (tr EA Shils), *The Dual State: A Contribution to the Theory of Dictatorship*, 1st edn (OUP, 2017).

[18] T Moustafa and T Ginsburg, *The Function of Courts in Authoritarian Politics* in T Ginsburg and T Moustafa (eds), *Rule by Law: The Politics of Courts in Authoritarian Regimes* (CUP, 2008) 14–15.

[19] As illustrated eg by cases of Nazi Germany or Pinochet's dictatorship in Chile – in both cases there was neither open struggle against, nor purges within, the judiciary, and the pressure on judges was rather indirect; Graver (n 16) 44–46.

[20] The crisis in the rule of law in Pakistan in 2007–08 provides an example: after having been revoked from the office by the President Pervez Musharraf, Chief Justice of the Supreme Court Iftikhar Muhammad Chaudhry began a successful fight for his reinstatement, which finally resulted in the resignation of Mr Musharraf; see ZS Ahmed and MJ Stephan, 'Fighting for the rule of law: civil resistance and the lawyers' movement in Pakistan' (2010) 17(3) *Democratization* 492 at https://doi.org/10.1080/13510341003700360.

[21] Fraenkel's model of the 'dual state', this term denominates the political sphere in an undemocratic government where, admittedly, there is a certain element of factual order and predictability in the behaviour of officials, yet still no legal rules govern the political sphere, the latter being regulated by

authoritarianism, the courts are only 'safe' insofar as they are willing to share and support the governmental policies and – as a result – they accept the supremacy of justice (or other values decreed by the rulers as 'fundamental for the nation') over applicable law.[22] This means that the loss of the independence of the courts and judges is actually an unavoidable consequence of moving away from (liberal) democracy, and at most only the measures used by the government for this purpose may differ.

Currently, judges, not for the first time in the history of Poland, are experiencing the correctness of the universal truth that maintaining judicial independence can be expensive.[23] The factors favouring the deterioration of the situation of judges in society are: the low culture of dispute resolution, the relative ease of influencing society by means of electronic media, and – which seems particularly important – the degree of trust in state institutions. Nowhere in the world does the judiciary have strong legitimacy, but it must constantly strive for it. Admittedly, the way courts properly carry out (or not) their public duties is not completely insignificant in terms of their perception by society, which may contribute to the level of support for politicians promising to strengthen political influence on the judiciary.

We believe, however, that the main reason for which the struggle for the Polish judiciary over last five years has been so uncompromised lies in the history of our modern statehood. In the common mind, administration of justice and law enforcement are associated with either foreign rule (Germany and Russia throughout the nineteenth and at the beginning of the twentieth centuries)[24] or more or less authoritarian regimes before and after World War II, in which the judiciary was not truly independent. Old clichés combined with the modern means of social influence greatly facilitate the government's attacks on judges and courts, based on arguments of its allegedly being detached from reality, corrupt, subject to undisclosed influences and neglecting the interests of individuals. The thing, however, is not the (rather questionable) veracity of these allegations, but the real danger of deepening the state

'arbitrary measures' and discretionary prerogatives of the dominant officials. Hence the expression 'Prerogative State' (*Massnahmenstaat*); Fraenkel (n 17) 3. The other side of the coin is the so-called 'normative state', standing for the sphere of individuals' everyday life, still subject to either the traditionally prevailing or the newly enacted law; ibid 57. Both 'states' build up a 'dual state', where the law gives way to, and may not overrule, political orders. Being very far from brutality and atrocities of the Third Reich, today's 'illiberal democracies' tend to take after the aforementioned way of functioning of the political sphere, which makes this intellectual model fit to them.

[22] cf an interview of a German broadcaster and media publisher 'Deutsche Welle' (DW) with the current Prime Minister of Poland Mr Mateusz Morawiecki, the latter stating that '[o]f course the law is not the most important. The life of people and security is'; see AS Brändlin, 'Mateusz Morawiecki: EU "completely misunderstood the situation"' at www.dw.com/en/mateusz-morawiecki-eu-completely-misunderstood-the-situation/a-37547967; a backup copy at https://archive.org/details/DW_20171228_000200_Conflict_Zone_-_Guest_Mateusz_Morawiecki.

[23] cf J Clifford Wallace, 'An Essay on Independence of the Judiciary: Independence from What and Why' (2001–2003) 58(2) *New York University Annual Survey of American Law* 241, 245.

[24] Rarely was a judicial profession truly appreciated in the Polish society. During the era of partitions of Poland by three powers: Russia, Austria, and Prussia (Germany), which lasted from 1795 to 1914, members of the native Polish population were appointed as magistrates practically only in the Austrian part (besides the German Austrians), whereas in both Russia and Prussia there were virtually no Polish judges (with only single exceptions in Russian lower courts). Together with imposed codes of law (as the old Polish law was practically abandoned), this way of doing things created a constant prejudgment toward the courts as something odd, suspect, and hardly understandable.

of anomie. Even though the government's fight against the judiciary has so far taken the forms of both symbolic (slander in mass and social media) and legal violence (repressions through disciplinary and criminal law instruments), which resembles similar events from the past century, the dynamics of the current conflict does not rule out even its worst evolution. The Turkish example indicates that this is possible.[25]

Before proceeding to the detailed considerations, it seems worth explaining why in the title of our contribution we refer to 'authoritarianism' instead of a commonly used term 'illiberal democracy'. First of all, we are fully aware that, for the time being, Poland may well be perceived as a (still) democratic state and it will probably remain such as long as the elections are not openly manipulated by the government. Indeed, various terms may be used to denote the phenomenon, for example the departure from democracy in Poland after 2015, for example abusive constitutionalism, populist constitutionalism, bad faith constitutionalism, de-constitutionalism, autocratic legalism, constitutional retrogression, constitutional capture, authoritarianisation, constitutional decay; other specialist terms include, for instance, constitutional rot, democratic deconsolidation, democratic backsliding, authoritarian backsliding, rule of law backsliding, illiberal democracy, majoritarian autocracy, and authoritarian constitutionalism.[26] However, the thing is not in the name, but in an overall direction of the march, whereas the thunderous slogans about strengthening the rule of the people conceal a completely different purpose. Even the electoral process in Poland is in fact reminiscent of a plebiscite rather, where there is no space for free competition of views and opinions on what is beneficial for the nation and state, and the renewal of the mandate of the government majority in the parliament serves just as a *placet* for them to exercise arbitrary rule for the next term of office. The lack of respect for the judiciary as one of the true bearers of authority is also a litmus test of dubious democratism of the current form of government, and hence it fully authorises the use of the term 'authoritarianism'.

The rest of the present chapter will be divided into three sections. The upcoming one briefly presents the most important features of the legal regulation of the Polish judiciary. The meaning of its functioning from the point of view of the democratic system of government will be explained. The following part of the chapter will contain a closer insight into the reasons and consequences of the weakening independence of the Polish judiciary since 2015. The last part of the contribution is in turn devoted to the problem of legitimacy of the judiciary in the region of Eastern Central Europe (ECE). We are of the opinion that the Polish legal elites have been

[25] A step-by-step slipping of the Turkish judiciary into dependence on the government has been evidenced in many contributions, see E Özbudun, 'Pending Challenges in Turkey's Judiciary' (Istanbul: Istanbul Policy Center-Sabanci University-Stiftung Mercator Initiative, 2015) at www.iai.it/en/pubblicazioni/pending-challenges-turkeys-judiciary; B Saatçioğlu, 'De-Europeanisation in Turkey: The case of the rule of law' (2016) 21(1) *South European Society and Politics* 133; M Yilmaz, *A török politikai rendszer átalakulása 2002 és 2018 között* (Transformation of the Turkish political system between 2002 and 2018), PhD diss. (Budapesti Corvinus Egyetem, 2019) at http://phd.lib.uni-corvinus.hu/1061/1/Yilmaz_Mehmet_dhu.pdf.

[26] TG Daly, 'Democratic Decay: Conceptualising an Emerging Research Field' (2019) 11 *Hague Journal on the Rule of Law* 9, 11.

disregarding the open debate on the role of law in society, by treating it as an instrument of governance, which resulted in a huge deficit of knowledge and understanding for the functions of judges and courts in society. This certainly does not make it easier for judges to reclaim their individual independence, as well as the independence of the judiciary as a whole, although it can also be a chance for more serious self-reflections.

The main thesis of this chapter indicates that there are moments in history in which the legitimacy of the judiciary may no longer be gained by sound carrying out of judicial activities. Irrespective of the legal constraints imposed upon judges, there is a need for their active and continuous participation in the public debate. Without increasing the level of this participation, the whole field will be captured by the populist demagogues; it will no longer be possible to strengthen the legitimacy of the judiciary, in recent years dramatically weakened in Poland and other ECE countries by the return of authoritarianism. A common slogan of majoritarian rulers that the judiciary should abide by every law enacted by Parliament as it does not have the necessary democratic mandate to contest it, is in our view ill-founded. Judges' mandate to oppose authoritarian rule imposed on the people in the name of the people comes directly from the Constitution as the supreme expression of the sovereign will in any modern Nation-State.

II. POINT OF DEPARTURE: POLISH JUDICIARY IN 2015

A substantive analysis of the Polish rule of law crisis would be hardly conceivable without considering the state of affairs at the time when it began, that is, in October 2015. After a period of communist rule, which during the last decade of the Polish People's Republic had been becoming more and more façade-like, the Polish judiciary seemed to be stronger than ever before. Undoubtedly, it had undergone a profound transformation in both the institutional and substantive dimension.

The most important part of the institutional reforms amounted to creating the structure of institutions of the judicial self-government, which – in a wider sense of the term – included the National Council of the Judiciary (*Krajowa Rada Sądownictwa*). It was one of the central postulates of the 'Solidarity' movement as regards judicial reforms, put forth as early as in 1980–81.[27] In this way, the judges were to be freed from the sword of Damocles over their heads: the possibility of dismissal at any time by the State Council (a collective head of the Communist state) at the request of the Minister of Justice due to the lack of a 'guarantee of the proper performance of the

[27] M Celej, 'Działalność Krajowej Rady Sądownictwa w latach 1990–2015' (2015) 1 *Krajowa Rada Sądownictwa* 22; K Grajewski, 'Postulat utworzenia rady do spraw sądownictwa podczas obrad Okrągłego Stołu' (2017) 3 *Krajowa Rada Sądownictwa* 25, 28. The ideas of democratisation of the administration of justice were worked out on a step-by-step basis, mainly by the Section of the Administration of Justice Employees of the 'Solidarity' Trade Union, starting from October 1990; see K Niewiński, *PZPR a sądownictwo w latach 1980–1985. Próby powstrzymania solidarnościowej rewolucji*, PhD dissertation (Uniwersytet w Białymstoku, 2016) 63.

judge's duties'.[28] A new independent body, mostly composed of the judges elected by their peers, was to become a guardian of judicial independence, taking part in the procedure of judges' nominations, as well as their promotions to higher-tier courts. The idea was put into operation as the result of the findings of the Round Table at the beginning of 1989. The National Council of the Judiciary was established very quickly; the then Constitution was amended in April 1989, and at the beginning of 1990 the Council commenced its regular work.[29] It has to be stressed, then, that the creation of the aforementioned body was not imposed upon the state as the result of the systemic transformation, for example by the CE standards or the like, but a carefully reflected domestic concept stood behind it.[30]

Structure of the judicial self-government understood in a stricter sense comprised general assemblies of judges (*zgromadzenia ogólne sędziów*) at the level of courts' districts, which delegated their members to the courts' colleges (*kolegia sądów*). Again, they were roughly based on the original concepts of the 'Solidarity' movement worked out already in 1981;[31] the assemblies were to put an end to a bad practice of the communist times of the total control of the Ministry of Justice over the judiciary, the emblematic example of which was appointments and dismissals of presidents of courts without any opinion or consultation by the local judicial community. This idea was also implemented into legislation as a result of legislative changes resulting from the political conference of the Round Table in 1989, although not without profound controversies between the bargaining partners – and not entirely.[32]

Generally speaking, organs of judicial self-government have become an important element of the administration of justice, giving the opportunity to express positions on important matters, and – most importantly – taking part in the process of the appointment and dismissal of chief judges.[33] Irrespective of an initial far-reaching programme of endowing the judges' assemblies themselves with the personnel governance prerogatives, the lawgiver finally decided to leave these matters to the Minister of Justice, though under control of the self-governmental organs: until the 2017 reforms, the appointment of presidents and vice-presidents of the courts was preceded by an obligatory opinion of the respective judges' assembly (at the level of the regional court's district or, as appropriate, the appellate circuit).[34] At the same time, the dismissal of presidents and vice-presidents in the course of the six-year term of office took place upon the consent of the National Council of the Judiciary; if this

[28] Grajewski (n 27) 26.

[29] Celej (n 27) 22.

[30] Grajewski (n 27) 28–29; A Śledzińska-Simon, 'The Rise and Fall of Judicial Self-Government in Poland: On Judicial Reform Reversing Democratic Transition' (2018) 19(7) *German Law Journal* 1839, 1842.

[31] In accordance with the original concepts, the whole composition of the courts' college, responsible for the current governance and key personal decisions concerning the court's staff, was to be elected by the general assemblies of judges of the given district, with the presidents of the courts and their deputies as non-voting members; Niewiński (n 27) 114.

[32] K Trembicka, 'Stagnacja czy zmiana? Wymiar sprawiedliwości przy Okrągłym Stole' (2018) 3 *Przegląd Sejmowy* 143, 149.

[33] Śledzińska-Simon (n 30) 1847.

[34] See Articles 23–25 of the Law of 27 July 2001 on the Structure of Common Courts (*ustawa z dnia 27 lipca 2001 r. – Prawo o ustroju sądów powszechnych*), the then consolidated text: Dz. U. of 2015 item 133, as amended; cf Niewiński (n 27) 386–87.

opinion was negative, changes in the position of the president and vice president of the court were in principle not possible.[35]

Institutional changes brought by the systemic turnover of 1989–90 were also important in terms of the transformation of the courts' structure. It was gradually rebuilt: instead of the hitherto system comprising district (*sądy rejonowe*) and voivodeship (*sądy wojewódzkie*) courts, and the Supreme Court (SC) carrying out both appellate and extraordinary judicial control, the lawgiver introduced a more complex chain of ordinary courts: district, regional (*okręgowe*), and appellate (*apelacyjne*) courts, whereas the SC became responsible solely for appeals in cassation and other means of the supervision over the correctness of the interpretation and application of law. Until 1997, all the key court procedures (civil and criminal ones) were amended so as to cut the ties with old Soviet-styled models and model them again on Western patterns.

Finally, after the entering into force of the new democratic Constitution of 1997, the administrative courts – in Poland quite detached from the ordinary courts – were enhanced through the establishment of the two-tier structure: instead of a one-instance Supreme Administrative Court (*Naczelny Sąd Administracyjny*), the voivodeship administrative courts (*wojewódzkie sądy administracyjne*) became the first-instance courts in public law matters, while the SAC became the higher court, and its President was endowed with wide prerogatives pertaining to the whole court staff administration and budget of the administrative courts. Unfortunately, no comparable operation took place as to the common courts, still subject to the administrative supervision of the Minister of Justice.

Last but not least, the lawgiver put an end to the criticised terms of office of the Supreme Court justices, which was one of the main means of securing the judges' leniency to the communist party. In 1990 the whole composition of the SC was renewed: judges underwent a re-appointment procedure involving the newly created National Council of the Judiciary, which resulted in the replacement of about 81 per cent of the composition of this Court. As for 2020, all those appointed for the first time before 1990 either retired or were deceased.[36] Admittedly, the judges of common courts kept their mandate untouched. Still, with the passing of time those who had acted against the fundamental rights and freedoms left the judiciary after 1990, usually due to retirement or by changing profession. Today's judiciary, 30 years after the collapse of the Soviet Block, has nothing in common with the past.

[35] Article 27 of the Law (n 34).

[36] Under the Act of 20 December 1989 amending the Law on the structure of common courts, the Act on the Supreme Court, the Act on the Supreme Administrative Court, the Act on the Constitutional Tribunal, the Act on the structure of military courts and the Law on Notaries (*ustawa z 20 grudnia 1989 r. o zmianie ustaw – Prawo o ustroju sądów powszechnych, o Sądzie Najwyższym, o Naczelnym Sądzie Administracyjnym, o Trybunale Konstytucyjnym, o ustroju sądów wojskowych i Prawo o notariacie*), Dz.U. No. 73, item 436, the five-year term of office of SN judges was abolished, and their irremovability was introduced. The five-year term of office of the Supreme Court at that time was shortened and ended on 30 June 1990 (Article 9 of the Act). The new composition of the Court was appointed by the President of the Republic of Poland on 4 June 1990. A total of 57 judges were appointed to the four chambers, including 22 from the previous composition of the Supreme Court.

In substantive terms, the opposition representing the 'Solidarity' social movement took much care regarding the constitutional guarantees of judicial independence. In and after 1990, it was effected in various ways.

Firstly, the Round Table established the division of powers and independence of the judiciary as the principles underpinning the new democratic rule of law. There were differences in this matter, since the communist party, although it verbally in 1989 rejected the previously binding principle of uniformity of state power, was unwilling to fully accept the resulting consequences. There was no agreement as to the assessment of Polish People's Republic as a law-abiding state: while according to the opposition's viewpoint the independence of judges and courts was not respected at all, the communist rulers declared their will to 'deepen the independence of the judiciary', which, in their opinion, truly existed. Quite interestingly, Mr Jarosław Kaczyński – one of the participants of the Round Table talks – proclaimed at that time that the courts needed to be 'neutral towards the political forces that currently controlled the executive'.[37]

Secondly, a solid foundation for the respect and the guarantees of the fundamental rights and freedoms have been created over years. The 1997 Constitution, aimed at consolidating democracy and the rule of law,[38] declares the rule of law in the sense close to the German idea of the '*Rechtsstaat*'.[39] It was not an empty declaration; a common understanding of this principle resulted from dozens of rulings of the Constitutional Tribunal. Also the courts, including the Supreme Court, vested – as all the adjudicative state organs – with a prerogative of the direct application of the Constitution,[40] had numerous occasions to refer to the rules and directives derived from, or forming part of, the rule of law principle. The Polish Constitution imposes limits on the scope of the public authorities' competence,[41] at the same time it provides for the principle of separation of powers.[42] As to the constitutional review, it has been entrusted to a special body – the Constitutional Tribunal – directly characterised by the Polish fundamental law (though not without substantive doubts) as a judicial authority.[43] It is significant from the point of view of the Polish dispute over the status

[37] Trembicka (n 32) 148.

[38] Constitution of the Republic of Poland of 2 April 1997, Dz. U. 1997 No. 78, item 483, as amended. Full text of the Constitution available at www.sejm.gov.pl/prawo/konst/angielski/kon1.htm.

[39] Article 2: The Republic of Poland shall be a democratic state ruled by law and implementing the principles of social justice. For a wide review of the content of the rule of law in the Polish legal system, cf S Wronkowska (ed), *Zasada demokratycznego państwa prawnego w Konstytucji RP* (Wydawnictwo Sejmowe, 2006).

[40] Article 8: The provisions of the Constitution shall apply directly, unless the Constitution provides otherwise.

[41] Article 7: The organs of public authority shall function on the basis of, and within the limits of, the law.

[42] Article 10: (1) The system of government of the Republic of Poland shall be based on the separation of and balance between the legislative, executive and judicial powers. (2) Legislative power shall be vested in the Sejm and the Senate, executive power shall be vested in the President of the Republic of Poland and the Council of Ministers, and the judicial power shall be vested in courts and tribunals.

[43] Article 188. Whether or not the Tribunal should be viewed as the only State organ competent to carry out constitutional review, used to be one of the most debatable issues among Polish academia. Some Polish authors allowed the refusal to apply legal provisions contrary to the Constitution, which would bring the Polish model of constitutional control closer to the American *judicial review*, although this view has so

of the judiciary that there exists a general constitutional obligation to comply with international law,[44] as well as an express supremacy of ratified international treaties and secondary law of the European Union.[45] From this point of view, the Polish government, which by citing the Constitution ostentatiously underestimates the importance of numerous interventions of international and European institutions in defence of the independence of the courts and judges from other branches of government, may have a problem with crediting its position, at least in external relations. The constitutional framework for the role of a judge is marked with a primordial significance of its separation from the other state authorities. Its sole function shall be the administration of justice.[46] The exposed political position of judges, who are subject only to the Constitution and statutory law in the exercising of their duties, correlates with this legal rule.[47] Consequently, the judges undoubtedly cannot accept any orders or suggestions regarding the content of their judgments. This stability and separation of other authorities serves the final aim of the realisation of the right to the court, enshrined in Article 45 of the Constitution, in line with both the European and international standards.

Thirdly, much effort was done to cut off judges from political circles and undue influences. Not only were judges prevented from any party membership (which, to be sure, used to be practised during the communist times), but furthermore, the 1997 Constitution, aimed at consolidating democracy and the rule of law,[48] expressly limited public activity of judges outside the office they hold.[49] Ongoing disputes over the extent of the judges' commitment to silence on 'political' matters cast a shadow over attempts to debate on newly introduced judicial reforms. Preventing judges from public activities incompatible with the independence of courts and judges is a harsh price of life tenure: Polish law does not accept the term of office at any level of the judiciary, and the judges are generally appointed for life by the President of the Republic of Poland at the request of the National Council of

far not gained the support of majority; R Hauser and J Trzciński, 'O formach kontroli konstytucyjności prawa przez sądy' (2008) 52(2) *Ruch Prawniczy, Ekonomiczny i Socjologiczny* 9; cf W Kręcisz, 'Stanowisko sądów powszechnych wobec bezpośredniego stosowania Konstytucji RP' in K Działocha (ed), *Bezpośrednie stosowanie Konstytucji Rzeczypospolitej Polskiej* (Warszawa, 2005) 114.

[44] Article 9: The Republic of Poland shall respect international law binding upon it.

[45] Article 91: (1) After promulgation thereof in the Journal of Laws of the Republic of Poland (Dziennik Ustaw), a ratified international agreement shall constitute part of the domestic legal order and shall be applied directly, unless its application depends on the enactment of a statute. (2) An international agreement ratified upon prior consent granted by statute shall have precedence over statutes if such an agreement cannot be reconciled with the provisions of such statutes. (3) If an agreement, ratified by the Republic of Poland, establishing an international organization so provides, the laws established by it shall be applied directly and have precedence in the event of a conflict of laws.

[46] See Articles 173 and 175(1).

[47] Article 178(1): Judges, within the exercise of their office, shall be independent and subject only to the Constitution and statutes.

[48] Constitution of the Republic of Poland of 2 April 1997, Dz. U. 1997 No. 78, item 483, as amended. Full text of the Constitution available at https://www.sejm.gov.pl/prawo/konst/angielski/kon1.htm.

[49] Article 178(3): A judge shall not belong to a political party, a trade union or perform public activities incompatible with the principles of independence of the courts and judges.

the Judiciary.[50] The latter is a mixed body, but with a predominance of judges;[51] in the literature, as well as in the jurisprudence of the Constitutional Tribunal before 2015, there was a well-established view that 15 judges to the Council should be elected by their peers.[52]

From a general perspective, it seems to be uncontroversial to say that the Polish judiciary before the entry into force of the 2017 reforms of the Law and Justice party that are discussed below fulfilled all the requirements of independence in both collective and individual aspects of the notion. Of course, it would be hard to deny that there were some problems and deficiencies. First and foremost, the courts' jurisdiction used to be extended by the lawgiver without looking at the social cost of such an operation. On the one hand it was the result of the worldwide judicialisation of politics and the social life, and on the other hand – a side effect of a freely taken decision to impose obligations on the courts, the implementation of which by other authorities, in conditions of limited confidence in their impartiality and independence, could cause opposition among the people or reduce the already low trust in state institutions. In this way, for instance, the judges became deeply involved in the electoral administration (characteristically, not only in an examination of the validity of the elections and referenda),[53] adjudication in all the minor offences, which before 1990 had been assigned to quasi-judicial bodies (*kolegia do spraw wykroczeń*) controlled by the local state administration[54] – not to mention a rapidly expanding registration matters (land and mortgage register, company registers), etc.

Together with the rising number of cases,[55] the aforementioned overburdening of the courts and the judges with extrajudicial or trivial work resulted in slowing down

[50] See Article 179.

[51] Article 187(1): The National Council of the Judiciary shall be composed as follows: (1) the First President of the Supreme Court, the Minister of Justice, the President of the Supreme Administrative Court and an individual appointed by the President of the Republic; (2) 15 judges chosen from amongst the judges of the Supreme Court, common courts, administrative courts and military courts; (3) 4 members chosen by the Sejm from amongst its Deputies and 2 members chosen by the Senate from amongst its Senators.

[52] See eg T Ereciński, 'Pozycja ustrojowa Krajowej Rady Sądownictwa' in A Dębiński, A Grześkowiak and K Wiak (eds), *Ius et lex: księga jubileuszowa ku czci Profesora Adama Strzembosza* (Katolicki Uniwersytet Lubelski, 2002) 266; L Garlicki, *Konstytucja Rzeczypospolitej Polskiej. Komentarz*, vol IV, (Warszawa: Wydawnictwo Sejmowe, 2005), Article 187 No 3; M Jabłoński, 'Uwagi o ewolucji gwarancji niezawisłości i niezależności sędziów i sądów powszechnych' in J Trzciński and B Banaszak (eds), *Studia nad prawem konstytucyjnym, Acta Universitatis Wratislaviensis. Prawo CCLVII* (Uniwersytet Wrocławski, 1997) 124–25; D Górecki et al, *Polskie prawo konstytucyjne*, 4th edn (Wolters Kluwer Polska, 2012) 219; H Zięba-Załucka, *Władza ustawodawcza, wykonawcza i sądownicza w Konstytucji Rzeczypospolitej Polskiej* (LexisNexis, 2002) 295–97; CT judgment of 18 July 2007, case No K 25/07, OTK-A 2007, No 7, item 80.

[53] See A Sokala and M Święcki, 'Administracja wyborcza w III Rzeczypospolitej Polskiej (struktura organizacyjna i charakter prawny)' in F Rymarz (ed), *Iudices electionis custodes (sędziowie kustoszami wyborów). Księga pamiątkowa Państwowej Komisji Wyborczej* (Wydawnictwo Krajowego Biura Wyborczego, 2007) 167.

[54] Trembicka (n 32) 153; Niewiński (n 27) 21.

[55] Even within the period of five years 2011–15, the number of new cases in the Polish courts rose from 13.5 to 15.2 million; the number of the matters resolved was more or less equal to it, except for 2013, when it was significantly lower than the incoming cases. As the result, in 2015 the 'old' cases pending before the courts rose up to circa 2.3 million; see *Analiza statystyczna działalności sądów powszechnych: rok 2015 na tle lat 2011–2014 – wybrane zagadnienia* (Ministerstwo Sprawiedliwości, 2016) at https://isws.ms.gov.pl/pl/baza-statystyczna/publikacje/download,2779,2.html 4.

the proceedings and a growing social dissatisfaction and criticism. With the passing of time, there was an appetite for conspiracy theories. Unfortunately, the lack of serious political will to improve the functioning of the administration of justice over the recent years created a climate to use the judiciary as a scapegoat. Still, we have every right to argue that there were no systemic problems with the rule of law or corruption among the judges, and courts' activities until 2015 were fully acceptable in the light of an average European output. The reasons for the current fierce struggle with the judiciary have to be sought mostly outside, not inside it.

III. POLISH JUDGES AND THE TRAP OF 'ILLIBERAL LEGALISM'. DIAGNOSIS OF THE CAUSES AND EFFECTS OF POLITICAL CHANGES IN POLAND IN 2015–20

The state of social emotions, with strong resentment beneath, could easily be intensified and exploited by today's populist leaders:[56] it is precisely the case with Poland. Systemic problems with the rule of law in Poland do not result from the courts' faults or negligence but rather from the social disrespect for, and distrust of, the legal mechanisms. We argue that not only does the society not treat the rule of law seriously, even worse: it does not understand its meaning.

Although the doctrine of the rule of law has been evolving gradually throughout centuries, and it still does not have uniform content in various Nation-States, it is possible to point out its core elements which matter virtually everywhere. First, it is followed by the existence of a system of law binding without exception on all those who are under the jurisdiction of a given state; secondly, the dispersing, dividing and balancing each of the state authorities in such a way that the rights and freedoms of individuals can be protected, and the allegation of arbitrariness of actions and omissions of the legislature or the executive – duly assessed by courts which remain separate and independent of the other authorities.[57]

The preservation of the system based on the rule of law is today an unquestionable duty of states, explicitly enshrined in numerous acts of international law and thus constituting one of the principles of the *jus gentium*;[58] one can be tempted to declare

[56] T Drinóczi and A Bień-Kacała, 'Illiberal Constitutionalism: The Case of Hungary and Poland' (2019) 20 *German Law Journal* 1140, 1145.

[57] D von der Pfordten, 'On the foundations of the Rule of Law and the Principle of the Legal State/ Rechtsstaat', in JR Silkenat, JE Hickey Jr and PD Barenboim (eds), *The Legal Doctrines of the Rule of Law and the Legal State (Rechtsstaat)* (Springer, 2014) 15 et seq; M Loughlin, *The rule of law in European jurisprudence* (Venice Commission Study 512/2009), CLD-DEM(2009)006, at www.venice.coe.int/webforms/ documents/default.aspx?pdffile=CDL-DEM(2009)006-e, with further reference to other sources.

[58] There are, to be sure, doubts about the exact scope of respect for the rule of law among contemporary members of the international community. Some authors tend to believe that the community of elementary values and principles constituting the rule of law may be considered to include only Western states, while other states either by definition reject or modify it according to their own perceptions of the role and place of law; cf R Gosalbo-Bono, 'The Significance of the Rule of Law and Its Implications for the European Union and the United States' (2010) 72 *University of Pittsburgh Law Review* 229, 288–90. It should be noticed, however, that the rule of law is recognised in a number of contemporary international treaties, not necessarily 'Western' ones, eg the UN International Covenant on Civil and Political Rights (signed and ratified by 172 states), UNTS 999, 171; 1057, 407; here, in spite of the silence of the Covenant as to the rule of law itself, its expression may be found especially in the provision regarding the right to a fair trial 'according to the law', namely Article 14(1); N Kaufman Hevener and SA Mosher, 'General

a universal obligation on this basis, in a sense of an obligation of customary international law (*consuetudo*). Without the rule of law, it would be difficult to imagine the peaceful cooperation of states ready to guarantee to their citizens the right to enjoy a minimum of rights in a globalised world, thus realising their individual freedom to establish cross-border legal relations, which are so necessary in the field of trade and everyday human life.[59]

Formally speaking, Polish society in 1989 was ready to accept the rule of law as one of foundations of liberal democracy and massively rejected the authoritarian regime. However, these attitudes were not accompanied by a profound reflection on what a nation Poland is and what it should be. It was caused by the fact that after the collapse of communism, the body of law – as many times before in history – did not emerge naturally from the country's own tradition but was based on Western 'legal transplants'. The changes were rapid and, to some extent, revolutionary. Within this framework, law was not treated as an autonomous value but rather as a means of social engineering. The prevailing belief was that communism, along with all normative content, was a foreign system imposed on Poles by the Soviet Union.

With this assumption, it was easy to treat any systemic deficiencies until 1989, such as the lacking rule of law, human rights guarantees, and the independence of the judiciary, as simply crossed out as the system changed and the necessary black-letter rules found themselves in the hastily revised legal provisions. The enactment of the Constitution of the Republic of Poland, developed by a group of experts over the years 1989–97,[60] was treated as a final chord in the composition of the Third Republic, permanently included in the European western community of nations. Hardly anyone among jurists paid attention to a relatively weak societal foundation of the new regime[61] and the disturbing, authoritarian models of Polish constitutionalism from the past preceding World War II. Discussions on the regime transition

Principles of Law and the UN Covenant on Civil and Political Rights' (1978) 27(3) *The International and Comparative Law Quarterly* 596, 610 (with further reference to national constitutions of the then UN states); as to an express provision on the rule of law, see eg Article 2(2)(h) of the Charter of the Association of Southeast Asian Nations (ASEAN), UNTS 2624, 223; on the international rule of law, see KJ Keith, 'The International Rule of Law' (2015) 28(3) *Leiden Journal of International Law* 403, at https://doi.org/10.1017/S0922156515000199. A Watts, 'The International Rule of Law' (1993) 36 *German Yearbook of International Law* 15; J Crawford, 'International Law and the Rule of Law' (2003) 24 *Adelaide Law Review* 3.

[59] The idea of 'perpetual peace' by Immanuel Kant, based on the peaceful federation of states (*foedus pacificum*) whose constitutions establish a 'republican rule' seems to be heading in this direction. Kant seemed to understand this as, first and foremost, a guarantee of the minimum freedom of individuals and their formal equality before the law, and this irrespective of the concrete form of government; moreover, these rights were to be universally recognised in all the states concerned. Equal guarantees of the rights and freedoms of individuals everywhere create a 'cosmopolitan right' (*hospitalitas*), which is – figuratively speaking – their right to be free and equally treated everywhere, enforceable against any sovereign; see I Kant, *Perpetual peace and other essays* (Hackett Publishing, 1983) 107.

[60] In a nutshell, cf R Mojak, 'Geneza, prawnoustrojowe zasady i prawne procedury tworzenia i uchwalenia Konstytucji Rzeczypospolitej Polskiej z 2 kwietnia 1997 r.' (2018) *Gdańskie Studia Prawnicze* 40.

[61] As rightly remarked by one of the authors, the process by which the Constitution was ratified has contributed to the crisis of legitimacy. It was ratified on 25 May 1997 by a bare majority of 52.7% in a public referendum in which only 43% of eligible voters participated. Thus, fewer than one-quarter of the electorate actually approved the supreme law of the land; DH Cole, 'Poland's 1997 Constitution in Its Historical Context' (1998) *Saint Louis-Warsaw Trans-Atlantic Law Journal* 1, 2 at www.repository.law.indiana.edu/facpub/589.

covered the European aspirations of the country's elite and the associated modernising efforts of the entire society. Meanwhile, the old ghosts have just returned with the frostbite of the concepts and disputes, which seem to have long been forgotten.

A great danger for the emerging rule of law in Poland soon became the myth of the Polish interwar statehood (1918–39). The dream of its restoration was strongly manifested in both the Solidarity movement and the democratic state it had founded. Some parts of the political and legal elites of the post-authoritarian state openly put forth a utopian project of removing the legal system in force and directly replacing it with the provisions as from the date of the outbreak of World War II.[62] Was it a dream of a liberal democratic state, with the substantive rule of law and the courts independent from the political authorities? Not at all. From 1926 to 1939 Poland was consolidating itself as an authoritarian dictatorship.[63] To be sure, the scale of the political persecutions can hardly be compared with any of the European fascist regimes, not to mention Hitler's Germany or Stalin's Soviet Union; nonetheless, the then state as a whole was not law-abiding.[64] The division of branches of government, the separation of judiciary, as well as the guarantees for the stability of the judicial tenures were not respected. In 1929 and 1932 purges in the Polish judiciary touched approximately 600 judges, including the Presidents of the Supreme Court, Aleksander Mogilnicki and Władysław Seyda.[65] Only rarely do these regrettable events arouse the interest of historians of law.

In view of what has been written, it is easier to understand the current state of affairs. The government, whose members for years used to glorify interwar Poland as a model for the present, also in terms of the legal system, is suspected of implementing an undemocratic agenda. Nation's sovereignty as the reason for actions against the 'postcommunist' Constitution in the mouth of the rulers somehow resembles the sense of Schmittian 'political':

> Hobbes has drawn these simple consequences of political thought without confusion and more clearly than anyone else. He has emphasized time and again that the sovereignty of law means only the sovereignty of men who draw up and administer this law. The rule of a higher order, according to Hobbes, is an empty phrase if it does not signify politically that certain men of this higher order rule over men of a lower order.[66]

[62] A particularly illustrative example of this attitude was the conference organised some years ago by the Polish upper house (*Senat*) entitled symbolically 'Restoration of legal continuity between the Third Republic of Poland and the Second Republic of Poland – implications and consequences'; see M Lipińska and E Przychodaj (ed.), *Przywrócenie ciągłości prawnej między III Rzecząpospolitą Polską i II Rzecząpospolitą Polską – implikacje i konsekwencje* (Senat, 1999).

[63] G Ławnikowicz, 'Z rozważań nad polskim autorytaryzmem. Pewność stanowiska sędziego w Konstytucji kwietniowej' (2019) 66(1) *Annales Universitatis Mariae Curie-Skłodowska Lublin-Polonia, Sectio G* 237, 238.

[64] Even the last Polish pre-war Constitution, called the 'April' one (as it was deemed to be in force as from 23 April 1935), was adopted by the *Sejm* in 1934 with a simple procedural trick, without the necessary quorum, and hence formally it has never been in force. Still, both courts and scholarly authors have constantly referred to it in terms of the binding law of the country; cf GM Kowalski, 'The Amendment of August 1926 to the first Polish Constitution of the Second Republic' (2014) 7(2) *Krakowskie Studia z Historii Państwa i Prawa* 317.

[65] A Mogilnicki, *Wspomnienia adwokata i sędziego* (Wolters Kluwer, 2016) 330.

[66] C Schmitt (tr G Schwab), *The Concept of the Political* (University of Chicago Press, 2007) 67.

Illiberal democracy – in Poland and elsewhere – does not mean carrying out the will of the people. It means the rule of those who 'best know what it really is'. Hence it is at odds with both the substantive rule of law and the judge's mandate in the state where the latter is a constitutional principle.

Putting aside, however, these dilemmas regarding the allocation of the power with the people, Polish political practice asks a question whether a Polish sovereign (whoever its nature is) can freely decide on how to shape its law, what its content should be and how it is to be applied. Although it goes beyond the scope of this chapter, one can sketch the direction of such an answer: the international recognition of the rule of law as one of the general principles of law limits the margin of discretion of the state when it comes to establishing, interpreting, and applying internal law. Even if the international community today is not competent to impose on any government the concept or interpretation of its internal legal order in accordance with the requirements derived from the 'core' of the rule of law (and, as a consequence, there are states disregarding this principle), it is precisely because of a widespread international concept of the rule of law that the basic standards of the states' behaviour can be set and, furthermore, sanctions against members of the international community for violating the necessary minimum guarantee for individuals in this respect have become possible at all.[67] The arguments of national authorities against the international interventions in the defence of the rule of law based on the traditional considerations of the state sovereignty and the will of the majority cannot be found as justified.

From the legal point of view, the increasingly dramatic position of Polish judges towards the authorities coming from the popular elections has its source in these two constitutional issues, which have just been mentioned: the subordination of courts to the Constitution and statutes, as well as the judges' obligation to maintain restraint – not to carry out public activities that cannot be reconciled with the principles of independence of courts and judges. The example of Poland shows that the questions asked by philosophers long ago have not become outdated: can a judge be allowed to engage in public debate and openly protest when political authorities, in the name of an alleged democratic mandate, violate the constitutional status of the independence of the courts and the independence of the judge? Is s/he obliged to comply with every law only because it was adopted by a representative body?

The first act of the drama of the Polish judiciary was the total loss of independence and authority of the Constitutional Tribunal. It is worth reminding those not oriented in Polish realities that it was the first victim of the transformation of the Polish system after the 2015 elections. Without attempting to describe in detail the whole battle, which resulted in actual paralysis of the Tribunal's functioning, and then its takeover by persons clearly associated with the ruling camp, it is enough to outline only the milestones of the dispute over the independence of this body.[68]

[67] Even if at international level such sanctions will be only dispersed and relative in nature (stronger only in the field of the law of international organisations); see M Pilich, 'The Rule of Law from the Perspective of International Law' in *Studia i Analizy Sądu Najwyższego. Materiały naukowe. T. VIII: Przyszłość Europy opartej na rządach prawa/The Future of Europe Based on the Rule of Law* (Sąd Najwyższy, 2019) 125, 136–37, 151.

[68] The general outline of the Polish Constitutional Court's decay has been reported in English by Wojciech Sadurski and Marcin Matczak; see W Sadurski, *Poland's Constitutional Breakdown* (OUP, 2019) 58; M Matczak, *Poland's Constitusional Crisis: Facts and Interpretations* (FLJS, 2018) at www.fljs.org/content/

1. The pretext to attack the Polish Constitutional Court was an obvious excess of the *Sejm* (the parliament's lower House) of the 7th term of office (2011–15).[69] At its last meeting after the parliamentary election, on 8 October 2015, the MPs of the former PO-PSL governing coalition elected not three, but five judges of the Constitutional Tribunal, by which the outgoing *Sejm* entered into the sphere of prerogatives of the Sejm of the next 8th term with regard to two judges. Although it was formally allowed by the transitional provision of the Act on the Constitutional Tribunal adopted a few months earlier,[70] its constitutionality was questionable. Aware of this, a group of the MPs of the currently governing Law and Justice (PiS) party had submitted before the 2015 election an application to the Constitutional Court in order to examine the legal basis for the selection of 'excess' judges, but later the application was simply withdrawn.[71] Instead of this, the Sejm of the new term of office, already filled by the majority of members of the 'United Right' coalition led by the PiS party, adopted the first amendment to the Act (19 November 2015), which took place without any real debate.[72] The new Act covered, among others, an unconstitutional rule that the term of office of a judge of the Constitutional Tribunal begins from the day of taking the oath, and not, as it was commonly believed so far, from the day of election by the Sejm; a special procedure was also introduced for submitting, giving opinions and selecting candidates for the position of Constitutional Tribunal judges whose term of office expired in 2015. It was a deliberate action which, as it soon turned out, aimed at an 'alternative concept of remedying unconstitutionality'.[73]
2. Pursuant to the provisions of the amending Act, already on 25 November 2015 (that is, before their formal entry into force![74]) the Sejm adopted resolutions depriving the legal force of the election of all five judges of the Constitutional Tribunal, that is, also three correctly appointed by the *Sejm* of the 7th term. Of no use were the voices of protest, indicating that the powers of the *Sejm* were

poland%E2%80%99s-constitutional-crisis-facts-and-interpretations; see also M Gersdorf and M Pilich, 'Judges and Representatives of the People: a Polish Perspective' (2020) 16(3) *European Constitutional Law Review* 345.

[69] The detailed analysis of facts and interpretations (in Polish), see P Radziewicz and P Tuleja (eds), *Konstytucyjny spór o granice zmian organizacji i zasad działania Trybunału Konstytucyjnego* (Warszawa, 2017).

[70] Article 137 of the Act of 25 June 2015 on the Constitutional Tribunal (*ustawa z dnia 25 czerwca 2015 r. o Trybunale Konstytucyjnym*), Dz. U. Item 1064, as amended.

[71] Application No. K 29/15, submitted to the Constitutional Tribunal on 23.10.2015, withdrawn on 10.11.2015 at https://trybunal.gov.pl/s/k-2915.

[72] The draft Bill on the Amendment of the Act on Constitutional Tribunal (Parliamentary Document No. 12) had been submitted to the Sejm (lower House) on 13.10.2015, which means that the whole procedure in matter of an utmost significance lasted only six days until the final voting; see the course of legislative procedure at www.sejm.gov.pl/Sejm8.nsf/PrzebiegProc.xsp?nr=12 (in Polish). The Act of 19 November 2015 on the Amendment of the Act on Constitutional Tribunal (*ustawa z dnia 19 listopada 2015 r. o zmianie ustawy o Trybunale Konstytucyjnym*), Dz. U. Item 1928, was promulgated on 20.11 and entered into force on 5.12.2015.

[73] A Bojańczyk, *Miniprzewodnik po sprawie ustawy o Trybunale Konstytucyjnym. Drugie orzeczenie TK: Delikatne tąpnięcie czy kataklizm ustrojowy?* at https://publica.pl/teksty/bojanczyk-delikatne-tupniecie-czy-kataklizm-ustrojowy-54337.html.

[74] See n 71.

exceeded again, as well as the immediate request to the Constitutional Tribunal by a group of opposition deputies exactly repeating the content of the withdrawn application of Law and Justice MPs. On 2 December 2015, just on the eve of the hearing at the Constitutional Tribunal, the *Sejm* adopted a resolution on the election of five judges, including three so-called 'double judges' for positions legally filled by the *Sejm* of the previous term.[75] Judges so elected took an oath at the Presidential Palace shortly after midnight on 3 December 2015.[76] The judgment of the Constitutional Tribunal handed down later on the very same day confirmed that the constitutional mandate of the Sejm of the 8th term of office was limited to electing only three and not five judges, so that the election of those three was in line with the Constitution;[77] in the next ruling, the constitutionality of the provisions introduced into the Act on the Constitutional Tribunal by the government majority was questioned, mainly due to the limitation of the independence of the Constitutional Tribunal as a judicial body.[78] However, the Chancellery of the Prime Minister illegally suspended the promulgation of both of these rulings until mid-December 2015; it was the first in the history of the Third Republic, although unfortunately not the last and not the most vivid example of actions putting the executive over the judiciary.

3. While the events described in points 1 and 2 already constituted an absolutely obvious and flagrant violation of constitutional norms, the further course of events proved that all changes in matters crucial for the Polish political system would be carried out without looking at the legal status, and only in order to achieve a specific end result: the taking over of all state institutions by the ruling camp as soon as possible. This is in particular the case of the next amendment to the Act on the CT, prepared instantly after handing down judgments of the Tribunal of 2015,[79] as well as the entirely new Act on CT of 2016.[80] The rulings of the Constitutional Tribunal in all cases pertaining to these statutory regulations, aimed at the maximum restraining judicial freedom and preparing the election of a new President of the Constitutional Tribunal, were neutralised in the same way: first by refusing publishing and then by adopting entirely new provisions.

[75] Two legally elected judges were Ms Julia Przyłębska and Mr Piotr Pszczółkowski; three elected against the Constitution: Mr Henryk Cioch, Mr Lech Morawski, and Mr Mariusz Muszyński. The acts of election had been challenged before the Constitutional Tribunal but, for the reason of their nature stepping outside the sphere of its jurisdiction, the Tribunal discontinued proceedings; cf CT ruling of 7 January 2016, U 8/15, OTK 2016/A/1.

[76] 'Prezydent odebrał ślubowanie od sędziów Trybunału Konstytucyjnego' (3 December 2015), at www.prezydent.pl/aktualnosci/wydarzenia/art,75,prezydent-odebral-slubowanie-od-sedziow-tk.html.

[77] Judgment of the Constitutional Tribunal of 3 December 2015, K 34/15, Dz.U. Item 2129, OTK 2015/11A/185.

[78] Judgment of the Constitutional Tribunal of 9 December 2015, K 35/15, Dz.U. Item 2147, OTK 2015/11A/186.

[79] The draft Bill on the Amendment of the Act on Constitutional Tribunal (Parliamentary Document No. 122) had been submitted to the Sejm (lower House) on 15.12.2015 – this time, parliamentary 'debate' took just a week; see the course of legislative procedure at www.sejm.gov.pl/Sejm8.nsf/PrzebiegProc.xsp?nr=122 (in Polish). The Act of 22 December 2015 on the Amendment of the Act on Constitutional Tribunal (*ustawa z dnia 22 listopada 2015 r. o zmianie ustawy o Trybunale Konstytucyjnym*), Dz. U. Item 2217, was promulgated on 20.11 and entered into force on 5.12.2015.

[80] *Ustawa z dnia 22 lipca 2016 r. o Trybunale Konstytucyjnym* (Dz.U. Item 1157, as amended).

Finally, under the pressure of the European Union, the disputed judgments were published, but reluctantly: after a very long time, with an unprecedented government annotation that the judgments were issued 'in violation of the provisions of the Act' and concerned 'a normative act that had lost its binding force'.[81] At this point, the concession was rather symbolic, because the effect sought by the ruling majority was actually achieved. Critical opinions of universally respected international bodies were no basis for political majority to reflect on the unacceptable direction of reforms.[82]

4. The above facts clearly indicate the fall of the authority of law, which is no longer a framework for political decisions in any matters, even regarding the functioning of a distinct branch of government – the judiciary. However, even worse, the Constitutional Tribunal itself lost all authority in the eyes of a large part of the legal community, and this was primarily due to the behaviour of its members (with or without respect to the Constitution). During a symposium at the University of Oxford on 9 May 2017, one of the 'double judges', Prof Lech Morawski, openly admitted that he is acting not only on behalf of the President of the Constitutional Tribunal, but also the government.[83] Another group of members of the Tribunal elected contrary to the Constitution, Mr Mariusz Muszyński is known for his press philippics, in which he always presents a position consistent with the narrative of the ruling coalition.[84] In turn, the President of the Tribunal, Ms Julia Przyłębska, was described by the political leader of the governing camp Mr Jarosław Kaczyński in a press interview as his 'great social discovery', which quite clearly indicates the close contacts between both, and due to the President's authority over the Court's activities, it generally undermines independence of this body as the whole.[85] Loyalty to the government becomes the hallmark of the suitability of candidates for new judges of this body – so important that even meeting the statutory requirements to run for office lose their usual importance.[86] Even though the selection of candidates for the highest judicial offices according

[81] See judgments of 9 March 2016, K 47/15, Dz.U. 2018, Item 1077, OTK 2016/A/2; of 11 August 2016, K 39/16, Dz.U. 2018, Item 1078, OTK 2016/A/71; of 7 November 2016, K 44/16, Dz.U. 2018, Item 1079, OTK 2016/A/86.

[82] cf opinions of the European Commission for Democracy Through Law (Venice Commission): of 11 March 2016, No. 833/2015, CDL-AD(2016)001, and of 14 October 2016, No. 860/2016, CDL-AD(2016)026, available at www.venice.coe.int/.

[83] 'An Oxford symposium on the Polish constitutional crisis sparks public debate' (12 May 2017), see www.law.ox.ac.uk/news/2017-05-11-oxford-symposium-polish-constitutional-crisis-sparks-public-debate.

[84] See M Muszyński, 'Nieudolni pogromcy Trybunału Konstytucyjnego (Inept suppressors of the Constitutional Tribunal)' (17 November 2017) at www.rp.pl/Opinie/311169885-Muszynski-Nieudolni-pogromcy-Trybunalu-Konstytucyjnego.html; M Muszyński, 'Muszyński ws. niepublikowania wyroków TK: To pewne – premier miała rację (Muszyński on the non-promulgation of judgments of the CT: It is certain – Prime Minister was right)' (2 January 2018) at www.rp.pl/Opinie/301029940-Muszynski-ws-niepublikowania-wyrokow-TK-To-pewne--premier-miala-racje.html.

[85] 'Mam wielu przyjaciół w polityce i poza nią (I have many friends in politics and beyond)' (13 May 2019) at www.tvp.info/42604906/mam-wielu-przyjaciol-w-polityce-i-poza-nia.

[86] At the beginning of 2016, the current judge of the Tribunal, Professor Jakub Stelina, prepared an opinion supporting the government's position in the dispute regarding the admissibility of adjudicating on the constitutionality of the Act of 22 December 2015 on the Constitutional Tribunal directly on the basis of the provisions of the Constitution; see at www.arch.ms.gov.pl/pl/informacje/download,8072,6.

to their political preferences is not completely unusual in history, such unambiguous demonstrations by constitutional judges of their political affiliations would be unthinkable in virtually every country of the Western world.

5. In recent years, there has been far-reaching interference in the jurisprudence of the Constitutional Tribunal in the proceedings before the Tribunal, by excluding three judges from adjudication: Stanisław Rymar, Piotr Tuleja and Marek Zubik, whenever requested by the Prosecutor General, Zbigniew Ziobro.[87] The pretext for such decisions was the (never heard) application of the Prosecutor General for examination of the constitutionality of the election of these judges by the Sejm.[88] This created an artificial dispute about the legality of the choice of judges, which – in addition to manipulating adjudicating panels – fulfilled many other functions important from the point of view of the ruling camp: it provided arguments to counterbalance in the public discourse the unconstitutionality of the choice of three 'double judges', as well as it served as a reinforcement of pressure on the judges who were still members of the Constitutional Tribunal elected before 2015.
6. The Constitutional Tribunal is eagerly used by the ruling majority to interfere in the judicial activities. The commencement of several cases before the Constitutional Tribunal was motivated solely or mostly by a desire to prevent the effects of uncomfortable court proceedings. This was especially the case when the President of the Republic of Poland pardoned legally convicted high-ranking Law and Justice politicians managing the Central Anti-Corruption Bureau, Mariusz Kamiński and Maciej Wąsik; the adoption by the Supreme Court of a resolution explaining the effects of exercising the right of pardon by the President for pending criminal proceedings[89] resulted in a very quick submission by the Speaker of the *Sejm* of an application for settlement of an alleged competence dispute between the President of the Republic of Poland and the Supreme Court;[90] thanks to this trick, the political majority managed to suspend the proceedings in the case pending before the Supreme Court (which is still unsolved due to the Tribunal's failure to hear the application).[91] Another, quite similar 'competence dispute' with the Supreme Court was

html. As the Dean of the Faculty of Law and Administration at the University of Gdańsk, he ostentatiously resigned after the Faculty Council had passed a resolution opposing violations of the Constitution by the government; 'Dziekan podał się do dymisji po głosowaniu nad uchwałą o "naruszaniu konstytucji"' (28 November 2018) at www.tvp.info/40188585/dziekan-podal-sie-do-dymisji-po-glosowaniu-nad-uchwala-o-naruszaniu-konstytucji. Recently elected judges of the Constitutional Tribunal: Mrs Krystyna Pawłowicz and Mr Stanisław Piotrowicz, both former MPs of the Law and Justice party, became famous for their very active participation in the work on controversial court laws (including the very radical Act of 2017 on the Supreme Court, vetoed by the President of the Republic) as well as their participation in the current composition of the National Council for the Judiciary, backed by the government. Interestingly, at the time of running for office, neither of the latter two persons met the age requirement, exceeding the 65-year threshold set by the current parliamentary majority; see www.rp.pl/Prawo-i-Sprawiedliwosc/191119771-Kandydaci-PiS-za-starzy-do-TK-Wedlug-wlasnych-kryteriow.html.

[87] M Kryszkiewicz, *Podwójne standardy w TK. Składy zależne od woli Zbigniewa Ziobry*, see https://prawo.gazetaprawna.pl/artykuly/1078563,podwojne-standardy-w-tk-wylaczenie-sedziow.html.

[88] Available at https://trybunal.gov.pl/s/u-117.

[89] SC Resolution of the panel of 7 Justices of 31 May 2017, I KZP 4/17, OSNKW 2017/7/37.

[90] Application No. Kpt 1/17, documents available at https://trybunal.gov.pl/s/kpt-117.

[91] SC ruling of 1 August 2017, II KK 313/16, unpublished, available at www.sn.pl.

> initiated by the Speaker of the *Sejm*[92] in order to stop the Supreme Court from adopting a resolution interpreting the provisions on the inappropriate composition of the court panel protecting the right to a fair trial, which followed the judgment of the Court of Justice of the European Union unfavourable to the policy of the Polish authorities. This time, however, the procedure has not brought the intended effects that the political majority hoped for: a resolution of the Supreme Court has been adopted.[93] However, even apart from examples of the participation of the Constitutional Tribunal in the obstruction of court proceedings, it is not difficult to see the close cooperation between the Polish Constitutional Court and the government majority in many other matters that have a direct impact on the functioning of the judiciary.[94] In this way, the Polish Constitutional Court clearly became a tool in the political struggle of the current government majority for the full and unrestricted power, as well as a weapon against the independence of the courts in administering justice.

The facts indicated above, although far from a complete description of reality, allow us to formulate a well-founded thesis that at present Polish constitutional judiciary no longer exists in practice. The situation can be compared to some extent in the case of Dollfussian Austria, in which the Constitutional Tribunal fell victim to the political machinations of the federal government in 1933.[95] Of course, it could be argued

[92] Competency dispute between the Sejm of the Republic of Poland and the Supreme Court and between the President of the Republic of Poland and the Supreme Court, appl. No. Kpt 1/20, at https://trybunal.gov.pl/s/kpt-1-20.

[93] Resolution of the panel of the SC, Joined Civil, Criminal, and Labor and Social Insurance Chambers of 23 January 2020, BSA I-4110-1/20, OSNKW 2020/2/7. In order to denounce its legal effects, the government had to institute another proceedings before the Constitutional Tribunal, this time in matters of constitutionality of an alleged 'legal instrument' included in the resolution, which after all is just a court decision and not the piece of legislation; see CT judgment of 20 April 2020 r., U 2/20, OTK 2020/A/61.

[94] Fearing that the mandates of the President and Vice-President and one of the judges of the Constitutional Tribunal could be questioned in the dispute regarding compensation from the Polish State Treasury for not properly examining a constitutional complaint, a group of Law and Justice deputies filed a request to review the constitutionality of one of the provisions of the Code of Civil Procedure; it was very quickly (within just over two months) settled in accordance with the application, so that the court would not be able to issue a judgment in favour of the plaintiff; cf CT judgment of 11 September 2017, K 10/17, OTK 2017/A/64. In turn, thanks to two subsequent judgments of the Constitutional Tribunal: from 2017 and 2019, the political power secured the possibility of exercising decisive influence on the majority of the composition of the National Council of the Judiciary in order to take full control over the system of appointment and promotion of judges. The 2017 judgment, directed to be heard by a panel of only five judges (only elected by Law and Justice, including two persons deprived of a constitutional mandate to hold their office), not only introduced a derogation from previous constitutional case law, but above all was an attempt to legitimise clearly unconstitutional shortening of the term of office of current members of the Council who are judges; see CT judgments of 20 June 2017, K 5/17, OTK 2017/A/48; of 25 March 2019, K 12/18, OTK 2019/A/17.

[95] The resignation of the speaker of the pre-war Austrian Parliament (*Nationalrat*) and his two deputies became a pretext for suspending the work of the legislative body and taking over its functions by the government. It was the most important step towards dictatorship. Soon thereafter, seven members of the Constitutional Tribunal (*Verfassungsgerichtshof*) resigned of their office in exchange for a likely promise from the federal government that they would be appointed judges of a replacement body – the Federal Tribunal (only three of them were actually appointed). The other judges did not form a quorum capable of hearing the case that caused the executive to take this action. They just accepted their fate, without even trying to challenge the legal provision which had led to this stalemate situation; K Heller, *Der Verfassungsgerichtshof: Die Entwicklung der Verfassungsgerichtsbarkeit in Österreich von den Anfängen bis zur Gegenwart* (Verlag Österreich, 2010) 251.

that the situation of Poland after 2015 and Austria after 1933 is incomparable in all respects: Poland is not a state in a state of deep political, socio-economic crisis, nor are there any serious postulatory forces – at least formally – abolishing parliamentarism, control constitutionality of law, civil rights or the rule of law. However, putting aside direct analogies, in both cases one can notice the ostentatious lack of respect for the law as an intrinsic value and the same will to subordinate the independent institutions to the current political majority, so that power is to be concentrated in an absolutely undemocratic way in one hand.

The fall of constitutional justice is closely linked to the condition of the judiciary as a whole. This is not only because there is no buffer between the courts and the legislative authority, which is naturally a constitutional court. The fate of the latter concentrates, as in a lens, the negative attitude of the government and its parliamentary majority towards all independent institutions and indicates the direction in which the entire Polish third power is heading. The authoritarian *modus operandi* of political authorities can be observed in several areas.

1. The new Law on the Prosecutor's Office of 2016[96] subordinates the public prosecutor's office to the management of the Prosecutor General, which is currently the Minister of Justice. The prosecutor, who is not only an applicant party in the criminal trial, but also holds a jurisdictional function in the pre-trial phase, now has an absolute obligation to comply with all official instructions of his or her superiors, including directly the Prosecutor General or his deputy, the National Prosecutor. This obligation also extends to the key decisions in a given cases, such as the presentation of charges, a request for pre-trial detention, as well as an indictment; moreover, all such actions can be performed even by the superior of the prosecutor conducting the case without the consent of the latter. In conjunction with the controversial judicial reforms discussed below, the principle of equality of arms of the prosecutor and the accused, which is the basic premise of a fair trial, has become a fiction more than ever before in the history of Poland after 1989. This fact violated the intra-EU principle of mutual trust between systems of justice and, as a consequence, became the reason for disturbing the intra-EU extradition procedure on the basis of the European Arrest Warrant.[97]
2. The laws adopted in 2017 abolished the abovementioned judicial self-government. The pro-democratic reforms initiated in 1989–90 have been undone; in a sense, therefore, the situation in the judiciary has returned to the state it existed at the end of the Polish People's Republic. Of course, this happens not by simply abolishing the institutions established as a result of the transformation of the past, but as a result of a gradual and thus incomprehensible to many observers change in their model. The systemic decomposition of the National Council of the Judiciary, as well as of judicial self-government bodies in the strict sense (above all assemblies of judges at particular levels of the judiciary) can be treated as an extremely sad symbol.[98]

[96] Law of 28 January 2016 on the Prosecution Office (*ustawa z dnia 28 stycznia 2016 r. o prokuraturze*), consolidated text: Dz. U. of 2019 Item 740.
[97] Case C-216/18 PPU *LM* (n 12).
[98] Śledzińska-Simon (n 30) 1841–42.

3. A key element ensuring the influence of elected authorities on the judiciary was the change in the way of appointing and dismissing presidents and vice presidents of common courts. After 1989, it was decided by the assemblies of judges and the National Council of the Judiciary. An amendment to the Law on the Structure of Common Courts adopted in 2017[99] granted the Minister of Justice, within six months of its entry into force, the power to decide by one person on the dismissal of presidents and vice presidents and the appointment of new ones in their place without any motivated reasons and consultation of judicial bodies. The Minister of Justice-Prosecutor General exercised this right eagerly, dismissing over 120 out of over 700 presidents and vice presidents of the Polish common courts. The decisions taken were at least controversial, as some of the appointees were eg disciplinarily convicted or their competence and authority in the professional environment could be doubted.[100] In a significant number of cases, changes were made by means of short letters sent from the Ministry by fax, without any other form of communication.[101] After the transition period, completely different nomination rules came into force, based on the high discretion of the reasons for dismissal of the president or vice president of the court, the reduced role of the National Council of the Judiciary (currently informally controlled by the Ministry of Justice), as well as the elimination of the institution of negative opinions of assemblies of judges.[102] At present, the Minister of Justice is free to decide on the amount of service allowances to be granted to presidents and vice presidents. Presidents of courts have enormous powers vis-à-vis judges, deciding on their professional status and being able to demand disciplinary proceedings, as well as managing the organisational structure of courts (appointing and dismissing faculty presidents).[103] The new organisation of the common judiciary undoubtedly strengthens the pressure of the executive on judges, contributing to a reduction in the guarantee of their independence.[104]
4. The controversy regarding the representativeness of judges in the National Council of the Judiciary served the ruling camp as an excuse to justify the

[99] Act of 12 July 2017 Amending the Law On the Structure of Common Courts And Some Other Laws (*ustawa z dnia 12 lipca 2017 r. o zmianie ustawy – Prawo o ustroju sądów powszechnych oraz niektórych innych ustaw*), Dz. U. Item 1452.

[100] For example, one of the appointees unsuccessfully applied for the post of judge 52 times, but her achievements were negatively assessed by the National Council of the Judiciary; B Grabowska-Moroz and M Szuleka, *Od kadr się zaczyna. Zmiana prezesów i wiceprezesów sądów powszechnych w okresie od sierpnia 2017 r. do lutego 2018 r.* (*It begins with the staff. Change of presidents and vice presidents of common courts in the period from August 2017 to February 2018*) (Helsińska Fundacja Praw Człowieka. 2018), at www.hfhr.pl/wp-content/uploads/2018/04/HFPC-Od-kadr-sie-zaczyna.pdf s 21.

[101] K Nowakowska, 'Dziesiątki odwołanych prezesów sądów. Część dowiedziała się o tym z faksu i dalej pracuje (Dozens of presidents of courts dismissed. Some learned about it from the fax and are still working)', at https://prawo.gazetaprawna.pl/artykuly/1093130,odwolania-prezesow-sadow.html.

[102] Such rules run against the established case law of the Constitutional Tribunal and thus they may well be unconstitutional; cf Śledzińska-Simon (n 30) 1845–46.

[103] Śledzińska-Simon (n 30) 1846, 1856.

[104] See SC, Opinion No. BSA I/II-021-161/17 of 28.04.2017, at www.sejm.gov.pl/Sejm8.nsf/druk.xsp?nr=1491 (in Polish).

decomposition of this body and to change the model for the selection of its members who are judges, which was entrusted to the lower house of the Polish Parliament – *Sejm* instead of assemblies of judges. The work proceeded in two stages: after vetoing the originally adopted law,[105] The President of the Republic submitted his own project. Despite the claim that the intention of this action was to remove the flaws of the original draft bill, the bill adopted as a result of the presidential initiative[106] did not change the basic assumptions that guided the authors of the vetoed law: election of the Council's judicial members by the *Sejm*, as well as shortening the term of office of previously elected members of the NCJ. Finally, it also turned out to be contrary to the basic principles of European Union and international law. Numerous opinions of both the domestic[107] and foreign bodies, including the Venice Commission,[108] the EU Commission[109] and the United Nations Organization,[110] unequivocally pointed to the unacceptable, from the point of view of the independence of the courts, dependence of the Council on the parliamentary majority. In any case, the criticism did not prevent the ruling camp from carrying out the intended operation, as a result of which the composition of the National Council of the Judiciary comprised judicial members in various ways associated with the Ministry of Justice or directly dependent on him due to their functions.[111] The non-transparency of

[105] Act of 12 July 2017 amending the act on the National Council of the Judiciary and certain other acts (*ustawa z dnia 12 lipca 2017 r. o zmianie ustawy o Krajowej Radzie Sądownictwa oraz niektórych innych ustaw*), vetoed by the President of the Republic on 31 July 2017, see www.sejm.gov.pl/Sejm8.nsf/PrzebiegProc.xsp?nr=1423.

[106] Act of 8 December 2017 amending the Act on the National Council of the Judiciary and certain other acts (*ustawa z dnia 12 lipca 2017 r. o zmianie ustawy o Krajowej Radzie Sądownictwa oraz niektórych innych ustaw*), Dz. U. of 2018, Item 3.

[107] See SC, Opinion No. BSA III-021-364/17 of 23.10.2017, at www.sn.pl/aktualnosci/SiteAssets/Lists/Wydarzenia/NewForm/021-364-17%20Opinia%20SN%20do%20projektu%20ustawy%20o%20KRS.pdf (in Polish).

[108] Venice Commission (n 10) 5–7.

[109] Commission Recommendation (EU) 2017/1520 of 26 July 2017 regarding the rule of law in Poland complementary to Recommendations (EU) 2016/1374 and (EU) 2017/146 (OJ L 228, 2.9.2017, p. 19) paras 26–28, 45; Commission Recommendation (EU) 2018/103 of 20 December 2017 regarding the rule of law in Poland complementary to Recommendations (EU) 2016/1374, (EU) 2017/146 and (EU) 2017/1520 (OJ L 17, 23.1.2018, p. 50) para 27.

[110] See UN Human Rights Council, *Report of the Special Rapporteur on the independence of judges and lawyers on his mission to Poland*, 05.04.2018, A/HRC/38/38/Add.1 at https://undocs.org/pdf?symbol=en/A/HRC/38/38/Add.1.

[111] For example, two current members of the Council, Mr Dariusz Drajewicz and Mr Jarosław Dudzicz, both judges of the District Courts (*Sądy Rejonowe*), were delegated up to the Regional Courts (*Sądy Okręgowe*) and appointed to managerial positions in the latter; such promotions, associated with a significant increase in remuneration, occurred during the period of operation of the extraordinary transitional provisions of the Act Amending the Law on the Structure of Common Courts, giving the Minister of Justice a free hand in the exchange of managerial staff in courts. In total, 12 out of 18 judicial candidates for the Council were connected in various ways with the Ministry and the current Minister of Justice, and these ones actually were accepted by the Sejm; see the data summary on the SSP Iustitia website at www.iustitia.pl/nowa-krs/2102-kandydaci-do-krs-i-ich-pelnomocnicy (in Polish). In January 2020, during the debate in the Senate on the so-called 'Muzzle Act', the Minister of Justice-Prosecutor General Mr Zbigniew Ziobro openly admitted that the parliamentary majority personally shaped the National Council of the Judiciary in such a way as to obtain the desired political effect: 'We submitted candidatures of such judges who in our opinion were ready to cooperate within the framework of the reform of the judiciary (*Myśmy zgłosili*

the elections was not accidental: although it was not possible for a long time to verify the lists of support for candidates,[112] evidence disclosed at the beginning of 2020 (almost two years after the submission of applications) showed that, among others, one of the members of the new Council did not obtain the required number of 25 signatures of the judges supporting him, and in several other cases the signatures could be put in blank by the group of the same judges delegated to the Ministry of Justice.[113] The Council was therefore composed even in violation of such a defective law as adopted by the *Sejm*.

5. Moreover, the very functioning of the National Council of the Judiciary as a body has dramatically deformed the relationship between judicial and executive branches of government. In one of the recent rulings, the Supreme Court expressed a critical assessment of the current composition of the Council, pointing to its eloquent silence in many cases of the obvious violation of the independence of the judiciary by the current authorities, regard being had to the simultaneous and hence non-accidental coincidence of its positions with the current line of government narrative.[114] The former Chairman of the National Council of the Judiciary, judge Leszek Mazur, did not see anything wrong in participating in a purely political event, which was the ceremony of giving an award to the President of Law and Justice Jarosław Kaczyński (16.02.2020); he stood up applauding the speech of the ruling majority leader.[115] As part of its official duties, the Council clearly submitted to the will of the Minister of Justice – the Prosecutor General: when considering the candidacy of a former employee of the Ministry of Justice as a judge of the Supreme Court, voting was conducted twice. The first time the candidacy was rejected, but after the personal speech of the Minister of Justice in its defence, the voting was repeated and this time the

takich sędziów, którzy naszym zdaniem byli gotowi współdziałać w ramach reformy sądownictwa)'; M Wilgocki, '"Myśmy zgłosili". Ziobro przypadkiem zdradził, kto poparł sędziów do KRS?' at https://wyborcza.pl/7,75398,25603501,mysmy-zglosili-ziobro-przypadkiem-zdradzil-co-jest-na-utajnionych.html.

[112] The ruling majority has used absolutely every opportunity, legal or not, to hide the content of the documents from the public. When the Supreme Administrative Court finally ordered to disclose them at the request of an interested MP, the President of the Office for Personal Data Protection, Mr Jan Nowak (once a Warsaw councilor of Law and Justice) initiated a proceeding regarding an alleged breach of the confidentiality of personal data and issued a security order prohibiting the publishing of the lists, which further was referred to by the Chancellery of the Sejm in order to avoid presenting documentation of candidates for NCJ members to the interested persons, including courts; see SAC judgment of 28 June 2019, I OSK 4282/18, http://orzeczenia.nsa.gov.pl/doc/EA1208209B; D Flis, 'Jan Nowak, prezes UODO, wstrzymał ujawnienie list poparcia kandydatów do KRS. Ekspert: "To anarchia"' (30 July 2019) at https://oko.press/jan-nowak-prezes-uodo-wstrzymal-ujawnienie-list-poparcia-kandydatow-do-krs-ekspert-to-anarchia/.

[113] A Łukaszewicz, 'Listy poparcia do KRS są jawne – co z nich wynika' (16 February 2020) at www.rp.pl/Sedziowie-i-sady/302169946-Listy-poparcia-do-KRS-sa-jawne---co-z-nich-wynika.html; M Jałoszewski, 'Iustitia: Listy do KRS poparli niemal wyłącznie beneficjenci rządów PiS. Publikujemy pełen wykaz' at https://oko.press/iustitia-listy-do-krs-poparli-niemal-wylacznie-beneficjenci-dobrej-zmiany-pis/.

[114] SC judgment of 5.12.2019, III PO 7/18, for the English translation see www.sn.pl/aktualnosci/SiteAssets/Lists/Komunikaty_o_sprawach/AllItems/III-PO-0007_18_English.pdf para 50.

[115] 'Szef KRS klaskał podczas przemówienia prezesa PiS. Oto, jak to tłumaczy' (17 February 2020) at https://dorzeczy.pl/kraj/129933/szef-krs-klaskal-podczas-przemowienia-prezesa-pis-oto-jak-to-tlumaczy.html.

candidate was confirmed with one voice only. The media noted that personal participation in the meeting of the Minister of Justice – officially a member of the Council by virtue of his office – against the background of his previous practice was absolutely unique.[116]

6. The judicial reform implemented by the PiS party also severely affected the Supreme Court. The struggle for his independence had many stages. On the one hand, it was decided to purge among the judges in office as on the day of the entry into force of the new Act on the SC of 8 December 2017.[117] On the other hand, efforts were made to introduce to the Court persons loyal to the authorities, first of all to the two newly created Chambers: Disciplinary and Extraordinary Control and Public Affairs ones. Admittedly, the implementation of the SC's reform was slowed down by judgments of the Court of Justice of the European Union[118] but it has never been put off. The recruitment of new judges to the Supreme Court did not meet the basic criteria of the rule of law in a formal sense. During the 2018 competition before the current National Council of the Judiciary, the Supreme Court Act was amended twice in order to deprive candidates of the right to appeal to the court;[119] moreover, the President appointed judges of the Chamber of Extraordinary Control and Public Affairs[120] despite the full awareness that the Supreme Administrative Court had asked the CJEU whether it is in accordance with European law.[121] Finally, due to the appointment of judges and their dependence on the executive, the functioning of the Disciplinary Chamber of the Supreme Court was questioned in both the European and the national case law.[122] Following the judgment of the Court of Justice, the status of all SC judges appointed with the participation of the new NCJ was assessed as not guaranteeing the right to a fair trial.[123]

[116] 'Pawłowicz przeciwna Zaradkiewiczowi na posiedzeniu KRS. Jaki: Jestem zażenowany' at https://dorzeczy.pl/kraj/75272/Pawlowicz-przeciwna-Zaradkiewiczowi-na-posiedzeniu-KRS-Jaki-Jestem-zazenowany.html.

[117] Consolidated text of the Act, see Dz.U. 2019, item 825; the purge was prevented by the CJEU proceedings ended with the judgment of 24 June 2019, Case C-619/18 *European Commission v Republic of Poland* (n 12).

[118] See orders in Case C-619/18: of the Vice-President of the Court of Justice of 19 October 2018, ECLI:EU:C:2018:852; CJEU Grand Chamber of 17 December 2018 [2020] 1 CMLR 5.

[119] The right of challenge of the NCJ resolution before the court initially was limited by the Act of 20 July 2018 amending the Law on the structure of common courts and some other acts (*ustawa z dnia 20 lipca 2018 r. o zmianie ustawy – Prawo o ustroju sądów powszechnych oraz niektórych innych ustaw*), Dz.U. z 2018 r. poz. 1443; finally it was wholly abolished by the Act of 26 April 2019 amending the Act on the National Council of the Judiciary and the Law on the structure of administrative courts (*ustawa z dnia 26 kwietnia 2019 r. o zmianie ustawy o Krajowej Radzie Sądownictwa oraz ustawy – Prawo o ustroju sądów administracyjnych*), Dz.U. z 2019 r. poz. 914. The Court of Justice challenged the legality of both amendments with its judgment of 2 March 2021, Case C-824/18 *A.B. and Others v Krajowa Rada Sądownictwa and Others* EU:C:2021:153.

[120] See the press release in the website of the President's Chancellery, 'Prezydent powołał nowych sędziów Sądu Najwyższego' (10 October 2018) at www.prezydent.pl/aktualnosci/nominacje/art,96,prezydent-powolal-nowych-sedziow-sadu-najwyzszego.html.

[121] SAC ruling of 26 July 2019, II GOK 2/18, followed by the CJEU judgment of 2 March 2021 [GC], C-824/18, *A.B. et al.*, EU:C:2021:153.

[122] See CJEU judgment of 19 November 2019, Joined Cases C-585/18, C-624/18 and C-625/18, *AK* (n 12).

[123] See the resolution of the SC Joined Chambers of 23 January 2020 (n 93).

7. The recently mentioned reaction of the judiciary to the appointment of judges in procedures that do not meet the basic criteria for compliance with the Constitution, international law and the legal order of the European Union caused a very sharp reaction from the power camp. The so-called 'Muzzle Act'[124] aims at preventing the courts, including the Supreme Court, from using an interpretation which was found necessary and legitimate in the Supreme Court judgments implementing European law. First of all, it provides for the initiation of disciplinary proceedings against judges who in any way – judicial or not – will question the composition of the court with the participation of persons appointed with the participation of the new Council for the Judiciary, and even criticism of governmental reforms of the judiciary may be sanctioned. The Act, which has been in force since 14 February 2020, in principle provides for two types of sanctions: transfer to another place of service or dismissal of a judge from office.[125]

In the literature, the situation we face in Poland is sometimes called the 'autocratic legalism'. It is a state of affairs in which both the democratic mandate and legal means are abused to implement the undemocratic political agenda; in other words, a democratically elected leader commits a coordinated and constant attack on institutions whose function is to control his actions, and on regulations that set the basis for his responsibility, even if he or she does so in the name of his democratic mandate.[126] As can be seen from the above description, the key part of these efforts is the acquisition of independent control institutions – that is, in principle, the judiciary – by court-packing. First of all, constitutional courts are taken over, in the case of which the nomination procedures are changed or the manner of performing their functions is modified.[127]

However, as usually happens with definitions in social sciences, they rely on considerable simplifications. This is easily seen by comparing the Polish and Hungarian situations. In the case of Hungary, Viktor Orbán's Fidesz has continuously had a constitutional mandate since 2010, even if some of the seats in at least two elections (2014, 2018) were won by the party due to manipulation of the electoral law and the unequal conditions of the campaign for opposition parties. This fact enormously strengthens powers of political actors for legal amendments: the most controversial reforms are introduced in a way that knocks the courts out of any arguments against the application of newly enacted laws. There is no point in expecting the Hungarian Constitutional Court – skilfully 'silenced' by the court-packing

[124] Act of 20 December 2019 Amending the Act – Law On The Structure of Common Courts, The Act On the Supreme Court and Some Other Acts (*ustawa z dnia 20 grudnia 2019 r. o zmianie ustawy – Prawo o ustroju sądów powszechnych, ustawy o Sądzie Najwyższym oraz niektórych innych ustaw*), Dz. U. 2020 Item 190.

[125] cf K Gajda-Roszczynialska and K Markiewicz, 'Disciplinary Proceedings as an Instrument for Breaking the Rule of Law in Poland' (2020) 12 *Hague J Rule Law* 451; M Pilich, 'Disobedience of Judges as a Problem of Legal Philosophy and Comparative Constitutionalism: A Polish Case' (2021) *Res Publica*, https://doi.org/10.1007/s11158-021-09501-8.

[126] KL Scheppele, 'Autocratic Legalism' (2018) 85 *The University of Chicago Law Review* 545, 548–49.

[127] Drinóczi and Bień-Kacała (n 56) 1140, 1146.

and the subsequent constitutional amendments[128] – to react against constitutional deficiencies of the legislation, where any Act of the Hungarian Parliament can be introduced into the country's Fundamental Law, which actually ends any debate on the validity of such or any other resolution.[129] It is difficult for a judge, who by nature must be a legalist, to question the formally valid result of lawmaking. This may be the reason for András Sajó and Juha Tuovinen to claim that the main source of legitimacy in political rhetoric is the sovereignty of the people. Popular legitimation is on what illiberal regimes rely, and the rule of law is regularly reduced to legalism.[130]

We believe that Polish judges are in a much more difficult situation than their Hungarian colleagues: this is the position between Scylla of the allegiance to the binding Constitution and Charybdis of the observance of the Acts adopted by the majority in parliament, which may well infringe the Constitution, while there is no possibility of verifying this hypothesis. For the Polish judges, article 178(1) of the Constitution[131] does not help in finding a way between these two options. By treating their function seriously, that is by acting in accordance with the Constitution, for example through pro-constitutional reinterpretation of provisions or the application of prevailing provisions of international and European law, judges are in a real danger of being subject to disciplinary and even criminal liability, which is being increasingly enforced.[132] In turn, trying to please the rulers and enforce all legislation without looking at its compliance with the Constitution, in accordance with the principle so criticised by Gustav Radbruch that 'an order is an order' and 'a law is a law',[133] judges compromise the oath and do not fulfill their obligations towards society, deepening the mistrust in their office. Unlike in Hungary, the government in Poland has no powers to amend the Constitution; it has, however, the influence on the Constitutional Tribunal.

[128] For a concise overview of legislative changes that led to the dismantling of constitutional checks in Hungary, see G Halmai, *Abuse of Constitutional Identity. The Hungarian Constitutional Court on Interpretation of Article E(2) of the Fundamental Law*, https://me.eui.eu/gabor-halmai/wp-content/uploads/sites/385/2018/05/Abuse_Halmai_final.pdf.

[129] Drinóczi and Bień-Kacała (n 56) 1152, 1155–56.

[130] A Sajó and J Tuovinen, 'The Rule of Law and Legitimacy in Emerging Illiberal Democracies' (2018) 64(4) *OER Osteuropa Recht* 507–08.

[131] See n 48.

[132] Judges in Poland have been subject to the rising pressure through a system of disciplinary responsibility. As an example, the recent disciplinary prosecution of several judges who referred questions to the CJEU could serve as an example. This, for instance, was the case of Ms A Bator-Ciesielska, a judge of the Regional Court (*Sąd Okręgowy*) in Warsaw; see *Justice under pressure* (n 14) 14. As to the criminal liability of judges for their office duties, it is not a pure fiction, too. A very significant example of how the executive is able to instrumentalise the criminal law is the so-called 'Police case': a group of former managers of chemical plants in Police (a town in the northwestern Poland) had been charged with acting to the detriment of the company. The prosecutor's office applied to the Szczecin District Court for the pre-trial detention of the suspects. Following a final refusal to apply this measure, proceedings were instituted against the superiors of the judges deciding in arrest cases for the failure to perform official duties. The case resulted in a defamatory practices of summoning judges to be heard by the public prosecutor, though so far to no avail; cf A Zadworny, 'Prokuratura wzywa na przesłuchania sędziów, którzy nie chcieli aresztować prezesów ZCh Police' (16 March 2018) at https://szczecin.wyborcza.pl/szczecin/7,34939,23150183,prokuratura-wzywa-na-przesluchania-sedziow-ktorzy-nie-chcieli.html.

[133] G Radbruch (tr B Litschewski Paulson and SL Paulson), 'Statutory Lawlessness and Supra-Statutory Law' (2006) 26(1) *Oxford Journal of Legal Studies* 1, see esp 6: 'Positivism, with its principle that "a law is a law", has in fact rendered the German legal profession defenceless against statutes that are arbitrary and criminal. Positivism is, moreover, in and of itself wholly incapable of establishing the validity of statutes.'

It is a paradox that the latter no longer serves to ensure compliance of the law with higher legal rules; the purpose of this institution, as a result of the changes made, is actually to discourage judges from asking whether there is any inconsistency of ordinary laws with the Constitution. This seems to be confirmed in light of all available statistical data: while in 2014 the Constitutional Tribunal received a total of 530 cases, and in 2015 a record number of 623 new applications were brought to it, in 2017 this impact dropped just to 282. The decrease in the number of legal questions submitted by the courts in cases pending before them is very telling: in 2015 as many as 135 such cases were submitted to the Court, while in 2017 – only 21.[134] More recent data is difficult to access because the Court has stopped publishing its activity reports annually. However, even based on the data available on the Constitutional Tribunal website, it can be concluded that this negative trend is continuing.

What is even worse, the Polish Constitutional Tribunal consciously limits its official activities. As an example of such an approach, one could give the matter of a highly controversial Law sanctioning the service of uniformed officers for the benefit of a totalitarian state; it radically reduced the retirement benefits for all persons who served for any period of time in units belonging to the supporters of the Polish People's Republic (regardless of the nature of such service, as well as the positive result of verification after the start of 1990 and service in free Poland). The constitutional question regarding this Act was submitted by the Regional Court in Warsaw at the end of January 2018 in connection with the case before it. The date of the hearing was finally set, after numerous prompts from the courts and other entities (the Ombudsman), for whom the issue is a priority: there are circa 24,000 such instances in the Polish courts, and they mostly concern older people for whom the right to obtain a judgment within a reasonable time is of particular importance. However, the judgment has not been delivered yet and, after the last decisions taken by the President of the Tribunal, it seems to be quite unreasonable to expect it to be done.[135]

The course of affairs is no wonder: this decision does not suit those in power who treat the bill as a kind of historical justice: settlement with communism, despite the awareness that collective responsibility is simply unfair. However, in the sense of the rule of law as one of the fundamental values of the Polish Constitution, this is an absolute deception and the ultimate proof of the loss of the real independence by the Constitutional Tribunal. For these reasons, it is not surprising that, waiting in vain for a swift judgment in an important case, some courts took suspended proceedings and gave judgments without looking at the CT.[136] Judges who might still have had

[134] B Szepietowska, 'Działalność orzecznicza Trybunału Konstytucyjnego w latach 2014–2017' in *Funkcjonowanie Trybunału Konstytucyjnego w latach 2014–2017* (Fundacja Batorego, 2018) 19–20.

[135] The hearings in Case P 4/18 took place twice: on 15 July and 18 August 2020. The judgment should have been handed down on 20 October 2020 but shortly before that date Ms Julia Przyłębska simply decided that the constitutional proceedings would be reopened once again. No date of hearing has been designated so far; see at https://trybunal.gov.pl/s/p-418; M Kryszkiewicz and P Nowosielska, 'TK bada ustawę dezubekizacyjną od trzech lat. Zacznie od nowa' (27 January 2021) at https://serwisy.gazetaprawna.pl/orzeczenia/artykuly/8077922,ustawa-dezubekizacyjna-prace-w-tk-od-nowa.html.

[136] Recently, the Court of Appeal in Warsaw ordered the Regional Court to consider the cases of retired officers affected by the Act of 16 December 2016 without further waiting for the judgment in Case P 4/18. It is argued that there is a right to a fair trial that cannot be put off indefinitely. Furthermore, the way the Constitutional Tribunal operates raises doubts about its acting in good faith, which indicates to the

any doubts about the legitimacy of questioning the role of this body will certainly not forget this lesson.

The current crisis of the rule of law in Poland and Hungary shows some disadvantages of the centralised constitutional review based on the Kelsenian doctrine.[137] It works well only in countries marked with a high standards of political culture, in which there is a constant dialogue between the courts and the constitutional court, as well as legislative proceedings are open and transparent. Such factors are fundamental to building a discursive legal community. Adopting the concept of discourse in the sense given to this concept by Jürgen Habermas and Robert Alexy,[138] we are of the opinion that law in modern society cannot be seen as a dictate of the current parliamentary majority. The law as a discourse is subordinated to certain idealising assumptions: the participating parties should be able to assume that they mean the same thing by the same words and expressions, should consider themselves as rationally accountable, and be able to suppose that when they arrive at a mutually acceptable resolution, supporting arguments sufficiently justify a (defeasible) confidence that any claims to truth, justice, etc that underlie their consensus will not later turn out to be false or mistaken.[139]

The discursive concept of law, which is close to our beliefs, assumes the rationality of law resulting from the exchange of positions and the development of solutions that are universally acceptable. As Habermas rightly puts it, the majority decision must be premised on a competent discussion of the disputed issues, that is, on a discussion conducted according to the communicative presuppositions of a corresponding discourse. Only then can its content be seen as a rationally motivated but fallible result of the process of argumentation that has been interrupted in view of institutional pressures to decide, but in principle is resumable. Habermas believes that doubts as to the legitimacy of majority decisions in cases of irreversible consequences are revealing in this regard. They are based on the view that the outlawed minority give their consent to the empowerment of the majority only with the proviso that they themselves retain the opportunity in the future of winning over the majority with better arguments and thus of revising the previous decision.[140]

subordinate court that it has the Constitution at its disposal and can directly apply it; P Nowosielska, 'Ustawa dezubekizacyjna. Sądy apelacyjne nie czekają na TK' (20 January 2020), at https://serwisy.gazetaprawna.pl/praca-i-kariera/artykuly/1449335,ustawa-dezubekizacyjna-wyroki-sadow-apelacyjnych.html.

[137] H Kelsen, *Wesen und Entwicklung der Staatsgerichtsbarkeit. Überprüfung von Verwaltungsakten durch die ordentlichen Gerichte*, Berlin-Leipzig 1929; idem, *Wer soll der Hüter der Verfassung sein?*, 2nd edn (Tübingen, 2019).

[138] J Habermas (tr W Rehg), *Between Facts and Norms. Contributions to a Discourse Theory of Law and Democracy* (The MIT Press, 1996); R Alexy (tr R Adler and N MacCormick). *A Theory of Legal Argumentation: The Theory of Rational Discourse as Theory of Legal Justification* (Clarendon Press, 1989).

[139] Summary of basic assumptions of the discourse in Habermas's philosophical system, see L Morawski, *Główne problemy współczesnej filozofii prawa. Prawo w toku przemian*, wyd. 1 (PWN, 1999) 107–08, with further references.

[140] Habermas (n 13) 179.

In the light of the facts discussed above, the process of legislating and controlling its constitutionality in Poland no longer meets the conditions of rationally conducted discourse. Courts cannot assume that the same words and concepts are understood in the same way by the parliament and the constitutional court subject to the right-wing political majority. The meaning of constitutional concepts is freely modified in such a way that reflects the current aspirations of the ruling parties to give them their own meaning in accordance with the current tactics of political struggle; its final goal seems to be to consolidate the changes made in the institutional and personal dimension.

An example of this modification is the principle of democracy, presented by the Polish government as equivalent to the 'restoration of sovereign control' over the entire state. Top politicians of the Law and Justice party tend to argue that it is the only way to prevent the courts from becoming just another political power, able to push through its interests against those of the whole nation.[141] Apart from the argument that the people also may be a tyrant,[142] with this assumption, it is impossible to talk about the realisation of the justified expectation that the principles of the independence of the judiciary and the judges enshrined in the Constitution will function at the level which would be acceptable from the point of view of the principles of Polish constitutionalism. The Constitution expresses the principle of democracy limited by the separation of powers and guarantees of the rights and freedoms of the individual. Polish statehood is a constitutional democracy which does not give parliament a superior position over judicial power, and even more so it does not allow control over the judiciary by political parties. Thus, the growing party control of

[141] Shortly before his first electoral victory in the 2015, the leader of Law and Justice, Mr Jaroslaw Kaczyński openly announced this idea, allegedly justified by placing the will of most citizens in his grouping: '[I]n fact, the final goal is the change in Poland … What namely is the main method of defense of the system today? At the same time, by the "system" I do not understand democratic institutions …. I understand everything that happens beyond the curtain …. This system can be challenged … only if the public authority is changed, while this authority can be changed if the pursuit of change … is properly located …. There is no democratic system in the world that is not based on political parties …. Political parties … are entities that have one feature … that is of extremely important from the point of view of democracy …: namely, they are subject to civic control, democratic control …. This control is flawed …, but are the companies subject to a democratic control whatsoever? No! … Are the services, various types of intra-state corporations …, e.g. the judiciary, subject to any control? If so, then only by the political parties!' (*Tak naprawdę ostatecznym celem jest zmiana w Polsce … Otóż jaka jest dzisiaj główna chyba metoda obrony systemu? Przy czym przez system ja nie rozumiem instytucji demokratycznych …. Rozumiem to wszystko, co dzieje się poza kurtyną … Ten system może być podważony …, tylko wtedy, gdy zostanie zmieniona władza publiczna, natomiast ta władza może być zmieniona wtedy, jeżeli dążenie do zmiany … zostanie odpowiednio ulokowane … Nie ma na świecie systemu demokratycznego, który nie byłby oparty o partie polityczne …. Partie polityczne … są podmiotami, które mają jedną cechę … z punktu demokracji niezwykle ważną …: otóż są jednak poddane kontroli obywateli, kontroli demokratycznej …. Ta kontrola jest ułomna …, ale czy koncerny są poddane jakiejkolwiek kontroli demokratycznej? Żadnej! … Czy służby, różnego rodzaju korporacje wewnątrzpaństwowe …, np. sądownictwo, są poddane jakiejś kontroli? Jeśli tak, to tylko przez partie!*)' *Jarosław Kaczyński w Klubie Ronina [Jarosław Kaczyński in the Ronin's Club]* (8 June 2015) at http://youtu.be/4c7Y9uyUL7U 5'33"–15'42".

[142] See JS Mill, *On Liberty*, 4th edn (Longmans, 1869) 12: 'The will of the people … practically means the will of the most numerous or the most active *part* of the people; the majority, or those who succeed in making themselves accepted as the majority; the people, consequently, *may* desire to oppress a part of their number.'

the entire apparatus of power means the disappearance of the actual separation of powers, in which the judiciary, separated from representative authorities, performs their function of control and restraint.[143]

In recent years, the implementation of the programme of 'repairing' the judiciary has significantly taken form far from the theory of discourse. It was disclosed gradually, and only after Law and Justice secured a decisive influence on the Constitutional Tribunal; it somewhat proves the full awareness of the reformers that their actions are not in line with the current state system. Needless to say, none of the bills mentioned so far have been consulted with the judges; this also concerned the package of presidential projects: on the reform of the Supreme Court and the National Council of the Judiciary[144] adopted on 8 December 2017, despite the fact that they were the result of mass social protests in defence of the courts' system in the summer of 2017.

The Polish example shows how the courts in a state appropriated by the ruling majority are deprived of the power to decide on the interpretation of applicable law. *Cuius regio eius interpretatio*: paraphrase of this known principle of the Augsburg Peace[145] in our opinion accurately reflects the desire of the ruling coalition led by the PiS party to appropriate the concepts of the legal system and change their meaning in a manner convenient for achieving their own political goals. The point is to eliminate any positions competing in the discourse, and thus to give oneself the exclusive right to decide what the argument and reason in the dispute are, just as during the Reformation, when the unilateral determination of the status quo by the monarchs invalidated any discourse and tore down the communities in so many Western realms. Today courts in the Republic of Poland – an emblemising example of the democratic decay – cease to be an equal partner in the constant dialogue with the legislator and the Constitutional Tribunal; moreover, as it turns out, their legitimacy for exercising public authority is gradually being undermined. The law subjected to the arbitrary will of the theoretically representing majority group becomes the rule of conduct, regardless of whether it can be rationally argued under the Constitution still in force. The danger to the rule of law constituting the skeleton of constitutional democracy is becoming more than real.

Moving towards the summary of the present part of the analysis, it should be emphasised that the term 'autocratic legalism' is apt insofar as it is used as a metaphor describing the destruction of democracy by law, while disregarding the meaning of the term 'legalism' established in the theory of constitutionalism. In fact, at present it would be difficult to define Poland as a 'legalist' state, even within the meaning of the rule 'by law' (regarding the formal rule of law), replacing the existing substantive rule of law.

[143] R Piotrowski, 'Sędziowie i granice władzy demokratycznej w świetle Konstytucji RP' (2018) 53(1) *Ruch Prawniczy, Ekonomiczny i Socjologiczny* 215, 216.

[144] See the Acts referred to in nn 106 and 117.

[145] The slogan *cuius regio eius religio* (Latin,'"whose land, his religion') was coined early in the 17th century by the Protestant canon lawyer Joachim Stephani to describe the key principle of the Peace of Augsburg of 29 September 1555, which gave the Imperial estates the freedom of deciding between Catholicism (Roman Catholic Church) and Lutheranism (Protestantism; Protestant churches) in their own territories; R Potz, '*Cuius regio, eius religio*' in G Dunphy and A Gow (eds), *Encyclopedia of Early Modern History Online* (Brill, 2015) at http://dx.doi.org/10.1163/2352-0272_emho_SIM_018148.

In recent years, Polish legislation has ceased to meet the basic requirements of internal morality according to Lon Fuller's assumptions.[146] It no longer creates a framework for the political life, where ad hoc decisions of the governing party's top management have the supreme position. If the law does not comply with them, then the state apparatus appropriated by the party is able to get over it by any means. It may be the adoption of the parliamentary Act changing the state of law, even if it clearly violates fundamental constitutional principles;[147] a judgment of the Constitutional Tribunal contrary to the case law established over 25 years, also potentially faulty due to the panel composition;[148] legal opinion containing a position which is isolated and impossible to defend;[149] finally, there may be completely arbitrary action that the political authorities generally do not care for at all.[150] The courage of judges to issue rulings contrary to the expectations of the party, just 30 years after the fall of communism, has become precious again – all the more as the courts are treated not as a separate authority, but as just an 'intra-state corporation'. What is behind this rhetoric?

IV. LEGITIMACY OF THE JUDICIARY: A HARD CASE OF POLAND

Since 2015, Polish anti-constitutional populist backsliding has been marked by uncompromising struggle against the judiciary. It was not casual but seems to be concerted from the outset. Several statements of the leader of the ruling camp Mr Jarosław Kaczyński,[151] as well as by the programming documents of the 'Allied Right' of summer 2015[152] may serve as evidence of this argument.

[146] Fuller's concept of the 'internal morality of law', which seems to be universal, has been based on eight principles that proclaim law should be general, publicly promulgated, clear, non-contradictory, possible to comply with, relatively constant through time, non-retroactive, and the official actions should be congruent to a declared rule; LL Fuller, *The Morality of Law* (Yale University Press, 1969) 41.

[147] See the Acts amending the procedure of appointment of the SC Justices in the course of an ongoing competition, switching off the right to the court (n 119).

[148] See the CT judgment No K 5/17 (n 94).

[149] See the opinion by Prof Michał Warciński according to which all the resolutions of the Sejm of 2015 regarding the election of CT judges were null and void *ab initio* due to the provision of the 2015 Act on the Constitutional Tribunal granting the competence to submit candidatures for judges to the Presidium of the Sejm 'and' the group of at least 50 MPs; the conjunction 'and' allegedly pointed to the need for joint action of both bodies. The literal interpretation of the provision was obviously incorrect, as it only listed the nomination bodies and was far from regulating the election procedure. The opinion's massive criticism, however, did not prevent its author from soon becoming a judge of the Constitutional Tribunal, proposed and elected by the deputies of the Law and Justice; cf M Warciński, 'Spór o Trybunał: Prezydent nie może przyjąć ślubowania' (9 December 2015) at www.rp.pl/Opinie/312099994-Spor-o-Trybunal-Prezydent-nie-moze-przyjac-slubowania.html.

[150] See the case of non-promulgated (until 2018) judgments of the CT.

[151] During his meeting with voters in the 'Klub Ronina' (n 141), Mr Jarosław Kaczyński openly expressed the opinion that the courts 'do not exercise their duties …, make harm to the people … and sometimes they hand down judgments which are outrageous, just unprecedented', as well as ascribed to the entire Supreme Court an intention to fight his political camp, especially due to the case of his close associate, Mr Mariusz Kamiński, allegedly initiated as a revenge for the fight for 'cleansing the judiciary'. All this made, as Kaczyński argued, the change in the judiciary critically necessary.

[152] In July 2015, Mr Janusz Wojciechowski, a current EU Commissioner and a former prominent politician of the Law and Justice party, listed certain goals of the 'Allied Right' in the field of administration

After the won elections of 2015, the role of the centre coordinating actions directed at courts and judges was taken over by the Minister of Justice – the Prosecutor General together with a group of his collaborators: politicians, judges delegated to the Ministry of Justice, and prosecutors promoted to a newly established top-level unit called the National Prosecutor's Office. This group waged a kind of 'hybrid war': fierce propaganda mixed with slander, directed at the defamation of the judges' community, attributing to it dirty intentions and ultimately discouraging citizens from the administrations of justice.

Evidence is not lacking. It was the former Deputy Minister of Justice (now the MEP) Mr Patryk Jaki, who popularised the term 'extraordinary caste' as a collective term for judges in the social media controlled by the ruling camp;[153] it has been eagerly picked up and is constantly used in a network of pro-government state and private media. The government indirectly inspired and financed the 'Fair Courts' outdoor campaign, closely modeled upon the *modus operandi* of the Hungarian Government.[154] Even the public utterances of the Polish Prime Minister Mateusz Morawiecki, in which the judges were collectively referred to as collaborators of the communist regime and compared to officers of the French State (Vichy France) or Frankist Spain, stepped far beyond of what might be expected from the head of an EU Member State's government.[155]

of justice, and among them: (i) the merger of the posts of the Prosecutor General and the Minister of Justice; (ii) enacting an institution of the 'extraordinary appeal'; (iii) introducing the lay judges to the higher courts. He, as well as the other speakers (especially Ms Beata Kempa, a former Deputy Minister of Justice), expressed a high level of distrust in the courts, by calling them a 'State within the State' or an 'absolute power', as well as calling to the 'smashing the corporate solidarity of the persons exercising the legal professions'; see transcripts of speeches by J Wojciechowski and B Kempa in *Myśląc Polska: Konwencja Programowa Prawa i Sprawiedliwości oraz Zjednoczonej Prawicy. Katowice, 3-5 lipca 2015 r. (Thinking Poland: The Program Policy Conference of the Law and Justice and the Allied Right. Katowice, 3–5 July 2015)* (the publication of The Alliance of European Conservatives and Reformists [AECR] and PiS), Katowice 2015 at http://pis.org.pl/document/archive/download/127 151–52, 154.

[153] In one of his interviews for the governmental broadcaster TVP Info, Mr Jaki said: 'The Disciplinary Chamber, independent from judges, will finally help us to separate the good grain from the ryegrass in this profession. The judicial power is just a service to a citizen and judges should treat their duty just in this way. Judges should serve to the citizens and not consider themselves to be an "extraordinary caste" [...]. I am convinced that the judicial milieu will stand on their heads in order to prevent us from the change of the system of judiciary. We want to reform the system from the very foundations. The judges have always been unpunished and this is why it will end (*Izba Dyscyplinarna, niezależna od sędziów, która sprawi, że wreszcie w tym zawodzie oddzielimy ziarno od plew. Władza sądownicza to usługa dla obywatela, i sędziowie tak powinni traktować swój zawód. Sędziowie mają służyć obywatelom, a nie uważać się za nadzwyczajną kastę [...]. Jestem przekonany, że środowisko sędziowskie będzie stawało na głowie, żeby przeszkodzić nam w zmianie systemu sądownictwa. Chcemy zreformować system od podstaw. Sędziowie zawsze byli bezkarni, dlatego to się skończy*)'; P Jaki, 'Problemy sądownictwa to przewlekłość i jakość orzecznictwa (Problems of judiciary are the length and quality of judgments)' (26 January 2017) at www.tvp.info/28796106/problemy-sadownictwa-to-przewleklosc-i-jakosc-orzecznictwa.

[154] M Gersdorf and M Pilich (n 67) 367–68.

[155] cf eg M Morawiecki, 'Prime Minister Mateusz Morawiecki: Why my government is reforming Poland's judiciary' (13 December 2017) at www.washingtonexaminer.com/prime-minister-mateusz-morawiecki-why-my-government-is-reforming-polands-judiciary; 'Poland lobbies EU leaders on investigation into court reforms' (15 December 2017) at https://www.irishtimes.com/news/world/europe/poland-lobbies-eu-leaders-on-investigation-into-court-reforms-1.3328844; 'NYU Law News: Polish Prime Minister discusses the state of Europe and Poland with J.H.H. Weiler' (21 April 2019) at www.law.nyu.edu/news/Poland-prime-minister-morawiecki-weiler-jean-monnet-center.

A famous case was the disclosure in 2019 of an alleged informal group of judges close to the Ministry of Justice, including those occupying administrative positions in the Ministry, who were involved in the transfer of data on their colleagues-members of the associations of judges to the mass media associated with the right-wing parties in order to take appropriate propaganda actions against these persons. An intermediary was an ex-wife of one of the group's members. There are many indications that the group had contacts with the troll factory through accounts on popular social networking sites. After detecting the scandal, Mr Łukasz Piebiak, deputy minister of justice responsible for supervising the judiciary, resigned.[156] Controlled disclosure has been limited though not completely ended.

The impression of declaring a ruthless war was to be intensified by the creation of the Department of Internal Affairs in the National Prosecutor's Office in March 2016, to which 10 prosecutors were delegated with the sole task of supervising criminal proceedings in matters of judges and prosecutors. So far, it is difficult to say that the allegations of the corrupted judges, of which there are about 10,000 in Poland, have proven to be true. As of September 2018, 110 criminal cases were conducted in the aforementioned Department (generally, causing a road accident or drunk driving and several cases for other acts, including corruption offences); of the aforementioned number, 61 cases concerned prosecutors, while only 49 cases related to acts committed by judges. Admittedly, there were some spectacular cases (accusation of theft for one of the appellate judges), which, however, can still be treated as an exception to the rule of compliance with legal order by judges.[157]

The events described here are difficult to understand without taking into account the specific context of the development of the Polish legal system over the last two centuries. It is not only about the period of communism, which, although quite long-lasting, took different forms in Poland than in the former Soviet Union. In our opinion, the emphasis should be placed primarily on the constant lack of continuity and legal stabilisation of the Polish state: starting from the nineteenth century period of the partitions of the Polish territory by three neighbouring powers, each with its own legal system (Prussia, Russia and Austria), through the interwar period of 1918–39 and the communist era until the political breakthrough in 1989–90 and the ongoing systemic transformation, the law and its enforcement were associated with imposed coercion, on which the will of the people had very little or virtually no influence. Law came and went like the tides, and hence judges and all state officials, too, were treated as something alien and temporary. It comes as no surprise that Polish society as a whole generally treats public life, authorities and the entire legal system with great distrust: starting from generalised distrust towards others (constantly approximately 75 per cent), and ending with a slightly smaller, but constantly declared percentage of negative responses in surveys about various institutions, such as the Sejm and

[156] K Sobczak and P Rojek-Socha, 'Hejt przeciw sędziom – dymisja wiceministra Piebiaka' at www.prawo.pl/prawnicy-sady/wiceminister-lukasz-piebiak-mial-stac-za-akcja-dyskredytowania,460697.html.

[157] A Łukaszewicz, 'Specwydział prokuratury: z wielkiej chmury mały deszcz' (Specialised department of the prosecutor's office: a lot of fuss over nothing) (11 September 2018) at www.rp.pl/Prokuratorzy/309109910-Specwydzial-prokuratury-z-wielkiej-chmury-maly-deszcz.html.

Senate (53 per cent), courts (50 per cent), and political parties (63 per cent).[158] Under such circumstances, manipulating social moods in order to incite resentment against judges as the modern 'enemies of the people' does not seem difficult.

One of the clichés used to this end is the alleged participation of judges in communist repression and lack of self-cleaning after the political breakthrough. It is hard to deny that settlements with the past were imperfect but still, those really involved in communist repression mostly left the judiciary after 1990, undertaking other legal professions or eventually getting retired. In the second half of the 1990s, there were also cases of their being punished in various procedures (eg, in disciplinary or lustration proceedings), even if it is true that this did not happen often and quickly.[159] That is why a collective name of a 'communist judge' is generally unfair. After all, those nominated during the existence of the Polish People's Republic hardly belonged to the supporters of the Communist regime just because of their appointment, and it would be absurd to expect them to refrain from adjudicating and be replaced immediately in 1990 by new cadres which democratic Poland simply did not have. There is nothing strange in the extension of the judicial mandates after the collapse of undemocratic forms of government, as the examples of both Spain[160] and the Federal Republic of Germany[161] show.

Attacks on modern judiciary, over 30 years after the political breakthrough, make very little sense, as justice has already been dispensed by the time lapse: the average age of a judge in Poland is currently around 40 years. In the district courts (the lowest tier) the parties already meet people who completed their legal education at the earliest at the beginning of the 1990s and there is no reason to doubt their full commitment to the values of constitutional democracy. A higher age of judges in senior courts is quite natural but it should not be forgotten that at the end of the Polish People's Republic, today's appellate or Supreme Court judges could at most occupy low positions in the judiciary, and the probability that they adjudicated in any political matter is close to zero.[162] Their latter have been positively verified by the passage of time since the democratic system was established.

[158] As evidenced by the results of public opinion polls conducted in 2018 by one of the leading Polish analytical centers, *Centrum Badania Opinii Społecznej* (abbrev CBOS – the Public Opinion Research Center); cf CBOS, 'O nieufności i zaufaniu' at www.cbos.pl/SPISKOM.POL/2018/K_035_18.PDF.

[159] Śledzińska-Simon (n 30) 1842–43. Attempts to prosecute judges in the years 1990–97 brought very moderate results. Only after 1997 did the amended Law on the System of Common Courts enable the Minister of Justice to apply to the National Council of the Judiciary for bringing the accusation against judges who before 1990 misappropriated the judge's oath; out of 47 such cases, 37 judges were subject to financial sanctions, while six persons were brought before criminal courts (none of the latter cases, however, ended with a final conviction); cf M Stanowska and A Strzembosz, *Sędziowie warszawscy w czasie próby 1981–1988* (Warszawa, 2005) 288–89, 296–97.

[160] J Urias, 'Spain has a Problem with its Judiciary' (15 January 2020) at https://verfassungsblog.de/spain-has-a-problem-with-its-judiciary/.

[161] For the lack of settlements with judges in post-war Germany, cf B Diestelkamp, 'Die Justiz nach 1945 und ihr Umgang mit der eigenen Vergangenheit' (1986) 5 *Rechtshistorisches Journal* 153, 156. A different story of the judiciary in the former German Democratic Republic might be explained by the superior position of West Germany as an established democracy taking over full responsibility for new Eastern *Länder*. Moreover, even the reaction of the German Federal Court of Justice (*Bundesgerichtshof*) was assessed as lenient. This example shows that expecting a new regime to sanction all the judges for the slightest offence whatsoever against human rights and liberties is hardly imaginable in practice; cf Graver (n 16) 192–99.

[162] Out of more than 10,000 judges currently adjudicating in common courts, 1015 (about 10%) began adjudicating before 4 June 1989 (ie, before the landmark June elections) as judges or temporary judges.

Another weapon against the judiciary in Poland is putting the blame on it for its pretended striving for taking over power. There are no good reasons for such considerations. The Constitution of the Republic of Poland of 1997 describes the status of the judiciary in a correct way, quite in line with the Western constitutionalism. By definition alone, as Alexis de Tocqueville has shown, judges are not involved in a dispute with elected authorities, even by ruling on the responsibility of the state agents; after all, the authority of a judge consists in something else: s/he is to monitor compliance with the law, acting within its limits, and only on the application of an authorised party.[163] Equally false, from a legal point of view, comes the criticism of 'juristocracy' as dangerous to democracy. The rising importance of the judiciary today is quite natural for various reasons, in particular as a side effect of both an increase in the number of legal regulations (so-called 'inflation of the law') and the need for creating legal rules where the statutory law is not sufficient to determine the effects of human behaviour in an increasingly complex social reality.[164] The very concept of 'juristocracy', associated with the judicial activism,[165] has very little to do with Polish courts, which are rather conservative in terms of literal law interpretation. Attempts to exercise the judicial review of constitutionality, as well as to create new legal rules through a broader interpretation of the law, may be considered as infrequent and modest. In the light of our observations, accusing Polish judges of attempts to take over part of the power to legislate has no justification in the facts.

Least but not last, the courts are silenced with an argument that they do not hold any mandate coming from popular elections; therefore it is advisable to be abstemious in presenting opinions about adopted laws and to submit to the will of the legislative authority. While it is difficult to deny that the Nation is a sovereign in Poland (article 4(1) of the Constitution), it cannot be rationally argued that in order to take a position of a true state authority, the judiciary should derive its mandate directly from the will of the voters.[166] Precisely because constitutional democracy rests on the foundation of the rule of law and, by the same token, on the limitation by law of every

At least 36 judges of the Supreme Court began their careers in common and administrative courts before 1989, although the vast majority already after the darkest period of martial law (1981–82). From the current composition of the Supreme Court, 10 judges were appointed to the Supreme Court in the 1990s, 22 in the 2000s, and 69 in the 2010s; 'Ilu sędziów zaczynało orzekanie jeszcze w PRL-u? Sprawdzamy słowa prezydenta', at https://konkret24.tvn24.pl/polityka,112/ilu-sedziow-zaczynalo-orzekanie-jeszcze-w-prl-u-sprawdzamy-slowa-prezydenta,987116.html.

[163] 'The first characteristic of judicial power in all nations is the duty of arbitration. But rights must be contested in order to warrant the interference of a tribunal; and an action must be brought to obtain the decision of a judge. As long, therefore, as the law is uncontested, the judicial authority is not called upon to discuss it, and it may exist without being perceived … The judicial power is by its nature devoid of action; it must be put in motion in order to produce a result.'; A de Tocqueville, (tr JT Schleifer, ed E Nolla), *Democracy in America* vol 1, (Liberty Fund, 2012) 117–18 at https://oll.libertyfund.org/titles/2735.

[164] Piotrowski (n 143) 220–21.

[165] R Hirschl, *Towards Juristocracy: The Origins and Consequences of the New Constitutionalism* (Harvard University Press, 2004); C Guarneri and P Pederzoli in CA Thomas (ed), *From Democracy to Juristocracy? The Power of Judges: A Comparative Study of Courts and Democracy* (OUP, 2002); T Vallinder, 'The Judicialization of Politics. A World-Wide Phenomenon: Introduction' (1994) 15(2) *International Political Science Review / Revue Internationale De Science Politique* 91.

[166] Even though in some countries (as, for instance, the US) there are actually exceptions to this rule, consisting in the selection of justices of peace or magistrates, competent in some minor cases.

authority, including the legislative, the legitimacy of judicial power is indirect, relying on duly established and promulgated law.[167]

The legitimacy of the judiciary occurs when a properly elected representative body has established, within the framework of the Constitution, legal rules conferring judicial power on the basis of these legal regulations, and then appropriate persons have been appointed in the procedures provided for by the law to exercise the power of adjudicating. The demos has appointed independent judges and courts to hear cases pursuant to the Constitution and statutory law (articles 173 and 178 of the Constitution), in accordance with the rule of law (article 2), and at the same time it ordered the Constitution to be applied directly as the supreme law of the country (article 8). Whereas the Constitution includes the principle of separation of powers (article 10), the demos has the obligation to accept that the courts are duly empowered, within province of their jurisdiction, to adequately deter representatives of the majority from exceeding their electoral mandate flowing from the system of constitutional norms. The judiciary is therefore a legitimised authority, and judges are also representatives of the nation within the meaning of article 4(2) of the Constitution, not less than the members of the legislative are; furthermore, an additional legitimising factor is precisely the separation of powers, without which representatives of the current majority could do everything, and the concepts of constitution and law would lose all meaning.[168]

The silence of judges and acceptance of the reforms, which distort the Polish constitutional system and undermine the foundations of Poland's participation in the European community of nations, do not help much in obtaining or, alternatively, strengthening legitimacy. The passivity potentially leads to a deepening of the phenomenon of social and legal delegitimisation of the judicial authority. Judges threatened with disciplinary penalties for their judicial decisions, whose voice in the courtroom is outright ignored,[169] have not only the right, but also the obligation to speak outside of it. It should be emphasised here that limiting the activity of judges to issuing judgments only and imposing the obligation of silence on them outside the courtroom means more than just a detriment to the future of Polish democracy, devoid of a voice of reason: it is a serious and unjustified restriction of human rights and freedoms, which a judge does not give up upon taking office.[170]

A particularly interesting case study in this respect was a public demonstration organised by the judges' associations together with other NGOs, called 'March of

[167] CD Classen, *Demokratische Legitimation im offenen Rechtsstaat. Zur Beeinflussung des Demokratieprinzips durch Rechtsstaatlichkeit und internationale Offenheit* (Tübingen, 2009) 20; cf J Kostrubiec, 'Istotna prawnej legitymizacji władzy' (2001) *Studenckie Zeszyty Naukowe* 8, 18–19.

[168] See RM Małajny, 'Podział władzy państwowej jako przesłanka jej legitymizacji' (2014) 22(3) *Przegląd Sejmowy* 26–28; cf also the concept of the 'constitutional recapture' by TT Koncewicz, 'The Capture of the Polish Constitutional Tribunal and Beyond: Of Institution(s), Fidelities and the Rule of Law in Flux' (2018) 43 *Review of Central and East European Law* 116, 143.

[169] See K Gajda-Roszczynialska and K Markiewicz (n 125) 467.

[170] See ECHR judgments: of 26 February 2009, *Kudeshkina v Russia*, appl. No. 29492/05, at http://hudoc.echr.coe.int/fre?i=001-91501; of 23 June 2016 (GC), *Baka v Hungary*, appl. No. 20261/12 at http://hudoc.echr.coe.int/fre?i=001-163113; s 8 of the *Basic Principles on the Independence of the Judiciary Adopted*

a Thousand Robes': in order to object to the drafted restrictions of the independence of judiciary; representatives of the legal professions, including judges, quietly walked through the streets of Warsaw in costumes in which they usually appear in the courtroom. Tens of thousands of people set off on a several kilometre road from the seat of the Polish Supreme Court to the complex of parliament buildings.[171] Judges from several countries, mainly belonging to the European Union, gave their support to Polish colleagues.[172]

The demonstration case has contributed to the debate that took place in *The Irish Times*. According to the editors, the role of the judges is not to go out, even if the organisers emphasise the lack of political goals. The main argument put forward by the author of the editorial comment is thus diminishing the credibility of the judiciary. Demonstrating against government policies, especially foreign ones, violates the principle that judges should speak through their judgments.[173]

The editorial position aroused a wave of criticism from the academic community, both in Ireland and Poland. Professor Ronan McCrea (University College, London) argued that judges have every right to defend their independence from political authorities, without which their mission in the state loses its sense; such activities cannot be termed political activities. Furthermore, due to the scale of interconnections between the Member States of the European Union, nowadays it is no longer possible to precisely distinguish between the domain of national authorities and the matter of EU law.[174] Meanwhile, two scholars from the University of Warsaw stated that the 'political' nature of judges' activities should be qualified in the sense of classical Greek philosophy as action in the community of citizens (*politeia*), and not as participation in the struggle for power. Support for Polish colleagues from the judges of other Member States contributes to the creation of a 'European community of values', in line with the objectives of the Treaty on European Union: an ever closer union of nations based on solidarity. Values that are not defended together cease to be common.[175]

Paradoxically, both the opposing positions can be described as legitimate. The author of *The Irish Times* editorial is basically correct in saying that judges should first of all speak through their judgments. After all, in modern, rule-of-law

by the Seventh United Nations Congress on the Prevention of Crime and the Treatment of Offenders held at Milan from 26 August to 6 September 1985 and endorsed by General Assembly resolutions 40/32 of 29 November 1985 and 40/146 of 13 December 1985, at www.ohchr.org/en/professionalinterest/pages/independencejudiciary.aspx.

[171] A Barteczko and P Florkiewicz in C Oziel (ed), 'Thousands protest against Poland's plan to discipline judges' at www.reuters.com/article/us-poland-judiciary-toga-march/thousands-protest-against-polands-plan-to-discipline-judges-idUSKBN1ZA0PD.

[172] 'European judges support Polish independent judges, joining the silent march on 11.01.2020 – update' at www.iustitia.pl/en/3588-european-judges-support-polish-independent-judges-joining-the-silent-march-on-11-01-2020-update.

[173] 'The Irish Times view on Irish judges protesting in Poland: crossing a line', at www.irishtimes.com/opinion/editorial/the-irish-times-view-on-irish-judges-protesting-in-poland-crossing-a-line-1.4134097?fbclid=IwAR1AdLY7DT7q6x4BE0KbmB_leS7XqTdM6L31O_2IZOXhOeWUP4gCOx_Iks4.

[174] R. McCrea, 'Irish judges have every right to back protests in Poland' (14 January 2020) at www.irishtimes.com/opinion/irish-judges-have-every-right-to-back-protests-in-poland-1.4142089.

[175] P Marcisz and J Urbanik, 'Judges and protests in Poland' (14 January 2020) at www.irishtimes.com/opinion/letters/judges-and-protests-in-poland-1.4138384.

representative democracies, the belief that the power of judging is separate from both law-making and law enforcement is taken for granted. As already stated, courts have not been called to participate in the normal political process. Judges rejecting these limits would lose their legitimacy to hold control over legality of actions undertaken by other authorities. It might be argued that the lack of a direct democratic mandate obliges judges to exercise restraint over legislative changes implemented by representative authorities. Outside of the province of their usual competence, judges have neither the resources nor the power to actively influence the course of public affairs.[176]

On the other hand, however – what we think is particularly important in the circumstances of the Polish case – defence of the 'inner morality' of law is a core obligation of the judiciary in a constitutional democracy. There is no doubt that the potential of the despotism of the 'political' authorities, which may feel entitled to arbitrarily influence the sphere of the courts' jurisdiction, as well as to staff the judicial offices according to their will, is much more real than despotism of judiciary. Courts subordinate to the executive lose their identity, becoming only an extension of the police arm of the state; they provide order but do not truly resolve disputes – and in any case society may not believe that they do so. In other words, the lack of independence, just like the attempts to corrupt judges, by definition leads to the deprivation of the judiciary of public trust.[177] This is the path that contemporary Poland follows.

V. FINAL CONSIDERATIONS

The end of April 2020, when the term of office of Ms Małgorzata Gersdorf as the Chief Justice of the Polish Supreme Court since 2014 was over, symbolically sets the crossroads where the Polish judiciary is standing. The time of regaining the freedom to interpret and apply the law is over, the era of limiting the sphere of competence of courts and their constant delegitimisation begins. There are many reasons for this and they are not limited to the aggressive, nationalist and authoritarian course that the elected Polish authorities have adopted over the past years in and after 2015. The historically conditioned attitudes of legal nihilism, which characterise Polish social and political culture, play an important role here, too. That is why just to limit itself

[176] 'Whoever attentively considers the different departments of power must perceive, that, in a government in which they are separated from each other, the judiciary, from the nature of its functions, will always be the least dangerous to the political rights of the Constitution; because it will be least in a capacity to annoy or injure them. The Executive not only dispenses the honors, but holds the sword of the community. The legislature not only commands the purse, but prescribes the rules by which the duties and rights of every citizen are to be regulated. The judiciary, on the contrary, has no influence over either the sword or the purse; no direction either of the strength or of the wealth of the society; and can take no active resolution whatever. It may truly be said to have neither **force** nor **will**, but merely judgment; and must ultimately depend upon the aid of the executive arm even for the efficacy of its judgments'; see A Hamilton, 'The Federalist No. 78: The Judiciary Department' in I Shapiro (ed), *The Federalist Papers* (Yale University Press, 2009) 391–97.

[177] Clifford Wallace (n 23) 244–46; A Barak, *The judge in a democracy* (Princeton University Press, 2006) 77.

to an exchange of legal arguments in the courtroom, might be too little to improve the position of the Polish judiciary. Legal legitimisation takes place on the foundation of social legitimacy, not the other way around.

We believe then that rights of judges to speak out and counteract anti-constitutional actions of other branches of government should no longer be treated as unusual and contrary to the nature of constitutional democracy. The only way for judges seems to be to symbolically go back to the sources of the crisis and try to work together to tame and make society aware of the illusions it is fed by the political class. New channels of communication with society are needed desperately; speaking through judgments is not enough. Outside the courtroom, the judge is also a citizen and has the right and even the duty to defend the value of the legal system against populism. *Tempora mutantur et nos mutamur in illis....*

Index

www.ingramcontent.com/pod-product-compliance
Ingram Content Group UK Ltd.
Pitfield, Milton Keynes, MK11 3LW, UK
UKHW020230290926
15470UKWH00002B/448